Physics
for Scientists and Engineers
An Interactive Approach

Custom Volume 2

PHYS 102

Custom Edition for
University of British Columbia

NELSON EDUCATION

Contents

Learning Objectives

When you have completed this chapter you should be able to:

1. Explain triboelectric charging, and predict static electricity situations.

2. State the SI unit of charge, and solve problems involving charge and current relationships.

3. Use Coulomb's law to calculate the electric forces exerted by point charges.

4. Calculate the net electric force exerted by multiple point charges using vector superposition.

5. Define electric field, and determine the electric field for various arrangements of point charges.

6. Differentiate between conductors, insulators, and dielectrics.

7. Define electric dipoles, and calculate the electric field for a dipole.

8. Apply electric dipole physics to molecular physics.

9. Define charge density, and use calculus to find the electric field in situations involving uniform charge density.

For additional Making Connections, Examples, and Checkpoints, as well as activities and experiments to help increase your understanding of the chapter's concepts, please go to the text's online resources at www.physics1e.nelson.com.

Chapter 19
Electric Charges and Forces

During a spectacular lightning discharge, there is a massive flow of electric charge (Figure 19-1). Scientists do not completely understand how clouds become electrically charged or how lightning strokes are initiated. In this chapter, we will examine the forces that charged objects exert and apply electric fields to various natural and technological phenomena.

Figure 19-1 A lightning strike results in the flow of a huge electric charge.

LOOK AHEAD

19-1   Static Electricity

Static electricity surrounds us in ways that are both obvious and subtle. If on a dry day you scuff your shoes across a carpeted floor, your body will become charged. When you then reach for a metal doorknob, current will suddenly flow to discharge your body.

Static electricity, which is stationary charge on insulated objects, is one of the oldest recorded topics in physics. Thales of Miletus (circa 624–546 BCE) made observations of static electricity. Indeed, the word "electricity" comes from the Greek word for amber, which is one of the first materials found to be easily charged with static electricity.

A key discovery was that electric charges come in two forms—positive and negative. As far as we know, the universe is overall electrically neutral, that is, it has equal amounts of positive and negative charge. Electric charges exert forces on each other: like electric charges (e.g., two negative charges) repel, and unlike charges (one negative and one positive) attract each other.

You probably associate static electricity with rubbing two objects against each other. In fact, charge can be transferred when two different materials come into contact and are then separated. When we rub two materials together, points on the surface of one object repeatedly contact and separate from points on the surface of the other object, causing positive charge to build up on one of the objects and negative charge on the other. This process is called triboelectric charging.

However, rubbing two materials together will result in significant charging only when the two materials have different electrical properties, with one holding on to electrons weakly compared to the other. Qualitatively, we can indicate the relative ability of materials to retain electrons by placing the materials in a triboelectric series, like the one in Table 19-1. For example, if we rub a rubber balloon with hair, the table indicates that the hair will become positively charged and the balloon will become negatively charged. No significant charging will result from rubbing together two materials that are in the centre of the table, near the positive to negative transition, or two materials that are close together in the table and are both in the positive or negative column. For example, rubbing cotton with wood will leave the wood with a tiny amount of positive charge at most.

Metals can be charged by the photoelectric effect, in which incident photons provide the energy needed to strip some electrons from the surface of the metal. Heating can also cause charging in some materials.

How do separated charges behave? When a charged object is placed in contact with an object with the opposite charge sign, or with an object with a much different concentration of charge, a flow of charges results.

Table 19-1   The triboelectric series for some common materials

Positive	Negative
Leather	
Glass	
Hair	
Nylon	
Wool	
Silk	
Paper	
Cotton	
	Wood
	Acrylic
	Rubber
	Polyester
	Polystyrene foam
	Plastic wrap
	Polyethylene
	Polyvinyl chloride (PVC)
	Silicon

The insulating medium between the objects may break down, allowing a sudden flow of charge, often with a visible spark.

Even if there is no actual flow of charges, one charged object can influence the distribution of charges on other objects. When you move a positively charged object near a fluid object, where both positive and negative charge carriers can move, the negative charges (electrons) on the second object are attracted by the positive charge and move closer to the first object. Similarly, positive charges on the second object are repelled and shift away from the positively charged object. In solids, usually only the electrons are free to actually move.

When a flexible, nonconducting object is charged, the charges in the different parts of the object repel each other. This repulsion makes people's hair stand on end when they have either a positive or a negative charge (Figure 19-2). Therefore, objects can be charged by conduction (when charges actually flow between objects) and by induction (no actual contact).

ONLINE ACTIVITY

The e-resource that accompanies every new copy of this textbook contains an Online Activity using the PhET simulation "Balloons and Static Electricity." Work through the simulation and accompanying questions to gain an understanding of static electrical charging and forces.

Figure 19-2 The child became charged by triboelectricity as she slid down the plastic tube, causing her hair to stand on end.

Courtesy of Marc Nantel

✓ **CHECKPOINT**

C-19-1 Clothes Dryer Charges

Some polyester shirts and wool socks have been tumbled together in a clothes dryer. Which of the following statements is correct? Refer to Table 19-1.

(a) The socks are negatively charged, and the shirts are positively charged. The socks stick to each other, and the shirts stick to each other.

(b) The socks are positively charged, and the shirts are negatively charged. The socks stick to each other, and the shirts stick to each other.

(c) The socks are negatively charged, and the shirts are positively charged. The socks stick to the shirts but not to the other socks.

(d) The socks are positively charged, and the shirts are negatively charged. The socks stick to the shirts but not to the other socks.

C-19-1 (d) From Table 19-1, wool is on the positive side, and polyester is on the negative side, which tells us how they are charged when they are rubbed together. Since unlike charges attract (and like repel), we expect the positively charged socks to stick to the negatively charged shirts. You might think that charge would flow to immediately neutralize the clothes in contact with each other, but the rate of flow is actually very low.

19-2 Electric Charge

The SI unit for electric charge is the coulomb (C), named in honour of Charles Augustin de Coulomb (1736–1806). In terms of the SI base units, one coulomb is equal to one ampere times one second: $1\,\mathrm{C} = 1\,\mathrm{A} \cdot \mathrm{s}$. Current is the rate of flow of charges.

KEY EQUATION
$$I = \frac{\Delta q}{\Delta t} = \frac{dq}{dt} \tag{19-1}$$

where I is the current (in amperes), and Δq is the amount of charge (in coulombs) that flows past a point in a time Δt (in seconds). We can think of the units of charge and time as infinitesimally small giving the differential form.

The magnitude of the electric charge on a proton or an electron is called the elementary charge, and is usually represented by the symbol e. The coulomb is vastly larger than the elementary charge: $e = 1.60 \times 10^{-19}\,\mathrm{C}$.

✓ **CHECKPOINT**

C-19-2 Charge and Current

Suppose that some dust grains have become charged such that each particle has a charge of $0.0200\,\mathrm{C}$. What current is flowing if 100 of these dust grains pass a point in $0.100\,\mathrm{s}$?

(a) $0.500\,\mathrm{A}$

(b) $2.00\,\mathrm{A}$

(c) $20.0\,\mathrm{A}$

(d) $200.\,\mathrm{A}$

C-19-2 (c) With each charge being 0.0200 C, if we have 100 of the charges, we will have a total charge of 2.00 C flowing in 0.100 s. Thus, the current is 2.00 C/0.100 s = 20.0 A.

 EXAMPLE 19-1

How Many Charges per Second?

A current of $0.250\,\mu\mathrm{A}$ is flowing in a circuit. How many elementary charge units are passing a point in this circuit each second?

SOLUTION

First, we convert the current into amperes:

$$\frac{0.250\,\mu\mathrm{A}}{1} \times \frac{1 \times 10^{-6}\,\mathrm{A}}{1\,\mu\mathrm{A}} = 2.50 \times 10^{-7}\,\mathrm{A}$$

A current of $1\,\mathrm{A}$ means that the amount of charge flowing is $1\,\mathrm{C}$ every second. Therefore, the rate of flow of charge is

$$\frac{2.50 \times 10^{-7}\,\mathrm{C}}{1\,\mathrm{s}} \times \frac{1\,e}{1.60 \times 10^{-19}\,\mathrm{C}} = \frac{1.56 \times 10^{12}\,e}{1\,\mathrm{s}}$$

4

Therefore, we would have 1.56×10^{12} elementary charge units (in this case, they would be negatively charged electrons) flowing past a point in the circuit every second.

Making sense of the result:

The elementary unit of charge, e, is truly a tiny charge, so it is reasonable that we would find a huge number flowing every second.

LO 3

19-3 Coulomb's Law

We saw in Chapter 11 that every mass in the universe attracts every other mass with a force directed along a line joining the centres of the two masses, and with a magnitude given by the following equation:

$$|\vec{F}_G| = \frac{GMm}{r^2} \qquad (11\text{-}1)$$

In an analogous way, every electric charge exerts a force on every other electric charge, with the force being attractive when the charges are of opposite sign (i.e., one positive and one negative charge) and repulsive when the two charges are of the same sign.

The electric force, $\vec{F}_{1\to2}$, that a point electric charge q_1 exerts on a second point charge q_2 is given by Coulomb's law:

KEY EQUATION
$$\vec{F}_{1\to2} = \frac{1}{4\pi\varepsilon_0}\frac{q_1 q_2}{r^2}\hat{r}_{1\to2} \qquad (19\text{-}2)$$

Here, q_1 and q_2 are the two electric charges, expressed in coulombs with the appropriate positive or negative sign. The distance between the point charges is r (expressed in metres). A unit vector, $\hat{r}_{1\to2}$, points in the direction from charge 1 toward charge 2. (Recall that a unit vector is a dimensionless vector of magnitude 1.) The constant that plays the role that G does in the universal gravitational force is the term $\frac{1}{4\pi\varepsilon_0}$, which is called Coulomb's constant. In Chapter 20, we will show why we prefer to express this constant in terms of ε_0, which is a constant of nature called the permittivity of free space and has a value of 8.85×10^{-12} C²/N·m². Coulomb's law is only applicable to static situations (charges not moving).

EXAMPLE 19-2

Charge on Hanging Masses

Two 100 g balls with equal but unknown charge Q are hanging from massless strings, each making an angle of 15.0° with the vertical, as shown in Figure 19-3. The strings are 40.0 cm long. Find the magnitude of Q. Can you determine the sign of the charges from the information provided?

Note that Equation (19-2) gives us the direction of the force exerted by q_1 on q_2. This force is in the same direction as a unit vector pointing from q_1 toward q_2 when both charges are of the same sign, and is in the opposite direction when one charge is positive and one is negative. We can use Newton's third law to find the force that q_2 exerts on q_1. This force has the same magnitude but the opposite direction as the force that q_1 exerts on q_2.

 PEER TO PEER

I find I make fewer mistakes when applying Coulomb's law in situations involving multiple charges if I draw the directions of the arrows for each electric force using the fact that like charges repel and unlike charges attract. I then just use Coulomb's law to find the magnitude of each force, putting in the directions myself.

Coulomb's law applies to point charges. Later in the chapter, we will see how to apply Coulomb's law to situations with multiple point charges, and then in situations with distributions of charges. We will relate electric force and electric field for point charges; one way to consider the inverse square relationship is that the field is spread over a sphere of area $4\pi r^2$ as distance r increases.

✓ CHECKPOINT

C-19-3 Electric Force Directions

Charge q_1 is a negative charge (say $-Q$) placed in the xy-plane at position ($x = 0$ m, $y = -1$ m), and charge q_2 is a positive charge (say $+Q$) placed at (0 m; $+1$ m). In terms of the ijk unit vector notation, what is the direction of the force acting on charge q_2?

(a) The direction is in the $+\hat{i}$-direction.
(b) The direction is in the $-\hat{i}$-direction.
(c) The direction is in the $+\hat{j}$-direction.
(d) The direction is in the $-\hat{j}$-direction.

C-19-3 (d) First, find the direction of the unit vector pointing from q_1 toward q_2, which must be in the $+\hat{j}$-direction. Since one charge is positive and the other is negative, there is a net negative sign in the equation for Coulomb's law. Thus, the direction of the force on q_2 must be opposite to the direction of the unit vector. This makes sense because unlike charges attract, so the top charge (2) will be pulled downward, in the $-y$-direction.

SOLUTION

As shown in Figure 19-4, there are three forces acting on each ball: a repulsive electric force, a downward gravitational force, and a tension force, $\vec{T}$, directed along the string.

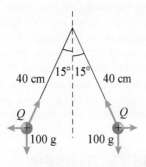

40 cm $\quad$ 15° 15° $\quad$ 40 cm

Q $\quad$ Q

100 g $\quad$ 100 g

Figure 19-3 The charged balls repel each other. Tension and gravity provide the other forces that together keep the system in static equilibrium.

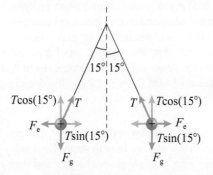

15° 15°

$T\cos(15°)$ $\quad$ T $\quad\quad$ T $\quad$ $T\cos(15°)$

F_e $\quad\quad$ F_e

$T\sin(15°)$ $\quad\quad$ $T\sin(15°)$

F_g $\quad\quad$ F_g

Figure 19-4 Forces acting on the suspended charged balls

The system is in static equilibrium, so these forces must add to zero. Therefore, the vertical component of the tension must balance the gravitational force:

$$T \cos(15.0°) = mg$$

Solving for the magnitude of the tension gives

$$T = \frac{mg}{\cos(15.0°)} = \frac{(0.100 \text{ kg})(9.81 \text{ m/s}^2)}{\cos(15.0°)} = 1.02 \text{ N}$$

Similarly, the horizontal component of the tension must balance the horizontal electric force. This horizontal component is

$$T \sin(15.0°) = (1.02 \text{ N})\sin(15.0°) = 0.263 \text{ N}$$

Applying Coulomb's law for the electric force, we have

$$0.263 \text{ N} = \frac{1}{4\pi\varepsilon_0}\frac{Q^2}{r^2} \quad \text{and} \quad Q^2 = 4\pi\varepsilon_0 r^2 \times 0.263 \text{ N}$$

We can use trigonometry to find the distance, r, between the charges:

$$r = 2 \times 0.400 \text{ m} \times \sin(15.0°) = 0.207 \text{ m}$$

Now we can solve for the unknown charge Q:

$$Q^2 = (4\pi)\, 8.85 \times 10^{-12}\, \frac{C^2}{N\, m^2}\, (0.207 \text{ m})^2 \times 0.263 \text{ N}$$

$$Q = 1.25 \times 10^{-12} \text{ C} = 1.25 \text{ pC}$$

However, we cannot determine the sign of the charges from the information provided. The charges could be both negative or both positive because the electric force would be repulsive in either case.

Making sense of the result:

This configuration is used in an electroscope to measure electric charges. If the balls had been separated at a greater angle, then we would find a greater value for Q. Note that in most everyday situations, static charges are a tiny fraction of a coulomb. In this solution, we used the fact that like charges repel to determine the direction of the electric forces. We could have obtained this result more formally using unit vector notation.

LO 4

19-4 Multiple Point Charges

When there are more than two point charges, we find the net force on any one charge by using Coulomb's law to find the force from each of the other charges, and then add these forces as vectors. Calculating the net force in this way is an application of the superposition principle. The superposition principle, widely used in physics, states that in a linear system you can find the response due to individual stimuli (in this case, the electric force due to one charge) and then add the individual contributions to find the total response. You can often use symmetry to simplify the situation because some components will cancel and do not need to actually be calculated.

The following example illustrates the process of combining electric forces for multiple point charge situations. The technique is the same as the technique you used for net forces in the dynamics chapter, except that you now use Coulomb's law to calculate the forces.

✓ CHECKPOINT

C-19-4 Zero Net Electric Force

As shown in Figure 19-5, the charge $-2Q$ is located on the x-axis at a distance D to the right of another charge, $+Q$. Is there a point anywhere on the x-axis where we could place a third positive charge, $+q$, such that it would experience zero net electric force?

 $+Q$ $\quad\quad$ $-2Q$

$\longleftarrow D \longrightarrow$

Figure 19-5 C-19-4

(a) No, there is no such point.
(b) Yes, and it would be between the charges.
(c) Yes, and it would be to the left of the $+Q$ charge.
(d) Yes, and it would be to the right of the $-2Q$ charge.

C-19-4 (c) Nowhere between the two charges will we be able to find a point with zero net force. This is because the $+q$ charge is attracted to the $-2Q$ and repelled by the $+Q$ charge. In both cases resulting in a force to the right so they could not balance. If we are to the left of the $+Q$ charge, then we would feel a repulsion from the $+Q$ charge (a force to the left) and an attraction toward the $-2Q$ charge (a force to the right). At the right distance, these two can cancel to produce zero net force. In the region to the right of the $-2Q$ charge, the force from that charge is always stronger because the charge is greater and the distance to it is smaller.

EXAMPLE 19-3

Net Force from Three Charges

Charge q_1 is $+1.00\,\mu C$. Located 0.500 m to the right of q_1 is charge q_2 $(+2.00\,\mu C)$. At a distance of 1.50 m in the $+y$-direction from charge q_1 is charge q_3 $(-3.00\,\mu C)$. Find the magnitude and direction of the net electric force on charge q_1.

SOLUTION

Let us define a coordinate system with charge q_1 at the origin, as shown in Figure 19-6. We now apply the vector form of Coulomb's law. Since we want to find the net force acting on q_1, we draw unit vectors for direction from q_2 and q_3 to q_1. When we draw the directions of the corresponding forces, we need to keep in mind that the charge product q_2q_1 is positive and the charge product q_3q_1 is negative. Consequently, the direction of the force that q_3 exerts on q_1 will be opposite to that of $\hat{r}_{3\to1}$.

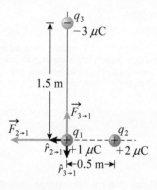

Figure 19-6 Forces acting on q_1

We will first calculate the force that q_2 exerts on q_1:

$$\vec{F}_{2\to1} = \frac{1}{4\pi\varepsilon_0}\frac{q_2q_1}{r_{21}^2}\hat{r}_{2\to1}$$

$$= \frac{1}{4\pi\varepsilon_0}\frac{(+2.00\times10^{-6}\,\text{C})(+1.00\times10^{-6}\,\text{C})}{(0.500\,\text{m})^2}\hat{r}_{2\to1}$$

$$= 0.0719\,\text{N}\,\hat{r}_{2\to1}$$

Since the unit vector points in the $-x$-direction, we express the force as $-0.0719\,\text{N}\,\hat{i}$.

Similarly, for the force that q_3 exerts on q_1 we have

$$\vec{F}_{3\to1} = \frac{1}{4\pi\varepsilon_0}\frac{q_3q_1}{r_{31}^2}\hat{r}_{3\to1}$$

$$= \frac{1}{4\pi\varepsilon_0}\frac{(-3.00\times10^{-6}\,\text{C})(+1.00\times10^{-6}\,\text{C})}{(1.50\,\text{m})^2}\hat{r}_{3\to1}$$

$$= -0.0120\,\text{N}\,\hat{r}_{3\to1}$$

The $\hat{r}_{3\to1}$ is in the $-y$-direction, and the force $\vec{F}_{3\to1}$ is in the $+y$-direction:

$$\vec{F}_{3\to1} = +0.0120\,\text{N}\,\hat{j}$$

Thus, the net force acting on q_1 can be written as

$$\vec{F}_{\text{net}\to1} = -0.0719\,\text{N}\,\hat{i} + 0.0120\,\text{N}\,\hat{j}$$

The magnitude of the net force is

$$\sqrt{(-0.0719)^2 + (+0.0120)^2} = 0.0729\,\text{N}.$$

The direction will be above the $-x$-axis at an angle ϕ given by

$$\tan\phi = \frac{0.0120}{0.0719};\quad \phi = 9.46°$$

Making sense of the result:

Charge 2 will repel charge 1, so charge 1 will experience a force directed to the left. Charge 3 will attract charge 1, so charge 1 will experience an upward force. These directions are consistent with what we found. The separation of charges 1 and 3 is three times the separation for charges 1 and 2, and the same magnitude of charge 3 is 1.5 times the magnitude of charge 2. Thus, the inverse square distance factor, 1/9, will more than offset the greater charge magnitude. When we combine the two forces, we should get a net force that is to the left and upward, with the leftward component dominating, which is consistent with our result.

LO 5

19-5   Electric Field

When a charge experiences an electric force, you could consider that the force is caused by a so-called action-at-a-distance, with the force caused directly by various other charges located at different displacements. Another way to explain the force is that the other charges create an electric field, and the charge responds to that electric field. Both views are valuable frameworks. When dealing with a few charges, it is often easiest to consider a vector superposition of individual electric forces. However, as we will see in Chapter 21, we can define an energy density present in an electric field, and it is helpful in situations involving distributions of many charges to think in terms of the electric field.

Recall that we can think of the vector of the acceleration due to gravity, $\vec{g}$, as being a gravitational field, as described in Chapter 11. If we place a mass m in this field, we observe a gravitational force $m\vec{g}$. If we want to calculate the gravitational field in a region, we can find the gravitational force on some test mass, divide by that mass, and the result would be the field, $\vec{g}$.

We can define an electric field in an analogous way: place a small positive test charge q in a region, measure the electric force on it, $\vec{F}$, and divide that force by the test charge to obtain the field, $\vec{E}$. In the same way that current is defined in terms of a flow of positive charges by convention only, again, electric field direction is by convention always defined in terms of the force on a positive test charge. Therefore, electric field is simply defined as the electric force per unit charge.

KEY EQUATION
$$\vec{E} = \frac{\vec{F}}{q} \qquad (19\text{-}3)$$

For an electric field at a distance r from a single point charge Q, we can combine Coulomb's law with Equation (19-3):

KEY EQUATION
$$\vec{E} = \frac{1}{4\pi\varepsilon_0} \frac{Q}{r^2}\hat{r} \qquad (19\text{-}4)$$

where $\hat{r}$ is a unit vector pointing away from the charge Q.

The electric field points *away* from a positive charge and *toward* a negative charge. The electric field is strongest near the charge, and decreases as the inverse square of the distance from the centre of the charge. These characteristics are illustrated in Figure 19-7. When we have multiple charges we draw electric field lines that start on positive charges and end on negative charges.

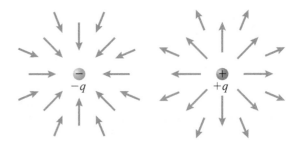

Figure 19-7 The electric field vectors for various points around a negative charge (left) and a positive charge (right)

✓ **CHECKPOINT**

C-19-5 Charged Particle in an Electric Field

A negatively charged particle is moving in the $+x$-direction, but is slowing down. What is the direction of the electric field?
(a) $+x$-direction
(b) $-x$-direction
(c) $+y$-direction
(d) $-y$-direction

C-19-5 (a) The particle is moving in the +x-direction but slowing, so the acceleration must be in the −x-direction. From Newton's second law, the force must therefore be in the −x-direction as well. From $\vec{F} = q\vec{E}$, if the charge (q) is negative, then $\vec{F}$ and $\vec{E}$ must be in opposite directions. Therefore, the electric field is in the +x-direction.

MAKING CONNECTIONS

Inkjet and Laser Printers

Inkjet printers use electric fields to deflect tiny charged drops of ink to form the desired character or image (Figure 19-8). The drops are formed by rapidly heating and vaporizing ink in a chamber or by using a piezoelectric crystal to compress the ink chamber. In both cases, the drops carry charges, and their vertical motion is precisely controlled by electric fields. Modern inkjet printers have ink drops as small as a picolitre, and the ink is typically moving at 10 to 50 m/s when it leaves the print head. The electric fields used for deflection are typically of the order of 100 kN/C. The concept of inkjet printing was first proposed by Lord Kelvin in 1867, but the technology did not become commercially viable until the mid–1970s.

Laser printers use electric charge as well but in a different way. Laser light temporarily changes the conductivity of a photosensitive coating on a drum inside the printer, creating a pattern of static charge on the drum. Toner particles are electrostatically attracted to the charged areas of the drum. When a sheet of paper contacts the drum, most of the toner particles adhere to the paper, transferring the image. A heater then fuses the powdery toner to the paper, making the image indelible.

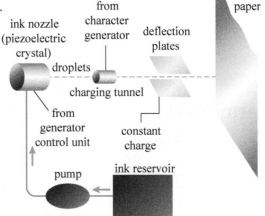

Figure 19-8 Inkjet printers use electric fields to deflect charged ink drops.

North America's First Electron Microscope

The resolution of an optical microscope is limited according to the wavelength of the light that it uses. The effective wavelength of electrons—the de Broglie wavelength (Chapter 31)—can be much shorter than the wavelength of visible light. In 1938, two University of Toronto graduate students, James Hillier (1915–2007) and Albert Prebus (1913–1997), built the first electron microscope in North America. The instrument, which was capable of magnifications of 20 000×, was a major advance over earlier European attempts and is sometimes credited as the first successful electron microscope. Electron microscopes use electric fields to accelerate the electrons that form the image and to position the beam of electrons when scanning an object. Scanning electron microscopes (SEMs) have many applications in science, engineering, and medicine. Figure 19-9 is an image of a virus taken with a modern electron microscope.

CLIPAREA1 Custom media/Shutterstock

Figure 19-9 A modern electron microscope image of a virus

---

applying an electric field produces very little, if any, current. Examples of good insulators are glass, ceramic, and paper, although many other materials such as various plastics are relatively good insulators.

Some molecules are polarized, although they have no net charge. In polar molecules, some electrons that are shared in bonds with the atoms in the molecule are pulled more strongly to one or more of the atoms, causing an uneven distribution of charge within the molecule. For example, in a water molecule, the oxygen atom attracts the shared electrons more strongly, so it is negatively charged, and the hydrogen atoms are positively charged. In the presence of an external electric field, the charged atoms in polar molecules shift somewhat. This slight shift of charge causes an additional electric field that opposes the external electric field. Materials that respond to electric fields in this way are called dielectrics. There is very little current in dielectrics: charge displaces within the polar molecules but does not leave the molecules with a net overall charge. In Chapter 21, we will examine an important application of dielectric materials in electronics.

The term "dielectric" was first proposed by the historian and philosopher of science William Whewell (1794–1866). He also introduced a number of other terms, including anode, cathode, physicist, and scientist.

✓ CHECKPOINT

C-19-6 Fields in Dielectrics

Two parallel horizontal conductors are separated by a liquid dielectric. The top conductor is positively charged, and the bottom conductor is negatively charged. How are the molecules in the dielectric material aligned?
(a) The positive ends of the molecules are toward the top.
(b) The positive ends of the molecules are toward the bottom.
(c) The positive ends of the molecules are toward the right.
(d) There is no net alignment of the molecules.

C-19-6 (b) The dielectric molecules are attracted toward the negative external charges (and the dielectric negative ends of the molecules are attracted to the positive external charges).

LO 6

19-6 Conductors, Insulators, and Dielectrics

We can classify materials according to how readily charge in the materials moves in response to an electric field. Some of the electrons in a conductor, such as copper, move readily when we apply an electric field, resulting in significant current flow. In contrast, the electrons and protons in insulators are so tightly bound in the atoms that

---

LO 7

19-7 Electric Dipoles

A particularly important configuration of charges is an electric dipole, two charges of equal magnitude but opposite sign that are separated by some distance, d. Even though the net charge is zero, a dipole produces an electric field because of the separation of the charges. The superposition principle applies for electric fields. In situations with multiple point charges, we can find the electric field at a point due to each charge separately, and then do a

EXAMPLE 19-4

Electric Field of a Dipole

Consider a dipole lying along the x-axis and centred at the origin. Derive an expression for the electric field at a point on the y-axis.

SOLUTION

Let r represent the distance from the point on the y-axis to the origin (the centre of the dipole). Draw the dipole and the electric field vectors for each charge, as shown in Figure 19-10. The magnitudes of these two electric field vectors are the same because the magnitudes of the charges are identical, as are the distances to the point. Therefore, by symmetry, the downward component of one field vector exactly cancels the upward component of the other, and the net electric field is the sum of

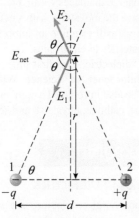

Figure 19-10 An electric dipole with charges $-q$ and $+q$ separated by distance d

the two x-components (both of which point in the $-x$-direction). Symmetry can often be used to simplify applications of the superposition principle for electric forces and fields.

The magnitudes of each of the two electric field vectors are

$$|\vec{E_1}| = |\vec{E_2}| = \frac{1}{4\pi\varepsilon_0}\frac{q}{\left(r^2 + \left(\frac{d}{2}\right)^2\right)} = \frac{1}{4\pi\varepsilon_0}\frac{q}{\left(r^2 + \frac{d^2}{4}\right)}$$

The net electric field is to the left ($-\hat{i}$-direction), and its magnitude is

$$|\vec{E}_{net}| = 2|\vec{E_1}|\cos\theta$$

We can express the angle θ in terms of d and r:

$$\cos\theta = \frac{d/2}{\sqrt{r^2 + \frac{d^2}{4}}}$$

Combining these results we have

$$\vec{E}_{net} = \left(-\frac{1}{4\pi\varepsilon_0}\right)\frac{qd}{\left(r^2 + \frac{d^2}{4}\right)^{3/2}}\hat{i}$$

Making sense of the result:

The direction of the field is the same as the direction from the positive to the negative charge, which makes sense. At large distances from the dipole ($r \gg d$), the electric field is approximately proportional to $1/r^3$, and the field from a single charge is proportional to $1/r^2$. Thus, the electric field from a dipole weakens faster with increasing distance, which makes sense because the fields from the two opposite charges partially cancel each other.

vector addition to obtain the net electric field at the point. In Example 19-4, we demonstrate this process for the electric field of a dipole.

We saw in the above example that the electric field for a dipole goes down as the inverse cube of the distance. It is common to define an electric dipole moment, $\vec{p}$, for charges $+q$ and $-q$ separated by a displacement vector $\vec{d}$ that points from the negative charge to the positive charge:

$$\vec{p} = q\vec{d} \tag{19-5}$$

The SI units for electric dipole moments are coulomb-metres. With this definition, we can write the result from Example 19-4 as

$$\vec{E}_{net} \approx \frac{1}{4\pi\varepsilon_0}\frac{\vec{p}}{r^3} \qquad \text{when } r \gg d \tag{19-6}$$

 CHECKPOINT

C-19-7 Dipole Moments

A proton and an electron are separated by 10 nm. What is the dipole moment?

(a) 1.6×10^{-27} C m directed toward the proton

(b) 1.6×10^{-27} C m directed toward the electron

(c) 3.2×10^{-27} C m directed toward the proton

(d) 3.2×10^{-27} C m directed toward the electron.

C-19-7 (a) The dipole moment is $\vec{p} = q\vec{d}$, where $\vec{d}$ is a displacement vector from the negative to the positive charge, and q is the magnitude of each charge (1.6×10^{-19} C).

ELECTRICITY, MAGNETISM, AND OPTICS

19-8 Electric Dipoles in Molecular Physics

Electric dipoles are of crucial importance in molecular physics. The 1936 Nobel Prize in Chemistry was awarded to Petrus Josephus Wilhelmus Debye (1884–1966) for his work on dipole moments. A convenient unit for dipole moments of molecules, the debye (D), was named in his honour (1 D = 3.34×10^{-30} C m).

Electrically, polar molecules can be approximated by a dipole moment. Among the strongest molecular dipoles are simple ionic compounds such as sodium chloride (NaCl), with a dipole moment of 9.0 D, and potassium bromide (KBr), with a dipole moment of about 10.4 D. Molecules of diatomic elements, such as chlorine (Cl_2), have no separation of charge and, hence, zero dipole moment. A number of other nonionic molecules, including CO and CO_2, have near zero dipole moments.

When an external electric field is applied to a substance with a dipole moment, the molecules will align with the field if the molecules are free to rotate. Such movement is the basis for heating in microwave ovens. In a typical household microwave oven, the electric field is applied at a frequency of 2.45 GHz. Water is a polar molecule, with a dipole moment of approximately 1.8 D. As the molecules try to align with the alternating electric field, they rapidly rotate back and forth, and the resulting thermal motion heats the food. Effective heating by this technique depends on a polar molecule (e.g., microwaves heat water more effectively than fats) and an appropriate applied frequency. The technique is called dielectric heating (because it works effectively on dielectrics, materials with polar molecules and electric insulator properties). There are many other applications of electric dipoles in science and technology.

✔ CHECKPOINT

C-19-8 Heating Polar Molecules

Polar molecules experience the most heating in an alternating electric field when their dipole moments are

(a) 0.0 D;
(b) 5.0 D;
(c) 8.0 D;
(d) 11 D.

C-19-8 (d) A higher dipole moment will result in more effective alignment of the molecule and, therefore, with an alternating field, more thermal motion and heating.

19-9 Electric Fields from Continuous Charge Distributions

So far, we have calculated electric fields produced by a finite number of discrete point charges. Now, we will consider electric field due to a charge spread uniformly over a linear element (and later over a surface). First, we need to introduce the concept of linear charge density. When a total charge Q is uniformly distributed along a thin rod of length L, we can define a linear charge density, μ, as follows:

$$\mu = \frac{Q}{L} \qquad (19\text{-}7)$$

Linear charge density has units of C/m.

✔ CHECKPOINT

C-19-9 Linear Charge Density

When a charge of 25 μC is uniformly distributed on a thin rod that is 2.5 cm long, the linear charge density is

(a) 1.0 mC/m;
(b) 10 mC/m;
(c) 10 C/m;
(d) 1.0 kC/m.

C-19-9 (a) Divide the charge expressed in coulombs by the length in metres to get the linear charge density of 0.0010 C/m.

To find the net electric field around a continuously distributed charge, we need to use calculus. We write an expression for the field produced by each infinitesimal charge element dq, and then integrate over all of the charge. Often, symmetry allows us to simplify the calculation because components in one or more directions cancel out.

Consider a thin, uniformly charged rod with linear charge density μ. If we define an x-axis along the length of the rod, a length element dx of the rod will have a charge dq given by

$$dq = \mu \, dx \qquad (19\text{-}8)$$

The contribution from this element of charge to the electric field at a point a distance r from the element is

$$d\vec{E} = \frac{1}{4\pi\varepsilon_0}\frac{dq}{r^2}\hat{r} \qquad (19\text{-}9)$$

Note that the unit vector $\hat{r}$ points away from the charge element. Therefore, the electric field element points away from the charge element when dq is positive, and toward the charge element when dq is negative.

We then integrate over the entire charged object to find the total electric field:

KEY EQUATION
$$\vec{E}_{\text{net}} = \int d\vec{E} = \int_{\text{object}} \frac{1}{4\pi\varepsilon_0}\frac{dq}{r^2}\hat{r} \qquad (19\text{-}10)$$

ELECTRICITY, MAGNETISM, AND OPTICS

EXAMPLE 19-5

Electric Force from a Charged Rod

A thin, horizontal rod of length 2.00 m carries a total positive charge of 98.0 μC distributed uniformly along its length. A single small charge, Q, of $+2.00$ μC, is 1.00 m from the right end of the charged rod. Find the total electric force acting on the charge Q.

SOLUTION

As we can see from Figure 19-11, every element of the charge on the rod produces a contribution to the electric field that is in the $+x$-direction, so these contributions all simply add together.

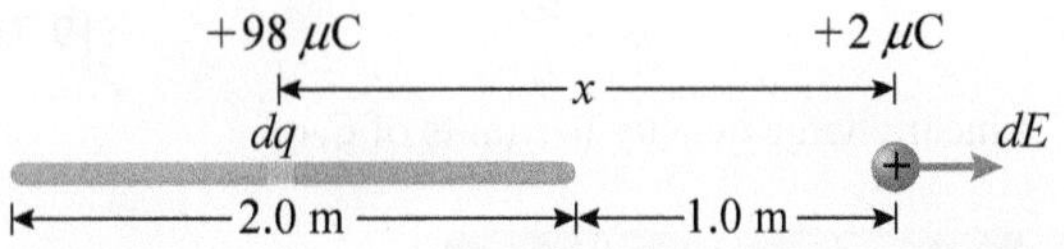

+98 μC   +2 μC

x

dq dE

2.0 m   1.0 m

Figure 19-11 To find the net electric field from a charged rod, we integrate the contributions from the various infinitesimal elements of the rod

First, we will express the charge element dq in terms of the linear charge density of the rod and a length element dx:

$$\mu = \frac{\text{charge}}{\text{length}} = \frac{98.0 \times 10^{-6}\,\text{C}}{2.00\,\text{m}} = 4.90 \times 10^{-5}\,\text{C/m}$$

$$dq = \mu\,dx = 4.90 \times 10^{-5}\,dx$$

Note that we have omitted units in the intermediate steps for clarity. Since all elements of charge on the rod produce force elements with the same direction, we can simplify Equation (19-5) to solve for just the magnitude of the electric force:

$$E_{\text{net}} = \frac{1}{4\pi\varepsilon_0} \int_1^3 \frac{\mu\,dx}{x^2}$$

$$= \frac{\mu}{4\pi\varepsilon_0} \int_1^3 \frac{dx}{x^2}\,dx$$

$$= \frac{4.90 \times 10^{-5}}{4\pi\varepsilon_0}\left[-\frac{1}{x}\right]_1^3$$

$$= \frac{4.90 \times 10^{-5}}{4\pi\varepsilon_0}\left[-\frac{1}{3} - \left(-\frac{1}{1}\right)\right]$$

$$= \frac{4.90 \times 10^{-5}\,\text{C/m}}{4\pi[8.85 \times 10^{-12}\,\text{C}^2/(\text{N}\cdot\text{m}^2)]}\left[+\frac{2}{3}\right]$$

$$= 294\,\text{kN/C}$$

To find the force on the charge Q, we use the relationship between electric field and force:

$$F = qE = (2.00 \times 10^{-6}\,\text{C})(2.94 \times 10^5\,\text{N/C}) = 0.588\,\text{N}$$

Since Q is a positive charge, the direction of the force is the same as for the electric field, that is, in the $+x$-direction.

Making sense of the result:

To check the order of magnitude of the force, we can replace the charge along the rod with a point charge of 98 μC at a distance of 2 m (average position) from the other charge. Applying Coulomb's law then gives a force of 0.4 N, which indicates that the answer we obtained is reasonable. (Note that this approximation underestimates the actual force because the force depends on the inverse square of the distance between the charges.)

We can use similar calculus techniques to find the net force on a charged object placed near a line of charge, but usually it is easier to solve such problems in two steps: first, calculate the electric field and second, use the relationship between force, charge, and electric field.

We can define surface charge density, σ, as the charge per unit area of a surface. We give both regular and differential forms of the surface charge density relationship below:

$$\sigma = \frac{Q}{A} = \frac{dq}{dA} \qquad (19\text{-}11)$$

In Example 19-6, we demonstrate the use of superposition, integration, symmetry, and surface charge density in finding the electric field of a charged ring and an infinite plane.

EXAMPLE 19-6

Electric Field from a Charged Ring and an Infinite Plane

(a) A horizontal ring of radius r carries a uniform charge and has a total charge of $+Q$. What is the electric field at a point a distance y vertically above the plane of the ring?

(b) Use your result from part (a) to find the electric field a distance y above an infinite plane with surface charge density σ.

12

SOLUTION

(a) The situation is shown in Figure 19-12, where we have shown the electric field dE from an infinitesimal charge element dq. We can consider the infinitesimal element as approximating a point charge dq, and we obtain the following relationship for the magnitude of the contribution of the electric field from dq:

$$dE = \frac{1}{4\pi\varepsilon_0} \frac{dq}{(y^2 + r^2)}$$

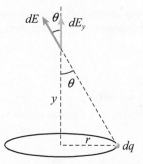

Figure 19-12 Example 19-6. A narrow ring carries a uniform charge.

At this point, it is important to consider the symmetry of the situation. Since the ring is uniformly charged, the components of the electric field in the xz-plane will all cancel, and the net electric field must be vertical. The vertical component is given by

$$dE_y = dE \cos\theta = \frac{1}{4\pi\varepsilon_0} \frac{y \, dq}{(y^2 + r^2)^{3/2}}$$

where we have used

$$\cos\theta = \frac{y}{(y^2 + r^2)^{1/2}}$$

Calculating the integral, and using the facts that both y and r are constant in this situation and that the integral of the charge element around the ring is simply the total charge on the ring Q, we have the following for the net electric field:

$$E = \int dE_y = \frac{1}{4\pi\varepsilon_0} \frac{y \, Q}{(y^2 + r^2)^{3/2}}$$

This expression gives the magnitude of the electric field. Its direction is vertically upward when the ring charge Q is positive and downward when it is negative.

(b) In this situation, we want to consider the electric field at a distance y above an infinite plane that is uniformly charged with surface charge density. The approach we will take is to imagine the plane as being made up of an infinite number of rings of charge of increasing radius. We then integrate over those rings.

If we consider a ring of radius r and width dr, then the charge on just that ring (the entire ring, not just a little piece of it as we did for dq), which we will call dQ, is given by $dQ = 2\pi dr\sigma$.

As in part (a), the symmetry of the situation means that the net electric field must be in a vertical direction. We can use the result from part (a) to find the contribution to this electric field just due to this ring:

$$dE = \frac{1}{4\pi\varepsilon_0} \frac{y \, dQ}{(y^2 + r^2)^{3/2}} = \frac{1}{4\pi\varepsilon_0} \frac{y \, 2\pi r dr\sigma}{(y^2 + r^2)^{3/2}}$$

To find the total electric field (due to all the rings), we need to integrate over all r values to infinity:

$$E = \int dE = \frac{2\pi\sigma}{4\pi\varepsilon_0} \int_{r=0}^{r=\infty} \frac{y \, rdr}{(y^2 + r^2)^{3/2}}$$

In calculating the integral, we can make the following substitution:

$$u = y^2 + r^2 \quad \text{and} \quad du = 2rdr$$

This allows us to calculate the integral:

$$E = \frac{\pi\sigma y}{4\pi\varepsilon_0} \int_{u=y^2}^{u=\infty} \frac{du}{u^{3/2}} = \left[-2\frac{\pi\sigma y}{4\pi\varepsilon_0} u^{-1/2} \right]_{y^2}^{\infty}$$

$$= -2\frac{\sigma y}{4\varepsilon_0}\left(0 - \frac{1}{y} \right) = \frac{\sigma}{2\varepsilon_0}$$

The electric field is vertical (upward when the charge is positive) and has the magnitude given.

Making sense of the result:

At first glance, it may be surprising that the strength of the electric field does not depend on the distance y that you are above the charged plane. Qualitatively, what is happening here is that, although the element of the charged plane nearest to you does produce a stronger electric field, the contributions from more distant parts of the plane are at a larger angle when you are close and have less contribution. The net result is independent of the distance from the charged infinite plane. In Chapter 20, you will see an alternative way to get the same result.

Most everyday forces are electromagnetic in nature. Electric charges are either positive or negative. Like charges repel, and unlike charges attract.

Static electricity is the surface charging of an object. Some materials hold on to their electrons more firmly than other materials, and contact followed by separation causes triboelectric charging. The triboelectric series is used to predict which materials take on positive charges and which take on negative charges when rubbed.

Conductors are materials in which a current flows in response to an applied electric field. Insulators are materials in which virtually no current flows. Dielectrics do not have a net current flow, but they do have charges that can be displaced when an electric field is applied.

Charge and Current

The SI unit of charge is the coulomb, C. Current is the amount of charge that flows past a point in a given time:

$$I = \frac{\Delta q}{\Delta t} \qquad (19\text{-}1)$$

Coulomb's Law

The electric force that one charge exerts on another is given by Coulomb's law:

$$\vec{F}_{1 \to 2} = \frac{1}{4\pi\varepsilon_0} \frac{q_1 q_2}{r^2} \hat{r}_{1 \to 2} \qquad (19\text{-}2)$$

where q_1 and q_2 are the two charges, r is the distance between the centres of the charges, $\hat{r}_{1 \to 2}$ is a unit vector that points from q_1 to q_2, and ε_0 is the permittivity of free space.

Superposition Principle

For systems of point charges, we can find the electric force or electric field separately for each charge, and then vectorially add the results to find the net force or field.

Electric Field

The electric field equals the net electric force on a small positive point charge divided by the magnitude of the point charge:

$$\vec{E} = \frac{\vec{F}}{q} \qquad (19\text{-}3)$$

Dipole Moment

For two opposite charges of equal magnitude ($+q, -q$) separated by displacement $\vec{d}$, the dipole moment is

$$\vec{p} = q\vec{d} \qquad (19\text{-}5)$$

Linear Charge Density

Linear charge density is the charge per unit length:

$$\mu = \frac{Q}{L} = \frac{dq}{d\ell} \qquad (19\text{-}7)$$

Electric Fields for Continuous Charge Distributions

For continuous charge distributions, the net electric field is given by

$$\vec{E}_{\text{net}} = \int_{\text{object}} \frac{1}{4\pi\varepsilon_0} \frac{dq}{r^2} \hat{r} \qquad (19\text{-}10)$$

Often, we can use symmetry to simplify the calculations.

When dealing with surfaces, a surface charge density is used in the calculations:

$$\sigma = \frac{Q}{A} = \frac{dq}{dA} \qquad (19\text{-}11)$$

Applications: static charging, electrostatic damage to electronics, inkjet and laser printers, electron microscopes, microwave heating

Key Terms: conductor, coulomb, Coulomb's law, current, dielectric, dipole moment, electric dipole, elementary charge, electric field, insulator, linear charge density, permittivity of free space, static electricity, superposition principle, surface charge density, triboelectric charging, triboelectric series

QUESTIONS

1. You remove a piece of polyethylene tape from a glass surface. Which statement best describes what will happen? Table 19-1 may be helpful in answering this question.
   (a) You need rubbing for triboelectric charging, so no electrostatic charge results.
   (b) The tape becomes positively charged, and the glass becomes negatively charged.
   (c) The glass becomes positively charged, and the tape becomes negatively charged.
   (d) Both the tape and the glass take on a positive charge.

2. You rub a balloon through your hair, and it becomes charged. You rub a second similar balloon through your hair. When the two balloons are tied to electrically insulating strings, what happens when you hold the end of the strings away from the balloon?
   (a) The balloons move away from each other.
   (b) The balloons come together and discharge.
   (c) The balloons come together, but each retains its charge.
   (d) The balloons come together, and each charges to a higher value.

14

3. Use Table 19-1 to determine which of the following combinations will have the greatest triboelectric charge when rubbed together.
   (a) paper and polystyrene
   (b) plastic wrap and glass
   (c) hair and wool
   (d) PVC and polyethylene tape

4. Refer to Table 19-1 when answering this question. Which of the following statements applies when you rub plastic wrap and glass together?
   (a) There is very little charging.
   (b) The glass becomes positively charged, and the plastic wrap becomes negatively charged.
   (c) The glass becomes negatively charged, and the plastic wrap becomes positively charged.
   (d) Both the glass and the plastic wrap become positively charged.

5. A charge of 50 μC flows past a point in 0.05 s. What is the resulting current?
   (a) 10 μA
   (b) 10 mA
   (c) 1 mA
   (d) 10 A

6. A positive charge q is placed near a larger, stationary positive charge $5q$. What happens when you let go of charge q?
   (a) It accelerates toward the larger charge.
   (b) It moves away from the larger charge with constant velocity.
   (c) It moves away from the larger charge with constant acceleration.
   (d) It moves away from the larger charge but with an acceleration that decreases the farther it moves away.

7. You have two charges, q and $4q$. Charge q exerts a force of magnitude F on charge $4q$. What is the magnitude of the force that $4q$ exerts on q?
   (a) $F/4$
   (b) F
   (c) $2F$
   (d) $4F$

8. You have two fixed charges, $+Q$ on the left and $+4Q$ on the right. Where could you place a third small charge, $+q$, along a line joining the two charges such that it would experience zero net electrostatic force?
   (a) at a point beyond the $+Q$ charge to the left
   (b) at a point 1/4 of the way between the charges, closer to the $+Q$ charge
   (c) at a point 1/3 of the way between the charges, closer to the $+Q$ charge
   (d) There is no location where it would experience zero electrostatic force.

9. Two charges, $+Q$ and $+Q$, are located a distance L apart. A second pair of charges, $+2Q$ and $-2Q$, is placed at a distance $2L$ apart. Which situation has the larger electrostatic force?
   (a) The force is the same in the two situations.
   (b) The force is greater in the case with the $+Q$ charges.
   (c) The force is greater in the case with the $+2Q$ charges.
   (d) Since the charges are both positive, the force is zero in both cases.

10. A proton is moving in the $+x$-direction, and its speed is increasing with a constant acceleration. What can you conclude about the external electric field?
    (a) The electric field is in the $-x$-direction and constant.
    (b) The electric field is in the $-x$-direction and increasing.

(c) The electric field is in the $+x$-direction and constant.
(d) The electric field is in the $+x$-direction and increasing.

11. A positive charge is located at the origin of an xyz-coordinate system. What is the electric field direction at the point $(x = 0, y = -1, z = 0)$?
    (a) $-\hat{\imath}$
    (b) $+\hat{\imath}$
    (c) $-\hat{\jmath}$
    (d) $+\hat{\jmath}$

12. An electron is located at the origin of an xyz-coordinate system. What is the direction of the electric field at the point $(x = 1, y = 0, z = 0)$?
    (a) $-\hat{\imath}$
    (b) $+\hat{\imath}$
    (c) $-\hat{\jmath}$
    (d) $+\hat{\jmath}$

13. You are midway between two charges, $+Q$ to the left ($-x$-direction) and $-Q$ to the right ($+x$-direction). What is the direction of the electric field at your location?
    (a) $-\hat{\imath}$
    (b) $+\hat{\imath}$
    (c) There is zero net electric field at your location.
    (d) $+\hat{\jmath}$

14. If you slightly increase the distance between a proton and an electron, what happens to the dipole moment?
    (a) The dipole moment is slightly larger.
    (b) The dipole moment is slightly smaller.
    (c) There is no dipole moment before or after.
    (d) The dipole moment has not changed because the charges are still the same.

15. Consider two oppositely charged vertical parallel plates with equal magnitudes of charge. The left plate is positively charged. The space between the conductors is filled with a dielectric. How are the molecules in the dielectric material aligned?
    (a) The positive ends of the molecules are toward the left.
    (b) The positive ends of the molecules are toward the right.
    (c) The positive ends of the molecules are toward the bottom.
    (d) There is no net alignment of the molecules.

16. A radio wave has an electric field of approximately 0.150 N/C. What is the approximate electric force on an electron that is in the path of the radio wave?
    (a) 0.15 N in a direction opposite to the direction of the electric field
    (b) 0.15 N in the same direction as the direction of the radio wave electric field
    (c) 2.4×10^{-20} N in a direction opposite to the direction of the electric field
    (d) 2.4×10^{-20} N in the same direction as the direction of the radio wave electric field

PROBLEMS BY SECTION

For problems, star ratings will be used, (✶, ✶✶, or ✶✶✶), with more stars meaning more challenging problems.

Section 19-2   Electric Charge

17. ✶ If 250 billion elementary charges pass a point in one second, what is the current?

15

18. ✶✶ When you rub a gold sphere with rabbit's fur, the gold takes on a negative charge (and the rabbit fur positive). Suppose the gold sphere has a mass of 100.0 g and it obtains a net charge of 0.500 μC. Estimate the ratio of the number of electrons added to the gold sphere to the number originally there.

Section 19-3 Coulomb's Law

19. ✶✶ One estimate of the mean separation between the proton and the electron in a hydrogen atom is 53.0 pm (if we picture them as classical particles).
    (a) What is the Coulomb force between the proton and the electron?
    (b) Set this force equal to ma, where the acceleration is a classical centripetal acceleration. What is the speed of the electron?

20. ✶✶ A $+35.0$ nC charge is place at the origin of a coordinate system, and a -25.0 nC charge is placed at the point $(0.100$ m, -0.0500 m).
    (a) Determine the magnitude and the direction of the force that the positive charge exerts on the negative charge. Use ijk notation for your result.
    (b) Determine the magnitude and direction of the force of the negative charge on the positive charge.

Section 19-4 Multiple Point Charges

21. ✶✶ A -2.00 μC is 3.00 cm to the left of a $+1.00$ μC charge. Where must a $+4.00$ μC be placed to make the net electric force on the $+1.00$ μC zero?

22. ✶✶✶ A square has charge $+Q$ on three of the corners and charge $-Q$ on the bottom-right corner. A charge $+q$ is placed at the exact centre of the square. What is the net force on this charge?

Section 19-5 Electric Field

23. ✶✶ Strong electric fields can be present inside biological cell membranes. The field in a particular cell at a certain location is 5.00 N/μC (note the units). What force magnitude would result on an ion that has a charge of $+2e$?

24. ✶✶ Consider a point midway between two point charges, a $+24.0$ pC charge on the right and a -12.0 pC charge on the left. The charges are separated by 0.240 mm. What is the electric field at this midway point?

Section 19-7 Electric Dipoles

25. ✶✶ An electric dipole consists of one positive and one negative elementary charge. The magnitude of the dipole moment is 1.75 D. What is the separation of the two charges? Express your answer in nanometres.

26. ✶✶ In Example 19-4, we found an expression for the electric field for a dipole when we were at a perpendicular distance from the dipole. Derive a similar expression for the case when you are at a distance in line with the dipole direction. What is the approximate expression for this case when the distance from the dipole is much greater than the dimensions of the dipole?

Section 19-9 Electric Fields from Continuous Charge Distributions

27. ✶✶ A thin, fixed rod is 25.0 mm long and carries a total positive charge of 75.0 nC distributed uniformly along its length. A single small charge $Q = 1.00$ μC is placed 100.0 mm from the left end of the charged rod. What is the total electric force on the charge Q?

28. ✶✶ A thin, fixed rod is 40.0 mm long and carries a total positive charge of $+40.0$ μC. The rod is located on the x-axis, with its centre at the origin of the coordinate system. What is the electric field at a point on the y-axis directly above the centre of the rod and a distance of 120. mm from the rod?

COMPREHENSIVE PROBLEMS

29. ✶ There are a number of different types of lightning with different characteristics. One estimate for a large bolt of positive polarity lightning is that it transfers 350 C of charge and has an average current of 120 kA. Estimate how long the lightning current flows.

30. ✶ Many first-year university textbooks write Coulomb's law with a simplified form for the constant, calling the whole expression k. What is the value of k?

31. ✶✶ Suppose that Earth and the Moon had opposite charges of equal magnitude. What would that magnitude be if the electrostatic force equalled the gravitational attraction between Earth and the Moon?

32. ✶✶ Charges Q and q are stationary at opposite corners of a square with side a as shown in Figure 19-13. Assume that Q is a positive charge. Derive an expression for the value of charge q in terms of the variables of the question so that there is no net force on charge Q. As part of your answer, clearly indicate whether charge q is positive or negative.

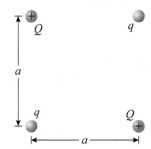

Figure 19-13 Problem 32

33. ✶✶ Three equal charges of $+0.250$ μC are at the vertices of an equilateral triangle with sides 3.25 cm. What is the magnitude of the force on each charge? What is the direction of each force?

34. ✶✶ In Figure 19-14, a small charge with a mass of 1.0 g and a charge of -0.80 μC is attached to the end of a massless string. The charge hangs at an angle of 30° when a uniform electric field, E, is applied in the horizontal direction.
    (a) What is the direction of the electric field?
    (b) Draw an FBD for the small mass.
    (c) Calculate the magnitude of the electric field.

16

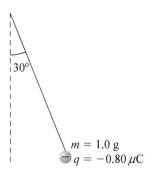

m = 1.0 g
q = −0.80 μC

Figure 19-14   Problem 34

35. ✱✱ Four electric charges are arranged as shown in Figure 19-15. Find the electric field at point P.

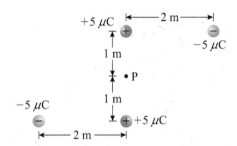

Figure 19-15   Problem 35

36. ✱✱✱ The charges in Figure 19-16 are held rigidly in their positions. Determine the direction and magnitude of the net electric field at point P. Assume the charges and other quantities are known to two significant figures (e.g. 2.0 μC). (Hint: Use symmetry to simplify the calculation.)

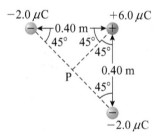

Figure 19-16   Problem 36

37. ✱ A proton has an instantaneous acceleration of 4.0×10^8 m/s² in the +x-direction. What electric field could account for this acceleration?

38. ✱ The electric field near Earth's surface points downward and has a magnitude of approximately 150 N/C. What is the force on an electron due to this electric field? Find the ratio of this force to the gravitational force on the electron.

39. ✱✱ A positive ion with a charge of $+3e$ is fixed at the origin of a coordinate system. An electron is located at $x = 0.20$ μm on the x-axis. Where is the electric field zero?

40. ✱✱ A cathode ray tube (CRT) display accelerates an electron from rest to 2.50×10^7 m/s within a distance of 0.950 cm in the acceleration region.

(a) What is the electric field in the CRT acceleration chamber?

(b) Does the electric field point in the direction of acceleration of the electron or in the opposite direction? Explain.

41. ✱✱✱ In the deflection area of an inkjet printer there is an electric field of 95.0 kN/C. Assume that one drop has a volume of 2.00 pL (picolitre) and that the density of the ink is the same as the density of water. A drop moves horizontally at a speed of 25.0 m/s and travels between deflecting plates with a length of 1.25 cm. What is the magnitude of the charge on the drop when the vertical deflection is 0.225 mm? Neglect gravitational acceleration, aerodynamic drag, and any effect from Earth's electric field.

42. ✱✱✱ Consider two dipoles, each with the same dipole moment p (from $+q$ and $−q$ charges separated by distance d). The dipoles are both aligned with the x-axis and are located a distance D apart. The negative end of the right dipole faces the positive end of the left dipole.

(a) Derive an expression for the net force between the dipoles.

(b) What does this expression reduce to for the large-distance approximation of $D \gg d$?

43. ✱✱✱ Dipoles placed in an electric field experience a torque unless they are aligned with the field. For an electric field of 30.0 kN/C directed in the +x-direction, find the torque exerted on a dipole that is aligned in the y-axis direction, with a charge of $−e$ at $y = −25$ nm and $+e$ at $y = +25$ nm.

44. ✱✱✱ In 1909, Robert Millikan (1868–1953) used his famous 1909 oil drop experiment to estimate the elementary charge. In this experiment, small drops of oil were charged, and an electric field was adjusted to help the drops stay suspended. From the required field, the charge on various drops was calculated—they were all whole-number ratios of the elementary charge. The actual analysis has to take into account buoyant forces and other details, but we will simplify it for this problem. Assume that the density of the oil used in the experiment is 820 kg/m³, a drop has a radius of 1.10 μm, and a drop has a charge of $+2e$. What applied electric field is necessary to keep the drop suspended against gravity?

45. ✱✱ A charge of 25.0 μC is uniformly distributed around a thin ring of radius 4.00 cm that is in the xy-plane and centred at the origin. What is the electric field at a point 10.0 cm directly above the centre of this ring? (Hint: Use symmetry to simplify the situation.)

46. ✱✱✱ A charge, α, is uniformly distributed over a circular plate of radius R. Derive an expression for the electric field at a distance d above the centre of the plate.

DATA-RICH PROBLEM

47. ✱✱✱ Table 19-2 lists the electric field at various locations along the +x-axis. The negative sign means that the electric field points in the −x-direction. Assuming that the field was created by a single point charge, determine the value and location of this charge.

Table 19-2   Data for Problem 47

Position, x(m)	Electric Field, E (kN/C)
2.0	−281
3.0	−222
4.0	−180
5.0	−147
6.0	−125
7.0	−106
8.0	−92
9.0	−80

OPEN PROBLEM

48. ✷✷✷   In this problem, we will consider several aspects of atmospheric electricity and lightning discharges. Look up information or make reasonable estimates as required.

(a) First, consider how charging might take place. Lightning-producing clouds are typically very high (10 km or more above surface), and during the active phase of these storms, there are extensive updrafts and downdrafts. In addition, the clouds usually have a mix of hail and water droplets. Explain a possible production mechanism for charging by triboelectricity. Do you expect the top of the clouds to be positively or negatively charged?

(b) As shown in the opening image of this chapter, the lightning strike does not take place in one direct line but in a series of near paths. Explain what you think might be happening.

(c) Weather services register lightning strikes (e.g., you can look up recent Canadian strikes on the Atmospheric Environment Service website). Try to find similar information for other countries. Where does the highest number of lightning strikes per day occur?

(d) List some guidelines for protecting human life during a lightning storm. Certain animals are more frequently killed by lightning. Which animals do you think might be at greater risk? Why?

(e) What are some concerns regarding airplanes and lightning discharges?

 See the text online resources at www.physics1e.nelson.com for Open Problems and Data-Rich Problems related to this chapter.

Chapter 20
Electric Potential and Gauss's Law

Learning Objectives

When you have completed this chapter you should be able to:

1. Calculate electric potential energy for configurations of charges.

2. Define and calculate electric potential for groups of point charges.

3. Draw electric field lines and equipotential lines for collections of electric charges.

4. Use calculus to determine electric fields from electric potentials.

5. Define and use the electron volt as a unit of energy.

6. Draw diagrams of the electric field around conductors.

7. Calculate line, surface, and volume charge densities.

8. Define and calculate the electric flux.

9. State and explain Gauss's law.

10. Use Gauss's law to find the electric field in a variety of situations.

11. Explain charge distribution on conductors and the relative magnitude of the electric field in different regions just outside a conducting surface.

Canada is home to the world's most powerful cyclotron, called TRIUMF (Figure 20-1). TRIUMF is an abbreviation of the original name of the laboratory, the Tri-University Meson Facility, which now has 17 Canadian universities as members. This cyclotron can accelerate protons to almost three-quarters the speed of light. A cyclotron uses a magnetic field to direct charged particles in a circular path inside an acceleration chamber, which is divided into two semicircular sections. Twice during each circuit of the chamber, the charged particles are accelerated by an electric field produced by an electric potential difference between the two sections. The TRIUMF cyclotron accelerates more than a thousand trillion protons each second. While much of the work at TRIUMF focuses on understanding subatomic physics, the cyclotron has a number of other purposes. For example, TRIUMF produces radioisotopes for medical research, and proton beams from the cyclotron have been used to image cancers and to treat eye cancers. Scientists at TRIUMF conduct research in materials science, superconductivity, and hydrogen energy storage mechanisms. Outstanding undergraduate science students are eligible to apply for a TRIUMF summer award.

Courtesy of TRIUMF

Figure 20-1 A portion of the cyclotron area at TRIUMF, the largest and most powerful cyclotron-based accelerator in the world.

For additional Making Connections, Examples, and Checkpoints, as well as activities and experiments to help increase your understanding of the chapter's concepts, please go to the text's online resources at www.physics1e.nelson.com.

ELECTRICITY, MAGNETISM, AND OPTICS

20-1 Electric Potential Energy

Since electrostatic forces are conservative, electric potential energy exists. We can equivalently consider the potential energy as equal to the positive of the work done by an external agent to produce a configuration of charges, or the negative of the work done by the electric field in moving the charges to the configuration. These are equivalent since the external agent must apply a force that is equal in magnitude but opposite in direction to the electric force exerted on a charge by the other charges in the configuration.

Consider the following situation: a positive charge Q is fixed in position, and a second positive charge q is gradually brought toward it. Since like charges repel, a force in the direction of motion is needed to bring the two charges closer together, say, from distance r_1 to r_2 as shown in Figure 20-2. The work done by this external applied force is positive. The force needed varies with the distance between the charges according to Coulomb's law. The Coulomb force on charge q is directed to the left, so the force needed to move the charge is to the right (shown as F in the diagram). The electric potential energy for a charge configuration represents the work that must be done to assemble the distribution.

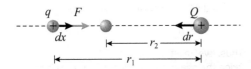

Figure 20-2 A force F must be applied to the right to move a positive charge q toward a fixed positive charge Q.

Since r decreases as the x-coordinate of charge q increases, $dx = -dr$. We can use this relationship when integrating to find the work W_a done by the agent moving the charge.

$$W_a = \int \vec{F} \cdot d\vec{x} = \int_{r_1}^{r_2} \frac{1}{4\pi\varepsilon_0} \frac{Qq}{r^2}(-dr) \qquad (20\text{-}1)$$

When we take the constant terms out of the integral and integrate, we have

$$W_a = -\frac{Qq}{4\pi\varepsilon_0} \int_{r_1}^{r_2} \frac{1}{r^2}\,dr = -\frac{Qq}{4\pi\varepsilon_0}\left[-\frac{1}{r}\right]_{r_1}^{r_2} = \frac{Qq}{4\pi\varepsilon_0}\left[\frac{1}{r_2} - \frac{1}{r_1}\right]$$

$$(20\text{-}2)$$

Since r_2 is less than r_1, the work required to move the charge is positive as expected. Since the external agent did positive work to move charge q, we must have increased the potential energy of the configuration. Equation (20-3) below gives the electric potential energy difference when we move a charge q from a distance r_1 to r_2 from a fixed charge Q. Note that this equation applies for like and

unlike charges as long as the signs of the charges are properly used in the equation:

$$\Delta U_E = \frac{Qq}{4\pi\varepsilon_0}\left[\frac{1}{r_2} - \frac{1}{r_1}\right] \qquad (20\text{-}3)$$

All potential energies are relative. For example, when a mass is on a table, we can use the surface of the table as the zero reference for gravitational potential energy, resulting in the mass having zero potential energy. However, if we use the floor as the zero reference, the mass has positive potential energy. We saw in Chapter 11 that, generally, the most convenient way to define the zero of gravitational potential energy is for the zero level to be when the masses are infinitely far apart. A similar convention is often adopted for electrostatic potential energy—zero when the charges are infinitely far apart. When $r_1 \to \infty$, Equation (20-3) gives the following expression for the potential energy when charges q and Q are a distance r apart:

KEY EQUATION
$$U_E = \frac{Qq}{4\pi\varepsilon_0 r} \qquad (20\text{-}4)$$

Since the existence of potential energy depends on the nature of the field (it being conservative), many physicists prefer to calculate the work W_E done by the electric force when the charge moves (which will be negative in this case), and then set the potential energy $U_E = -W_E$.

✓ CHECKPOINT

C-20-1 Electric Potential Energy

Consider a situation similar to Figure 20-2 but with charge q being negative. The negative charge is moved from a very great distance along the x-axis to a position a short distance from the positive charge. If the potential energy was zero when the charges were infinitely separated, then

(a) positive work must be done by an external agent to move the charge to that position, and the potential energy of the system is positive;

(b) positive work must be done by an external agent to move the charge to that position, and the potential energy of the system is negative;

(c) negative work must be done by an external agent to move the charge to that position, and the potential energy of the system is positive;

(d) negative work must be done by an external agent to move the charge to that position, and the potential energy of the system is negative.

C-20-1 (d) The charges are of opposite sign and therefore attract each other. The applied external force counteracts this force and must be in the +x-direction, and the distance moved is along the negative x-direction. Therefore, the net amount of work is negative. This results in a negative potential energy.

Equation (20-4) gives the potential energy for a pair of charges. With three charges, there is a potential energy contribution from each pairing of the charges, where r_{ij} represents the distance between charge i and charge j.

$$U_{total} = \frac{q_1 q_2}{4\pi\varepsilon_0 r_{12}} + \frac{q_1 q_3}{4\pi\varepsilon_0 r_{13}} + \frac{q_2 q_3}{4\pi\varepsilon_0 r_{23}} \qquad (20\text{-}5)$$

We can readily extend this idea to larger numbers of charges, keeping in mind that we must have a term in the potential energy equation for each pairing and that we do not duplicate any pair (i.e., we would not count both a 12 and a 21 pairing). Example 20-1 shows how to apply the technique to four charges.

EXAMPLE 20-1

Electric Potential Energy for Four Charges

(a) Find the total work required to move four charges (+2.00, +3.00, +4.00, +5.00 nC) from initial positions infinitely far apart to the corners of a square with sides of 0.150 m, as shown in Figure 20-3.

(b) Define the zero of electric potential energy to be when the charges are infinitely far apart. What is the electric potential energy of the charge configuration shown in Figure 20-3?

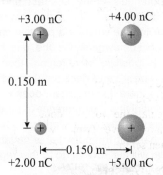

Figure 20-3 Four charges are located at the corners of a square.

SOLUTION

(a) You might at first consider calculating work using force and displacement. However, the forces vary with distance moved, so you would need to integrate, which becomes much more cumbersome once we add the third and fourth charges because the force vectors have different directions. One strength of energy approaches to solving problems is that the potential energy for conservative forces depends only on the actual configuration of the system, and is not affected by how the system got to that configuration. Therefore, we will use electric potential energy, expanding Equation (20-5) to the situation for four charges: We will number the charges 1 to 4 in same order as the charge magnitudes (i.e. the 2 nC charge is number 1).

$$U_{total} = \frac{q_1 q_2}{4\pi\varepsilon_0 r_{12}} + \frac{q_1 q_3}{4\pi\varepsilon_0 r_{13}} + \frac{q_1 q_4}{4\pi\varepsilon_0 r_{14}} + \frac{q_2 q_3}{4\pi\varepsilon_0 r_{23}} + \frac{q_2 q_4}{4\pi\varepsilon_0 r_{24}} + \frac{q_3 q_4}{4\pi\varepsilon_0 r_{34}}$$

$$= \frac{1}{4\pi\varepsilon_0}\left(\frac{q_1 q_2}{r_{12}} + \frac{q_1 q_3}{r_{13}} + \frac{q_1 q_4}{r_{14}} + \frac{q_2 q_3}{r_{23}} + \frac{q_2 q_4}{r_{24}} + \frac{q_3 q_4}{r_{34}}\right)$$

Note that we have included a term for each charge pair combination, and we have used the r_{ij} notation; for example, r_{34} represents the distance between charges 3 and 4. We use Pythagoras's theorem to obtain the distance between charges on opposite corners of the square. All the terms being summed have identical units, so we can move these units into the common factor for clarity:

$$U_{total} = \frac{1.00 \times 10^{-18}\ \text{C}^2/\text{m}}{4\pi \times 8.85 \times 10^{-12}\ \text{C}^2/(\text{N} \cdot \text{m}^2)}$$

$$\times\left(\frac{2.00 \times 3.00}{0.150} + \frac{2.00 \times 4.00}{0.212} + \frac{2.00 \times 5.00}{0.150}\right.$$

$$\left. + \frac{3.00 \times 4.00}{0.150} + \frac{3.00 \times 5.00}{0.212} + \frac{4.00 \times 5.00}{0.150}\right)$$

$$= 3.85 \times 10^{-6}\ \text{N} \cdot \text{m}$$

$$= 3.85\ \mu\text{J}$$

Thus, we must do 3.85×10^{-6} J of positive work to bring the charges into this configuration from an initial position of infinite separation.

(b) The electric potential energy of the configuration is simply the work required to create the configuration, which is $+3.85 \times 10^{-6}$ J, or 3.85 μJ.

Making sense of the result:

We expect the work required to be positive because the positive charges repel and it takes positive work to push them closer together. The potential energy is only a few microjoules, which is reasonable because the charges are tiny.

LO 2

20-2 Electric Potential

The **electric potential**, V, is the electric potential energy per unit charge. We can define a zero point for electric potential energy, so the same is true for electric potential. Normally, we define electric potential energy to be zero for infinitely separated charges, but in Chapter 21, when we discuss capacitors, we will invoke alternative definitions for zero potential.

KEY EQUATION
$$V = \frac{U}{q} \qquad (20\text{-}6)$$

The unit of electric potential is the volt (V). We can see from Equation (20-6) that 1 V = 1 J/C. At first, it might seem confusing to use the same symbol V for the quantity electric potential as well as for the unit used to measure it. However, there is a subtle difference in how we write the two symbols: unit symbols should be written as roman (upright) text, and symbols for variables are written as italic (slanted) text.

It is critical to always keep in mind that electric potentials are relative and subject to definition of a zero point.

In electric circuits, this zero point is called ground because in an electrical system it may well be directly connected to a conducting plane placed in the ground. We consider two points, A at +2 V and B at +5 V. Both points are positive with respect to the zero point of potential, but when compared to each other point A has a negative potential difference compared to point B.

We can combine Equation (20-6) with Equation (20-4) to obtain an expression for the electric potential at a distance r from a point charge Q:

$$V = \frac{Q}{4\pi\varepsilon_0 r} \qquad (20\text{-}7)$$

The electric potential and definition of the zero point expressed in Equation (20-7) are positive in the region near a positive charge, negative near a negative charge, and zero at an infinite distance from the charge Q. It is important to

ONLINE ACTIVITY

Exploring Electric Potentials

The e-resource that accompanies every new copy of this textbook contains an Online Activity using the PhET simulation "Charges and Fields." Work through the simulation and accompanying questions to gain an understanding of electric potentials.

EXAMPLE 20-2

Electric Potential for Three Charges

(a) Find the electric potential at point P in Figure 20-4.
(b) How much work is required to move a +1.00 μC charge to point P from an infinite distance?

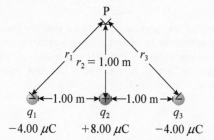

Figure 20-4 Example 20-2. Three charges are in a line; the middle charge is positive.

SOLUTION

(a) According to the superposition principle, we can find the electric potential at point P due to each of the charges separately, and then simply add the three individual potentials algebraically. We use Equation (20-7) with the appropriate charge and the distance from each charge to point P. Distances r_1 and r_3 are both $\sqrt{2}$ m.

realize that normally electric potential varies with position, and it is often written as $V(r)$ or $V(x)$ to show this dependence. The electric field is often written in a similar way to specifically show its dependence with position.

We apply the superposition principle to situations involving multiple charges, using Equation (20-7) to find the contributions to the potential from each charge. Since these contributions are scalar quantities, it is easy to add them to obtain a net electric potential, as demonstrated in Example 20-2.

PEER TO PEER

I must admit that at first I found the whole idea of electric potentials pretty abstract and confusing. Then I suddenly realized one day that really potentials are telling me whether a positive charge would want to go somewhere. On the one hand, if the potential is positive in a region, then a positive charge is repelled and does not want to go there. It will only go there if some agent does work to move it there. Multiplying the difference in potential by the charge tells you how much work you need to do. On the other hand, if the potential is negative, a positive charge will just love to go to that region and will accelerate to get there.

$$V = \frac{q_1}{4\pi\varepsilon_0 r_1} + \frac{q_2}{4\pi\varepsilon_0 r_2} + \frac{q_3}{4\pi\varepsilon_0 r_3}$$

$$= \frac{1}{4\pi\varepsilon_0}\left(\frac{-4.0\times10^{-6}\,\text{C}}{1.41\,\text{m}} + \frac{+8.0\times10^{-6}\,\text{C}}{1.00\,\text{m}} + \frac{-4.0\times10^{-6}\,\text{C}}{1.41\,\text{m}}\right)$$

$$= \frac{1\,\text{C/m}}{4\pi\times8.85\times10^{-12}\,\text{C}^2/(\text{N}\cdot\text{m}^2)}$$

$$\times (-2.828\times10^{-6} + 8.0\times10^{-6} - 2.828\times10^{-6})$$

$$= +2.11\times10^4\,\text{V}$$

(b) When the +1.00 μC charge is infinitely far away, it will have an electric potential of zero, so the potential difference between that location and point P is +21.1 kV. Since the electric potential is the electric potential energy per unit charge, the electric potential energy when the 1.00 μC charge is at point P is

$$(+1.00\times10^{-6}\,\text{C})(+2.11\times10^4\,\text{V}) = +0.0211\,\text{J}$$

Therefore, the work required to move the charge from infinitely far away to point P is 0.0211 J, or 21.1 mJ.

Making sense of the result:

Although there are equal amounts of positive and negative charge in the initial configuration, the net electric potential is positive because point P is closer to the positive charge than to the negative charges. You may be surprised by how large a potential difference is produced by a small fraction of a coulomb of charge. In part (b), we are moving a positive charge to a region with a more positive electric potential; therefore, the work required is positive.

Example 20-2 demonstrates a useful strategy for finding the work required to move a charge: (1) find the electric potentials at the initial and final points, (2) subtract to determine the electric potential difference, and (3) multiply the potential difference by the charge being moved.

✓ CHECKPOINT

C-20-2 Work Required to Move a Charge

Two charges, $+Q$ and $-Q$, are located a fixed distance apart along the x-axis, with $+Q$ on the left. A small positive point charge q is moved along the line joining the charges, from a point near the $+Q$ charge to a point near the $-Q$ charge. The work required to move the charge is
(a) positive;
(b) negative;
(c) zero;
(d) either positive or negative depending on where the zero point is for the electric potential.

C-20-2 (b) Since the positive charge q is repelled by the $+Q$ charge and attracted to the $-Q$ charge, a force must be applied in the opposite direction to the motion to keep positive charge from accelerating. In terms of electric potential difference, the electric potential is positive near the $+Q$ charge and negative near the $-Q$ charge because the closer charge dominates in each case. Thus, the potential difference is negative, and when multiplied by a positive charge $+q$, yields a negative value for the work required.

ONLINE ACTIVITY

Fields and Potentials for a Dipole

The e-resource that accompanies every new copy of this textbook contains an Online Activity using the PhET simulation "Charges and Fields." Work through the simulation and accompanying questions to gain an understanding of fields and potentials for a dipole.

So far, we have only considered a small number of discrete point charges. The same strategies can be used to integrate over continuous distributions of charge to obtain the electric potential, with an infinitesimal charge distribution dq playing the role of the point charge. Since electric potentials are scalar quantities, the integrations are considerably easier than the electric field calculations for charge distributions considered in Chapter 19.

20-3 Equipotential Lines and Electric Field Lines

It is useful to draw lines, called **equipotential lines**, through points of equal electric potential. We see from Equation (20-7) that for a single point charge equipotential lines are concentric circles centred on the point charge. When the charge is positive, the potentials are positive, with increasing values as one approaches the charge. Figure 20-5 shows these equipotential lines along with electric field vector arrows, which point outward from a positive charge. (Recall from Chapter 19 that electric fields point in the direction of the electric force on a positive test charge.)

Note that the electric field arrows are perpendicular to the equipotential lines. In fact, we can easily show that electric field lines are always perpendicular to lines or surfaces made up of points that are at equal electric potentials. Assume for a moment that the electric field $\vec{E}$ is not perpendicular to the equipotential lines. Then there would be a component of the electric field along the equipotential line and, hence, a force acting on any charge moving along the line. But this force does work as the charge moves along the line, which makes the electric potential different at each point, so the line cannot be an equipotential line. This contradiction shows that all electric field lines cross equipotential lines perpendicularly.

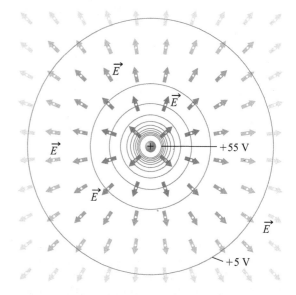

Figure 20-5 Equipotential lines and electric field vectors around a single $+1$ nC charge. The plotted equipotential lines are for intervals of 5 V starting at $+5$ V as shown. Note that here the colour intensity of the vector arrows, rather than their length, represents the strength of the electric field.

C-20-3 Zero Net Electric Potential

Two fixed charges have equal magnitude but unknown signs. At the point (2, 0) in the xy-plane, the net electric field points in the $-x$-direction, and the net electric potential is zero. What can you conclude about the signs and locations of the two fixed charges? Draw a diagram of the situation to help you answer this question.

(a) The two charges must both be negative, one to the left and one to the right along the x-axis.

(b) The two charges must have opposite signs and must both be along the x-axis at equal distance from the point where the potential is zero, with the positive charge to the right.

(c) The two charges must have opposite signs and must both be along the x-axis at equal distance from the point where the potential is zero, with the positive charge to the left.

(d) The charges must have opposite signs and be along a vertical line, with the positive charge at the point (2, $+y$) and the negative charge at the point (2, $-y$).

C-20-3 (b) The only way to have zero electric potential is when the charges have opposite signs and are equal distances from the measurement point. For the electric field to point to the left, we must have the positive charge on the right.

Figure 20-6 shows a positive central charge with two lesser negative charges symmetrically placed on

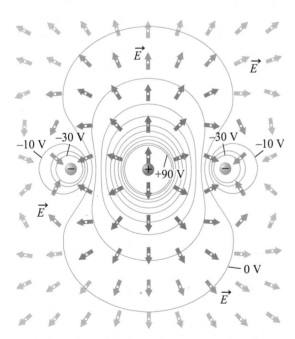

Figure 20-6 Equipotential and electric field vectors for a situation with a positive charge (+4 nC) in the centre and equal negative (−1 nC) charges symmetrically on each side. The plotted equipotential lines are at intervals of 10 V, starting with the equipotential line closest to the positive charge at +90 V. You can produce your own plots like this using the PhET simulation called "Charges and Fields."

each side. The positive charge is +4 nC, and the negative charges are −1 nC. We have plotted only 12 equipotential lines at 10 V intervals. There would be higher and higher potentials near each charge. Note that very near each charge the contribution from that charge dominates, and the equipotential lines approach concentric circles. Farther away, the influence of other charges on the net potential becomes apparent.

20-4 Electric Field from Electric Potential

In Chapter 11, we showed how the gravitational force and the gravitational field can be calculated from the change in gravitational potential energy using partial derivatives. This technique is valid for any conservative force field. The force components can be calculated as follows:

$$F_x = -\frac{\partial U}{\partial x}; \quad F_y = -\frac{\partial U}{\partial y}; \quad F_z = -\frac{\partial U}{\partial z} \quad (20\text{-}8)$$

where U is the potential energy function.

Keep in mind that these partial derivatives are taken with respect to one coordinate variable while holding the others constant. For example, for the potential energy given by $U = 20y - 10$ (in J), the x- and z-components of the corresponding force are zero, and the component in the y-direction is −20 N.

Electric potentials are commonly used in place of electric potential energy when dealing with electric fields. Recall that electric potential is the electric potential energy per unit charge, and electric field is electric force per unit charge. If we divide both sides of Equations (20-8) by charge, we get the following relationships:

KEY EQUATION $\quad E_x = -\dfrac{\partial V}{\partial x}; \quad E_y = -\dfrac{\partial V}{\partial y}; \quad E_z = -\dfrac{\partial V}{\partial z} \quad (20\text{-}9)$

If you know the electric potential at all points, then you can use these relationships to find the electric field at all points. Since electric potentials are scalar quantities, and we can calculate them using the superposition principle, this approach is often the easiest way to calculate electric fields, even in complex situations.

The relationship between the electric field and electric potential suggest that the SI units for electric field are V/m. From the definition of electric field in terms of electric force per unit charge, we had units of N/C. In fact, the definitions of these SI units are such that 1 N/C = 1 V/m.

C-20-4 Electric Potential and Electric Field

The electric potential (in V) in a certain region is given by $V = 3x^2 - 5$. What is the electric field at the origin of the coordinate system?

(a) All components are zero.
(b) The y- and z-components are 0, and the x-component is in the $+x$-direction.
(c) The y- and z-components are zero, and the x-component is in the $-x$ direction.
(d) The x-component is zero, and the y- and z-components are both infinite.

C-20-4 (a) Since y and z do not appear explicitly in the expression for potential, clearly, those components of the electric field are zero everywhere. Taking the partial derivative with respect to the x-coordinate gives $E_x = -6x$, which has a zero value at the origin.

EXAMPLE 20-3

Electric Field from Electric Potential

In a region of space, the electric potential (in V) is given by

$$V = \frac{25.0}{x^2 + y^2} + 80.0.$$

(a) Is the potential defined everywhere?
(b) Derive expressions for the components of the electric field.
(c) Find the electric field at the point (1.5 m, 0 m, 0 m).
(d) Sketch the magnitude of the x-component of the electric field along the x-axis as a function of distance from the origin.

SOLUTION

(a) The potential is defined everywhere except at the origin, where it becomes infinite. The electric potential is positive everywhere and decreases as the distance from the origin in the xy-plane increases. The potential approaches a value of $+80.0$ V for large absolute values of either the x- or y-coordinate.

(b) To obtain the components of the electric field, we use Equation (20-9). Rewriting the electric potential as $V = 25(x^2 + y^2)^{-1} + 80$ makes it easier to take the partial derivatives. For the x-component of the electric field we have

$$E_x = -\frac{\partial V}{\partial x} = -25(-1)(x^2 + y^2)^{-2}(2x) + 0 = +50x(x^2 + y^2)^{-2}$$

Similarly, $E_y = -\dfrac{\partial V}{\partial y} = +50y(x^2 + y^2)^{-2}$

Since z does not appear in the expression for the electric potential, the partial derivative with respect to z is 0, so $E_z = 0$.

(c) Substituting $x = +1.5$ m, $y = 0$ m, and $z = 0$ m into the expressions from part (b), we obtain

$$E_x = 50x(x^2 + y^2)^{-2} = 50(+1.5)(1.5^2 + 0^2)^{-2} = +14.8 \text{ V/m}$$

$$E_y = 0 \text{ V/m}$$

$$E_z = 0 \text{ V/m}$$

Therefore, the electric field at the point (1.5 m, 0 m, 0 m) has a magnitude of 14.8 V/m and points in the $+x$-direction.

(d) Figure 20-7 shows plots of the magnitude of the electric potential and the magnitude of the electric field along the x-axis. Note that the magnitudes of both V and E_x are infinite at $x = 0$.

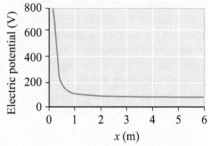

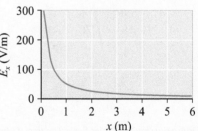

Figure 20-7 (a) A plot of the electric potential (V) as a function of position along the $+x$-axis. (b) A plot of the x-component of the electric field along the $+x$-axis

Making sense of the result:

The first term in the potential function decreases as the square of the distance in the xy-plane from the origin. The constant term does not affect the electric field because the derivative of a constant is zero. Since the electric potential is positive along the x-axis and increases closer to the origin, we expect a positive test charge on the positive x-axis to be repelled with the x-component of the electric field in the positive direction, as obtained above. Careful examination of the two plots shows that the values of E_x correspond to the negative of the slope of the V plot, as expected, because the slope corresponds to the derivative of the potential function.

You may wonder whether we can reverse the process used above and determine the resultant electric potential for a given electric field. Indeed, you can perform an integral along a path between two points to find the potential difference between the points. In a conservative field, the path taken does not matter, only the end points. We let V_a and V_b represent the electric potentials at points a and b, and $d\vec{r}$ represents a small element of a path from point a to point b. The electric potential difference between the two points is given by the following integral:

KEY EQUATION
$$V_b - V_a = -\int_a^b \vec{E} \cdot d\vec{r} \qquad (20\text{-}10)$$

Of course, absolute electric potential can have an arbitrary constant voltage added; this constant is determined by the definition of the zero point.

Pay careful attention to the signs of the various quantities. You should always check whether the result that you obtain makes sense with what you know about the electric fields and potentials. For example, for the situation in Figure 20-8, an electric field points straight down. By definition, the path element $d\vec{r}$ points along the path going from a to b. Since $\vec{E}$ and $d\vec{r}$ have almost opposite directions, the dot product of the vectors is negative. The right side of Equation (20-10) also has a negative sign, so the net sign is positive, indicating that V_b is greater than V_a.

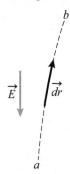

Figure 20-8 In this situation, the electric field points from the top toward the bottom. The element $d\vec{r}$ always points along the integration path going from point a to point b.

Remember that you can take any path in a conservative field, so you are free to choose a path for which the dot product and integral are easy to calculate. For example, *when the electric field is constant, you can choose a straight path from point a to point b*. Then the angle between the field and path vectors is constant, making the dot product easy to integrate.

20-5 The Electron-volt

Rearranging Equation (20-6), we see that, when we move a charge q through an electric potential difference ΔV, the change in electric potential energy, ΔU, is

KEY EQUATION
$$\Delta U = q\Delta V \qquad (20\text{-}11)$$

We have used the notations ΔV and ΔU because we are considering the *changes* in potential and potential energy. When we move a positive charge to a region with higher electric potential, the electric potential energy of the charge increases. However, the electric potential energy of a negative charge decreases when the charge moves to a region of higher electric potential.

When zero work is done by external forces, a loss in electric potential energy must correspond to a gain in some other form of energy, usually kinetic energy. In the TRIUMF cyclotron described at the beginning of this chapter, charged particles are accelerated by changes in electric potential. You can also describe the acceleration in terms of forces exerted on the charged particles in electric fields, but in many situations it is easier to use an energy-potential approach.

In many devices, electrons, protons, and singly charged ions experience changes in electric potential. A small unit of energy called the **electron volt** (eV) is convenient to use in these situations. One electron volt is the energy change when one elementary charge moves through a potential difference of exactly 1 V. For example, cathode ray tubes typically accelerate electrons using a potential difference of approximately 30 000 V, so one electron would have an energy change of 30 000 eV (or 30 keV). Charged particles (often electrons) are accelerated when they pass through a high electric potential difference in a variety of other technological devices, including X-ray machines and electron microscopes.

✓ CHECKPOINT

C-20-5 Change in potential

A doubly charged positive ion (charge of $+3.2 \times 10^{-19}$ C) loses 24 keV in going from point A to point B. Which of the following statements describes the potential difference between the points?

(a) Point A is at a higher potential than point B by 24 kV.
(b) Point B is at a higher potential than point A by 24 kV.
(c) Point A is at a higher potential than point B by 12 kV.
(d) Point B is at a higher potential than point A by 12 kV.

C-20-5 (c) Here, a positively charged (positive q) particle loses electric potential energy (ΔU) is negative, so the change in potential (ΔV) must be negative. Therefore, point A is at a higher potential than point B. Since the particle has a charge of 2e, the voltage difference must just be 12 kV.

It is important to remember that the electron volt is a unit of energy, and the volt is a unit of electric potential difference (energy per unit charge). To convert electron volts to joules, we use the magnitude of the elementary charge, 1.60×10^{-19} C for q:

$$1 \text{ eV} = 1.60 \times 10^{-19} \text{C} \times 1 \text{ V} = 1.60 \times 10^{-19} \text{J}$$

The electron volt is a tiny amount of energy by macroscopic standards, but a convenient amount on the atomic scale. For example, it takes approximately 13.6 eV to ionize hydrogen and approximately 5.2 eV to remove the first electron from sodium. Those working with atomic spectra usually state energy level differences in electron volts.

Proton beams, such as those produced at TRIUMF, are used in the treatments of certain types of cancer. Proton beams are preferable to X-rays for cancer treatment for a number of reasons, the main one being that the beam width and the effective depth in the body are better controlled. The proton beam damages the DNA of the cancer cells, thereby reducing the ability of the cancerous cells to reproduce. The proton beam for this type of treatment usually needs to be in the energy range of approximately 75 MeV to 225 MeV, that is, each proton has an energy of between 75 million electron volts and 225 million electron volts.

EXAMPLE 20-4

Proton Beam Therapy

TRIUMF can produce protons with energies between 5 MeV and 120 MeV in the lower energy beam (called BL2C). Consider a beam of 100 MeV protons used for treating cancer.

(a) What is the energy of one of these protons, in joules?
(b) The energy of the protons is built up after many passages through an accelerating potential of 94.0 kV. How many passes are needed to produce 100 MeV protons?
(c) The protons are accelerated by an electric potential difference across a gap between two halves of the cyclotron chamber. Which side of this acceleration region has the higher electric potential?

SOLUTION

(a) Since one electron volt equals 1.60×10^{-19} J,

$$100 \text{ MeV} \times \frac{1.00 \times 10^6 \text{ eV}}{1 \text{ MeV}} \times \frac{1.60 \times 10^{-19} \text{ J}}{1 \text{ eV}} = 1.60 \times 10^{-11} \text{ J}$$

(b) The proton has a charge of one elementary charge $(1.60 \times 10^{-19}$ C). Therefore, the energy gained when it passes through an accelerating potential of 94.0 kV is 94.0 keV. Therefore, the number of passes required is

$$100 \text{ MeV} \times \frac{1.00 \times 10^6 \text{ eV}}{1.00 \text{ MeV}} \times \frac{1 \text{ pass}}{94.0 \text{ keV}} \times \frac{1.00 \text{ keV}}{1.00 \times 10^3 \text{ eV}}$$

$$= 1064 \text{ passes}$$

Therefore, to three significant figures 1060 passages through the accelerating region are needed.

(c) Protons are positively charged; therefore, they are accelerated toward a more negative region. The end of the acceleration region must be at a lower electric potential.

Making sense of the result:

This example demonstrates how convenient the electron volt unit is when dealing with charged particles. Since higher positive electric potentials are more positive regions, it makes sense that positively charged particles lose electric potential energy and gain kinetic energy as they move toward more negative regions.

MAKING CONNECTIONS

Ion Propulsion Rockets

The underlying principle of any rocket engine is conservation of linear momentum: fuel is expelled in one direction with a high relative velocity, and the rocket moves in the opposite direction with the total momentum of the rocket-plus-fuel system unchanged. Most rocket engines, such as those used in space launches, burn fuel for exhaust propulsion. Ion propulsion systems are more environmentally friendly and ultimately more efficient. These systems are relatively simple: the engine ionizes a material, such as xenon gas, using electric energy from solar cells on the spacecraft. The positive ions are then accelerated through a large electric potential difference. High ejection velocities are possible, making ion propulsion quite efficient. Ion propulsion is also safer and more reliable than chemical rockets, which burn fuel in violent oxidation reactions. Ion propulsion systems are in use, but the thrusts available are still tiny compared to chemical propellants. At present, ion propulsion technology is best suited for long-duration voyages where a spacecraft can maintain a tiny thrust for a long time. NASA's *Dawn* mission (Figure 20-9) uses ion propulsion to move the space vehicle into the orbits required to provide close-up views of the two largest asteroids, Ceres and Vesta, from 2007 to 2015.

Figure 20-9 NASA's *Dawn* spacecraft uses ion propulsion engines for thrust to put it into orbits around the asteroids Ceres and Vesta.

20-6 Electric Fields and Conductors

An ideal conductor allows charges to flow without resistance. An infinitesimally small electric force moves a charge along this conductor. Consequently, when a static charge is on a conductor, there is no electric field component directed along the conductor. Therefore, electric fields are always perpendicular to the surfaces of conductors when no current flows. Note that this orientation applies in static situations, but not when there are moving charges or changing electric fields, which we will consider in Chapter 26. The direction (outward or inward) depends on the charge on the conductor, with positively charged conductors having electric field lines directed outward.

✓ CHECKPOINT

C-20-6 Electric Field Near Conductors

Which part of Figure 20-10 shows the electric field close to a negatively charged conducting surface?

C-20-6 (c) The electric field must be perpendicular to the surface of a conductor (at least an ideal one), so (a) and (d) are excluded. Since the electric field points inward for a negatively charged surface, the answer is (c).

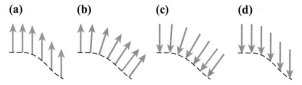

Figure 20-10 C-20-6

The electric potential must be exactly the same everywhere on an ideal conductor. For example, the voltage measured at each end of a conducting wire with zero resistance is the same. Superconductors are the only known materials with zero resistance, but some metals, such as copper and silver, are close enough to being ideal conductors that the potential difference across them can be considered negligible for most situations.

PEER TO PEER

The idea that the electric field is the rate of change of electric potential is a really powerful and useful idea. It means that if different parts of an object, such as a wire, are at the same voltage (potential), then there is no electric field in that object. Also, when an electric field is constant, you can find a potential difference by simply multiplying the field by the distance. Say the field between two plates is 20 V/m, and the plates are 0.10 m apart. Then the potential difference is 2.0 V.

Consider an ideal conducting spherical shell that has a static charge on it. How is this charge distributed? There must be no electric field inside the material of the conductor; otherwise, the charge carriers in the conductor would move and the charge could not be static. In fact, charges on conductors always stay on the outer surface of the conductor. Later in the chapter, we will see why the charge does not stay on the inner surface of a conducting shell.

20-7 Charge Densities

In Chapter 19, we developed the idea of a linear charge density, μ, defined as the charge per unit length of a linear conductor, such as a narrow wire. We similarly define surface charge density, σ, as the charge per unit area of a surface and volume charge density, and ρ, as the charge per unit volume. In a section 20-9, we will use these definitions to determine the electric field near a charged object.

EXAMPLE 20-5

Surface Charge Density on a Conductor

A solid conducting sphere has a radius of 12.0 cm and a total charge of 25.0 μC. Find the charge density on the surface of this sphere.

SOLUTION

From Section 20-6, we know that all the charge on a conductor goes to its outer surface. The surface area of the sphere is

$$A = 4\pi r^2 = 4\pi (0.120 \text{ m})^2 = 0.181 \text{ m}^2$$

Therefore, the surface charge density is simply

$$\sigma = \frac{Q}{A} = \frac{25.0 \ \mu C}{0.181 \text{ m}^2} = 138 \ \mu C/m^2 = 1.38 \times 10^{-4} \text{ C/m}^2$$

Making sense of the result:

Remember that μC is a small unit of charge, so the charge density expressed in C/m^2 is expected to be small.

PEER TO PEER

Whenever you have a charge density question, ask yourself whether it deals with a conductor or an insulator. With an insulator, you must have some assumption (such as evenly distributed charge). With a conductor, all the charge on it goes to the outer surface.

C-20-7 Surface Charge Density

Which of the following has the largest surface charge density, assuming that the total charge on each object is the same?

(a) the surface of a solid conducting sphere of radius r

(b) the surface of a solid insulating sphere of radius r

(c) the surface of a solid conducting cube with all sides of length r

(d) Both (a) and (b) always have exactly the same surface charge density.

C-20-7 (c) For conducting objects, all the charge goes on the outer surface. For nonconducting objects, the charge can be distributed inside as well as on the surface. So, for objects with the same shape, the surface charge density is less on the insulating objects than on the conducting objects. A sphere of radius r has a surface area of $4\pi r^2$, and a cube with sides r has a total surface area of $6r^2$. Therefore, the surface charge density is more on the cube because the same charge is spread over a smaller surface area.

20-8 Electric Flux

In Section 20-9, we will introduce Gauss's law, which allows us to calculate (at least in cases with symmetry) the electric field for a known charge distribution. Gauss's law is expressed in terms of a quantity called the electric flux, Φ_E, so before we introduce Gauss's law, we need to introduce flux. When we draw electric field lines closer together, where the magnitude of the electric field is higher, we can consider the electric flux as a measure of how many electric field lines pass through a given area.

A qualitative analogy be helpful. Imagine a heavy rain that is being pushed by a strong wind so that the rain falls at an angle, as shown in Figure 20-11. We are interested in how much rain will be collected by each of the four buckets in a given time. The amounts depend on the rainfall rate, the area of the circular opening of each bucket, and the angle of the falling rain relative to these areas. In Figure 20-11, bucket B will collect the most rainwater (or rain flux). The flux into bucket A is less because the collecting area is less, and the flux into bucket D is less because the rate of rainfall is less. The flux into bucket C is less because the angle of the rainfall results in fewer drops entering the bucket per unit area of the bucket opening.

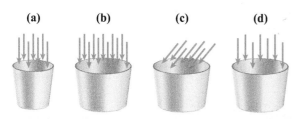

Figure 20-11 A rainfall analogy to electric flux

Electric flux is a scalar quantity defined as the vector dot product of the electric field, $\vec{E}$, and an area vector, $\vec{A}$, that has a direction perpendicular to the surface (by convention directed outward from the surface) and a magnitude equal to the area over which electric flux is being calculated:

$$\Phi_E = \vec{E} \cdot \vec{A} \qquad (20\text{-}12)$$

Although we introduced an analogy with a flat surface, electric flux can be calculated over a curved surface as well.

C-20-8 Electric Flux

The cube in Figure 20-12 is oriented in an electric field pointing in the y-direction. Which of the following statements best describes the electric flux through the faces of the cube?

(a) The only surfaces with nonzero flux are the faces parallel to the yz-plane, and the net flux for the entire cube is zero.

(b) The only surfaces with nonzero flux are the faces parallel to the xy-plane, and the net flux for the entire cube is negative.

(c) The only surfaces with nonzero flux are the faces parallel to the xz-plane, and the net flux for the entire cube is zero.

(d) The only surfaces with nonzero flux are the faces parallel to the xz-plane, and the net flux for the entire cube is negative.

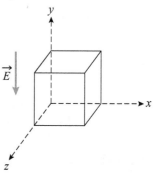

Figure 20-12 C-20-8

C-20-8 (c) Because of the vector dot product, the four faces parallel to the electric field vector all have zero flux. Just the top and the bottom faces of the cube have nonzero electric flux. Since the direction of the area vector is defined as perpendicular to the surface and pointing outward, the electric flux is negative for the top face of the cube (where the vectors $\vec{E}$ and $\vec{A}$ are opposite) and positive for the bottom face (where the vectors are in the same direction). Since the magnitudes of these two fluxes are equal, the net flux through the cube is zero.

In most situations, the electric field varies over the area. We then use an integral over the surface. This integral also accommodates situations in which the angle between the area and the electric field varies (e.g., when the surface is not flat).

 $\qquad \Phi_E = \oint \vec{E} \cdot d\vec{A} \qquad (20\text{-}13)$

EXAMPLE 20-6

Electric Flux Through a Circle

Derive an expression for the electric flux through a circle of radius r_0 in the xy-plane, centred at the origin. The electric field makes an angle of 30° with the z-axis, as shown in Figure 20-13. Assume that the magnitude of the electric field for points in the xy-plane is given by $\left|\vec{E}\right| = \dfrac{E_0}{r}$, where r is the distance from the origin.

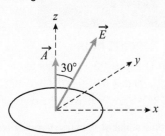

Figure 20-13   Example 20-6

SOLUTION

We will use the definition of electric flux in the derivation of the expression:

$$\Phi_E = \oint \vec{E} \cdot d\vec{A}$$

Since the angle between the electric field and area vectors is a constant 30°, the dot product gives a factor of $\cos(30°)$. Thus, we can write the electric flux through the circle as

$$\Phi_E = \cos(30°) \oint_{circle} E\, dA = \frac{\sqrt{3}}{2} \oint_{circle} E\, dA$$

There are several options for specifying the area element dA. We will take an infinitesimally thin ring as the differential area element and integrate over concentric rings to make up the circle. As shown in Figure 20-14, each ring has an approximate area of $dA = 2\pi r dr$.

Therefore, the electric flux is

$$\Phi_E = \frac{\sqrt{3}}{2} \oint_{circle} E\, dA = \frac{\sqrt{3}}{2} \oint_0^{r_0} \frac{E_0}{r} 2\pi r\, dr$$

$$= \pi\sqrt{3}E_0 \int_0^{r_0} dr = \pi\sqrt{3}E_0 r_0$$

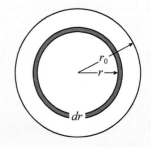

Figure 20-14   We can integrate over the circle by adding rings of length $2\pi r$ and width dr.

Making sense of the result:

You might be surprised that we obtained a finite answer because the electric field is infinite at the origin. However, the flux depends on the angle, area, and electric field, and the region with an infinite electric field has an infinitesimal area, so the total flux through the circle is finite. The electric field goes down with distance from the centre, but the corresponding circular area increases with the square of the radius, so the net flux depends on increases with the radius of the circle, r_0.

LO 9

20-9   Gauss's Law

Gauss's law states that the electric flux through any closed surface is given by the enclosed charge within the region bounded by that surface divided by the permittivity of free space, ε_0, which is a constant of nature:

KEY EQUATION
$$\oint \vec{E} \cdot d\vec{A} = \frac{q_{enc}}{\varepsilon_0} \qquad (20\text{-}14)$$

where the circle on the integral symbol (called a surface integral) indicates that the integral is taken over a closed surface, and q_{enc} represents the charge *enclosed* by that surface. If both positive and negative charges are enclosed by the surface, it is the net value which appears in Equation 20-14 (e.g. if there was a +3 C charge and a −1 C charge we would use +2 C).

Although Gauss's law is true for any closed surface, it is only useful for calculating the electric field in situations involving symmetry.

✓ CHECKPOINT

C-20-9 Gauss's Law

Which of the following surfaces will have the greatest net electric flux passing through it if they all enclose the same net electric charge?

(a) a small sphere

(b) a large sphere

(c) a cube

(d) The flux is the same for all three surfaces.

C-20-9 (d) By Gauss's law, the net electric flux through any of the closed surfaces depends only on the enclosed charge, which is the same for all three surfaces.

When applying Gauss's law, you can choose any convenient closed surface, including an irregularly shaped surface. However, choosing a symmetrical surface can greatly simplify the calculations. We will consider spherical symmetry in this section, and in the next section we will apply Gauss's law with several other types of symmetry.

In Chapter 19, we obtained the electric field at a distance r from a point charge Q using Coulomb's law and the definition of the electric field as the force on a small positive test charge divided by that charge. We now apply Gauss's law to the same situation. In Figure 20-15, an electric field is symmetric about a single positive charge, Q. At a given distance r from the charge, the magnitude of the electric field is the same in any direction. Therefore, we choose a sphere centred on the charge Q as the closed surface for application of Gauss's law.

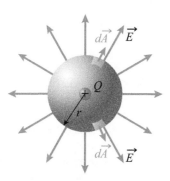

Figure 20-15 A spherical surface surrounding a single positive point charge, Q. The surface area elements, $d\vec{A}$, points radially outward everywhere and are parallel to the electric field at the surface.

Applying Gauss's law to the spherical surface gives

$$\oint \vec{E} \cdot d\vec{A} = \frac{q_{enc}}{\varepsilon_0} \qquad (20\text{-}15)$$

The directions of the electric field and the surface area element $d\vec{A}$ vary around the sphere, but both are always directed radially outward so they are always parallel to each other. Therefore, the dot product in the equation for Gauss's law produces a constant factor of $\cos(0°)$, which is simply 1. By symmetry, we know that the magnitude of

the electric field is the same all over the spherical surface, so E can be taken outside the integral:

$$E \oint dA = \frac{Q}{\varepsilon_0} \qquad (20\text{-}16)$$

Since the integral of dA over the closed surface is simply the surface area of the sphere, we have

$$E(4\pi r^2) = \frac{Q}{\varepsilon_0} \qquad (20\text{-}17)$$

and

$$E = \frac{1}{4\pi\varepsilon_0}\left(\frac{Q}{r^2}\right) = \frac{Q}{4\pi\varepsilon_0 r^2} \qquad (20\text{-}18)$$

Equation (20-18) is the same expression for the magnitude of the electric field at a distance r from a single point charge Q that we obtained using Coulomb's law in Chapter 19. We now see why the constant in Coulomb's law is often written $\frac{1}{4\pi\varepsilon_0}$.

Coulomb's law is an inverse square law—the strength of the electric field due to a point charge is inversely proportional to the square of the distance from the charge. We can show that this behaviour is in accordance with Gauss's law. Figure 20-16 shows a single positive point charge Q enclosed by two concentric spheres, one of radius r and one of radius $3r$. The electric field lines that start on the positive charge pass through both spheres. The smaller sphere has more electric field lines per unit area, so the electric field is stronger at its surface than at the surface of the larger sphere. The larger sphere has 9 times the surface area of the smaller sphere, but the number of electric field lines per unit area (a measure of the strength of the electric field) is only 1/9 as much, so the electric flux through each sphere is the same, as predicted by Gauss's law.

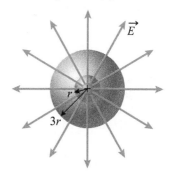

Figure 20-16 Gaussian spheres with different radii do not have the same surface area or electric field strengths, but the electric flux through them is the same.

We can obtain all aspects of Coulomb's law through the combination of the definition of electric field (force per charge) and Gauss's law. In one of the most brilliant contributions to physics, James Clerk Maxwell (1831–79) described all aspects of static and changing electromagnetic fields (and, therefore, electromagnetic waves such as light) in only four powerful equations. Gauss's law is one of these relationships.

20-10 Applications of Gauss's Law

Using symmetry, we can readily apply Gauss's law to calculate electric fields around uniform charge distributions that are spherical, linear, or planar. Often, a calculation for a theoretical infinitely long object will give a good approximation of the electric field, except near the ends, for an actual object, such as a straight wire or a charged plate.

Consider the very long line of positive charge (wire) with uniform linear charge density μ shown in Figure 20-17. We want to find the electric field at a distance r from the line. If we assume that the line of charge is essentially infinite, we know from symmetry that the electric field must point radially away from the line of charge and have the same magnitude E at every point that is at the same radial distance r from the line of charge.

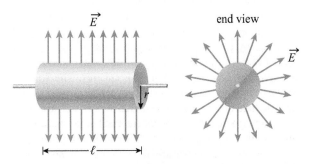

Figure 20-17 A long line of charge with a Gaussian cylinder of radius r and arbitrary length ℓ. The electric field points radially outward from the wire in all directions, but is shown only at the horizontal surfaces of the cylinder here.

Next, we choose a cylinder of arbitrary length ℓ as our closed Gaussian surface. We can find the total electric flux through the cylinder by adding the flux through the flat ends and the curved side of the Gaussian cylinder:

$$\Phi_{\text{left cap}} + \Phi_{\text{curved surface}} + \Phi_{\text{right cap}} = \frac{q_{\text{enc}}}{\varepsilon_0} \quad (20\text{-}19)$$

For each of the parts of the electric flux we have

$$\Phi_{E} = \oint \vec{E} \cdot d\vec{A} \quad (20\text{-}20)$$

For the left end, $d\vec{A}$ points left, which is perpendicular to the electric field, so the vector dot product yields a flux of zero. Similarly, the electric flux through the right end is also zero. On the curved part of the cylindrical surface, $d\vec{A}$ points radially outward everywhere, the same direction as the local electric field, $\vec{E}$. Therefore, the dot product is simply the product of the magnitudes of the two vectors, and

$$\Phi_{E} = E \int dA = E(2\pi r \ell) \quad (20\text{-}21)$$

The amount of charge enclosed by the cylindrical Gaussian surface is simply $\mu\ell$, so Gauss's law gives

$$\frac{\mu\ell}{\varepsilon_0} = E(2\pi r \ell) \quad (20\text{-}22)$$

Now we can easily solve for E, the magnitude of the electric field at a distance r from an infinite line with a charge density μ. The direction of the electric field is radially away from the line of charge, as discussed above:

$$E = \frac{\mu}{2\pi r \varepsilon_0} \quad (20\text{-}23)$$

It makes sense that the electric field depends proportionally on the charge per unit length. Note that the electric field is inversely proportional to the radial distance r, not the square of the distance, as it is for a point charge. If the charge were negative, the results would be exactly the same except that the electric field would point toward the line of charge instead of away from it.

✓ **CHECKPOINT**

C-20-10 Coaxial Cable

Coaxial cables are commonly used for transmitting signals, such as TV and audio. A coaxial cable consists of a central wire, a layer of insulation, a concentric cylindrical second conductor, and an outer layer of insulation. Which of the following statements best describes the electric field between the conductors and outside a length of coaxial cable that has a charge of $+q$ on the inner wire and $-q$ on the outer conductor?

(a) The electric field is directed away from the wire in both regions.

(b) The electric field is directed toward the wire in both regions.

(c) The electric field is zero in the region between the conductors and directed outward outside the cable.

(d) The electric field is directed radially away from the central wire in the space between the conductors and is zero outside the cable.

C-20-10 (d) By Gauss's law, the net electric flux outside the cable must be zero because the total enclosed charge is zero inside a Gaussian box that encloses both the inner wire and the outer conductor. In the space between the conductors, the electric field is directed outward because the inner wire has a positive charge.

Here is a summary of the strategy used to solve problems using Gauss's law:

1. Without some symmetry, Gauss's law is of little use in calculating the electric field, so determine whether the situation has symmetry about a point, line, or plane.

2. Choose an appropriate Gaussian surface according to the symmetry of the situation (spherical or cylindrical). For example, a line of charge has cylindrical symmetry, and a charged sphere or single point charge has spherical symmetry. In the case of planes of charge, we often use cylindrical Gaussian surfaces, although boxes could also be used. The Gaussian surface must be centred around a point or axis of symmetry. The size of the Gaussian surface is determined by the distance to the point where the electric field is to be calculated.

3. Draw a diagram of the situation, including the electric field and the Gaussian surface. Indicate the directions of $d\vec{A}$ on the diagram. Remember that area vectors always point outward perpendicular to the surface.

4. Divide the Gaussian surface into different segments if necessary, ensuring that the entire closed Gaussian surface is included.

5. Note which segments have the electric field perpendicular to the area vector (and hence zero flux) and which have parallel field and area vectors.

6. Calculate the net charge enclosed by the Gaussian surface. Remember that only the charge inside the surface needs to be considered.

7. Use Gauss's law to solve for the magnitude of the electric field. Be sure to state the direction of the field.

8. Check that your answer makes sense.

In Example 20-7, we apply this technique to a planar charge.

EXAMPLE 20-7

Electric Field from an Infinite Plane of Charge

Derive an expression for the electric field a distance d from a very large (assumed infinite) plane of charge that has uniform surface charge density σ.

SOLUTION

We will assume that the charge is positive, although other than reversing the direction of the electric field, the analysis is the same for either sign. To use the planar symmetry of the situation, we draw a cylindrical Gaussian surface that extends an equal distance d above and below the plane of charge, as shown in Figure 20-18. This placement equalizes the flux through the two ends of the cylinder.

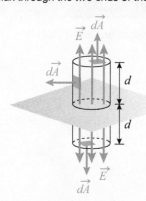

Figure 20-18 A thin, infinite plane of charge with a Gaussian surface extending equal distances above and below the surface. For clarity, the electric field vectors are shown only where they pass through the surface of the Gaussian cylinder.

According to Gauss's law, the net electric flux must equal the enclosed charge divided by the permittivity, ε_0. The cross-sectional area of the Gaussian surface is A, so the enclosed charge is simply σA. Therefore,

$$\Phi_{\text{top cap}} + \Phi_{\text{curved surface}} + \Phi_{\text{bottom cap}} = \frac{q_{\text{enc}}}{\varepsilon_0} = \frac{\sigma A}{\varepsilon_0}$$

In each region, we calculate the electric flux according to the relationship

$$\Phi_{E} = \oint \vec{E} \cdot d\vec{A}$$

In the figure, we indicate the directions of $\vec{E}$ and $d\vec{A}$ for the three parts of the Gaussian cylinder. For the two ends, $\vec{E}$ and $d\vec{A}$ are parallel, and the magnitude of the electric flux is the same on both. Along the curved side of the cylinder, $\vec{E}$ and $d\vec{A}$ are at right angles, so the electric flux through these curved surfaces of the cylinder is zero.

From the symmetry, we can see that the magnitude of the electric field has a constant value, E, at every point in the ends of the cylinder. Therefore, the flux through each end is simply EA. Applying Gauss's law, we have

$$\Phi_{\text{top cap}} + \Phi_{\text{curved surface}} + \Phi_{\text{bottom cap}} = EA + 0 + EA = \frac{\sigma A}{\varepsilon_0}$$

and

$$E = \frac{\sigma}{2\varepsilon_0}$$

Making sense of the result:

You may be surprised that the strength of the electric field does not depend on the distance from the infinite uniform plane of charge. The contributions to the electric field from distant points almost entirely cancel at points near the plane of charge, but for greater distances from the plane, these contributions cancel less completely, leaving a perpendicular component. This effect exactly offsets the decrease in strength from the point on the plane nearest the measurement point, so the net effect is that the electric field does not depend on distance from the plane. This result is the same result that we obtained in Chapter 19 using direct integration. Gauss's law provides a shorter way to obtain the result for this configuration.

CHAPTER 20 | ELECTRIC POTENTIAL AND GAUSS'S LAW 539

Gauss's law can also be expressed in terms of derivatives, rather than integrals. You will encounter the differential form of Gauss's law if you take advanced physics courses in electricity and magnetism. Gauss's law is not used just to calculate electric fields. Often, we measure the electric field from an object and then use Gauss's law to calculate the charge on the object. Usually, it is easier to measure electric fields (often from the electric potential at two separated points) than to measure electric charge directly.

LO 11

20-11 Charges, Conductors, and Electric Fields

We argued earlier that in a static situation, an ideal conductor must have zero electric field inside it and the electric field at the surface of the conductor must be exactly perpendicular to the surface. In this section, we will use Gauss's law to examine the charge distribution in conductors and the electric fields just outside conductors.

Consider the positively charged conducting spherical shell shown in Figure 20-20. From the symmetry of the situation, we know that the charge must be distributed symmetrically and the magnitude of the electric field must be the same in all points at a distance r from the centre of the shell. We also know that the electric field inside the conductor must be zero.

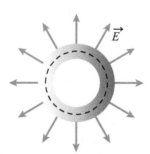

Figure 20-20 Since the electric flux through any spherical Gaussian surface inside the conductor is zero, the enclosed charge must be zero. We can conclude that all charge must reside on the outer surface.

If we draw a spherical Gaussian surface inside the conducting shell, the electric flux through the surface is zero because the electric field in the conductor is zero. Gauss's law then requires that the enclosed charge be zero.

Therefore, the charge on the conducting shell must all reside on the outer surface of the conductor.

In fact, static charges on all conductors always lie on the outer surfaces. Consequently, the electric field lines begin on the outer surface, and there is no static electric field in the cavity inside the conductor, as shown in Figure 20-20.

These charge distributions are examples of electrostatic equilibrium. Electrostatic equilibrium refers to a situation where the charges in the conductor have reached stable equilibrium positions.

C-20-11 Electric Potential of a Charged Conducting Shell

Which statement correctly describes the electric potential around a positively charged spherical conducting shell?

(a) The electric potential is positive and constant inside, and positive and decreasing outside.

(b) The electric potential is zero inside, and positive and decreasing outside.

(c) The electric potential is zero inside, and positive and constant outside.

(d) The electric potential is positive and increasing, both inside and outside.

C-20-11 (a) All the charge goes to the outer surface of the conducting shell. By Gauss's law, the electric field inside the shell is zero. The potential inside the shell is constant but not necessarily zero. Outside the shell, Gauss's law requires an electric field pointing away from the shell, so there must be a positive potential that decreases as the distance from the shell increases.

Although the absence of charges inside a closed conducting surface is strictly true only in electrostatic situations, such surfaces are often effective shields that block electromagnetic waves from penetrating the surface, provided that any holes in the surface are small compared to the wavelength of the electromagnetic waves. Such shielding enclosures are called Faraday cages, after Michael Faraday. In 1816, Faraday used them to demonstrate that no charge was present inside a conducting shell. Actually Benjamin Franklin had made the same discovery earlier while experimenting with charge distributions in 1755.

Suppose we place an uncharged conducting sphere in an external electric field directed downward, as shown in Figure 20-21. The conductor has no net charge, but it does have mobile charge carriers that are free to move within the conductor. We must still have zero net electric field inside the conductor—the mobile charge carriers in the conductor move to positions such that their own electric fields exactly cancel the external electric field. Free electrons move to the top of the sphere, producing a negative charge there and leaving a net positive charge at the bottom of the sphere, a phenomenon called induced charge separation. Note that the electric field lines in Figure 20-21 are distorted by the presence of the conductor: some electric

field lines end at the negative induced charges on the conductor, and an equal number of electric field lines start at the positive induced charges. The total electric field in the conductor is exactly zero in electrostatic equilibrium.

The induced charge can also be explained in terms of electric forces. The external electric field in Figure 20-21 exerts an upward force on negative charges and a downward force on positive charges.

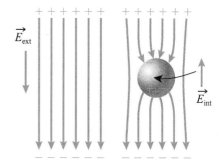

Figure 20-21 Charge separation induced in a conductor by an external electric field

Now consider two conducting spheres with different radii connected with a conducting wire, as shown in Figure 20-22. Recall that the electric field is stronger where the electric field lines are closer together and weaker where the electric field lines are widely separated. Electric charge is placed on one of the spheres. Some of that charge will flow through the conducting wire so that both spheres are charged. In electrostatic equilibrium, the charge must be distributed so that the electric potential is the same on the two spheres (otherwise, charges would flow in the conducting wire and the system would not be in electrostatic equilibrium).

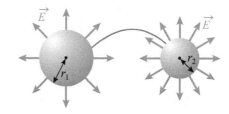

Figure 20-22 Two conducting spheres with different radii connected with a conducting wire

To see how the charge is distributed, first consider the simpler case of a single conducting sphere of radius r_0 that carries charge Q (Figure 20-23). We draw a Gaussian sphere around the conducting sphere at some distance r, with $r > r_0$. By the symmetry of the situation, the electric field has a constant magnitude at any particular distance, and $\vec{E}$ and $d\vec{A}$ are everywhere directed outward and are, therefore, parallel. All the charge is enclosed, so we can apply Gauss's law to find the magnitude of the electric field at a distance r:

$$\oint \vec{E} \cdot d\vec{A} = \frac{q_{enc}}{\varepsilon_0} \qquad (20\text{-}24)$$

$$E(4\pi r^2) = \frac{Q}{\varepsilon_0}$$

$$E = \frac{1}{4\pi\varepsilon_0} \frac{Q}{r^2} \qquad (20\text{-}25)$$

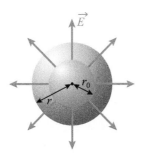

Figure 20-23 A conducting sphere (red) of radius r_0 carries a positive charge Q. The charge is on the outer surface, and the electric field lines start there. We can draw a Gaussian sphere of radius r to find the electric field at that distance.

Equation (20-25) is identical to the expression we obtained in Chapter 19 for the electric field around a point charge Q. Thus, for electric fields and forces outside a uniformly charged sphere, we can treat the sphere as a point charge. We obtain the electric potential V by integrating the electric field over a path from the reference point of zero potential (normally at infinite distance). Since the electric field is the same for a uniformly charged sphere and for a point charge that has the same electric charge Q, the expression we obtained for the electric potential at a distance r from a point charge also applies for the potential from a charged conducting sphere:

$$V = \frac{Q}{4\pi\varepsilon_0 r} \qquad (20\text{-}26)$$

We now return to the two spheres in Figure 20-22. As argued earlier, to be in electrostatic equilibrium the electric potential on each sphere must be the same:

$$\frac{Q_1}{r_1} = \frac{Q_2}{r_2} \qquad (20\text{-}27)$$

where Q_1 and Q_2 are the charges on the spheres of radii r_1, and r_2, respectively.

Comparing the magnitude of the electric field at the surface of the two spheres, we find

$$\frac{E_1}{E_2} = \frac{\dfrac{1}{4\pi\varepsilon_0}\dfrac{Q_1}{r_1^2}}{\dfrac{1}{4\pi\varepsilon_0}\dfrac{Q_2}{r_2^2}} = \frac{Q_1 r_2^2}{Q_2 r_1^2} = \frac{Q_1 r_2^2}{\dfrac{Q_1 r_2}{r_1} r_1^2} = \frac{r_2}{r_1} \qquad (20\text{-}28)$$

We have derived Equation (20-28) for the specific case of two conducting spheres, but the relationship is true in general: The electric field has a larger magnitude when the radius of curvature of a charged conducting surface is smaller. That is, the electric field is stronger near points, and has low values beside flat or nearly flat regions of the surface, as illustrated in Figure 20-24.

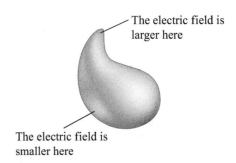

Figure 20-24 The electric field is stronger near sharply curved points.

Because the electric field is much greater in sharply pointed regions, it may become large enough to ionize material near those points. Corona discharge is electric discharge due to ionization of material in a fluid (such as air) surrounding a conductor. This discharge happens near pointed regions on conductors. This effect is used in ozone generators, in electrostatic precipitators that remove particulates in smokestacks, and in forced-air heating systems (see the Making Connections feature below).

 MAKING CONNECTIONS

Electrostatic Precipitators

Undesired by-products of power plant and industrial combustion processes are particulates in the exhaust gases. Electrostatic precipitators can reduce particulate concentrations. The gas containing particulates passes through a chamber region with high voltages applied to a grid with

many sharp points (like a screen with spikes or barbed wire points). Figure 20-25 shows the configuration of a typical electrostatic precipitator. The electric field is high enough near these points to cause corona discharge, which makes some of the particulates electrically charged. When the exhaust then passes near electrode plates with the opposite electric polarity, the charged particles precipitate onto the plates, thus cleaning the exhaust gases. Mechanical or fluid cleaning periodically removes the buildup of particulates from the plates. A similar process can be used in electrostatic cleaners as part of hot-air heating systems in the home and in free-standing air-cleaning units. The idea of charging dust to remove it was devised in the nineteenth century, but the first modern electrostatic precipitator was not patented until 1907, by Dr. Frederick Cottrell. The Research Corporation that Cottrell set up using revenues from these patents continues to fund university scientific research.

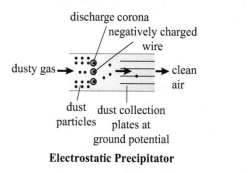

Electrostatic Precipitator

Figure 20-25   An electrostatic precipitator

When charges of the same sign are moved closer together, positive work is required by an external agent to move them so the electric potential energy increases.

Electric potential, V, is electric potential energy per unit charge. We usually talk of electric potential differences between two points. If the term "electric potential" is used, the zero point should always be specified (usually at an infinite distance).

The electron volt (eV) is a unit of energy that corresponds to the change in electric potential energy when one elementary charge unit moves through a potential difference of one volt.

Electric fields are vector quantities obtained by finding the electric force on a small positive test charge, and then dividing by the charge (units of N/C). These fields also correspond to the negative of the rate of change of electric potential (giving units of V/m).

Equipotential lines and surfaces join points of equal electric potential. Electric field lines show the direction of the electric field at a point and always cross equipotential lines perpendicularly. Electric field lines are drawn more closely together in regions of high electric field intensity.

The surface of an ideal electrical conductor must be at one common electric potential. There is no electric field inside a conductor in electrostatic equilibrium. Electric fields are exactly perpendicular to the surface of a conductor.

Because there is no electric field inside a conductor, all parts of that region must be at the same electric potential.

Charge placed on a conductor distributes itself entirely on the outer surface of the conductor.

For an irregularly shaped conductor, the electric field is stronger in regions where the surface is more pointed.

Electric Potential Energy

The electrostatic potential energy represented by a configuration with two charges, Q and q, a distance r apart is

$$U_{\text{E}} = \frac{Qq}{4\pi\varepsilon_0 r} \tag{20-4}$$

We can use the superposition principle to find the total potential energy for configurations of many point charges.

Electric Potential

Electric potential (V) is measured in volts and is defined as electric potential energy per unit charge.

$$V = \frac{U}{q} \tag{20-6}$$

We sometimes write ΔV and ΔU to remind ourselves that differences are important and a zero level must be defined.

$$\Delta U = q\Delta V \tag{20-11}$$

The electric potential for a point a distance r from a single point charge Q is

$$V = \frac{Q}{4\pi\varepsilon_0 r} \tag{20-7}$$

The superposition principle can be used to find the potential due to collections of point charges.

Electric Field from Electric Potential

If we know the electric potential distribution, we can use partial derivatives to find the electric field components:

$$E_x = -\frac{\partial V}{\partial x}; \quad E_y = -\frac{\partial V}{\partial y}; \quad E_z = -\frac{\partial V}{\partial z} \tag{20-9}$$

We can integrate the electric field to find the potential difference between two points:

$$V_b - V_a = -\int_a^b \vec{E} \cdot d\vec{r} \tag{20-10}$$

Gauss's Law

Gauss's law allows us to calculate the electric field in situations involving spherical, cylindrical, and planar symmetry:

$$\oint \vec{E} \cdot d\vec{A} = \frac{q_{\text{enc}}}{\varepsilon_0} \tag{20-14}$$

where the left-hand quantity is the electric flux integrated over some closed surface, and the vector dot product is taken between the electric field and an element of area perpendicular to the surface $d\vec{A}$. The total net electric charge enclosed by the surface is q_{enc}, and ε_0 is a constant of nature called the permittivity of free space.

Applications: atmospheric electricity, radiation treatment using particles from particle accelerators, electron microscopes, electrostatic precipitators for dust control, cathode ray tube devices, ozone production by corona discharge, shielding from electromagnetic fields and waves

Key Terms: corona discharge, electric flux, electric potential, electric potential difference, electric potential energy, electron volt, electrostatic equilibrium, equipotential lines, Gauss's law, induced charge, permittivity of free space, surface integral, surface charge density, volt, volume charge density

QUESTIONS

1. An electron ($-e$ charge) is in orbit about a hydrogen nucleus ($+e$ charge) at a distance r_0. What is the electric potential energy of this system?

   (a) $-\dfrac{1}{4\pi\varepsilon_0}\dfrac{e^2}{r_0}$

   (b) $+\dfrac{1}{4\pi\varepsilon_0}\dfrac{e^2}{r_0}$

   (c) $-\dfrac{1}{4\pi\varepsilon_0}\dfrac{e^2}{r_0^2}$

   (d) $+\dfrac{1}{4\pi\varepsilon_0}\dfrac{e^2}{r_0^2}$

2. You have two unknown point charges, Q_1 and Q_2. You observe that the electric potential is zero exactly halfway between the two charges. What conclusion can you make?

   (a) The two charges have the same magnitude and the same sign.

   (b) The two charges have the same magnitude and the opposite sign.

   (c) There is no way that you can have zero potential at the midpoint.

   (d) The magnitudes of both charges are zero.

3. An electron is moving past a positive ion on the path shown in Figure 20-26. At which of the following points does the electron–ion system have highest speed?

   (a) A

   (b) B

   (c) C

   (d) D

Figure 20-26 Question 3

4. An electron goes from a region at -10 kV to a region at $+30$ kV. What is the electron's change in kinetic energy?

   (a) -40 keV

   (b) $+20$ keV

   (c) $+30$ keV

   (d) $+40$ keV

5. You have two fixed charges, $+Q$ on the left and $-4Q$ on the right, separated by a distance of 3 m. Where is one location with zero electric potential?

   (a) at a point 1 m to the left of the $+Q$ charge

   (b) at a point 1 m to the right of the $+Q$ charge

   (c) at a point 1 m to the left of the $-4Q$ charge

   (d) at a point 1 m to the right of the $-4Q$ charge

6. Which of the following statements is correct?

   (a) Electric field and electric potential are both vectors, and electric flux is a scalar.

   (b) Electric field and electric potential are both scalars, and electric flux is a vector.

   (c) Electric field is a vector, and electric potential and electric flux are scalars.

   (d) Electric field, electric potential, and electric flux are vector quantities.

7. A proton is moving in the $+x$-direction, and its speed is increasing but its acceleration is constant. Which of the following statements is correct?

   (a) The proton is moving into a region with higher electric potential.

   (b) The proton is moving into a region with lower electric potential.

   (c) The acceleration is constant, so there is no change in electric potential.

   (d) The scenario is impossible.

8. A positive charge is located at the origin of an xyz-coordinate system. What can you conclude about the electric potential at the points A(0, -1, 0) and B(0, $+1$, 0)?

   (a) Points A and B are both at a negative electric potential.

   (b) Points A and B are both at a positive electric potential.

   (c) Point A is at a negative electric potential, and point B is at a positive electric potential.

   (d) Point A is at a positive electric potential, and point B is at a negative electric potential.

9. When an electric potential increases with distance in the x-direction according to $V = 3x^2 + 20$, what is the electric field at the point $x = y = z = 1$ m?

   (a) The electric field components are $+20$ N/C in the y- and z-directions and -6 N/C in the x-direction.

   (b) The electric field components are $+20$ N/C in the y- and z-directions and $+6$ N/C in the x-direction.

   (c) The electric field components are zero in the y- and z-directions and $+14$ N/C in the x-direction.

   (d) The electric field components are zero in the y- and z-directions and -6 N/C in the x-direction.

10. When you slightly increase the distance between a proton and an electron in a hydrogen atom, what happens to the electric potential energy of the system?

    (a) The electric potential energy increases.

    (b) The electric potential energy decreases.

    (c) The electric potential energy is negative both before and after but does not change in magnitude.

    (d) The electric potential energy is zero both before and after.

11. A single positive charge is placed inside a small cube. What can be said about the net electric flux over the surfaces of the cube?

    (a) The net electric flux is negative, and the value depends on where in the cube the charge is placed.

    (b) The net electric flux is positive, and the value depends on where in the cube the charge is placed.

    (c) The net electric flux is negative, and the value is independent of the position of the charge inside the cube.

    (d) The net electric flux is positive, and the value is independent of the position of the charge inside the cube.

12. An ion contains a nuclear charge of $+5e$ and has a total electronic charge of $-4e$. What is the electric field at a distance r well outside the atom? Assume spherical symmetry.

    (a) The electric field is $\dfrac{1}{4\pi\varepsilon_0}\dfrac{e}{r^2}$ in a direction radially inward toward the atom.

    (b) The electric field is $\dfrac{1}{4\pi\varepsilon_0}\dfrac{e}{r^2}$ in a direction radially outward away from the atom.

    (c) The electric field is $\dfrac{1}{4\pi\varepsilon_0}\dfrac{5e}{r^2}$ in a direction radially inward toward the atom.

    (d) The electric field is $\dfrac{1}{4\pi\varepsilon_0}\dfrac{9e}{r^2}$ in a direction radially outward away from the atom.

CHAPTER 20 | ELECTRIC POTENTIAL AND GAUSS'S LAW   545

13. You draw a spherical Gaussian surface just outside an electric dipole (equal positive and negative charges separated by a small distance). What can you conclude about the electric flux through that surface?
  (a) As long as the dipole is completely inside the surface, the flux is zero.
  (b) The flux is only zero when the surface is centred on the midpoint of the dipole.
  (c) The flux is approximately but not exactly zero, even when the surface is centred on the midpoint of the dipole.
  (d) None of the above are true.

14. Some charge is placed on a closed (and hollow) tin can. Where is the charge located?
  (a) The charge is located equally throughout the metal of the can.
  (b) All the charge is on the inside surface.
  (c) All the charge is on the outside surface.
  (d) All the charge is on the two ends (none on the curved surface).

15. Two conducting spheres with different radii are joined by a wire, and a negative charge is placed on the system. Which statement correctly describes the electric field and electric potential just outside the surface of each sphere?
  (a) The electric field points toward the surface in both cases and is stronger on the smaller sphere. The electric potential is negative and the same for both spheres.
  (b) The electric field points away from the surface in both cases and is stronger on the smaller sphere. The electric potential is zero for both spheres.
  (c) The electric field points toward the surface in both cases and is stronger on the larger sphere. The electric potential is negative and the same for both spheres.
  (d) The electric field points toward the surface in both cases and is of the same strength. The potential is negative in both cases and higher for the smaller sphere.

16. When the charge on a conducting sphere is doubled, how does the electric potential *inside* the sphere change?
  (a) The electric potential is now four times as large.
  (b) The electric potential is now two times as large.
  (c) The electric potential is now approximately $\sqrt{2}$ times as large.
  (d) The electric potential is zero in both cases.

PROBLEMS BY SECTION

For problems, star ratings will be used, (✻, ✻✻, or ✻✻✻), with more stars meaning more challenging problems.

Section 20-1 Electric Potential Energy

17. ✻ We assume that an electron and a proton are on average separated by 53.0 pm. What is the electric potential energy of a hydrogen atom?

18. ✻✻ How much work is required to move four charges from infinite initial separation into the following configuration along the x-axis: $+1.00\ \mu$C at $+2.00$ m, $+2.00\ \mu$C at $+3.00$ m, $+3.00\ \mu$C at $+4.00$ m, and $+4.00\ \mu$C at $+5.00$ m?

Section 20-2 Electric Potential

19. ✻✻ Four $+2.00$ nC charges are located at the corners of a square that is 10.0 cm on each side. What is the electric potential at the exact centre of the square?

20. ✻✻ In Figure 20-27, a $-3.00\ \mu$C charge is 0.500 m to the right of a $+6.00\ \mu$C charge. Point P_1 is located 0.250 m to the right of the negative charge, and point P_2 is located a further 0.250 m to the right.
  (a) What is the electric potential at point P_1?
  (b) What is the electric potential at point P_2?
  (c) How much work is required to move a -1.00 nC charge from point P_2 to P_1?

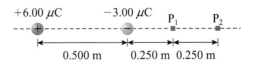

Figure 20-27 Problem 20

Section 20-3 Equipotential Lines and Electric Field Lines

21. ✻ Figure 20-28 shows plots of some equipotential lines. Sketch in the corresponding electric field lines, and indicate the relative strength of the electric field vectors in different regions.

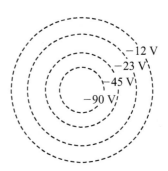

Figure 20-28 Problem 21

22. ✻✻ The central $+2$ nC charge in Figure 20-29 is flanked on the left and right (at equal distances) by -1 nC charges. Qualitatively sketch the electric field lines and equipotential lines for the system.

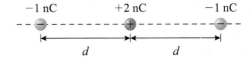

Figure 20-29 Problem 22

Section 20-4 Electric Field from Electric Potential

23. ✻✻ An electric potential in SI units has the form $V = -100.0 + 25.0y$.
  (a) Write expressions for the three components of the electric field.
  (b) What is the electric field at the point (1.00 m, 2.00 m, 0.00)?

24. ✻ In Chapter 19, we noted that high electric fields can be present inside biological cell membranes. The field in a particular cell over a small region is assumed to have a constant value of 5.00 N/μC. What is the potential difference over a 2.00 μm distance?

25. ✷✷ An electric field vector is $\vec{E} = -20\hat{i}$ N/C.
(a) Describe the equipotential surfaces.
(b) When $V = +25.0$ V at the origin, where is $V = 75.0$ V?

Section 20-5   The Electron Volt

26. ✷✷ The electron beam in a typical scanning electron microscope produces kinetic energies of 25.0 keV.
(a) Assuming that relativistic effects can be ignored, what is the speed of the electrons?
(b) What potential difference is required to produce electrons of this energy?
(c) This accelerating potential difference is applied over a distance of 2.50 cm. What is the electric field in that region?

27. ✷ A particular chemical reaction requires 2.45 eV to create a new molecule.
(a) What is this energy per molecule expressed in units of joules?
(c) What is this energy in thermochemical calories? (1 calorie = 4.184 J)

Section 20-6   Electric Fields and Conductors

28. ✷ A conducting solid oval carries a negative charge (Figure 20-30). Sketch the electric field vectors, if any, (a) inside, (b) on the surface, and (c) slightly away from the surface.

Figure 20-30   Problem 28

Section 20-7   Charge Densities

29. ✷ A charge of +165 μC is uniformly distributed around a very thin ring of radius 4.00 cm. What is the linear charge density along the ring?

30. ✷ A thin plate has the dimensions 3.50 cm × 12.0 cm and carries a charge density of 45.0 μC/m². How many elementary charge units (i.e., 1.60×10^{-19} C) are on the entire plate?

31. ✷ A nonconducting sphere has a radius of 2.75 cm and a total charge of +3.00 μC uniformly spread throughout the sphere. What is the volume charge density?

Section 20-8   Electric Flux

32. ✷✷ In a certain region, the electric field points in the +y-direction and has a magnitude of 35.0 N/C. What is the electric flux through a circle of radius 1.00 cm that lies in the xz-plane?

33. ✷✷ An electric field $\vec{E}$ is parallel to the axis of a hemispheric shell, as shown in Figure 20-31. What is the electric flux through the surface?

Figure 20-31   Problem 33

Section 20-9   Gauss's Law

34. ✷✷ A +25.0 nC point charge is surrounded by a concentric conducting spherical shell of radius 2.40 cm that carries a charge of −20.0 nC. Derive expressions for the electric field as a function of radial distance both inside and outside the shell.

35. ✷✷ A solid, nonconducting sphere of radius r_0 has a uniform charge density ρ (assume a positive charge). Derive expressions for the electric field as a function of radial distance r both inside and outside the sphere.

Section 20-10   Applications of Gauss's Law

36. ✷✷ A solid, nonconducting very long cylinder of radius r_0 has a uniform charge density ρ. Derive expressions for the electric field as a function of radial distance r both inside and outside the cylinder.

37. ✷✷✷ Two long, concentric conducting cylinders have radii 4.50 cm and 8.50 cm (Figure 20-32). The inner cylinder carries a charge per unit length of +15.0 μC/m, and the outer cylinder carries a charge per unit length of −10.0 μC/m. Derive and plot expressions for the electric field as a function of radial distance r in all three regions: inside the inner cylinder, the space between the two cylinders, and outside the outer cylinder.

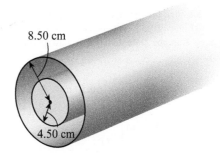

8.50 cm

4.50 cm

Figure 20-32   Problem 37

Section 20-11   Charges, Conductors, and Electric Fields

38. ✷✷✷ A relatively large Van de Graaff generator has a conducting sphere of radius 0.600 m. Assume that a total charge of 94.0 μC is present on the sphere.
(a) What is the electric field inside the conducting sphere?
(b) What is the electric potential at the surface of the conductor?
(c) What is the electric potential inside the conducting sphere?
(d) Calculate and plot the electric potential as a function of distance outside the conductor.
(e) What is the electric field just outside the conductor?

COMPREHENSIVE PROBLEMS

39. ✶ Two protons are 3.00 fm apart. What is the electrostatic energy of this configuration?

40. ✶✶ Three +2.00 nC charges are placed at the vertices of an equilateral triangle with 25.0 cm sides.
(a) What is the electric potential energy of this charge distribution?
(b) How much work is needed to bring the charges from an infinite distance into this configuration?

41. ✶✶ Two positive charges in space, each with a charge of +25.0 μC and a mass of 5.00 mg, are initially held in a fixed separation of 35.0 mm. They are released and allowed to separate under mutual repulsion. What speed will they each attain when they are very far apart? (Hint: Use an energy approach. By conservation of linear momentum, you know that the situation must result in symmetric motions relative to the centre of mass.)

42. ✶✶ An electric dipole has two charges, +1.00 nC and −1.00 nC, separated by a distance of 0.250 μm. What is the electric potential energy of the configuration?

43. ✶✶ An electron is accelerated through a constant electric field until it reaches a speed of 3.0×10^5 m/s. What is the potential difference between the starting and ending positions?

44. ✶✶ Consider the distribution of the four point charges shown in Figure 20-33. What is the electric potential, V, at a point halfway between charges A and B?

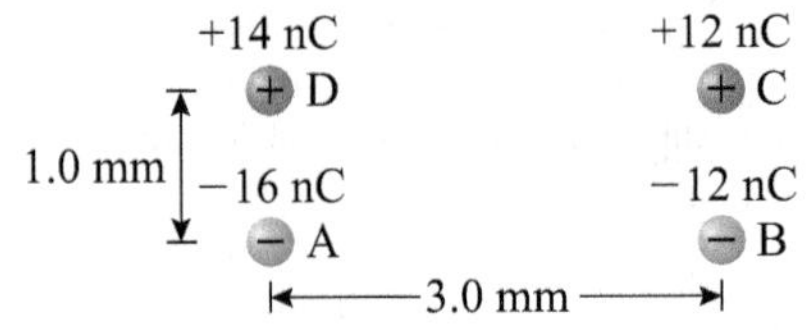

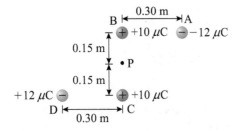

Figure 20-33 Problem 44

45. ✶✶ Consider the arrangement of four electric charges shown in Figure 20-34. Find the electric potential at point P, assuming that the potential has a zero point at infinite distance.

Figure 20-34 Problem 45

46. ✶✶✶ Three identical charges +q are placed at three of the four corners of a square with sides d.
(a) What is the electric potential at the corner that is missing a charge?
(b) What is the work required to move a fourth charge +q from an infinite distance to the corner that is missing a charge?

(c) Check your answer to part (b) by calculating the difference between the electrostatic potential energy in the cases of three charges and four charges.

47. ✶✶ In the famous Rutherford scattering experiment, α-particles were fired at a thin gold foil. When the α-particles passed near a nucleus, they were deflected by large angles. For the purpose of this question we are going to consider the situation of an α-particle directed exactly at a gold nucleus. Calculate how close an α-particle could get before it "bounces back" due to electric repulsion. Use energy considerations to solve this problem. Gold has 79 protons in the nucleus. An α-particle is made up of 2 protons and 2 neutrons. The α-particle had a speed of 1.50×10^7 m/s when it was a large distance away. Assume that the gold nucleus is sufficiently massive that it does not move. Treat the gold nucleus as though it were a point charge of the same total charge for purposes of solving this problem.

48. ✶✶ A constant electric field is defined by the following vector:

$$\vec{E} = 4.00\hat{\imath} + 25.0\hat{k} \text{ N/C}$$

What is the electric flux through a 1.00 m × 1.00 m area that is in the xy-plane and is centred on the origin?

49. ✶✶ The electric field near Earth's surface points downward and has a magnitude of approximately 150 N/C. If the field were due to a thin layer of charge spread evenly over Earth's surface, what would the magnitude and sign of the electric charge be?

50. ✶✶ (a) Determine the sign and direction of the electric field required for an electron to have an upward electric force that just balances the downward force of gravity.
(b) With this field, we define the electric potential as 0 V at the surface. What is the potential at a height of 3.00 m? Assume a constant field.

51. ✶✶ A cathode ray tube display accelerates an electron from rest to 2.25×10^7 m/s within a distance of 1.25 cm in the acceleration region.
(a) What is the magnitude of the electric potential difference in this accelerating region?
(b) What is the increase in the kinetic energy of the electrons, in eV?

52. ✶✶ (a) A proton is travelling at a speed of 2.50×10^7 m/s. What is the kinetic energy, in eV? Ignore relativistic effects.
(b) Repeat part (a) with an electron.

53. ✶✶✶ A conducting sphere of radius 12.0 cm has a spherical cavity of radius 5.00 cm in its centre. The sphere carries a total charge of +240 nC. Derive expressions for the electric field magnitude and the electric potential as a function of radial distance, r.

54. ✶✶ A nonconducting plate carries a uniformly distributed charge of 600.0 nC. The plate is 18.00 cm long, 40.00 cm wide, and 0.500 cm thick.
(a) Use Gauss's law to approximate the electric field at a point 1.00 cm above the surface of the plate.
(b) What is the electric field at a point 5.00 cm above the plate?

55. ✶✶✶ The diameter of the central wire in a very long triple conductor coaxial cable is 4.00 mm. Concentric around the wire is a middle cylindrical conductor with a diameter of 2.60 cm and an outer conductor with a diameter of 5.00 cm. At some instant, the wire carries a charge density of $+15.0\ \mu C/m$, the middle conductor carries a charge density of $-7.00\ \mu C/m$, and the outer conductor carries a charge density of $-8.00\ \mu C/m$. Derive expressions for the electric field as a function of radial distance in each of the following regions:

(a) between the wire and the central conductor;

(b) between the middle and outer conductors;

(c) outside the outer conductor.

56. ✸✸ Consider a nonconducting sphere of radius r_0 and uniform charge density ρ.

(a) Derive an expression for the electric field as a function of radial distance for $r < r_0$.

(b) Derive an expression for the electric field as a function of radial distance for $r > r_0$.

57. ✸✸ Figure 20-35 shows a plot of an electric potential as a function of distance along the x-axis. From this information, determine the x-component of the electric field at each of the following displacements:

(a) $x = 0.5$ m;

(b) $x = 1.5$ m;

(c) $x = 3.0$ m;

(d) $x = 4.5$ m.

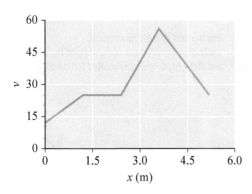

Figure 20-35   Problem 57

58. ✸✸✸ (a) We assume that dry air breaks down electrically when the electric field exceeds 2.50×10^6 V/m. Determine the maximum charge that can be placed on a conducting sphere with each of the following radii: (i) 10.0 cm and (ii) 20.0 cm.

(b) For each case in part (a), determine the surface charge density.

59. ✸✸ As mentioned earlier in the chapter, electrostatic dust precipitators have a section where there are spikes to make high electric fields to ionize the dust grains (followed by high voltages to collect the charged dust later). Assume that the spikes can be approximated by a hemisphere at the top of a rod as shown in Figure 20-36, with a diameter of

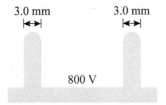

Figure 20-36   Problem 59

3.00 mm. When the plate is held at a potential of 800 V, what is the electric field near a spike surface? (Assume for this purpose that it is the same field as for an entire sphere of the same radius.)

60. ✸✸ Imagine that the attractive force between the Sun and Earth were electrostatic rather than gravitational. Assume that Earth has a negative charge and the Sun has a positive charge of equal magnitude.

(a) What charge would produce an electric force equal the actual gravitational force?

(b) Suppose that the charge is distributed evenly over the surface of Earth. What would the surface charge density be?

(c) What would the electric field just above Earth's surface be?

(d) What would the electric potential on Earth's surface be?

61. ✸✸✸ Three drops each have a radius of 250 μm and a charge of 50 nC. Assume that the drops are perfectly spherical (this is a good approximation because of surface tension).

(a) What is the electric potential just outside the surface of one drop?

(b) The three drops coalesce, with the total charge now equally spread over the resultant larger drop. What is the new electric potential?

(c) What is the electric field just outside the drop in each case?

62. ✸✸✸ (a) A positive charge Q is placed at some distance d to the left of an infinite conducting plate that is at zero electric potential (grounded). What sign of charge is induced in the conducting plate at the point nearest Q?

(b) Sketch electric field lines for the situation.

(c) In more advanced electromagnetism courses, a technique called the "method of images" is used. In this case, we can imagine a charge of the opposite sign $-Q$ (an "image charge") placed behind the plate at an equal distance d from the plate. We know this is the correct placement because it will lead to a zero potential along the conducting plate. We can replace the plate with the image charge and consider the two charges when calculating electric potentials. Use this idea to sketch electric equipotential lines.

(d) If $Q = 2.50$ nC and $d = 0.150$ m, what is the electric potential at a point halfway between the charge Q and the plate?

63. ✸✸ Use calculus to find the electric potential at distances $a/2$ and $2a$ from an infinite line of charge having a linear charge density μ (measured in coulombs per metre). Assume that zero electric potential is defined at distance a from the line of charge.

64. ✸✸✸ A thin ring of charge of radius a is in the xy-plane centred on the origin. The ring has linear charge density μ. Derive an expression for the electric potential at the point $(0, 0, z)$. In your final expression, include a constant of integration, representing the zero definition of electric potential.

65. ✸✸✸ Using calculus on differential elements of charge, derive an expression for the electric potential at a point located a distance z above the centre of a disk of radius a. Assume that the disk has a surface charge density of σ (measured in coulombs per square metre).

ELECTRICITY, MAGNETISM, AND OPTICS

DATA-RICH PROBLEM

66. ✱✱✱ Table 20-1 lists data on electric potential as a function of radial distance. The object is some sort of a sphere.
   (a) Plot the electric potential data.
   (b) From the data, determine the approximate electric field, and plot the electric field data. Indicate the direction of the electric field.
   (c) Is the object conducting or nonconducting? Justify your answer.
   (d) What is the radius of the object?
   (e) Calculate the approximate charge distribution for the object: If the charge is all on a surface, calculate the surface charge density. If the charge is uniformly spread throughout the object, calculate the volume charge density, assuming that it is constant. Is the charge positive or negative?
   (f) How far from the object would you need to be for the electric potential to be 500 V?

Table 20-1 Data for Problem 66

R (m)	Electric potential (V)
0.0	7000
0.1	7000
0.2	7000
0.3	7000
0.4	7000
0.5	6300
0.6	5250
0.7	4500
0.8	3940
0.9	3500
1.0	3150
1.1	2865
1.2	2625
1.3	2425
1.4	2250
1.5	2100
1.6	1970
1.7	1855
1.8	1750

OPEN PROBLEM

67. ✱✱✱ If you scuff along a carpeted floor on a dry day, and then approach a metal object, such as a doorknob, a spark can jump from your finger. In this problem, you will estimate the amount of charge on your finger as a result of this scenario.
   (a) When the electric field reaches a certain value, breakdown will occur. That is what happens when the spark jumps. Use a reliable source to determine a value for breakdown in dry air.
   (b) Perform an experiment in which you scuff across a carpet and produce a spark when you point toward a doorknob. From that experiment, estimate the distance that the spark jumps from your finger to the doorknob.
   (c) Using your answer from (b) and assuming that the potential on the doorknob is approximately zero, estimate the original electric potential on your finger.
   (d) Approximate the end of your finger as a sphere, and estimate its radius. When the charge is equally spread on the surface of the sphere, what is the charge density on the tip of your finger?

 See the text online resources at www.physics1e.nelson.com for Open Problems and Data-Rich Problems related to this chapter.

Chapter 21
Capacitance

Every day defibrillators save many lives. Fibrillation is a series of rapid, irregular muscle contractions. Fibrillation of the heart can be fatal because it prevents proper blood flow and can seriously damage heart tissue. A defibrillator uses an electric shock to momentarily stop the heart and give it a chance to resume beating normally. Figure 21-1 shows a common type of external defibrillator. A miniature internal defibrillator can be implanted in patients who have chronic problems with heart fibrillation. A key part of the defibrillator circuit that delivers a controlled pulse of electric current to the patient is the capacitor, which is a device that can store charge and electrostatic energy. In this chapter, you will learn how capacitors are made, how they operate, and how these relatively simple devices have innumerable applications in modern technologies.

LOOK AHEAD

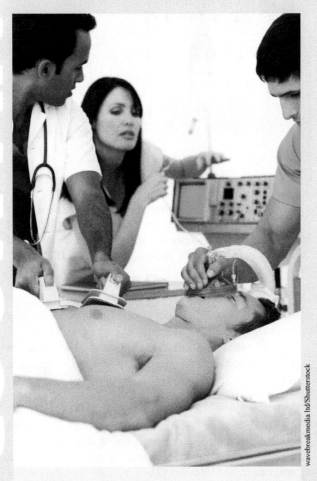

Figure 21-1 A paddle-type defibrillator

wavebreakmedia ltd/Shutterstock

Learning Objectives

When you have completed this chapter you should be able to:

1 Define capacitance and capacitor, and perform calculations relating capacitance, charge, and potential difference.

2 Prove that the electric field is constant inside a parallel-plate capacitor, and calculate its value.

3 Calculate capacitance for parallel plates and other configurations.

4 Perform calculations for situations with combinations of capacitors in series and in parallel.

5 Explain why the presence of a dielectric increases the capacitance, and calculate capacitance in the presence of dielectrics.

6 Derive an expression for the electrostatic potential energy stored in a capacitor, and use that expression to calculate energies for stored capacitors with and without dielectrics.

7 Explain how capacitors are used in various applications.

ELECTRICITY, MAGNETISM, AND OPTICS

For additional Making Connections, Examples, and Checkpoints, as well as activities and experiments to help increase your understanding of the chapter's concepts, please go to the text's online resources at www.physics1e.nelson.com.

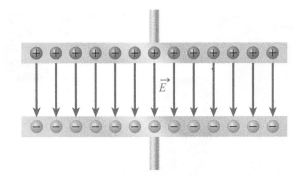

21-1 Capacitors and Capacitance

A capacitor is a device that can store charge and electrostatic energy. You have probably used capacitors numerous times without realizing it. For example, an electronic camera flash uses a capacitor to store the energy that is released during the flash. Turn indicators on some automobiles use a circuit with capacitors and resistors to control the rate at which the signals flash. Electronic cameras and camcorders form images by storing charge on an array of tiny photosensitive capacitors.

Capacitors come in many shapes and sizes and can be made with a variety of materials (Figure 21-2); however, most capacitors consist of two closely spaced parallel plates. When the capacitor is charged, one of these plates carries a positive charge and the other plate carries a negative charge of the same magnitude. The words "capacitor" and "capacity" have the same root, which reflects the key feature of capacitors: their ability to store charge.

Figure 21-2 An assortment of modern capacitors

The first capacitors were invented independently around 1745 by the German scientist Ewald Georg von Kleist (1700–48) and the Dutch professor Pieter van Musschenbroek (1692–1761). The very first models consisted simply of a glass jar of water with a metal wire or chain suspended from an insulating stopper. The water acted as one plate and the experimenter's hand as the other plate. Researchers soon found that coating the inside and outside of the jar with metal foil increased the amount of charge that it could store. These glass jar capacitors were called Leyden jars after the university where Musschenbroek conducted his research. Benjamin Franklin was possibly the first to make a capacitor with flat, parallel plates. Michael Faraday is generally credited with the first clear explanation of the charge storage process in capacitors.

Ideally, the material between the plates of a capacitor is totally nonconducting. Some capacitors simply have air between the plates, but most capacitors have a solid dielectric material (see Chapter 19). Since unlike charges

attract, electrostatic forces hold the charge on the plates of a capacitor when the source of the charge is disconnected from the capacitor. An ideal capacitor would stay charged forever, but an actual capacitor discharges because charge gradually leaks through the dielectric between its plates or through the air between its terminals.

ONLINE ACTIVITY

Capacitor Basics

The e-resource that accompanies every new copy of this textbook contains an Online Activity using the PhET simulation "Capacitor Lab." Work through the simulation and accompanying questions to gain an understanding of capacitor basics.

The electric field between the plates of the capacitor in Figure 21-3 is directed from the positively charged plate to the negatively charged plate because that would be the direction of the force on a small positive test charge placed between the plates. As we will prove in the next section, this field is essentially constant: it is the same everywhere between the plates except very near the edge of a plate.

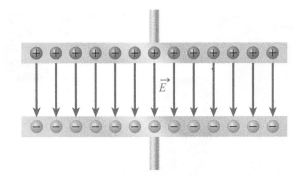

© David J. Green - electrical/Alamy

Figure 21-3 An idealized parallel-plate capacitor

Recall from the previous chapter that the electric potential difference between two points can be found by integrating the vector dot product of the electric field along a path joining the points:

$$V_b - V_a = -\int_a^b \vec{E} \cdot \vec{dr} \qquad (20\text{-}10)$$

Since the electric field is constant in both direction and magnitude between the plates of a capacitor, we can take $\vec{E}$ outside the integral, giving a simple expression for the potential difference, V, between the two plates a distance d apart:

KEY EQUATION
$$V = Ed \qquad (21\text{-}1)$$

Keep in mind that it is always the positively charged plate that is at the higher electric potential. If we add more charge to the plates, the electric field must increase in magnitude, and Equation (21-1) indicates that the electric potential difference increases correspondingly. The rate at which changes in charge on a plate, Q, affect the potential difference, V, depends on the physical dimensions of the capacitor (described in the next section) and is called the capacitance, C. Note that Q in the following equation is the magnitude of charge on one of the plates; the sum of the charges on both plates is zero because the plates have opposite charges of equal magnitude.

KEY EQUATION
$$Q = CV \qquad (21\text{-}2)$$

It is important to realize that capacitance is the ratio of charge to potential difference, but the capacitance does not change when you change the potential difference. Capacitance is determined by the dimensions and physical properties of the materials in the capacitor. A useful way to think about capacitance is that it is a measure of how much charge can be stored for a certain voltage. High capacitance means that you can store more charge at the same voltage than in a capacitor with less capacitance.

The SI unit of capacitance is the farad (F), named in honour of Michael Faraday. As you can see from Equation (21-2), one farad is equal to one coulomb per volt. A farad is a huge amount of capacitance for everyday purposes; most capacitors that you will use in the lab or encounter in household devices are measured in pico-farads (pF) or microfarads (μF). By convention, capacitance is rarely measured in nanofarads.

Capacitors are charged by connecting them to a source of electric potential difference, such as the battery in the circuit shown in Figure 21-4. The symbol for a capacitor is simply two parallel lines, representing the plates. Some textbooks show capacitors with one thick or curved line, but in all cases the lines are the same length. The end connected to the positive terminal of the battery is positively charged. We have indicated the polarity in Figure 21-4, but it is not usual to show this on the symbol.

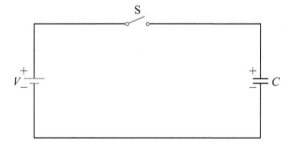

Figure 21-4 When the switch (S) is closed, the capacitor (C) will charge to the same voltage as the ideal battery (V). The end connected to the positive terminal of the battery is the positively charged capacitor side.

 ONLINE ACTIVITY

Capacitor Electric Fields

The e-resource that accompanies every new copy of this textbook contains an Online Activity using the PhET simulation "Capacitor Lab." Work through the simulation and accompanying questions to gain an understanding of capacitor electric fields.

✅ **CHECKPOINT**

C-21-1 Capacitance

Capacitors A and B are charged by connecting them to identical batteries. Capacitor A has a higher capacitance, even though the distance between the plates is the same for both capacitors. Which of the following statements is correct?

(a) Both capacitors have the same voltage, but A has more charge stored and a larger electric field between the plates.

(b) Both capacitors have the same voltage and electric field, but A has more charge stored.

(c) Both capacitors have the same voltage and electric field, but A has less charge stored.

(d) Capacitor A has a higher voltage, more charge stored, and a larger electric field.

LO 2

21-2 Electric Fields in Capacitors

In this section, we will show that the electric field is essentially constant in the region between the plates of a capacitor. Consider a parallel-plate capacitor with a positively charged top plate. We will draw a Gaussian cylinder with one end inside the top metal plate and the other end in the space between the plates, as shown in Figure 21-5.

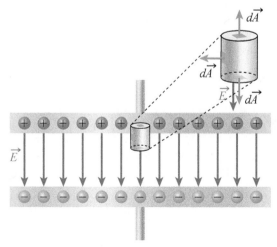

Figure 21-5 Gaussian cylinder in a parallel-plate capacitor

Recall from Chapter 20 that Gauss's law relates the total flux through our Gaussian surface to the enclosed charge:

$$\oint \vec{E} \cdot d\vec{A} = \frac{q_{enc}}{\varepsilon_0} \qquad (20\text{-}15)$$

The total flux equals the sum of the flux through the flat ends and the curved side of the Gaussian cylinder. However, the electric field is zero inside the conductive top plate, so the flux through the top end of the cylinder is zero. Also, the area vector $d\vec{A}$ and the electric field vector $\vec{E}$ are perpendicular to each other for the entire curved side of the cylinder, so the vector dot product makes the net flux on this surface zero. We are left with only the flux through the end that is located between the capacitor plates. Since the area vector for this end is parallel to the electric field, Gauss's law for this situation reduces to

$$EA_e = \frac{\sigma A_e}{\varepsilon_0} \qquad (21\text{-}3)$$

where A_e is the area of the end, and σ is the surface charge density of the plate.

Therefore, the magnitude of the electric field in the space between the plates is simply

$$E = \frac{\sigma}{\varepsilon_0} \qquad (21\text{-}4)$$

This relationship applies as long as our Gaussian surface is located anywhere along the plates and ends anywhere between the plates. Therefore, the electric field between the plates of a parallel-plate capacitor is essentially constant. When you go on to more advanced courses in electromagnetism, you will learn about the variations in the electric field near the ends of the capacitor. However, through most of the capacitor the field is approximately constant, and we will assume that in this textbook.

Most of the time, we do not deal directly with the surface charge density, so Equation (21-4) is rarely used in capacitor problems. If we assume that the area of one plate of the capacitor is A, we can rewrite Equation (21-4) in terms of the total charge, Q, on one plate:

$$E = \frac{Q}{\varepsilon_0 A} \qquad (21\text{-}5)$$

Multiplying both sides of this equation by the distance between the plates, d, and using the fact that the potential difference between the plates, V, is equal to Ed, we have

$$V = \frac{Qd}{\varepsilon_0 A} \qquad (21\text{-}6)$$

This equation is consistent with our basic capacitor equation, $Q = CV$, when the capacitance of a parallel-plate capacitor is given by

KEY EQUATION
$$C = \frac{\varepsilon_0 A}{d} \qquad (21\text{-}7)$$

This expression for capacitance makes sense because we expect plates with a larger area to be able to store more charge (i.e., have a greater capacitance). Also, with a closer spacing of the plates, the positive and negative charges can more effectively "hold" each other in place; hence the capacitance is greater. Equation (21-7) is exact for a parallel-plate capacitor with a vacuum between the plates, and is a close approximation for capacitors with air between the plates. Later in the chapter, we will see how a dielectric between the plates changes the capacitance.

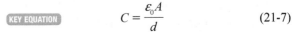

CHECKPOINT

C-21-2 The Electric Field between Parallel Plates

Two parallel conducting plates are separated by 4.00 mm; one has a voltage of +400 V, and the other is grounded (0 V). Which statement correctly describes the electric field between the plates?

(a) The electric field is 100 kV/m near the midpoint, essentially zero just outside the grounded plate, and essentially infinite just outside the +400 V plate.

(b) The electric field is zero at the midpoint, 100 kV/m pointing away from the +400 V plate, and for the grounded plate the same magnitude but pointing toward the grounded plate.

(c) The electric field is 50 000 V/m at the midpoint, almost 100 kV/m near the +400 V plate, and near zero just outside the grounded plate.

(d) The electric field is constant throughout the entire region at a value of 100 kV/m.

C-21-2 (d) The electric field is essentially constant inside a parallel-plate capacitor. To obtain the value, you divide the potential difference by the plate spacing. Remember that electric potentials (voltages) are always referenced to some zero level, and the answer to this question would not change if we had said the plates were $+200$ V and -200 V, $+100$ V and -300 V, or any other combination with the same potential difference.

EXAMPLE 21-1

A Parallel-Plate Capacitor

A capacitor that has two parallel plates of dimensions $8.00\ \text{cm} \times 10.00\ \text{cm}$ separated by 2.00 mm of air is connected to a 24.0 V battery. Find

(a) the capacitance;
(b) the charge on one plate;
(c) the electric field in the capacitor;
(d) the surface charge density on the plates.

SOLUTION

(a) We can find the capacitance from the relationship for a parallel-plate capacitor:

$$C = \frac{\varepsilon_0 A}{d} = \frac{8.85 \times 10^{-12}\ \text{C}^2\text{N}^{-1}\text{m}^{-2} \times 0.0800\ \text{m} \times 0.100\ \text{m}}{0.002\ 00\ \text{m}}$$

$$= 3.54 \times 10^{-11}\ \text{F} = 35.4\ \text{pF}$$

Remember that electric potential is electric potential energy per charge; therefore, $1\ \text{V} = 1\ \text{J/C} = 1\ (\text{N}\cdot\text{m})/\text{C}$. Hence, $1\ \text{C}^2/(\text{N}\cdot\text{m}) = 1\ \text{C/V} = 1\ \text{F}$.

(b) To determine the charge on one plate, we need the capacitance and the applied voltage. The voltage is given, and we now know the capacitance:

$$Q = CV = 3.54 \times 10^{-11}\ \text{F} \times 24.0\ \text{V}$$

$$= 8.50 \times 10^{-10}\ \text{C} = 0.850\ \text{nC}$$

(c) The electric field is essentially constant between the plates of a parallel-plate capacitor. Therefore, we can find the field by dividing the potential difference by the plate spacing:

$$E = \frac{V}{d} = \frac{24.0\ \text{V}}{0.002\ 00\ \text{m}} = 1.20 \times 10^4\ \text{V/m} = 12.0\ \text{kV/m}$$

(d) If we rearrange Equation (21-4), we can solve for the surface charge density (remember that all plate charge will go to the surface):

$$\sigma = E\varepsilon_0 = 12\ 000\ \text{V/m} \times 8.85 \times 10^{-12}\ \text{C}^2\text{N}^{-1}\text{m}^{-2}$$

$$= 1.06 \times 10^{-7}\ \text{C/m}^2$$

Making sense of the result:

These results demonstrate that typical plate dimensions and separations for parallel plates in air lead to modest values for the capacitance, usually in the picofarad range. You may be surprised by how large the electric field is, but do not confuse a field of thousands of volts per metre with the potential difference (just 24 V here). Remember that in this capacitor, the field extends only a few millimetres.

LO 3

21-3 Calculating Capacitance

By far, the most common capacitance configuration is that of a parallel plate. We saw in the last section how the capacitance depends on the area and spacing of the plates for a parallel-plate configuration. While most commercial capacitors do not look like parallel plates, they are essentially parallel plates with the conducting plates and insulating layer rolled into a cylindrical shape.

It is important to realize that capacitance is a feature of various configurations of conductors, and not just parallel plates. Capacitance is defined as the ratio of the stored charge, Q, to the potential difference, V, between the plates:

$$C = \frac{Q}{V} \tag{21-8}$$

This definition of capacitance is equivalent to the definition in Section 21-1, as we can easily see by comparing Equations (21-2) and (21-8).

✓ CHECKPOINT

C-21-3 Capacitance and Field

Two surfaces (not necessarily planes) have an essentially constant electric field of 1000 V/m between them when a charge of 200 μC is applied to one surface and a charge of $-200\ \mu$C is applied to the other surface. The spacing between the surfaces is 5.00 mm. What is the capacitance?

(a) $10\ \mu\text{F}$
(b) $40\ \mu\text{F}$
(c) $250\ \mu\text{F}$
(d) $40\ \text{F}$

C-21-3 (b) Since the electric field is essentially constant, the potential difference must be $Ed = 5$ V. The capacitance is $Q/V = 200\ \mu\text{C}/5$ V $= 40\ \mu\text{F}$.

Here is a procedure for finding the capacitance of any configuration of two plates:

■ Assume some arbitrary charge, Q, on the plates, and use Gauss's law to determine the electric field in the space between the plates.

■ Integrate the electric field between the two plates to obtain the potential difference, V.

■ Take the ratio of the charge Q to the potential difference V to obtain the capacitance.

Example 21-2 demonstrates the application of this procedure.

EXAMPLE 21-2

Capacitance for Coaxial Cylinders

Consider a system of two coaxial cylinders. The inner cylinder is solid and has radius r_1, and the outer cylindrical conductor is thin and has radius r_2. The inner cylinder carries a charge of $+Q$ over a length L, and the outer cylinder carries a charge of $-Q$ over the same length.

(a) What is the capacitance of this configuration?
(b) When $L = 0.500$ m, $r_1 = 4.00$ mm, and $r_2 = 5.00$ mm, what is the capacitance?

SOLUTION

(a) As we saw in the previous chapter, all the charge on the inner solid conductor will be on its outer surface. The outer conductor is thin, and its charge is on its outer surface as well, but we are assuming that the radii of its inner and outer surfaces are essentially the same. As shown in Figure 21-6, the electric field reflects the symmetry of the cylinders and is directed radially outward (from positive to negative charge).

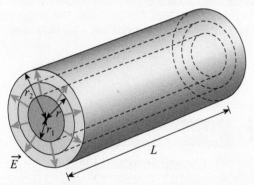

Figure 21-6 Example 21-2. Gaussian cylinder of radius r drawn on coaxial cylindrical conductors

To find the capacitance, we apply the three-stage process of first finding the electric field by Gauss's law, then the potential difference between the surfaces, and finally the charge-to-potential difference ratio.

The system has linear symmetry, so we draw a concentric Gaussian cylinder with length L and radius r intermediate between r_1 and r_2. We can ignore flux through the ends of the Gaussian cylinder because the surface area vector and the electric field are perpendicular, making the vector dot product vanish. Over the curved side of the Gaussian cylinder, the electric field is of constant magnitude (at the same r) and is everywhere parallel to the area vector element, so we simplify the integral as shown below. Note that the enclosed charge is only the charge on the inner conductor, $+Q$.

$$\oint \vec{E} \cdot d\vec{A} = E \oint dA = \frac{q_{enc}}{\varepsilon_0} = \frac{Q}{\varepsilon_0}$$

The area of the curved part of the cylinder is simply the circumference times the length. Thus,

$$E(2\pi r L) = \frac{Q}{\varepsilon_0}$$

$$E = \frac{Q}{\varepsilon_0 2\pi r L}$$

Now we have an expression for the magnitude of the electric field between the two conductors as a function of radial distance. Although this electric field is not constant, we can still integrate it over a path between the cylindrical conductors to find the potential difference. Since $\vec{E}$ and $d\vec{r}$ both point radially outward, their dot product becomes a simple multiplication. Therefore, the potential difference between the plates is

$$V_{r_2} - V_{r_1} = -\int_{r_1}^{r_2} \vec{E} \cdot d\vec{r} = -\int_{r_1}^{r_2} \frac{Q}{\varepsilon_0 2\pi r L}\, dr = -\frac{Q}{2\pi \varepsilon_0 L} \int_{r_1}^{r_2} \frac{1}{r}\, dr$$

Since $\int \frac{1}{r}\, dr = \ln(r)$,

$$V_{r_2} - V_{r_1} = -\frac{Q}{2\pi \varepsilon_0 L}\left[\ln(r_2) - \ln(r_1)\right]$$

$$= -\frac{Q}{2\pi \varepsilon_0 L} \ln\left(\frac{r_2}{r_1}\right)$$

To find the capacitance, we simply take the ratio of the magnitude of the charge to magnitude of the potential difference. Note that we ignore the signs of the charge and the potential difference:

$$C = \frac{Q}{V} = \frac{Q}{\dfrac{Q}{2\pi \varepsilon_0 L} \ln\left(\dfrac{r_2}{r_1}\right)} = \frac{2\pi \varepsilon_0 L}{\ln\left(\dfrac{r_2}{r_1}\right)}$$

(b) Substituting the given quantities yields

$$C = \frac{2\pi \varepsilon_0 L}{\ln\left(\dfrac{r_2}{r_1}\right)} = \frac{2\pi \times 8.85 \times 10^{-12}\, \text{C}^2 \text{N}^{-1}\text{m}^{-2} \times 0.500\ \text{m}}{\ln\left(\dfrac{0.005\,00\ \text{m}}{0.004\,00\ \text{m}}\right)}$$

$$= 1.25 \times 10^{-10}\, \text{F} = 125\ \text{pF}$$

Making sense of the result:

Since the electric field in part (a) is directly proportional to the charge and inversely proportional to the length, this field really depends only on the linear charge density (the charge per unit length). It makes sense that the electric field decreases in magnitude as the radial distance increases (to conserve electric flux). In the expression for the potential difference, we found that the potential at the outer conductor is less than the potential at the inner conductor. This makes sense because the inner conductor carries the positive charge. To determine whether the capacitance in part (b) is reasonable, we could approximate the coaxial conductors as a parallel-plate capacitor of area $2\pi r L$ with spacing equal to $r_2 - r_1$:

(continued)

$$C \approx \frac{\varepsilon_0 A}{d} \approx \frac{\varepsilon_0 2\pi r L}{d}$$

$$\approx \frac{8.85 \times 10^{-12}\, C^2 N^{-1} m^{-2} \times 2\pi \times 0.0045\ m \times 0.50\ m}{0.001\ m}$$

$$\approx 1.25 \times 10^{-10}\, F$$

Most audio and communications signals are transmitted along coaxial cables with a structure similar to that in Example 21-2. Capacitance is an important consideration for such signal transmissions. Note that we found that the capacitance of coaxial configurations increases linearly with length. Figure 21-7 shows a common type of flexible coaxial cable.

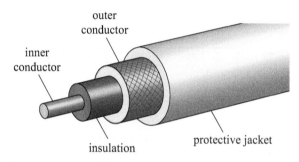

Figure 21-7 The structure of coaxial cables that are frequently used for signal transmission

21-4 Combining Capacitors

If you had only, say, 1 μF capacitors and wanted to make a 0.25 μF capacitance, could you do it? What if you needed a 5.0 μF capacitor? In fact, you can indeed combine capacitors in parallel, in series, and in series–parallel combinations to produce different equivalent capacitances. Combinations of capacitors are often used in circuits in which a required value is not available as a standard part.

Capacitors connected in parallel add in the same way that resistors add in series. When you add a capacitor in parallel to another capacitor, you *increase* the net capacitance.

KEY EQUATION
$$C_{\text{parallel}} = C_1 + C_2 \qquad (21\text{-}9)$$

Similarly, capacitors connected in series add like resistors added in parallel. When you insert a capacitor in series with another capacitor, you *decrease* the net capacitance.

KEY EQUATION
$$\frac{1}{C_{\text{series}}} = \frac{1}{C_1} + \frac{1}{C_2} \qquad (21\text{-}10)$$

Recall that components in series are connected such that the current must flow through one component followed by each of the others, and the voltages across the individual components sum to the total applied voltage. When components are connected in parallel, they all share the same voltage; one end of each individual component is connected to the same common terminal, and the other end of each parallel component is connected to a second common terminal.

Consider two capacitors, C_1 and C_2, connected in parallel to a battery, as shown on the left in Figure 21-8. On the right is an equivalent circuit with C_{eq} charged by the same battery. If the circuit really is equivalent, then the same total charge must be redistributed by the battery in both cases:

$$Q_1 + Q_2 = Q_{\text{eq}} \qquad (21\text{-}11)$$

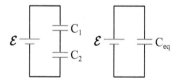

Figure 21-8 A parallel combination of two capacitors charged by battery $\mathcal{E}$ (left) and the equivalent capacitance form of the circuit (right)

The charge on each capacitor is given by $Q = CV$. Since the capacitors are in parallel, the voltage across each capacitor is equal to the battery voltage $\mathcal{E}$, as is the voltage across the equivalent capacitor. Therefore,

$$C_1\mathcal{E} + C_2\mathcal{E} = C_{\text{eq}}\mathcal{E} \qquad (21\text{-}12)$$

We simply divide by $\mathcal{E}$ to get the relationship for capacitors in parallel. Another way to think about capacitors in parallel is this: you are connecting their plates together, thus increasing the total area of the plates. It makes sense that the capacitances will add together in the same way.

When capacitors are combined in series, as in Figure 21-9, all the capacitors have the same charge, and that charge must be the same as on the equivalent single capacitor. The voltages across the individual capacitors must sum to be the applied voltage. See the Peer to Peer box to see how this can be used to derive the relationship for combining capacitors in series.

Figure 21-9 A series combination of two capacitors charged by a battery $\mathcal{E}$ (left) and the equivalent capacitance form of the circuit (right)

PEER TO PEER

I had a difficult time remembering that the rules for adding capacitors are opposite to the rules for adding resistors. Finally, the relationship between voltage and capacitance and the relationship between voltage and resistance helped me out. In series, the current is the same and voltages add. So, for resistors $IR_1 + IR_2 = IR_{eq}$; therefore, resistances in series add. But the voltage for a capacitor is given by Q/C, so when adding voltages for capacitors, you have $\frac{Q}{C_1} + \frac{Q}{C_2} = \frac{Q}{C_{eq}}$. Then, you just divide by the constant charge Q to get the formula for capacitors in series.

To understand why the charges on capacitors in series must be the same, consider what a capacitor is—two conducting plates separated by an insulating region. The energy of the battery will cause a flow of charges, charging the left plate of C_1 positively and the right plate of C_3 negatively, as shown in Figure 21-10. The insulating regions of each capacitor prevent the flow of current through the

capacitor, so overall, the regions marked A and B on the figure must remain electrically neutral. The right plate of capacitor C_1 will get some negative charge (electrons) attracted to the positive charges on the other plate of that capacitor. Since region A stays neutral overall, the left end of C_2 must develop an equal magnitude of positive charge. Similar arguments show that all the series capacitors have the same charge magnitudes.

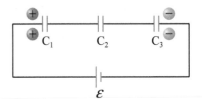

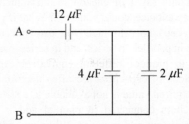

Figure 21-10   Charge on capacitors connected in series

EXAMPLE 21-3

Capacitor Combination

What is the net capacitance between terminals A and B of the circuit in Figure 21-11 when $C_1 = 12.0\ \mu F$, $C_2 = 4.00\ \mu F$, $C_3 = 3.00\ \mu F$, and $C_4 = 6.00\ \mu F$?

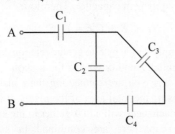

Figure 21-11   Example 21-3

SOLUTION

Capacitors C_3 and C_4 are in series because they are connected end to end with no branching to other components at the junction. (Whether they are drawn in a straight line does not matter.) We first find the equivalent capacitance for these two capacitors. For simplicity of notation, we leave out the units until the final step, noting that all the capacitances in this circuit are measured in microfarads:

$$\frac{1}{C_{series}} = \frac{1}{C_3} + \frac{1}{C_4} = \frac{1}{3.00} + \frac{1}{6.00} = \frac{3}{6.00}$$

$$C_{series} = 2.00\ \mu F$$

It is helpful when simplifying combinations of components to redraw the circuit diagram after each step. Figure 21-12 shows the circuit with C_3 and C_4 replaced by the series equivalent of $2.00\ \mu F$.

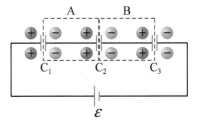

Figure 21-12   The circuit of Example 21-3 redrawn using the series equivalent for C_3 and C_4

From this revised circuit diagram, it is clear that the next step is to combine the $2.00\ \mu F$ and $4.00\ \mu F$, which are in parallel:

$$C_{parallel} = 2.00\ \mu F + 4.00\ \mu F = 6.00\ \mu F$$

Finally, this equivalent $6.00\ \mu F$ capacitor is in series with the $12\ \mu F$ capacitor, so the net equivalent capacitance is

$$\frac{1}{C_{eq}} = \frac{1}{12.0} + \frac{1}{6.00} = \frac{3}{12.0}$$

$$C_{eq} = 4.00\ \mu F$$

(continued)

Making sense of the result:

When finding equivalents for combinations of capacitors, you should check your results at each stage, remembering that parallel capacitors always add to a greater value than any of the individual capacitors, and series capacitors yield an equivalent that is less than any of the individual capacitors. The calculations satisfy these criteria.

 CHECKPOINT

C-21-4 Combining Capacitors

You have only 6 μF capacitors and need a 2 μF capacitor. How could you get the capacitance you need?
(a) Place three 6 μF capacitors in series with each other.
(b) Place three 6 μF capacitors in parallel with each other.
(c) Place two 6 μF capacitors in series with each other.
(d) It is not possible.

C-21-4 (a) With three 6 μF capacitors in series, $1/C_{eq} = 3/6 \ \mu F$, so the equivalent capacitance, C_{eq}, is 2 μF.

LO 5

21-5 Dielectrics and Capacitors

Chapter 19 introduced dielectrics, which are materials with atoms that align in the presence of an external electric field such that the electric field due to the polar molecules opposes the external field. Although there is no flow of electric charge, the distribution of the charge on these molecules (which are either polar to start with or become polarized in the applied electric field) is slightly changed.

 ONLINE ACTIVITY

Capacitors and Dielectrics

The e-resource that accompanies every new copy of this textbook contains an Online Activity using the PhET simulation "Capacitor Lab." Work through the simulation and accompanying questions to gain an understanding of capacitors and dielectrics.

Figure 21-13 shows a capacitor with a dielectric material inserted between its plates. The top plate is positively charged, so the electric field due to the charge on the plates (the solid arrow) points from top to bottom. The molecules of the dielectric (represented by ovals) orient themselves so that their negative end (shaded blue) is slightly closer to the positively charged top plate on the capacitor. Therefore, the electric field from the polarized dielectric molecules points upward (dashed arrow). The net electric field is the difference between these two electric fields. Thus, the presence of the dielectric reduces the net electric field produced between the plates of a capacitor by a given amount of charge on the plates.

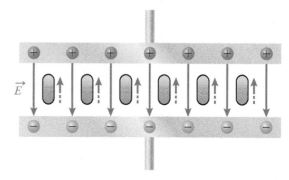

Figure 21-13 A capacitor with a dielectric material between the parallel plates. The internal electric field of the dielectric (dashed red arrows) opposes the field produced by the charges on the capacitor plates (solid red arrows).

If the net electric field is less but the spacing between the plates is unchanged, then the electric potential difference is less for the same amount of charge. Therefore, the capacitance must be greater. The presence of a dielectric between the plates always increases the capacitance. Inserting a dielectric between the plates of a capacitor increases the charge on the plates if they are hooked up to a battery (which holds the voltage constant) or reduces the potential difference if the plates have been disconnected (in which case the charge on the plates is unchanged).

To calculate capacitance in the presence of dielectrics, we simply replace the permittivity of free space, ε_0, with the permittivity of the dielectric material, ε. Permittivity is a measure of the response of a material to an applied electric field depending on the dielectric properties. For example, for a parallel-plate capacitor with a dielectric material between the plates:

$$C = \frac{\varepsilon A}{d} \qquad (21\text{-}13)$$

The dielectric constant (symbol κ) is the dimensionless ratio of the permittivity of the material to the permittivity of free space:

$$\kappa = \frac{\varepsilon}{\varepsilon_0} \qquad (21\text{-}14)$$

Good dielectrics have higher κ values. Table 21-1 lists the dielectric constants for a variety of materials, many of which are used in capacitors. In addition to the dielectric constant, it is important to consider how strong the field can be before electric breakdown occurs and conduction takes place through the dielectric, and this is given in the right-hand column of the table.

Table 21-1 Dielectric constants and maximum electric field strength before electrical breakdown for various materials

Dielectric material	Dielectric constant (κ)	Typical Breakdown Field Strength (MV/m)
Dry air	1.0006	3
Aluminum oxide	7–9	700
Ceramic	10–100	10
Glass	4–10	10
Mica	6.9	150
Mylar	3.1	400
Nylon	3.5	15
Paper	3–4	15
Plexiglas	3.4	40
Polyethylene	2.3	20
Rubber	2–7	10
Skin	30–40	
Tantalum oxide	20–30	500
Water	80	30 (pure water)
Waxed paper	4	50

✓ CHECKPOINT

C-21-5 A Dielectric in a Capacitor

An air-filled parallel-plate capacitor with capacitance C is charged using a battery of voltage $\mathcal{E}$, which is then disconnected. When a dielectric with dielectric constant 2 is inserted to totally fill the space between the plates,
(a) the capacitance is C, and the voltage is $2\mathcal{E}$;
(b) the capacitance is $2C$, and the voltage is $\mathcal{E}$;
(c) the capacitance is $2C$, and the voltage is $\mathcal{E}/2$;
(d) the capacitance is $2C$, and the voltage is $2\mathcal{E}$.

C-21-5 (c) The dielectric will increase the capacitance by a factor equal to the dielectric constant, so the capacitance becomes $2C$. Since the battery is disconnected, the charge must stay the same on the capacitor. Since $Q = CV$, Q is constant, and C is doubled, the new voltage must be $\mathcal{E}/2$.

LO 6

21-6 Energy Storage in Capacitors

As mentioned at the beginning of this chapter, one of the main applications of capacitors is storing electrostatic energy. We now develop the key relationships for energy storage in capacitors. The electric potential, V, is defined

as the electrostatic potential energy per unit charge, so you might expect that the energy stored in a capacitor carrying a charge Q would be QV, where V is the voltage across the fully charged capacitor. However, the voltage across the capacitor is zero when charging starts and reaches V only as the last of the charge moves onto the plates.

Consider the electrostatic potential energy of a capacitor of capacitance C as it is charged with Q coulombs of charge. Let V represent the changing voltage on the capacitor. As a small element of charge dq is added, V increases, as does the electric potential energy, U. From the definition of electric potential, we have

$$\int dU = \int_0^Q V\, dq$$

We can express V in terms of the charge q at any given moment:

$$V = \frac{q}{C}$$

Therefore, the electrostatic energy, U, stored in the capacitor when it carries charge Q is given by

$$U = \int_0^U dU = \int_0^Q \frac{q}{C}\, dq = \frac{1}{C}\frac{Q^2}{2}$$

We can use the basic capacitor relationship $Q = CV$ to substitute for either of the variables on the right side of this equation.

Electrostatic potential energy of a charged capacitor

$$\boxed{\text{KEY EQUATION}} \quad U = \frac{1}{2}\frac{Q^2}{C} = \frac{1}{2}CV^2 = \frac{1}{2}QV \qquad (21\text{-}15)$$

✓ CHECKPOINT

C-21-6 Potential Energy in a Capacitor

A capacitor with air between the plates is charged with a battery, which is then disconnected. If a dielectric (with a dielectric constant greater than that of air) is then slid into the space between the plates, the electrostatic potential energy stored in the capacitor
(a) increases;
(b) decreases;
(c) does not change;
(d) may increase or decrease depending on the sign of the dielectric constant.

C-21-6 (b) Dielectric constants are always positive and have values of 1 and above, so answer (d) does not make sense. When the dielectric is inserted, the capacitance increases. Because the capacitor had previously been disconnected from the battery, no charge can flow and, therefore, charge Q is unchanged. From the equation for the potential energy of a charged capacitor, this means that the energy must have decreased. How is this change of energy possible? The dielectric is pulled into the space; therefore, negative work is done by the person who is guiding the dielectric into the space, and the potential energy of the capacitor decreases. Note that the answer would be different if the capacitor had remained connected to the battery.

The National Ignition Facility

The National Ignition Facility, operated by Lawrence Livermore National Laboratory in the United States, seeks to produce energy by nuclear fusion. In nuclear fusion, light atoms combine into heavier atoms; for example, hydrogen atoms fuse to form helium. Such fusion is the source of energy for the Sun and other stars and could be the basis for power reactors. Fusion reactors are inherently safer than current nuclear fission reactors. However, a key challenge in producing controlled nuclear fusion is creating the incredible pressures and temperatures needed to initiate nuclear fusion. The National Ignition Facility creates these conditions by directing 192 powerful laser beams on a small pellet containing hydrogen. This facility has the world's most powerful laser array. High-energy density capacitors play a crucial role in this facility, storing and then rapidly releasing the energy needed for the powerful laser pulses (Figure 21-14).

Lawrence Livermore National Laboratory

Figure 21-14 The target area at the National Ignition Facility. The arm on the right positions the target to a precision of less than the width of a human hair.

EXAMPLE 21-4

Defibrillator

A defibrillator uses a 5000 V power supply to charge a 32.0 μF capacitor. How much energy is stored in this capacitor when fully charged?

SOLUTION

Since we know the voltage and the capacitance, we choose the form of Equation (21-15) that expresses the electrostatic potential energy in terms of these two quantities:

$$U = \frac{1}{2} CV^2 = \frac{1}{2}(32 \times 10^{-6}\,\text{F})(5000\,\text{V})^2 = 400\,\text{J}$$

Making sense of the result:

The stored energy is significant — it is approximately equivalent to the energy needed to lift an 40 kg person 0.5 m. Since the energy is not required continuously, storing energy in a capacitor makes it possible to use a power supply that is smaller, lighter, and less expensive than a power supply that supplies energy directly to the defibrillator paddles.

We can think of the energy in a capacitor as being stored in the electric field in the space between the plates of a capacitor. Consider an air-filled parallel-plate capacitor with plate area A and spacing d. For this capacitor, the electric field is related to the potential difference by $V = Ed$. Therefore, the electrostatic potential energy can be written as

$$U = \frac{1}{2} CV^2 = \frac{1}{2} C(Ed)^2 \qquad (21\text{-}16)$$

As we saw earlier in this chapter, the capacitance of this type of capacitor is given by

$$C = \frac{\varepsilon_0 A}{d} \qquad (21\text{-}7)$$

Substituting for C in Equation (20-16) gives

$$U = \frac{1}{2}\left(\frac{\varepsilon_0 A}{d}\right)(Ed)^2 = \frac{1}{2}\varepsilon_0 A dE^2 \qquad (21\text{-}17)$$

The area of the plates times the spacing of the plates, Ad, equals the volume between the plates, which is the volume containing the electric field. So, Equation (21-17) shows that the electrostatic energy stored in the capacitor depends on the volume between the plates and the square of the electric field.

It is common, especially in more advanced physics courses, to work in terms of energy density, u, which is defined as energy per unit volume (see Section 26-5). Dividing Equation (21-17) by the volume gives us an expression for the energy density between the capacitor plates:

KEY EQUATION

$$u = \frac{1}{2}\varepsilon_0 E^2 \qquad (21\text{-}18)$$

This expression for energy density is generally true for electric fields in a vacuum and can be applied, for example, to the energy density of electromagnetic waves in a vacuum.

ELECTRICITY, MAGNETISM, AND OPTICS

21-7 Applications of Capacitors

Most capacitor applications involve charging or discharging. Let us be clear on what a battery does when it charges a capacitor: The battery provides the energy to move existing charges; it does not create or destroy electric charge. Once the capacitor starts to charge, the flow of more electrons onto the negatively charged plate is opposed by electrostatic repulsion. The battery provides the energy needed to overcome this repulsion and thus provides the electric potential energy stored in the capacitor when it is charged. When a capacitor is discharged by connecting the two plates with an external conductor, electrons flow from the negative plate to the positive plate, eventually resulting in zero net charge on each plate.

Storing Charge

Probably the most direct application of capacitors is the storage of charge. Dynamic random access memory (DRAM), a common type of electronic memory, has arrays of microscopic capacitors, with a high bit or low bit indicated by whether the stored charge is above or below some critical value. In the charge coupled device (CCD) image sensor, tiny capacitors each store charge corresponding to the brightness of a pixel of the image (Figure 21-15).

Figure 21-15 The CCD image sensor is an array of photosensitive capacitive cells.

Storing Energy

A charged capacitor can be used to store electrostatic potential energy, energy that we can get back by allowing partial or full discharge of the capacitor. Capacitors store energy for many electrical devices, including the defibrillator mentioned at the beginning of the chapter. Similarly, camera flash units store the energy needed for a bright flash in capacitors. A wide variety of "instant on" electronic devices store enough energy to start up in a capacitor even when they are switched off.

The Nd:YAG Laser

Nd:YAG lasers, like the one in Figure 21-16, are widely used in medicine, dentistry, industrial machining, and cosmetic surgery. Nd:YAG lasers use a neodymium (Nd) doped yttrium aluminum garnet (YAG) crystal as the lasing medium. An optical flash lamp close to the crystal adds energy to the crystal atoms, populating excited (higher-energy) states. A number of other types of lasers use similar optical pumping systems. The energy to fire the flash lamp is built up in a capacitor, which can then quickly deliver a pulse of energy to the flash tube.

Figure 21-16 The Nd:YAG laser uses a flash tube to energize the crystal that produces the laser light.

Filtering

In scientific instrumentation, as well as in everyday applications such as audio amplifiers, one needs to filter signals. A filter circuit allows certain frequencies through while blocking others. For example, when you use an audio equalizer or even simple bass and treble controls, you are adjusting the settings of various filters.

Most filters use capacitors, often in combination with resistors. Resistors oppose the flow of current in a circuit: the greater the resistance (symbol R), the less the current that flows for a given applied voltage, as you will see in the discussion of current and resistance in Chapter 22. A low-pass filter lets only low frequencies through. The simplest low-pass filter consists of just a single resistor and a single capacitor, as shown in Figure 21-17. When the frequency of the signal is low, most of the input signal is passed on to the output. When the frequency is high, however, the capacitor cannot rapidly change its voltage as needed for the output voltage to follow the input voltage, and the signal is largely blocked. A cut-off frequency separates the signal frequencies that are largely passed from those that are largely blocked. For the simple RC low-pass filter in Figure 21-17, the cut-off frequency is

$$f_{\text{cutoff}} = \frac{1}{2\pi RC} \qquad (21\text{-}19)$$

Note that the product RC has units of time.

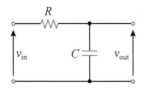

Figure 21-17   The RC low-pass filter

A high-pass filter passes high frequencies and blocks low frequencies. Switching the positions of the capacitor and the resistor in an RC low-pass filter turns it into a high-pass filter. Since the capacitor completely blocks direct current (zero frequency) signals, the majority of electronic devices use capacitors in this high-pass configuration to separate regions of the circuit that have different direct current (DC) voltages.

DC Power Supplies

For efficiency and ease of conversion to different voltages, most power systems transmit electricity as alternating current (AC) with a sinusoidal waveform. In North America, most household circuits have a voltage of 120 V. However, most electronic devices require a lower DC voltage. The power supplies for these devices convert household AC voltage into lower-voltage DC. The essential parts of a power supply are a transformer, which steps down the AC voltage; diodes, which allow the current to flow in only one direction; and a capacitor, which alternately stores and releases charge so that the DC output is approximately constant. Most DC power supplies use electrolytic capacitors, a type of capacitor that allows relatively large capacitances to fit in compact packages (Figure 21-18). Most high-quality power supplies also have a regulator section to help maintain constant voltage under varying conditions.

Uniform Electric Fields

Since the electric field inside a parallel-plate capacitor is essentially constant, this configuration is often used in applications that require uniform electric fields. Such

Figure 21-18   Electrolytic capacitors of the type used in a DC power supply

fields are used to select, direct, and accelerate electrons and other subatomic particles, such as in particle accelerators at major scientific facilities, cathode ray tube (CRT) display devices, X-ray machines, and mass spectrometers.

✅ CHECKPOINT

C-21-7 Particle Physics Experiment

A capacitor in a particle physics experiment provides a uniform electric field of 14 000 V/m directed upward. The plate separation is 1.0 cm. When the bottom plate is at -100 V relative to the ground, what is the potential of the top plate?

(a) -240 V
(b) -140 V
(c) $+140$ V
(d) $+800$ V

C-21-7 (a) The potential difference, ΔV, equals Ed, where d is the plate spacing. Substituting the given values, $d = 0.01$ m and $E = 14\ 000$ V/m, we get $\Delta V = 140$ V. Since the electric field points upward, the bottom plate must be more positive. Therefore, the potential at the top plate must be -100 V $- 140$ V $= -240$ V.

Timing Circuits

Many general-purpose timing circuits use the time required to charge, or discharge, a capacitor to a certain level to control the timing. In these devices, a voltage comparison circuit detects when the voltage across a capacitor reaches the threshold value. Although high-precision timing requires other approaches (such as the use of piezoelectric crystals in resonant circuits), for many technological and scientific applications capacitor timers are sufficient and cost-effective.

Transducers

A transducer is a device that provides an electrical signal that depends on some physical parameter. For example, a microphone is a transducer that transforms sound pressure waves into electrical signals. Many transducers, including

MAKING CONNECTIONS

Touch-Sensitive Screens

Touch-sensitive screens on devices such as smart phones and tablets have revolutionized portable electronics. Although several different mechanisms are used for touch screens, including thermal, light, and resistive sensing, the majority of modern touch screens use capacitive effects. Transparent conducting grids lie above the display and the glass layer. In one design, lines for an electrically driven grid are separated by an insulator from sensing lines, forming, in essence, an array of capacitors. When you touch the screen, essentially grounding that point, you alter the charge stored at that point, and the electronics detect which capacitor has been grounded (Figure 21-19).

© Chris Rout/Alamy

Figure 21-19 The iPad and the iPhone use touch screens that depend on capacitive effects.

some types of microphones, pressure sensors, and fluid-level sensors, make use of capacitive effects. Recall that the capacitance depends on the area of the plates, the separation of the plates, and the dielectric properties of any material between the plates:

$$C = \frac{\varepsilon A}{d} \qquad (21\text{-}13)$$

A capacitive-based transducer may work by changing any of these three parameters. For example, in most capacitive pressure sensors, the distance between two plates changes according to the pressure on the transducer. In some position sensors, the effective area of the plates changes as one plate slides relative to the other. The capacitance of a fluid-level sensor can change as the level of a dielectric fluid between the plates of the capacitor changes.

Transistor Capacitors

While passive elements such as resistors and capacitors are fabricated as part of integrated circuits, it is the active semiconductor devices—diodes and transistors—that play the central role. The most important type of transistor for integrated circuits is the metal oxide semiconductor field effect transistor (MOSFET), which is essentially a capacitor with an insulating layer separating two charge regions. Physicist Julius Edgar Lilienfeld (1882–1963) sought the first ever patent for a field effect transistor (FET) in 1925; it was awarded by the Canadian government in 1927. When compared to the other major type of transistor (BJT, or bipolar junction transistor), FET and especially MOSFET devices have significantly lower power requirements. However, it would be many decades before mass production of MOSFETs became practical. Lilienfeld also invented the electrolytic capacitor.

Biological Measurements

Natural systems show capacitive effects, which are widely used in biological research and development. For example, the first accurate measurement of the thickness of the cell wall was done using a capacitive measurement. Samples of different types of cells have capacitances that vary according to the DNA content.

ELECTRICITY, MAGNETISM, AND OPTICS

A common type of capacitor consists of two parallel conducting plates separated by a small gap, which may be filled with air or a dielectric. Capacitors are used to store charge and energy, and have many applications, for example, timing and measurement circuits.

Capacitance is a measure of how much charge can be stored for a given applied potential difference and is measured in farads (F).

The Capacitor

The relationship between the stored charge, Q, the applied electric potential difference, V, and the capacitance, C, is

$$Q = CV \qquad (21\text{-}2)$$

Electric Fields

Except for small differences near the ends of the capacitor, the electric field is essentially constant in the area between the plates. The relationship between the potential difference across the plates, V, the plate spacing, d, and the magnitude of the electric field magnitude, E, is

$$V = Ed \qquad (21\text{-}1)$$

Parallel-Plate Capacitors

The capacitance for parallel-plate capacitors depends on the plate area, A, plate spacing, d, and the permittivity of the region between the plates, ε:

$$C = \frac{\varepsilon A}{d} \qquad (21\text{-}13)$$

Calculating Capacitance

The term "capacitance" can be applied to configurations other than parallel plates. For a general configuration, capacitance can be calculated by finding the ratio of charge to potential difference between the conductors. Gauss's law is used to find the electric field between the conductors, which is then integrated over a path between the conductors to find the potential difference.

Combining Capacitors

When capacitors are connected in parallel, the capacitances add:

$$C_{\text{parallel}} = C_1 + C_2 \qquad (21\text{-}9)$$

When capacitors are connected in series, each of the capacitors has the same charge and

$$\frac{1}{C_{\text{series}}} = \frac{1}{C_1} + \frac{1}{C_2} \qquad (21\text{-}10)$$

Dielectrics and Capacitors

Adding a dielectric between the plates of a capacitor increases its capacitance, and

$$C = \frac{\varepsilon A}{d} \qquad (21\text{-}13)$$

where ε is the permittivity of the dielectric.

The dielectric constant, κ, is a dimensionless ratio of the permittivity of the dielectric to the permittivity of a vacuum:

$$\kappa = \frac{\varepsilon}{\varepsilon_0} \qquad (21\text{-}14)$$

Energy Storage

The energy stored in a capacitor (capacitance C) carrying a charge Q with a voltage V is

$$U = \frac{1}{2}\frac{Q^2}{C} = \frac{1}{2}CV^2 = \frac{1}{2}QV \qquad (21\text{-}15)$$

Energy is stored in the electric field between the plates. The energy density in this field is

$$u = \frac{1}{2}\varepsilon_0 E^2 \qquad (21\text{-}18)$$

Applications: capacitive measurements of biological cells, energy storage in capacitors (e.g., camera flash units and defibrillators), capacitance-based measurements (e.g., fluid levels), touch screens, charge coupled devices (CCDs) for images, timing, filtering of signals

Key Terms: capacitance, capacitor, charging, cut-off frequency, dielectrics, dielectric constant, discharging, energy density, farad, filter, high-pass filter, low-pass filter, permittivity

QUESTIONS

1. A capacitor is connected to a 40 V battery. It is observed that the charge on one of the plates is 160 μC. What is the capacitance?
   (a) 0.25 μF
   (b) 4.0 μF
   (c) 640 μF
   (d) 4.0 F

2. A capacitor has capacitance C and applied voltage V. What is the net total charge on the capacitor?
   (a) 0
   (b) CV
   (c) C/V
   (d) $2CV$

3. The spacing between the plates of a 10 μF capacitor is 1.0 mm. It is connected to a 10 V battery for charging. What is the electric field in the capacitor?
(a) 10 V/m
(b) 100 V/m
(c) 1 000 V/m
(d) 10 000 V/m

4. Two parallel plates have been charged with equal magnitude and opposite polarity charges. The plates are then disconnected from the charging source, and the spacing between the plates is decreased. Which of the following statements correctly describes what happens?
(a) The capacitance and the electric potential both decrease.
(b) The electric potential increases, and the capacitance decreases.
(c) The capacitance increases, and the potential difference decreases.
(d) The capacitance and the electric potential both increase.

5. Consider two cylindrical capacitors: A has radii 2.5 cm and 2.6 cm and length 2.0 m; B has radii 1.0 cm and 3.0 cm and length 1.0 m. Rather than using the exact relationship for cylindrical capacitors, you want to approximate them as parallel-plate capacitors. Which of the following statements is best?
(a) You cannot approximate them at all as a parallel-plate configuration.
(b) You can approximate A very well, but B will probably be a poor approximation.
(c) You can approximate B very well, but A will probably be a poor approximation.

6. A coaxial cable is made up of two concentric cylinders. You have two cables, A and B, with the same distance between the cylinders (i.e., from the outside of the inner cylinder to the outer cylinder, which is considered to be thin). Both cables also use the same dielectric material. However, the diameter of cable B is larger than that of cable A. How does the capacitance per length compare with the two cables?
(a) They both have exactly the same capacitance per length.
(b) A has a larger capacitance per length.
(c) B has a larger capacitance per length.
(d) A has slightly more capacitance per length.

7. You need a slightly smaller capacitance than the value of a capacitor that you are using. How should you add a capacitor to accomplish this?
(a) Add a much smaller capacitor in series.
(b) Add a much smaller capacitor in parallel.
(c) Add a much larger capacitor in series.
(d) Add a much larger capacitor in parallel.

8. You have a single 1 μF capacitor in a circuit. When you connect a 10 μF capacitor in parallel with the 1 μF capacitor, what is the new effective capacitance?
(a) 0.1 μF.
(b) 0.9 μF.
(c) 1.1 μF.
(d) 11 μF.

9. An air-filled parallel-plate capacitor initially has some capacitance, C. It is charged using a battery of voltage X, which is left connected. A dielectric with dielectric constant 2 is then inserted, totally filling the space between the plates. Which of the following statements describes the new condition?

(a) The capacitance is C, and the voltage is $2X$.
(b) The capacitance is $2C$, and the voltage is X.
(c) The capacitance is $2C$, and the voltage is $X/2$.
(d) The capacitance is $2C$, and the voltage is $2X$.

10. An air-filled parallel-plate capacitor is charged with a battery, which is kept connected. A dielectric (with a dielectric constant greater than that of air) is then inserted into the space between the plates. What change, if any, is there for the electrostatic potential energy stored in the capacitor?
(a) The electrostatic potential energy increases.
(b) The electrostatic potential energy decreases.
(c) The electrostatic potential energy does not change.
(d) It depends on whether the dielectric constant is positive or negative.

11. When the voltage applied to the plates of a capacitor is doubled, what happens to the energy stored in the device?
(a) The energy is one-quarter the previous value.
(b) The energy is one-half the previous value.
(c) The energy is double the previous value.
(d) The energy is four times the previous value.

12. Two capacitors have identical dielectrics and plate spacing, and they are connected to the same battery. However, capacitor A has a plate area that is four times the plate area of capacitor B. How do the electric potential energy values stored in the capacitors compare?
(a) The electric potential energy of A is 16 times the electric potential energy of B.
(b) The electric potential energy of A is 4 times the electric potential energy of B.
(c) The electric potential energy of A is 2 times the electric potential energy of B.
(d) The electric potential energy of B is 2 times the electric potential energy of A.

13. The power supply you have constructed has too much "ripple," which means that the voltage goes down too much from a constant value during the 1/60 s period until it is refreshed from the transformer–rectifier network. Which statement correctly describes how the situation might be improved?
(a) You could add a capacitor in series with the existing capacitor.
(b) You could add a capacitor in parallel with the existing capacitor.
(c) Changing the capacitor value will not help the situation.
(d) Replacing the capacitor with a large resistor will help most.

14. In a particle physics experiment, you use the area between capacitor plates to create an electric field for exerting a force on electrons. You find that the force is too strong. What could you do to help the situation?
(a) Increase the plate area and leave everything else the same.
(b) Decrease the plate spacing and leave the applied voltage constant.
(c) Decrease the applied voltage and leave the plate spacing the same.
(d) Add a second capacitor in parallel, and keep the applied voltage the same.

15. You are using a simple low-pass filter, which consists of a resistor and a capacitor. The cut-off frequency is 500 Hz. However, you need the filter to cut off at about 250 Hz. If you keep the capacitor unchanged, how should you change the resistor value?

60

(a) Make the resistor value $R/2$.

(b) Make the resistor value $2R$.

(c) Make the resistor value $4R$.

(d) It is impossible to do by changing the resistor. You need to change the capacitor value.

16. You have purchased an old car and find that the turn signals flash too slowly. How can you increase the rate (i.e., the number of flashes per second) of the flasher circuit?

(a) You want to increase the capacitance and can do this by adding another capacitor in parallel with the existing one.

(b) You want to increase the capacitance and can do this by adding another capacitor in series with the existing capacitor.

(c) You want to decrease the capacitance and can do this by adding another capacitor in parallel with the existing capacitor.

(d) You want to decrease the capacitance and can do this by adding another capacitor in series with the existing capacitor.

PROBLEMS BY SECTION

For problems, star ratings will be used, (✷, ✷✷, or ✷✷✷), with more stars meaning more challenging problems.

Section 21-1 Capacitors and Capacitance

17. ✷ You need to store a charge of 6.00 mC when a 12.0 V battery is applied to a capacitor. What must be the capacitance?

18. ✷✷ A capacitor has a charge of 30 μC when a voltage X is applied to it. When the voltage is increased to $X + 10$ V, the new charge on the capacitor is 40.0 μC.

(a) What is the voltage X?

(b) What is the capacitance?

Section 21-2 Electric Fields in Capacitors

19. ✷✷ A capacitor has plates separated by a 2.00 mm air gap. A charge of magnitude 56.0 μC is on each plate. The electric field between the plates is 2400. V/m.

(a) What must be the electric potential difference between the plates?

(b) What is the capacitance?

20. ✷✷ An air-filled parallel-plate capacitor has a plate spacing of 1.50 mm and an electric potential difference of 65.0 V.

(a) What is the electric field between the plates?

(b) Calculate the surface charge density on each plate.

(c) The effective dimensions of the plate are 4.00 cm $\times$ 5.00 cm. What is the total charge on each plate?

Section 21-3 Calculating Capacitance

21. ✷✷ An air-filled parallel-plate capacitor consists of two circular plates of radius 7.50 cm. To achieve a capacitance of 115 pF, what must be the separation of the plates?

22. ✷✷✷ Consider a spherical capacitor that is made up of two spheres of radii 8.00 cm and 9.00 cm. The inner sphere is negatively charged with 450.0 nC, and the outer sphere is positively charged to the same magnitude. Air fills the region between the conductors.

(a) Use Gauss's law to find an expression (as a function of radial distance r) for the electric field in the region between the two spheres. Include the direction of the field.

(b) What is the electric field in the region outside both spheres?

(c) What is the potential difference between the two spheres?

(d) Calculate the capacitance.

(e) Estimate the capacitance by approximating the configuration as a set of parallel plates.

Section 21-4 Combining Capacitors

23. ✷✷ Explain how you could combine an unlimited supply of 500 pF capacitors in order to obtain each of the following:

(a) 0.002 μF;

(b) 0.0001 μF;

(c) 0.001 25 μF.

24. ✷✷ If you had only four capacitors, of values 1.00 μF, 2.00 μF, 3.00 μF, and 4.00 μF, what would be the smallest and the largest capacitances that you could obtain by combinations of these capacitors? In each case, draw the circuit and show the calculation for the equivalent capacitance.

Section 21-5 Dielectrics and Capacitors

25. ✷✷ A parallel-plate capacitor has rectangular plates 6.50 cm $\times$ 8.50 cm, spaced 2.00 mm apart. It has a dielectric material totally filling the space between the plates. The capacitor has a capacitance of 169 pF. Which of the materials in Table 21-1 could be the dielectric?

26. ✷✷ A parallel-plate capacitor has a capacitance of 0.002 00 μF when the space between the plates is filled with air. The plate spacing is 0.200 mm. It is connected throughout to an ideal 24.0 V battery.

(a) What is the charge on each plate?

(b) What is the electric field strength in the space between the plates?

(c) A dielectric with $\kappa = 3.50$ is inserted, totally filling the space between the plates. What is the charge on each plate now?

(d) What is the net electric field between the plates now?

Section 21-6 Energy Storage in Capacitors

27. ✷✷ You have two identical 5.00 μF capacitors and a single 12.0 V ideal battery. What is the total electrostatic energy stored in the system under each of the conditions below?

(a) The two capacitors are placed in series, and that combination is charged with the 12.0 V battery.

(b) The two capacitors are placed in parallel, and that combination is charged with the 12.0 V battery.

28. ✷✷ An air-filled capacitor charged with an ideal battery of voltage V has a total stored electrostatic energy U.

(a) The space between the plates is now filled with a dielectric of dielectric constant κ. The battery is left connected throughout. What is the amount of stored electrostatic energy now?

(b) Answer part (a) for the case in which the battery has been disconnected prior to insertion of the dielectric material.

Section 21-7 Applications of Capacitors

29. ✷✷ A pulsed laser that uses optical flash pumping produces 25.0 mJ per output pulse. Assume that the system is only 20% efficient, so five times as much energy must be stored in a capacitor to fire the flash each time. The capacitance of the capacitor is 50.0 μF. What is the minimum applied voltage needed to charge this capacitor?

30. ✶✶✶ A simple RC high-pass filter is to have a cut-off at 200 Hz.
    (a) Sketch the circuit, with input and output marked.
    (b) Calculate the resistance needed if only a 1.00 μF capacitor is available.

COMPREHENSIVE PROBLEMS

31. ✶ Prove that the permittivity of free space, ε_0, can be expressed in units of F/m.

32. ✶✶ Capacitors can be made on semiconductor integrated circuits essentially as parallel-plate capacitors, although it is difficult to achieve high capacitance values (and also challenging to create precise values). Assume that you want a 13.0 pF capacitor and that the layers of the integrated circuit allow you to have a spacing of 1.50 μm. Assume that the material has a dielectric constant of 3.10. What is the necessary area of the plates on this integrated circuit capacitor?

33. ✶✶ A single cell in a computer memory chip has a capacitance of 90.0 fF (femtofarads) and operates at a voltage of 3.3 V when charged.
    (a) What is the charge on the cell?
    (b) Express this charge in terms of the number of electrons.

34. ✶✶ An air-filled capacitor is to use circular plates of radius 5.00 cm that are separated by 3.00 mm. It is to have a maximum electric field of 1.0 kV/m in the space between the plates. Calculate
    (a) the capacitance;
    (b) the maximum voltage that should be applied;
    (c) the maximum charge that can be stored;
    (d) the maximum energy that can be stored.

35. ✶✶ A capacitor consists of two thin coaxial cylinders. The inner radius is 1.00 cm, the outer radius is 2.50 cm, and the length of both is 2.00 m. They carry equal amounts of charge per unit length but have opposite polarities. What is the capacitance per metre for the system?

36. ✶✶ While it may at first seem strange, you can consider a single charged sphere as having a capacitance.
    (a) Derive an expression for the capacitance of two concentric spheres (assume both are thin) of radii r_1 and r_2. Assume that a vacuum fills the space between the spheres.
    (b) Now, find the limit as we let the second sphere be of infinite radius. This will give you a result for the capacitance of a single sphere.
    (c) What would need to be the radius for a sphere in order for its capacitance to be 100 pF?

37. ✶✶ A parallel-plate capacitor has plates of area A and separation d. Two different dielectrics (κ_1, κ_2) are inserted (Figure 21-20), each filling half the space. Derive an expression for the capacitance. (Hint: Treat the setup as two capacitors in parallel.)

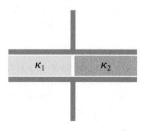

Figure 21-20 Problem 37

38. ✶✶✶ One form of transmission line consists of two long conducting wires (of radius r) separated by a separation distance D. Assume that D is much larger than r and that one wire has a linear charge density of $+\mu$ (measured in coulombs per metre) and the other wire has a linear charge density of $-\mu$.
    (a) Calculate the capacitance per length of the transmission line. In the early days of television the signal from the antenna to the television was carried on this type of transmission line.
    (b) Find a numerical value for the capacitance per unit length for $D = 7.50$ mm and $r = 0.320$ mm.

39. ✶✶✶ Five 2.00 μF capacitors are connected in series, and that combination is charged with a 9.00 V ideal battery.
    (a) What is the charge on one plate of each capacitor?
    (b) What is the voltage across each capacitor?
    (c) How much energy is stored in one capacitor?

40. ✶✶✶ What is the effective capacitance between points A and B in the circuit shown in Figure 21-21?

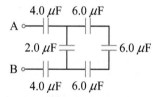

Figure 21-21 Problem 40

41. ✶✶✶ An air-filled parallel-plate capacitor is to be used to create an approximately constant electric field that will accelerate electrons with an acceleration of 7.00×10^{15} m/s². Assume that the spacing between the plates is 4.00 mm.
    (a) What is the required electric field strength?
    (b) What must be the applied voltage?
    (c) Will the acceleration of the electrons be in the direction of the higher or lower electric potential plate?
    (d) What time would be required for the electrons to accelerate from rest to a speed of 2.50×10^7 m/s, assuming that there is sufficient space between plates to reach this speed?
    (e) What distance would the electrons travel in reaching this speed? Is it possible to reach this speed with the given plate spacing?

42. ✶✶ A 0.100 μF capacitor is charged to 15.0 V. It is then connected in parallel to a second 0.100 μF capacitor, which was originally uncharged. Calculate the charge and voltage on each capacitor afterward.

43. ✶✶ Consider the circuit shown in Figure 21-22. The voltage is shown at a variety of points in the circuit. You are given the capacitance of the leftmost capacitor. Find the value of each of the other capacitors.

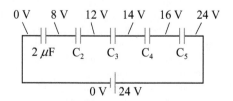

Figure 21-22 Problem 43

44. ✷✷ A 2.00 μF capacitor is charged to 12.0 V. It is then disconnected from the battery and connected across an uncharged 4.00 μF capacitor. Calculate the resulting charge and voltage on each capacitor.

45. ✷✷✷ A 4.00 cm by 5.00 cm parallel plate capacitor uses a dielectric with a dielectric constant of 4.0. The capacitor is designed so that when a potential difference of 60.0 V is applied, the charge stored on each plate has a magnitude of 150. nC. Calculate
(a) the necessary capacitance;
(b) the spacing between the plates;
(c) the energy that will be stored in the capacitor under these conditions;
(d) the electric field due to charge on the plates (not the net field considering the dielectric).

46. ✷✷ An air-filled parallel-plate capacitor has a plate area of 0.100 m², a plate spacing of 2.50 mm, and an applied voltage of 120. V. What is the energy density in the space between the plates of the capacitor?

47. ✷✷ What is the energy density just outside the surface of a conducting sphere of radius 3.50 cm that contains 3.50 nC of charge?

48. ✷✷✷ A charge coupled device (CCD) chip has an active area of 12.0 mm × 9.00 mm and a resolution of 9.0 megapixels; the pixels are square. Note that here we are using the binary definition of megapixel: 1 megapixel = 2^{20} pixels = 1 048 576 pixels.
(a) What are the dimensions of the device, expressed in pixels (i.e., x pixels × y pixels)? Round to the nearest integer number of pixels.
(b) What are the dimensions of each pixel, in micrometres?
(c) Using your answer in (b) as the plate area, and assuming a dielectric constant of 3.1 and a plate spacing of 1.00μm, what is the capacitance of each pixel cell? (Note: This is a very simplified model of a CCD.)

49. ✷✷ The outer layers of biological cells (lipid bilayers) act as capacitors, with the two sides holding opposite charge (the inside of the cell is negatively charged). Cells come in a variety of sizes, but assume a spherical cell of radius 5.00 μm and a dielectric constant of 4.00. Assume an electric potential difference between the layers of 75.0 mV.
(a) The thickness of the bilayer is 20.4 nm. What is the capacitance of the cell? (Hint: Model it as two thin spherical shells.)
(b) What is the charge on each side?
(c) How many elementary charges does this represent?

50. ✷✷ You are camping in a remote location and would like to have power at night. However, you do not want to carry a heavy battery to store the energy from the lightweight solar collectors that you are planning to carry in. The solar array that you have can generate 5.50 W in full sunlight. The array produces a potential difference of 12.0 V.
(a) How much capacitance is needed to store the energy produced by solar array in 6.0 h of full sunlight?
(b) The largest electrolytic capacitors you have available are 1000 μF each. How many would be needed in parallel?
(c) How long could the stored energy power a netbook that uses 8.00 W?

51. ✷✷ Current high-energy capacitor designs (e.g., like those used in the National Ignition Facility) achieve energies of about 2.00 J for every cubic centimetre of the capacitor. If one of these capacitors were in the shape of a cylinder

of radius 5.00 cm and length 10.0 cm, and had a maximum voltage rating of 750 V, what would its capacitance be?

DATA-RICH PROBLEM

52. ✷✷✷ Table 21-2 shows a relationship between electric potential (in V) versus radial distance, r (in cm).
(a) Describe a situation that could correspond to these data.
(b) What is the electric field at $r = 6$ cm?
(c) What is the electric field at $r = 12$ cm?
(d) What is the electric field just outside $r = 10$ cm?
(e) If this is some sort of capacitor, what is the voltage between the two plates?
(f) What charge must be on the inner plate to be consistent with the electric field in part (d)?
(g) Use your data from parts (e) and (f) to estimate the capacitance.

Table 21-2 Data for Problem 52

Radial distance (cm)	Voltage (V)
0	27 000
2	27 000
4	27 000
6	27 000
8	27 000
10	27 000
12	22 500
14	19 300
16	16 900
18	15 000
20	13 500
22	13 500
24	13 500
26	13 500
28	13 500

OPEN-ENDED PROBLEM

53. ✷✷✷ In this question, you will make reasonable estimates to determine whether it is feasible to power an electric vehicle with charged capacitors instead of batteries.
(a) Estimate (or look up specifications for) the energy required for an electric vehicle to drive 50 km during one day. List any assumptions that you make for your estimate.
(b) Design an optimally efficient (in terms of energy storage per volume) capacitor. Include the design (e.g., shape and size), materials (e.g., dielectric used), and estimates of the working electric potential and energy storage per capacitor unit. Provide comments on all aspects of your design.

(c) To provide the energy estimated in part (a), what volume and mass of capacitors are required, considering your capacitor design in part (b)? Comment on how reasonable these requirements are.

(d) Current technology uses lithium ion batteries for electric automobile energy storage. Look up, or estimate, the volume and mass requirements using that technology to provide the same amount of energy.

(e) Comment on the general advantages and disadvantages (with an electric automobile context) of capacitor-based energy storage compared to lithium ion batteries or fuel cells.

 See the text online resources at www.physics1e.nelson.com for Open Problems and Data-Rich Problems related to this chapter.

Chapter 22
Electric Current and Fundamentals of DC Circuits

In 1791, an Italian physician and physicist, Luigi Galvani (1737–98), discovered bioelectricity. Shortly thereafter, his associate, Alessandro Volta (1745–1827), invented the first battery. Less than 250 years later, we rely heavily on ubiquitous access to electric power. Terms such as "electricity," "electric current," "electric resistance," "electric power," "energy generation," and "transmission" have entered our everyday vocabulary. Sometimes, we use them interchangeably even though they mean different things. Electric phenomena are the basis of our lives on both microscopic (e.g., physiological phenomena and electron motion) and macroscopic levels (e.g., our use of external electric appliances). To appreciate the importance of electric phenomena in our lives, we only need to recall the havoc in northeastern Canada and the United States on the hot summer day of August 14, 2003. On that day, more than 55 million people in Ontario and in the northeast of the United States were left without electric power due to the failure of a transmission grid as a result of a 3500 MW (3.5×10^9 W) power surge (Figure 22-1). In this chapter, we examine the nature of electric current and its applications in direct current (DC) circuits.

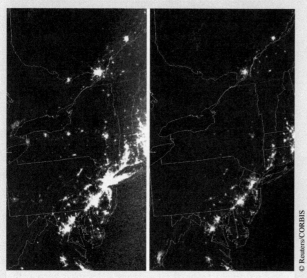

© Reuters/CORBIS

Figure 22-1 The "Northeast Blackout" of 2003 affected more than 55 million people in North America and was the second most widespread blackout in history. A view of the 2003 blackout from space: Ontario and the northeastern United States before (left) and during (right) the blackout.

 For additional Making Connections, Examples, and Checkpoints, as well as activities and experiments to help increase your understanding of the chapter's concepts, please go to the text's online resources at www.physics1e.nelson.com.

ELECTRICITY, MAGNETISM, AND OPTICS

22-1 Electric Current: The Microscopic Model

In Chapter 20, we saw that electric charges can move through a metal conductor to charge or discharge a capacitor. Various experiments, such as studies of the Hall effect (described in Chapter 23) and the Tolman–Stewart experiment conducted in 1916, have shown that the moving charges in metals are electrons. Thus, we can describe the electric current in metals as an **electron current** or an **electron flow**. In some materials, such as plasmas and ionic solutions, the charge carriers may include positive and negative ions.

We model a metal as a crystal lattice of positively charged ions immersed in a cloud, or sea, of free (delocalized) electrons. In most metals, each atom loses one outer (valence) electron, thus turning the atom into a positive ion (Figure 22-2). The solid metal is held together by the electrostatic attraction forces between the positive lattice and a negative free electron cloud. These forces are called **metallic bonds**. The presence of free electrons in a metal explains why a metal is a good conductor of both thermal energy and electricity. Metal ions are comprised of the metal nuclei and bound electrons. The nuclei of metal atoms consist of protons and neutrons that are approximately 2000 times heavier than electrons ($m_p \approx m_n \approx 2000\, m_e$), so the thermal motion of the metal ions is negligible compared to the thermal motion of the much lighter free electrons. (We will calculate the average speed for thermal motion of electrons in Chapter 32.) Therefore, we consider the heavy lattice ions almost static compared to the fast but randomly moving free electrons. The **free** (or **conduction**) **electron density** (n_e) of a material is defined as the number of free electrons per cubic metre of the material. Table 22-1 lists free electron densities for some familiar metals.

Table 22-1 Conduction electron density in metals

Metal	Conduction electron density, n_e (m^{-3})
Aluminum	6.0×10^{28}
Copper	8.4×10^{28}
Gold	5.9×10^{28}
Iron	8.4×10^{28}
Nickel	9.0×10^{28}
Silver	5.8×10^{28}
Zinc	6.0×10^{28}

EXAMPLE 22-1

Estimating Free Electron Density in Aluminum

Estimate the free electron density in aluminum, given that the density of aluminum is $\rho = 2.7 \times 10^3 \dfrac{\text{kg}}{\text{m}^3}$.

SOLUTION

Assuming that every atom of aluminum contributed one free electron to the free electron cloud (Al: $1s^2, 2s^2, 2p^2, 3s^2, 3p^1$), the free electron density is equal to the number of aluminum atoms per cubic metre. That number can be calculated from the molar mass (M_{Al}) and density (ρ_{Al}) of aluminum, and the number of atoms in one mole of aluminum (Avogadro's number N_A):

$$n_e = \frac{\rho_{Al}}{M_{Al}} \cdot N_A = \frac{2.7 \times 10^6\, \dfrac{\text{g}}{\text{m}^3}}{27\, \dfrac{\text{g}}{\text{mol}}} \cdot 6.022 \times 10^{23}\, \text{mol}^{-1}$$

$$= 6.0 \times 10^{28}\, \text{m}^{-3}$$

Making sense of the result:

Our estimated value for the free electron density in aluminum agrees with the observed value listed in Table 22-1. Thus, the free electron cloud model produced a prediction supported by an experiment.

As long as there is no external electric field applied on conduction electrons, their average velocity is zero as they randomly collide with ions of the metal lattice. However, when an external electric field is applied, the resulting net force acting on the electron cloud is directed opposite to the direction of the electric field (Figure 22-3). If the electrons were located in a vacuum, the electric field would have continuously accelerated them to very fast speeds. However, since electrons are located in a metal, they have

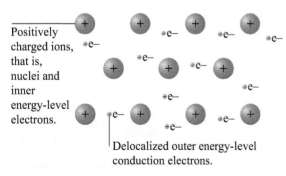

Positively charged ions, that is, nuclei and inner energy-level electrons.

Delocalized outer energy-level conduction electrons.

Figure 22-2 The sea-of-electrons model in a metal. Delocalized conduction electrons are immersed in an ionic lattice of a metal.

to move through the crystal lattice, undergoing multiple scattering, which slows them down, making the average velocity of an electron cloud quite small. This average velocity is called the **drift velocity**, $\vec{v}_d$. For metals, the magnitude of the drift velocity is on the order of 10^{-4} m/s.

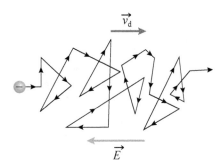

Figure 22-3 An external electric field applies an electric force on electrons in a metal, so they start moving with nonzero average velocity.

Let us estimate the number of electrons, N_e, passing through a cross-sectional area, A, of a cylindrical wire in a time interval, Δt, as a result of an applied external electric field, $\vec{E}$ (Figure 22-4). Note that there is an electric field inside a wire carrying an electric current, in contrast to the electrostatic case, in which the electric field inside a conductor is always zero, as described in Chapter 20.

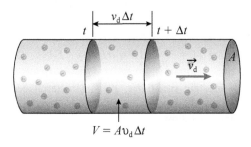

Figure 22-4 The movement of electrons in a conductor under the influence of an external electric field

Since the electron cloud moves a distance $\Delta x = v_d \Delta t$ during the time interval Δt, the number of passing through the cross-sectional area A over this time is

$$N_e = n_e V = n_e A \Delta x = n_e A v_d \Delta t \qquad (22\text{-}1)$$

An **electron current** is defined as the number of electrons passing through a cross-sectional area per unit time. Thus,

KEY EQUATION
$$I_e = \frac{N_e}{\Delta t} = n_e v_d A \qquad (22\text{-}2)$$

Using the value for the conduction electron density of aluminum from Table 22-1 and a drift velocity of 10^{-4} m/s for electrons, we can estimate the electron current through an aluminum wire with a cross-sectional area of 1 mm²:

$$I_e = n_e v_d A = \left(6 \times 10^{28}\, \frac{1}{\text{m}^3}\right)\left(10^{-4}\, \frac{\text{m}}{\text{s}}\right)(10^{-6}\, \text{m}^2)$$
$$= 6 \times 10^{18}\, \text{s}^{-1} \qquad (22\text{-}3)$$

It is generally more convenient to measure the current in terms of the amount of electric charge rather than the number of electrons carried through the wire per unit time. The flow of charge is called **electric current,** I. Historically, it was thought that positive charges (protons) and not electrons moved in a wire. For this reason, by convention, electric current is defined as the motion of positively charged particles. Therefore, the directions of electric and electron currents are opposite. Since the electric charge carried by one electron is $q_e = -e = -1.6 \times 10^{-19}$ C, where e is the elementary charge, the relationship between electric current and electron current is as follows:

KEY EQUATION
$$I = I_e \cdot e = (n_e v_d A)e = n_e v_d A (1.6 \times 10^{-19}\, \text{C}) \qquad (22\text{-}4)$$

Electric current is a scalar quantity, even though it describes the motion of charged particles.

The unit of current is the ampere (a base unit of SI), named in honour of the French scientist Andre-Marie Ampère (1775–1836).

We can use Equations (22-3) and (22-4) to estimate the electric current in the aluminum wire in Example 22-1:

$$I = (6.0 \times 10^{18}\, \text{s}^{-1})(1.6 \times 10^{-19}\, \text{C}) \approx 1.0\, \frac{\text{C}}{\text{s}} = 1.0\, \text{A}$$

The **current density**, J, in a conductor is the amount of electric current flowing per unit of cross-sectional area:

KEY EQUATION
$$J = \frac{I}{A} = \frac{n_e v_d A e}{A} = n_e v_d e$$
$$[J] = \frac{\text{C}}{\text{s} \cdot \text{m}^2} = \frac{\text{A}}{\text{m}^2} \qquad (22\text{-}5)$$

✓ CHECKPOINT

C-22-1 Relating Current Density in a Wire to its Physical Properties

Which statement must always be true regarding two copper wires carrying currents I_1 and I_2 with current densities J_1 and J_2, respectively? Explain.

(a) If $I_1 = 2I_2$ and $J_1 = J_2$, then $R_1 = \frac{1}{2}R_2$.

(b) If $I_1 = 2I_2$ and $J_1 = J_2$, then $R_1 = \sqrt{2}\, R_2$.

(c) If $I_1 = 2I_2$ and $J_1 = J_2$, then $R_1 = 4R_2$.

(d) If $I_1 = 2I_2$ and $J_1 = J_2$, then $R_1 = \frac{1}{\sqrt{2}}R_2$.

(e) If $I_1 = I_2$ and $J_1 = J_2$, then $(n_e)_1 = (n_e)_2$.

C-22-1 (b) Using Equation (22-5): $J = \dfrac{I}{A} = \dfrac{I}{\pi R^2} \Rightarrow R = \sqrt{\dfrac{I}{\pi J}} \Rightarrow \dfrac{R_1}{R_2} = \sqrt{\dfrac{I_1}{I_2}} = \sqrt{2}$

CHAPTER 22 | ELECTRIC CURRENT AND FUNDAMENTALS OF DC CIRCUITS   573

67

MAKING CONNECTIONS

Turn on the Light: A Microscopic View of Electric Current

The drift velocity of electrons in metals is of the order of magnitude of 10^{-4} m/s. Why, then, do lights turn on almost instantly when you turn on a light? The answer is that a metal wire is full of conduction electrons even before you turn the light on, and what propagates through the wire is a vibrational wave in the free electron cloud, not the cloud itself. This vibrational wave propagates through the metal lattice at a speed close to the speed of light, thus making the light turn on almost instantaneously.

LO 2

22-2 Electric Conductivity and Resistivity: The Microscopic Model

When a copper wire is connected to a charged capacitor, there is an excess of positive charge at the end of the wire connected to the positive plate of the capacitor (high potential) and an excess of negative charge (electrons) at the end of the wire connected to the negative plate (low potential). The nonuniform charge distribution on the wire's surface creates an internal electric field inside it, $\vec{E}$, directed from high to low external potential. This internal electric field accelerates electrons in the direction opposite to $\vec{E}$:

$$\vec{a} = \frac{\vec{F}}{m_e} = -\frac{e\vec{E}}{m_e} = (-1.6 \times 10^{-19}\,\text{C})\frac{\vec{E}}{m_e} \quad (22\text{-}6)$$

Thus, the collective motion of electrons in the direction opposite to the internal electric field, $\vec{E}$, is superimposed on the random motion of electrons caused by their collisions with the lattice ions (Figure 22-2). The result is the drifting of the electrons in the direction opposite to $\vec{E}$ (Figure 22-3). We can estimate the drift velocity if we assume that, on average, electrons spend τ seconds moving freely between collisions. This value can be measured experimentally and is a property of the metal. As discussed earlier, in the absence of an electric field, the average velocity of the free electrons is zero. During the time between collisions, electrons experience an electrostatic force $\vec{F} = -e\vec{E}$ that causes them to accelerate, gaining drift speed:

$$v_d = \frac{eE}{m}\tau \quad (22\text{-}7)$$

Substituting the above expression into the equations for electron (Equation (22-3)) and electric current (Equation (22-4)), we find the following:

$$I_e = n_e\frac{eE}{m}\tau A = \frac{n_e e\tau A}{m}E$$

KEY EQUATION
$$I = I_e e = \frac{n_e e^2 \tau A}{m}E \quad (22\text{-}8)$$

Equation (22-8) shows that the values of both electron and electric currents are proportional to the electric field. All the other variables in Equation (22-8) are fully determined by the electrons and the physical properties of the metal wire. Let us rewrite the above equation in terms of current density, to exclude the specific dimensions of the wire:

KEY EQUATION
$$J = \frac{I}{A} = \frac{n_e e^2 \tau}{m}E = \sigma E$$

where
$$\sigma = \frac{n_e e^2 \tau}{m} \quad (22\text{-}9)$$

Equation (22-9) describes a causal relationship between the electric field and the current density inside the wire. In this equation, σ is **electric conductivity**, which represents how much electric current flows through the wire in response to a given electric field. Electric conductivity is an internal property of a material. The greater the electric conductivity, the better the material conducts electric current.

Multiplying Equation (22-9) by the cross-sectional area of the wire, A, gives an expression for the electric current:

$$I = JA = \frac{n_e e^2 \tau}{m}AE = \sigma EA = \frac{1}{\rho}EA \quad (22\text{-}10)$$

The **electric resistivity**, ρ, of a material describes how strongly the material opposes the electric current. It is defined as follows:

$$\rho = \frac{1}{\sigma} = \frac{m}{n_e e^2 \tau} \quad (22\text{-}11)$$

The shorter the time (τ) between collisions of electrons within the crystal lattice, the more collisions take place and, consequently, the more kinetic energy of the electrons will be converted into thermal energy. This energy transfer explains why wires heat up when electric current flows through them.

When the temperature rises, the average kinetic energy of the electrons increases. Therefore, the resistivity of a metal also increases with temperature, and the conductivity decreases. As the metals heat up, the time between collisions, τ, decreases, which affects both ρ and σ, as can be seen from Equation (22-11). For most metals, the dependence of resistivity on temperature is linear for a limited range of temperatures:

$$\rho = \rho_0 + \alpha\rho_0(T - T_0) = \rho_0[1 + \alpha(T - T_0)]$$
$$= \rho_0[1 + \alpha\Delta T] \quad (22\text{-}12)$$

C-22-2 Dimensional Analysis in Action

Which of the following equations has incorrect dimensions?

(a) $[I] = \dfrac{C^2 \cdot s \cdot V}{kg \cdot m^2}$

(b) $[J] = \dfrac{C^2 \cdot s \cdot V}{kg \cdot m^4}$

(c) $[\rho] = \dfrac{kg \cdot m^3}{C^2 \cdot s}$

(d) $[\sigma] = \dfrac{C^2 \cdot s}{kg \cdot m^3}$

(e) $[I_c] = \dfrac{C \cdot s \cdot V}{m^3 \cdot kg}$

C-22-2 (e) $[I_c'] = \dfrac{I}{l} = \dfrac{A}{C/s} = \dfrac{C}{s} = \dfrac{q_b}{t_b} \neq \dfrac{V \cdot s \cdot C}{m^3 \cdot kg}$

where ρ is the resistivity at temperature T, measured in degrees Celsius, ρ_0 is the resistivity at the baseline temperature T_0 (often chosen to be 20°C), and α is the temperature coefficient of resistivity.

The resistivities, conductivities, and temperature coefficients for various materials are given in Table 22-2.

A **superconductor** is a material with a resistivity that abruptly drops to zero below a critical temperature (less than 100 K for all presently known superconductors). We will discuss superconductivity in Chapter 24.

22-3 Ohm's Law and Combinations of Resistors

We want to be able to analyze circuits that contain various combinations of electrical resistors. First, we derive a relationship between electric current, voltage, and resistance.

In Chapter 20, we saw that in the case of a constant and uniform electric field in a wire of length l, the relationship between electric field strength and electric potential is given by $E = V/l$. Substituting for E in Equation (22-10), we obtain

$$I = \sigma EA = \frac{1}{\rho} EA = \frac{1}{\rho}\frac{V}{l}A = \frac{A}{\rho l}V = \frac{V}{R} \quad (22\text{-}13)$$

In this equation, we introduce a new variable, R, for **electric resistance**:

$$R = \rho \frac{l}{A} \quad (22\text{-}14)$$

where A is the cross-sectional area of the material, l is its length, and ρ is its resistivity.

If we know the resistivity of a material, we can calculate the resistance of a wire or cylinder of the material with any arbitrary length or cross-sectional area. From Equation (22-14) we deduce that a wire with a shorter length or a larger cross-sectional area has a lower resistance than a longer or narrower wire.

Table 22-2 Resistivities, conductivities, and temperature coefficients for different metals

Material	$\rho(\Omega \cdot m)$ at 20°C	$\sigma(\Omega \cdot m)^{-1}$ at 20°C	Temperature coefficient α (K^{-1})
Aluminum	2.65×10^{-8}	3.77×10^{7}	3.8×10^{-3}
Copper	1.72×10^{-8}	5.95×10^{7}	4.3×10^{-3}
Gold	2.24×10^{-8}	4.10×10^{7}	3.4×10^{-3}
Iron	9.7×10^{-8}	1.00×10^{7}	5.0×10^{-3}
Lead	2.06×10^{-7}	4.55×10^{6}	3.9×10^{-3}
Nichrome	1.10×10^{-6}	9.09×10^{5}	4.0×10^{-3}
Nickel	6.85×10^{-8}	1.43×10^{7}	6.41×10^{-3}
Platinum	1.06×10^{-7}	9.43×10^{6}	3.92×10^{-3}
Silver	1.59×10^{-8}	6.30×10^{7}	3.8×10^{-3}
Tin	1.09×10^{-7}	9.17×10^{6}	4.5×10^{-3}
Tungsten	5.60×10^{-8}	1.79×10^{7}	4.5×10^{-3}
Zinc	5.90×10^{-8}	1.69×10^{7}	3.7×10^{-3}

Source: The Engineering Toolbox http://www.engineeringtoolbox.com/index.html
http://www.engineeringtoolbox.com/resistivity-conductivity-d_418.html

ELECTRICITY, MAGNETISM, AND OPTICS

Equation (22-13) was derived for a very special case—an electrical wire with a uniform cross-sectional area—but it can be generalized for a large variety of electrical components, such as resistors. The equation shows a very important relationship between electric current flowing through a wire and the voltage across it: the amount of electric current is directly proportional to the voltage. Introducing electric resistance allows us to describe the proportionality between electric current and voltage, and the physical properties of the wire in a very succinct form, called **Ohm's law**: Electric current across an ohmic circuit element, such as a resistor, is directly proportional to the voltage applied across it (Figure 22-5(a)):

Ohm's Law

$$I = \frac{V}{R}$$

$$[I] = \frac{V}{\Omega} = A \tag{22-15}$$

This relationship was discovered by Georg Simon Ohm (1787–1854), a German scientist. The unit of electric resistance, the ohm (Ω), is named in his honour. Ohm's law is widely used in designing and analyzing electric circuits. However, you have to remember that electric resistivity, ρ, and electric resistance, R, for many materials depend on temperature. Thus, the slope of the I-V curve (the common name for the $I(V)$ graph) might change if the material heats up as the current increases (Figure 22-5(b)). Such heating could make the relationship nonlinear. Ohm's law accurately describes how current through the element of a circuit depends on the voltage across it only when the temperature of the element remains constant. For example, the resistance of the filament of an incandescent light bulb increases markedly when current heats it enough to produce visible light; therefore, it is a nonohmic circuit element. It also explains why the light bulbs usually burn out just as they are turned on. A diode is another example of a nonohmic circuit element (Figure 22-5(c)).

The dependence of resistance on temperature can be derived from Equations (22-12) and (22-14):

$$I = \frac{V}{R} = \frac{VA}{\rho_0[1 + \alpha(T - T_0)]l} = \frac{V}{R_0[1 + \alpha(T - T_0)]}$$

$$\tag{22-16}$$

Components with resistance, such as the ones shown in Figure 22-6(a), are found in all electrical and electronic devices. Often an electric circuit for a particular application will need circuit elements that have constant specified resistances. These circuit elements are called **resistors**. The symbol for resistor used in circuit diagrams is shown in Figure 22-6(b). To mark the value of resistance on small circuit elements, engineers and scientists use colour coding (Figure 22-6(c)).

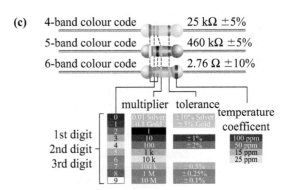

Figure 22-6 (a) Miniature electrical resistors inside a digital watch. (b) The symbol for a resistor in a circuit diagram. (c) Colour coding scheme of electrical resistors. In order to find the value of the resistor you first look at the left bands (25, 460, 276 in our examples) and then multiply this value by the corresponding power of 10 expressed by the following band. This value can be found in the second column of the diagram above (1000, 1000 and 0.01 in our examples). The value of the resistance is the product of the two: 25 kΩ, 460 kΩ and 2.76 Ω for the resistors in the example.

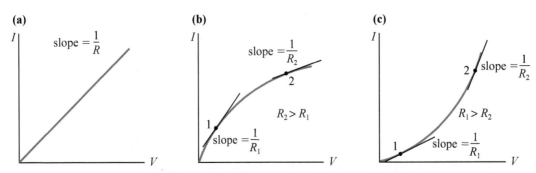

Figure 22-5 The dependence of current on applied voltage across (a) an ohmic circuit element and two nonohmic circuit elements, (b) an incandescent light bulb, and (c) a diode

EXAMPLE 22-2

Applying Ohm's Law to a Current-Carrying Wire

A potential difference of 100 mV is applied across a 5.0 m-long metal wire that has a diameter of 0.50 mm. The resulting electric current is 66.7 mA.

(a) Find the resistance of the wire.
(b) Find the resistivity of the wire, and suggest what metal it could be made of.

SOLUTION

(a) We assume that the metal wire obeys Ohm's law. Therefore, we can find its resistance, R, using Equation (22-15):

$$R = \frac{V}{I} = \frac{100 \text{ mV}}{66.7 \text{ mA}} = \frac{100 \times 10^{-3} \text{ V}}{66.7 \times 10^{-3} \text{ A}} = 1.50 \ \Omega$$

(b) Rearranging Equation (22-14), we can find the resistivity of the wire:

$$\rho = \frac{RA}{l} = \frac{(1.5 \ \Omega) \cdot \pi (0.25 \times 10^{-3} \text{m})^2}{5.0 \text{ m}} = 5.9 \times 10^{-8} \ \Omega \cdot \text{m}$$

Comparing this value to the resistivities listed in Table 22-2, we find that the wire could be made of zinc.

Making sense of the result:

Resistance and resistivity are different physical quantities. The resistance provides a description of how a particular piece of wire resists the flow of electric current. The resistivity is the resistance of a hypothetical wire that is 1 m long and has a cross-sectional area of 1 m².

 CHECKPOINT

C-22-3 Ranking Resistances of Metal Wires

Which of the following statements correctly represents the ranking of the resistances of the five copper wires shown in Figure 22-7? How would you rank the resistivities of these wires?

(a) $R_B > R_A = R_E > R_C > R_D$
(b) $R_B > R_A > R_E > R_C > R_D$
(c) $R_C > R_A = R_E > R_B > R_D$
(d) $R_D > R_C > R_E = R_A > R_B$
(e) $R_D > R_A = R_E > R_C > R_B$

each with resistance R. What is the effective resistance of a combination of these resistors? The answer depends on how the resistors are connected.

Resistors Connected in Series When two or more resistors are connected in series (Figure 22-8(a)), the circuit is called a **series circuit**. In that case, the same electric current flows through each resistor because the current that exits the first resistor must enter the second resistor. Connecting two identical resistors in series affects their total length while leaving the other parameters unchanged. It is convenient to define equivalent resistance of electric circuits that are comprised of two or more resistors. The **equivalent resistance** is the

(a) **(b)** **(c)**

L, R $2L, R$ $2L, 2R$

(d) **(e)**

$L, 2R$ $4L, 2R$

Figure 22-7 C-22-3

Now we are ready to explore how Ohm's law can be applied to a combination of resistors. Let us model a resistor as a wire of length l, cross-sectional area A, and resistivity ρ. Imagine that we have two identical resistors,

(a)

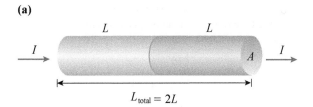

(b)

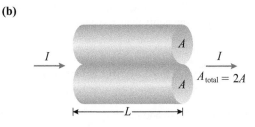

Figure 22-8 Electrical resistors connected (a) in series and (b) in parallel

resistance of a resistor that, when connected in series to the circuit's battery will produce an electric current equal to the electric current in the original circuit. To find the value of the equivalent resistance in a series circuit, R_{series}, we use Equation (22-14):

$$R_{series} = \rho \frac{2L}{A} = 2\rho \frac{L}{A} = 2R \qquad (22\text{-}17)$$

Although this expression was derived for a special case of two identical resistors, we will show later that it applies to any number of different resistors connected in series:

KEY EQUATION
$$R_{series} = \sum_{i=1}^{N} R_i \qquad (22\text{-}18)$$

Equation (22-18) indicates that connecting resistors in series increases their equivalent resistance. The term "equivalent" here indicates that resistors connected in series behave as one equivalent resistor that has a resistance equal to the sum of all the individual resistances.

Resistors Connected in Parallel A circuit in which the electric current has more than one continuous path for electrons to flow (**electric circuit branch**) is called a **parallel circuit**. A parallel circuit has **junction points**, which are points where electric current can split up and flow through different branches of the circuit. When two resistors are connected in parallel (Figure 22-8(b)), some of the current will flow through the first resistor, and the rest will flow through the second resistor. Connecting identical resistors in parallel increases the effective cross-sectional area while leaving the length of the path for electrons unchanged. To find the value of the equivalent resistance for two identical resistors connected in parallel, $R_{parallel}$, we again use Equation (22-14):

$$R_{parallel} = \rho \frac{L}{2A} = \frac{1}{2}\rho \frac{L}{A} = \frac{R}{2} \qquad (22\text{-}19)$$

Although we used a special case of two identical resistors to derive this equation, we will show later that the equivalent resistance for any number of different resistors connected in parallel is given by

KEY EQUATION
$$\frac{1}{R_{parallel}} = \sum_{i=1}^{N} \frac{1}{R_i} \qquad (22\text{-}20)$$

Equation (22-20) indicates that connecting resistors in parallel reduces the equivalent resistance.

Power in DC Circuits

In Chapter 20, we defined electric potential difference as the potential energy gained by a unit charge when it moves from one point to another: $V = \frac{U_{el}}{q}$. In Section 22-2, we saw that a current of free electrons in a material heats

PEER TO PEER

I always thought that in a parallel circuit, the current splits equally between the circuit's parallel branches. Then I realized that this is only true when the branches have equal resistance. The current will split in a way such that the more resistance the branch has, the less current will flow through it. For example, if 6 A of current enters the junction and splits between two branches of 2 Ω and 4 Ω, the branch that has twice the resistance will receive half the current. Thus, the current will split into 4 A and 2 A, respectively. Keeping this in mind always helps me determine whether my circuit solution is reasonable.

the material through collisions with its atoms. We define **power**, P, as the rate of energy transfer. For the thermal energy dissipated as a result of electric charges flowing through a material,

$$P = \frac{Q_{heat}}{\Delta t} \qquad (22\text{-}21)$$

where Q_{heat} is heat dissipated during the time interval, Δt.

When current flows in a material, the electric potential energy of the electrons is converted first to kinetic energy and then into heat, which is dissipated by the material. Therefore,

$$P = \frac{Q_{heat}}{\Delta t} = \frac{qV}{\Delta t} = IV \qquad (22\text{-}22)$$

Using Ohm's law, Equation (22-22) can be rewritten as follows:

KEY EQUATION
$$P = IV = I^2R = \frac{V^2}{R}$$

$$[P] = \frac{J}{s} = \text{watt (W)};$$

$$1W = 1A \cdot 1V \qquad (22\text{-}23)$$

Consequently, the heat dissipated by a conductor of resistance R carrying electric current I over the time period Δt can be expressed as

KEY EQUATION
$$Q_{heat} = I^2R\Delta t \qquad (22\text{-}24)$$

This relationship was discovered independently by two scientists: British physicist James Prescott Joule (1818–89) and Russian-German-Estonian physicist Heinrich Lenz (1804–65), and is often called Joule–Lenz's law.

From this example we conclude that in a parallel electric circuit, the power output of the circuit equals the sum of the nominal power outputs of its components.

Household Electrical Wiring: How Much Is Too Much?

All your household appliances are connected in parallel to the external source of electric energy through the electrical outlets in the walls (Figure 22-9). By connecting more appliances in a parallel circuit, you are reducing the equivalent resistance of the combined load, thus increasing the current drawn from the electrical outlet: $I_{outlet} = I_1 + I_2 + I_3 + \cdots$

$$= \frac{V}{R_1} + \frac{V}{R_2} + \frac{V}{R_3} + \cdots = V \left(\frac{1}{R_1} + \frac{1}{R_2} + \frac{1}{R_3} \cdots \right) = \frac{V}{R_{parallel}}.$$

In North America, common electrical outlets are designed to supply currents of up to 15 A. Larger currents in such circuits can overheat the wires enough to damage the insulation and possibly cause a fire. For this reason, strict safety regulations are in place that require all household circuits to be protected by a fuse or a circuit breaker, which will cut off the current when the circuit is overloaded.

In an electric circuit, the total power output of the circuit equals the sum of the power outputs of all the appliances. Therefore, to avoid reaching the maximum allowable current, the sum of all the power values produced by the appliances should not exceed 1800 W. For a parallel circuit at your home:

$$P_{max} = IV = (I_1 + I_2 + I_3 + \cdots)V$$

$$= I_1 V + I_2 V + I_3 V + \cdots = \frac{V^2}{R_1} + \frac{V^2}{R_2} + \frac{V^2}{R_3} + \cdots$$

$$= P_1 + P_2 + P_3 + \cdots$$

$$P_{max} = IV = (15 \text{ A})(120 \text{ V}) = 1800 \text{ W}$$

$$P_1 + P_2 + P_3 + \cdots \leq P_{max}$$

In a series circuit connected to an energy source V, the power output of the circuit will also be equal to the sum of the power outputs of its elements. However, the power output of each of the elements will be less than the nominal power output they were designed for, as the potential difference across each one of them will be less than V (which was used to calculate the nominal power output).

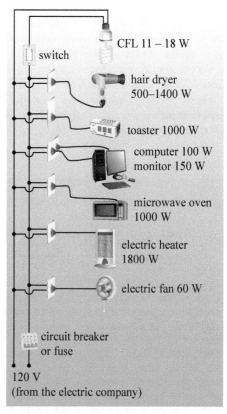

Figure 22-9 All your household appliances are connected in parallel to the external source of electric energy through the electrical outlets in the walls.

The power output increases when the number of electrical appliances connected in parallel increases:

KEY EQUATION
$$P_{parallel} = \sum_{i=1}^{N} P_i \qquad (22\text{-}25)$$

The electric energy used by a load (such as a toaster or other appliance) in a circuit depends on the power drawn from the source and on the length of time, Δt, that the circuit operates:

$$E_{el} = P\Delta t \qquad (22\text{-}26)$$

Electrical utility companies commonly measure energy consumption in kilowatt hours (kW·h) (Figure 22-10), although some companies now use megajoules (MJ) for their billing. By converting hours to seconds, we can convert a kilowatt hour into joules:

$$1 \text{ kW} \cdot \text{h} = (1000 \text{ W})(3600 \text{ s}) = 3.6 \times 10^6 \text{ J} = 3.6 \text{ MJ}$$

$$(22\text{-}27)$$

BC Hydro Electric Charges

Apr 07 to Jun 04 (Residential Conservation Rate 1101)	
Basic charge: 59 days @ $0.13410/day	7.91*
Usage charge:[1]	
Step 1: 935 kW.h @ $0.06270/kW.h	58.62*
Step 2: 0 kW.h @ $0.08780/kW.h	0.00
Rate Rider at 4.0%	2.66*
Innovative Clean Energy Fund Levy at 0.4%	0.28
Regional transit levy: 59 days @ $0.06240/day	3.68*
* GST	3.64
	$76.79

Your total consumption for the billing period is 935 kW.h

Figure 22-10 A residential electricity bill

PEER TO PEER

I knew that on an electrical bill the energy is written as $kW \cdot h$, but only recently did I notice that it stands for the product of the two, not the ratio (i.e., it is *not* kW per hour). When measuring energy consumption in everyday life, the unit J is inconvenient because it is too small. So we use $kW \cdot h$ instead: $1 \, kW \cdot h = 3.6 \times 10^6 \, J$ (Equation 22-27). To show the ratio of two numbers, we use the term "per" (e.g., kilometres per hour), but when we want to show the product of two numbers, we just write them side by side (e.g, kilowatt hours).

MAKING CONNECTIONS

The Invention of the Incandescent Light Bulb

Humphry Davy (1778–1829) built the first electric light bulb in 1809. Over the next century, a number of inventors developed a variety of designs, which led to the mass production of affordable and reasonably reliable incandescent light bulbs. Among these inventors were Sir Joseph Wilson Swan (1828–1914) in England, who invented a bulb using a carbon filament, and Henry Woodward and Mathew Evans in Canada, who ended up selling their incandescent light bulb patent to an American, Thomas Alva Edison (1847–1931). Edison had the financial backing needed to improve and commercialize their design. Today, the filaments in incandescent lamps are made of tungsten, which can withstand higher temperatures and therefore produce more light than carbon filaments. The energy efficiency of tungsten bulbs is 2% to 10% because only a tiny fraction of the light they emit is in the range of visible light. Traditional incandescent light bulbs are gradually being replaced by more efficient bulbs, such as halogen incandescent light bulbs, fluorescent lamps, and light-emitting diodes.

EXAMPLE 22-3

Power Rating of a Light Bulb

The antique 30 W light bulb in Figure 22-11(a) was designed to be connected to a 200 V battery. What is the power output of this light bulb when it is operated by a 100 V battery (Figure 22-11(b))?

SOLUTION

The power output of the light bulb depends on the resistance of its filament and the voltage of the energy

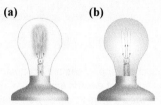

(a)   **(b)**

Figure 22-11 This antique incandescent light bulb uses a carbon filament. The grey colour results from sublimated carbon that is gradually deposited on the inner surface of the bulb. This light bulb is powered by (a) a 200 V source and (b) a 100 V source.

source. The nominal resistance of the carbon filament of this light bulb is

$$R = \frac{V_1^2}{P_1} = \frac{(200 \, V)^2}{30 \, W} = \frac{4.0 \times 10^4 \, V^2}{30 \, W} = 1.33 \, k\Omega$$

When the light bulb is connected to a source with a lower voltage, the power output is reduced:

$$P_2 = \frac{V_2^2}{R} = \frac{(100 \, V)^2}{1.33 \, k\Omega} = \frac{1.0 \times 10^4 \, V^2}{1.33 \times 10^3 \, \Omega} = 7.5 \, W$$

Making sense of the result:

Since the power depends on the square of the voltage, decreasing the voltage across the light bulb by half reduces the power output of the bulb by a factor of 4.

MAKING CONNECTIONS

You Are Grounded!

You probably have heard the term "electrical grounding" and may have wondered what it meant. **Electrical grounding** was invented as a safety measure to protect people, who, when accidentally touching a faulty electrical appliance, become a path for the electric current and being shocked by it. For example, consider the heating element inside your electric toaster. When the toaster is operating properly, electric current flows through the heating element, thus heating your bagel. If for any reason the heating element comes into contact with the metal case of the toaster, the case will become a part of the circuit. If you accidentally touch the case, your body will become a part of the circuit as well, providing a path for electric current from a high-voltage power source (high potential energy) to the ground (low potential energy): the current will flow through the device, through the metal case, and through you into the ground. This will expose you to high voltage.

While the current through your body might be low due to your high internal resistance, it is still very dangerous. A person will feel a shock if only 5 mA of current flows

ELECTRICITY, MAGNETISM, AND OPTICS

through the body; 100 mA of current could be lethal. The danger of relatively low electric current is very important because a circuit breaker is built to break the circuit when the current levels reach much higher values in order to prevent fires (15 A for Canadian households), while not protecting people from being shocked. By connecting the toaster to the ground, the current will have an alternative (parallel) path to flow from the toaster case to the ground circuit. If the ground circuit has less resistance than the circuit through your skin, you will be safe. This low-resistance return path for electric current (grounding circuit) protects you from being shocked by the toaster. Since the resistance of a ground circuit is much higher than the resistance of the original circuit when the toaster is operating properly, the electric current only flows through the ground circuit when there is a problem.

LO 4

22-4 Analysis of DC Circuits and Kirchhoff's Laws

A **direct current (DC)** circuit is a circuit in which electric current flows in one direction. A simple DC electric circuit consists of circuit elements, such as batteries, resistors, switches, capacitors, and diodes, connected by conducting wires that allow the flow of electric current. We will use the concepts of electric current I, resistance R, power P, and voltage V to describe the operation of these circuits. First, we consider the source of electric potential energy.

Source of Electromotive Force Electric batteries and generators are sources of electric energy. Historically, they were called the **sources of electromotive force** (emf). However, as you will see below, electromotive force is not

a real force but is a measure of electric potential energy per unit charge. To avoid confusion while adhering to the tradition, we will use the abbreviation emf to refer to a constant voltage produced by a source. Figure 22-12 shows representations of an ideal battery and a real battery.

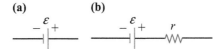

Figure 22-12 Schematic representations of ideal and real batteries. (a) An ideal battery (b) A real battery that has a nonzero internal resistance r

The simple DC circuit in Figure 22-13(a) consists of a battery connected to a light bulb with conducting wires. As a result of the energy stored in the battery, an electric current, I, flows through the circuit. We assume that the resistance of the wires compared to the resistance of the light bulb is negligible, but the emf source (the battery) is real, which means it has an internal resistance, r. We apply Ohm's law (Equation (22-15)) to each segment of this circuit, and summarize the results in Table 22-3.

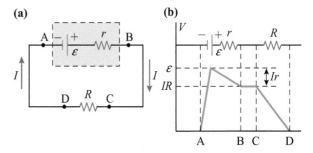

Figure 22-13 Analysis of a simple DC circuit consisting of a non-ideal emf source (a battery), a light bulb, and connecting wires. (a) A schematic representation of a real-life circuit real-life circuit (b) A schematic representation of the energy use in the circuit

Table 22-3 Analysis of a simple DC circuit containing a nonideal emf source (a battery), a light bulb, and connecting wires for Figure 22-13

Segment	I (A)	R (Ω)	V (V)	Meaning
AB	I	R	$V_{AB} = V_B - V_A = (\varepsilon - Ir)$	The positive terminal, B, has a higher potential than the negative terminal, A; therefore V_{AB} is positive. Moving charged particles (electric current) will use some of the potential energy Ir from the emf source ε to move through it. Thus, the voltage output between the terminals of the emf source V_{AB} will be reduced by Ir as compared to emf ε.
BC	I	0	$V_{BC} = V_B - V_C = I(0\ \Omega) = 0\ \text{V}$	No energy is used by the current to flow through this segment: zero potential difference.
CD	I	R_{bulb}	$V_{CD} = V_C - V_D = IR_{bulb}$	Electric current converts electric potential energy into heat, thus dissipating electric energy.
DA	I	0	$V_{DA} = V_D - V_A = I(0\ \Omega) = 0\ \text{V}$	No energy is used by the current to flow through this segment: zero potential difference.
Total: ABCDA	I	$R_{bulb} + r$	$IR_{bulb} - (\varepsilon - Ir) = 0$ $IR_{bulb} - \varepsilon + Ir = 0$ $IR_{bulb} = V_{AD} = \varepsilon - Ir$	Since electric charges complete an entire circuit, their total change in electric potential must be zero: $\Delta V_{total} = 0$.

The analysis presented in Table 22-3 is an application of the law of conservation of energy to a simple DC circuit. As with gravitational potential energy, if one returns to the starting point, the sum of all the gains and losses of potential energy along the way must be zero.

Since any real (non-ideal) emf source has some internal resistance, we represent it by connecting an internal resistance, r, in series to an ideal source that has zero internal resistance (Figure 22-13(b)).

Figure 22-13(c) shows potential differences across different elements of the circuit. This diagram clearly identifies the segments where the sources of energy are located. When a positive electric charge moves from point A to point B, it gains energy. Since the internal resistance of the source is nonzero, the energy gain per unit charge is $\varepsilon - IR$. On the other hand, there is no change in energy when the charge moves along segments BC and DA; and the electric potential energy of the charge is converted into thermal energy over the segment CD.

The analysis above shows that the emf and the voltage across the terminals of a source will differ by an amount that depends on the current and the internal resistance of the source:

$$V_{AB} = \varepsilon - Ir \qquad (22\text{-}28)$$

Since the light bulb is connected to the emf source with conducting wires that have negligible resistance, the potential difference across the light bulb equals the potential difference across the terminals of the emf source:

$$IR_{bulb} = \varepsilon - Ir$$

$$I = \frac{\varepsilon}{(R_{bulb} + r)} \qquad (22\text{-}29)$$

The thermal energy dissipated by this circuit includes the energy dissipated by the light bulb and by the battery:

$$I\varepsilon = I^2 R_{bulb} + I^2 r \qquad (22\text{-}30)$$

This example illustrates how the law of energy conservation applies to electric circuits.

Meters in an Electric Circuit To confirm that our analysis of a circuit is correct, we can use an **ammeter** to measure the currents through various circuit elements and a **voltmeter** to measure the potential differences across them. An ammeter has to be connected in series with the circuit elements so that the same current flows through the ammeter and through the element, as shown in Figure 22-14(a). An ammeter has a very low internal resistance to minimize its effect on the circuit. However, a voltmeter has to be connected in parallel to a circuit element to measure the voltage across it. A voltmeter (Figure 22-14(b)) has a very high internal resistance, producing a minimal effect on the circuit. Both ammeter and voltmeter measurements have to be made on an operating circuit.

An ohmmeter (Figure 22-14(c)) measures the electrical resistance of a circuit element when the element is disconnected from a circuit. A device that can be set

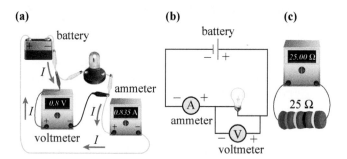

Figure 22-14 (a) An ammeter and a voltmeter connected to an electric circuit (b) A circuit diagram showing the ammeter and the voltmeter (c) An ohmmeter connected to a resistor

to measure current, voltage, or resistance is called a **multimeter**.

You can solve many problems dealing with simple DC circuits. However, to develop a real physics intuition, you have to have some hands-on experience with constructing and analyzing circuits. Today, you can gain such experience—even if you do not have a real-life circuit in front of you—by trying the online activity below.

ONLINE ACTIVITY

Simple and Not So Simple DC Circuits

The e-resource that accompanies every new copy of this textbook contains an Online Activity using the PhET simulation "Circuit Construction Kit." Work through the simulation and accompanying questions to gain an understanding of DC circuits.

Kirchhoff's Laws

Series Circuits Figure 22-15 shows three different light bulbs connected in series with an ideal battery (zero internal resistance) and a switch. When the switch is closed, it has negligible resistance and the potential difference across it is zero. As a consequence of the law of energy conservation, the potential difference across the battery, V_B, must be equal to the sum of potential differences across all circuit elements. Therefore,

$$V_B = V_1 + V_2 + V_3 \qquad (22\text{-}31)$$

Equation (22-31) can be generalized to state that the algebraic sum of all the potential differences (voltages) across all circuit elements around a closed circuit loop must be zero:

KEY EQUATION
$$\sum_{closed\ loop} \Delta V = 0 \qquad (22\text{-}32)$$

This loop rule, called **Kirchhoff's second law**, after German physicist Gustav Kirchhoff (1824–87), is a consequence of the law of energy conservation.

Next, we note that the same current I flows through all the elements of our series circuit. Applying Ohm's law to each light bulb and once again using R_{series} for the equivalent resistance of the entire series circuit, we obtain

$$V_B = IR_1 + IR_2 + IR_3 = I(R_1 + R_2 + R_3)$$

Since $\quad V_B = IR_{series}$,

$$IR_{series} = I(R_1 + R_2 + R_3)$$

$$R_{series} = R_1 + R_2 + R_3$$

We can apply the same analysis to any number of different resistors connected in series, thus proving a general formula for resistors connected in series we discussed earlier:

KEY EQUATION $$R_{series} = \sum_{i=1}^{N} R_i \qquad (22\text{-}18)$$

✅ **CHECKPOINT**

C-22-4 Three Light Bulbs in a Series Electric Circuit

The three light bulbs in Figure 22-15 are connected in series. The middle light bulb is the brightest, and the bulb on the left is the dimmest. For these light bulbs,

(a) $R_1 > R_3 > R_2$; $I_1 = I_2 = I_3$;
(b) $R_1 = R_2 = R_3$; $I_1 < I_3 < I_2$;
(c) $R_1 > R_3 > R_2$; $I_1 < I_3 < I_2$;
(d) $R_1 = R_2 = R_3$; $I_2 < I_3 < I_1$;
(e) $R_2 > R_3 > R_1$; $I_1 = I_2 = I_3$.

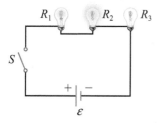

Figure 22-15 Three non-identical light bulbs connected in series

C-22-4 (e) The light bulbs are connected in series; therefore, the same amount of current flows through them. Since $P = I^2R$ (Equation (22-23)), the greater the resistance of the light bulb, the greater the potential difference across it and the higher the power it generates, thus dissipating more heat.

Parallel Circuits Figure 22-16 shows three light bulbs connected in parallel to an ideal battery. Each light bulb is connected directly to the battery and thus forms a separate branch of the circuit. A point where different branches join together is called a **junction**, or a **node**. Figure 22-17 shows currents flowing through two different junctions. As discussed earlier, the current does not necessarily divide equally among the parallel branches, but the amount of current entering any branch must equal the current exiting it, and the current entering any junction must equal the current exiting it. In the junction rule, we use a plus sign before the currents entering the junction and a minus sign before the currents exiting the junction.

KEY EQUATION $$\sum_{junction} I_i = 0 \quad \text{or} \quad \sum_{junction} I_{entering} = \sum_{junction} I_{exiting}$$
$$(22\text{-}33)$$

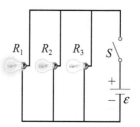

Figure 22-16 Three light bulbs connected in parallel

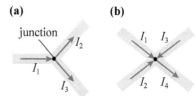

Figure 22-17 The amount of current entering a junction equals the amount of current leaving it.

This junction rule, called **Kirchhoff's first law**, is a consequence of the **law of electric charge conservation**, which states electric change can neither be created nor destroyed.

Applying Kirchhoff's junction rule to our parallel circuit, we see that the current leaving the battery must equal the sum of the currents in the three branches:

$$I_B = I_1 + I_2 + I_3 \qquad (22\text{-}34)$$

Since each light bulb is connected directly to the battery, the potential difference across each bulb must be equal to the potential difference across the battery's terminals. Applying Ohm's law to substitute for the currents in Equation (22-34), we find

$$\frac{V_B}{R_{parallel}} = \frac{V_B}{R_1} + \frac{V_B}{R_2} + \frac{V_B}{R_3}$$

$$\frac{1}{R_{parallel}} = \frac{1}{R_1} + \frac{1}{R_2} + \frac{1}{R_3}$$

We can apply the same argument to any number of different resistors connected in parallel, thus proving a general formula for resistors connected in parallel we discussed earlier:

KEY EQUATION $$\frac{1}{R_{parallel}} = \sum_{i=1}^{N} \frac{1}{R_i} \qquad (22\text{-}20)$$

ELECTRICITY, MAGNETISM, AND OPTICS

NEL CHAPTER 22 | ELECTRIC CURRENT AND FUNDAMENTALS OF DC CIRCUITS 583

77

CHECKPOINT

C-22-5 Three Light Bulbs in a Parallel Electric Circuit

The three light bulbs in Figure 22-16 are connected in parallel to a battery. The left light bulb is the brightest, and the light bulb in the middle is the dimmest. For these light bulbs,

(a) $R_1 > R_3 > R_2$; $I_1 = I_2 = I_3$;
(b) $R_1 = R_2 = R_3$; $I_1 > I_3 > I_2$;
(c) $R_1 > R_3 > R_2$; $I_1 < I_3 < I_2$;
(d) $R_1 = R_2 = R_3$; $I_2 < I_3 < I_1$;
(e) $R_2 > R_3 > R_1$; $I_1 > I_3 > I_2$.

C-22-5 (e) The light bulbs are connected in parallel; therefore, they have the same potential difference across them. Since $P = \dfrac{V^2}{R}$ (Equation (22-23)), the lower the resistance of the light bulb, the more current will flow through it and the more power it and will produce, thus dissipating more heat.

CHECKPOINT

C-22-6 The Relative Brightness of Two Light Bulbs in Series and Parallel Electric Circuits

A 25 W light bulb and a 40 W light bulb are first connected in series. Then they are connected in parallel. Which statement describes their relative brightness?

(a) The 25 W light bulb is brighter in a series circuit and dimmer in a parallel circuit.
(b) The 25 W light bulb is brighter in a parallel circuit and dimmer in a series circuit.
(c) The 25 W light bulb is always brighter.
(d) The 40 W light bulb is always brighter.

C-22-6 (b) The light bulbs are designed to be used in a parallel circuit; therefore, the higher the nominal power (power rating), the less the resistance of the light bulb (higher-rated light bulbs have thicker filaments).

We can use the properties of series and parallel circuits to find the simplest way to determine the power developed in the components of the circuits. In a series circuit, the same current flows through each component, so it is convenient to use the equation $P = I^2R$ to determine the power dissipated by each component. However, the branches in a parallel circuit are all connected to the same battery; thus, the potential differences across them must be the same and equal to the potential difference across the battery. Therefore, it is more convenient to use $P = \dfrac{V^2}{R}$ to determine the thermal energy (heat) dissipated by each branch.

 PEER TO PEER

I never thought that a power rating for a light bulb (nominal power) is the power it will generate only when connected to the power source for which the light bulb was rated. If the light bulb is designed to generate 40 W while connected to a 110 V source, it will generate less power if it is connected to a lower-voltage source. Thus, the nominal power is not necessarily the power that the light bulb generates.

 EXAMPLE 22-4

Resistors in Series and in Parallel

Two different combinations of resistors are shown in Figure 22-18. Each combination then is connected to a 12.0 V battery which is connected to points A and B respectively. The current through the battery in the first circuit is twice the current in the second circuit.

(a) What is the value of R in the second circuit?
(b) Find the currents in each branch of the two circuits.

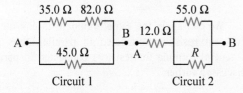

Figure 22-18 Example 22-4

SOLUTION

(a) In the first circuit diagram, the two resistors in the top branch are connected in series, so their equivalent resistance is

$$(R_{eq})_{top1} = 35.0\ \Omega + 82.0\ \Omega = 117\ \Omega$$

Since the top and the bottom branches are connected in parallel, their equivalent resistance is

$$\frac{1}{R_{eq1}} = \frac{1}{117\ \Omega} + \frac{1}{45.0\ \Omega}$$

$$\frac{1}{R_{eq1}} = 0.0308\ \Omega^{-1}$$

$$R_{eq1} = 32.5\ \Omega$$

ELECTRICITY, MAGNETISM, AND OPTICS

In the final answer, three significant figures are kept in accordance with the significant figure rules.

We now use Ohm's law to find the current flowing through the battery (again, we round the final answer to three significant figures):

$$I_{battery} = \frac{V_{battery}}{R_{eq1}} = \frac{12.0 \text{ V}}{32.5 \text{ }\Omega} = 0.36923 \text{ A} \approx 0.369 \text{ A}$$

Since the current in the second circuit is half the current in the first one, $I_2 = 0.185$ A. To produce this current by connecting the combination of resistors to a 12.0 V battery, the equivalent resistance in the second circuit must be

$$R_{eq2} = \frac{12.0 \text{ V}}{0.18462 \text{ A}} = 64.998 \text{ }\Omega \approx 65.0 \text{ }\Omega$$

To find R, we write an equation for the equivalent resistance in the second circuit:

$$R_{eq2} = 64.998 \text{ }\Omega$$

$$64.998 \text{ }\Omega = 15.0 \text{ }\Omega + \left[\frac{1}{55.0 \text{ }\Omega} + \frac{1}{R}\right]^{-1}$$

$$49.998 \text{ }\Omega = \frac{(55.0 \text{ }\Omega)R}{R + 55.0 \text{ }\Omega}$$

$$(49.998 \text{ }\Omega)R + 2749.89 \text{ }\Omega^2 = (55.0 \text{ }\Omega)R$$

$$R = 549.803 \text{ }\Omega \approx 549 \text{ }\Omega$$

(b) To find the currents flowing through each branch, we apply Ohm's law to each one. For diagram (a), both branches have a potential difference of 12.0 V across them. Therefore, the currents through the branches are as follows:

$$I_{top1} = \frac{12.0 \text{ V}}{117 \text{ }\Omega} = 0.103 \text{ A}$$

$$I_{bottom1} = \frac{12.0 \text{ V}}{45.0 \text{ }\Omega} = 0.267 \text{ A}$$

For diagram (b), the potential difference across each resistor is less than 12.0 V because the parallel combination of resistors is connected in series with the 12.0 Ω resistor. Therefore,

$$I_{top2} = \frac{12.0 \text{ V} - (0.185 \text{ A})(15.0 \text{ }\Omega)}{55.0 \text{ }\Omega} = 0.168 \text{ A}$$

$$I_{bottom2} = \frac{12.0 \text{ V} - (0.185 \text{ A})(15.0 \text{ }\Omega)}{549.803 \text{ }\Omega} = 0.0168 \text{ A}$$

Making sense of the result:

To verify our calculations, we can check that the sum of the currents in each circuit equals the current flowing through the battery:

$$I_{battery1} = I_{top1} + I_{bottom1} = 0.369 \text{ A} \quad \text{and}$$

$$I_{battery2} = I_{top2} + I_{bottom2} = 0.185 \text{ A}$$

Example 22-4 demonstrates two important properties of parallel circuits:

■ In a parallel circuit, the ratio of the currents through parallel branches is equal to the inverse ratio of the resistances of these branches. Consequently, a branch with less resistance has greater current. In the example above,

$$\frac{I_{top2}}{I_{bottom2}} = \frac{R_{bottom2}}{R_{top2}}$$

$$\frac{0.168 \text{ A}}{0.0168 \text{ A}} = \frac{549 \text{ }\Omega}{55.0 \text{ }\Omega}$$

■ The equivalent resistance in a parallel circuit is less than the lowest resistance of its branches. In the example above, the equivalent resistance of the parallel components of the second circuit is 50.0 Ω, which is less than either 55.0 Ω or 549 Ω. (See problems 33, 43, and 44 at the end of the chapter.)

Resolving Compound Electric Circuits Most practical circuits that you will deal with have both series and parallel connections of multiple resistors. In this section, we describe a strategy for finding a single equivalent resistance for these circuits. This strategy works for many, but not all, circuits. For circuits that cannot be analyzed in this way, you can use Kirchhoff's rules as described in the next section.

A Strategy for Resolving Compound DC Circuits

1. Draw the circuit diagram, label all the circuit elements, and record all the known quanitites.

2. Identify all the resistors connected in series. Calculate the equivalent resistance of each set of series-connected resistors using Equation (22-18):

$$R_{series} = R_1 + R_2 + R_3 + \cdots R_N = \sum_{i=1}^{N} R_i$$

3. Draw a simplified circuit diagram, and replace each series combination of resistors with its equivalent resistance.

4. Identify all the resistors connected in parallel. Calculate the equivalent resistance of each set of parallel-connected resistors using Equation (22-20):

$$\frac{1}{R_{parallel}} = \frac{1}{R_1} + \frac{1}{R_2} + \frac{1}{R_3} + \cdots \frac{1}{R_N} = \sum_{i=1}^{N} \frac{1}{R_i}$$

5. Draw a further simplified circuit diagram, and replace each parallel combination of resistors with its equivalent resistance.

6. Repeat steps 4 and 5, if necessary, for series and parallel combinations that include the equivalent resistances until you have simplified the DC circuit to one final equivalent resistance.

EXAMPLE 22-5

Analyzing a Compound Electric Circuit

Figure 22-19 shows a compound electric circuit that has nine identical $2.0\ \Omega$ resistors connected to a 12 V ideal battery.

(a) Find the equivalent resistance for the circuit.
(b) Find the total electric current flowing from the battery.
(c) Identify the resistors that have the greatest potential difference across them.

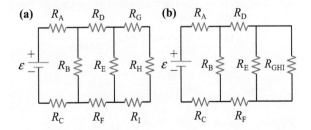

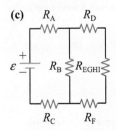

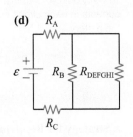

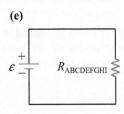

Figure 22-19 Example 22-5

SOLUTION

(a) Although the resistors are identical, the currents flowing through them likely differ. Therefore, we give each resistor a separate label: R_A, R_B, R_C, and so on. Then, we identify the resistors connected in series: R_G, R_H, and R_I. The equivalent resistance of these resistors is

$$R_{GHI} = R_G + R_H + R_I = 6.0\ \Omega$$

We can simplify the circuit using this equivalent resistance (Figure 22-21(b)). Since there are no more resistors connected only in series, we now find the equivalent resistance for the two resistances connected in parallel, R_E and R_{GHI}:

$$\frac{1}{R_{EGHI}} = \frac{1}{R_E} + \frac{1}{R_{GHI}} = \frac{1}{2.0\ \Omega} + \frac{1}{6.0\ \Omega} \Rightarrow \frac{1}{R_{EGHI}} = \frac{2}{3\ \Omega}$$

$$\Rightarrow R_{EGHI} = \frac{3}{2}\ \Omega$$

We can simplify the circuit further using the equivalent resistance R_{EGHI} (Figure 22-21(c)). In this simplified circuit, R_D, R_F, and R_{EGHI} are connected in series. Their equivalent resistance is

$$R_{DEFGHI} = 2.0\ \Omega + 2.0\ \Omega + \frac{3}{2}\ \Omega = \frac{11}{2}\ \Omega = 5\frac{1}{2}\ \Omega$$

Continuing this procedure, we eventually get a circuit that has only one equivalent resistance (Figure 22-19(e)):

$$R_{ABCDEFGHI} = 5\frac{7}{15}\ \Omega$$

(b) We apply Ohm's law to find the current output of the battery:

$$I_{battery} = \frac{\varepsilon}{R_{ABCDEFGHI}} = \frac{12\ V}{5\frac{7}{15}\ \Omega} = \frac{90}{41}\ A$$

(c) To identify the resistors that have maximum potential difference across them, we use Ohm's law once again. Since all the resistors have the same resistance, the one with the largest current flowing through it will have the greatest potential difference across it. Based on the diagram, you can see that all the current from the battery flows through resistors R_A and R_C, and only part of this current flows through the other resistors. Therefore, the potential difference across resistors R_A and R_C is the highest among them all:

$$V_A = V_C = I_{battery}(2.0\ \Omega) = \left(\frac{90}{41}\ A\right)(2\ \Omega) = 4\frac{16}{41}\ V$$

Making sense of the result:

Notice the problem solving strategy: we identify a part of a circuit that can be simplified and continue step by step simplification until we arrive at the final circuit that contains a battery and an equivalent resistance. You can check your calculations using PhET or other circuit simulation software by constructing and measuring the circuit.

CHECKPOINT

C-22-7 Ranking the Relative Brightness of Light Bulbs

The circuit in Figure 22-20 has six identical light bulbs and an ideal battery. Initially, switch S is open. Which of the following statements correctly describes what happens to the brightness of bulbs A and D when the switch is closed?

(a) Bulb A gets brighter, and bulb D turns off.
(b) Bulb A gets dimmer, and bulb D gets brighter.
(c) Bulb A turns off, and bulb D gets brighter.
(d) The brightness of bulbs A and D remains the same.
(e) Both bulbs A and D get dimmer.

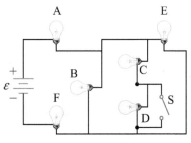

Figure 22-20 C-22-7

C-22-7 (a) By closing switch S, you will create a zero-resistance path for the electric current that will bypass light bulb D. Thus, the equivalent resistance of the circuit will decrease. Assuming that all light bulbs have equal resistance R, the equivalent resistance initially equals $R_{eq1} = 2\frac{2}{5}R$. After the switch is open, the equivalent resistance will be $R_{eq2} = 2\frac{1}{3}R$. Decreasing equivalent resistance means increasing the current through bulb A and decreasing the current to zero through bulb D.

Consider a circuit with two parallel branches, one of which has zero resistance. The equivalent resistance of such a circuit is also zero:

$$\frac{1}{R_{parallel}} = \frac{1}{R_1} + \frac{1}{R_2}$$

$$R_{parallel} = \frac{R_1 \cdot R_2}{R_1 + R_2} = \frac{0 \cdot R_2}{R_2} = 0 \qquad (22\text{-}35)$$

According to Ohm's law, a zero–equivalent resistance electric circuit connected to a real battery produces a very high electric current. The current will travel through the zero-resistance branch, causing overheating. We say that the branches with nonzero resistance are "shorted out" by the branch with no resistance. A **short circuit** can damage power supplies and cause a fire or shock hazard.

The potential differences across the parallel branches of this circuit are also zero:

$$V_{across\ branch1} = R_1 \cdot I_1 = 0 \cdot I = 0\ \text{V}$$

$$V_{across\ branch2} = R_2 \cdot I_2 = R_2 \cdot 0 = 0\ \text{V} \qquad (22\text{-}36)$$

Applications of Kirchhoff's Circuit Laws

The technique of analyzing a circuit by replacing series and parallel combinations of resistances with equivalent resistances might not work for some circuits, such as those with configurations of components that cannot be separated into series and parallel connections. For such circuits, we apply Kirchhoff's circuit laws, which we introduced earlier in this section (Equations (22-32) and (22-33)):

Kirchhoff's Circuit Laws

KEY EQUATION
$$\sum_{junction} I_i = 0 \quad \text{or} \quad \sum_{junction} I_{entering} = \sum_{junction} I_{exiting}$$

$$(22\text{-}33)$$

KEY EQUATION
$$\sum_{closed\ loop} \Delta V = 0 \qquad (22\text{-}32)$$

As we discussed earlier, Kirchhoff's first law is a consequence of the electric charge conservation, and it states that the algebraic sum of the currents at a junction is zero provided the sign notation for the currents mentioned earlier is used. Kirchhoff's second law is a consequence of energy conservation, and it states that the algebraic sum of potential differences (voltages) across the circuit elements around a closed circuit loop is zero. To demonstrate a step by step procedure for applying Kirchhoff's laws, we analyze the circuit shown in Figure 22-21. Our goal is to find the current flowing through each circuit branch and the potential difference across each circuit element.

Circuit Analysis Using Kirchhoff's Laws

1. Identify the loops. For example, the circuit in Figure 22-21 has three loops, two of which are independent loops.

2. Identify and label all the junctions and branches. In Figure 22-21, there are three parallel branches (top, middle, and bottom) connecting the two junctions, A and B.

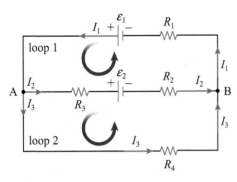

Figure 22-21 Circuit analysis using Kirchhoff's laws

3. Label the currents in each branch. Do not worry about current direction. You can choose it arbitrarily. If your choice happens to be opposite to the actual direction of the current, the value of the current you calculate will be negative. In Figure 22-21, we have three different currents: I_1, I_2, and I_3. Remember that the current through each series component in a branch is the same. For example, the current leaving the battery ε_1 in Figure 22-21 is labelled I_1 because it is the same current as the current entering R_1 from junction B.

4. Apply Kirchhoff's first law (junction rule) to each junction. In general, the number of independent equations you obtain from applying the junction rule is one fewer than the number of junctions. In our example, the equations for junctions A and B are the same: $I_1 = I_2 + I_3$.

5. Apply Kirchhoff's second law (loop rule) to as many loops as needed to include each branch of the circuit at least once. Choose a starting point in each loop, and make sure that you go around the entire loop. Follow the same direction (clockwise or counterclockwise)

in each loop, and use the sign convention listed in Table 22-4. For example, in loop 1, we have chosen the positive terminal of the battery as the starting and ending point and counterclockwise as the direction.

For our example, the application of the Kirchhoff's second law produces the following equations:

Loop 1: $-I_2R_3 - \varepsilon_2 - I_2R_2 - I_1R_1 + \varepsilon_1 = 0$

Loop 2: $I_2R_3 - I_3R_4 + I_2R_2 + \varepsilon_2 = 0$

6. Identify the number of unknowns, and choose an equal number of independent equations. For the example circuit, we have three unknowns (currents I_1, I_2, and I_3), so we need three independent equations. Solve the equations in general form. Do not substitute known values right away.

$$\begin{cases} -I_2R_3 - \varepsilon_2 - I_2R_2 - I_1R_1 + \varepsilon_1 = 0 \\ I_2R_3 - I_3R_4 + I_2R_2 + \varepsilon_2 = 0 \\ I_1 = I_2 + I_3 \end{cases}$$

$$\begin{cases} -I_2(R_3 + R_2) - \varepsilon_2 - I_1R_1 + \varepsilon_1 = 0 \\ I_2(R_3 + R_2) - I_3R_4 + \varepsilon_2 = 0 \\ I_1 = I_2 + I_3 \end{cases}$$

$$\begin{cases} -I_2(R_3 + R_2) - \varepsilon_2 - (I_2 + I_3)R_1 + \varepsilon_1 = 0 \\ I_2(R_3 + R_2) - I_3R_4 + \varepsilon_2 = 0 \\ I_1 = I_2 + I_3 \end{cases}$$

$$\begin{cases} I_2 = \dfrac{\varepsilon_1 - I_3(R_1 + R_4)}{R_1} \\ I_2 = \dfrac{I_3R_4 - \varepsilon_2}{R_2 + R_3} \\ I_1 = I_2 + I_3 \end{cases}$$

Table 22-4 Sign conventions for applying Kirchhoff's laws

Sign convention	Potential difference across the resistor	Potential difference across the source
Positive: 1. The direction of the traverse around the loop is opposite to the direction of the current through the resistor (R). 2. The direction of the traverse around the loop is from the positive terminal to the negative terminal of the emf source.	IR	ε
Negative: 1. The direction of the traverse around the loop coincides with the direction of the current through the resistor (R). 2. The direction of the traverse around the loop is from the negative terminal to the positive terminal of the source.	$-IR$	$-\varepsilon$

$$
\begin{cases}
I_1 = \dfrac{\left(\dfrac{\varepsilon_1(R_2 + R_3) + \varepsilon_2 R_1}{R_1 R_4 + R_1 R_2 + R_1 R_3 + R_2 R_4 + R_3 R_4}\right)R_4 - \varepsilon_2}{R_2 + R_3} \\[3em]
\qquad + \dfrac{\varepsilon_1(R_2 + R_3) + \varepsilon_2 R_1}{R_1 R_4 + R_1 R_2 + R_1 R_3 + R_2 R_4 + R_3 R_4} \\[3em]
I_2 = \dfrac{I_3 R_4 - \varepsilon_2}{R_2 + R_3} = \dfrac{\left(\dfrac{\varepsilon_1(R_2 + R_3) + \varepsilon_2 R_1}{R_1 R_4 + R_1 R_2 + R_1 R_3 + R_2 R_4 + R_3 R_4}\right)R_4 - \varepsilon_2}{R_2 + R_3} \\[3em]
I_3 = \dfrac{\varepsilon_1(R_2 + R_3) + \varepsilon_2 R_1}{R_1 R_4 + R_1 R_2 + R_1 R_3 + R_2 R_4 + R_3 R_4}
\end{cases}
$$

7. Use dimensional analysis to check whether the expressions for the unknowns make sense. In our example, all the final variables (I) should have units of current (amperes or volts/ohm).

8. Use limiting cases to check your final answers. Example 22-6 demonstrates this technique.

9. Use Ohm's law and the calculated values for the currents to find potential differences across the circuit elements.

EXAMPLE 22-6

Analyzing a Multiloop and Multibattery Electric Circuit

Assume that the components in Figure 22-21 have the following values:

$$\varepsilon_1 = 10 \text{ V}; \quad \varepsilon_2 = 15 \text{ V (ideal batteries)}$$

$$R_1 = 5.0 \ \Omega; \quad R_2 = 10 \ \Omega; \quad R_3 = 15 \ \Omega; \quad R_4 = 20 \ \Omega$$

(a) Find the current through each branch of the circuit.
(b) Find the potential differences across each circuit element.
(c) How will your answers to parts (a) and (b) differ if the batteries are real batteries?

SOLUTION

(a) Substituting the given values into the expressions derived for the currents in the three branches, we obtain the following:

$$
I_2 = \frac{I_3 R_4 - \varepsilon_2}{R_2 + R_3} = \frac{\left(\dfrac{\varepsilon_1(R_2 + R_3) + \varepsilon_2 R_1}{R_1 R_4 + R_1 R_2 + R_1 R_3 + R_2 R_4 + R_3 R_4}\right)R_4 - \varepsilon_2}{R_2 + R_3}
$$

$$= -\frac{7}{29} \text{ A}$$

$$I_3 = \frac{\varepsilon_1(R_2 + R_3) + \varepsilon_2 R_1}{R_1 R_4 + R_1 R_2 + R_1 R_3 + R_2 R_4 + R_3 R_4} = \frac{13}{29} \text{ A}$$

$$I_1 = I_2 + I_3 = \frac{6}{29} \text{ A}$$

These results indicate that our choice of current directions for I_1 and I_3 was correct, and current I_2 flows in the opposite direction to the one chosen in the diagram.

(b) To find the potential differences across each resistor, we use Ohm's law:

$$V_{R_1} = I_1 R_1 = \left(\frac{6}{29} \text{ A}\right)(5.0 \ \Omega) = 1\frac{1}{29} \text{ V}$$

$$V_{R_2} = I_2 R_2 = \left|-\frac{7}{29} \text{ A}\right|(10 \ \Omega) = \frac{70}{29} \text{ V} = 2\frac{12}{29} \text{ V}$$

$$V_{R_3} = I_2 R_3 = \left|-\frac{7}{29} \text{ A}\right|(15 \ \Omega) = \frac{105}{29} \text{ V} = 3\frac{18}{29} \text{ V}$$

$$V_{R_4} = I_3 R_4 = \left(\frac{13}{29} \text{ A}\right)(20 \ \Omega) = \frac{260}{29} \text{ V} = 8\frac{28}{29} \text{ V}$$

(c) If the batteries are real, we have to account for their internal resistance. This can be done by adding their internal resistances in series to each battery. For the circuit, it is equivalent to replacing resistances R_1 and R_2 with R_1' and R_2':

$$
\begin{cases}
R_1' = R_1 + r_1 \\
R_2' = R_2 + r_2
\end{cases}
$$

Making sense of the result:

To check your calculations, you can use Wolfram Alpha (www.wolframalpha.com) or other software for solving simultaneous equations. However, checking the calculations does not tell you if your initial equations are correct. To check these equations, we can apply dimensional analysis, analysis of limiting cases, and the law of conservation of energy.

Dimensional analysis: The currents should all have dimensions of amperes:

(continued)

$$[I_3] = \frac{\varepsilon_1(R_2 + R_3) + \varepsilon_2 R_1}{R_1 R_4 + R_1 R_2 + R_1 R_3 + R_2 R_4 + R_3 R_4}$$

$$= \frac{V \cdot \Omega + V \cdot \Omega}{\Omega^2} = \frac{V}{\Omega} = A$$

$$[I_2] = \frac{I_3 R_4 - \varepsilon_2}{R_2 + R_3} = \frac{A \cdot \Omega - V}{\Omega} = \frac{V}{\Omega} = A$$

$$[I_1] = I_2 + I_3 = A + A = A$$

Dimensional analysis helps identify errors, but does not guarantee that the solution is correct.

Limiting case analysis: Let us consider the limiting case, where no source of energy is present in the circuit. If we replace the two batteries with conductors, all the currents become zero. The expressions derived above equal zero when the two emfs are zero. So, these equations are valid for this limiting case. If only the first battery, ε_1, is removed from the circuit, then the equivalent resistance of the circuit becomes

$$R_{eq1} = 10\ \Omega + 15\ \Omega + \frac{1}{\dfrac{1}{5.0\ \Omega} + \dfrac{1}{20\ \Omega}} = 29\ \Omega$$

and the current flowing through the battery is

$$I_2 = \frac{\varepsilon_2}{R_{eq1}} = \frac{15\ V}{29\ \Omega} = \frac{15}{29}\ A$$

Let us check that by substituting $\varepsilon_1 = 0$ in the general solution we get the same answer:

$$(I_2)_{\varepsilon_1 = 0} = \frac{\left(\dfrac{\varepsilon_2 R_1}{R_1 R_4 + R_1 R_2 + R_1 R_3 + R_2 R_4 + R_3 R_4}\right)R_4 - \varepsilon_2}{R_2 + R_3} = \frac{15}{29}\ A$$

Energy analysis: You can check that the potential differences across each branch between junctions A and B are equal, as we would expect because the branches are parallel.

Top branch:

$$V_{AB} = I_1 R_1 - \varepsilon_1 = \left(\frac{6}{29}\ A\right)(5.0\ \Omega) - 10\ V$$

$$= \left(\frac{30}{29} - 10\right)V = -8\frac{28}{29}\ V$$

Middle branch:

$$V_{AB} = -I_2 R_3 - \varepsilon_2 - I_2 R_2 = -\left(-\frac{7}{29}\ A\right)(15\ \Omega)$$

$$-15\ V - \left(-\frac{7}{29}\ A\right)(10\ \Omega) = -8\frac{28}{29}\ V$$

Bottom branch:

$$V_{AB} = -I_3 R_1 = \left(-\frac{13}{29}\ A\right)(20\ \Omega) = -8\frac{28}{29}\ V$$

The values for V_{AB} are identical across each branch, which tells us that we solved the problem correctly. Note that when finding potential difference V_{AB} along a particular branch, we traverse the branch from point A to point B.

PEER TO PEER

It is important to remember that you always have to try and make sense of your values, especially when the intermediate calculations are long and tedious. It is easy to make a mathematical error. A careful analysis of your answer will help you catch it.

LO 5

22-5   RC Circuits

Online Activity 22-1 examines a circuit with a capacitor, a battery, a light bulb, and two switches. The brightness of the light bulb in this circuit changes with time, indicating that the current through the circuit is time-dependent. Since the voltage across the capacitor and across the light bulb are both related to the current in the circuit, these voltages also vary with time. We will now use Kirchhoff's laws to derive mathematical expressions describing how the current and voltage change as a capacitor charges and discharges.

Charging a Capacitor

Consider the circuit in Figure 22-22. Let us first close switch S_1 while switch S_2 remains open. By closing this switch, we complete a series circuit that includes an initially uncharged capacitor (C), a resistor (R), and an emf source (ε). Closing switch S_1 starts the process of charging the capacitor. Applying Kirchhoff's loop rule to the circuit, we obtain

$$\varepsilon - IR - V_C = 0 \qquad (22\text{-}37)$$

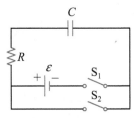

Figure 22-22   A simple RC circuit

In Chapter 21, we discussed how the potential difference across a capacitor, V_C, is related to the charge on each of its plates (q) and to its capacitance (C):

$$V_C = \frac{q}{C}$$

In this section, we consider what happens during the charging and discharging of a capacitor. During these processes the values of electric current in the circuit, the charge on capacitor's plates, and the voltage across the plates are continuously changing. We will use lower case letters for these instantaneous values. Do not confuse I, which stands for a constant value of electric current, and $i(t)$, which represents an instantaneous value of electric current. Since $i(t) = \dfrac{dq}{dt}$, we can substitute for I and V_C in Equation (22-37) to obtain

$$\varepsilon - \frac{dq}{dt}R - \frac{q}{C} = 0 \qquad (22\text{-}38)$$

As the electric charge on the capacitor's plates varies with time, we denote it as $q(t)$. Then we can rearrange the above equation as follows:

$$\varepsilon - \frac{dq(t)}{dt}R - \frac{q(t)}{C} = 0$$

$$\frac{dq(t)}{dt} = \frac{\varepsilon}{R} - \frac{q(t)}{RC}$$

$$\frac{dq(t)}{dt} = -\frac{q(t) - \varepsilon C}{RC}$$

$$\frac{dq(t)}{q(t) - \varepsilon C} = -\frac{dt}{RC} \qquad (22\text{-}39)$$

This is a differential equation. Noticing that the quantity εC is constant, we can use the following substitution:

$$x(t) \equiv q(t) - \varepsilon C \Rightarrow dx(t) \equiv dq(t) \qquad (22\text{-}40)$$

As a result, Equation (22-39) can be rewritten as follows:

$$\frac{dx(t)}{x} = \frac{dt}{RC} \qquad (22\text{-}41)$$

Moreover, at time $t = 0$, the capacitor had no charge on its plates, so $q(t = 0) = 0 \Rightarrow x(t = 0) = -\varepsilon C$, and at time t, the plates had a charge of $\pm q(t)$. Therefore, $x(t) = q(t) - \varepsilon C$. Integrating both sides of Equation (22-41) gives

$$\int_{-\varepsilon C}^{q - \varepsilon C} \frac{dx(t)}{x} = -\int_{0}^{t} \frac{dt}{RC}$$

$$\ln(x(t))\Big|_{-\varepsilon C}^{q(t) - \varepsilon C} = -\frac{t}{RC}$$

$$\ln(q(t) - \varepsilon C) - \ln(-\varepsilon C) = -\frac{t}{RC}$$

$$\ln\frac{q(t) - \varepsilon C}{-\varepsilon C} = -\frac{t}{RC}$$

$$\frac{q(t) - \varepsilon C}{-\varepsilon C} = e^{-\frac{t}{RC}}$$

$$q(t) = (-\varepsilon C)e^{-\frac{t}{RC}} + \varepsilon C = \varepsilon C(1 - e^{-\frac{t}{RC}}) \quad (22\text{-}42)$$

Recall that the maximum amount of charge, q_{max}, on the capacitor's plates is $V_{max}C$. In our circuit, the maximum potential difference across the plates equals the potential difference across the battery, so $V_{max} = \varepsilon$. Therefore, while a capacitor is charging, the charge on the capacitor's plates can be expressed as follows:

KEY EQUATION
$$q(t) = q_{max}\left(1 - e^{-\frac{t}{RC}}\right) = q_{max}\left(1 - e^{-\frac{t}{\tau}}\right) \qquad (22\text{-}43)$$

Let us check the dimensions of the product RC:

$$[RC] = \Omega \cdot F = \frac{V}{A} \cdot \frac{C}{V} = \frac{C}{A} = \frac{C}{C/s} = s \qquad (22\text{-}44)$$

The product of the capacitance and the resistance of a series RC circuit has dimensions of time. It is called the **time constant** of the circuit, $\tau = RC$. The exponent in Equation (22-43) is therefore dimensionless: $\left[\dfrac{t}{\tau}\right] = 1$.

Differentiating Equation (22-45), we find the dependence of electric current on time:

$$i(t) = \frac{dq(t)}{dt} = \frac{d\left(q_{max}\left(1 - e^{-\frac{t}{\tau}}\right)\right)}{dt} = \frac{\varepsilon C}{RC}e^{-\frac{t}{\tau}} = \frac{\varepsilon}{R}e^{-\frac{t}{\tau}}$$
$$(22\text{-}45)$$

The ratio $\dfrac{\varepsilon}{R}$ represents the maximum current in this RC circuit (the current in the absence of a capacitor). This current flows in the circuit only at the initial moment when the switch is being closed ($t = 0$) and the capacitor begins charging. Thus,

KEY EQUATION
$$i(t) = I_0 e^{-\frac{t}{RC}} = I_0 e^{-\frac{t}{\tau}} \qquad (22\text{-}46)$$

Equation (22-46) describes the dependence of electric current on time during the charging of a capacitor in an RC circuit. In Chapter 21, we found that the energy stored in a charging capacitor depends on the square of the charge stored by it. Substituting for $q(t)$ in Equation (21-15), $U = \dfrac{1}{2}\dfrac{Q^2}{C}$, gives an expression for the energy stored in a capacitor as a function of time:

$$U_C = \frac{(q(t))^2}{2C} = \frac{\left(q_{max}\left(1 - e^{-\frac{t}{RC}}\right)\right)^2}{2C} \qquad (22\text{-}47)$$

Graphs of $q(t)$ and $i(t)$ are shown in Figure 22-23.

The voltage across the capacitor asymptotically approaches its maximum value, $V_{max} = \varepsilon C$. At the same time, the current in this RC circuit decreases exponentially but never reaches zero. For exponential decay or growth, it is common to describe the relationship using the time constant. In the case of charging a capacitor, $\tau = RC$.

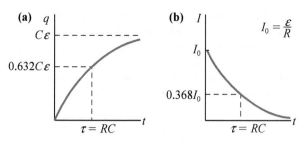

(a)

q
$C\varepsilon$ - - - - - - - - - -
$0.632C\varepsilon$ - - - -
$\tau = RC$ t

(b)

I
$I_0 = \dfrac{\varepsilon}{R}$
I_0
$0.368I_0$ - - - - -
$\tau = RC$ t

Figure 22-23 (a) Graph of charge versus time and (b) graph of current versus time for a charging capacitor in a series RC circuit

The time constant is the time that it takes the capacitor to charge to about 63% of its maximum value, q_{max}:

$$q(\tau) = q_{max}\left(1 - e^{-\frac{\tau}{\tau}}\right) = q_{max}\left(1 - \frac{1}{e}\right) \approx 0.632\, q_{max}$$

$$(22\text{-}48)$$

At the same time ($t = \tau$), the current across the capacitor is a factor of e less than the maximum current, I_0:

$$i(\tau) = I_0 e^{-\frac{\tau}{\tau}} = \frac{I_0}{e} \approx 0.368\, I_0 \qquad (22\text{-}49)$$

The relationships described above explain the observed light bulb brightness in a series RC circuit. When the capacitor begins charging, the current is near its maximum and the light bulb is bright. Then the light bulb gets progressively dimmer, and eventually stops glowing.

Therefore, the charge on the plates of a capacitor when it is charging can be expressed as follows:

KEY EQUATION
$$q(t) = q_{max}\left(1 - e^{-\frac{t}{RC}}\right) \qquad (22\text{-}50)$$

For most practical purposes, a capacitor can be considered fully charged after 5 to 10 time constants have elapsed.

Discharging a Capacitor

Let us now assume that the capacitor in Figure 22-22 is fully charged, and we open switch S_1 and close switch S_2. The capacitor and resistor are now connected in a loop with S_2, leaving out the emf source (ε). With these

EXAMPLE 22-7

Charging a Capacitor

A 500 μF capacitor is connected to a 9.00 V battery through a 2.00 kΩ resistor, thus completing a simple RC series circuit.

(a) How long does it take for the capacitor to reach 99% of q_{max}? Express your answer in terms of the time constant, τ.
(b) How much charge will have accumulated on the capacitor's plates when $t_1 = \tau$, $t_2 = 2\tau$, and $t_3 = 3\tau$?
(c) Find the current in the circuit at the times in part (b).

SOLUTION

(a) For this circuit,

$$\tau = RC = (2 \times 10^3\ \Omega)(500 \times 10^{-6}\,\text{F}) = 1.00\ \text{s}$$

$$0.99\, q_{max} = q_{max}\left(1 - e^{-\frac{t}{RC}}\right)$$

$$0.99 = 1 - e^{-\frac{t}{RC}}$$

$$e^{-\frac{t}{RC}} = 0.01$$

$$t = -RC\ln(0.01) = -\tau\ln(0.01) = 4.61\tau$$

$$t = -(2 \times 10^3\ \Omega)(500 \times 10^{-6}\,\text{F})\ln(0.01)$$

$$= 4.61\ \text{s}$$

(b)

$$q_{max} = \varepsilon C = (9\ \text{V})(500 \times 10^{-6}\,\text{F}) = 4.5 \times 10^{-3}\,\text{C}$$

$$q(\tau) = q_{max}\left(1 - e^{-\frac{\tau}{RC}}\right) = q_{max}\left(1 - e^{-\frac{RC}{RC}}\right)$$

$$= q_{max}\left(1 - \frac{1}{e}\right) \approx 0.632\, q_{max} = 2.84 \times 10^{-3}\,\text{C}$$

$$q(2\tau) = q_{max}\left(1 - e^{-\frac{2\tau}{RC}}\right) = q_{max}\left(1 - e^{-\frac{2RC}{RC}}\right)$$

$$= q_{max}\left(1 - \frac{1}{e^2}\right) \approx 0.865\, q_{max} = 3.89 \times 10^{-3}\,\text{C}$$

$$q(3\tau) = q_{max}\left(1 - e^{-\frac{3\tau}{RC}}\right) = q_{max}\left(1 - e^{-\frac{3RC}{RC}}\right)$$

$$= q_{max}\left(1 - \frac{1}{e^3}\right) \approx -0.950\, q_{max} = 4.28 \times 10^{-3}\,\text{C}$$

(c)

$$I_0 = \frac{\varepsilon}{R} = \frac{(9.00\ \text{V})}{2000\ \Omega} = 4.50 \times 10^{-3}\,\text{A}$$

$$I(\tau) = I_0 e^{-\frac{\tau}{RC}} = I_0 e^{-\frac{RC}{RC}} = I_0\left(\frac{1}{e}\right) \approx 0.368\, I_0 = 1.66 \times 10^{-3}\,\text{A}$$

$$I(2\tau) = I_0 e^{-\frac{2\tau}{RC}} = I_0 e^{-\frac{2RC}{RC}} = I_0\left(\frac{1}{e^2}\right) \approx 0.135\, I_0 = 0.609 \times 10^{-3}\,\text{A}$$

$$I(3\tau) = I_0 e^{-\frac{3\tau}{RC}} = I_0 e^{-\frac{3RC}{RC}} = I_0\left(\frac{1}{e^3}\right) \approx 0.050\, I_0 = 0.224 \times 10^{-3}\,\text{A}$$

Making sense of the result:

It is often helpful to calculate the time constant of the circuit first ($\tau = 1$ s in this example). You can see that the capacitor acquired 99% of its maximum charge before $t = 5\tau = 5$ s.

connections, the capacitor will start discharging. Applying Kirchhoff's loop rule to the circuit, we obtain

$$-V_C - IR = 0$$

$$-\frac{q(t)}{C} - IR = 0 \qquad (22\text{-}51)$$

We can derive equations for the charge on the capacitor's plates and the current through the circuit by using the same method as for the example above. For the discharging capacitor,

$$-\frac{q(t)}{C} - \frac{dq(t)}{dt}R = 0 \qquad (22\text{-}52)$$

At time $t = 0$, the capacitor was fully charged: $q(0) = C\varepsilon = q_{max}$. Again, we find the solution by rearranging the differential equation and integrating both sides:

$$\frac{dq(t)}{q(t)} = -\frac{dt}{RC}$$

$$\int_{\varepsilon C}^{q(t)} \frac{dq(t)}{q(t)} = -\int_0^t \frac{dt}{RC}$$

$$\ln q(t) - \ln(\varepsilon C) = -\frac{t}{RC}$$

$$\ln \frac{q(t)}{\varepsilon C} = -\frac{t}{RC}$$

$$q(t) = q_{max} e^{-\frac{t}{RC}} = q_{max} e^{-\frac{t}{\tau}} \qquad (22\text{-}53)$$

Therefore, the charge on the plates of a capacitor when it is discharging can be expressed as follows:

KEY EQUATION $\quad q(t) = q_{max} e^{-\frac{t}{RC}} = q_{max} e^{-\frac{t}{\tau}} \qquad (22\text{-}54)$

Consequently, the current is

$$I(t) = \frac{dq(t)}{dt} = \frac{d\left(q_{max} e^{-\frac{t}{RC}}\right)}{dt}$$

$$= -\frac{\varepsilon C}{RC} e^{-\frac{t}{RC}} = -\frac{\varepsilon}{R} e^{-\frac{t}{RC}} = -\frac{\varepsilon}{R} e^{-\frac{t}{\tau}}$$

The ratio $\dfrac{\varepsilon}{R}$ once again represents the maximum current in this RC circuit. This current flows at the instant that switch S_2 is being closed ($t = 0$). Thus,

$$I(t) = -I_0 e^{-\frac{t}{RC}} = -I_0 e^{-\frac{t}{\tau}} \qquad (22\text{-}55)$$

The negative value for current in this equation indicates that it flows in an opposite direction to the current when the capacitor was charging.

Equations (22-54) and (22-55) describe the time dependence of the current and charge during the discharge of a capacitor in an RC circuit. As above, we use these equations to find an expression for the electric potential energy stored in the capacitor at any given moment:

$$U_C = \frac{(q(t))^2}{2C} = \frac{\left(q_{max} e^{-\frac{t}{RC}}\right)^2}{2C} = \frac{(q_{max})^2 e^{-\frac{2t}{RC}}}{2C} \qquad (22\text{-}57)$$

Figure 22-24 shows $q(t)$ and $i(t)$ graphs for a capacitor discharging through a resistor. Comparing the graphs in Figures 22-23 and 22-24, we see that $i(t)$ graphs are the same: the current starts with its maximum value and then diminishes exponentially with time. However, $q(t)$ graphs for charging and discharging a capacitor have opposite trends.

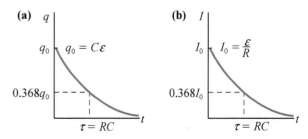

Figure 22-24 (a) Graph of charge versus time and (b) graph of current versus time for a discharging capacitor in a series RC circuit. The absolute value of current is shown in the graph.

The analysis above can be extended to circuits that have a combination of resistors and capacitors by calculating the equivalent resistance and the equivalent capacitance of the combinations.

C-22-8 Discharging a Capacitor

The five circuits in Figure 22-25 consist of identical capacitors and resistors. At $t = 0$ s, the switch is closed and the capacitors start discharging. In which circuit will the capacitors discharge to 5% of their maximum charge in the shortest time? Explain.

(a) circuit 1
(b) circuit 2
(c) circuit 3
(d) circuit 4
(e) circuit 5

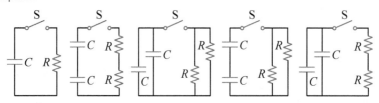

Figure 22-25 C-22-8

C-22-8 (d) The circuit time constant $\tau = RC$ shows how fast the capacitor in the circuit is going to be charging or discharging. The time constants of the circuits are
$$\tau_1 = RC; \ \tau_2 = 2R\frac{C}{2} = RC; \ \tau_3 = \frac{R}{2}2C = RC; \ \tau_4 = \frac{RC}{4} = \frac{R}{2}\frac{C}{2}; \ \tau_5 = 2R2C = 4RC$$

 MAKING CONNECTIONS

How Do Touch-Sensitive Lamps Work?

Touch-sensitive lamps commonly have a power-level switch controlled by an RC circuit. Your body has some capacitance. When you touch the metal body of a touch-sensitive lamp, you add capacitance to the control circuit and usually some static charge from your body, as well. These changes in the capacitance trigger the control circuit such that it changes the voltage supplied to the lamp's bulb. Often, touch-sensitive switches cycle through three power levels: off-low-medium-high, then back to off.

Metals have free electrons that can drift in the direction opposite to the external electric field. Moving electric charges create electric current. Electric current flowing through a conductor carries energy that can be converted into heat, which is dissipated by the conductor. There is a fundamental relationship between electric current through a resistor, its resistance, and the voltage across it. DC circuits have currents that flow in only one direction through the components. Ohm's law, equivalent resistances, and Kirchhoff's laws can be used to analyze circuits that contain a number of components such as resistors, capacitors, and emf sources.

Electric Current: The Microscopic Model

Electron current in a metal wire i is related to electric current in it and electric current density, J. They depend on electron density n_e, drift speed v_d, and cross-sectional area A:

$$I = I_e \cdot e = (n_e v_d A)e = n_e v_d A(1.6 \times 10^{-19} \text{C}) \qquad (22\text{-}4)$$

Electric conductivity and resistivity, ρ, describe how well a specific metal conducts current; these properties are temperature-dependent:

$$\sigma = \frac{1}{\rho} = \frac{n_e e^2 \tau}{m} \qquad (22\text{-}9)$$

$$\rho = \rho_0[1 + \alpha \Delta T] \qquad (22\text{-}12)$$

where α is the temperature coefficient of resistivity, T is temperature, and ρ_0 is the resistivity at a baseline temperature.

Electric Current, Resistance, and Voltage: The Macroscopic Model

Electric current I through a resistor R and the voltage across it V are related by Ohm's law:

$$I = \frac{V}{R} \text{ (for ohmic resistors only)} \qquad (22\text{-}15)$$

The resistance of a conductor depends on its resistivity ρ, length l, and cross-sectional area A:

$$R = \rho \frac{l}{A} \qquad (22\text{-}14)$$

A resistor R that carries electric current I dissipates thermal energy Q_{heat} according to Joule–Lenz's law:

$$Q_{heat} = I^2 R \Delta t \qquad (22\text{-}24)$$

In a series RC circuit, electric current across the capacitor changes as

$$i(t) = I_0 e^{-\frac{t}{RC}} \qquad (22\text{-}46)$$

Electric charge on the capacitor's plates:

$$q(t) = q_{max}\left(1 - e^{-\frac{t}{RC}}\right) \quad \text{charging} \qquad (22\text{-}50)$$

$$q(t) = q_{max}\left(e^{-\frac{t}{RC}}\right) \quad \text{discharging} \qquad (22\text{-}54)$$

Analysis of Compound Electric Circuits: Equivalent Resistance

For resistors connected in series:

$$R_{series} = \sum_{i=1}^{N} R_i \qquad (22\text{-}18)$$

For resistors connected in parallel:

$$\frac{1}{R_{parallel}} = \sum_{i=1}^{N} \frac{1}{R_i} \qquad (22\text{-}20)$$

Kirchhoff's Laws for Analysis of Multiloop DC Circuits

Junction rule (conservation of current):

$$\sum_{junction} I_{entering} = \sum_{junction} I_{exiting} \qquad (22\text{-}33)$$

Loop rule (energy conservation):

$$\sum_{closed\ loop} \Delta V = 0 \qquad (22\text{-}32)$$

Applications: electrical appliances, residential and commercial electrical wiring, physiological applications

Key Terms: ammeter, conduction electron density, current density, direct current (DC) circuit, drift velocity, electric circuit junction, electric current, electric conductivity, electric resistivity, electrical grounding, electron current, free electron density, electron flow, equivalent resistance, junction points, Kirchhoff's first law, Kirchhoff's second law, law of electric charge conservation, metallic bonds, multimeter, node, ohmmeter, Ohm's law, parallel circuit, power, series circuit, short circuit, superconductor, time constant, voltmeter

QUESTIONS

1. Which of the following statements is true? Explain your answer.
   (a) The directions of electron and electric currents in metals are always the same.
   (b) If the resistivities of two wires are the same, then their resistances must also be the same.
   (c) The free electron density in a metal depends on its temperature.
   (d) Resistivity and conductivity of a metal depend on the metal's temperature.
   (e) The electron drift speed depends on the resistivity of the metal.

2. In a box labelled "spare 40 W and 60 W bulbs," there are two clear incandescent light bulbs. One bulb has a thicker filament than the other. Which bulb is likely to be rated at 40 W?
   (a) thicker filament
   (b) thinner filament
   (c) It is impossible to know without trying each one.

3. In circuit I, a light bulb is connected to a battery. In circuit II, 10 light bulbs, all identical to the light bulb in circuit I, are connected in series to an identical battery. In circuit III, 10 light bulbs are connected in parallel to an identical battery. Which statement correctly describes the relative power outputs of these circuits? Explain your answer.
   (a) circuit I > circuit II > circuit III
   (b) circuit III > circuit I > circuit II
   (c) circuit I = circuit II = circuit III
   (d) circuit II > circuit I > circuit III
   (e) circuit III > circuit II > circuit I

4. In circuit I, a light bulb is connected to a battery. In circuit II, 10 light bulbs, all identical to the light bulb in circuit I, are connected in series to the same type of battery. Which circuit in Question 3 will produce the most light? Explain.
   (a) circuit I
   (b) circuit II
   (c) circuit III
   (d) Circuits II and III will both produce 10 times more light than circuit I.

5. The resistance of a long copper wire is R. You cut the wire into N equal pieces and connect the pieces in parallel. What is the resistance of this combination?
   (a) N^2R
   (b) NR
   (c) R
   (d) R/N
   (e) R/N^2

6. How much energy is consumed by a 60 W bulb if you leave it on for 10 h?
   (a) 60 kW·h
   (b) 60 kJ
   (c) 600 J
   (d) 3600 kW·h
   (e) 2.16 MJ

7. How much energy is stored in a fully charged 12 V car battery rated at 100 A·h?
   (a) 12 MW·h
   (b) 1.2 MW·h
   (c) 1.0 MW·h
   (d) 4320 kJ
   (e) 432 kW·h

8. What is the ratio of the filament resistance of a 70 W light bulb designed for North America (110 V) and a 140 W light bulb designed for Europe (220 V)?
   (a) 2:1
   (b) 1:2
   (c) 2:2
   (d) 4:1
   (e) 1:4
   (f) 1:1

9. You have six identical 4.0 Ω resistors and one 3.0 V battery. How can you connect the resistors to the battery such that the current flowing from the battery is 4.5 A?
   (a) Attach all the resistors in series, and connect them to the battery.
   (b) Attach all the resistors in parallel, and connect them to the battery.
   (c) Attach two resistors in series and the rest in parallel, and then connect them to the battery.
   (d) Attach three resistors in series and the rest in parallel, and then connect them to the battery.
   (e) It is not possible.

10. Which of the following statements is false?
    (a) According to Ohm's law, an increase in a circuit's equivalent resistance means a decrease in the circuit's power output.
    (b) A voltmeter is always connected in parallel to the circuit element across which we want to measure a voltage.
    (c) An ammeter is always connected in series to the circuit element through which we want to measure a current.
    (d) A short circuit means a circuit that has a very large electric resistance, thus becoming a fire hazard.
    (e) If a piece of metal wire is heated, its resistivity will increase and its conductivity will decrease.

11. You need a 6.0 Ω resistor, but you only have four 4.0 Ω resistors. How many resistors should you use and how should you connect them to produce a total resistance of 6.0 Ω?
    (a) three 4.0 Ω resistors connected in series
    (b) three 4.0 Ω resistors connected in parallel
    (c) two 4.0 Ω resistors connected in parallel and then connected in series to a 4.0 Ω resistor
    (d) two 4.0 Ω resistors connected in series and then connected in parallel to a 4.0 Ω resistor
    (e) two 4.0 Ω resistors connected in parallel, connected in series to two 4.0 Ω resistors connected in series.

12. What is the operating resistance of a 100 W (110 V) light bulb?
    (a) 1.11 Ω
    (b) 12.1 Ω
    (c) 121 Ω
    (d) 12.1 kΩ
    (e) 121 kΩ

13. Figure 22-26 shows an electric circuit consisting of six identical light bulbs, each with an operating resistance of 10.0 Ω, connected to a 20.0 V battery. What is the equivalent resistance of this circuit?
    (a) 60 Ω
    (b) 22.5 Ω
    (c) 21.7 Ω
    (d) 18.8 Ω
    (e) 18.4 Ω

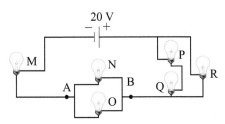

Figure 22-26 Question 13

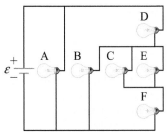

Figure 22-28 Question 18

14. What is the electric current flowing through the battery in Figure 22-26?
    (a) 1.07 A
    (b) 1.0 A
    (c) 0.92 A
    (d) 0.89 A
    (e) 1.09 A

15. In the circuit shown in Figure 22-26, what is the value of the potential difference between points A and B?
    (a) 9.24 V
    (b) 10.0 V
    (c) 18.46 V
    (d) 5.45 V
    (e) 4.62 V

16. Rank the brightness of the light bulbs in Figure 22-26. Use your answers to questions 13, 14, and 15.
    (a) $M > N > O > P = Q > R$
    (b) $M > N = O < P = Q > R$
    (c) $M > R > N = O > P = Q$
    (d) $M = N = O > P = Q < R$
    (e) $M > N > O > R > P = Q$

17. A 12.0 V battery is connected to a combination of nine identical 400.0 Ω resistors shown in Figure 22-27. What is the current flowing through this battery?
    (a) 3.33 mA
    (b) 1.33 A
    (c) 8.92 mA
    (d) 11.0 mA
    (e) 533 A

19. A 5 μF capacitor is connected through a 10 kΩ resistor to a 12 V battery. It takes this capacitor 0.002 s to be charged to 95% of its maximum charge in this series circuit. How long would it take the same capacitor to get 95% charged (if initially uncharged) when the 12 V battery is replaced by a 6 V battery?
    (a) 0.004 s
    (b) 0.002 s
    (c) 0.001 s
    (d) less than 0.001 s
    (e) more than 0.001 s

20. An RC electric circuit is shown in Figure 22-29. Initially, switch S is open and the capacitors are completely uncharged. After the switch has been closed for 3 min, how much energy will be stored in the 5 μF capacitor?
    (a) 0.3 mJ
    (b) 0.6 mJ
    (c) 1.5 mJ
    (d) 36 mJ
    (e) 72 mJ

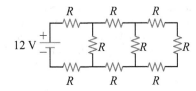

Figure 22-27 Question 17

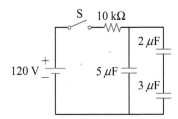

Figure 22-29 Question 20

18. Six identical 5 Ω light bulbs—A, B, C, D, E, and F—are connected as shown in Figure 22-28; $\varepsilon = 24$ V. Which of the following ranks the amount of current flowing through the light bulbs from the largest to the smallest?
    (a) $I_D, I_A, I_B, I_F, I_C = I_E$
    (b) $I_A, I_D, I_B = I_F, I_C = I_E$
    (c) $I_A, I_D, I_B, I_F, I_C = I_E$
    (d) $I_A, I_D, I_B, I_F = I_C = I_E$
    (e) $I_D, I_A, I_B, I_F = I_C = I_E$

21. A series RC circuit consists of a resistor, a battery, wires, and a capacitor. You are worried that the wires might not withstand the current flowing through them as the capacitor charges. When are the wires more likely to burn?
    (a) right at the beginning of the experiment, when the capacitor just starts charging
    (b) in the middle of the experiment, when the capacitor is about 32% charged
    (c) in the middle of the experiment, when the capacitor is about 67% charged
    (d) at the end of the experiment, when the capacitor is almost fully charged

PROBLEMS BY SECTION

For problems, star ratings will be used, (✳, ✳✳, or ✳✳✳), with more stars meaning more challenging problems.

Section 22-1   Electric Current: The Microscopic Model

22. ✳ Estimate the conduction (free) electron density in copper given that the atomic mass of copper is 63.546 amu and the density of copper at 293 K is 8.96 g/cm³. Compare your estimate with an experimentally established value.

23. ✳ An electric current of 2.0 A is flowing through a copper wire that has a diameter of 2.0 mm.
    (a) At what rate are electrons flowing through the wire?
    (b) Find the electric current density in the wire.
    (c) How much electric charge will be carried through the cross section of the wire in 2.0 s?

24. ✳ Your classmate heard the professor mention that the average drift speed of electrons in metals is about 0.1 mm/s. This did not make sense to your friend: "If this were true," he said, "I would have to keep my key in the ignition switch of my car for more than 4 h in order for the electrons to flow from the negative terminals of the battery to the starter motor and back to the positive terminal of the battery." How will you respond to him?

Section 22-2   Electric Conductivity and Resistivity: The Microscopic Model

25. ✳ An electric current of 2.0 A flows through a copper wire at 15°C. The wire has a circular cross section and is 2.0 mm in diameter.
    (a) Using the information in Table 22-2, find the conductivity and the resistivity of the wire.
    (b) Using Table 22-1, find the drift velocity of the conduction electrons in the wire.
    (c) Estimate the mean time, τ, that free electrons in the wire spend between collisions.
    (d) Find the electric field inside the wire.
    (e) How would your answers to parts (a) to (d) change if the electric current through the wire doubled (i.e., 4.0 A instead of 2.0 A)?
    (f) Suppose the cross-section of the wire were changed from circular to square with the same area. What effect would this change have on the quantities in parts (a) to (d)?
    (g) How will the quantities in parts (a) to (d) change when the temperature of the wire is raised from 15°C to 35°C while the current remains constant?

Section 22-3   Ohm's Law and Combinations of Resistors

26. ✳ The resistance of the tungsten filament in a common size of incandescent light bulb is 15 Ω. The diameter of the filament is 0.1 mm. What is the length of the filament wire?

27. ✳ The mass of the copper wire in a coil is 1.78 g, and its resistance is 34 Ω. Estimate the length and the cross-sectional area of the wire in the coil.

28. ✳ (a) Compare the relative change of the resistances and resistivities of an aluminum wire and a Nichrome wire that are both heated to 500°C. Neglect the thermal expansion of the wires.
    (b) How would your answers change if the lengths of the wires were doubled?
    (c) How would your answers change if you took the thermal expansion of the wires into account?

29. ✳ How much current flows through a 1.0 kW electric toaster connected to a 120 V outlet? (The voltage is AC, not DC, but the physics is the same.) How many toasters can you operate at the same time before you blow a fuse? (Assume that the maximum allowed current is 15 A.)

30. ✳ You have two conductors: Conductor 1 is a 10 m-long tin wire that has a 1 mm² square cross-sectional area. Conductor 2 is a strip of tin foil that you have shaped into a strip with the dimensions 10 mm × 200 mm, and a thickness of 100 μm. Compare the resistance of both conductors, assuming that the current flows along the longest dimension of the tin strip.

31. ✳ A wire made of a manganese alloy has a length of 56 cm and a diameter of 0.40 mm. The resistivity of the alloy is $\rho = 0.45 \, \mu\Omega \cdot m$.
    (a) Find the resistance of the wire.
    (b) Find the current through the wire when the potential difference across it is 3.0 V.

32. ✳ Will a 3 m-long aluminum wire melt if you heat it enough to triple its resistance? Explain your answer.

33. ✳✳ Prove that an equivalent resistance of any number of parallel resistors will never exceed the resistance of the branch that has the least resistance among all parallel branches:

$$R_{\text{parallel}} < (R_{\text{min}})_{\text{in parallel branch}}$$

34. ✳ Use Figure 22-9 to determine three possible different combinations of household electrical appliances that can be used simultaneously without exceeding the maximum current of 15 A.

35. ✳✳ You decide to decrease your electricity bill by reducing the usage of your toaster from 5 min/day to 3 min/day. Your toaster has a wattage of 1 kW, and you pay 6.5¢ per kW·h.
    (a) How much energy will you save per year?
    (b) How much less will you pay for your electricity bill per year than before?
    (c) Suggest more effective ways of reducing your electricity bill.

Section 22-4   Analysis of DC Circuits and Kirchhoff's Laws

36. ✳ Ohm's law is sometimes expressed as $I = \dfrac{V}{R}$, $I = \dfrac{\varepsilon}{R}$, or $I = \dfrac{\varepsilon}{R + r}$. Explain when each equation applies and the differences between them.

37. ✳ You have four identical ideal 1.5 V batteries. How should you connect these batteries to produce
    (a) a 1.5 V emf source that will outlast a single battery;
    (b) a 3.0 V emf source that will outlast a single battery;
    (c) a 4.5 V emf source;
    (d) a 6.0 V emf source?
    Check your answer by using PhET computer simulations used earlier in Online Activities.

38. ✳✳ A series electric circuit consists of a real battery ($\varepsilon = 12$ V; $r = 3.0$ Ω) and an ohmic resistor with $R = 20$ Ω.
    (a) Draw a schematic diagram for the circuit.
    (b) Derive an expression to determine how much current will flow through the battery in the circuit, and calculate the current.

(c) Derive an expression to determine the potential difference across the battery, and calculate its value.

(d) Without doing the calculations, describe what will happen to the answers above if another identical resistor ($R = 20\ \Omega$) were connected
  (i) in parallel with the original resistor;
  (ii) in series with the original resistor.

(e) Modify the expressions derived in parts (b) and (c) to determine whether your predictions in part (d) were correct. Calculate the current through the circuit and the potential difference across the battery.

39. ✷✷ Figure 22-30 shows an electric circuit that consists of nine resistors (all multiples of $R = 5.0\ \Omega$) connected to a 12 V ideal emf source.

(a) Calculate the equivalent resistance of the circuit and the electric power dissipated by it.

(b) Find the electric current that flows through each resistor.

(c) Calculate the potential differences across each resistor.

(d) Calculate the power dissipated by each resistor.

(e) Compare your answer in question (d) to the electric power dissipated by the circuit you found in part (a). What does your comparison tell you?

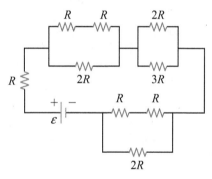

Figure 22-30   Problem 39

40. ✷✷ An ammeter is always connected in series (it has a very small internal resistance), and a voltmeter is always connected in parallel (it has a very large internal resistance). Assume that the resistance of an ammeter is $1\ \mu\Omega$ and the resistance of a voltmeter is $10.0\ k\Omega$. If a series circuit consists of a 12 V battery and a $5.0\ \Omega$ resistor, what will be the effect of measuring the electric current in this circuit and the electric voltage across the resistor using the ammeter and the voltmeter? Calculate the percentage change of electric current and voltage before and after the meters are connected.

41. ✷✷ Seven identical resistors, resistance R, are connected as shown in Figure 22-31. What is the equivalent resistance between points A and B?

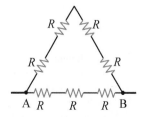

Figure 22-31   Problem 41

42. ✷✷✷ Twelve identical resistors, resistance R, are connected as shown in Figure 22-32. What is the equivalent resistance between points A and B?

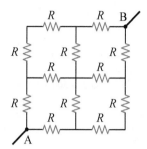

Figure 22-32   Problem 42

43. ✷✷✷ Twelve identical $3.0\ \Omega$, resistors are connected as shown in Figure 22-33. What is the equivalent resistance between points A and B?

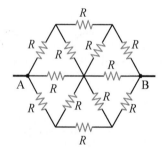

Figure 22-33   Problem 43

44. ✷✷✷ Figure 22-34 shows a multiloop electric circuit. The components have the following values:

$$\varepsilon_1 = 10\ V; \quad \varepsilon_2 = 20\ V\ \text{(ideal batteries)}$$

$$R_1 = 10\ \Omega; \quad R_2 = 15\ \Omega; \quad R_3 = 15\ \Omega; \quad R_4 = 20\ \Omega$$

(a) Find the currents through all the branches of the circuit.

(b) Find the potential differences across each circuit element.

(c) How will your answers to parts (a) and (b) differ if the batteries are real batteries?

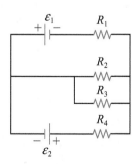

Figure 22-34   Problem 44

CHAPTER 22 | **ELECTRIC CURRENT AND FUNDAMENTALS OF DC CIRCUITS**   599

Section 22-5 RC Circuits

45. ✳ A series RC circuit consists of a 300.0 μF capacitor, a 12 V battery, and a 5.0 kΩ resistor.
(a) How long does it take for the capacitor to reach 99.9% of q_{max}? Express your answer in terms of the time constant, τ.
(b) How much charge will be accumulated on the capacitor's plates after $t_1 = \tau$, $t_2 = 2\tau$, and $t_3 = 3\tau$?
(c) What will be the value of electric current in the circuit in each of the above cases?

46. ✳ An initially uncharged 500 μF capacitor is being connected in series to a 2500 V emf source with a 10 kΩ resistor.
(a) How long will it take for the voltage across this capacitor to reach 95% of its maximum value? What is its maximum value?
(b) When the capacitor reaches 95% of its maximum voltage, the charging circuit is removed and the capacitor is left charged but can slowly discharge through the moist air with a resistance of 1000 MΩ. How long will it take to discharge the capacitor to 20 V?

COMPREHENSIVE PROBLEMS

47. ✳ A high-quality dry-cell D battery (1.5 V) can provide 0.67 A for about 5 h before dying.
(a) Compare the cost of energy you get from buying a dry-cell D battery to the cost of the energy you get from the electrical outlet in your wall. (Assume that the cost of 1 kW·h is 10¢ and one D dry-cell battery costs $1.)
(b) How much would an average Canadian household pay per month for their electric bill if they were to use dry cells to satisfy all their electricity needs?

48. ✳ When operating, the resistance of the filament of a 60 W incandescent light bulb is 240 Ω. However, if you were to measure the resistance of the filament using a regular ohmmeter, you would find it to be about 12 times smaller (20 Ω).
(a) How can you explain this phenomenon? (Hint: Think what happens to the light bulb when it is plugged in.)
(b) Do appropriate calculations to show that when operating, the tungsten filament does have the appropriate resistance.
(c) Based on your calculations, estimate the temperature of the incandescent light bulb when operating.

49. ✳ Four resistors connected to a battery have the resistances indicated in Figure 22-35; $R = 5\,\Omega$. The battery is an ideal emf source that maintains a constant potential difference across it of 10 V. A voltmeter is used to measure the following potential differences: V_{AB}, V_{AG}, V_{BH}, V_{HF}, V_{FG}, V_{HD}, V_{EF}, V_{CD}, V_{DE}, V_{BE}, and V_{CF}. Determine the readings of the voltmeter.

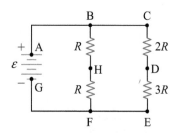

Figure 22-35 Problem 49

50. ✳✳ An electric circuit consists of six resistors and a real battery with $\varepsilon = 9.0$ V and an internal resistance $r = 0.5\,\Omega$ (Figure 22-36). Find the battery current, the voltage across each resistor, and the terminal voltage of the battery.

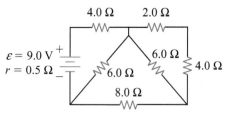

Figure 22-36 Problem 50

51. ✳ Figure 22-37 shows two different electric circuits.
(a) Compare the current flowing through the batteries in both circuits.
(b) Compare the potential differences across points A and B in each circuit. What does your comparison tell you?
(c) Compare the brightness of the light bulbs in both circuits.

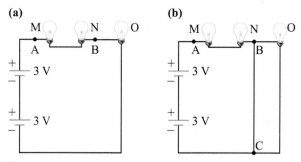

Figure 22-37 Problem 51

52. ✳ In Figure 22-38, a metal net is connected to an emf source through points A and B. The conductivity of the external (solid lines) frame of the net is very high, and the resistance of each internal (dashed) segment is r. What is the resistance of the net between points A and B?

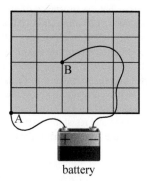

Figure 22-38 Problem 52

53. ✳✳✳ You have an aluminum wire and a tungsten wire that have the same resistance at room temperature. The temperature resistivity coefficient of aluminum is approximately half the temperature resistivity coefficient of tungsten (see Table 22-2). When answering the questions below, assume that when their temperatures are equal the wires lose thermal energy to the surrounding at the same rate. For each part, provide a detailed explanation.

(a) When the wires are connected in parallel to the battery, which wire will have a higher temperature when the system reaches equilibrium?

(b) When the wires are connected in series to the battery, which wire will have a higher temperature when the system reaches equilibrium?

54. ✶✶ Twelve identical 4.0 Ω resistors are connected to form a cube as shown in Figure 22-39. What is the equivalent resistance between points A and B?

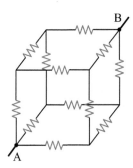

Figure 22-39 Problem 54

55. ✶✶✶ Figure 22-40 shows a multiloop electric circuit. The values of the components are as follows:

$\varepsilon_1 = 15.0$ V; $\varepsilon_2 = 20.0$ V (ideal batteries)

$R_1 = 10.0$ Ω; $R_2 = 10.0$ Ω; $R_3 = 15.0$ Ω; $R_4 = 20.0$ Ω;

$R_5 = 20.0$ Ω; $R_6 = 10.0$ Ω

(a) Find the currents through each branch of the circuit.

(b) Find the potential difference across each circuit element.

(c) How will your answers to parts (a) and (b) differ if the batteries are real batteries?

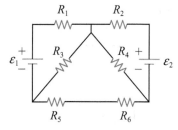

Figure 22-40 Problem 55

56. ✶✶ Design an electric circuit that can be described by the following system of equations:

$$\begin{cases} I_1 + I_2 + I_3 = 0 \\ -V_1 + I_1 R_1 - I_3 R_3 = 0 \\ I_3 R_3 - I_2 R_2 + V_2 = 0 \end{cases}$$

57. ✶✶✶ Analyze the DC circuit shown in Figure 22-41 by finding the currents flowing through each light bulb and the potential differences across each light bulb. All the emf sources in this circuit are ideal. The values of the emf sources and resistances are as follows:

$\varepsilon_1 = 25.0$ V; $\varepsilon_2 = 10.0$ V; $\varepsilon_3 = 12.0$ V

$R_1 = 10.0$ Ω; $R_2 = 5.0$ Ω; $R_3 = 15.0$ Ω; $R_4 = 20.0$ Ω;

$R_5 = 10.0$ Ω

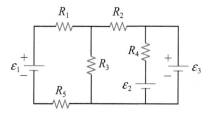

Figure 22-41 Problem 57

58. ✶✶ A capacitor is connected to a battery through a resistor and allowed to charge fully, such that the voltage across the capacitor is V. The distance between the plates of the capacitor is quadrupled, and the capacitor remains connected to the battery. Describe what happens to the charge (Q) of the capacitor, its electric field (E), and the voltage across it (V) as a result of the increase in distance. Explain why this happens. Include appropriate diagrams to support your explanation.

59. ✶✶ The switch in the circuit shown in Figure 22-42 has been closed for a long time.

(a) Find the potential difference across each circuit element.

(b) When the switch is reopened, what is the time constant of the circuit?

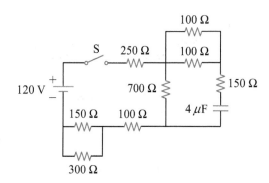

Figure 22-42 Problem 59

60. ✶✶✶ A pacemaker uses an RC circuit for timing.

(a) If the pacemaker is to operate at 72 beats/min, and if the circuit "fires" when the capacitor is 65% charged, what must the time constant be?

(b) When $C = 7.50$ μF, what value of resistance should be used?

61. ✶✶✶ Assume that a capacitor used for smoothing in a DC power supply is to discharge by no more than 0.100 V (from an initial value of 10.0 V) during 1/60 s. The power supply has specifications of output voltage of 10.0 V and a supplied current of 250.0 mA.

(a) What is the effective "resistance" of the circuit connected to the power supply?

(b) What must the minimum value for the smoothing capacitor be?

(c) How much energy is stored in the capacitor when it is fully charged?

(d) How much energy has been drawn from the capacitor when it has had its voltage reduced by 0.100 V?

DATA-RICH PROBLEM

62. ✳✳✳ Figure 22-43 is a voltage versus time graph for a circuit using a 5.00 μF capacitor and an unknown resistor.
   (a) What is the time constant?
   (b) What is the approximate value of the resistor?
   (c) What is the approximate voltage of the charging source?

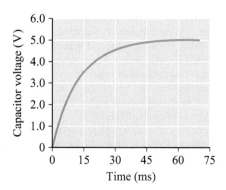

Figure 22-43   Problem 62

 See the text online resources at www.physics1e.nelson.com for Open Problems and Data-Rich Problems related to this chapter.

Chapter 23

Magnetic Fields and Magnetic Forces

A Magnetic Stripe That Changed Our Lives

You have probably used a plastic card bearing a magnetic stripe, such as a credit card, a debit card, a student identification card, a driver's licence, or a transit pass (Figure 23-1). Have you ever wondered how these cards work? Magnetic stripes are made of iron-based magnetic particles approximately 5 μm across embedded in a thin film. To record information on the magnetic stripe, groups of these particles are magnetized in a specific direction. The card is read by measuring the magnetic field along the stripe.

The process of attaching a magnetic stripe to a plastic card was invented in the 1960s by the IBM engineer Forrest Parry, who was working on developing a security system for the U.S. government. Parry found that it was quite difficult to attach a magnetic stripe to a plastic card without warping the stripe or having its surface damaged or contaminated by the adhesives used to glue it in place. The solution came from Parry's wife, Dorothea Tillia, who suggested using an iron to bond the stripe to the card.

The concept of the modern credit card was invented by Frank McNamara in 1949. It was intended to be used by salesmen who had to travel a lot and did not want to carry large amounts of cash to pay for their meals and entertainment. Hence, the first credit card was the "Diners' Club" card.

Figure 23-1 The magnetic stripe on the back of a credit card

Learning Objectives

When you have completed this chapter you should be able to:

1. Describe magnetic fields using the concept of magnetic field lines.

2. Calculate the magnitude and direction of the magnetic force acting on a charged particle moving inside a uniform magnetic field.

3. Describe the trajectory of a charged particle moving inside crossed electric and magnetic fields.

4. Calculate the magnitude and direction of a magnetic force and a magnetic torque applied by a magnetic field on current-carrying wires and current-carrying loops.

5. Calculate the magnitude and direction of a magnetic field created by moving electric charges using the Biot–Savart law.

6. Calculate the magnitude and direction of a magnetic field created by moving electric charges using Ampère's law.

7. Describe the magnetic forces between two current-carrying wires quantitatively and qualitatively.

8. Describe the magnetic properties of materials and their applications.

9. Describe some everyday applications of electromagnetic phenomena.

For additional Making Connections, Examples, and Checkpoints, as well as activities and experiments to help increase your understanding of the chapter's concepts, please go to the text's online resources at www.physics1e.nelson.com.

ELECTRICITY, MAGNETISM, AND OPTICS

23-1 Magnetic Field and Magnetic Force

Earlier chapters describe electric and gravitational fields and illustrate how field lines can be used to represent the direction and strength of a field. The concepts of fields and field lines were originally developed by the British scientist and engineer Michael Faraday (1791–1867) to model a magnetic field. In 1845, Faraday used **magnetic field lines** (which he called "lines of force") to describe the space surrounding a permanent magnet.

You can map the **magnetic field** created by a small permanent magnet by moving a compass around it. The needle of the compass is itself a small magnet, and it deflects differently, depending on its location relative to the magnet.

ONLINE ACTIVITY

Magnetic Field Lines Created by a Permanent Magnet

The e-resource that accompanies every new copy of this textbook contains an Online Activity using the PhET simulation "Magnet and Compass." Work through the simulation and accompanying questions to gain an understanding of magnetic field lines created by a permanent magnet.

The end of the compass needle pointing toward Earth's North Pole is called a north-seeking pole, or simply a north pole. Similarly, the end of the compass needle pointing toward Earth's South Pole is called a south-seeking pole, or a south pole (Figure 23-2(a)). Earth's magnetic field is likely caused by electric currents flowing in its molten outer core. This magnetic field is similar to the field that would be produced by a giant bar magnet located inside Earth's core. Earth's magnetic north pole would be located near the south pole of this imaginary bar magnet, and Earth's magnetic south pole would be near the magnet's north pole. The magnetic and geographical poles do not coincide. In fact, the magnetic poles are gradually moving relative to the geographic poles.

Another way of displaying the magnetic field patterns is to use iron filings. In a magnetic field, suspended iron filings behave as tiny magnets and orient themselves in the direction of the field lines. To visualize a 3-D magnetic field, we can use iron filings suspended in oil (Figure 23-2(b)). Figures 23-2(c)–(e) show magnetic field lines created by different magnet configurations.

Like an electric field, a magnetic field is a vector physical quantity. We defined the direction and magnitude of an electric field in terms the electrostatic force that it exerts on a test charge. The electric field and the electrostatic force are always collinear, and $\vec{F}_E = q\vec{E}$,

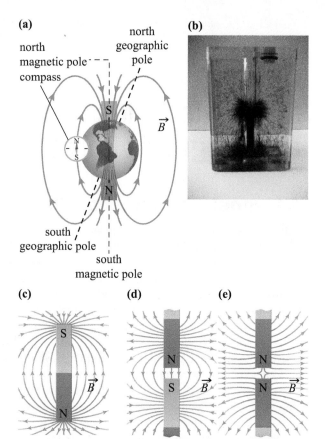

Figure 23-2 (a) Earth's magnetic field can be visualized as the magnetic field of a giant bar magnet. (b) Magnetic field lines created by iron fillings suspended in oil. (c), (d), and (e) Magnetic field patterns indicated by iron fillings.

where $\vec{F}_E$ is an electrostatic force, q is an electric charge, and $\vec{E}$ is the electric field. Although the electrostatic force $\vec{F}_E$ and the magnetic force $\vec{F}_B$ on a charged particle are both proportional to the particle's charge, the **magnetic force** also depends on the velocity of the particle and is *not* collinear with the magnetic field. The forces exerted on charged particles by electric and magnetic fields thus differ significantly:

- The magnitude of the magnetic force $\vec{F}_B$ on a charged particle is proportional to particle's speed. A faster-moving particle experiences a greater magnetic force, and a particle at rest does not experience any magnetic force.

- Unlike the electrostatic force, the magnetic force depends on the direction of the motion of a charged particle relative to the direction of the magnetic field. For a given speed, a charged particle moving perpendicular to the magnetic field lines experiences the greatest magnetic force, and a charged particle moving parallel to the magnetic field lines experiences no magnetic force. When the particle moves at an angle θ to the magnetic field lines, the force exerted by the magnetic field is proportional to $\sin\theta$ (Figure 23-3).

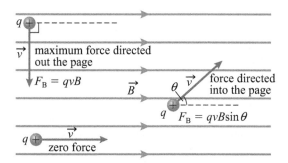

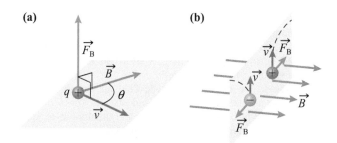

Figure 23-3 The magnetic force acting on a charged particle moving inside a uniform magnetic field at different angles relative to the magnetic field lines

Figure 23-4 (a) The direction of the magnetic force on a charged particle q moving with velocity $\vec{v}$ in a magnetic field $\vec{B}$. (b) Magnetic forces on positively and negatively charged particles moving inside a uniform magnetic field $\vec{B}$. (We indicate magnetic field vectors with green arrows, magnetic forces with blue arrows, and velocities with red arrows.)

■ The magnetic force is always perpendicular to a particle's velocity $\vec{v}$ and to the magnetic field $\vec{B}$: $\vec{F}_B \perp \vec{v}$ and $\vec{F}_B \perp \vec{B}$. In Figure 23-3 it is directed in or out of the page. Consequently, the magnetic force does zero work on the particle:

$$dW = (\vec{F}_B \bullet d\vec{r}) = (\vec{F}_B \bullet \vec{v}\,dt) = (\vec{F}_B \bullet \vec{v})dt = 0$$

Thus, the magnetic force cannot change the particle's kinetic energy (just as the gravitational force acting on an object in a circular orbit does not change its kinetic energy, Chapter 11). However, the magnetic force can affect the *direction* of the particle's motion.

Can you think of any case in which a force applied on an object does not change its speed, but only affects the direction of its motion? (See Section 4-3)

Calculating the magnitude and direction of the magnetic force requires knowing not only the magnetic field $\vec{B}$ and the particle's charge q, but also its velocity $\vec{v}$. Moreover, the three vectors $\vec{v}$, $\vec{B}$, and $\vec{F}_B$ are never located all in the same plane. Therefore, problems involving magnetic forces are always three-dimensional. The magnetic force acting on a charged particle can be described succinctly using a cross product (Figure 23-4):

KEY EQUATION
$$\vec{F}_B = q\vec{v} \times \vec{B} \qquad (23\text{-}1)$$

which means $\vec{F}_B = qvB\sin\theta$

Equation (23-1) indicates that the magnetic forces acting on oppositely charged particles moving in the same direction in a uniform magnetic field are indeed opposite. Remember that cross products are anticommutative: $\vec{v} \times \vec{B} = -\vec{B} \times \vec{v}$.

When a charged particle is moving inside crossed magnetic and electric fields, it experiences both electrostatic and magnetic forces.

KEY EQUATION
$$\vec{F} = \vec{F}_E + \vec{F}_B = q\vec{E} + q\vec{v} \times \vec{B} \qquad (23\text{-}2)$$

The expression for the combined force is called the **Lorentz force**, in honour of the Dutch physicist Hendrik Lorentz (1853–1928), who formulated it in 1892. However, Equation (23-2), albeit not in the present form, appeared 31 years earlier in the works of the Scottish mathematician and theoretical physicist James Clerk Maxwell (1831–79).

The SI unit of magnetic field is the **tesla** (T), named for the Serbian-American inventor, physicist, and engineer Nikola Tesla (1856–1943). A particle carrying a charge of 1 C moving with a speed of 1 m/s perpendicular to a magnetic field of 1 T will experience a magnetic force of 1 N:

$$1\,\text{N} = 1\,\text{C} \cdot 1\,\frac{\text{m}}{\text{s}} \cdot 1\,\text{T} \quad \text{or} \quad 1\,\text{T} = 1\,\frac{\text{N} \cdot \text{s}}{\text{C} \cdot \text{m}}$$

The tesla can be also expressed as follows:

$$1\,\text{T} = 1\,\frac{\text{N} \cdot \text{s}}{\text{C} \cdot \text{m}} = 1\,\frac{\text{N}}{\text{C/s} \cdot \text{m}} = 1\,\frac{\text{N}}{\text{A} \cdot \text{m}} \qquad (23\text{-}3)$$

A magnetic field of 1 T is quite strong. The magnetic fields that we typically encounter have strengths of less than 1 mT.

Another commonly used unit for magnetic fields is the gauss (G), named after the German mathematician and physical scientist Carl Friedrich Gauss (1777–1855): $10^4\,\text{G} = 1\,\text{T}$ or $1\,\text{G} = 10^{-4}\,\text{T}$

 MAKING CONNECTIONS

Strengths of Magnetic Fields

Earth: The strength of the magnetic field at Earth's surface ranges from about 30 μT (0.3 G) in an area including most of South America and South Africa to over 60 μT (0.6 G) in areas near the magnetic poles (in northern Canada and southern Australia).

The solar wind: The solar wind is a stream of plasma that flows away from the Sun. The magnetic field of the solar wind ranges between 5 and 10 nT (approximately 1000 times weaker than Earth's magnetic field).

(continued)

ELECTRICITY, MAGNETISM, AND OPTICS

Magnetic resonance imaging (MRI): MRI is a technique for producing diagnostic images of tissue inside the body. MRI scanners generally use powerful magnetic fields in the range of 0.5 to 3.0 T.

Atoms: The effective magnetic field felt by an electron inside an alkali atom can exceed 1000 T. These atomic magnetic fields are responsible for fine structure splitting of atomic spectra measured in laboratories.

Earth's magnetosphere: Earth's magnetosphere, a region in space dominated by the magnetic field, was detected in 1958 during the *Explorer 1* mission. The magnetosphere is located above the ionosphere and extends as far as 25 Earth radii. Two main phenomena affect Earth's magnetosphere: Earth's internal magnetic field (30 to 60 μT) and the solar wind (5 to 10 nT).

Laboratory experiments: To date, the strongest continuous magnetic field created in a lab is a 45 T field at the National High Magnetic Field Laboratory of Florida State University. Pulsed electromagnets have created fields of over 100 T for a few milliseconds.

Tokamaks: These experimental fusion reactors use magnetic fields of 8 to 10 T to confine extremely hot plasma. The word "tokamak" is a Russian acronym for toroidal chamber with magnetic coils.

Neutron stars: The magnetic field on the surface of a neutron star is calculated to be of the order of magnitude of 10^8 T, making neutron stars the strongest known naturally occurring magnetic fields.

✓ CHECKPOINT

C-23-1 Ranking the Magnitudes of Magnetic Forces

Four charged particles, $q_1 = q$, $q_2 = -q$, $q_3 = 2q$, and $q_4 = -2q$, moving with velocities $\vec{v}_1 = 3v\hat{i}$, $\vec{v}_2 = 3v\hat{j}$, $\vec{v}_3 = -2v\hat{i}$, and $\vec{v}_4 = 3v\hat{j}$, enter a uniform magnetic field $\vec{B} = -2B_0\hat{i}$. Which of the following correctly ranks the magnitudes of the magnetic forces acting on these particles?

(a) $F_{B_1} < F_{B_2} < F_{B_3} < F_{B_4}$
(b) $F_{B_1} > F_{B_2} > F_{B_3} > F_{B_4}$
(c) $F_{B_1} = F_{B_2} > F_{B_3} = F_{B_4}$
(d) $F_{B_1} > F_{B_2} = F_{B_3} > F_{B_4}$
(e) $F_{B_1} = F_{B_3} < F_{B_2} < F_{B_4}$

C-23-1 (e) The magnetic force can be calculated using Equation (23-1).

"Hand" rules are useful shortcuts for determining the direction of a magnetic force without calculating a cross product. Here are two commonly used versions of the **right-hand rule** (Figure 23-5).

Right-hand rule 1: Point your four right-hand fingers in the direction of motion of a positively charged particle, and curl them in the direction of the magnetic field. Your stretched-out thumb points in the direction of the magnetic force acting on the particle (Figure 23-5(a)).

Right-hand rule 2: Position your right-hand so that your fingers point in the direction of the magnetic field and your thumb points in the direction of the velocity of a positively charged particle. When you then bend your fingers 90°, they point in the direction of the magnetic force (Figure 23-5(b)).

Check for yourself that both versions of the right-hand rule are equivalent. For a negatively charged particle, the direction of the magnetic force is opposite to the direction indicated by the right-hand rule. (Alternatively, you can use corresponding left-hand rules for negative charges.)

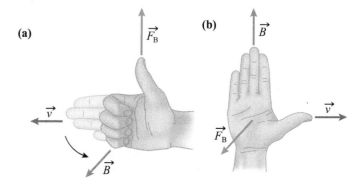

Figure 23-5 Right-hand rules for the direction of a magnetic force acting on a charged particle. (a) Right-hand rule 1 (b) Right-hand rule 2

👥 PEER TO PEER

Don't be intimidated if your professor uses a right-hand rule that you're not aware of. There are a number of different ways to use the right-hand rule. Make sure that you use a right-hand rule correctly, and find the one that works for you. All produce the same result as long as you use them properly. Remember that a right-hand rule applies to a positively charged particle. A negatively charged particle will produce the opposite result.

Since problems involving the calculation of magnetic forces involve three dimensions, it is useful to have conventions to represent 3-D situations as 2-D diagrams. We represent a vector directed away from us into the page as a cross (like the end view of the tail of an arrow). Similarly, we represent a vector coming out of the page toward us as a dot (the front view of the tip of an arrow) (Figure 23-7).

EXAMPLE 23-1

The Right-Hand Rule and the Cross Product

A positively charged particle q enters a region with a uniform magnetic field $\vec{B} = B_0\hat{i}$. The particle's initial velocity is $\vec{v} = 3v_0\hat{j}$ (Figure 23-6). Determine the magnetic force acting on the particle just as it enters the magnetic field.

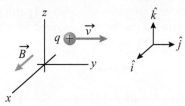

Figure 23-6 A positively charged particle moves inside a uniform magnetic field.

SOLUTION

Method 1: Using the Right-Hand Rule

Applying the right-hand rule, we find that the magnetic force points in the negative z-direction:

Its magnitude is given by:

$$F_B = qvB\sin\theta = q3v_0B_0\sin(90°) = 3qv_0B_0$$

In vector form, the magnetic force can be represented as $\vec{F}_B = -3qv_0B_0\hat{k}$.

Method 2: Using a Cross Product

$$\vec{F}_B = q\vec{v} \times \vec{B} = q3v_0\hat{j} \times B_0\hat{i} = q3v_0B_0\begin{pmatrix} \hat{i} & \hat{j} & \hat{k} \\ 0 & 1 & 0 \\ 1 & 0 & 0 \end{pmatrix}$$

$$= q3v_0B_0(\hat{i}(1\cdot0 - 0\cdot0) - \hat{j}(0\cdot0 - 1\cdot0) + \hat{k}(0\cdot0 - 1\cdot1))$$

$$= -3qv_0B_0\hat{k}$$

Making sense of the result:

As expected, both solutions produce the same result. Method 1 appears to be more straightforward; however, in general, an algebraic approach is more versatile.

(a) $\vec{B}$ out of page:

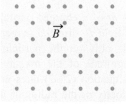

(b) $\vec{B}$ into page:

(c) $\vec{B}$ out of page:

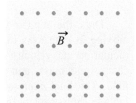

(d) $\vec{B}$ into page:

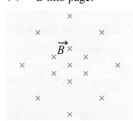

Figure 23-7 Representations of magnetic fields perpendicular to the page. (a) A uniform magnetic field is directed out of the page. (b) A uniform magnetic field is directed into the page. (c) A nonuniform magnetic field is directed out of the page. (d) A nonuniform magnetic field is directed into the page.

A **uniform magnetic field** is a magnetic field that is not changing in space (Figures 23-7(a) and (b)), and a **constant magnetic field** is a magnetic field that is not changing in time. A uniform field is not necessarily constant nor is a constant field necessarily uniform.

✓ CHECKPOINT

C-23-2 Determining the Direction of the Magnetic Force

An electron is moving at speed v in the positive x-direction. The magnetic field $\vec{B}$ points in the negative x-direction. What is the magnetic force experienced by the electron?

(a) $F_B = qvB$ points in the positive y-direction.
(b) $F_B = qvB$ points in the negative y-direction.
(c) $F_B = qvB$ points in the positive z-direction.
(d) $F_B = qvB$ points in the negative z-direction.
(e) $F_B = 0$.

C-23-2 (e) A magnetic field that is parallel or antiparallel to the charged particle's velocity exerts no force on the particle (Equation (23-1)).

23-2 The Motion of a Charged Particle in a Uniform Magnetic Field

As noted earlier, the magnetic force acting on a charged particle can change the *direction* of its motion but not its speed. In this section, we use Newton's laws and the description of the magnetic force (Equation (23-2)) to investigate the trajectory of a charged particle moving in a uniform magnetic field.

A Charged Particle Moving Perpendicular to a Uniform Magnetic Field

Consider an electron moving with velocity $\vec{v}$ entering a uniform magnetic field $\vec{B}$, directed *perpendicular* to the electron's velocity (Figure 23-8). Since the magnetic force acting on the electron is perpendicular to its velocity (Equation (23-1)), the electron moves along a circular path (Section 4-3), accelerating at the rate of $a_R = \dfrac{v^2}{R}$. Applying Newton's second law to this circular motion, we get

$$\sum \vec{F} = m\vec{a}$$

$$qvB\sin\theta = ma_R$$

$$qvB\sin(90°) = m\frac{v^2}{R}$$

$$qvB = m\frac{v^2}{R}$$

Therefore, the radius of the electron's trajectory can be expressed as follows:

KEY EQUATION
$$R = \frac{mv}{qB} = \frac{p}{qB} \qquad (23\text{-}4)$$

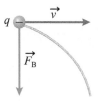

Figure 23-8 An electron moving in a uniform magnetic field directed perpendicular to its velocity has a circular trajectory.

Equation (23-4) indicates that the radius of the electron's trajectory is proportional to the magnitude of its momentum, $\vec{p}$. The radius of the motion is inversely proportional to the particle's charge and the magnitude of the magnetic field.

We now consider a stream of identical particles all moving in the same direction but with different speeds. For these identical particles, the mass-to-charge ratio is the same. Therefore, when the stream of charged particles enters a uniform magnetic field perpendicular to its direction, the particles move along circles of different radii (Equation (23-4)), defined by the particle's momentum and charge, and the magnitude of the magnetic field.

For circular trajectories of a charged particle, we can define the period, T, as the time required for a particle to complete one revolution:

$$T = \frac{2\pi R}{v} \qquad (23\text{-}5)$$

Combining Equations (23-4) and (23-5) yields

KEY EQUATION
$$T = \frac{2\pi R}{v} = \frac{2\pi mv}{vqB} = 2\pi\frac{m}{qB} \qquad (23\text{-}6)$$

The period, T, depends only on the ratio m/qB and is not affected by the particle's speed. Since the relationship between magnitudes of angular and linear velocities is $v = \omega R$,

$$\omega = \frac{v}{R} = \frac{qBR}{mR} = \frac{qB}{m}$$

KEY EQUATION
$$f_{cyc} = \frac{\omega}{2\pi} = \frac{qB}{2\pi m} \qquad (23\text{-}7)$$

Thus, the angular velocity ω of a charged particle moving in a uniform magnetic field $\vec{B}$ directed perpendicular to its velocity depends only on the particle's charge and mass, and the magnitude of the magnetic field. The final expression in Equation (23-7) does not include the particle's linear velocity or the radius of its trajectory. The angular velocity of the particle, ω, divided by 2π has the unit of 1/s or Hz: $[\omega] = \dfrac{1}{s} \equiv$ Hz, and is called the **cyclotron frequency**, f_{cyc} (recall that $\omega = 2\pi f$ (Equation (13-5))). A **cyclotron** is a type of particle accelerator that accelerates charged particles moving along circular trajectories (see Section 23-3).

A Charged Particle Moving at an Angle to a Magnetic Field

Let us consider what happens when a charged particle enters a uniform magnetic field at an arbitrary angle θ to the field lines. We can resolve the particle's velocity into components perpendicular ($\vec{v}_\perp$) and parallel ($\vec{v}_\parallel$) to the magnetic field (Figure 23-9):

$$\vec{v} = \vec{v}_\parallel + \vec{v}_\perp, \quad v = \sqrt{v_\parallel^2 + v_\perp^2} \qquad (23\text{-}8)$$

where $v_\parallel = v\cos\theta$ and $v_\perp = v\sin\theta$.

The magnetic force acting on the particle due to the perpendicular component of the particle's velocity causes

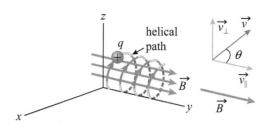

Figure 23-9 A positively charged particle moving at angle θ to a uniform magnetic field follows a helical trajectory.

the particle to move along a circular path with a radius given by Equation (23-4). The velocity component parallel to the magnetic field lines is not affected by the magnetic field. The magnetic force can be expressed as

$$\vec{F}_B = q\vec{v} \times \vec{B} = q(\vec{v}_\parallel + \vec{v}_\perp) \times \vec{B}$$

$$= q\vec{v}_\parallel \times \vec{B} + q\vec{v}_\perp \times \vec{B} = q\vec{v}_\perp \times \vec{B} \qquad (23\text{-}9)$$

The charged particle follows a helical path, a combination of circular motion in a plane perpendicular to the magnetic field and uniform linear motion parallel to it:

In the plane perpendicular to the magnetic field—circular motion

$$R = \frac{mv\sin\theta}{qB}$$

In the direction parallel to the magnetic field—motion with constant velocity:

$$\vec{v}_\parallel = \text{const}$$

The distance along the magnetic field travelled by a charged particle during one revolution (pitch):

$$d = v_\parallel T = v\cos\theta \frac{2\pi m}{qB} = \frac{2\pi mv\cos\theta}{qB} \qquad (23\text{-}10)$$

PEER TO PEER

When I realized that the motion of a charged particle in a magnetic field can be considered as a combination of linear and circular motions, it became much easier for me to solve problems. I now apply all I learned about circular motion in earlier chapters to the motion of charged particles in magnetic field.

Auroras

Spectacular auroras occur in regions 10° to 20° of latitude from the magnetic poles: the aurora borealis (Northern Lights) in the northern hemisphere (Figure 23-10(a)) and the aurora australis in the southern hemisphere. Auroras happen when fast-moving electrons and protons enter the magnetosphere, which is the region of strong magnetic fields with a boundary at approximately 15 to 25 Earth radii above Earth's surface. These charged particles follow magnetic field lines moving along helical paths (Figure 23-10(b)), as described above. When they collide with oxygen and nitrogen atoms at altitudes of 30 to 300 km above Earth's surface, they transfer part of their energy to atmospheric atoms and molecules, which then emit visible light. The colour of the aurora depends on the atoms that were struck and on the altitude of the collision.

(a)

iStockphoto/Thinkstock

(b)

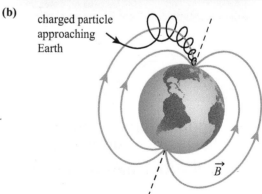

Figure 23-10 (a) The aurora borealis in Northern Canada (b) Schematic representation of auroras

EXAMPLE 23-2

A Charged Particle Moving in a Uniform Magnetic Field

A particle with a charge of 1.3 nC and a mass of 1.4×10^{-9} kg moves with velocity $\vec{v} = (1.5 \times 10^4\,\hat{i} + 1.2 \times 10^4\,\hat{j})$ m/s as it enters a uniform magnetic field $\vec{B} = (1.4\hat{i})$ T.

(a) Determine the magnetic force acting on the particle as it enters the field.

(b) Describe the path of the particle, and determine its radius.

(c) Find the time it takes for the particle to complete one revolution.

(d) Find the distance the particle travels along the magnetic field lines as it completes one revolution.

SOLUTION

(a) Part (a) can be solved in a way similar to the previous example:

$$\vec{F}_B = q\vec{v} \times \vec{B} = (1.3 \times 10^{-9})\begin{pmatrix} \hat{i} & \hat{j} & \hat{k} \\ 1.5 \times 10^4 & 1.2 \times 10^4 & 0 \\ 1.4 & 0 & 0 \end{pmatrix} \text{N}$$

$$= [(1.3 \times 10^{-9})10^4\,(\hat{i}(1.2 \cdot 0 - 0 \cdot 0) - \hat{j}(1.5 \cdot 0 - 0 \cdot 1.4)$$

$$+ \hat{k}(1.5 \cdot 0 - 1.4 \cdot 1.2))] \text{ N}$$

$$= 1.3 \times 10^{-5}(-1.68\,\hat{k})\,\text{N} = -2.184 \times 10^{-5}\,\hat{k}\,\text{N}$$

(b) The particle moves along a helical path because the $\hat{i}$ component of the particle's velocity is parallel to the magnetic field and therefore unaffected by the field. So, the particle moves along a circular trajectory in the yz-plane while moving with a constant velocity in the x-direction. The radius of the helix can be found using Equation (23-4):

$$R = \frac{mv}{qB} = \frac{(1.4 \times 10^{-9}\,\text{kg})(1.2 \times 10^4\,\text{m/s})}{(1.3 \times 10^{-9}\,\text{C})(1.4\,\text{T})} = 9.2 \times 10^3\,\text{m}$$

(c) We can use Equation (23-6) to find the period of the particle's motion:

$$T = \frac{2\pi m}{qB} = \frac{2(3.14)(1.4 \times 10^{-9}\,\text{kg})}{(1.3 \times 10^{-9}\,\text{C})(1.4\,\text{T})} = 4.8\,\text{s}$$

(d) It will take the particle 4.8 s to complete one revolution. During this time, the particle will move a distance d along the x-axis. This distance is called the **pitch of the helix**:

$$d = Tv_x = (4.8\,\text{s})(1.5 \times 10^4\,\text{m/s}) = 7.2 \times 10^4\,\text{m}$$

✓ CHECKPOINT

C-23-3 Location of Auroras

Auroras do not occur near the equator because

(a) charged particles never reach the equator;

(b) the magnetic field lines are strongest near the equator;

(c) the magnetic field lines near the equator are directed toward Earth;

(d) there is no magnetosphere near the equator.

(e) None of the above are true.

C-23-3 (e): Charged particles emitted by the Sun follow a helical path around B lines reaching north and south poles, but not the equator.

LO 3

23-3 Applications: Charged Particles Moving in a Uniform Magnetic Field

The behaviour of charged particles in a magnetic field has a number of applications in medicine, industry, and scientific research. In this section, we see how the physics of this behaviour is used in several important devices.

Velocity Selector

Charged particles produced in a lab or arriving from the Sun often have a range of velocities. A **velocity selector** uses perpendicular electric and magnetic fields to filter a beam of charged particles, leaving only those with a particular desired velocity.

The velocity selector in Figure 23-11 has a chamber with crossed uniform electric and magnetic fields. When a positively charged particle enters this chamber, the electric force

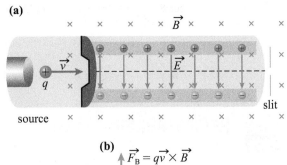

Figure 23-11 (a) An operation of a velocity selector (b) A free body diagram for a positively charged particle moving inside a velocity selector

610   SECTION FOUR | ELECTRICITY, MAGNETISM, AND OPTICS   NEL

104

acting on the particle is directed along the electric field lines (downward). However, the magnetic force is directed upward, perpendicular to the magnetic field lines. Particles with a velocity such that the magnetic force balances the electric force pass through the chamber without changing their velocity, as indicated by the dashed line. All other charged particles are deflected either upward or downward, depending on which force is stronger for each particular particle. The magnetic force can be opposite to the electric force only for the particles entering the region with the velocity perpendicular to both $\vec{B}$ and $\vec{E}$. When the electric and magnetic forces balance,

$$F_E = F_B$$

$$qE = qvB \tag{23-11}$$

$$E = vB$$

and

$$v = \frac{E}{B} \tag{23-12}$$

Thus, only the particles whose velocity satisfies Equation (23-12) pass straight through the velocity selector.

✓ CHECKPOINT

C-23-4 Operation of the Velocity Selector

Which of the following statements represents the operation of a velocity selector?

(a) The polarity of the electric and magnetic fields in the velocity selector depends on the charge of the selected particles.

(b) The ratio $\frac{E}{B}$ of the velocity selector depends on the mass of the charged particles to be selected.

(c) If in the velocity selector $E \neq vB$, the particle moves in a circular trajectory.

(d) If a positive particle is moving faster than the speed chosen in the velocity selector, the particle is deflected in the direction of the electric field.

(e) If a negative particle is moving faster than the speed chosen in the velocity selector, the particle is deflected in the direction of the electric field.

C-23-4 (e) The speed of the particle has no effect on the electric force acting on it, but it has an effect on the magnetic force. Since the particle in the velocity selector is negatively charged, the magnetic force acting on it will be larger than the electric force. The magnetic force in that case is directed in the direction of the electric field.

Mass Spectrometers

The charged particles that pass through a velocity selector all have the same velocity, but they do not necessarily have the same masses or charges. A **mass spectrometer** sorts particles by their mass-to-charge ratios, making it a powerful tool for chemical analysis.

As shown in Figure 23-12, a mass spectrometer has a velocity selector connected to a chamber with a uniform magnetic field. Charged particles leaving a velocity selector have a known speed. When they enter the second chamber, the uniform magnetic field causes them to move along

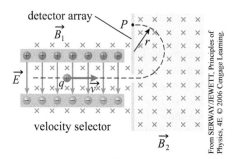

Figure 23-12 An operation of a mass spectrometer

From SERWAY/JEWETT, Principles of Physics, 4E. © 2006 Cengage Learning.

semicircular trajectories with radii that depend on their mass and charge. Combining Equations (23-4) and (23-12):

$$R = \frac{mv}{qB_2} = \frac{mE}{qB_1B_2} \tag{23-13}$$

where B_1 represents the magnetic field inside the velocity selector chamber 1, and B_2 represents the magnetic field inside chamber 2.

Thus, by measuring the radius of a particle's trajectory, we can determine its mass-to-charge ratio:

$$\frac{m}{q} = \frac{RB_1B_2}{E} \tag{23-14}$$

If the magnetic fields in the two chambers are equal which is not always the case, $B_1 = B_2 = B$,

$$\frac{m}{q} = \frac{RB^2}{E} \tag{23-15}$$

Some mass spectrometers might not have a separate velocity selector chamber as shown in Figure 23-12. These devices (Figures 23-12 and 23-73) have an advantage of being lighter and lower in cost. We will consider this model of a mass spectrometer in the comprehensive problems at the end of the Chapter, Problem 74.

✓ CHECKPOINT

C-23-5 The Motion of Charged Particles Inside a Mass Spectrometer

An electron beam travels through a mass spectrometer of the type shown in Figure 23-12. Then a beam of protons travels through the same mass spectrometer. What is true about the trajectories of the electrons and protons inside the mass spectrometer?

(a) The electron beam has a smaller radius of curvature than the proton beam. The beams bend in opposite directions.

(b) The electron beam has a larger radius of curvature than the proton beam. The beams bend in the same direction.

(c) The electron beam has a smaller radius of curvature than the proton beam. The beams bend in the same direction.

(d) The electron beam has a larger radius of curvature than the proton beam. The beams bend in opposite directions.

C-23-5 (a) Electrons and protons have the opposite charges but very different masses; the mass of a proton is about 2000 times larger than the mass of an electron. Thus, a proton beam will have a radius 2000 times smaller than an electron beam. The beams will also bend in different directions.

CHAPTER 23 | **MAGNETIC FIELDS AND MAGNETIC FORCES**   611

Determining the Electron's Charge-to-Mass to Ratio

Experiments by the British scientist J.J. Thomson (1856–1940) culminated in 1897 with the discovery of the electron. Thomson was able to measure the electron's charge-to-mass ratio using a cathode ray tube (CRT), like the one shown in Figure 23-13. Thomson's apparatus consisted of a vacuum tube containing an electrode that emits electrons (a cathode), a fluorescent screen, plates to apply an electric field, and coils to apply a magnetic field. Electrons emitted by the cathode passed through a slit into a region of crossed magnetic and electric fields; then they struck a fluorescent screen, causing it to glow at the point of impact. Thomson determined the radius of the path of the electrons from the position of the glowing point. Then he calculated the $\dfrac{m_e}{e}$ ratio for the electron:

$$\frac{m_e}{e} = \frac{RB}{v} \tag{23-16}$$

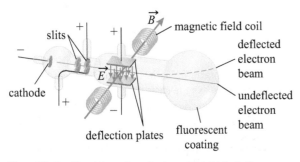

Figure 23-13 Thomson used a cathode ray tube, similar to the one shown here, to determine the charge-to-mass ratio for the electron.

Although Thomson's equipment produced only an approximate value for the ratio $\dfrac{m_e}{e}$, it was nonetheless clear evidence that "cathode rays" are tiny negatively charged particles. Almost 15 years later, American physicist Robert A. Millikan (1868–1953) devised an ingenious method to use electric fields to determine the mass and charge of the electron. Millikan's experiment is described in Chapter 30.

CHECKPOINT

C-23-6 The Cathode Ray Tube

Which particle *cannot* be measured by using the crossed magnetic and electric field method suggested by Thomson? Explain.

(a) electron
(b) proton
(c) α-particle
(d) neutron
(e) hydrogen ion

C-23-6 (d) Neutrons have no electric charge, so they will move along the cathode ray tube undeflected.

Uranium Enrichment During World War II

The mass spectrometer played a crucial role in the Manhattan Project, which is the name given to the secret project to develop the atomic bomb during World War II. Uranium-235 is the only naturally occurring isotope that undergoes nuclear fission when bombarded with thermal (low-energy) neutrons. However, only 0.711% of the uranium in ore is uranium-235 (most of the remainder is the much more stable isotope uranium-238). The Manhattan Project had to develop ways to separate the isotopes. One of the methods used was a form of multistage mass spectrometer, called a calutron (Figure 23-14). Today, more effective methods of isotope separation are used. Canada produces approximately 20% of the world's uranium. Approximately 50% of the electrical power in Ontario and 15% of the overall power generation in Canada are generated using unenriched uranium.

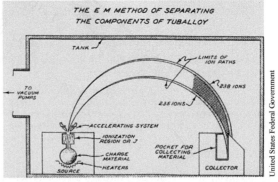

Figure 23-14   (a) The Oakridge Nuclear Plant (b) An original drawing of a calutron used to separate uranium isotopes in the Manhattan Project

Cyclotrons

Cyclotrons use electric and magnetic fields to accelerate charged particles to very high kinetic energies. A uniform electric field acts on a charged particle that moves a distance d along the electric field lines, and changes the particle's kinetic energy:

$$\Delta KE = W$$

$$W = (\vec{F}_E \cdot \vec{d}) = qEd = q\Delta V$$

$$\Delta KE = qEd = q\Delta V \qquad (23\text{-}17)$$

Increasing the distance d and strengthening the electric field E increase the gain in the particle's kinetic energy. However, building very long accelerators and using extremely strong electric fields is costly and technologically difficult. The cyclotron reduces some of these challenges by using crossed electric and magnetic fields to accelerate charged particles as they follow a spiral path (Figure 23-15).

A cyclotron consists of two hollow semicircular chambers called "dees," labelled D_1 and D_2 in Figure 23-15(a). A high-frequency voltage is applied across the gap between the dees, and a uniform magnetic field is directed perpendicular to the plane of the dees. An ion source feeds ions to the centre of the cyclotron (point P). When an ion enters a region of the uniform magnetic field, it starts moving along a circular path, repeatedly crossing the gap between the dees. The alternating voltage source across the gap ensures that the ion experiences an electric field in the direction of its motion, thus increasing its kinetic energy. Example 23-3 discusses how the frequency of the alternating voltage across the gap is calculated. After exiting the gap between the dees, the ion is subjected to a uniform magnetic field only, perpendicular to its velocity. As a result, the ion continues to move along a circular path. However, since the speed of the ion is higher than it was before the ion entered the gap, the radius of the ion's trajectory increases. When the ion enters the second gap between the dees, the potential difference between the dees has reversed, so the electric field once again points in the direction of the ion's motion and the ion gains additional kinetic energy. After the ion exits the gap between the dees, it is moving even faster, causing an additional increase in the radius of its trajectory. Eventually, the trajectory radius increases enough that the ion travels along the edge of the dee and passes through the exit slit.

The exit kinetic energy of the ion is

$$KE = \frac{mv^2}{2} = \frac{m}{2}\left(\frac{RqB}{m}\right)^2 = \frac{R^2 q^2 B^2}{2m} \qquad (23\text{-}18)$$

Cyclotrons can accelerate charged particles to speeds approaching the speed of light. For example, the giant TRIUMF cyclotron (www.triumf.info/), located in Vancouver, British Columbia, accelerates negatively charged hydrogen ions (called H⁻ ions) to 224 000 km/s, approximately 75% of the speed of light (Figure 23-16). These high-energy particles can be used to produce beams of neutrons and short-lived particles called mesons. TRIUMF is so efficient at creating pi-mesons that it is often called a meson factory. The high-energy particles are also used to treat several forms of cancer.

(a)

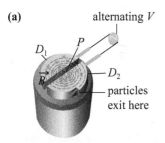

alternating V

(b)

Figure 23-15 (a) A schematic representation of a cyclotron (b) The first cyclotron, which was invented by E.O. Lawrence and M.S. Livingston in 1934

LAWRENCE BERKELEY LABORATORY/SCIENCE PHOTO LIBRARY

Courtesy of TRIUMF

Figure 23-16 The cyclotron at TRIUMF is the largest cyclotron in the world. It accelerates 1000 trillion protons per second to speeds of 75% of the speed of light. TRIUMF's cyclotron accelerates H⁻ ions: it can extract multiple beams with varying energy levels at very high efficiency, making TRIUMF's accelerator one of the most versatile accelerators in the world.

EXAMPLE 23-3

The Cyclotron Frequency of the TRIUMF Cyclotron

The magnetic field used in the cyclotron at TRIUMF to accelerate H⁻ ions for the purpose of medical research has a strength of 0.3 T.

(a) Calculate the cyclotron frequency of the TRIUMF cyclotron.
(b) Calculate the period of one revolution.
(c) How will increasing the magnetic field approximately 1.5 times, to 0.46 T, affect the cyclotron frequency?

SOLUTION

(a) As per Equation (23-7), the cyclotron frequency is defined as the inverse of the time it takes a charged particle to complete one revolution inside a cyclotron (a circular trajectory of radius R). In the case of the TRIUMF cyclotron, the charged particles are H⁻ ions. Therefore, their charge is -1.6×10^{-19} C, and their mass is approximately equal to the mass of one proton (the mass of two electrons is negligible):

$$m_p \sim 1800\, m_e \rightarrow m_{H^-} = m_p + 2\, m_e \sim 1.67 \times 10^{-27}\, \text{kg}$$

Therefore, the cyclotron frequency, f_{cyc}, is

$$f_{cyc} = \frac{qB}{2\pi m} = \frac{|-1.6 \times 10^{-19}\, \text{C}|(0.3\, \text{T})}{2\pi(1.67 \times 10^{-27}\, \text{kg})} = 4.6 \times 10^6\, \text{s}^{-1}$$

$$f_{cyc} = 4.6 \times 10^6\, \text{Hz}$$

The cyclotron frequency is always positive, thus we use the absolute value of the charge in calculations.

(b) The period of one revolution is the inverse of the cyclotron frequency:

$$T = \frac{1}{f_{cyc}} = (4.6 \times 10^6\, \text{s}^{-1})^{-1} = 2.2 \times 10^{-7}\, \text{s}$$

(c) As discussed in part (a), the cyclotron frequency is proportional to the magnetic field and to the charge-to-mass ratio of the accelerated particles (Equation (23-7)). Therefore, if the magnetic field were to increase 1.5 times, the cyclotron frequency would increase in the same proportion.

Making sense of the result:

The cyclotron frequency does not depend on the radius of the particle's motion. Thus, the oscillating voltage between the dees can have a constant frequency, equal to the cyclotron frequency.

MAKING CONNECTIONS

Cyclotron Use in Medicine

Canada is one of the world leaders in the production of medical isotopes. For example, MDS Nordion, a leading Canadian company that produces radioisotopes for cancer treatment, has recently started building its fourth cyclotron. The new cyclotron will help meet a growing demand for the radioisotopes iodine-123 and palladium-103. Palladium-103 is used to treat prostate cancer, and iodine-123 is primarily used in the diagnosis of thyroid cancer and neurological disorders (such as Alzheimer's and Parkinson's disease). MDS Nordion supplies over two-thirds of the world's reactor-produced isotopes. It is estimated that nearly 20 million nuclear medicine procedures are conducted worldwide each year. MDS Nordion currently operates two commercial cyclotrons at the TRIUMF site located on the University of British Columbia campus, and a third in Fleurus, Belgium.

The Hall Effect

Magnetic fields can also be used to determine the sign of charge carriers. Let us consider a wide conducting strip carrying electric current placed in a uniform magnetic field B perpendicular to it (Figure 23-17). As discussed in Section 22-1, charge carriers can be considered to move with an average drift speed, v_{drift}. Let us assume that an electric current flows clockwise (Figure 23-17(a)), which can be represented by negative charges moving counter-clockwise or by positive charges moving clockwise. When positive charge carriers are moving clockwise, the magnetic field pointing perpendicular to the conducting strip (directed into the strip) exerts an upward magnetic force on the positive charges, so they move toward the top of the conducting plate. The positive charge carriers leave an excess of negative charges behind and create a potential difference across the conductor. The top of the conductor

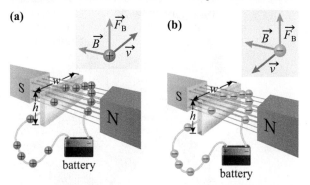

Figure 23-17 The Hall effect. A magnetic field perpendicular to the direction of an electric current creates a potential difference in the direction perpendicular to both the electric current and the magnetic field. (a) The Hall effect in the case of positive charge carriers. (b) The Hall effect in the case of negative charge carriers. The Hall potential difference is indicated with red for the higher potential and blue for the lower potential.

has a *higher* potential than the bottom. When negative particles are moving counterclockwise, the same magnetic field exerts an upward magnetic force on them, shifting them toward the top of the conductor, leaving an excess of positive charges behind. Then the top of the conductor becomes negatively charged and has a *lower* potential than the bottom. This effect, called the **Hall effect**, is named after Edwin Hall (1855–1938), who discovered it in 1879.

However, almost 50 years before Hall, Faraday realized that moving electric charges in a uniform magnetic field create a potential difference in the direction perpendicular to the magnetic field and the charge flow. In the 1830s, Faraday made an unsuccessful attempt to measure the electric voltage between the sides of the Waterloo Bridge across the Thames River in London, England. Faraday expected that salt water flowing through Earth's magnetic field as the tide ebbed would produce a potential difference across the river (Figure 23-18).

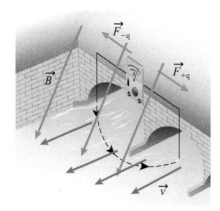

Figure 23-18 In 1831, Faraday tried to measure the potential difference across the Waterloo Bridge over the Thames River due to the motion of ions in Earth's magnetic field. This schematic representation of Faraday's original experiment shows the magnetic field, velocity, and magnetic forces acting on positive and negative ions.

EXAMPLE 23-4

The Thames River as a Natural Dynamo

Estimate the maximum potential difference across the Waterloo Bridge in London, England. The width of the Thames River at the bridge is approximately 265 m. The average flow rate of the Thames at London is approximately 65 m^3/s. Assume that the average depth of the river near the bridge is 2.5 m. London is close enough to the sea that the tides affect the flow of the river at Waterloo Bridge and the salinity of the water—the river here is brackish.

SOLUTION

Let us consider a charged particle moving in brackish Thames River waters, and assume that the vertical component of the Earth's magnetic field in this area equals 45 μT. The magnitude of the magnetic force acting on such a particle is given by the magnetic component of the Lorentz force, Equation (23-2): $F_B = qvB$.

Since the magnetic force is perpendicular to both the magnetic field and the direction of water flow, the force is parallel to the bridge. This magnetic force acts in opposite directions on positive and negative ions, creating a potential difference of $\Delta V = Ed$. In a state of equilibrium, the electrostatic force attracts oppositely charged ions and is equal to the magnetic force pulling them apart:

A potential difference across a conductor is called the **Hall voltage**. A metal conductor has only one type of charge carrier. Therefore, the Hall voltage can be calculated using the fact that in a steady state, the electric field across the conductor creates an electric force equal and opposite to the magnetic force acting on the charge carriers. In a metal conductor with cross-sectional area $w \times h$ (as in Figure 23-17),

$$F_B = qv_{drift}B$$

$$F_E = qE_{Hall} = q\frac{\Delta V_{Hall}}{w}$$

$$qE = qvB$$

therefore, $\Delta V = vBd$

$$E = \frac{\Delta V}{d} \qquad (23\text{-}19)$$

The average speed of the water flowing past the bridge equals the flow rate divided by the cross-sectional area of the river:

$$v \approx \frac{65 \text{ m}^3/\text{s}}{(2.5 \text{ m})(265 \text{ m})} \approx 0.10 \text{ m/s}$$

The flow rate is greatest when the tide is ebbing. As an approximation, we assume that the maximum speed of the water is approximately 0.3 m/s (three times the average value). Then the potential across the bridge is

$$\Delta V = vBd \approx \left(0.3 \frac{\text{m}}{\text{s}}\right)(0.045 \text{ mT})(265 \text{ m}) = 0.0036 \text{ V} = 3.6 \text{ mV}$$

Notice that ion concentration in the Thames River does not affect the potential difference caused by the Hall effect.

Making sense of the result:

The potential difference across the river is quite small. To detect this voltage, Faraday would have needed a voltmeter sensitive enough to measure a few millivolts.

$$F_E = F_B, \quad \text{thus} \quad qv_{drift}B = q\frac{\Delta V_{Hall}}{w}$$

$$v_{drift} = \frac{\Delta V_{Hall}}{wB}$$

$$\Delta V_{Hall} = wv_{drift}B = w\frac{J}{ne}B = w\frac{I/A}{ne}B = w\frac{I}{whne}B$$

KEY EQUATION $\qquad \Delta V_{Hall} = \frac{IB}{hne} \qquad (23\text{-}20)$

CHAPTER 23 | MAGNETIC FIELDS AND MAGNETIC FORCES   615

where I is the electric current, B is the magnetic field, h is the dimension of the conductor perpendicular to both the current and the magnetic field, n is the charge density, and e is the charge of the charge carrier.

The Hall effect is used in magnetic field sensors, proximity switches, position and speed detectors, and current sensors. A Hall effect sensor is a transducer that varies its output voltage in response to changes in a magnetic field. To determine the strength of a magnetic field, a Hall effect sensor measures voltage across a conductor in a direction perpendicular to the current flowing in the conductor, then uses this voltage, the current, and the width of the conductor to calculate the magnetic field.

EXAMPLE 23-5

Using the Hall Effect to Describe Electric Properties

A Hall probe containing a strip of copper 1.5 mm thick and 1.0 cm wide is placed in a uniform magnetic field of 1.5 T. The probe measures a Hall voltage of 0.108 μV when the current through the probe is 10.0 A. Determine

(a) the drift speed of the electrons in the copper strip;
(b) the strength of the electric field across the strip;
(c) the density of the charge carriers in the strip.

SOLUTION

(a) Equation (23-20) can be used to find the drift speed of the electrons inside the probe:

$$v_{drift} = \frac{\Delta V_{Hall}}{wB} = \frac{0.108 \times 10^{-6}\,V}{(1.5 \times 10^{-3}\,m)(1.5\,T)} = 4.8 \times 10^{-5}\,m/s$$

(b) The strength of the electric field inside the wire due to the Hall effect is

$$E = \frac{\Delta V_{Hall}}{w} = \frac{(0.108\,\mu V)}{(1.5 \times 10^{-3}\,m)} = 72\,\mu V/m$$

(c) Then the density of the charge carriers can be expressed as follows:

$$n = \frac{I}{ev_{drift}A}$$

$$= \frac{10\,A}{(1.6 \times 10^{-19}\,C)(4.8 \times 10^{-5}\,m/s)(1.5 \times 10^{-3}\,m)(1.0 \times 10^{-2}\,m)}$$

$$= 8.7 \times 10^{28}\,m^{-3}$$

Making sense of the result:

The values of the drift speed (4.8×10^{-5} m/s) of the charge carriers in copper and of the charge density in copper (8.7×10^{28} m^{-3}) agree with the experimentally measured values listed in Table 22-1 in Chapter 22.

23-4 The Magnetic Force on a Current-Carrying Wire

As discussed earlier, a charged particle moving inside a magnetic field experiences a magnetic force. Therefore, a magnetic field exerts a force on each charged particle moving inside a current-carrying wire. The net magnetic force acting on the wire depends on the net motion of the electrons and, hence, on the drift velocity of the electrons.

Figure 23-19 shows a series of experiments to study the effect of a magnetic field on a current-carrying wire placed between the poles of a permanent magnet. As expected, a wire carrying no current is unaffected by the magnetic field. Since free electrons inside the wire move randomly, the effect of the magnetic field on the electrons averages to zero. However, when electric current flows in the wire, the effect of a magnetic field becomes pronounced. The direction of conventional current is defined in terms of the flow of positively charged carriers. Thus, to find the direction of the magnetic force on the wire, we use the same right-hand rule that we used to find the direction of a magnetic force acting on a positively charged carrier. Note that a

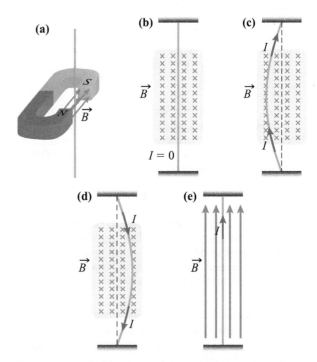

Figure 23-19 The effect of a magnetic field on a current-carrying wire. (a) A wire suspended vertically between the poles of a permanent magnet. (b) A wire carrying no current ($I = 0$) in a uniform magnetic field perpendicular to the wire. (c) A wire carrying an upward nonzero current in a uniform magnetic field perpendicular to the wire. (d) A wire carrying a downward nonzero current in a uniform magnetic field perpendicular to the wire. (e) A wire carrying a nonzero current in a uniform magnetic field parallel to the wire.

magnetic field directed parallel or antiparallel to the current does not exert any force on the wire.

We now derive an expression for the magnitude of the magnetic force on a current-carrying wire of length l and cross-sectional area A (Figure 23-20). Let us assume that all charge carriers have the same charge e and are moving with the same drift velocity $\vec{v}_{drift}$. Then the magnetic force acting on each charge carrier is

$$\vec{F}_B = e\vec{v}_{drift} \times \vec{B}$$

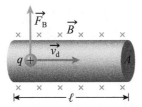

Figure 23-20 Calculating the effect of the magnetic field on a straight current-carrying wire. To calculate the net force on a segment of the wire, we calculate the magnetic force on each moving charge (considering that the charges move with an average drift velocity $\vec{v}_{drift}$) and then add the forces acting on all the charges in this segment.

Since the volume of the wire is Al, the total charge on the charge carriers in the wire is $q = nAl$, where n is the charge density in the wire.

The net magnetic force acting on the wire is

$$\vec{F} = nlA\vec{v}_{drift} \times \vec{B} \qquad (23\text{-}21)$$

Substituting $I = nv_{drift}$, and recalling that the direction of the drift velocity of positive charge carriers coincides with the direction of the electric current, we get

$$\vec{F} = nAv_{drift}\vec{l} \times \vec{B} = I\vec{l} \times \vec{B}$$

KEY EQUATION $$\vec{F} = I\vec{l} \times \vec{B} \qquad (23\text{-}22)$$

where $\vec{l}$ is a small segment of the wire in the direction of the electric current I.

For the above calculation we assumed that the wire is straight.

We now consider a wire of arbitrary shape (Figure 23-21), which consists of an infinite number of small segments, $d\vec{l}$. The magnetic force acting on each

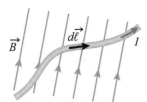

Figure 23-21 Calculating the effect of the magnetic field on a current-carrying wire of an arbitrary shape. The wire can be split into small straight segments $d\vec{l}$, and the effects of the magnetic field on each segment can be added to find the net force on the wire.

individual segment is expressed by Equation (23-22). To find the net magnetic force on the wire, we integrate the forces on the infinitesimal segments:

KEY EQUATION $$\vec{F} = \int_a^b I d\vec{l} \times \vec{B} = -I \int_a^b \vec{B} \times d\vec{l} \qquad (23\text{-}23)$$

Note that *the electric current flowing through all the wire segments is the same.* The negative sign on the right-hand side of the equation results from the noncommutative nature of the cross product: $d\vec{l} \times \vec{B} = -\vec{B} \times d\vec{l}$. Equation (23-23) provides a way to define the ampere: a uniform magnetic field of 1 T perpendicular to the wire carrying an electric current of 1 A exerts a force of 1 N on a 1 m length of wire:

$$1\text{ A} = \frac{1\text{ N}}{1\text{ m} \cdot 1\text{ T}} \qquad (23\text{-}24)$$

✓ **CHECKPOINT**

C-23-7 The Magnetic Force Acting on a Current-Carrying Wire

An electric current of 1 A flows through a long, straight vertical conductor located near Earth's surface. The horizontal component of Earth's magnetic field in this location is 0.4 mT. What is the magnetic force per metre of this conductor?

(a) 0
(b) 0.0004 N
(c) 4 N
(d) 2500 N

C-23-7 (b) Use Equation (23-22).

 PEER TO PEER

At first, I was stressed out by the electricity and magnetism equations. However, later I realized that I should start with understanding the problem and finding the approximate answer conceptually before jumping into the calculations. Understanding the problem first made it much easier for me.

LO 5

23-5 The Torque on a Current-Carrying Loop in a Magnetic Field

Let us consider a rectangular loop of wire, with the dimensions a and b, carrying a current in a clockwise direction (Figure 23-22(a)). This loop is placed in a uniform magnetic field of magnitude B directed to the right.

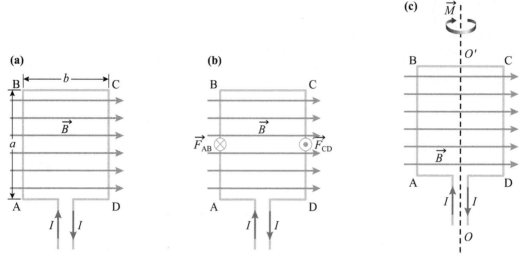

Figure 23-22 (a) A rectangular current-carrying loop in a uniform magnetic field (b) Magnetic forces acting on opposite sides of the carrying-current loop (c) A couple moment M (torque) acting on a current-carrying loop in a uniform magnetic field

The magnetic field is parallel to the sides BC and DA of the loop; therefore $\vec{F}_{BC} = \vec{F}_{DA} = 0$. Sides AB and CD are perpendicular to the magnetic field. Since an electric current in AB flows in the opposite direction to the electric current in CD, the magnetic forces on the two opposite sides of the loop are opposite to each other: the magnetic force on AB is directed into the page, and the magnetic force on CD is directed out of the page (Figure 23-22(b)). Mathematically, this result can be expressed as follows:

$$\vec{F}_{ABCD} = \vec{F}_{AB} + \vec{F}_{BC} + \vec{F}_{CD} + \vec{F}_{DA}$$

$$= I\vec{l}_{AB} \times \vec{B} + I\vec{l}_{BC} \times \vec{B} + I\vec{l}_{CD} \times \vec{B} + I\vec{l}_{DA} \times \vec{B}$$

$$= \vec{F}_{AB} + \vec{F}_{CD}$$

Forces $\vec{F}_{AB}$ and $\vec{F}_{CD}$ are equal in magnitude and opposite in direction:

$$F_{AB} = F_{CD} = IaB \qquad (23\text{-}25)$$

Since forces $\vec{F}_{BC}$ and $\vec{F}_{DA}$ are applied to opposite sides of the loop and are perpendicular to its plane, they create a torque on the loop, causing it to rotate about the OO'- axis (Figure 23-22(c)). The magnitude of this torque is

$$\tau_{ABCD} = \tau_{AB} + \tau_{CD}$$

$$= \frac{b}{2}F_{AB} + \frac{b}{2}F_{CD} = \frac{b}{2}IaB + \frac{b}{2}IaB = abIB = AIB$$

KEY EQUATION $\qquad \tau_{ABCD} = IAB \qquad (23\text{-}26)$

where A is the area of the loop: $A = ab$.

The torque exerted on the loop by the magnetic field is proportional to the area of the loop, the electric current and the magnitude of the magnetic field. It is common to describe the orientation of the loop by a vector $\vec{A}$,

such that its magnitude represents the area of the loop and its direction is defined by a right-hand rule: when the fingers of your right-hand are curled in the direction of the electric current, the direction of the thumb indicates the direction of the vector $\vec{A}$ (Figure 23-23).

Figure 23-23 A right-hand rule for determining the orientation of a current-carrying loop using vector $\vec{A}$ and magnetic dipole moment $\vec{\mu}$

As discussed in Chapter 8, torque is a vector quantity that points along the object's axis of rotation, indicating clockwise or counterclockwise rotation. The direction of rotation is called the "sense of the torque vector." For the loop in Figure 23-24, for example, the direction of $\vec{\tau}$ is perpendicular to both vectors $\vec{A}$ and $\vec{B}$:

KEY EQUATION $\qquad \vec{\tau}_{ABCD} = I\vec{A} \times \vec{B} \qquad (23\text{-}27)$

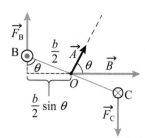

Figure 23-24 The top view of a vertical rectangular loop carrying a current submerged in a uniform horizontal magnetic field. The loop is free to rotate about its vertical axis of symmetry.

Figure 23-25 A rectangular loop carrying current in a uniform magnetic field. The maximum torque on this current-carrying loop is 0.15 N·m.

The magnitude of the torque is determined by the properties of the loop and the external magnetic field. To describe these properties, we introduce the concept of a **magnetic dipole moment**, $\vec{\mu}$, (Figure 23-24) defined as follows:

$$\vec{\mu} = I\vec{A} \qquad (23\text{-}28)$$

The concept of a magnetic dipole helps clarify a key difference between electric and magnetic fields. An electric dipole, a combination of two equally but oppositely charged objects, in a uniform electric field experiences a torque that acts to align the dipole with the electric field lines: $\vec{\tau}_E = \vec{p} \times \vec{E}$ (Chapter 20), where $\vec{p}$ is the electric dipole moment. However, there is no evidence that magnetic charge or magnetic monopoles exist. A **magnetic dipole** is a current-carrying loop or a permanent magnet, not a combination of two magnetic monopoles. A magnetic field exerts a torque on a magnetic dipole, directed such that the magnetic dipole moment aligns with the magnetic field:

KEY EQUATION
$$\vec{\tau}_B = \vec{\mu} \times \vec{B} \qquad (23\text{-}29)$$

You may have noticed that a current-carrying loop behaves like a permanent magnet, with the polarity of the loop depending on the direction of the current. Only the magnetic field component parallel to the plane of the loop results in a torque on it. When a loop positioned parallel to a uniform magnetic field starts rotating, the effect of the magnetic field on the loop changes (Figure 23-24).

The component of the magnetic field parallel to the surface of the rotating loop can be expressed as $B\sin\theta$, where θ is an angle between the normal to the loop and the magnetic field (Figure 23-25). Then the net torque (a couple moment) produced by the magnetic force is

$$\tau = blaB\sin\theta = AIB\sin\theta \qquad (23\text{-}30)$$

Consequently, the net torque varies as the loop rotates, reaching a maximum value when the magnetic field is parallel to the plane of the loop ($\theta = 90°$) and a minimum value when the magnetic field is perpendicular to it ($\theta = 0°$):

$$\tau_{max} = blaB, \quad \text{when } \theta = 90°$$

$$\tau_{min} = blaB\sin(0°) = 0, \quad \text{when } \theta = 0° \qquad (23\text{-}31)$$

Although we derived this expression for a rectangular loop, we can show that it holds true for any loop.

✓ **CHECKPOINT**

C-23-8 Interactions of a Current-Carrying Loop and a Magnetic Field

A current-carrying loop hangs from a light thread (Figure 23-26). A permanent magnet is brought close to the loop so that the north pole of the magnet faces the loop. Which statement best describes the interaction between the magnet and the loop?

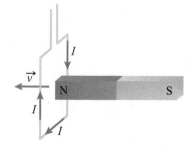

Figure 23-26 C-23-8

(a) There is no interaction because electric currents do not repel or attract magnets.
(b) They will attract.
(c) They will repel.
(d) There is not enough information to determine.

C-23-8 (b) The loop is a magnetic dipole oriented such that it is attracted to the magnet.

MAKING CONNECTIONS

Can You Build an Electric Motor?

Many everyday appliances use electric motors, for example, microwave ovens, food processors, fans, DVD players, and washing machines. These motors all apply the concept of a magnetic torque on a current-carrying loop. Although some motors, such as those in DVD players and computer hard drives, involve complex precision technology, you can build a simple DC motor with a flashlight, a battery, a few pieces of wire, a small permanent magnet, a pair of scissors, a few paper clips, tape, and any convenient cylinder, such as a thick marker, as shown in Figure 23-27.

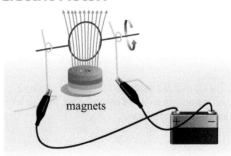

Figure 23-27 A simple DC motor

EXAMPLE 23-6

The Magnetic Torque on a Simple Electric Motor

Estimate the maximum value of the magnetic torque in the simple electric motor shown in Figure 23-27, given that the magnetic field created by the magnets is 0.4 T, the battery has a voltage of 3 V, the number of copper wire loops is 2, and the area of each loop is 5 cm². Assume that the resistance of all the wire used in the motor is 1 Ω.

SOLUTION

The magnetic torque acting on a current-carrying loop in a magnetic field can be found using Equation (23-26):

$$\tau_{max} = 2IAB = 2\frac{V}{R}AB = 2\frac{3\text{ V}}{1\text{ }\Omega}(5\times10^{-4}\text{ m}^2)(0.4\text{ T})$$

$$= 2\times6\times10^{-4}\frac{\text{V}\cdot\text{m}^2\cdot\text{T}}{\Omega} = 1\times10^{-3}\text{ N}\cdot\text{m}$$

Making sense of the result:

This simple experiment helps us make two interesting observations: First, the low resistance of the wire allows a relatively large current to flow from the battery. Nevertheless, the magnetic torque is very small. Therefore, in order for this motor to work, the loop has to be very light. The second observation is more profound. We discussed earlier that magnetic force cannot do work on a moving charge because it is directed perpendicular to the charge's velocity (Equation (23-1)). In the case of an electric motor, it appears to do work on a moving current-carrying wire. How can this happen? The solution to this apparent paradox is that the physics involved is really more complex than finding the magnetic force on the electrons flowing in the wire, although that standard derivation does give the correct answer. In reality, the magnetic force on the electrons exerts a transverse force on them as in the Hall effect (Equation (23-20)). This charge separation creates an electric force across the wire, which exerts a force on the positively charged lattice atoms, doing the work.

LO 6

23-6   The Biot-Savart Law

Electric charges create electric fields, but we have yet to discuss the sources of magnetic fields. The nature of the sources of magnetic fields was a mystery for centuries. The equations we have derived so far show how magnetic fields affect moving charges, but not vice versa. Is it reasonable to assume that a magnetic field can be affected by an electric current? Could electric current be a source of a magnetic field? Although the answers to these questions might seem obvious today, two centuries ago they were at the forefront of scientific inquiry. The first step in solving this mystery was made by the Danish scientist Hans Christian Oersted (1777–1851).

In 1820, Oersted was able to show that a compass needle deflects from magnetic north when an electric current is switched on or off in a nearby wire. This discovery motivated the French scientists Jean-Baptiste Biot (1774–1862) and Félix Savart (1791–1841) to conduct experiments not only to confirm that electric current is the source of magnetic fields, but to find a mathematical expression for the relationship between them. The Biot–Savart law describes how to calculate a magnetic field generated by an infinitesimally small element of a steady electric current (Figure 23-28):

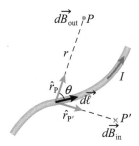

Figure 23-28 Using the Biot–Savart law to find a magnetic field created by a long current-carrying wire

$$d\vec{B} = \frac{\mu_0}{4\pi} \frac{Id\vec{l} \times \hat{r}}{r^2} = \frac{\mu_0}{4\pi} \frac{Id\vec{l} \times \vec{r}}{r^3} \quad (23\text{-}32)$$

In this equation, $d\vec{l}$ is an infinitesimally small element of the wire carrying current I, so $d\vec{l}$ is directed in the direction of the conventional current; r is the distance from the element $d\vec{l}$ to an arbitrary point at which the magnetic field is calculated; $\hat{r}$ is the unit vector in the direction of $\vec{r}$; and μ_0 is a constant called the **permeability constant of free space** and has a value of $4\pi \times 10^{-7}$ T·m/A. The term 4π was introduced in the definition in order to make Maxwell equations of electromagnetism appear more elegant.

Let us examine the Biot–Savart law more closely:

- Since the expression for $d\vec{B}$ includes the cross product of $d\vec{l}$ and $\vec{r}$, $d\vec{B}$ is always perpendicular to the element of electric current that created it, as well as to the position vector $\vec{r}$ connecting $d\vec{l}$ and the point at which the magnetic field is calculated. The direction of the magnetic field can be observed experimentally by spreading iron filings near a long, straight current-carrying wire (Figure 23-29).

- $d\vec{B}$ is inversely proportional to the square of the distance from the point for which the field is calculated to the infinitesimal element of electric current creating the field.

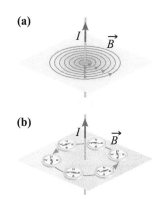

Figure 23-29 (a) A magnetic field created by a long, current-carrying wire. Iron fillings spread near the current-carrying wire. (b) Compass needles indicate the direction of the magnetic field surrounding the current-carrying wire.

- Both $d\vec{B}$ and the resultant magnetic field are proportional to the current.

- Since $d\vec{B}$ is proportional to the cross product of $d\vec{l}$ and $\vec{r}$, the magnetic field depends on the sine of the angle between the infinitesimally small element of the wire $d\vec{l}$ and the position vector $\vec{r}$.

The Biot–Savart law for magnetism is analogous to Coulomb's law for electric fields. Both laws show that the strength of the field is proportional to its source: q for an electric field and the electric current element $d\vec{l} = Id\hat{l}$, where $\hat{l}$ is a unit vector in the $\vec{l}$ direction for a magnetic field. In both laws, the field strength is inversely proportional to the square of the distance from the source of the field.

However, there are also some important differences: electric field lines always start on positive charges and end on negative charges. Sources of electric field (positive and negative charges) can be separated, with a positive charge defined as a source and a negative charge as a sink. We cannot, however, separate the south and north poles of a magnet because, as far as we know, there are no magnetic monopoles. Since there is no magnetic monopole, magnetic field lines are continuous and closed: they have neither a beginning nor an end, and they surround the electric current that created them.

 EXAMPLE 23-7

The Magnetic Field Created by an Infinitely Long, Straight Current-Carrying Wire

Find the magnetic field created by the infinitely long, straight current-carrying wire at point P located a distance R from the wire (Figure 23-30).

SOLUTION

We use the Biot–Savart law to calculate the magnetic field at point P. Let us denote the current flowing through the wire I, and the shortest distance from the wire to the point where the magnetic field is to be calculated R. To use the Biot–Savart law (Equation (23-32)), we have to calculate the contribution of the current in the wire segment $d\vec{l}$ ($d\vec{l} = Id\hat{l}$)

(continued)

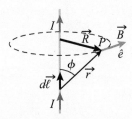

Figure 23-30 Calculating the magnetic field created by an infinitely long, straight current-carrying wire at point P located a distance R from the wire

to the magnetic field at point P. Then we add the effects of all the segments along the wire. The magnetic field produced by the wire segment $d\vec{l}$ has the direction $d\vec{l} \times \vec{r}$. The resultant vector is perpendicular to both $d\vec{l}$ and $\vec{r}$, and we denote its direction using a unit vector, $\hat{e}$:

$$d\vec{l} \times \vec{r} = \hat{e}r\sin\theta\, dl = \hat{e}R\, dl$$

Now we are ready to apply the Biot–Savart law:

$$d\vec{B} = \frac{\mu_0}{4\pi}\frac{I d\vec{l} \times \vec{r}}{r^3} = \frac{\mu_0 I}{4\pi}\frac{\hat{e}R\, dl}{(l^2 + R^2)^{3/2}} = \hat{e}\frac{\mu_0 IR}{4\pi}\frac{dl}{(l^2 + R^2)^{3/2}}$$

where $r = \sqrt{l^2 + R^2}$.

The magnitude of the magnetic field at point P can be expressed as follows:

$$\vec{B} = \int_{-\infty}^{\infty} \hat{e}\frac{\mu_0 IR}{4\pi}\frac{dl}{(l^2 + R^2)^{3/2}} = \hat{e}\frac{\mu_0 IR}{4\pi}\int_{-\infty}^{\infty}\frac{dl}{(l^2 + R^2)^{3/2}}$$

This integral can be calculated using two substitutions: $x = el/R$ and then $x = \cot\phi = \cos\phi/\sin\phi$:

First substitution: $\dfrac{l}{R} \equiv x$; $dl = R\, dx$

$$\vec{B} = \hat{e}\frac{\mu_0 IR}{4\pi}\int_{-\infty}^{\infty}\frac{dl}{(l^2 + R^2)^{3/2}} = \hat{e}\frac{\mu_0 IR}{4\pi R^3}\int_{-\infty}^{\infty}\frac{R\, dx}{(x^2 + 1)^{3/2}}$$

$$= \hat{e}\frac{\mu_0 IR^2}{4\pi R^3}\int_{-\infty}^{\infty}\frac{dx}{(x^2 + 1)^{3/2}} = \hat{e}\frac{\mu_0 I}{4\pi R}\int_{-\infty}^{\infty}\frac{dx}{(x^2 + 1)^{3/2}}$$

Second substitution: $x \equiv \cot\phi = \dfrac{\cos\phi}{\sin\phi}$; $dx = -\dfrac{d\phi}{\sin^2\phi}$

$$\vec{B} = \hat{e}\frac{\mu_0 I}{4\pi R}\int_{-\infty}^{\infty}\frac{dx}{(x^2 + 1)^{3/2}} = -\hat{e}\frac{2\mu_0 I}{4\pi R}\int_0^{\pi/2}\sin\phi\, d\phi = \hat{e}\frac{\mu_0 I}{2\pi R}$$

Making sense of the result:

It has been confirmed experimentally that the magnetic field created by current flowing through a long, straight wire is directed along concentric circles surrounding the wire (Figure 23-29). The magnitude of this field is described by the following equation:

$$B_{\text{outside straight wire}} = \frac{\mu_0 I}{2\pi R} \tag{23-33}$$

The direction of the magnetic field due to the electric current can be conveniently established using the following right-hand rule for the magnetic field (Figure 23-31): When you point your right thumb in the direction of the electric current and curl your fingers, the direction of the curled fingers is the direction of the magnetic field lines that form concentric circles around the current-carrying wire.

Figure 23-31 The right-hand rule for determining the direction of the magnetic field surrounding a long, straight current-carrying wire. The magnetic field lines create closed circular concentric loops. The magnitude of the magnetic field can be found using Equation (23-34).

EXAMPLE 23-8

The Magnetic Field Created by a Circular Current-Carrying Loop

Derive an expression for the magnetic field along the axis of symmetry of a circular loop of radius R that carries an electric current I.

SOLUTION

For convenience, we choose a coordinate system with the current-carrying loop in the yz-plane (Figure 23-32). We divide the loop into an infinitely large number of infinitesimally small current elements: $d\vec{l} = I d\vec{l}$. The Biot–Savart law

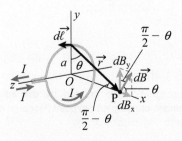

Figure 23-32 Using the Biot–Savart law to calculate the magnetic field created by a current-carrying loop along its axis of symmetry

can be used to calculate the contribution of each element to the magnetic field at point P on the axis of symmetry of the loop. Let x be the distance of this point from the centre of the loop, O. Then,

$$d\vec{B} = \frac{\mu_0}{4\pi}\frac{Id\vec{l}\times\hat{r}}{r^2} = \frac{\mu_0 I}{4\pi}\frac{d\vec{l}\times\hat{r}}{(x^2+R^2)}$$

First, consider the cross product of $d\vec{l}$ and $\vec{r}$. Since point P is on the loop's axis of symmetry, the unit vector $\hat{r}$ is perpendicular to any loop element $d\vec{l}$. Therefore, $|d\vec{l}\times\hat{r}| = dl$. The direction of the cross product, shown in Figure 23-32, is perpendicular to both $d\vec{l}$ and $\vec{r}$. The magnetic field created by this loop element has two components, B_y and B_z. Now consider another element of the loop $d\vec{l}''$ symmetrical to the element $d\vec{l}$ about the centre of the loop. Since the elements $d\vec{l}$ and $d\vec{l}''$ are antiparallel, the magnetic fields created by them have x-components that are equal and y-components that are equal in magnitude but opposite in direction. The same consideration is applicable to any pair of symmetrical loop elements: the magnetic field components perpendicular to the loop's axis of symmetry cancel out, and the components parallel to the axis add up. The dB_x components can be calculated as follows:

$$dB_x = \frac{\mu_0}{4\pi}\frac{I\cos\theta\,dl}{(x^2+R^2)} = \frac{\mu_0}{4\pi}\frac{Idl}{(x^2+R^2)}\cos\theta$$

$$= \frac{\mu_0}{4\pi}\frac{Idl}{(x^2+R^2)}\frac{R}{(x^2+R^2)^{1/2}}$$

$$= \frac{\mu_0}{4\pi}\frac{IRdl}{(x^2+R^2)^{3/2}}$$

To calculate the net magnetic field created by the entire loop, we integrate the contributions of all the loop elements:

$$\vec{B}_{loop} = \int_0^{2\pi R}\frac{\mu_0}{4\pi}\frac{IRdl}{(x^2+R^2)^{3/2}}$$

$$= \frac{\mu_0 IR}{4\pi(x^2+R^2)^{3/2}}\int_0^{2\pi R}dl = \frac{\mu_0 IR2\pi R}{4\pi(x^2+R^2)^{3/2}}$$

$$= \frac{\mu_0}{2}\frac{IR^2}{(x^2+R^2)^{3/2}}$$

Thus, the magnetic field created by a circular current-carrying loop along its axis of symmetry is collinear with this axis. The direction of the magnetic field can be determined using the right-hand rule for current, and its magnitude is

KEY EQUATION
$$B_{loop} = \frac{\mu_0}{2}\frac{IR^2}{(x^2+R^2)^{3/2}} \qquad (23\text{-}34)$$

Making sense of the result:

The magnetic field of a circular current-carrying loop along its axis of symmetry diminishes to zero when the distance from the centre of the loop is much larger than the size of the loop: $x \gg R$. The magnetic field in the centre of the loop ($x = 0$) is

KEY EQUATION
$$B_{loop\text{-}centre} = \frac{\mu_0}{2}\frac{IR^2}{R^3} = \frac{\mu_0}{2}\frac{I}{R} \qquad (23\text{-}35)$$

✓ **CHECKPOINT**

C-23-9 Ranking Magnetic Field Strengths Produced by Current-carrying Circular Loops

For the six circular loops in Figure 23-33, which of the following correctly ranks the magnetic fields in the centre of each loop?

(a) $B_D > B_B > B_A > B_C > B_F > B_E$
(b) $B_E > B_F = B_A > B_C = B_B > B_D$
(c) $B_D > B_B = B_C > B_A = B_F > B_E$
(d) $B_B > B_C = B_A > B_E = B_F > B_D$
(e) $B_B = B_D > B_C > B_A > B_E > B_F$

(a)

(b)

(c)

(d)

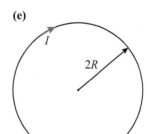
(e)

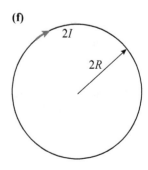
(f)

Figure 23-33   C-23-9

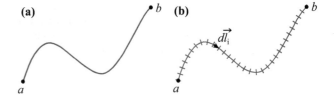

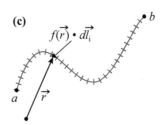

Figure 23-35 (a) An arbitrary line connecting two points *a* and *b* along the path of integration. (b) The line can be divided into infinitesimally small segments, $\vec{dl_i}$. (c) The integral along the path of integration can be considered as a sum of the products of $f(\vec{r})$ and $\vec{dl_i}$.

23-7 Ampère's Law

Although the Biot–Savart law provides a technique for determining the magnetic field around a wire of any arbitrary shape, the calculations can be somewhat daunting even for relatively simple shapes, as we saw in Examples 23-7 and 23-8. In this respect, the Biot–Savart law resembles Coulomb's law, which can be used to determine the electric field around any distribution of charge, but involves difficult calculations unless the charge distribution is highly symmetric. When a continuous charge distribution has certain symmetries, Gauss's law significantly simplifies the electric field calculations. Similarly, Ampère's law allows much easier calculations of magnetic fields when the path of the current is symmetric. Before we define Ampère's law, we need to introduce line integrals.

Overview of Line Integrals

In the previous chapters, we saw that the integral of a function $\int f(x)dx$ is an infinite sum of the products of the values of the function $f(x)$ and an infinitesimally small element dx along a path of integration from $x = a$ to $x = b$, where *a* and *b* are the limits of integration. Thus, dx is the lower limit of small steps, Δx, along the path of integration, and

$$\lim_{N \to \infty} \sum_{i=1}^{N} f(x)\Delta x_i = \int_a^b f(x)dx \qquad (23\text{-}36)$$

Consequently, an integral represents the area under the graph of $f(x)$ (Figure 23-34).

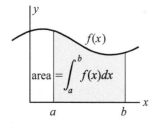

Figure 23-34 The area under the graph represents integration geometrically.

Sometimes, instead of varying an independent variable along a linear coordinate axis, it is useful to vary it along a 2-D or a 3-D curve (Figure 23-35). Such line integrals are defined as

$$\lim_{N \to \infty} \sum_{i=1}^{N} f(\vec{r}) \cdot \Delta \vec{l_i} = \int_a^b f(\vec{r}) \cdot \vec{dl} \qquad (23\text{-}37)$$

An integral defined by Equation (23-37) is a general case of a line integral along a straight line, such as the *x*-coordinate axis. The function $f(x)$ that we want to integrate can be either a scalar or a vector function. Each infinitesimally small element of the curve is considered an infinitesimally small vector element $\vec{dl}$ because it has both magnitude and direction. Consider a line integral where the magnetic field has a constant magnitude and is parallel to the line of integration. In this case, the integral of the scalar product of the magnetic field and the curve element can be simplified. Notice that although the magnetic field depends on $\vec{r}$, for simplicity, we will omit $\vec{r}$ from the notation of the magnetic field and will denote it as $\vec{B}$.

$$\int_a^b \vec{B} \cdot \vec{dl} = \int_a^b B \cdot dl = B\int_a^b dl = BL \qquad (23\text{-}38)$$

where L is the total displacement along the curve of integration.

Closed loop path integrals are integrals around a closed loop, so the initial and the final points of integration coincide. Such integrals are denoted by a small circle over the conventional integral sign, for example, $\oint \vec{B} \cdot \vec{dl}$. Closed loop path integrals are used to calculate the magnetic fields created by electric currents.

Ampère's Law

French physicist and mathematician André-Marie Ampère (1775–1836), for whom the unit of electric current is named, studied magnetic fields created by current-carrying wires. He noticed that the direction of a magnetic field is always perpendicular to the direction of the wire. He also realized that magnetic field lines should have a symmetry corresponding to the symmetry of the wire. The only way this symmetry can occur is if the magnetic field lines form concentric circles around the wire in the planes perpendicular to it (Figure 23-36).

path of integration $\overrightarrow{dl}$

Figure 23-36 The magnetic field created by a straight current-carrying wire

Ampère's law states:

1. The magnetic field in the space around an electric current is proportional to the electric current that serves as its source, just as an electric field is proportional to the charge that serves as its source.

2. For any closed loop path (Figure 23-36), the sum of the scalar products of the length element $\overrightarrow{dl}$ and of the magnetic field $\overrightarrow{B}$ (which can be expressed as the line integral along the closed path) is equal to the permeability of free space (or magnetic constant) μ_0 multiplied by the electric current enclosed by the loop:

KEY EQUATION
$$\oint \overrightarrow{B} \cdot \overrightarrow{dl} = \mu_0 \Sigma I_{enc} \qquad (23\text{-}39)$$

When electric currents enclosed by an integral path flow in opposite directions, they have opposite signs. The direction of the magnetic field can be determined using a right-hand rule: when you orient your right-hand such that the thumb points in the direction of the electric current, the curled fingers point in the direction of the magnetic field. It is especially convenient to apply Ampère's law when one can choose a path of integration along the magnetic field lines. Notice that only electric currents *enclosed* by the path of integration contribute to the magnetic field (similar to Gauss's law (Equation (20-15), where only electric charges enclosed

by the surface are used for calculating the electric flux contribute to the electric field).

Applications of Ampère's law

We now look at three common applications of Ampère's law.

An Infinitely Long, Straight Current-carrying Wire
For a path of integration, we choose a circle centred on the wire and perpendicular to it (Figure 23-36). The magnetic field at any point along this path is tangent to the integration path element $\overrightarrow{dl}$ Moreover, due to the symmetry of the problem, the magnitude of the magnetic field is constant along the path of integration. Thus, we can apply Ampère's law (Equation (23-39)) as follows:

$$\oint \overrightarrow{B}(\overrightarrow{r}) \cdot \overrightarrow{dl} = \mu_0 \Sigma I_{enc}$$

$$\oint B dl = 2\pi R B = \mu_0 I$$

$$B = \frac{\mu_0 I}{2\pi R}$$

The same result was obtained earlier using the Biot–Savart law (Equation (23-33)). However, the application of Ampère's law greatly simplifies the derivation.

 EXAMPLE 23-9

The Magnetic Field Around a Long, Straight Current-Carrying Wire

Find the magnetic field at a distance of 1 m from a long, straight wire carrying a current of 1 A.

SOLUTION

This problem can be solved using Equation (23-33):

$$B = \frac{\mu_0 I}{2\pi R} = \frac{\left(4\pi \times 10^{-7} \frac{\text{T}\cdot\text{m}}{\text{A}}\right)(1\text{ A})}{2\pi(1\text{ m})}$$

$$= 2 \times 10^{-7}\text{ T} = 2 \times 10^{-4}\text{ mT}$$

Making sense of the result:

It is worth noting that Earth's magnetic field is in the range of 30 to 60 mT, which is approximately 10^5 times stronger than the magnetic field 1 m from a long, straight wire carrying 1 A of electric current.

C-23-10 Ranking the Line Integrals

Figure 23-37 shows six different configurations of electric currents going into or coming out of the plane of the page. The closed loop path of integration is indicated by a dashed line in each diagram. Which of the following correctly ranks the magnitudes of the $(\vec{r} \cdot \vec{dl})$ integrals for these configurations?

(a) (c) > (e) > (a) = (b) = (d) > (f)
(b) (f) > (a) = (b) = (d) = (c) > (e)
(c) (c) > (e) > (a) > (b) > (f) > (d)
(d) (f) > (e) > (d) = (b) = (a) > (c)
(e) (a) > (d) > (b) = (c) = (d) > (f)

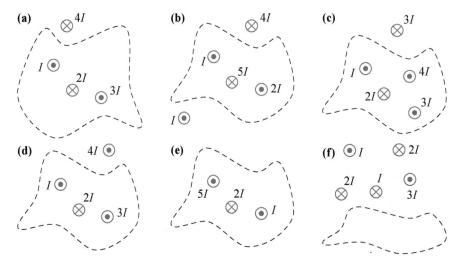

Figure 23-37   Checkpoint C-23-10

C-23-10 (a) According to Ampère's law, the path that encloses the most electric current has the highest value of the $(\vec{r}) \cdot (d\vec{l})$ loop integral along it.

EXAMPLE 23-10

The Magnetic Field Inside and Outside a Long, Current-Carrying Wire

Determine the magnetic field inside and outside a long wire of radius R carrying an electric current I.

SOLUTION

Figure 23-38(a) shows an electric wire of radius R carrying an electric current I. To find the magnetic field inside the wire, let us assume a constant current density across the wire. Let us choose an arbitrary point P a distance r from the centre of the wire, such that $r < R$. Now let us draw a circular loop of radius r with the wire at its centre. This loop goes through point P. To find how much current is enclosed by the loop, we calculate the current density inside the wire and multiply it by the cross-sectional area of the wire enclosed by it:

$$\sigma = \frac{I}{\pi R^2} \tag{23-40}$$

$$B_{\text{inside wire}} = \frac{\mu_0 I}{2\pi R} = \frac{\mu_0}{2\pi r}(\sigma \pi r^2)$$

$$= \frac{\mu_0}{2\pi r} \frac{I}{\pi R^2} \pi r^2 = \frac{\mu_0 I}{2\pi R^2} r, \, r \leq R$$

Making sense of the result:

The magnetic field *inside* the current-carrying wire is proportional to the distance from the centre of the wire. This relationship is shown in Figure 23-38(b). The magnetic field *outside* the wire is inversely proportional to the distance from its centre, as indicated by Equation (23-33):

$$B = \frac{\mu_0 I}{2\pi r}, \, r \geq R$$

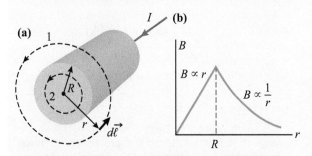

Figure 23-38   (a) The cross section of a current-carrying wire (b) A plot of B(r), the dependence of the magnitude of the magnetic field created by the current-carrying wire on distance from the centre of the wire

Coaxial Cables A **coaxial cable** is an electrical cable that consists of an inner conductor surrounded by an outer cylindrical conductor. The two conductors are separated by an insulating spacer of constant thickness, and the cable usually has an insulating jacket over the outer conductor (Figure 23-39). The term "coaxial" is used because the inner and outer conductors have the same axis of symmetry. Coaxial cables have many applications, in particular, for carrying high-frequency voltages such as for TV and radio signals. Coaxial cables have electrical characteristics that help reduce signal losses in long cable runs and shield against electromagnetic interference.

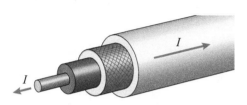

Figure 23-39 A cross section of a coaxial cable

Ampère's law can be used to show that the electromagnetic field carrying the signal exists only in the space between the inner and the outer conductors of the coaxial cable when the currents passed in the two conductors have equal magnitude but opposite direction. Outside the coaxial cable, the magnetic field created by the electric current flowing in one direction is equal and opposite to the magnetic field created by the opposite current (see problem 68).

Solenoids In Chapter 20, we found that two large, oppositely charged parallel metal plates create a uniform electric field in the space between them. A solenoid is a device that produces a nearly uniform magnetic field (Figure 23-40). Solenoids are widely used because the uniform magnetic field inside them is determined solely by their structure and the current flowing through them.

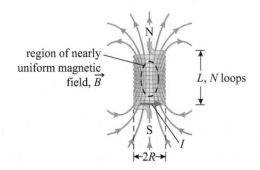

Figure 23-40 A solenoid of length L and radius r consists of N current-carrying loops.

Recall the expression for the magnetic field created in the centre ($x = 0$) of a current-carrying loop (Equation (23-35)):

$$B_{\text{loop-centre}} = \frac{\mu_0}{2} \frac{I}{R}$$

Now we draw magnetic field lines created by a single loop, by three neighbouring loops, and by four neighbouring loops (Figure 23-41).

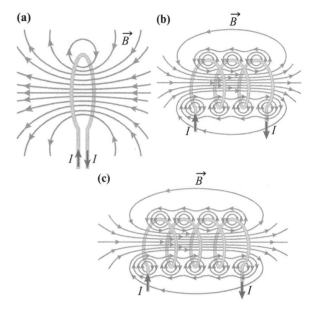

Figure 23-41 Calculating the magnetic field of a solenoid (a) The magnetic field created by a single loop (b) The magnetic field created by three adjacent loops (c) The magnetic field created by four adjacent loops

Magnetic field lines inside the loops (Figure 23-41) reinforce each other, and the magnetic field lines outside the loops nearly cancel each other. The more loops that are placed next to each other, the more their magnetic fields are reinforced inside the loops and cancel each other outside of them. A cross section of a 10-loop solenoid is shown in Figures 23-42a and 23-42b. The magnetic field is almost uniform in the centre of the solenoid and is relatively weak outside of it. Increasing the number of loops increases the magnetic field inside the solenoid and makes it more uniform. A solenoid is also called an **electromagnet** because it uses an electric current to produce a magnetic field. However, unlike permanent magnets, the magnetic field of a solenoid depends on its structure and on the amount and direction of the electric current that flows through it.

Figure 23-42(a) illustrates how Ampère's law can be used to calculate the magnetic field inside a long solenoid of length L and radius R, which has N loops and carries current I. The axis of a solenoid is directed along the x-axis. It is convenient to choose a rectangular path of integration with length a and width b. The magnetic field

(a)

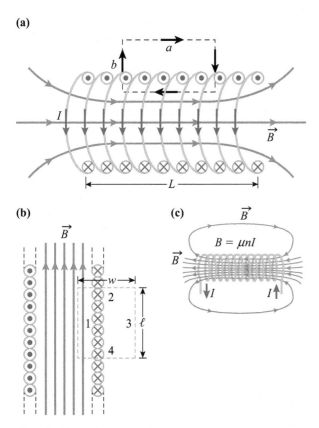

(b)

(c)

Figure 23-42 (a) The magnetic field created by a 10-loop solenoid, (b) a cross section of a very long solenoid, and (c) a very long solenoid consisting of *N* loops.

inside the solenoid is directed along its axis of symmetry, so the field is parallel to the long side of the rectangle, *a*, and perpendicular to the short side, *b*. The magnetic field outside the solenoid is negligible. Since Ampère's law is defined in terms of the dot product of the magnetic field and the path element $d\vec{l}$, this product is nonzero only for one side of the rectangle: the long side located inside the solenoid. Applying Ampère's law,

$$\oint \vec{B} \cdot d\vec{l} = \mu_0 \sum I_{\text{enc}}$$

$$\oint B\hat{i} \cdot d\vec{l} = \mu_0 \frac{INa}{L}$$

$$B \oint \hat{i} \cdot d\vec{l} = \mu_0 \frac{INa}{L}$$

$$Ba = \mu_0 \frac{INa}{L}$$

KEY EQUATION $B_{\text{solenoid}} = \mu_0 \frac{IN}{L} = \mu_0 In$ (23-41)

Therefore, the magnetic field inside the solenoid depends on the density of the solenoid's loops ($n = N/L$) and the value of the electric current *I*. Unlike the magnetic field created by a current-carrying loop, the magnetic field of a solenoid does not depend on the radius of the coils.

ONLINE ACTIVITY

The Magnetic Field of a Solenoid

The e-resource that accompanies every new copy of this textbook contains an Online Activity using the PhET simulation "Magnets and Electromagnets." Work through the simulation and accompanying questions to gain an understanding of how the current and the number of loops affect the magnetic field of a solenoid.

MAKING CONNECTIONS

Magnetic Resonance Imagining

Although magnetic resonance imaging (MRI) was invented less than 40 years ago, it is difficult to imagine a modern hospital without it. MRI technology produces images of body tissue and can show details of soft tissue that are not visible using other imaging technologies, such as X-rays and CT scans (Figure 23-43). In addition to the advantage of being good resolution for soft tissue we should mention that it does not involve ionizing radiation so does not carry the potential risks of X-rays. MRI machines generate these images by measuring changes in the magnetic fields of hydrogen nuclei in water molecules in the body (human bodies are 70% water). These changes are caused by nuclear magnetic resonance of the hydrogen nuclei: when a person is inside the scanner, the hydrogen nuclei (i.e., protons) align with a strong magnetic field in the scanning chamber. A radio wave at just the right frequency (the resonance frequency) for the protons to absorb energy pushes some of the protons out of alignment. The protons then snap back to alignment, producing a detectable rotating magnetic field as they do so. Since protons in different types of tissue (e.g., fat, muscle, or a tumour) realign at different speeds, these tissues can be distinguished in the MRI images. Most MRI systems use a superconducting magnet to generate the very strong magnetic fields required, typically 0.5 to 3.0 T (approximately 10 000 times greater than Earth's magnetic field).

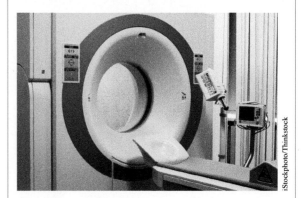

iStockphoto/Thinkstock

Figure 23-43 An MRI scanner

EXAMPLE 23-11

Coils in an MRI Magnet

Some MRI scanners need a magnetic field of 3.0 T. How many loops per metre does an electromagnet require to produce this magnetic field with a current of 15 A?

SOLUTION

We can use Equation (23-41) to calculate the turn density of the coil:

$$B = \mu_0 \frac{IN}{L} = \mu_0 In$$

Therefore,

$$n = \frac{B}{\mu_0 I} = \frac{3.0 \text{ T}}{(4\pi \times 10^{-7} \text{ T} \cdot \text{m/A})(15 \text{ A})} = 1.6 \times 10^5 \text{ loops/m}$$

Making sense of the result:

The number of loops per metre is very high. To have fewer turns and to reduce the size of the electromagnets, MRI scanners use a superconducting wire that allows significantly higher electric currents.

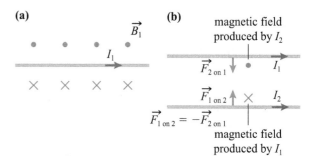

Figure 23-44 (a) Magnetic field produced by I_1 (b) Two parallel wires carrying currents that flow in the same direction attract each other (c) Two parallel current-carrying wires carrying opposite currents repel each other

---

LO 8

23-8 The Magnetic Force Between Two Parallel Conductors

Imagine two straight, parallel wires that are separated by a distance R and carry electric currents I_1 and I_2 in the same direction, as shown in Figure 23-44(b). We first consider the magnetic field created by the top wire. Using the right-hand rule (Figure 23-44(a)), we see that directly below the wire, the magnetic field created by I_1 is directed into the page and, hence, is perpendicular to the bottom wire. The magnitude of this field is given by Equation (23-33): $B = \dfrac{\mu_0 I_1}{2\pi R}$.

Applying the right-hand rule for the magnetic force exerted on a moving charge shows that the magnetic field from the top wire exerts an upward force on the bottom current-carrying wire. Consequently, the magnetic force experienced by I_2 due to the magnetic field created by I_1 is a force of attraction. The magnitude of this force can be calculated using Equation (23-22):

$$\vec{F}_{1 \text{ on } 2} = I_2 \vec{l} \times \vec{B}$$

$$F_{1 \text{ on } 2} = I_2 l \frac{\mu_0 I_1}{2\pi R} = \frac{\mu_0 I_1 I_2 l}{2\pi R} = \frac{\mu_0 I_1 I_2}{2\pi R} l$$

Similarly, the magnetic force experienced by I_1 due to the magnetic field created by I_2 is directed toward I_2 (force of attraction) and has a magnitude of

$$F_{2 \text{ on } 1} = I_1 l \frac{\mu_0 I_2}{2\pi R} = \frac{\mu_0 I_1 I_2 l}{2\pi R} = \frac{\mu_0 I_1 I_2}{2\pi R} l$$

The fact that these two forces are equal in magnitude and opposite in direction is not surprising because the interacting wires should obey Newton's third law. The magnitude of force per unit length is also equal for the two wires:

KEY EQUATION
$$\frac{F_{1 \text{ on } 2}}{l} = \frac{F_{2 \text{ on } 1}}{l} = \frac{\mu_0 I_1 I_2}{2\pi R} \qquad (23\text{-}42)$$

We also use the right-hand rule to show that whenever two parallel wires carry electric currents in opposite directions, they repel each other (Figure 23-44(c)).

The force between two straight, parallel wires provides a way to define the SI unit of electric current, the ampere: When two parallel wires each carry an electric current of 1 A and are a distance of 1 m from each other, the force between the wires per metre of wire is

$$\frac{F_{1 \text{ on } 2}}{l} = \frac{F_{2 \text{ on } 1}}{l} = \frac{\mu_0 I_1 I_2}{2\pi R} = \frac{\mu_0 (1 \text{ A})(1 \text{ A})}{2\pi (1 \text{ m})}$$

$$= \frac{4\pi \times 10^{-7}}{2\pi} \text{ N/m} = 2 \times 10^{-7} \text{ N/m}$$

C-23-11 The Magnetic Force Between Two Current-carrying Wires

Two straight, parallel wires carry electric currents of $I_1 = I$ and $I_2 = 2I$. Which of the following equations correctly describes the magnetic forces that the wires exert on each other?

(a) $F_{1 \text{ on } 2} = 4F_{2 \text{ on } 1}$

(b) $F_{1 \text{ on } 2} = 2F_{2 \text{ on } 1}$

(c) $F_{1 \text{ on } 2} = F_{2 \text{ on } 1}$

(d) $2F_{1 \text{ on } 2} = F_{2 \text{ on } 1}$

(e) $4F_{1 \text{ on } 2} = F_{2 \text{ on } 1}$

C-23-11 (c) Think of Newton's third law.

LO 9

23-9 The Magnetic Properties of Materials

We began this chapter with a discussion of how credit cards work. To store information on a credit card, an array of microscopic magnetic particles is arranged. Credit cards, magnetic tapes, computer hard drives, and refrigerator magnets all depend on the magnetic properties of matter. Materials can be classified into three broad groups based on their magnetic properties: paramagnetic, diamagnetic, and ferromagnetic. The behaviour of these three classes of materials arises from interactions at the atomic level, which we look at first.

The Bohr Magneton

At the beginning of the 20th century, the Danish physicist Niels Bohr (1885–1962) proposed a model for the structure of atoms (which will be discussed in more detail in later chapters). In Bohr's model, atoms consist of a nucleus made of protons and neutrons, with electrons orbiting around it. These orbiting electrons behave like microscopic current loops inside the atoms and give the atom a magnetic moment. In some materials, the atomic magnetic moments orient themselves along the external magnetic field, increasing its strength. We call this process magnetization and say that some materials can be magnetized by an external magnetic field.

To understand how atomic magnetic moments contribute to the magnetic properties of matter, we look at hydrogen, the simplest atom. A semiclassical model of the hydrogen atom consists of one electron orbiting a nucleus that consists of just one proton. As discussed in Section 23-5, the magnetic dipole moment of the current loop can be expressed as $\vec{\mu} = I\vec{A}$, where I is the electric current and A is the area of the loop (Equation (23-28)). Applying this definition to an electron orbiting the nucleus in the atom of hydrogen, we obtain the following:

$$\mu = IA = \frac{e}{T} A = \frac{e}{2\pi r/v} \pi r^2 = \frac{evr}{2} \qquad (23\text{-}43)$$

It is often convenient to express the dipole moment of the hydrogen atom in terms of the angular momentum of the electron moving in a circular orbit (Section 8-7), $L = rp = rmv$:

KEY EQUATION
$$\mu = \frac{evr}{2} = \frac{e}{2m} L \qquad (23\text{-}44)$$

Expression (23-44) shows that the magnetic dipole moment of a hydrogen atom is proportional to the angular momentum of its electron. Bohr suggested that this angular momentum must always be an integer multiple of $h/2\pi$, where h is Planck's constant, a fundamental physical constant with a value of 6.626×10^{-34} J·s. Bohr's postulate of the quantization of angular momentum is a cornerstone of quantum mechanics (Chapter 31). Until now, we have discussed angular momentum as being a continuous physical quantity. However, due to the extremely small value of Planck's constant, the quantum properties of matter only become relevant at the atomic scale.

Using the quantization of angular momentum, we can rewrite Equation (23-44) as

KEY EQUATION
$$\mu_n = \frac{e}{2m} L_n = \frac{e}{2m} \frac{h}{2\pi} n = \frac{eh}{4\pi m} n = \mu_B n$$

$$\text{where } n = 1, 2, 3, \ldots \qquad (23\text{-}45)$$

The quantity $\mu_B = \dfrac{eh}{4\pi m} = 9.274 \times 10^{-24} \dfrac{J}{T} = 9.274 \times 10^{-24}$ A·m² represents the fundamental unit of magnetic moment and is called the **Bohr magneton**. It is convenient to express magnetic moments of charged particles in terms of the Bohr magneton. Equation (23-45) can also be used to calculate the magnetic potential energy for a magnetic moment in a magnetic field:

$$U = -\vec{\mu} \cdot \vec{B} \qquad (23\text{-}46)$$

Electron Spin

In 1925, three young doctoral students—George Uhlenbeck, Samuel Goudsmit, and Ralph Kronig—independently came up with the then radical idea that an electron has an inherent property (similar to its mass or charge) that interacts with a magnetic field. This inherent property of an electron is called **electron spin**, and its magnitude is slightly greater than the Bohr magneton, $1.001 \, \mu_B$. The net magnetic moment of an atom is the sum of the magnetic moments of the electrons orbiting the nucleus and the spins of these electrons.

Paramagnetism

In most materials, the net magnetic moments in the atoms are zero. However, in certain materials, some atoms have nonzero magnetic moments on the order of magnitude of the Bohr magneton, μ_{B}. When these materials—called paramagnetic materials—are placed in an external magnetic field, the unbalanced atomic magnetic moments experience a magnetic torque of $\vec{\tau} = \vec{\mu} \times \vec{B}$. The unbalanced torques will try to align with the magnetic field to decrease the potential energy of the system, thus increasing the net magnetic field. This phenomenon is called **paramagnetism**.

Since the net magnetic dipole moment of the material $\vec{\mu}_{\text{net}}$, depends on the amount of material, it is more meaningful to discuss the net magnetic dipole moment of the material per unit volume. This quantity is called the **magnetization** of the material and is denoted by $\vec{M}$:

$$\vec{M} = \frac{\vec{\mu}_{\text{net}}}{V} \qquad (23\text{-}47)$$

This additional magnetic dipole moment produces an additional magnetic field, which can be calculated in the same way as the magnetic field produced by a current-carrying loop: $\vec{B}_{\text{add}} = \mu_0\vec{M}$. Then the total magnetic field inside such a material is given by

$$\vec{B} = \vec{B}_0 + \mu_0\vec{M}$$

where $\vec{B}_0$ is an external magnetic field.

It is common to describe the behaviour of paramagnetic materials using the **relative permeability** of the material, K_{m}, which indicates how much greater the magnetic field inside a paramagnetic material in an external magnetic field is relative to the external magnetic field:

KEY EQUATION $\qquad \vec{B} = \vec{B}_0 + \mu_0\vec{M} = K_{\text{m}}\vec{B}_0 \qquad (23\text{-}48)$

Table 23-1 shows the relative magnetic permeability K_{m} of different paramagnetic and diamagnetic materials K_{m} at room temperature (20°C). The relative magnetic

Table 23-1   Relative magnetic permeability K_{m} and magnetic susceptibility of paramagnetic and diamagnetic materials, χ_{m}, at room temperature (20°C)

Material	Relative magnetic permeability, K_{m}	Magnetic susceptibility, $\chi_{\text{m}} = K_{\text{m}} - 1$
Paramagnetic materials		
Iron oxide	1.007 20	0.007 20
Ammonium iron (III) sulfate (iron alum)	1.000 66	0.000 66
Uranium	1.000 40	0.000 40
Platinum	1.000 26	0.000 26
Tungsten	1.000 068	0.000 068
Cesium	1.000 051	0.000 051
Aluminum	1.000 022	0.000 022
Lithium	1.000 014	0.000 014
Magnesium	1.000 012	0.000 012
Sodium	1.000 007 2	0.000 007 2
Oxygen gas	1.000 001 9	0.000 001 9
Diamagnetic materials		
Bismuth	0.999 834	−0.000 166
Mercury	0.999 971	−0.000 029
Silver	0.999 974	−0.000 026
Carbon (diamond)	0.999 979	−0.000 021
Carbon (graphite)	0.999 984	−0.000 016
Lead	0.999 982	−0.000 018
Sodium chloride	0.999 986	−0.000 014
Copper	0.999 99	−0.000 010
Water	0.999 991	−0.000 009 1

Source: Adapted from HyperPhysics, http://hyperphysics.phy-astr.gsu.edu/hbase/tables/magprop.html

ELECTRICITY, MAGNETISM, AND OPTICS

permeabilities of these materials typically range from 1.000 01 to 1.003 00. Another way of thinking of the relative permeability is to use a coefficient that compares the magnetic field inside the paramagnetic material to the magnetic field in a vacuum immersed in the same external magnetic field. This view of relative permeability allows us to extend all the magnetic field derivations to current-carrying conductors embedded in paramagnetic materials. For such derivations, μ_0 should be replaced by the quantity **magnetic permeability**, μ:

$$\mu = \mu_0 K_{\mathrm{m}} \tag{23-49}$$

Be careful not to confuse the magnetic permeability of a material with the magnetic dipole moment, which is also denoted by μ.

Another convenient way of describing paramagnetic materials is to use **magnetic susceptibility,** χ_{m}, which shows by how much the magnetic permeability differs from 1. For paramagnetic materials, the magnetic susceptibility is positive (Table 23-1):

$$\chi_{\mathrm{m}} = K_{\mathrm{m}} - 1 \tag{23-50}$$

For paramagnetic materials, the magnetization of the material depends on the absolute temperature. In many cases, this dependence can be described by Curie's law, named after the renowned French scientist Pierre Curie (1859–1906):

$$M = C \frac{B}{T} \tag{23-51}$$

where C is the Curie constant, T is the absolute temperature, and B is the magnetic field.

Different materials have different Curie constants. Curie's law can be understood when we consider how the variables affect atomic magnetic moments: thermal motion tends to randomize atomic magnetic moments, and an external magnetic field tends to align the atomic magnetic moments along its direction.

Diamagnetism

Unlike paramagnetic materials, the net magnetic moments of atoms in diamagnetic materials are zero when there is no external magnetic field present. However, an external magnetic field affects the motion of the electrons within the atoms, creating magnetic dipole moments within the atoms. These induced magnetic dipole moments are always directed opposite to the external magnetic field. We explain the reason for this orientation when we talk about Faraday's law of electromagnetic induction in Chapter 24. **Diamagnetism** can be compared to the effect of polarization by an electric field (Section 19-6). For example, a neutral water molecule can become polarized in the presence of an electric field and act as an electric dipole.

Diamagnetic materials always have a negative susceptibility, as shown in Table 23-1. The relative permeability of diamagnetic materials is slightly less than 1. In contrast to paramagnetic materials, the susceptibility of diamagnetic materials is almost independent of temperature.

Ferromagnetism

Note that Table 23-1 does not include the metals that come to mind when we talk about magnetic materials: iron, nickel, cobalt, and their alloys. These materials constitute a third group of magnetic materials, called ferromagnetic materials. In ferromagnetic materials, strong magnetic interactions between atomic magnetic dipole moments make them align parallel to each other within small regions even when there is no external magnetic field, a phenomenon called **ferromagnetism**. These regions of aligned dipole moments are called **magnetic domains**. The magnetic moment of a magnetic domain can be of the order of magnitude of 1000 μ_{B} because most of the individual atomic magnetic moments within the domain are parallel.

When there is no external magnetic field $\vec{B}_0$, as shown in Figure 23-45, the magnetic domains are randomly oriented, and the net magnetic moment of the material is almost zero. However, in the presence of an external magnetic field $\vec{B}_0$, the domains orient themselves in the direction of the field, creating a strong magnetic field within the material.

The boundaries of magnetic domains in ferromagnetic materials are also affected by the external magnetic field: domains oriented in the direction of an external magnetic field grow as the external magnetic field increases. As a result, the relative magnetic permeability

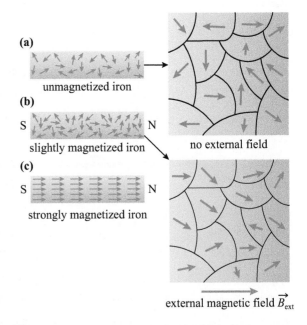

(a) unmagnetized iron

(b) S slightly magnetized iron N

(c) S strongly magnetized iron N

no external field

external magnetic field $\vec{B}_{\mathrm{ext}}$

Figure 23-45   (a) Magnetic domains inside a ferromagnetic material when there is no external magnetic field present. (b) Magnetic domains in the presence of a weak external magnetic field.
(c) Magnetic domains in the presence of a strong magnetic field.

Table 23-2 Initial and maximum relative magnetic permeability K_m of some ferromagnetic materials at room temperature (20°C)

Material	Treatment	Initial relative magnetic permeability, K_m	Maximum relative magnetic permeability, K_m
Iron, 99.8% pure	Annealed	150	5 000
Iron, 99.95% pure	Annealed in hydrogen	10 000	200 000
78 Permalloy	Annealed, quenched	8 000	100 000
Superpermalloy	Annealed in hydrogen, controlled cooling	100 000	1 000 000
Cobalt, 99% pure	Annealed	70	250
Nickel, 99% pure	Annealed	110	600

Source: Adapted from HyperPhysics, http://hyperphysics.phy-astr.gsu.edu/hbase/tables/magprop.html

of a ferromagnetic material, K_m is 1000 to 1 000 000 times greater than the relative permeability of a paramagnetic material (Table 23-2). Consequently, ferromagnetic materials, such as iron, are strongly attracted to a permanent magnet, and a paramagnetic material, such as aluminum, is not. Aluminum does experience some magnetic attraction, but it is thousands of times weaker than for iron in the same magnetic field.

When an external magnetic field increases, more and more domains in the ferromagnetic material align with the external magnetic field. As a result, the magnetization and the relative magnetic permeability of the ferromagnetic material increase. When all the magnetic domains have aligned with the external magnetic field, increasing the external field will not produce any further increase in relative permeability. At this point, the ferromagnetic sample has reached **saturation of magnetization**.

Figure 23-46 shows how the magnetization of a ferromagnetic material varies as the external magnetic field changes. This nonlinear behaviour is called magnetic **hysteresis**. As the external magnetic field increases, the magnetization of a ferromagnetic sample increases until it reaches its maximum value (saturation). However, when the external magnetic field is removed, the magnetization of the sample does not completely disappear. To decrease magnetization of the sample to zero, one has to apply a magnetic field in the opposite direction. The area inside the hysteresis curve indicates the relative amount of energy required to magnetize and demagnetize a sample: A ferromagnetic material that has a large area inside the hysteresis loop requires more energy to remagnetize it than a ferromagnetic sample with a smaller area. The more energy required to demagnetize a material, the better this material can serve as a permanent magnet.

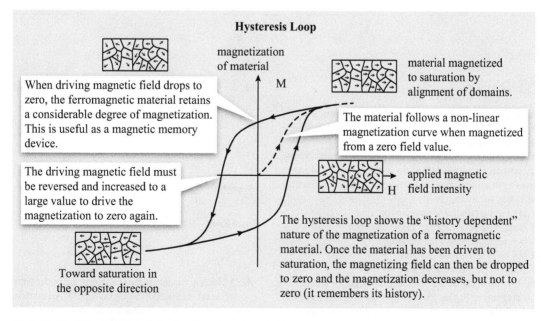

Figure 23-46 Magnetic hysteresis loop for a ferromagnetic material

FUNDAMENTAL CONCEPTS AND RELATIONSHIPS

Electric charges *moving* inside a magnetic field experience a magnetic force that is perpendicular to both the magnetic field and the velocity of the moving charge. Moving electric charges (electric currents) are the sources of magnetic fields.

The Magnetic Force

Charged particles moving inside a magnetic field experience a magnetic force that is perpendicular to both the particle's velocity and the direction of the magnetic field:

$$\vec{F}_B = q\vec{v} \times \vec{B} \qquad (23\text{-}1)$$

The Lorentz Force

Charged particles moving in electric and magnetic fields experience a Lorentz force:

$$\vec{F}_B = q\vec{E} + q\vec{v} \times \vec{B} \qquad (23\text{-}2)$$

Magnetic Fields

Moving electric charges (electric currents) are the sources of magnetic fields. A magnetic field produced by a small element of wire carrying a current can be calculated using the Biot–Savart law:

$$d\vec{B} = \frac{\mu_0}{4\pi} \frac{I d\vec{l} \times \hat{r}}{r^2} \qquad (23\text{-}32)$$

Ampère's Law

Ampère's law provides another way of calculating the magnetic field created by a wire carrying a current:

$$\oint \vec{B} \cdot d\vec{l} = \mu_0 \sum I_{enc} \qquad (23\text{-}39)$$

APPLICATIONS

Applications: mass spectrometers, electromotors, magnetic field sensors, proximity switches, position and speed detectors, current sensors, coaxial cables, solenoids

Key Terms: Ampère's law, Bohr magneton, constant magnetic field, coaxial cable, cyclotron, cyclotron frequency, diamagnetism, electromagnet, electron spin, ferromagnetism, Hall effect, Hall voltage, hysteresis, Lorentz force, magnetic dipole, magnetic dipole moment, magnetic domains, magnetic field, magnetic field lines, magnetic force, magnetic permeability, magnetic susceptibility, magnetization, mass spectrometer, paramagnetism, permeability constant of free space, pitch of a helix, relative permeability, right-hand rule, saturation of magnetization, tesla, uniform magnetic field, velocity selector

QUESTIONS

1. A charged particle moves in a straight line through a particular region of space. Could there be a nonzero magnetic field in this region? Explain.
2. An electron is travelling above and parallel to a conducting wire when a current is turned on in the wire. The electron curves upward and away from the wire. Initially, the current in the wire
   (a) is running parallel to the electron;
   (b) is running perpendicular to the electron;
   (c) is running opposite the electron;
   (d) has no effect on the electron.
   (e) None of the above are true.
3. Find the direction of the force on the negative charge for each diagram in Figure 23-47. Copy the diagram into your notebook, and indicate the direction of the force on your diagram.

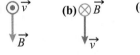
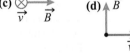
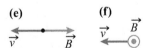

Figure 23-47 Question 3

4. A charged particle is moving along a circular path under the influence of a uniform magnetic field. An electric field that points in the same direction as the magnetic field is turned on. Describe the path that the charged particle will take.

5. A rectangular piece of a semiconductor is inserted in a magnetic field, and a battery is connected to its ends, as shown in Figure 23-48. When a sensitive voltmeter is connected between points D (back face) and C (front face), it is found that point D is at a higher potential than point C. What is the sign of the charge carriers in this semiconductor material? Explain.

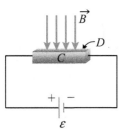

Figure 23-48 Question 5

6. Figure 23-49 shows several situations with two wires with currents of 2 A flowing out of or into the page. Rank the magnetic field at point P from greatest to least. Denote the downward-pointing field as negative and the upward-pointing field as positive. Assume that all the adjacent lines on the grid are separated by the same distance and that each situation is independent of the others.

Greatest 1____ 2____ 3____ 4____ 5____ 6____
7 ____ Least
Or, the magnetic field is the same in all cases. _____
Or, the magnetic field is zero in all cases. _____
If the magnetic field is the same for two or more cases, clearly indicate it on the ranking scheme. Explain your reasoning.

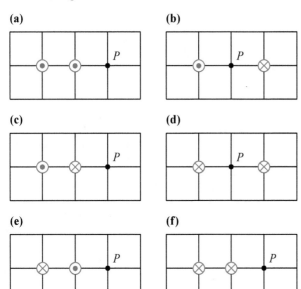

(a) **(b)** **(c)** **(d)** **(e)** **(f)** **(g)**

Figure 23-49 Question 6

7. The coil shown in Figure 23-50 attracts a permanent bar magnet. Which of the following statements correctly describes the polarity of the permanent bar magnet? Draw a diagram for this problem, and show your solution on the diagram.
   (a) The end of the bar magnet that is close to the coil is north; the opposite end is south.
   (b) The end of the bar magnet that is close to the coil is south; the opposite end is north.
   (c) The upper side of the bar magnet is north; the bottom side is south.
   (d) The upper side of the bar magnet is south; the bottom side is north.
   (e) Since we have a permanent magnet, we cannot determine its polarity in this example.
   (f) A permanent magnet (unlike a temporarily magnet) has zero polarity; it is neutral.

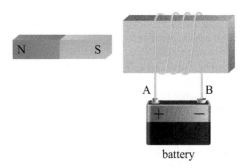

Figure 23-50 Question 7

8. The coil in Figure 23-51 repels the iron bar on the left by causing it to become a temporary magnet. Which of the following statements correctly describes the polarity of the temporary bar magnet in this situation? Draw a diagram for this problem, and show your solution on the diagram.
   (a) The end of the bar magnet that is close to the coil is north; the opposite end is south.
   (b) The end of the bar magnet that is close to the coil is south; the opposite end is north.
   (c) The upper side of the bar magnet is north; the bottom side is south.
   (d) The upper side of the bar magnet is south; the bottom side is north.
   (e) A temporary magnet cannot repel the coil, so this example does not make sense.

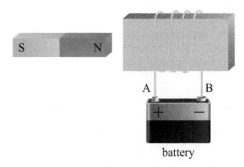

Figure 23-51 Question 8

9. A proton moving upward enters the magnetic field created by two bar magnets, as shown in Figure 23-52. The direction of the force exerted on the proton by the magnetic field is
(a) in the direction of the proton motion (upward);
(b) in the direction opposite to the proton motion (downward);
(c) left (i.e., toward the south pole of the left magnet);
(d) right (i.e., toward the north pole of the right magnet);
(e) into the page;
(f) out of the page.

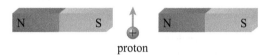

proton

Figure 23-52   Question 9

10. What would your answer be to question 9 if there was an electron instead of a proton?

11. An electric current in a long, vertical straight wire is flowing straight up (Figure 23-53). What is the direction of the magnetic field at point P?
(a) up (vertically)
(b) down (vertically)
(c) into the page
(d) out of the page
(e) to the right (horizontally)
(f) to the left (horizontally)

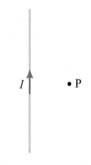

Figure 23-53   Question 11

12. Two long, parallel vertical wires carry electric currents of I and $3I$ in the same direction, as shown in Figure 23-54. The wires are separated by a distance d. At what point will the net magnetic field created by these wires equal zero?
(a) between the wires, a distance $d/3$ from the wire carrying current I and $2d/3$ from the wire carrying current $3I$
(b) between the wires, a distance $2d/3$ from the wire carrying current I and $d/3$ from the wire carrying current $3I$
(c) outside the wire carrying current I, a distance $d/3$ from this wire and $4d/3$ from the wire carrying current $3I$
(d) between the wires, a distance $d/4$ from the wire carrying current I and $3d/4$ from the wire carrying current $3I$
(e) between the wires, a distance $3d/4$ from the wire carrying current I and $d/4$ from the wire carrying current $3I$

Figure 23-54   Question 12

13. A negatively charged ion moving with speed v (Figure 23-55) enters three adjacent regions of uniform magnetic fields but of varying magnitudes. The magnetic field in each region is directed perpendicular to the plane of the paper. Which of the following correctly ranks the magnitudes of these magnetic fields?
(a) $B_3 > B_1 > B_2$
(b) $B_3 > B_2 > B_1$
(c) $B_2 > B_1 > B_3$
(d) $B_2 > B_3 > B_1$
(e) $B_1 > B_3 > B_2$
(f) $B_1 > B_2 > B_3$

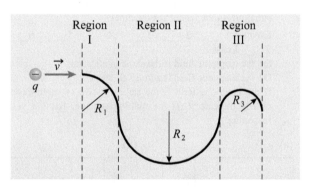

Figure 23-55   Question 13

14. What is true about the directions of the magnetic fields in question 13?
(a) Magnetic fields B_1 and B_3 are into the page, and magnetic field B_2 is out of the page.
(b) Magnetic fields B_1 and B_3 are out of the page, and magnetic field B_2 is into the page.
(c) All the magnetic fields are directed into the page.
(d) All the magnetic fields are directed out of the page.
(e) There is not enough information to determine the directions.

15. An electron is moving inside the cathode ray tube shown in Figure 23-13. What happens to the deflection of an electron when the magnetic field decreases by a factor of 2?
(a) The deflection remains the same.
(b) The deflection decreases by a factor of 2.
(c) The deflection decreases but not by a factor of 2.
(b) The deflection increases by a factor of 2.
(c) The deflection increases but not by a factor of 2.

16. Rank the magnitudes of the magnetic fields produced at the centres of curvature (points O) of the wires shown in Figure 23-56 from highest to lowest. All the wires carry an identical electric current. The radii of the circular segments are shown in the figure.

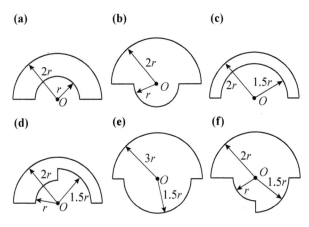

(a) 2r, r, O
(b) 2r, r, O
(c) 2r, 1.5r, O

(d) 2r, 1.5r, r, O
(e) 3r, 1.5r, O
(f) 2r, 1.5r, r, O

Figure 23-56 Question 16

17. Rank the magnitudes of the magnetic fields in the centres of the six squares shown in Figure 23-57. The magnetic fields are created by four different parallel (or antiparallel) currents I flowing through the vertices of each square.

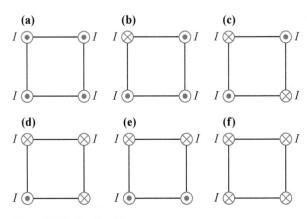

Figure 23-57 Question 17

18. Each wire in Figure 23-58 carries an electric current of 1 A into or out of the page. Each diagram indicates the path of a line integral $\oint \vec{B} \cdot \vec{dl}$ to be used while applying Ampère's law for calculating the magnitude of the resultant magnetic field. Rank the values of each line integral.

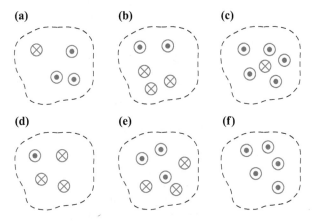

Figure 23-58 Question 18

PROBLEMS BY SECTION

For problems, star ratings will be used, (✷, ✷✷, or ✷✷✷), with more stars meaning more challenging problems.

Section 23-1 Magnetic Field and Magnetic Force

19. ✷ An electron moving with velocity $\vec{v} = (4.0\hat{i} - 8.0\hat{k}) \times 10^4$ m/s enters a region where a uniform magnetic field $\vec{B} = (0.80\hat{i} - 0.60\hat{j})$ T is present. Determine the force on the electron in algebraic notation, and find its magnitude.

20. ✷ An electron, accelerated to an energy of 100 eV, enters a region with a uniform magnetic field with a magnitude of 1.5×10^{-2} T. When a magnetic field is directed in the positive x-direction and an electron is moving in the positive z-direction, what are the direction and magnitude of the force acting on the electron? How would your answer change if instead of an electron, a proton with the same energy entered this region of the magnetic field? Explain.

21. ✷ A particle carrying a charge of 10 nC is moving at $0.001c$ along the positive x-direction in the region of a uniform magnetic field directed in the negative z-direction. The magnitude of the magnetic field is 1.5 T. Calculate the magnetic force on the particle.

22. ✷✷ A droplet has a mass of 2×10^{-4} g, a charge of 35 nC, and an initial horizontal velocity of $6 \times 10^5 \hat{j}$ m/s. The electric field in the vicinity of Earth is approximately 100 N/C directed downward, and the magnetic field in this area was measured to be approximately 45 μT directed parallel to Earth's surface. Find the magnitude and direction of a magnetic field that will keep the droplet moving in this direction. What assumptions did you make to solve the problem? (Hint: Do you need to take the gravitational force into account?)

Section 23-2 The Motion of a Charged Particle in a Uniform Magnetic Field

23. ✷ An electron, a proton, and an α-particle are moving with the same velocity. At some instant, they enter a region of a uniform magnetic field B pointing perpendicular to the direction of their motion.
    (a) Compare the radii of the orbits of the particles upon entering this region.
    (b) Compare the time it takes for each particle to complete one revolution (period of motion).

24. ✷ An electron moving perpendicular to a magnetic field of magnitude 2.4×10^{-2} T has a circular trajectory of radius r. The speed of the electron is 5% of the speed of light.
    (a) Determine the radius of the electron's trajectory.
    (b) Determine the period of revolution.

25. ✷ A proton enters a uniform magnetic field that causes it to follow a circular path of radius 0.1 mm. The field strength is 0.9 T.
    (a) Calculate the proton's speed.
    (b) Calculate the proton's angular frequency.

26. ✷✷ An electron of mass m and charge $-e$ moving with an initial velocity of $\vec{v} = v_{ox}\hat{i} + v_{oy}\hat{j}$ m/s enters a uniform magnetic field, $\vec{B} = B\hat{j}$. Derive an expression, in algebraic notation, for the velocity of the electron at any later instant, t.

27. ✷✷ A proton (mass m_p), a deuteron ($m_d = 2m_p$, $Q = e$), and an α-particle ($m_\alpha = 4m_p$, $Q = 2e$) are accelerated by the same potential difference, V, and then enter a uniform magnetic field, B, where they move in circular paths

ELECTRICITY, MAGNETISM, AND OPTICS

perpendicular to B. Express the radii of the paths for the deuteron and α-particle in terms of the proton's radius.

28. ✷✷ An electron is travelling at 100 km/s parallel to a long, straight horizontal conductor a distance of 3 cm from the conductor. A current of 12 A runs through the wire as the electron travels parallel to it, in the same direction as the electron's velocity. Find the strength and direction of the external electric field that will prevent the electron from deviating from its original path. Express your answer in V/m.

Section 23-3   Applications: Charged Particles Moving in a Uniform Magnetic Field

29. ✷ A magnetic field at the surface of a neutron star can reach 3.0×10^7 T. What would be the radii of curvature for the paths of three electrons moving in the vicinity of a neutron star with speeds of 5%, 10%, and 20% of the speed of light? What are the magnitudes of the magnetic forces acting on these electrons?

30. ✷ Charged particles, such as protons, found in cosmic rays, enter the Van Allen belt as they approach Earth. The average strength of the magnetic field of the lower Van Allen belt at a height of 3000 km is approximately 10^{-5} T. What is the radius of curvature and the cyclotron frequency of a proton entering the lower Van Allen belt at an angle of 30°? Describe the trajectory of the proton. Why do scientists say that a "proton was captured by the Van Allen belt"?

31. ✷ Cathode ray tube TVs used crossed electric and magnetic fields to deflect electrons before they struck a fluorescent screen. A beam of electrons moving with speed 6.0×10^7 m/s strikes a fluorescent screen located 0.5 m away. However, even when the magnetic field of the cathode ray is turned off, Earth's magnetic field is still present in that region. When an electron beam is moving along the x-axis, and Earth's magnetic field in the region has the components $(15\ \mu\text{T}, 20\ \mu\text{T}, 18\ \mu\text{T})$, what is the deflection, in mm, of the electron beam due to Earth's magnetic field?

32. ✷✷ The core of any microwave oven is a high-voltage system called a magnetron tube. The magnetron is a diode-type electron tube, which is used to produce electromagnetic waves with a frequency of 2450 MHz which are strongly absorbed by water. These waves are microwaves and have a wavelength of approximately 0.12 m. Determine the strength of the magnet needed to move the electrons in the oven at that frequency.

Section 23-4   The Magnetic Force on a Current-Carrying Wire

33. ✷ (a) Find the magnetic force per unit length on a long, straight wire carrying 10 A of electric current in the positive x-direction in a uniform magnetic field of 1.8 T directed in the negative y-direction.
(b) What happens to this force when the magnitude of the magnetic field is halved and the electric current in the wire doubles?

Section 23-5   The Torque on a Current-Carrying Loop in a Magnetic Field

34. ✷✷ A copper loop in the shape of an equilateral triangle ABC (AB = AC = BC = a), carrying an electric current I, is placed in a uniform magnetic field of magnitude B directed parallel to the side AC of the triangle (Figure 23-59).

(a) Find the magnitude of the magnetic force exerted on each side of the triangle.
(b) Find the net magnetic force exerted on this triangle by the magnetic field.
(c) Find the magnetic torque exerted on this triangle by this magnetic field.

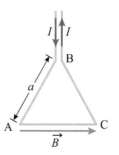

Figure 23-59   Problem 34

Section 23-6   The Biot–Savart Law

35. ✷✷ A long, straight conductor carrying a current I splits into two identical semicircular arcs of 5 cm radius (Figure 23-60). Calculate the magnitude and the direction of the magnetic field at the centre of the circle (point O).

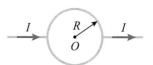

Figure 23-60   Problem 35

36. ✷✷ The magnitude of a magnetic field created by a long, straight wire carrying an electric current 25 cm from the wire is 10.0 μT.
(a) What is the current through the wire?
(b) What will happen to the magnitude of the magnetic field when the current in the wire doubles?

Section 23-7   Ampère's Law

37. ✷ A lightning bolt can generate electric currents of magnitude on the order of 10^4 A. What are the magnitudes of the magnetic fields generated 10 m, 100 m, and 1 km from a lightning bolt that generated a 10^4 A current? Compare these magnitudes to the magnitude of Earth's magnetic field.

38. ✷ A straight, vertical wire carries 10 A of electric current. Find the direction and magnitude of the magnetic fields created by this wire at a distance of (a) 10 cm, (b) 20 cm, and (c) 50 cm from the wire.

39. ✷✷ An electric cable has a diameter of 10 mm and carries an electric current of 25 A.
(a) Find the strength of the magnetic field at distances of 2 mm and 7 mm from the centre of the cable.
(b) Plot a graph of the magnitude of the magnetic field as a function of the distance from the centre of the cable for each distance.
(c) In Examples 23-9 and 23-10, we found expressions for the magnitude of the magnetic field inside and outside a long wire. Compare these expressions with the expressions for the magnitude of the electric field inside and outside of a uniformly charged insulating sphere. What does this comparison tell you?

Section 23-8 The Magnetic Force Between Two Parallel Conductors

40. ✱ Two straight, parallel superconducting cables can withstand a maximum tension of 10 kN/m without breaking. An engineer wants to use these cables in a device in which each cable is securely fastened and carries 20 kA of electric current. The currents will be flowing in opposite directions. What is the minimum separation required to keep the cables from breaking? Explain.

41. ✱ A rectangular loop of dimensions of 30 cm × 20 cm carries 10 A of electric current. Find the magnitudes and directions of the magnetic forces experienced by the sides of the loop.

Section 23-9 The Magnetic Properties of Matter

42. ✱ The magnetic field inside an air-filled solenoid is measured to be 1.2 T. Will the field inside the solenoid change if the air is pumped out of the core of the solenoid? If so, by how much will the magnetic field change? Explain.

COMPREHENSIVE PROBLEMS

43. ✱✱ A circular 100-loop coil with a radius of 0.10 m is located in a horizontal (xy) plane as shown in Figure 23-61. A 10 A current flows clockwise through the coil (as seen from above). The coil is in a uniform magnetic field of 1.0 T, directed in the positive y-direction with $\vec{B} = 1.0\hat{j}$.
(a) Calculate the magnetic moment of each loop of the coil.
(b) Calculate the magnetic moment of the entire coil.
(c) Calculate the magnetic torque experienced by the coil. Clearly identify the direction of the torque.
(d) How will your answers to parts (a) to (c) change if the direction of the current in the coil is reversed?
(e) How will your answers to parts (a) to (c) change if the direction of the magnetic field is changed to $\vec{B} = 1.0\hat{i}$ or $\vec{B} = 1.0\hat{k}$? Explain.
(f) The coil rotates from the position where its magnetic moment is parallel to the direction of the magnetic field to the position where its magnetic moment is perpendicular to it. What is the change in the potential energy of the coil? Explain.

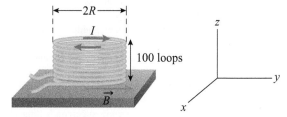

Figure 23-61   Problem 43

44. ✱✱ A current-carrying wire is located along the y-axis. An electric current of 5.0 A flows through this wire in the positive y-direction. Calculate the magnetic force per metre experienced by this wire when it is placed in the following magnetic fields:

(a) $\vec{B} = (0.55 \text{ T})\hat{i}$
(b) $\vec{B} = (0.55 \text{ T})\hat{j}$
(c) $\vec{B} = (0.55 \text{ T})\hat{k}$
(d) $\vec{B} = (0.55 \text{ T})\hat{i} - (0.55 \text{ T})\hat{k}$

45. ✱✱ A long wire carries a 5 A current toward the top of the page, as shown in Figure 23-62. An electron is travelling parallel to the wire with an initial separation of 2 cm and an initial velocity of 1.5×10^7 m/s toward the top of the page.
(a) What are the magnitude and direction of the magnetic force on the electron?
(b) What would your answers to part (a) be if instead of an electron, there was a proton moving in the same direction at the same speed?
(c) Draw the trajectories of the electron and the proton.

Figure 23-62   Problem 45

46. ✱✱✱ A charged particle carrying charge q and moving with a speed v enters a region of a uniform magnetic field $\vec{B}$ directed perpendicular to the particle's velocity. The particle spends time Δt in this region.
(a) Assume that Δt is small. Estimate the angle of deflection θ of the particle. When we assume that Δt is small, to what are we comparing Δt? Explain your answer.
(b) Suppose the charged particle is an electron moving with a speed of 1.5×10^7 m/s. What should be the size (length along the particle's original path) of the region of a uniform magnetic field of 2.0×10^{-2} T to produce a deflection of 0.15 rad?

47. ✱✱ A long, straight conductor carrying current I splits into two semicircular arcs. The resistance of the bottom arc is twice the resistance of the upper arc (Figure 23-63). Calculate the magnitude and the direction of the magnetic field in the centre of the circle (point O).

Figure 23-63   Problem 47

48. ✱✱ In Figure 23-64, three parallel, current-carrying wires pass through the vertices of an equilateral triangle. Two wires carry an electric current that is going into the page, and one wire carries an electric current that is coming out of the page. The magnitudes of the currents are 5 A, and the side of the equilateral triangle is 5 cm. Find the magnitude and direction of the magnetic field in the centre of the triangle (point O).

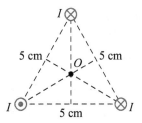

Figure 23-64 Problem 48

49. ✷✷✷ A 40-cm solenoid has a radius of 0.05 m and consists of 50 circular loops. An electric current of 1 A flows through the solenoid.
   (a) Determine the magnetic field in the centre of the solenoid.
   (b) Derive the formula for magnetic field along the axis of symmetry of the solenoid (Hint: you can check if your answer makes sense by using it to answer part (a)). Use this formula to find the magnetic field along the axis of the solenoid 15 cm off its centre.
   (c) Plot the graph of the magnetic field along the axis of symmetry of the solenoid as a function of the distance from its centre (use graphing software).
   (d) From the plot in (c) estimate at what distance from the centre of the solenoid the magnetic field will decrease by 5%.

50. ✷✷ Two parallel, current-carrying wires are separated by a distance d. The wires carry currents of equal magnitude. In Figure 23-65(a), both currents are going into the page, and in Figure 23-65(b), one current is going into the page and the other is coming out of the page. At what location(s) does the resultant magnetic field equal zero for each one of the cases? Explain.

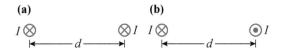

Figure 23-65 Problem 50

51. ✷✷ Two long, parallel vertical wires carry electric currents of I and $2I$ in opposite directions (Figure 23-66). Find the magnitude and direction of the magnetic fields at points A, B, C, and D when $I = 10$ A and the distance between the wires is 1 m.

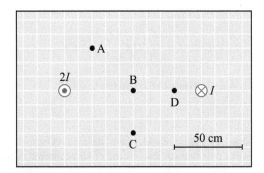

Figure 23-66 Problem 51

52. ✷✷ Two parallel wires separated by a distance of 50 cm carry currents in opposite directions (Figure 23-67). The left wire carries a current of 10 A. Point A is the midpoint

between the wires, and point B is 5 cm to the left of the 10 A current. The current I is adjusted so that the magnetic field at B is zero.
   (a) Find the strength of the magnetic field 10 cm to the left of A.
   (b) Find the direction and magnitude of the force per unit length on the left wire. Ignore gravity.

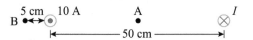

Figure 23-67 Problem 52

53. ✷✷✷ A rectangular loop of dimensions 30 cm × 20 cm carries 10 A of electric current (Figure 23-68). The loop is oriented in the xz-plane. Sixty centimetres from the centre of the loop is an infinitely long, straight vertical wire carrying 20 A of electric current in the positive z-direction. Find the resultant force acting on the loop.

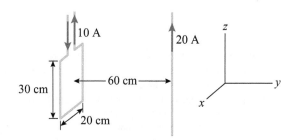

Figure 23-68 Problem 53

54. ✷✷✷ A long copper wire of length L carries an electric current I. This wire can be formed into a coil consisting of multiple loops while preserving the total length of the wire. Find the optimal number of the loops in such a coil to maximize the torque on the coil when it carries a current I in a uniform magnetic field B. Prove that the maximum value of this torque is $\tau = (1/4\pi)L^2IB$.

55. ✷✷ Two very long, straight, parallel wires carry 10 A (wire A) and 15 A (wire B) of electric current. The currents in the wires flow in the same direction. The wires are located 1 m from each other.
   (a) What is the magnitude of the magnetic force that wire A exerts on wire B?
   (b) What is the magnitude of the magnetic force that wire B exerts on wire A?
   (c) Compare your answers to parts (a) and (b) and explain them.

56. ✷✷ A straight, vertical wire carries a downward current of 1.5 A. The wire is placed in the area of a uniform magnetic field created by a strong superconducting electromagnet. The magnitude of this magnetic field reaches 0.65 T. Calculate the magnetic force per metre of the wire applied on it by the magnetic field when
   (a) the direction of the magnetic field is perpendicular to the direction of the wire;
   (b) the direction of the magnetic field is parallel to the wire;
   (c) the magnetic field is directed at 45° to the direction of the wire.
   Draw a diagram for each scenario.

57. ✱✱ A proton, moving (at $t = 0$) with the velocity $v_x = 2.0 \times 10^5$ m/s, $v_y = 0$, $v_z = 1.5 \times 10^5$ m/s, enters a uniform magnetic field of 0.45 T directed along the z-axis. Assume that the only force acting on the proton is a magnetic force.
   (a) Find the magnetic force acting on the proton as it enters the region of the magnetic field, and compare its magnitude with the gravitational force. Use your findings to justify the above assumption.
   (b) Describe the proton's trajectory as it travels inside the magnetic field region.
   (c) Find the proton's angular speed and its period of circular motion.
   (d) Find the radius of the proton's trajectory and the pitch of the helix.
   (e) How would your answers to parts (a) to (d) change if instead of a proton, an electron entered this region at the same velocity?

58. ✱✱✱ An α-particle travels in a circular path of radius 15 cm in a uniform magnetic field of 2.0 T.
   (a) Find the speed of the α-particle. Express the speed of the α-particle as a fraction of the speed of light. Is it justified to use classical physics to express the kinetic energy of this particle, or should relativity be used?
   (b) What is the kinetic energy of the α-particle in eV?
   (c) What is the potential difference that the α-particle should be accelerated through in order to achieve such a speed?

59. ✱✱ At a certain instant, an electron with kinetic energy of 20 eV is moving in the westward direction. The horizontal component of Earth's magnetic field in this region is 18 μT north, and its vertical component is 48 μT down.
   (a) What is the trajectory of the electron?
   (b) What is the radius of curvature of the electron's path?
   (c) Should the gravitational force on the electron be taken into account? Justify your answer.

60. ✱✱ A proton is moving in a circular orbit of radius 14 cm in a uniform 0.35 T magnetic field perpendicular to the velocity of the proton.
   (a) Find the linear speed of the proton.
   (b) Find the time it takes for the proton to complete one revolution.
   (c) Suddenly a uniform electric field is turned on in the direction opposite to the direction of the magnetic field. The magnitude of the electric field is 400 kV/m.
      (i) Draw a Free Body Diagram for the proton.
      (ii) Draw the trajectory of the proton when both fields are on. Explain your drawing.
      (iii) How would your answers to parts (i) and (ii) be different if instead of a proton an electron was moving in a uniform magnetic field of 0.35 T and the electric field mentioned above was turned on?

61. ✱✱ Due to health regulations, the magnetic field produced by a current-carrying wire at a distance of 30 cm is not allowed to exceed Earth's magnetic field (5.5×10^{-5} T).
   (a) What is the maximum current that this wire can carry?
   (b) What would the maximum current be if the regulations require the same limit at half the original distance (15 cm)?

62. ✱✱ A jumper cable used to start a vehicle with a dead battery carries a 65 A current. What is the magnitude of the magnetic field created by the cable (a) 10 cm away and (b) 25 cm away? Compare the values of the magnetic field to the magnitude of Earth's magnetic field.

63. ✱✱ A long, straight wire carrying an electric current of 50 A is placed in a uniform magnetic field of 5 mT directed toward the north magnetic pole. The wire is oriented such that the electric current flows from east to west. Find the points at which the net magnetic field is zero. (Hint: Think of the influence of Earth's magnetic field).

64. ✱✱ Figure 23-69 shows six sets of five equally spaced long, parallel wires carrying electric currents of equal magnitudes into or out of the page. Rank the magnitude of the magnetic forces acting on the central wire in each scenario, due to the currents in the other four wires, from greatest to smallest. Support your ranking with the appropriate calculations.

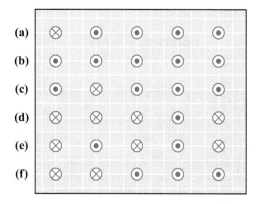

Figure 23-69 Problem 64

65. ✱✱✱ What is the magnetic field inside a 2 m-long solenoid of radius $r = 0.25$ m that has 1000 turns per metre and 10 A of current flowing through it? How does the magnetic field change if an iron core with $\chi_{iron} = 4.0 \times 10^3$ is inserted inside this solenoid?

66. ✱✱✱ Two charged particles moving with the same speed but in opposite directions pass each other at a distance d. The speed of the particles, v, is much less than the speed of light, $v \ll c$. Compare the magnetic and electric forces that the particles exert on each other at the instant when the particles are closest to each other. Perform the calculations for the three cases listed below.
   (a) The charged particles are two protons.
   (b) The charged particles are two electrons.
   (c) One charged particle is a proton, and the other charged particle is an electron.

67. ✱✱ A 15 A current flows through a 50 cm-long solenoid that has 1000 turns. By how much will the magnetic field inside this solenoid change if the air in its core is replaced by
   (a) water at 20°C;
   (b) oxygen at 20°C;
   (c) a vacuum?

68. ✱✱ A coaxial cable has an external radius of 5 mm and an internal radius of 2 mm, and carries an electric current of 5 A in each direction. Derive an equation to determine the magnitude and direction of the magnetic field generated by this cable at an arbitrary distance from its axis. Then use your equation to find the magnetic fields at the following distances from its axis:
   (a) 1 mm
   (b) 3 mm
   (c) 5 mm

ELECTRICITY, MAGNETISM, AND OPTICS

69. ✷✷✷ Use the Biot–Savart law to prove that the magnetic field at the centre of a wire shaped into a circular arc (Figure 23-70) is given by $B = \dfrac{\mu_0 I \phi}{4\pi R}$, where I is the electric current flowing through the wire, R is the radius of curvature, and ϕ is the angle subtended by the circular arc.

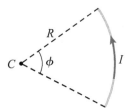

Figure 23-70   Problem 69

70. ✷✷✷ Each wire in Figure 23-71 carries an electric current of 5 A.
(a) In Figure 23-71(a), the radius of the arc is 10 cm. Find the strength of the magnetic field in the centre of the wire.
(b) In Figure 23-71(b), the radius of the arc is 20 cm. Find the strength of the magnetic field in the centre of the wire. (Hint: Use your result from part (a).)

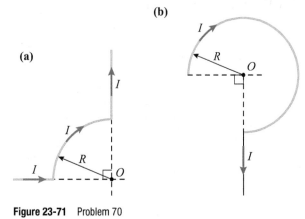

Figure 23-71   Problem 70

71. ✷✷✷ A straight wire of length L carries an electric current of magnitude I.
(a) Use the Biot–Savart law to prove that the magnetic field at point P_1, located a distance R from the centre of the wire along the line perpendicular to it, can be expressed as

$$B_{P_1} = \frac{\mu_0 I}{2\pi R}\,\frac{L}{(L^2 + 4R^2)^{1/2}}$$

(b) What result would you expect if the length of the wire were to become infinitely long? Show that the result you proved in part (a) satisfies the limiting case of an infinitely long wire.

(c) Use the Biot–Savart law to prove that the magnetic field at point P_2, located a distance R from the end of the wire along the line perpendicular to it, can be expressed as

$$B_{P_2} = \frac{\mu_0 I}{4\pi R}\,\frac{L}{(L^2 + 4R^2)^{1/2}}$$

(d) Show that the results you proved in parts (a) and (c) are consistent.

72. ✷✷✷ A copper wire is bent to create a square loop with sides of length d. An electric current of magnitude I flows counterclockwise through this loop. Find the magnitude and direction of the magnetic field created in the centre of this loop.

73. ✷✷✷ A toroidal (donut-shaped) coil is closely wound with one continuous wire as shown in Figure 23-72. Assume that the current in the wire is I, the number of turns in the coil is N, and the radius of the toroid (the distance between the inner and outer radii of the toroid) is R.
(a) Derive an expression for the magnetic field both inside and outside the toroid.
(b) Compare your answer for the magnetic field of a toroid to the magnetic field of a solenoid.
(c) What does your comparison in part (b) tell you?
(d) Calculate the magnetic field of a 1000-turn toroid of radius 0.5 m when 15 A of electric current flows through it.
(e) Compare your result in part (d) to the magnetic field inside a 1 m-long solenoid that has 1000 turns and a 15 A current flowing through it. What does your comparison tell you?

Figure 23-72   Problem 73

74. ✷✷✷ As discussed earlier, there are different versions of mass spectrometers. Figure 23-74 shows a mass spectrometer that does not have a velocity selection stage (compare it to the mass spectrometer shown in Figure 23-12). Derive an expression that shows how the radius of the charged particle in the mass spectrometer depends on the mass of the particle, its charge, magnetic field $\vec{B}$ and the potential difference V. What assumption have you made for your derivation? Compare the operation of two mass spectrometer models (Figure 23-12 and Figure 23-73) and discuss what are their advantages and disadvantages.

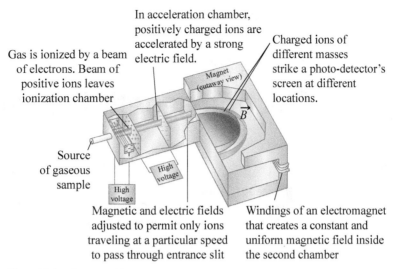

Gas is ionized by a beam of electrons. Beam of positive ions leaves ionization chamber

In acceleration chamber, positively charged ions are accelerated by a strong electric field.

Charged ions of different masses strike a photo-detector's screen at different locations.

Magnet (cutaway view)

$\vec{B}$

Source of gaseous sample

High voltage

High voltage

Magnetic and electric fields adjusted to permit only ions traveling at a particular speed to pass through entrance slit

Windings of an electromagnet that creates a constant and uniform magnetic field inside the second chamber

Figure 23-73   Problem 74

DATA-RICH PROBLEM

75. ✷✷✷   Could using a device such as an iPod be hazardous for a person who has a pacemaker? A paper called "Low frequency magnetic emissions and resulting induced voltages in a pacemaker by iPod portable music players," by Howard Bassen, attempts to provide an experimental answer to this question (www.pubmedcentral.nih.gov/articlerender. fcgi?artid=2265271). Use the information provided in the paper to give scientifically warranted recommendations regarding the use of portable music devices by people who have pacemakers.

 See the text online resources at **www.physics1e.nelson.com** for Open Problems and Data-Rich Problems related to this chapter.

Chapter 24
Electromagnetic Induction

Canada is the second-largest country in the world, and more than one-third of its CO_2 emissions come from transportation. For example, a round-trip flight from Vancouver to Toronto (6717 km) produces 1.536 tonnes of CO_2 emissions.[1] Consequently, the development of energy-efficient transportation is an important issue for Canadians. One promising technology is magnetic levitation (maglev) trains, which are suspended over conductive rails by electromagnetic forces (Figure 24-1). Maglev trains are powered by electric energy. In addition to reducing CO_2 emissions, (assuming the electricity is not fossil fuel generated) maglev trains are fast—they reach speeds comparable to modern jets: up to 590 km/h. They can travel at high speeds because levitating the train eliminates friction and vibrations from contact between wheels and the rails, thus reducing waste energy.

The first maglev vehicle patent was obtained in 1902 by an American, A. Zehden. However, this technology required very strong magnets, so practical maglev vehicles were not developed until the early 1960s. The world's first commercial maglev train was introduced in Birmingham, England, in 1984, but it was discontinued in 1995 due to technical difficulties. In 2002, German scientists and engineers from Transrapid International developed the first maglev system still in operation today: a maglev line between Shanghai's Pudong airport and its financial district (30.5 km). Other commercial maglev trains operate in Japan. Currently, there are a few maglev projects under construction in Europe, China, Japan, and the United States. These maglev trains use the law of electromagnetic induction discovered by Michael Faraday almost two centuries ago, and they might be a solution to the energy-efficient transportation problem.

Figure 24-1 Magnetic levitation (maglev) trains are high-speed trains that use the law of electromagnetic induction for their operation.

[1]www.less.ca

24-1 In Faraday's Lab

As described in Section 23-6, the first solid evidence for a connection between electric and magnetic phenomena was the discovery by Danish physicist and chemist Hans Christian Oersted. In 1821, while showing an experiment during a lecture, Oersted noticed that an electric current deflects the needle of a nearby compass, suggesting that the current generates a magnetic field. Oersted's findings intrigued a British scientist, Michael Faraday (1791–1867), who set out in the late 1820s to answer one of the most important questions in the history of physics: *If electric current is capable of generating a magnetic field, can a magnetic field generate an electric current?*

You can recreate Faraday's experiments either with available equipment or with the computer simulation in the Online Activity below.

ONLINE ACTIVITY

In Faraday's Lab

The e-resource that accompanies every new copy of this textbook contains an Online Activity using the PhET simulation "Faraday's electromagnetic lab: pickup coil." Work through the simulation and accompanying questions to gain an understanding of Faraday's experiments.

Faraday observed that moving a magnet toward a coil generated an electric current in one direction, and moving the same magnet away from the coil generated an electric current in the opposite direction. When the magnet was not moving relative to the coil, no current flowed in the coil. Faraday made several important observations from this series of experiments:

- A magnetic field can induce (generate) an electric current in a coil; thus, the phenomenon is called **electromagnetic induction** (Figure 24-2).

- The magnitude and the direction of the induced current depend on the rate of change of the magnetic field and the rate of change of the effective area of the loops in the coil. As soon as the change ceases the generation of electric current stops.

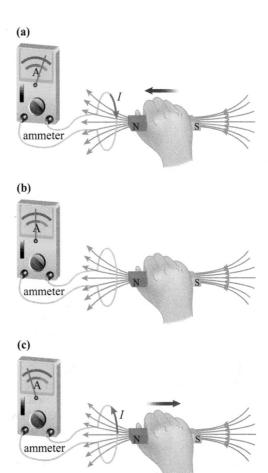

Figure 24-2 The effects of moving a magnet through a conducting loop. (a) When the magnet moves into the loop, an electric current is generated in the loop that is registered by an ammeter. (b) When the magnet is stationary relative to the loop, no current in the loop is detected. (c) When the magnet moves away from the loop, a current is generated again. The direction of the current depends on the relative motion of the magnet and the loop.

Faraday's original experiment (Figure 24-3) used two adjacent electric circuits called the primary and secondary circuits. The primary circuit consisted of a coil connected to a battery, while the secondary circuit consisted of a coil connected to an ammeter. The coils were made of insulated wire wound around opposite sides of an iron ring, which kept most of the magnetic field inside the coils. Faraday noticed that, when a steady electric current flowed through the primary circuit, the ammeter in the secondary circuit indicated zero current. However, when the circuit was switched on or off, the needle of the ammeter deflected for an instant, indicating the generation of an electric current in the secondary circuit. Faraday hypothesized

 CHECKPOINT

C-24-1 In Michael Faraday's Lab

Which of the following actions in Faraday's experiment will NOT induce electric current in the pickup coil, provided other parameters remain unchanged?

(a) gradually changing the number of loops
(b) gradually changing the strength of the magnet
(c) gradually changing the area of the loops
(d) using the most powerful stationary magnet available

C-24-1 (d) To generate an induced current, a magnetic flux has to be changing with time.

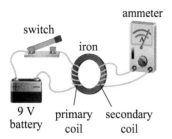

Figure 24-3 A modern version of Faraday's original experiment

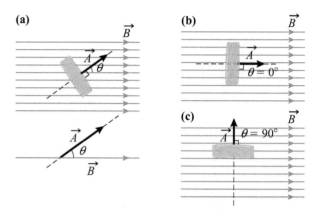

Figure 24-4 Magnetic flux through a closed loop can be expressed as $\Phi_B = BA \cos\theta$. (a) A magnetic field is directed at an angle θ to the normal to the loop. (b) The magnetic field is perpendicular to the plane of the loop $\Phi_B = BA \cos(0°) = BA$. (c) The magnetic field is parallel to the plane of the loop, $\Phi_B = BA \cos(90°) = 0$.

that the changing electric current in the primary circuit induced a changing magnetic field that, in turn, induced a changing electric current in the secondary circuit. The secondary coil is sometimes called a pick-up coil because it is picking up the signal of the varying magnetic field.

24-2 Magnetic Flux and Its Rate of Change

Faraday introduced the concept of **magnetic flux** to explain how a varying magnetic field generates electric current. You learned about electric flux in Chapter 20. To distinguish between electric and magnetic flux, we will use the subscripts E and B, respectively. In Section 23-5, we defined the orientation of a loop of wire with area vector, $\vec{A}$, where the magnitude of the vector represents the loop's area and the vector's direction is perpendicular to the plane of the loop. If a uniform magnetic field is directed at an arbitrary angle θ to the surface of the loop (Figure 24-4(a)), the magnetic flux through the loop is defined as follows:

$$\Phi_B = BA \cos\theta = BA_{eff} \qquad (24\text{-}1)$$

The product of the area of the loop and the cosine of the angle between the normal to the loop and the direction of the magnetic field ($A \cos\theta$) is called the **effective surface area** of the loop. The magnetic flux passing through the loop is a scalar quantity. It can be described more concisely using a scalar product:

KEY EQUATION $\qquad \Phi_B = BA \cos\theta = \vec{B} \cdot \vec{A} \qquad (24\text{-}2)$

When a uniform magnetic field is directed perpendicular to the plane of the loop (Figure 24-4(b)), the angle between the vectors $\vec{A}$ and $\vec{B}$ is 0°; thus, the magnetic flux Equation (24-2) becomes

$$\Phi_{B(\vec{B} \perp \vec{A})} = BA \cos(0°) = BA \qquad (24\text{-}3)$$

When magnetic field lines are parallel to the plane of the loop, the angle between $\vec{A}$ and $\vec{B}$ is 90°, and the magnetic flux through the loop is zero (Figure 24-4(c)):

$$\Phi_{B(\vec{B} \parallel \vec{A})} = BA \cos(90°) = 0 \qquad (24\text{-}4)$$

The SI unit for magnetic flux is the weber (Wb):

$$1 \text{ Wb} = 1 \text{T} \cdot \text{m}^2 \qquad (24\text{-}5)$$

Thus, 1 Wb of magnetic flux passes through each square metre of a surface perpendicular to a magnetic field of 1 T.

For a nonuniform magnetic field, magnetic flux is defined as follows:

$$\Phi_B = \vec{B}_{avg} \cdot \vec{A} = B_{avg}A \cos\theta = B_{avg}A_{eff} \qquad (24\text{-}6)$$

We can divide an arbitrary surface into infinitesimally small area elements, $d\vec{A}_i$, calculate magnetic flux $d\Phi_i$ through each element, and then integrate over the surface to determine the net flux:

$$\Phi_B = \int \vec{B} \cdot d\vec{A} = \int d\Phi \qquad (24\text{-}7)$$

For a three-dimensional surface (Figure 24-5), the direction of the normal to the surface element is always chosen to point outward. Therefore, a vector field directed inward through the surface generates a negative flux, and a field directed outward generates a positive flux. For a flat surface, the direction of the normal to the surface (and, hence, the sign of the magnetic flux) is chosen arbitrarily.

The breakthrough idea in Faraday's discovery of electromagnetic induction was his realization of the importance of the **rate of change of magnetic flux**. Since the coil can be represented as a stack of closed loops, we first

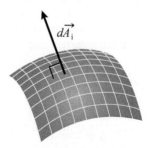

Figure 24-5 A three-dimensional surface can be divided into small surface elements $d\vec{A}_i$. The direction of each $d\vec{A}_i$ element is normal to the surface and points outward.

learn how to calculate the rate of change of the magnetic flux through a single loop:

$$\frac{d\Phi_B}{dt} = \frac{d\left(\vec{B} \cdot \vec{A}\right)}{dt}$$

$$\frac{d\Phi_B}{dt} = \frac{d[B(t)A(t)\cos(\theta(t))]}{dt}$$

$$\frac{d\Phi_B}{dt} = \underbrace{\frac{dB(t)}{dt}A(t)\cos(\theta(t))}_{B \text{ changes with time}} + \underbrace{\frac{dA(t)}{dt}B(t)\cos(\theta(t))}_{\text{Area changes with time}}$$

$$+ \underbrace{\frac{d\cos(\theta(t))}{dt}B(t)A(t)}_{\text{Angle } \theta \text{ changes with time}} \qquad (24\text{-}8)$$

EXAMPLE 24-1

Calculating the Rate of Change of a Magnetic Flux

A rectangular copper loop with the dimensions $l = 60$ cm and $w = 20$ cm is moving at a constant speed of 1 m/s out of the region of a uniform time-varying magnetic field, $B(t) = (0.001t + 0.005)$ T. The magnetic field is directed perpendicular to the loop (Figure 24-6).

(a) Derive an expression that describes how the rate of change of the magnetic flux through the loop varies with time.

(b) Find the rate of change of the magnetic flux through the loop at the instant when the loop is halfway out of the magnetic field region.

(c) Answer part (b) when the loop has moved completely out of the magnetic field region.

(d) Find the rate of change of the magnetic flux when the loop is stationary, while located within the magnetic field.

(e) Recalculate parts (a) to (d) for a coil consisting of three loops, all identical to the loop described above.

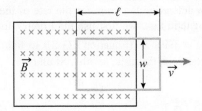

Figure 24-6 A rectangular copper loop is moving at a constant speed out of a uniform magnetic field region.

SOLUTION

(a) We use Equation (24-8) to calculate the rate of change of the magnetic flux. The plane of the loop is always perpendicular to the magnetic field, $\cos(0°) = 1$, so Equation (24-8) simplifies to

C-24-2 Magnetic Flux Through the Surface of a Closed Loop

The magnetic flux through the plane of a closed loop is zero ($\Phi_B = 0$). What can you conclude?

(a) There is no magnetic field in that space.

(b) Magnetic field lines are perpendicular to the plane of the loop.

(c) Magnetic field lines are parallel to the plane of the loop.

(d) The effective area of the loop is zero.

(e) Statements (a), (c), and (d) may be true.

(f) Statements (a), (b), (c), and (d) may be true.

C-24-2 (e) Use the definition of magnetic flux.

$$\frac{d\Phi_B}{dt} = \frac{dB(t)}{dt}A(t)\cos\theta + \frac{dA(t)}{dt}B(t)\cos\theta$$

Since the loop is pulled out of the magnetic field region with constant speed v, the effective area of the loop changes with time. If $t = 0$ s was the last instant when the loop was entirely inside the magnetic field region, at time t, its effective area is $A(t) = w(l - vt)$, provided $t \le \frac{l}{v}$. Therefore,

$$\frac{dA(t)}{dt} = \frac{d[w(l - vt)]}{dt} = -wv$$

Consequently, the rate of change of the magnetic field is

$$\frac{d\Phi_B}{dt} = \frac{dB(t)}{dt}A(t) - wvB(t) = \frac{dB(t)}{dt}w(l - vt) - wvB(t)$$

$$\frac{d\Phi_B}{dt} = \left(0.001\,\frac{T}{s}\right)(0.2\text{ m})\left(0.6\text{ m} - \left(1\,\frac{m}{s}\right)t\right)$$

$$- (0.2\text{ m})\left(1\,\frac{m}{s}\right)(0.001t + 0.005)\text{ T}$$

$$\frac{d\Phi_B}{dt} = \left(0.0002\,\frac{T\cdot m}{s}\right)\left(0.6\text{ m} - \left(1\,\frac{m}{s}\right)t\right)$$

$$- \left(0.2\,\frac{m^2}{s}\right)(0.001t + 0.005)\text{ T}$$

while $t \le \dfrac{l}{v} = 0.6$ s

This result applies only during the time when the loop is partially submerged in the magnetic field region. After 0.6 s, the loop is clear of the magnetic field and is no longer affected by it. As expected, the rate of change of the magnetic field is time-dependent.

(continued)

(b) The loop is halfway out of the magnetic field at $t = 0.3$ s, and

$$\left|\frac{d\Phi_B}{dt}\right|_{t=0.3\,s} = \left|\left(0.0002\,\frac{T\cdot m}{s}\right)\left(0.6\,m - \left(1\,\frac{m}{s}\right)(0.3\,s)\right)\right.$$
$$\left. - \left(0.2\,\frac{m^2}{s}\right)(0.001(0.3\,s) + 0.005)\,T\right|$$

$$\left|\frac{d\Phi_B}{dt}\right|_{t=0.3\,s} = \left|\left(6\times 10^{-5}\,\frac{T\cdot m^2}{s}\right) - \left(106\times 10^{-5}\,\frac{T\cdot m^2}{s}\right)\right|$$

$$= \left(100 \times 10^{-5}\,\frac{Wb}{s}\right) = 1.0\,\frac{mWb}{s}$$

(c) When the loop has moved completely outside the magnetic field region, the magnetic flux through the loop is $\Phi_B \equiv \text{const} \equiv 0$, and the rate of change is $\frac{d\Phi_B}{dt} \equiv 0$.

(d) When the entire loop is held stationary in the uniform magnetic field, the effective area of the loop remains constant. However, the magnetic flux through the loop is changing because the magnetic field depends on time. Consequently, Equation (24-8) simplifies to

$$\frac{d\Phi_B}{dt} = \frac{dB(t)}{dt}A(t) = \left(0.001\,\frac{T}{s}\right)(0.6\,m)(0.2\,m) = 0.12\,\frac{mWb}{s}$$

(e) When the number of loops is tripled, the effective area of the loop and thus the rate of change of the magnetic

flux also triples. Therefore, the answers to the previous parts triple as well.

Making sense of the result:

Since the solution to the problem depends on the expression derived in part (a), we can check it using dimensional analysis:

$$\left[\frac{d\Phi_B}{dt}\right] = \frac{Wb}{s}$$

$$\left[\left(0.0002\,\frac{T\cdot m}{s}\right)\left(0.6\,m - \left(1\,\frac{m}{s}\right)t\right) + \left(0.2\,\frac{m^2}{s}\right)(0.001t + 0.005)\,T\right]$$
$$= \frac{T\cdot m^2}{s} = \frac{Wb}{s}$$

The answer to part (c) is zero because the loop in (c) is unaffected by the magnetic field. The answers to parts (b) and (d) are nonzero because the rate of change of the magnetic flux in (b) is larger than in part (d). In part (d), the only cause of the change of the magnetic flux is the change of the magnetic field. Yet in part (b) the changes in both the magnetic field and in the effective area of the loop contribute to the change in the magnetic flux. Therefore, the final result in part (b) is larger than the result in part (a).

In general, when the number of loops in a coil is N,

$$\left(\frac{d\Phi_B}{dt}\right)_{coil} = N\left(\frac{d\Phi_B}{dt}\right)_{loop} \qquad (24\text{-}9)$$

LO 3, LO 4, LO 8

24-3 Faraday's Law of Electromagnetic Induction

In 1831, Faraday formulated a theory of electromagnetic induction to explain the results of his experiments: a time-varying magnetic flux through a conducting loop induces an emf ε across the loop. This emf has a magnitude equal to the rate of change of the magnetic flux through this loop and is directed such that it opposes the change of the magnetic flux that causes it.

The part of this law pertaining to the direction of induced current was rediscovered in 1834 by the Russian physicist Heinrich Lenz (1804–65) and is called **Lenz's law.**

The law of electromagnetic induction

$$\varepsilon_{ind} = -\left(\frac{d\Phi_B}{dt}\right) \qquad (24\text{-}10)$$

The minus sign in the law of electromagnetic induction emphasizes that the direction of the induced current is such that the magnetic field induced by it ($\vec{B}_{ind}$) *opposes* the change of the magnetic flux. It is important to note that if the direction of the induced emf were not opposed to the change of the magnetic flux, one would get a perpetual motion machine arising from the positive feedback. This "runaway" scenario contradicts the law of energy conservation. You might want to revisit the Online Activity on page 645 now, paying special attention to the direction and magnitude of the induced current.

To determine the units for the rate of the change of the magnetic flux, we first use the Lorentz force expression $\vec{F}_B = q\vec{v} \times \vec{B}$ (Equation (23-2)) to link the unit of magnetic field, the tesla, to other SI units:

$$[\vec{B}] = T = \frac{N}{C\cdot\dfrac{m}{s}} = \frac{kg\cdot\dfrac{m}{s^2}}{C\cdot\dfrac{m}{s}} = \frac{kg}{s\cdot C} \Rightarrow T \equiv \frac{kg}{s\cdot C}$$

Therefore, and

$$\left[\frac{d\Phi}{dt}\right] = \frac{Wb}{s} = \frac{T\cdot m^2}{s} = \frac{kg}{s\cdot C}\cdot\frac{m^2}{s} = \frac{kg\cdot m^2}{s^2\cdot C} = \frac{J}{C} = V$$

$$(24\text{-}11)$$

Thus, dimensional analysis confirms that a rate of change of magnetic flux corresponds to a potential difference. A conducting loop in a magnetic field acts as an emf source, as long as the magnetic flux keeps changing in time.

When a coil consists of N identical loops, the law of electromagnetic induction (Equation (24-10)) can be rewritten as follows:

KEY EQUATION
$$\varepsilon_{ind} = -\left(\frac{d\Phi_B}{dt}\right)_{coil} = -N\left(\frac{d\Phi_B}{dt}\right)_{loop} \quad (24\text{-}12)$$

Expressions (24-8) and (24-12) can be combined to obtain the following:

$$\varepsilon_{ind} = -N\left(\underbrace{\frac{dB(t)}{dt}A(t)\cos(\theta(t))}_{B \text{ changes with time}} + \underbrace{\frac{dA(t)}{dt}B(t)\cos(\theta(t))}_{Area \text{ changes with time}}\right.$$
$$\left. + \underbrace{\frac{d\cos(\theta(t))}{dt}B(t)A(t)}_{Angle \ \theta \text{ changes with time}}\right) \quad (24\text{-}13)$$

✓ CHECKPOINT

C-24-3 Induced Current in a Metal Ring

In which direction should the bar magnet in Figure 24-7 move to induce the electric current in the ring shown in the diagram?

(a) horizontally toward the ring
(b) horizontally away from the ring
(c) upward
(d) downward
(e) None of the above will generate an electric current in the ring.

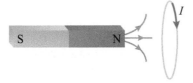

Figure 24-7 C-24-3

C-24-3 (b) Apply Lenz's law.

Eddy Currents

In 1851, almost 20 years after Faraday's original discovery, French physicist Léon Foucault (1819–68) noticed that when the magnetic flux through a large piece of conductor varies with time, the flux induces electric current loops inside the conductor (Figure 24-8(a)). Such currents are called **eddies** or **eddy currents**. According to Faraday's law, these induced currents oppose the change of the original magnetic flux. The faster the magnetic flux changes, the stronger the induced eddy currents. The direction of eddies can be determined using Lenz's law. Since all conductors (except for superconductors) have some resistance, eddy currents generated in them by the changing magnetic

flux will heat the conductors up. This heating means generation of thermal energy. Therefore, eddy currents can convert mechanical energy (e.g. motion of a conductor through the non-uniform magnetic field) into thermal energy (heat dissipated by the current-carrying conductors). (In some applications such as hand-crank generator flashlight, http://www.youtube.com/watch?v=Im14gk4L7XA, the electrical

(a)

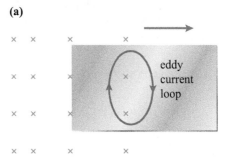

(b)

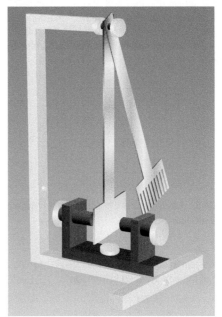

(c)

Figure 24-8 Eddy currents. (a) One of the eddy current loops inside a metal sheet moving to the right through a nonuniform magnetic field (b) Two metal pendulums are placed between the poles of two permanent magnets. As the pendulums swing, eddy currents generated in the pendulum that consists of a solid metal sheet (no slits) generate eddy currents that slow the motion of the pendulum (a consequence of Lenz's law). On the other hand, the pendulum that has slits in it does not slow down, since slits prevent generation of eddy currents. (c) A magnet levitates above a superconductor as a result of the Meissner effect.

CHAPTER 24 | ELECTROMAGNETIC INDUCTION   649

energy generated by the changing magnetic flux can be stored). However, in other applications, the energy dissipation from eddy currents is undesirable. To reduce energy losses, conductors are made with slits (Figure 24-8(b)) or are constructed with thin layers (laminations) that are insulated from each other by a nonconductive varnish. These techniques reduce undesirable eddy currents by making the area of the closed loops much smaller. Eddy currents are used in magnetic brakes and magnetic dampers, as discussed in the following section.

Since superconductors have zero resistance (and, hence, no thermal energy dissipation), eddy currents generated on the surface of a superconductor will flow indefinitely. Consequently, such eddy currents induce a magnetic field that *completely* opposes the external magnetic flux that induced them. Consequently, the superconductor expels the magnetic field from its interior. This phenomenon is called the Meissner effect (Figure 24-8(c)), named after the German physicist Walther Meissner (1882–1974), who discovered it in 1933.

 EXAMPLE 24-2

Emf Induced by a Time-dependent Magnetic Field

A rectangular stationary loop with dimensions $l = 60$ cm and $w = 20$ cm (Figure 24-9) and a resistance of 0.1 Ω is placed perpendicular to a uniform time-dependent magnetic field with $B(t) = (0.04t + 0.002)$ T. Calculate the direction and the magnitude of the electric current induced in the loop.

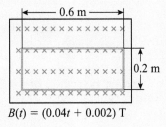

$$B(t) = (0.04t + 0.002) \text{ T}$$

Figure 24-9 A rectangular loop in a uniform magnetic field that changes with time

SOLUTION

First, we use expression (24-8) with $N = 1$ to find the magnitude of the emf induced in the loop:

$$|\varepsilon_{ind}| = N \left| \underbrace{\frac{dB(t)}{dt} A(t) \cos(\theta(t))}_{B \text{ changes with time}} \right|$$

$$= \left(\underbrace{\frac{d(0.04t + 0.02) \text{ T}}{dt} (0.2 \text{ m} \cdot 0.6 \text{ m}) \cos(0°)}_{B \text{ changes with time}} \right)$$

$$|\varepsilon_{ind}| = 0.04 \frac{\text{T}}{\text{s}} \cdot 0.12 \text{ m}^2 = 0.0048 \text{ V} = 4.8 \text{ mV}$$

To calculate the magnitude of the induced current, we use Ohm's law:

$$I_{ind} = \frac{\varepsilon_{ind}}{R} = \frac{4.8 \text{ mV}}{0.1 \text{ Ω}} = 48 \text{ mA}$$

Since the magnetic field increases with time, the magnetic flux increases with time. According to Lenz's law, the direction of the induced current is such that the induced magnetic field $\vec{B}_{ind}$ opposes the magnetic flux change. The direction of the original magnetic field $\vec{B}(t)$ is into the page in Figure 24-9, so the direction of the induced magnetic field $\vec{B}_{ind}$ will be opposite: out of the page. Therefore, the induced current flows counterclockwise.

Making sense of the result:

Since the original magnetic field $\vec{B}(t)$ changes with time linearly, its rate of change is constant. Consequently, the induced emf and induced current are also constant.

Additional examples in the online supplement to this textbook consider more complex time-dependent magnetic fields. Next, we consider **motional emf**, which is emf induced by the motion of a rectangular coil (consisting of N rectangular loops) inside or outside a region of a constant and uniform magnetic field. Let us first assume that each rectangular loop has a width w and length l. Let us calculate the induced emf in this rectangular coil when it enters or leaves a region of a uniform and constant magnetic field, $\vec{B}$ = const, that is directed perpendicular to the coil $\theta = 0°$. (See Figure 24-10(a) in Example 24-3 below.) Moreover, the coil is moving at a constant velocity $\vec{v}$ such that its plane is perpendicular to the direction of the magnetic field. We

can use Equation (24-13) to derive the expression for the induced emf:

$$\varepsilon_{ind} = -\left(\frac{d\Phi_B}{dt} \right)_{coil} = -N \left(\frac{d\Phi_B}{dt} \right)_{loop}$$

KEY EQUATION
(24-14)

$$= -NB \left(\underbrace{\frac{dA(t)}{dt}}_{\substack{\text{Area changes} \\ \text{with time}}} \right) = -NBvl$$

where N is the number of loops in the coil, and l is the length of the side of the coil that is in the field and perpendicular to both the field and the velocity.

EXAMPLE 24-3

Motional emf in a Rectangular Coil

A horizontal, rectangular (5 cm $\times$ 10 cm) coil has 100 turns and a total resistance of $10\ \Omega$. Initially, it is sitting with the right side of the coil at the edge of a vertical uniform magnetic field with $B = 0.4$ T as shown in Figure 24-10(a). The coil is then pulled to the right, out of the field.

(a) Determine the velocity of the coil needed to generate an emf of 0.5 V.

(b) Draw a graph that shows the dependence of the induced emf on time while the coil is leaving the magnetic field at the constant velocity $\vec{v}$ found in part (a).

(c) Find the direction and the magnitude of the electric current induced in the coil during this process.

(d) Find the magnitude of the external force $\vec{F}_{ext}$ needed to pull the coil with the constant velocity $\vec{v}$. Assume that friction is negligible.

(e) Sketch a graph that represents the dependence of the external force $\vec{F}_{ext}$ on time. Compare this graph with the emf graph in part (b).

SOLUTION

(a) Applying expression (24-2), we find the speed of the coil that will generate 0.5 V of induced emf:

$$v = \frac{\varepsilon_{ind}}{NBl} = \frac{0.5\ \text{V}}{(100)(0.4\ \text{T})(0.05\ \text{m})} = 0.25\ \text{m/s} = 25\ \text{cm/s}$$

(b) Moving at a constant speed of 25 cm/s, it takes 0.4 s for the coil to move 10 cm to get completely outside of the magnetic field region. During this time, the induced emf is constant (Equation (24-14)). However, as soon as the coil is clear of the magnetic field, the induced emf drops to zero (Figure 24-10(b)).

(c) To find the magnitude of the electric current induced in the coil while it is being pulled out of the field, we use Ohm's law:

$$I_{ind} = \frac{\varepsilon_{ind}}{R} = \frac{NBvl}{R} = \frac{0.5\ \text{V}}{10\ \Omega} = 0.05\ \text{A} = 50\ \text{mA}$$

Since the magnetic flux through the coil decreases as the coil leaves the field, Lenz's law requires the induced current to move in the clockwise direction to induce a magnetic field $\vec{B}_{ind}$ in the same direction as the original field (into the page).

(d) Since the coil is moving with a constant velocity, the net force acting on it must be zero. It might seem that there is no need to apply an external force $\vec{F}_{ext}$ to pull the coil out of the magnetic field. However, let us consider every side of the coil more carefully (Figure 24-10(c)). Side AB

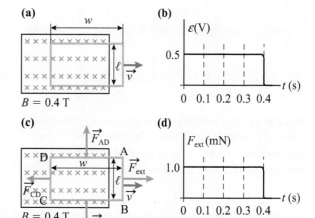

Figure 24-10   A rectangular coil leaves a uniform magnetic field

is never inside the magnetic field, so there is no magnetic force acting on it. However, there are magnetic forces acting on the other three sides. Using the right-hand rule for magnetic force (Section 23-1) and the direction of the current in the coil, we find that the magnetic forces acting on sides AD and BC are directed upward and downward, respectively (Figure 24-10(c)), and the magnetic force acting on side CD is directed to the left, resisting the coil's motion. The magnitude of the resultant horizontal magnetic force can be found using Equation (23-22):

$$F_B = N(IlB) = N\frac{NBvl}{R}lB = \frac{N^2B^2l^2v}{R} \quad (24\text{-}15)$$

Since the net force acting on the coil is zero, the external force pulling it must be directed right with a magnitude of

$$F_{ext} = \frac{NB^2l^2v}{R} = \frac{(100)^2(0.4\ \text{T})^2(0.05\ \text{m})^2(0.25\ \text{m/s})}{10\ \Omega}$$

$$= 0.1\ \text{N}$$

(e) Figure 24-10(d) shows how the magnitude of the pulling force $\vec{F}_{ext}$ depends on time.

Making sense of the result:

The induced emf is generated as long as the magnetic flux through the coil is changing, that is, while the coil is moving out of the region of a constant and uniform magnetic field. During this process, the magnetic force acting on the coil resists its motion.

Let us consider the energy transfer in Example 24-3. We generated an electric current by pulling the coil out of the region of a constant and uniform magnetic field. To pull the coil with constant velocity $\vec{v}$, we had to apply an external force $\vec{F}_{ext}$ (Figure 24-11), which did work on the coil (Equation (24-15)). The rate at which this work was done equals the generated power, P:

$$P = F_{ext}\,v = \frac{N^2B^2l^2v}{R}\,v = \left(\frac{NBlv}{R}\right)^2 R = \left(\frac{\varepsilon_{ind}}{R}\right)^2 R = I_{ind}^2 R$$

$$(24\text{-}16)$$

Expression (24-16) shows that the power delivered by the external force dissipates as thermal energy.

ELECTRICITY, MAGNETISM, AND OPTICS

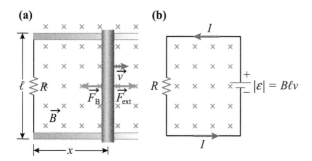

Figure 24-11 (a) A conducting bar is in a constant and uniform magnetic field. An applied force $\vec{F}_{app}$ slides the bar with constant velocity along the frictionless rails. (b) The equivalent circuit diagram for the conducting bar sliding with constant velocity

We now consider motional emf at the microscopic level. When a conductor is moving with a constant velocity $\vec{v}$ inside a uniform magnetic field $\vec{B}$ directed perpendicular to its velocity, the charged particles inside the conductor move with the same average velocity $\vec{v}$. Therefore, positive and negative charges inside this moving conductor experience magnetic forces acting in opposite directions (Figure 24-12). Consequently, the charges separate. Electrons are free to move inside a conductor, so they will be affected by this magnetic force. This will generate a potential difference across the conductor. The separation of charges continues until the magnitudes of the electric and magnetic forces equalize:

$$F_E = F_B \Rightarrow E_{ind}q = qvB_\perp \text{ Thus, } E_{ind} = vB_\perp$$

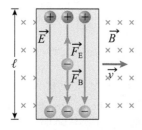

Figure 24-12 The separation of charges inside a rectangular conductor of length l moving inside a region of a uniform magnetic field $\vec{B}$, directed perpendicular to its velocity $\vec{v}$.

In a conductor of length l, an induced electric field $\vec{E}_{ind}$ causes an induced potential difference across the conductor:

KEY EQUATION $$\Delta V_{ind} = E_{ind}l = vB_\perp l \qquad (24\text{-}17)$$

Motional emf is induced as long as the velocity of a conductor moving in a magnetic field is directed at a nonzero angle to the field. The velocity of the conductor does not need to be constant or perpendicular to the magnetic field.

✓ **CHECKPOINT**

C-24-4 Charge Distribution on a Plate Moving Inside a Magnetic Field

A rectangular metal plate initially located outside of a constant and uniform magnetic field is given an initial push toward the magnetic field region and then let go. Which diagram in Figure 24-13 correctly represents the charge distribution on the plate as it moves into the magnetic field?

(a) diagram (a)
(b) diagram (b)
(c) diagram (c)
(d) diagram (d)
(e) diagram (e)
(f) diagram (f)

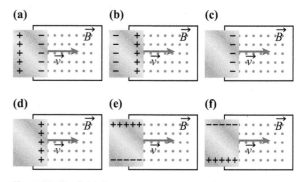

Figure 24-13 C-24-4

C-24-4 Diagram (f): Use the right-hand rule to determine the direction of the magnetic force on charged particles moving inside a magnetic field.

LO 4, LO 8

24-4 Applications of Faraday's Law of Electromagnetic Induction

Few scientific discoveries have had a more significant impact on our lives than Faraday's law of electromagnetic induction. In this section, we look at a few examples of how this law is applied in the multitude of devices used in homes, businesses, and industry every day.

AC Power Generators

Most of the electric power generated in the world is produced using generators that convert mechanical energy into electric energy using the same principle as the simple generator shown in Figure 24-14.

The core of an electric generator is a system of conductive loops that rotate in a uniform and constant magnetic field. As each loop rotates, the magnetic flux through it changes, inducing an emf in it. Consider a single loop of area A and resistance R rotating at an angular velocity ω

(a)

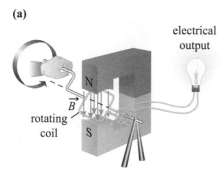

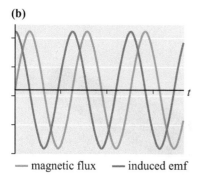

electrical output

rotating coil

$\vec{B}$

N

S

(b)

t

— magnetic flux   — induced emf

Figure 24-14 (a) The operation of an electric generator (b) The dependence of the magnetic flux through the rotating coil and of the induced emf on time

in a uniform magnetic field (Figure 24-14(a)). The angle between the magnetic field and the normal to the plane of the loop can be described as $\theta = \omega t$. Then the rate of change of the magnetic flux through the loop is

$$\frac{d\Phi}{dt} = \frac{dBA\,\cos(\theta)}{dt} = \frac{dBA\,\cos(\omega t)}{dt} = -BA\,\omega\sin(\omega t)$$

(24-18)

We use Faraday's law to find the magnitude of the induced emf in the loop:

$$\varepsilon_{ind} = BA\,\omega\sin(\omega t) = V_{max}\sin(\omega t)$$

$$V_{max} = BA\omega = 2\pi BAf$$

$$I = I_{max}\sin(\omega t)$$

(24-19)

where

$$I_{max} = \frac{BA\omega}{R} = \frac{2\pi BAf}{R}$$

Thus, such a generator produces an emf that varies sinusoidally with time, which is the most common type of **alternating emf**. An electric current generated by such a generator is called **alternating current** (AC). For a rotating coil with N loops, the expressions for emf and current become the following:

KEY EQUATION

$$\varepsilon_{ind} = NBA\,\omega\sin(\omega t)$$

$$I = I_{max}\sin(\omega t)$$

(24-20)

where

$$I_{max} = \frac{NBA\omega}{R} = \frac{2\pi NBAf}{R}$$

and the frequency of the alternating current (f) depends on the angular speed of the coil (ω), $f = \dfrac{\omega}{2\pi}$.

ELECTRICITY, MAGNETISM, AND OPTICS

MAKING CONNECTIONS

Sources of Electrical Energy

In North America, the standard frequency for AC current is 60 Hz; in Europe and some other countries it is 50 Hz. The most common source of mechanical energy for electric generators worldwide is steam from burning fossil fuels or from nuclear fission. However, in Canada, the most common source of this mechanical energy is hydroelectric—kinetic energy from falling water (approximately 60%). Coal supplies slightly less than 20%, and nuclear power supplies approximately 12%. The proportions vary considerably by province: in 2007, more than half of Ontario's energy came from nuclear power, and only 21% was hydroelectric. However, Alberta generates almost 90% of its electricity with coal and natural gas. More than 70% of the energy for generators in the United States is produced using fossil fuels and nuclear power.

The same principles of electromagnetic induction that underlie giant generators (Figure 24-15) feeding national power grids also apply to the diesel-powered backup generators for hospitals, gas-powered portable generators on

Diana Cardoso

Figure 24-15 The Churchill River Underground Power Plant in Newfoundland and Labrador is the second largest underground power plant in the world.

(continued)

construction sites, and even hand-powered flashlights, like those shown in Figure 24-16. The flashlight on the bottom right uses a stationary coil and a movable magnet. Shaking this flashlight makes the magnet slide back and forth through the coil, changing the magnetic flux and, hence, inducing current. On the hand-crank flashlights, turning the crank either rotates a coil inside a stationary magnet directly or winds a spring, which powers clockwork, which rotates the coil until the spring runs down. All of these flashlights use electromagnetic induction to convert human mechanical energy into electrical energy.

Figure 24-16 Several types of hand-powered generator flashlights

EXAMPLE 24-4

Exploring How an Electric Generator Works

An electric generator has a circular coil with 20 turns, each 60 cm in diameter. The coil makes 60 revolutions per second. What strength of magnetic field is required to produce a peak output voltage of 170 V?

SOLUTION

Using expression (24-20) we find

$$V_{max} = NBA\omega = 2\pi NBAf$$

$$B = \frac{V_{max}}{2\pi NAf} = \frac{V_{max}}{2\pi N\left(\pi \frac{d^2}{4}\right)(60 \text{ Hz})}$$

$$= \frac{170 \text{ V}}{2\pi(20 \text{ turns})\left(\pi \frac{(0.6 \text{ m})^2}{4}\right)(60 \text{ Hz})} = 0.08 \text{ T}$$

Making sense of the result:

A strong permanent magnet can produce a magnetic field strength in the order of 0.1 T, so a value of 0.08 T seems reasonable.

Transformers

Have you ever wondered why electric power delivered to our homes comes in the form of alternating current (AC) rather than direct current (DC)? At the end of the 19th century, the struggle between the proponents of AC and DC power generation was so fierce that it was dubbed the "war of currents." Thomas Alva Edison (1847–1931) advocated for DC power, and Nikola Tesla (1856–1943, Figure 24-17) and George Westinghouse (1846–1914) promoted AC power generation. The key issue that swayed the argument in favour of AC power was power transmission. For various practical reasons, large electric power plants are often located away from densely populated areas, so the electric current has to travel through wires over long distances to reach consumers. The amount of power dissipated as thermal energy in the transmission lines depends on the current and the resistance of the wires (Equation (22-23)):

$$P = I^2R$$

The longer the transmission line, the higher its resistance and the greater the proportion of electrical energy lost as thermal energy. Edison tried to minimize such losses by building electric power plants very close to the consumers, for example, in New York City. However, this approach turned out to be impractical.

Figure 24-17 The Nikola Tesla monument in Queen Victoria Park at Niagara Falls, Ontario, was unveiled on July 9, 2006. Tesla is standing on top of an AC motor, one of the 700 inventions he patented.

Tesla realized that AC voltages can be stepped up or down using a **transformer**. By using high voltages and much smaller currents, the thermal energy dissipation in transmission lines can be greatly reduced. In Edison's time, there was no practical way of changing the voltage of large amounts of DC. Transformers use changing magnetic flux, so they do not work with DC.

 ONLINE ACTIVITY

Operation of a Transformer

The e-resource that accompanies every new copy of this textbook contains an Online Activity using the PhET simulation "Faraday's Electromagnetic Lab: Transformer." Work through the simulation and accompanying questions to gain an understanding of the operation of transformers.

A transformer consists of two adjacent coils: a primary coil, which is connected to the power supply, and a secondary coil, which is connected to the load (Figure 24-18). Usually, the coils are wound on the same iron core. A transformer is based on the principle of **mutual inductance**: a changing magnetic field through the primary coil generates a time-varying magnetic field through the secondary coil. In the primary coil of a transformer, an AC current produces a time-varying magnetic field. This field creates a time-varying magnetic flux through the secondary coil, which induces a time-varying

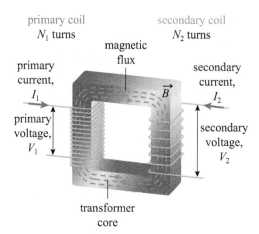

primary coil
N_1 turns

secondary coil
N_2 turns

magnetic flux

primary current, I_1

secondary current, I_2

$\vec{B}$

primary voltage, V_1

secondary voltage, V_2

transformer core

Figure 24-18 A step-down transformer

emf in the secondary coil. Let us denote the potential difference across the primary coil as V_1 and the potential difference across the secondary coil as V_2. Sinusoidal alternating currents continuously change their magnitude and direction, but due to symmetry considerations, the average values of V_1 and V_2 are zero. For power calculations, we need to use root-mean-square values for AC voltages and currents. You will learn more about root-mean-square values in Chapter 25.

Transformers transform lower voltages into higher voltages and back by converting electric energy into magnetic energy and vice versa. The law of energy conservation states that if there are no energy losses (such as dissipated thermal energy), the power delivered to the primary coil equals the power generated in the secondary coil. Using Equation (22-23),

$$P_1 = P_2$$
$$I_1 V_1 = I_2 V_2 \tag{24-21}$$

Since power dissipated through thermal energy is proportional to the square of the current ($P = I^2 R$), to reduce energy transmission losses, the current transmitted through the wires should be as low as possible. Therefore, power stations have transformers that step up the voltage (transforming low voltage into high voltage) and, consequently, lower the current in the transmission lines. Transmission voltages generally range from 138 kV to 765 kV. At the other end of the transmission line, the voltage is stepped down (transformed from high voltage to lower voltage) in several stages to the standard 120 V/240 V for most residential customers.

In the next section, we will discuss the phenomenon of mutual inductance in more detail and will prove that the function of a transformer (step-up or step-down) is defined by the ratio of the number of loops in its primary and secondary coils:

$$\frac{V_2}{V_1} = \frac{N_2}{N_1} \tag{24-22}$$

C-24-5 The Operation of a Transformer

Figure 24-19 shows a simple transformer: two coils wound around an iron core. The primary coil is connected to a DC power supply. The voltmeter shows the voltage induced in the secondary coil of the transformer. When was the voltmeter reading taken?

(a) The voltmeter reading was taken during the opening of a circuit, when the current in the circuit was decreasing.

(b) The voltmeter reading was taken during the closing of a circuit, when the current in the circuit was increasing.

(c) The voltmeter reading was taken when the current in the circuit was steady: the circuit has been closed for a while.

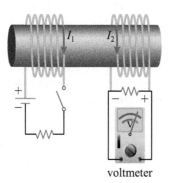

voltmeter

Figure 24-19 C-24-5

C-24-5 Use Lenz's law to verify that (a) is correct.

EXAMPLE 24-5

Transformer Ratio

A transformer is used to change a 120 V, 3 A current to 12 V in a power supply for a laptop computer.

(a) Is this a step-up or a step-down transformer? Explain.

(b) What is the ratio of the number of secondary coil turns to the number of primary coil turns in this transformer?

(c) What current would be induced in the secondary coil?

SOLUTION

(a) This is a step-down transformer because it transforms higher voltage into lower voltage.

(b) To find the ratio of the number of secondary coil turns to the number of primary coil turns, we use Equation (24-22):

$$\frac{V_2}{V_1} = \frac{N_2}{N_1} \Rightarrow \frac{N_2}{N_1} = \frac{12 \text{ V}}{120 \text{ V}} = 1{:}10$$

(c) The law of energy conservation can be used to find the current in the secondary coil (Equation (24-21)):

$$I_1 V_1 = I_2 V_2 \Rightarrow I_2 = \frac{I_1 V_1}{V_2} = \frac{(3 \text{ A})(120 \text{ V})}{12 \text{ V}} = 30 \text{ A}$$

Making sense of the result:

The secondary current is 10 times higher than the primary current, which is reasonable because the secondary voltage is 10 times lower than the primary voltage.

Electromagnetic Damping and Electromagnetic Braking

Electromagnetic dampers consist of a strong electromagnet or permanent magnet and a moving nonmagnetic metal part whose vibrations are to be damped. In the presence of a strong magnetic field, eddy currents are created inside the moving part. These eddy currents oppose the motion that induces them, and thus act to damp vibration in the moving part. Electromagnetic dampers are clean, easy to adjust, and less sensitive to temperature than hydraulic dampers. For example, when sheet metal is fed along a production line for coating, transverse vibrations in the sheets can make the coating uneven. Placing a powerful electromagnet near the sheets induces eddy currents that dampen the vibrations significantly.

Electromagnetic braking uses the same principle, slowing an object by inducing eddy currents that convert mechanical energy into thermal energy or electrical energy. The first electromagnetic brakes were used on mountain trains. Today, electromagnetic brakes are used on vehicles such as roller coasters, conventional and magnetic levitation trains, and hybrid vehicles. To slow the vehicle, the electric drive motor is switched to act as a generator. The motor then converts kinetic energy into electric energy and thermal energy. As a coil on the shaft of the motor rotates in a magnetic field inside the motor, a **back emf** is induced on the coil and fed to the battery, recharging it while slowing the rotation of the motor shaft.

The Electric Guitar

In both acoustic and electric guitars, sound is produced by the vibration of the strings. In an acoustic guitar, the sound of the strings is boosted by a soundboard and a resonant cavity (Chapter 15). In an electric guitar, electromagnetic induction produces an electric current that corresponds to the vibration of the strings. The signal is then amplified electronically to drive a speaker. The strings of an electric guitar are made of a ferromagnetic material (often steel or nickel). Electric guitars typically have two or three sets of pickups positioned along the strings (Figure 24-20(a)). Each set has six coils, one aligned directly underneath each of the six strings on

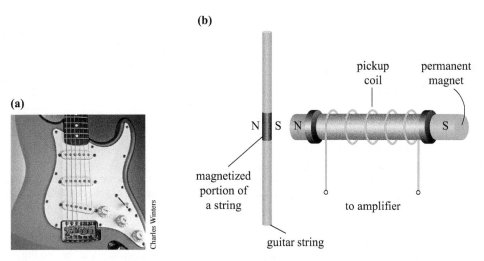

Figure 24-20 The operation of an electric guitar. (a) Pickup coils (metal circles) are located under the string of an electric guitar. (b) The moving steel string changes the flux from the permanent magnet, inducing a current in the pickup coil.

the guitar. The design of the coils and the position of the pickups affect the signal they produce, so the guitarist can change the sound of the guitar by choosing which pickups are connected to the amplifier. The vibrating ferromagnetic strings create time-varying magnetic fields through the pickup coils (Figure 24-20(b)), which then induce a changing emf and a changing electric current, which control the sound created by the speakers.

Metal Detectors

There are several types of metal detectors, and they all use electromagnetic induction. In the single-coil metal detector shown in Figure 24-21(a), a pulsing current is applied to the coil. This current induces a time-varying magnetic field and, hence, a time-varying magnetic flux through nearby objects. In metal objects, the varying flux induces eddy currents, which generate their own magnetic fields, shown in red in Figure 24-21(b). As a result, an electric current opposite in direction to the original electric current is generated in the coil. This change of current in the coil is used to detect the presence of metal.

In a two-coil metal detector (Figure 24-21(c)), the transmitter and receiver coils act as a transformer. The presence of metal near the receiver coil induces eddy currents that change the current in the receiver coil.

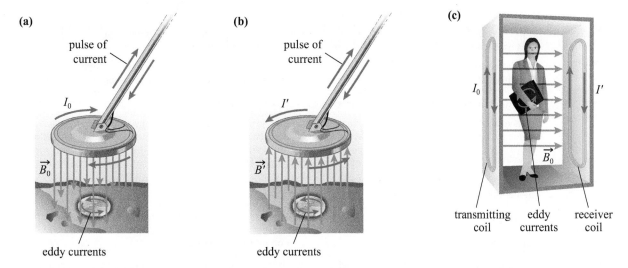

Figure 24-21 Metal detectors. (a) A single-coil metal detector consists of a transmitter coil that generates a pulsing magnetic field. (b) In the presence of a coin, for example, in the vicinity of the coil, the eddy currents induced in the coin affect the current in the transmitter coil and indicate the presence of metal. (c) A two-coil metal detector

24-5 Induced emf and Induced Electric Fields

We now take a closer look at the current induced in a circular conducting loop by a time-varying magnetic flux (Figure 24-22). As the magnetic field in the shaded area changes with time, it generates a changing magnetic flux through the loop. This changing magnetic flux induces an electric current in the loop. A galvanometer (G) connected in series with the loop can measure this current. The presence of an electric current indicates the presence of an electric field that applies an electric force on charge carriers. Since the loop is circular, the direction of the electric field must be tangent to the loop to force the charged particles to move along the circular loop (Figure 24-22(a)). An electric field is induced in the space surrounding the time-varying magnetic flux (Figure 24-22(b)). Note that this **induced electric field**, $\vec{E}_{ind}$, is independent of the presence of free electric charges in the space. The properties of an induced electric field differ substantially from the properties of an electrostatic electric field.

Table 24-1 compares the properties of the electrostatic field $\vec{E}$ created by a stationary electric charge and with the properties of an induced electric field $\vec{E}_{ind}$.

Say there is a positively charged particle q moving along a circular loop in a counterclockwise direction in Figure 24-22(a). Let us calculate the work done by the induced electric field on the particle. Both the force acting on the charged particle and the induced electric field lines are always tangent to the loop. From symmetry considerations, we deduce that at any given instant the magnitude of the induced electric field $\vec{E}_{ind}$ is the same at every

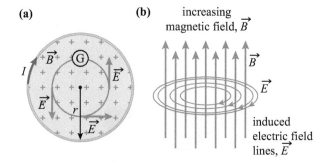

Figure 24-22 (a) A galvanometer, G, records a presence of electric current in the coil, induced by a magnetic field through the coil, $\vec{B}$, that changes with time. (b) Induced electric field lines surrounding the area of the increasing magnetic field

point along the circular loop. When the electric charge moves a distance ds along the loop, the work done on it is $dW = \vec{F} \cdot d\vec{s} = q\vec{E} \cdot d\vec{s}$. The work done on a charged particle is $W = q\varepsilon_{ind}$. Therefore,

$$\begin{cases} W_{\text{along closed loop}} = \oint dW = \oint q\vec{E}_{ind} \cdot d\vec{s} \\ \qquad\qquad = qE_{ind}\oint d\vec{s} = qE_{ind}2\pi r \\ W_{\text{along the loop}} = q\varepsilon_{ind} \end{cases} \qquad (24\text{-}23)$$

Since both expressions represent the work done on a charged particle moving along a closed circular loop, they must be equal, and

$$E_{ind} = \frac{\varepsilon_{ind}}{2\pi r} = \frac{1}{2\pi r}\left(-\frac{d\Phi_B}{dt}\right)$$

$$= -\frac{1}{2\pi r}\left(\frac{dB(t)}{dt}\right)\pi r^2 = -\frac{r}{2}\left(\frac{dB(t)}{dt}\right) \qquad (24\text{-}24)$$

Table 24-1 Comparison of electrostatic field $\vec{E}$ and induced electric field $\vec{E}_{ind}$

	Electrostatic field $\vec{E}$ (Figure 19-7)	**Induced electric field $\vec{E}_{ind}$ (Figure 24-24(b))**
Definition	The electrostatic field $\vec{E}$ at a point represents the **electrostatic force** per unit charge acting on a test charge at that point: $\vec{E} = \dfrac{\vec{F}_{q_0}}{q_0}$. The electrostatic field is a vector field directed parallel to the electrostatic force acting on a positively charged test particle.	An induced electric field $\vec{E}_{ind}$ at a certain point in space represents the **electromagnetic force** per unit charge acting on a test charge placed at that point: $\vec{E}_{ind} = \dfrac{\vec{F}_{q_0}}{q_0}$. The induced electric field is a vector field directed parallel to the electromagnetic force acting on a positively charged test particle.
Source	Electric charges	Time-varying magnetic fields
Field lines	Emanate from positive charges and point toward negative charges	Are closed loops without a beginning or an end point
Work done on a charged particle	Depends on initial and final position of the particle, but not on the path between them; hence, electrostatic fields are **conservative fields**.	Done on a charged particle moving along a closed loop and is nonzero; hence, induced electric fields are **nonconservative fields**.
Potential energy	The electrostatic potential energy is defined as $U_E = \dfrac{Qq}{4\pi\varepsilon_0 r}$.	We cannot associate potential energy with an induced electric field because it is a nonconservative field.

In this derivation, we expressed the magnetic flux through the loop as $\Phi_B = B(t)\pi r^2$. Equation (24-24) indicates that as long as the magnetic field varies with time, an induced electric field is created. The minus sign indicates that the induced electric field opposes the change in the magnetic flux. Since the change in the magnetic flux is proportional to the area of the loop (provided the loop is situated within the magnetic field region), a bigger loop means a greater induced emf and induced electric field. Therefore, the intensity of the induced field increases as one moves away from the centre of the loop, as long as the loop is located inside the region of changing magnetic field. (Notice how the density of electric field lines changes in Figure 24-2(b).)

Equation (24-23) can be extended to the general case of a closed path of an arbitrary shape:

$$\begin{cases} W_{\text{along the loop}} = \oint \vec{F} \cdot d\vec{s} = \oint q\vec{E}_{\text{ind}} \cdot d\vec{s} \Rightarrow \varepsilon = \oint \vec{E}_{\text{ind}} \cdot d\vec{s} \\ W_{\text{along the loop}} = q\varepsilon_{\text{ind}} \end{cases}$$

$$\oint \vec{E} \cdot d\vec{s} = -\frac{d\Phi_B}{dt}$$

This equation leads to a reformulation of **Faraday's law of electromagnetic induction**: A time-varying magnetic flux in a certain region of space always induces a *nonconservative* electric field $\vec{E}_{\text{ind}}$ in that region, even in the absence of electric charges. The magnitude of this induced electric field can be expressed as follows:

KEY EQUATION $\varepsilon_{\text{ind}} = \oint \vec{E}_{\text{ind}} \cdot d\vec{s} = -\frac{d\Phi_B}{dt}$ (24-25)

The direction of the induced electric field is such that the electric current generated by it induces a magnetic field that *opposes* the change in the magnetic flux.

✓ CHECKPOINT

C-24-6 Exploring Induced Electric Fields

A uniform but time-varying magnetic field $\vec{B}(t)$ induces an electric field that is constant in magnitude but has a varying direction. What must be true about the dependency of the magnetic field $\vec{B}$ on time?

(a) The magnetic field does not depend on time; it is constant.

(b) The magnetic field changes with time exponentially: $B(t) = Be^{-Ct}$, where C is a constant.

(c) The magnetic field changes with time at a constant rate.

(d) The magnetic field B changes with time as $B(t) = At^2 + Bt + C$, where A, B, and C are constants.

C-24-6 (c) Use Faraday's law of electromagnetic induction: An induced electric field is proportional to the rate of change of the magnetic field. Therefore, a magnetic field that changes with time at a constant rate induces a constant electric field.

24-6 Self-Inductance and Mutual Inductance

Understanding the concepts of induced emf and induced electric field leads us to another question: What effect does the presence of a loop have on a circuit consisting of a battery, a resistor, a coil, and a switch? To distinguish between the emf from a battery and an induced emf, we denote the battery emf as ε and the emf induced in a coil as ε_{ind}. Induced currents can be generated in any closed loop. However, they become especially important in circuits containing various coils, significantly affecting the behaviour of the circuit. Such elements of electric circuits are called **inductors** and are denoted in circuit diagrams by a helical symbol and the letter L (in honour of Heinrich Lenz), as shown in Figure 24-23. Let us consider an inductor that has a very low internal resistance ($R \approx 0\ \Omega$) and is connected in series to resistor R and a battery ε. This circuit is called a **series RL circuit**.

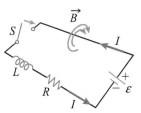

Figure 24-23   An RL circuit consists of a battery, a switch, a resistor, and a coil (also called an inductor and denoted as L).

First, we consider the circuit when the switch has been in position a for a long time, and a steady electric current flows through the RL circuit (Figure 24-24). Let us use a voltmeter (V_L) to measure the potential difference across

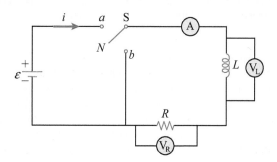

Figure 24-24   The RL circuit in this figure is designed such that when the switch is in position a, the battery, the resistor, and the inductor are part of the series circuit. When the switch is in position b, only the resistor and the inductor are part of the series circuit. When the switch is in position a, the potential difference across the inductor is zero: $\varepsilon_{\text{ind}} = 0$. When the current across the inductor is changing (the switch is being flipped from a to b or vice versa), the changing current in the circuit induces a nonzero emf across the inductor: $\varepsilon_{\text{ind}} \neq 0$.

the inductor ε_{ind} and an ammeter to measure the current I through it. Since a constant current flows through the inductor, it generates a constant magnetic field, so there is no change in the magnetic flux through the inductor. In that case, the inductor behaves like an ordinary wire with a very low resistance R. Therefore, the potential difference across this inductor is zero: $\varepsilon_{ind} \approx 0$.

Now let us examine what happens immediately after the switch has been flipped from position a to position b. Initially, the current in the circuit was I. However, as the battery was effectively removed from the circuit, the current in the circuit will start decreasing. The changing electric current in the circuit induces emf ε_{ind} in the coil. We apply Faraday's law to find the direction of the induced emf. Since the induced emf is directed such that it reduces the change in the magnetic flux through the coil, this emf induces electric current I_{ind} in the direction of the original current I. Thus, the magnetic field, $\vec{B}_{ind}$, by this current, is directed in the direction of the original magnetic field created by the decreasing current. If we flip the switch once again from position b to position a, induced emf will have an opposite direction. In this case, the induced electric current I_{ind} will be in the opposite direction to the current I in the circuit. The Online Activity below provides an opportunity to take a closer look at the behaviour of an RL circuit and build a deeper understanding of this phenomenon.

 ONLINE ACTIVITY

An Induced emf Across an Inductor in an RL Circuit

The e-resource that accompanies every new copy of this textbook contains an Online Activity using the PhET simulation "Circuit construction kit (AC + DC)". Work through the simulation and accompanying questions to gain an understanding of the behaviour of RL circuits.

An induced emf across an inductor, ε_{ind}, is often called a "back emf" because it opposes the change in the magnetic flux. A back emf has a nature different from the emf created by the battery. In a coil consisting of many loops, the magnetic field of each loop creates a back emf, which affects each of the other loops, multiplying the effect. Every loop affects itself as well as its neighbours. Therefore, the process of creating a back emf is called **self-induction**.

Recall from Chapter 23 that a solenoid is a coil with evenly spaced turns. Consider a solenoid of radius r and length l, consisting of N closely spaced loops. Using Faraday's law (Equation (24-10)) and the expression for the magnetic field of a solenoid (Equation (23-47)), the back emf can be expressed as follows:

$$\varepsilon_{ind} = -N\left(\frac{d\Phi_B}{dt}\right) = -N\frac{d}{dt}(BA) = -NA\frac{dB(t)}{dt}$$

$$B(t) = \mu_0 nI = \mu_0 \frac{N}{l}I \Rightarrow \frac{dB(t)}{dt} = \mu_0 \frac{N}{l}\frac{dI}{dt}$$

$$\varepsilon_{ind} = -N\pi r^2 \mu_0 \frac{N}{l}\frac{dI}{dt} = -\mu_0 \frac{N^2\pi r^2}{l}\frac{dI}{dt} = -L\frac{dI}{dt} \quad (24\text{-}26)$$

The back emf depends on the rate of change of the electric current through the solenoid and on its **inductance**, L:

$$\varepsilon_{ind} \equiv \varepsilon_L = -L\frac{dI}{dt} \quad (24\text{-}27)$$

While expression (24-27) is true for any inductor, the following derivation for inductance L only applies to a solenoid with circular coils:

$$L_{solenoid} = \mu_0 \frac{N^2\pi r^2}{l} = \mu_0 \frac{N^2 l\pi r^2}{l^2} = \mu_0 n^2 V \quad (24\text{-}28)$$

where $V = l\pi r^2$.

The inductance of a solenoid depends solely on its geometric and physical properties. The inductance is proportional to the volume V and to the square of the density of the loops. A solenoid with an iron core often has an inductance hundreds of times greater than an air-core solenoid of the same size. Using the expression for magnetic permeability (Equation (23-57)), the inductance of a circular solenoid can be expressed as

$$L_{solenoid} = K_m \mu_0 \frac{N^2 l\pi r^2}{l^2} = \mu n^2 V \quad (24\text{-}29)$$

where μ is the magnetic permeability of the core.

We can also calculate the inductance of a solenoid using the expression for its magnetic field (Equation (23-41)) and the law of electromagnetic induction:

$$\varepsilon_L = -N\frac{d\Phi_B}{dt} = -N\frac{d(\mu_0 nIA)}{dt} = -N\mu_0 nA\frac{dI}{dt} = -L\frac{dI}{dt}$$

$$L \equiv N\mu_0 nA = \mu_0 n^2 Al \quad (24\text{-}30)$$

Therefore, considering that for a circular coil $\Phi_B = \mu_0 nAI$, the inductance of a solenoid can be expressed as

$$L = N\mu_0 nA = \frac{N\Phi_B}{I} \quad (24\text{-}31)$$

Let us compare the functions of resistors and inductors in electric circuits. Since $I = \dfrac{\Delta V}{R}$, increasing the resistance in a circuit reduces the current that converts electric energy to thermal energy. The potential difference across a resistor is proportional to both the current and the resistance: $\Delta V = IR$ (Figure 24-25(a)). Current flows through a resistor from a higher potential to a lower potential. Inductors, however, act to oppose or impede the *change* in electric current. The potential difference across an inductor is proportional to its inductance and the rate of change of the electric current: $\Delta V = -L\dfrac{dI}{dt}$. Notice the direction of the induced potential difference in the inductor (Figure 24-25(b)). Thus, inductors behave somewhat like resistors to AC current. However, when a steady (DC) current flows through the inductor, the potential difference across the inductor is zero because $\dfrac{dI}{dt} = 0$. The inductor provides no resistance in a DC circuit. This explains why a transformer can burn out if you try to use DC instead of AC current.

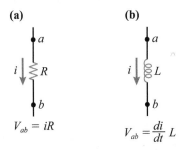

(a)

$V_{ab} = iR$

(b)

$V_{ab} = \dfrac{di}{dt} L$

Figure 24-25 Comparison of the resistive and inductive elements of an electric circuit. (a) In the case of a resistor, electric current flows from a higher potential to a lower potential: $V_a > V_b$. (b) In the case of an inductor, the induced current in the coil generates a potential difference V_{ab} such that $V_b > V_a$.

The SI unit for inductance is the henry (symbol H), named after renowned American physicist Joseph Henry (1797–1878). An inductance of 1 H corresponds to an inductor that self-induces an emf of 1 V when an electric current in it changes at a rate of 1 A/s:

$$1\ \text{H} = \frac{1\ \text{V}}{1\ \text{A/s}} \qquad (24\text{-}32)$$

✓ CHECKPOINT

C-24-7 The Direction of an Induced emf in an Ideal Inductor

Figure 24-26 shows an ideal inductor ($R = 0$). The potential at point a of the inductor is measured to be higher than the potential at point b. Which of the following current flow(s) could account for this potential difference?

(a) A steady current flows from a to b.
(b) A steady current flows from b to a.
(c) A decreasing current flows from a to b.
(d) An increasing current flows from a to b.
(e) A decreasing current flows from b to a.
(f) An increasing current flows from b to a.

$$a \quad \overset{V_a > V_b}{\underset{}{\longmapsto}} \quad b$$

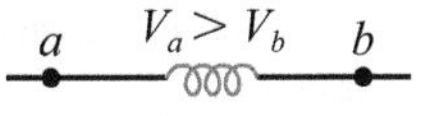

Figure 24-26 C-24-7

C-24-7 (d) and (e) according to Faraday's or Lenz's law

The transformer discussed earlier is an example of two **coupled inductors**. Consider two solenoids wound around an iron core such that the magnetic fluxes through them are equal, as shown in Figure 24-27. Let us assume that the solenoids have N_1 and N_2 loops, respectively, the average circumference of the iron core is l, and its cross-sectional area is A. Faraday's law of electromagnetic induction states that a time-varying electric current in the first solenoid $I_1(t)$ generates a time-varying magnetic field $\vec{B}(t)$ through the second solenoid, which induces an electric current in it. Let us calculate this induced current.

To calculate the magnetic field induced by the first solenoid, we apply Ampère's law (Equation (23-39)) to a closed contour L located inside the iron core:

$$\oint_L \vec{B} \cdot d\vec{l} = \mu_0 \sum I_{\text{enc}}$$

Since the magnetic field has the same magnitude at all points inside the iron core and is always directed along the tangent to the contour L, we rewrite the above equation as

$$Bl = \mu N_1 I$$

$$B = \frac{\mu N_1 I}{l}$$

where μ is the magnetic permeability of iron.

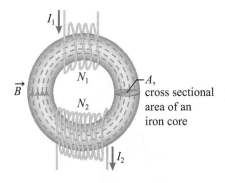

Figure 24-27 Two coils coupled through an iron core of average circumference l and cross-sectional area A

Using Faraday's law, the induced emf in the second solenoid can be expressed as

$$(\varepsilon_{\text{ind}})_2 = -N_2\left(\frac{d\Phi_B}{dt}\right)_2 = -N_2\frac{d(AB)}{dt} = -N_2 A \frac{dB}{dt}$$

$$= -N_2 A \frac{d}{dt}\frac{\mu N_1 I_1}{l} = -\frac{\mu A N_2 N_1}{l}\frac{dI_1}{dt}$$

Then, the emf induced in the second solenoid can be expressed as

$$(\varepsilon_{\text{ind}})_2 = -M_{12}\frac{dI_1}{dt} \qquad (24\text{-}33)$$

where

$$M_{12} = \mu A \frac{N_1 N_2}{l}$$

The coefficient M_{12}, called the **coefficient of mutual inductance**, indicates the strength of coupling between the two coils. Similarly, if we consider the emf induced in the first solenoid by the varying current in the second, we find that

$$\varepsilon_1 = -M_{21}\frac{dI_2}{dt}; \quad M_{21} = \mu A \frac{N_2 N_1}{l} \quad (24\text{-}34)$$

Comparing Equations (24-33) and (24-34) we see that

$$M_{12} = M_{21} = M \quad (24\text{-}35)$$

Thus, the coefficient of mutual inductance between two coils is denoted as M.

Now we consider two long, thin solenoids of length l wound over top of each other (Figure 24-28). The inner and outer solenoids have N_1 and N_2 coils, respectively, and their cross-sectional area is A. Once again, if a time-varying electric current flows through the inner solenoid I_1, it will induce an emf ε_2 in the outer coil:

$$(\varepsilon_{\text{ind}})_2 = -N_2\frac{d\Phi_B}{dt} = -N_2\frac{d(AB)}{dt} = -N_2 A\frac{dB}{dt}$$

$$= -N_2 A\frac{d}{dt}\frac{\mu N_1 I_1}{l} = -\frac{\mu A N_2 N_1}{l}\frac{dI_1}{dt}$$

and

$$(\varepsilon_{\text{ind}})_2 = -M\frac{dI_1}{dt}$$

where

$$M = \frac{\mu A N_2 N_1}{l} \quad (24\text{-}36)$$

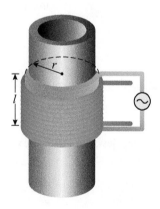

Figure 24-28 Two long, thin concentric solenoids wound on top of each other

Once again, we can show that the mutual inductance $M_{12} = M_{21} = M$. Comparing expression (24-36)

with the expression for the self-inductance of a solenoid (Equation (24-30)), we find

$$M = \frac{\mu A N_1 N_2}{l} = \sqrt{L_1 L_2} \quad (24\text{-}37)$$

In the derivation above we assumed that all the magnetic flux created by the first solenoid passes through the second solenoid. This is rarely true; therefore, formula (24-37) should be adjusted to include the coefficient of coupling between the inductors, k that varies from 0 to 1. Perfectly coupled coils have a coefficient of coupling of 1, and perfectly decoupled coils have a coefficient of coupling of zero:

$$M = k\sqrt{L_1 L_2} \quad (24\text{-}38)$$

MAKING CONNECTIONS

How Does an Electric Toothbrush Work?

Have you ever wondered how an electric toothbrush can be recharged when the charging stand and the battery-powered toothbrush are both sealed and have no exposed metal contacts to make a circuit (Figure 24-29)? The answer is **inductive charging**. The stand and toothbrush essentially operate like a transformer. The base connected to the AC power outlet serves as the primary coil, and a coil inside the toothbrush acts as the secondary coil. Every time you slide your toothbrush into the base, you couple these coils, allowing current to be induced in the toothbrush. The induced current recharges the toothbrush battery and also makes the handle of the toothbrush feel warm. So, the next time you brush your teeth, think of Michael Faraday, whose discovery of electromagnetic induction made the operation of your toothbrush possible.

Figure 24-29 An electric toothbrush uses an inductive charger, which operates like a transformer.

EXAMPLE 24-6

Calculating the Mutual Inductance of Two Coupled Solenoids

Two long, thin solenoids of equal length l and equal radius r are wound over top of each other (Figure 24-28). The inner and outer solenoids have N_1 and N_2 turns, respectively. An alternating electric current $I_1 = (I_1)_{max} \sin(\omega t)$ flows through the inner solenoid, where $(I_1)_{max}$ represents the maximum value of the current in the inner solenoid.

(a) Calculate the mutual inductance of the solenoids, and prove that it satisfies Equations (24-36) and (24-38).
(b) Find an expression for the emf induced in the outer solenoid.

SOLUTION

(a) Using Equation (24-31) for the inductance of a solenoid and substituting it into Equation (24-36) for the mutual inductance of two solenoids gives

$$M = \mu_0 A \frac{N_1 N_2}{l} = \sqrt{\left(\mu_0 A N_1 \frac{N_1}{l}\right)\left(\mu_0 N_2 A \frac{N_2}{l}\right)} = \sqrt{L_1 L_2}$$

In this derivation, we assumed that the cross-sectional area of each solenoid is A. Since the outer solenoid surrounds the inner solenoid, all the magnetic flux produced by the inner solenoid passes through the outer solenoid. Therefore $k = 1$, and the solution satisfies Equation (24-38).

(b) To find the emf induced in the outer solenoid, we use Faraday's law (Equation (24-33)) for a solenoid, taking into account that the cross-sectional area of a solenoid is πr^2:

$$(\varepsilon_{ind})_2 = -M\frac{dI_1}{dt} = -M\frac{d}{dt}(I_1)_{max}\cos(\omega t)$$

$$= (I_1)_{max}\,\omega\mu_0\pi r^2\frac{N_1 N_2}{l}\sin(\omega t)$$

Making sense of the result:

As expected, a sinusoidal emf is generated in the outer coil because it is being induced by a sinusoidal current, $I = (I_1)_{max}\sin(\omega t)$.

LO 7

24-7 RL Circuits

We now consider a circuit in which an inductor and a resistor are connected in series to a battery (Figure 24-30). Since an ideal inductor influences the circuit behaviour only when the current through it varies in time, the inductor shown in Figure 24-30 affects the current only for a relatively short time immediately after the switch is turned on or off. (See the Online Activity box on page 660 for simulations of such transient currents.)

Let us assume that the switch is being flipped to position a (from a neutral position, N) at time $t = 0$. Since all the circuit components are connected in series, the law of energy conservation and Kirchhoff's second law require that

$$\varepsilon + V_R + V_L = 0 \Rightarrow \varepsilon - IR + \varepsilon_{ind} = 0 \quad (24\text{-}39)$$

where

$$V_R = -IR \quad \text{and} \quad V_L = \varepsilon_{ind} = -L\frac{dI}{dt}$$

These expressions can be combined:

$$\varepsilon - IR - L\frac{dI}{dt} = 0$$

$$\frac{dI}{dt} = \frac{\varepsilon - IR}{L} \quad (24\text{-}40)$$

To solve this differential equation, we set $x = \varepsilon - IR$. Then $dx = d(\varepsilon - IR) = -RdI$, and Equation (24-40) can be rewritten as

$$x + \frac{L}{R}\frac{dx}{dt} = 0 \Rightarrow \frac{dx}{x} = -\frac{R}{L}dt \quad (24\text{-}41)$$

We solve this equation by integrating both sides. Since we are interested in knowing the behaviour of the current from time $t_i = 0$ to $t_f = t$, we choose these values as the limits of integration. The corresponding limits of integration for the variable x are denoted as x_i and x:

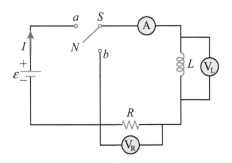

Figure 24-30 A series RL circuit consists of at least a resistor (R) and an inductor (L). Such a circuit might (when the switch is in position a) or might not (when the switch is in position b) include a battery. The ammeter registers electric current flowing through the resistor and an inductor, while the voltmeters (V_L and V_R) measure potential differences across the inductor and the resistor respectively.

$$\int_{x_i}^{x} \frac{dx}{x} = -\int_0^t \frac{R}{L}dt \Rightarrow \int_{x_i}^{x} \frac{dx}{x} = -\frac{R}{L}\int_0^t dt$$

$$\ln\frac{x}{x_i} = -\frac{R}{L}t \Rightarrow \frac{x}{x_i} = e^{-\frac{R}{L}t} \qquad (24\text{-}42)$$

Let us verify that Equation (24-42) has the proper units. The exponent should be a pure number, so the units of the ratio L/R should be time (seconds). Substituting for the inductance gives

$$\left[\frac{L}{R}\right] = \frac{\dfrac{V \cdot s}{A}}{\Omega} = \frac{\Omega \cdot s}{\Omega} = s$$

Using $x = \varepsilon - IR$ and taking into account that the current at $t = 0$ is zero, Equation (24-42) can be rewritten as

$$x = x_i e^{-\frac{R}{L}t} \Rightarrow \varepsilon - IR = (\varepsilon - I_i R)e^{-\frac{R}{L}t}$$

$$\varepsilon - IR = \varepsilon e^{-\frac{R}{L}t}$$

$$\varepsilon\left(1 - e^{-\frac{R}{L}t}\right) = IR$$

$$I(t) = \frac{\varepsilon}{R}\left(1 - e^{-\frac{R}{L}t}\right)$$

The ratio L/R has the units of time and is called the **time constant**, τ, of the RL circuit. Substituting for L/R in the above expression gives

$$I(t) = \frac{\varepsilon}{R}\left(1 - e^{-\frac{t}{\frac{L}{R}}}\right) = \frac{\varepsilon}{R}\left(1 - e^{-\frac{t}{\tau}}\right)$$

where $\tau = L/R$.
Figure 24-31(a) shows a graph of $I(t)$ versus time.

The $I(t)$ graph starts from zero, then the current increases exponentially with time, asymptotically approaching its maximum value of $\dfrac{\varepsilon}{R}$. This is the value of the current that would have been observed if there were no inductor in the circuit. This makes sense because as the time increases, the rate of change of current diminishes (the current approaches the steady state as the $I(t)$ slope becomes more horizontal); as a result, ε_L approaches zero. Another important observation is that at time $t = \tau$, the current reaches approximately 63% of its maximum value:

$$I(\tau) = \frac{\varepsilon}{R}\left(1 - e^{-\frac{\tau}{\tau}}\right) = \frac{\varepsilon}{R}(1 - e^{-1}) \approx \frac{\varepsilon}{R}(1 - 0.368)$$

$$= 0.632\frac{\varepsilon}{R} \qquad (24\text{-}43)$$

To examine how the potential difference across the inductor ε_L depends on time, we find the derivative of current with respect to time $\dfrac{dI(t)}{dt}$ and again use Equation (24-27):

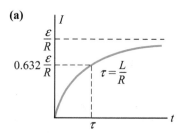

(a)

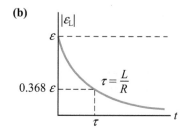

(b)

Figure 24-31 (a) The dependence of the electric current through the series RL circuit on time when the switch is flipped from position N to position a. (b) The dependence of the induced emf across the inductor on time when the closed switch is flipped from position N to position a.

$$\varepsilon_L = -L\frac{dI}{dt} = -L\frac{d}{dt}\left(\frac{\varepsilon}{R}\left(1 - e^{-\frac{t}{\tau}}\right)\right) = -\frac{L\varepsilon}{R\tau}e^{-\frac{t}{\tau}}$$

$$= -\frac{L\varepsilon}{R\frac{L}{R}}e^{-\frac{t}{\tau}} = -\varepsilon e^{-\frac{t}{\tau}}$$

Combining the results of the above equations, we obtain

$$I(t) = \frac{\varepsilon}{R}\left(1 - e^{-\frac{t}{\tau}}\right)$$

KEY EQUATION

$$\varepsilon_L = -\varepsilon e^{-\frac{t}{\tau}} \qquad (24\text{-}44)$$

where $\tau = L/R$.

From a graph of $\varepsilon_L(t)$, we see that at $t = 0$, $\varepsilon_L(0) = \varepsilon$, and $\varepsilon_L(t)$ diminishes exponentially with time (Figure 24-34(b)). Therefore, at $t = 0$, the emf across the inductor equals the value of emf supplied by the battery. Then, after τ seconds have passed, the value of ε_L is approximately equal to 37% of ε:

$$\varepsilon(\tau) = \varepsilon e^{-\frac{\tau}{\tau}} = \varepsilon e^{-1} \approx 0.368\varepsilon \qquad (24\text{-}45)$$

Both graphs are asymptotic: it takes an infinitely long time for the current to reach its steady-state value of ε/R and for the voltage across the inductor ε_L to reach zero. However, the time constants for most practical inductive circuits are short enough that the difference between the actual value and the final steady-state value is negligible after a few seconds.

We can use the same method to determine what happens to the circuit when the switch being moved to position b, after it has been in position a for a long time.

CHECKPOINT

C-24-8 Exploring RL Circuits

How long does it take for the current in the RL circuit in Figure 24-30 to reach 74% of its maximum value (Figure 24-31(a))?

(a) τ
(b) $1.34\,\tau$
(c) $1.50\,\tau$
(d) $2.00\,\tau$
(e) $2.67\,\tau$

C-24-8 (b) Use Equation (24-44) to check the answer.

Taking the instant when the switch is opened as $t = 0$, we have $I(0) = I_{max}$ and $I(\infty) = 0$. Then the expressions for the current in the circuit and the emf across the inductor can be rewritten as follows:

$$I(t) = \frac{\mathcal{E}}{R}e^{-\frac{t}{\tau}}$$

$$\mathcal{E}_L = \mathcal{E}e^{-\frac{t}{\tau}} \qquad (24\text{-}46)$$

Figure 24-32 shows how $I(t)$ and $\mathcal{E}_L(t)$ change immediately after the switch in a series RL circuit is open.

The time constant of the circuit τ determines how fast the current in the circuit reaches its steady state when the

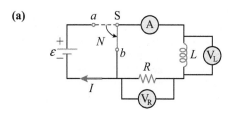

(a)

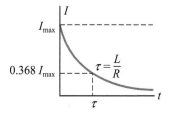

(b)

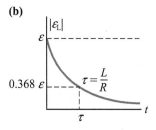

Figure 24-32 A switch in a series RL circuit is being moved from position a to position b. (a) The dependence of the electric current through this circuit on time, $I(t)$. (b) The dependence of the potential difference across the inductor on time, $\mathcal{E}_{ind}(t)$.

EXAMPLE 24-7

Exploring RL Circuits

In the RL circuit shown in Figure 24-33, the battery has an emf of 20 V, the resistor has a resistance of 10 Ω, and the inductor has an inductance of 40 mH.

(a) How long after the switch is set to position a does it take the current to reach 99% of its maximum value? Express your answer in seconds and in terms of the time constant.
(b) What is the current at this time?
(c) When the current reaches 99% of its maximum value, what is the emf across the inductor?
(d) After 20 s, the switch is moved to position b. How long will it take for the current to decrease to 10% of its maximum value?

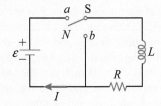

Figure 24-33 An RL circuit

SOLUTION

(a) To find how long it will take the current to reach 99% of its maximum value, we use Equation (24-44):

$$I(t) = \frac{\mathcal{E}}{R}\left(1 - e^{-\frac{t}{\tau}}\right)$$

$$0.99\,\frac{\mathcal{E}}{R} = \frac{\mathcal{E}}{R}\left(1 - e^{-\frac{t}{\tau}}\right)$$

$$e^{-\frac{t}{\tau}} = 0.01 \implies t = -\tau\ln(0.01)$$

$$t = 4.6\,\tau = 4.6\,\frac{L}{R} = 4.6\,\frac{40 \times 10^{-3}\,\text{H}}{10\,\Omega} = 4.6(4\,\text{ms}) = 18.4\,\text{ms}$$

The current will reach 99% of its maximum value after $4.6\,\tau$ or 18.4 ms.

(b) The maximum value of the current is

$$I_{max} = \frac{\mathcal{E}}{R} = \frac{20\,\text{V}}{10\,\Omega} = 2\,\text{A}$$

and 99% of this value is 1.98 A.

(c) When the current reaches 99% of its maximum value, the emf across the inductor can be calculated using Equation (24-46):

$$\mathcal{E}_L = \mathcal{E}e^{-\frac{t}{\tau}} = (20\,\text{V})e^{-\frac{18.4\,\text{ms}}{4\,\text{ms}}} = (20\,\text{V})e^{-4.6} = 0.20\,\text{V}$$

(continued)

(d) The switch is moved to position b after 20 s. Since this time interval is over 4000 times longer than the circuit time constant (4.6 ms), we can assume that at the time the switch was moved to position b, the current has reached its maximum value. Let t_{10} represent the time when the current reaches 10% of its initial value. Then, $I(t_{10}) = 0.1\,I_{max} = 0.1\dfrac{\varepsilon}{R}$. Substituting into Equation (24-46) gives

$$0.1\,I_{max} = \frac{\varepsilon}{R}e^{-\frac{t}{\tau}} \Rightarrow 0.1\frac{\varepsilon}{R} = \frac{\varepsilon}{R}e^{-\frac{t}{\tau}}$$

$$0.1 = e^{-\frac{t}{\tau}} \Rightarrow t = -\tau\ln(0.1) = 2.3\,\tau = 2.3(4.6 \text{ ms}) = 11 \text{ ms}$$

Making sense of the result:

Due to the presence of an inductor in an electric circuit, the current cannot reach its maximum value or diminish to zero instantaneously.

circuit is being connected to a battery and how quickly it diminishes to zero when a battery is being switched off. Since the time constant is directly proportional to L and inversely proportional to R $\left(\tau = \dfrac{L}{R}\right)$, when $\dfrac{L}{R} \gg 1$ the inductor dominates the circuit behaviour (inductive circuit), and when $\dfrac{L}{R} \ll 1$, the resistance dominates the circuit behaviour (resistive circuit).

LO 6, LO 8

24-8 Energy Stored in a Magnetic Field

Example 24-7 demonstrated that the current in an RL circuit continues to flow for some time after the battery is disconnected. This tells us that an inductor is supplying energy to the circuit, somewhat like a battery. In fact, the energy is stored in the magnetic field of the inductor.

Let us once again consider the RL circuit shown in Figure 24-36. When the switch is in position a, the law of energy conservation demands that Equation (24-40) holds true. Multiplying both sides of this equation by I, we obtain

$$\varepsilon I - I^2 R - LI\frac{dI}{dt} = 0$$

$$\varepsilon I = I^2 R + LI\frac{dI}{dt} \tag{24-47}$$

This equation describes the law of energy conservation for an RL circuit. The εI component represents the rate at which the energy is supplied by the battery to the circuit, that is, the electric power delivered to circuit. Some of this energy is delivered to the resistor at the rate of $I^2 R$, and the rest is delivered to the inductor at the rate of $LI\dfrac{dI}{dt}$. Since the latter expression represents the rate of energy transfer to the inductor, we define the energy stored in the magnetic field, U_B, as

$$\frac{dU_B}{dt} = LI\frac{dI}{dt}$$

$$dU_B = LI\,dI \tag{24-48}$$

Knowing the rate of energy transfer to the inductor, we calculate the energy stored in the inductor as the current in the circuit changes from zero to its maximum (steady-state) value:

$$\int_0^{U_B} dU_B = \int_0^I LI\,dI$$

 KEY EQUATION

$$U_B = \frac{LI^2}{2} \tag{24-49}$$

This important relationship indicates that the energy stored in the inductor is proportional to the inductance L and to the square of the current flowing through the inductor. This energy is stored in the magnetic field of the inductor when current flows through it. Notice that U_B is present only when charge is moving through the inductor. This magnetic energy expression is somewhat analogous to the kinetic energy, $KE = \dfrac{mv^2}{2}$, and to the potential energy stored in the electric field of a capacitor, $U_E = \dfrac{CV^2}{2}$ (Equation (21-15)).

Let us now examine Faraday's law of electromagnetic induction from the energy perspective. When electric current starts flowing through a solenoid, the current generates a magnetic field inside the solenoid. We determined (Equation (24-49)) that magnetic energy is stored within this magnetic field. This energy must have come from somewhere. As the current builds up in the circuit, the inductor acts to oppose that current increase by converting kinetic energy carried by the moving electric charges into magnetic energy stored in the inductor's magnetic field.

When the switch disconnects the battery, moving into position b (Figure 24-33), the current in the solenoid, already at its maximum value, starts to drop off. The energy stored in the inductor also begins to drop off according to Equation (24-49). Since the inductor acts to oppose the resulting decrease in current, the energy stored in the magnetic field is used to reduce the rate of decrease of electric current. The inductor uses the energy stored in its magnetic field to prevent the abrupt decrease of the current in the circuit. Therefore, the current induced by the inductor is directed such that the induced emf has the same direction as the emf from the original battery. As when the circuit was first switched on, the inductor opposes the *change* in electric current.

Let us calculate the energy stored in the magnetic field of a long solenoid with loop density n, radius R, and length L:

$$U_B = \frac{LI^2}{2} = \frac{1}{2}(\mu_0 n^2 lA)I^2 = \frac{1}{2}\mu_0 n^2 l(\pi R^2)\left(\frac{B}{\mu_0 n}\right)^2 = \frac{B^2}{2\mu_0}l(\pi R^2)$$

$$U_B = \frac{B^2}{2\mu_0}V \qquad (24\text{-}50)$$

where $V = \pi R^2 l$ is the volume of a solenoid.

Equation (24-50) shows that the energy stored in a solenoid is determined by its volume and the strength of the magnetic field inside it. For many practical applications, it is useful to know the energy density (amount of energy per unit volume):

KEY EQUATION
$$u_B = \frac{B^2}{2\mu_0} \qquad (24\text{-}51)$$

Although we derived Equation (24-51) for a particular type of solenoid, the equation is valid for any region of space that contains a magnetic field. Compare this equation to the equation describing the energy density of the electric field, $u = \frac{1}{2}\varepsilon_0 E^2$ (Equation (21-18)). Both types of energy density depend solely on the square of the magnitude of the respective field. We will apply this crucial observation when discussing the transfer of energy by electromagnetic waves in Chapter 25.

It will be instructive to compare what you have learned about RL circuits in this chapter with what you learned about RC circuits in Chapter 22, focusing on the functions of the resistors, capacitors, and inductors in the circuits. We will discuss circuits combining resistors, capacitors, and inductors in Chapter 25 in detail.

MAKING CONNECTIONS

Maglev Trains

There are three major technologies currently in use for magnetic levitation in maglev trains. The electromagnetic system (EMS) uses the attractive force between a support magnet located under the vehicle and a rail that is made of a ferromagnetic material. The attractive force between the steel rail and the supporting magnet (Figure 24-34(a)) lifts the vehicle upward. EMS technology is used in German maglev trains. The distance between the electromagnets and the rail is critical, so this system requires a control mechanism that continuously measures this distance and adjusts it by varying the current in the guidance magnet.

The electrodynamic system (EDS) is used in the maglev trains in Japan (Figure 24-34(b)). These trains carry magnets, and a large metal plate runs along the centre of the maglev track. When a train's magnet passes over the plate, eddy currents are created in the metal plate, generating a repulsive force between the track and train. The EDS maglev trains are naturally stable: if the train drops toward the rail, the repulsive force increases; if the train rises too high above the rail, the repulsive force decreases. However, the electromagnetic repulsion is present only when the vehicle is moving, and the vehicle must have wheels for takeoff and landing (unlike EMS trains). Moreover, the electric currents induced in the metal plates dissipate energy and create a significant drag force on the vehicle.

Inductrack, a variation of the EDS technology, uses permanent room-temperature magnets attached to the vehicle (instead of electromagnets or superconducting magnets) to produce a magnetic field that levitates the train over passive coils. Like EDS trains, inductrack maglev trains do not levitate until they are in motion (Figure 24-34(c)).

(a)

Electromagnetic Suspension

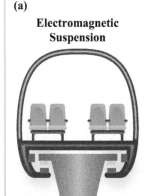

Electromagnets are located on the train cars, and they lift the train cars.

(b)

Electrodynamic Suspension

Electromagnets are located on the guideway, and they lift the train cars.

(c)

Inductrack

Permanent magnets levitate over passive coils.

Figure 24-34 (a) The electromagnetic suspension system is used in German maglev trains. (b) The electrodynamic suspension system is used in Japanese maglev trains. (c) Inductrack uses permanent magnets to levitate the train over passive coils.

A time-varying magnetic flux through a conducting loop induces an emf in it. To produce a magnetic flux that changes with time, we must either have a magnetic field that changes with time or a constant magnetic field but a loop whose effective area changes with time. The latter can be achieved, for example, by rotating the loop in the constant magnetic field.

Magnetic Flux Through a Surface

Magnetic flux is a scalar quantity (can be positive, negative, or zero) and is defined as an integral over the surface:

$$\Phi_B = \int \vec{B} \cdot d\vec{A} = \int d\Phi \qquad (24\text{-}7)$$

Magnetic flux changes with time when the magnetic field, the area of the loop, and/or the angle between the normal to the loop and the magnetic field vary in time (Figure 24-3).

Faraday's Law of Electromagnetic Induction

A time-varying magnetic flux through a conducting loop induces an emf in it:

$$\varepsilon = -\left(\frac{d\Phi_B}{dt}\right) \qquad (24\text{-}10)$$

Lenz's law: The directions of the induced emf and induced current always oppose (reduce) the change of the magnetic flux that caused it.

Energy Stored in a Magnetic Field

1. The energy stored in a magnetic field can be expressed as

$$U_B = \frac{LI^2}{2} \qquad (24\text{-}49)$$

2. The energy stored in a magnetic field per unit volume is

$$u_B = \frac{B^2}{2\mu_0} \qquad (24\text{-}51)$$

APPLICATIONS

Applications: AC current generator, AC circuits (RL, RC, and RLC circuits), electromagnetic brakes and dampers, transformers, metal detectors, electric guitars, magnetic levitation trains

Key Terms: alternating current, alternating emf, back emf, coefficient of mutual inductance, conservative fields, coupled inductors, eddies, eddy currents, effective surface area, electromagnetic force, electromagnetic induction, electrostatic force, Faraday's law of electromagnetic induction, induced electric field, inductance, inductive charging, inductors, Lenz's law, magnetic flux, motional emf, mutual inductance, nonconservative fields, rate of change of the magnetic flux, self-induction, series RL circuit, transformer

QUESTIONS

1. A rectangular metal loop is located in the region of a uniform magnetic field directed perpendicular to the plane of the loop (Figure 24-35) An induced electric current in the clockwise direction is detected in the loop. What must be true about this magnetic field?
   (a) The magnetic field is directed into the page and is steady.
   (b) The magnetic field is directed into the page and is increasing.
   (c) The magnetic field is directed into the page and is decreasing.
   (d) The magnetic field is directed out of the page and is steady.
   (e) The magnetic field is directed out of the page and is increasing.
   (f) The magnetic field is directed out of the page and is decreasing.
   (g) Only (a) and (b) are possible correct answers.
   (h) Only (c) and (e) are possible correct answers.
   (i) Only (d) and (f) are possible correct answers.
   (j) All the answers can be correct.

Figure 24-35 Question 1

2. Which of the following descriptions accurately describes a magnetic field that can produce a constantly increasing emf in a loop oriented perpendicular to its direction?
   (a) $B(t) = (3t + 278)$ mT
   (b) $B(t) = (5\sin(2\pi t))$ mT
   (c) $B(t) = (5\sin(3\pi t) + 10)$ mT
   (d) $B(t) = (5\cos(3\pi t) + 30)$ mT
   (e) $B(t) = (5t^2 + 15)$ mT

3. Which of the following scenarios describes a magnetic flux through a loop that does not change with time?
   (a) A uniform magnetic field changes with time, and the area of the loop and its orientation remain constant.
   (b) A loop is moving with constant velocity through a non-uniform and constant magnetic field.
   (c) A square loop is rotating about its diagonal in a uniform and constant magnetic field directed perpendicular to the loop's diagonal.
   (d) A loop is moving at a constant velocity (its orientation is not changing) in a uniform and constant magnetic field.
   (e) The area of a loop is increasing at a constant rate while it is in a uniform magnetic field whose magnitude is also increasing and whose direction is always parallel to the surface of the loop.

4. In which one of the following cases will there be an electric current induced in the ring in Figure 24-36?
   (a) The ring is moving in a horizontal direction in a uniform and constant magnetic field.
   (b) The ring is moving vertically in a uniform and constant magnetic field.
   (c) The ring is stationary, but the magnetic field is increasing.
   (d) The ring is stationary, but the magnetic field is decreasing.
   (e) The ring is spinning about a horizontal axis parallel to the B lines and going through its centre.
   (f) The ring is spinning about a horizontal axis perpendicular to the B lines and going through its centre.
   (g) The ring is spinning about a vertical axis perpendicular to the B lines and going through its centre.
   (h) The ring is moving diagonally (without spinning) at a constant velocity.
   (i) The ring is moving diagonally (without spinning) but at an increasing speed.
   (j) parts (b), (c), (d), (e), (f), (h), and (i)
   (k) parts (c), (d), (f), (g), and (i)
   (l) parts (c), (d), (f), and (g)
   (m) parts (a), (c), (d), (f), (g), and (i)
   (n) All of the above.

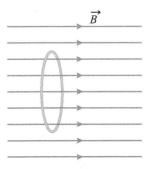

Figure 24-36 Questions 4 and 5

5. What will the direction of the current in the metal ring in Figure 24-36 be if the magnetic field starts increasing?
   (a) counterclockwise (if seen from the left)
   (b) clockwise (if seen from the left)
   (c) There will be no current generated in the ring, and the ring is stationary.

6. A metal ring is dropped between the poles of a horseshoe magnet (Figure 24-37). What is true about the electric current in the ring as observed if looking from the right?
   (a) The electric current is clockwise while entering the loop and counterclockwise while exiting.
   (b) The electric current is counterclockwise when entering the loop and clockwise while exiting.
   (c) The electric current is counterclockwise all the time.
   (d) The electric current is clockwise all the time.
   (e) There is no current in the ring.

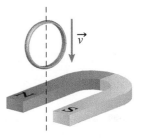

Figure 24-37 Question 6

7. A very light, 1 m-long metal rod is placed in a uniform and constant horizontal magnetic field $B = 1$ T, directed as shown in Figure 24-38. The rod is free to move along frictionless metal rails that have negligibly small resistance. A light bulb, requiring a potential difference of 10 V to light up, is attached to the metal rails as shown. What should the minimal speed of the rod be for the bulb to light up?
   (a) 0.01 m/s
   (b) 0.1 m/s
   (c) 1 m/s
   (d) 10 m/s
   (e) 100 m/s

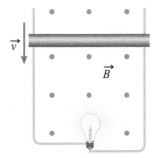

Figure 24-38 Question 7

8. Three light rectangular blocks with the same shape and approximately the same mass are placed on top of an aluminum inclined plane relatively far from each other (Figure 24-39). Block A is made of wood, block B is made of a magnetic material, and block C is made of copper. The coefficients of friction between the blocks and the incline are negligible. The blocks, initially at rest, are let go from the top of the incline. Which of the following statements most accurately describes what happens to the blocks?

(a) The copper block will come down last because copper is attracted to aluminum.

(b) The magnetic block will come down last because, during its motion, eddy currents will be created in the incline, which will slow it down significantly.

(c) The magnetic block will come down first because, during its motion, eddy currents will be created in the incline, speeding it up.

(d) The wooden block will come down last because wood will experience significant friction that will slow it down.

(e) Since friction is negligible, all the blocks will have the same acceleration. As a result, they will reach the bottom simultaneously.

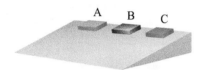

Figure 24-39   Question 8

9. A step-up transformer has $N_1 = 25$ loops and $N_2 = 25\ 000$ loops. The output voltage, V_2, has to be 120 000 V, and the output I_2 has to be 10 mA. What are the input V_1 and I_1?
   (a) $V_1 = 12$ V; $I_1 = 10$ mA
   (b) $V_1 = 12$ V; $I_1 = 1$ A
   (c) $V_1 = 12$ V; $I_1 = 10$ A
   (d) $V_1 = 120$ V; $I_1 = 10$ A
   (e) $V_1 = 120$ V; $I_1 = 1$ A
   (f) $V_1 = 120$ V; $I_1 = 10$ mA
   (h) $V_1 = 120$ V; $I_1 = 0.01$ mA

10. A current through an inductor starts increasing at a steady rate as shown in Figure 24-40. Which of the following is true about the potentials at points a and b?
    (a) $V_a = V_b$
    (b) $V_a < V_b$
    (c) $V_a > V_b$

Figure 24-40   Question 10

11. A circular copper loop is moving away from a long, straight wire-carrying current as shown in Figure 24-41. Which of the following statements correctly describes what is happening to the loop as a result of its motion?
    (a) A circular loop is attracted to the current-carrying wire because copper is magnetic and it is attracted to the current.
    (b) A current in the clockwise direction is induced in the loop, which makes the loop attracted to the current-carrying wire.
    (c) A current in the counterclockwise direction is induced in the loop, which makes the loop attracted to the current-carrying wire.

(d) A current in the clockwise direction is induced in the loop, which makes the loop repelled by the current-carrying wire.

(e) A current in the counterclockwise direction is induced in the loop, which makes the loop repelled by the current-carrying wire.

(f) There are no forces of attraction or repulsion between the loop and the wire because copper is a nonmagnetic material.

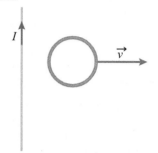

Figure 24-41   Question 11

12. A circular copper loop is moving along a long straight wire carrying current as shown in Figure 24-42. The speed of the loop is steadily increasing. Which of the following statements correctly describes what is happening to the loop as a result of its motion?
    (a) A counterclockwise current is induced in the loop, which causes the loop to be attracted to the current-carrying wire.
    (b) A clockwise current is induced in the loop, which makes the loop repelled by the current-carrying wire.
    (c) A current in the counterclockwise direction is induced in the loop, which makes the loop repelled by the current-carrying wire.
    (d) A current in the clockwise direction is induced in the loop, which makes the loop attracted by the current-carrying wire.
    (e) There are no forces of attraction or repulsion between the loop and the wire because the magnetic flux is constant.

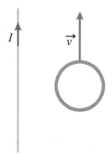

Figure 24-42   Question 12

13. A metal ring is moved over a permanent magnet, as shown in Figure 24-43(a). Which of the following statements correctly describes what happens to the ring and the direction of the current as seen from above?
    (a) A clockwise current is induced in the ring before it reaches the middle of the magnet, then the induced current flows in the counterclockwise direction.

(b) A counterclockwise current is induced in the ring before it reaches the middle of the magnet, then the current is induced in the clockwise direction.

(c) A clockwise current is induced in the ring only when the magnet is inside the ring.

(d) A counterclockwise current is induced in the ring before it reaches the magnet, then the current stops.

(e) A current is induced in the ring in the clockwise direction only when the ring leaves the magnet. (The magnet is no longer inside the ring.)

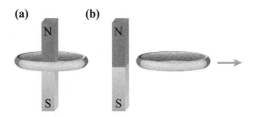

Figure 24-43   Questions 13 and 14

14. A metal ring is located near a permanent magnet, as shown in Figure 24-43(b). The ring is moved away from the magnet. Which of the following statements correctly describes the direction of the current in the ring as seen from above?

(a) There is an induced current in the clockwise direction.

(b) There is an induced current in the counterclockwise direction.

(c) There is no current induced in the ring.

15. Rank the inductances of the five solenoids shown in Figure 24-44 from the largest to the smallest.

Largest 1_____ 2_____ 3_____ 4_____ 5_____ Smallest

Or, the inductances are the same in all cases. _____

If the inductance is the same for two or more cases, clearly indicate it on the ranking scheme. Explain your reasoning.

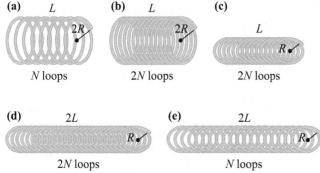

Figure 24-44   Questions 15, 16, and 17

16. The same electric current flows through the five solenoids shown in Figure 24-44. Rank the energy stored inside the solenoids from largest to smallest if a 1 A electric current flows through each solenoid.

Largest 1____ 2____ 3____ 4____ 5____ Smallest

Or, the stored energy is the same in all cases. _____

If the energy is the same for two or more cases, clearly indicate it on the ranking scheme. Explain your reasoning.

17. Rank the energy density inside the five solenoids in Figure 24-44 from largest to smallest when a 1 A electric current flows through each solenoid.

Largest 1_____ 2_____ 3_____ 4_____ 5_____ Smallest

Or, the energy density is the same in all cases. _____

If the energy density is the same for two or more cases, clearly indicate it on the ranking scheme. Explain your reasoning.

18. Two copper coils are facing each other as shown in Figure 24-45. Coil 1 is connected to a battery, so a constant current I_1 flows through it. At time $t = 0$, coil 2 starts moving to the right with a velocity $\vec{v}$. Which of the following statements correctly describes what happens as soon as coil 2 starts moving away from coil 1?

(a) There is an induced current in coil 2 in the clockwise direction if looking from the right.

(b) There is an induced current in coil 2 in the counterclockwise direction if looking from the right.

(c) There is no current induced in coil 2 because current I_1 is constant.

(d) All the above are possible, depending on the velocity of coil 2 relative to coil 1.

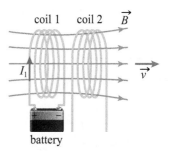

Figure 24-45   Question 18

19. Five series RL circuits (like the RL circuits in Figure 24-30) have different resistors, inductors, and batteries. The information for each circuit is shown in Table 24-2. The circuits were initially off; at time $t = 0$ s, they were turned on. Rank the times it takes for the current in each circuit to reach 75% of its maximum value from largest to smallest.

Largest 1_____ 2_____ 3_____ 4_____ 5_____ Smallest

Or, the time is the same for each circuit. _____

If the time is the same for two or more circuits, clearly indicate that on the ranking scheme. Explain your reasoning.

Table 24-2   Data for Question 19

	R	L	ε
Circuit 1	10 Ω	10 mH	10 V
Circuit 2	20 Ω	20 mH	10 V
Circuit 3	20 Ω	20 mH	20 V
Circuit 4	50 Ω	30 mH	25 V
Circuit 5	50 Ω	30 mH	30 V

165

20. Five different series RL circuits (like the RL circuits in Figure 24-30) have the same batteries (20 V each), the same resistors (20 Ω each), but different inductors: $L_1 = 10$ mH, $L_2 = 20$ mH, $L_3 = 30$ mH, $L_4 = 40$ mH, and $L_5 = 50$ mH. The circuits are initially turned off, then turned on. What is true about the values of the maximum current in these circuits?

(a) $I_1 > I_2 > I_3 > I_4 > I_5$
(b) $I_1 < I_2 < I_3 < I_4 < I_5$
(c) $I_1 = I_2 = I_3 = I_4 = I_5$

21. The light bulb in Figure 24-46 is a part of a series circuit powered by an AC source and containing an air-filled inductor. When an iron bar is moved inside the inductor's core, what happens to the brightness of the light bulb? Explain.

(a) The brightness remains the same.
(b) The brightness increases.
(c) The brightness decreases.

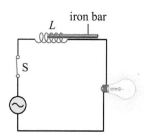

Figure 24-46 Question 21

PROBLEMS BY SECTION

For problems, star ratings will be used, (✶, ✶✶, or ✶✶✶), with more stars meaning more challenging problems.

Sections 24-1 and 24-2 In Faraday's Lab and Magnetic Flux and Its Rate of Change

22. ✶ A circular loop of area $A = 3$ cm² is in a region where there is a uniform and steadily decreasing magnetic field. The direction of the magnetic field is at a 30° angle to the loop's axis of symmetry. At time $t = 2$ s, the magnetic field has a magnitude of 10 mT, and at time $t = 6$ s, the magnetic field has a magnitude of 2 mT. Find the rate of change of the magnetic flux through the loop.

23. ✶ A rectangular copper loop with the dimensions $l = 50$ cm and $w = 25$ cm is moving at a constant velocity of 1.5 m/s out of a uniform magnetic field directed into the page. The magnetic field varies with time as $B = (0.002t + 0.001)$ T.

(a) Find the rate of change of the magnetic flux through this loop at the instant when the loop is three-quarters of its length out of the magnetic field.
(b) Answer part (a) when the loop has moved completely out of the magnetic field.
(c) How will your answers to parts (a) and (b) change if, instead of a single loop, there is a coil consisting of 20 loops?

24. ✶ A square copper loop 5 cm × 5 cm is located in an area of a uniform, time-varying magnetic field. The loop is directed perpendicular to the magnetic field. The magnetic field varies with time, as shown in Figure 24-47. Find the emf induced in the loop during the time intervals I, II, and III.

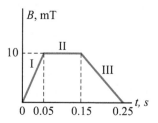

Figure 24-47 Problem 24

25. ✶ Two long, concentric (coaxial) copper solenoids have the same length $l = 50$ cm. Their radii are $R_1 = 2.0$ cm and $R_2 = 3.0$ cm, and their numbers of turns are 100 and 200, respectively. When the electric current in the inner solenoid changes at a rate of 0.5 A/s, what is the rate of change of the magnetic field through the outer solenoid?

26. ✶✶ A circular coil with 10 loops and the radius of 5 cm rotates about its diameter in a uniform and constant magnetic field with a magnitude of 10 mT. The axis of rotation of a coil is always perpendicular to the magnetic field. When the angular velocity of rotation is 4 rpm, what is the maximum rate of change of the magnetic flux through the coil?

Section 24-3 Faraday's Law of Electromagnetic Induction

27. ✶ The magnetic flux through a solenoid with 100 turns changes from 6×10^{-2} Wb to 8×10^{-4} Wb in 0.1 s. Find the induced emf in the coil.

28. ✶ A rectangular metal loop with the dimensions 5 cm × 10 cm is inserted in a uniform but changing magnetic field. The resistance of the loop is 3 Ω. Find the rate of change of the magnetic field so that 5 A of electric current is induced in the loop when

(a) the magnetic field is perpendicular to the surface of the loop;
(b) the magnetic field is directed at a 30° angle to the loop's normal;
(c) the magnetic field is directed parallel to the loop's surface.

29. ✶ To find the magnitude of the magnetic field between the poles of a large horseshoe magnet, a coil of wire consisting of 20 turns and with a cross-sectional area of 6 cm² is inserted between the poles of the magnet perpendicular to the magnetic field lines. When the coil is pulled out of the magnetic field in 0.02 s, an induced emf of 45 mV was measured in the coil. What is the magnitude of the magnetic field between the poles of the magnet?

30. ✶✶ A rectangular 4 cm × 8 cm metal coil has 50 turns and a resistance of 10 Ω. The coil is placed on a horizontal frictionless table and is completely submerged in a vertical uniform magnetic field, $B = 0.5$ T.

(a) How fast should the coil be pulled out of this uniform magnetic field so that the emf generated in the coil reaches 0.5 V? The velocity of the coil $\vec{v}$ is directed perpendicular to one of its sides (Figure 24-48).
(b) Draw a graph that shows the dependence of the induced emf on time while the coil is pulled out of the magnetic field at the constant velocity $\vec{v}$ found above.

(c) Find the direction and the magnitude of the electric current induced in the coil while it is pulled out of the magnetic field at a constant velocity $\vec{v}$.

(d) Find the force F that needs to be applied to pull the coil with this constant velocity $\vec{v}$.

(e) Draw the graph representing the dependence of F on time. Draw this graph under the graph you made for part (b) to see the correspondence.

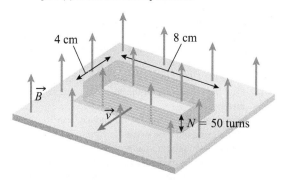

Figure 24-48   Problem 30

31. ✷✷ Another way of looking at Faraday's law of electromagnetic induction is to consider the induced charge in a wire placed in a magnetic field (due to the Lorentz force acting on moving electric charges submerged in magnetic fields). An induced charge in a coil with N loops and resistance R can be expressed as

$$\Delta Q = \frac{-N\Delta\Phi_B}{R}$$

Show that this relationship is a direct consequence of the law of the electromagnetic induction.

32. ✷✷✷ A conducting bar of length $l = 0.2$ m and mass $m = 0.1$ kg is submerged in a uniform and constant magnetic field $B = 0.5$ T (Figure 24-49). The bar is free to slide down two frictionless metal rails. At time $t = 0$ s, the bar is given an initial velocity $\vec{v}_i = 2$ m/s directed to the right. The resistance $R = 4\ \Omega$ comprises the resistance of the entire circuit.

(a) Find the velocity of the bar 1.0 s after it was pushed.

(b) Find the acceleration of the bar at $t = 1.0$ s

(c) Determine the distance travelled by the bar during the first second.

(d) Calculate the distance travelled by the bar before its speed decreases to $v_i/4$.

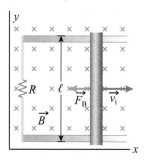

Figure 24-49   Problem 32

33. ✷✷ A metal rod of mass $m = 250$ g and length $L = 50$ cm is free to slide on two parallel, frictionless horizontal metal rails (Figure 24-50). The rails are connected at one end so that they and the rod form a closed circuit. The rod and the rails have a resistance of 2 Ω. A uniform magnetic field B, perpendicular to the plane of this circuit and directed vertically upward, is decreasing at a constant rate of 0.3 mT/s. At time $t = 0$ s, the magnetic field has a strength of 15 mT, and the rod is at rest at a distance of 150 cm from the connected end of the rails.

(a) Describe the forces acting on the rod at $t = 0$ s and thereafter.

(b) Derive an expression for the acceleration of the rod at $t = 0$ s in terms of the given quantities.

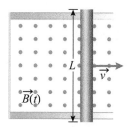

Figure 24-50   Problem 33

Section 24-4   Applications of Faraday's Law of Electromagnetic Induction

34. ✷✷ An engineering student proposes to use the law of electromagnetic induction to power aircraft equipment. The proposal uses the Boeing 757-200 as an example. The aircraft has a maximum cruising speed of 914 km/h and a wing span of 38.05 m. Suppose the aircraft is flying in the region where the vertical component of the magnetic field is 3.5×10^{-5} T. What is the potential difference generated across the wings? Is it sufficient to power the onboard equipment?

35. ✷✷ A simple AC generator, like the one described in Figure 24-14, consists of a single loop with an area of 100 cm² that rotates with a frequency of 60 Hz in a uniform magnetic field of 3.0×10^{-2} T.

(a) Find the maximum emf generated by this generator.

(b) Find the maximum emf that would be generated by this generator if instead of a single loop it had 100 loops.

(c) Describe mathematically how the output voltage depends on time. The output voltage is maximum when $t = 0$ s.

36. ✷✷ A horizontal copper disk 40 cm in diameter is placed in a constant and uniform magnetic field of 8.0×10^{-2} T directed vertically upward. The disk spins about a vertical axis through its centre, with an angular velocity of 10 rad/s.

(a) What is the magnitude of the emf induced between the centre of the disk and its rim?

(b) What is the magnitude of the induced emf between diametrically opposite points on the disk?

37. ✷✷ To reduce the 120 V AC voltage to 12 V AC to operate a standard doorbell, a step-down transformer is used.

(a) This transformer has 1000 turns in the primary coil. How many turns does it have in the secondary coil?

(b) When the doorbell button is pushed, 15 Ω of resistance is introduced in the secondary circuit. What are the values of the maximum and rms currents in the primary and in the secondary coils? Assume that the transformer used in the doorbell has 100% efficiency.

(c) How would your answers to part (b) change if the efficiency of the transformer were 90%?

167

Section 24-5 Induced emf and Induced Electric Fields

38. ✷✷ A circular loop of radius $R = 10$ cm is coaxial with a solenoid ($r = 0.05$ m, $l = 1.00$ m, and 750 turns), as shown in Figure 24-51. The current in the circuit decreases linearly from 1.0 A to 4.6 A over 0.5 s.
   (a) Calculate the induced emf in the loop.
   (b) Calculate the induced electric field in the loop.
   (c) When the resistance of the loop is 20 Ω, how much energy will be dissipated by the loop in 10 s?

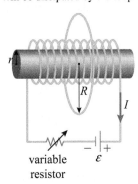

Figure 24-51 Problem 38

39. ✷✷ A solenoid with length L and radius R has N turns. The solenoid carries an electric current that varies with time as $I(t) = I_{max}\sin(2\pi ft)$, where I_{max} represents the maximum current, and f is the frequency of the AC source.
   (a) Derive an expression that describes the magnitude of the electric field outside the solenoid ($r > R$).
   (b) Derive an expression that describes the magnitude of the electric field inside the solenoid ($r < R$).
   (c) For parts (a) and (b), draw graphs showing the dependence of the magnitude of the electric field on r: $E(r)$ at a certain instant of time t. Explain your results.

Section 24-6 Self-Inductance and Mutual Inductance

40. ✷ The current through an air-filled coil is changing at a rate of 200 A/s. As a result of this change, the induced emf in it is measured to be 250 V.
   (a) What is the self-inductance of the coil?
   (b) How will the value of the self-inductance change if an iron core is inserted in this coil?
   (c) What is the rate of change of the magnetic flux through this coil?

41. ✷✷ Two electric circuits are located near each other. When the electric current in the first circuit changes at a rate of 200 A/s, an induced emf of 20 V is measured in the second circuit. What is the mutual inductance of the circuits?

42. ✷✷ Two coaxial air-filled solenoids of equal length ($L = 20$ cm) and equal radius ($r = 5$ cm) have 100 turns and 400 turns.
   (a) Find the mutual inductance of these solenoids.
   (b) How will your answer to part (a) change if iron cores are inserted in the solenoids?

43. ✷✷ A 2 m-long air-filled solenoid has a radius of 5 cm and 25 000 turns. A 500-turn coil is tightly wound over the outside of the solenoid, as shown in Figure 24-52.
   (a) Find the mutual inductance of the solenoid and the coil.
   (b) The current in the solenoid is changing according to
   $$I_{solenoid}(t) = \left(10\frac{A}{s}\right)t.$$ Find the emf induced in the coil.

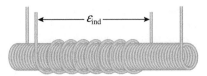

Figure 24-52 Problem 43

Section 24-7 RL Circuits

44. ✷✷ A series electric circuit consists of a 24 V battery, a switch, a 20 Ω resistor, and an inductor. The inductor is a 30 cm-long solenoid that has 1000 turns and a radius of 2.5 cm. After the switch is closed, it takes 0.28 ms for the current in the circuit to reach half of its maximum value.
   (a) Find the inductance of the solenoid using two different methods.
   (b) Derive an expression for the induced emf in the solenoid during the time when the current is changing from zero to its maximum value.
   (c) Find the value of the maximum current in the circuit.
   (d) Find the value of the voltage across the resistor when the induced emf in the solenoid is at one-half of its maximum value.
   (e) The switch is left on for a long time. What is the value of the induced emf in the solenoid at $t = 0.1$ s? What is the value of the voltage across the resistor at that time?

Section 24-8 Energy Stored in a Magnetic Field

45. ✷ Find the energy stored in the solenoid described in problem 44 when the current in the circuit
   (a) is at its maximum value;
   (b) is at one-half of its maximum value;
   (c) is zero.

COMPREHENSIVE PROBLEMS

46. ✷✷ A square loop of wire with a side length of 5 cm is bent along its diagonal such that its two triangular halves are located in perpendicular planes (Figure 24-53). The loop is then submerged in a uniform magnetic field B, directed perpendicular to the diagonal of the square loop and at a 45° angle to the planes of the bent square. The resistance of the loop is 3 Ω, and the magnetic field in the region changes with time according to $B(t) = (50t + 3)$ mT. Find the magnitude and the direction of the induced emf and the induced electric current in the loop during the time interval 0 s < $t < 5$ s.

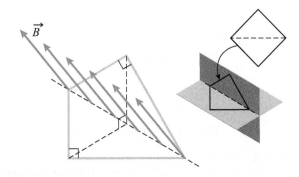

Figure 24-53 Problem 46

47. ✱✱ A horizontal, 10 cm-long aluminum rod is located inside a vertical, uniform, and constant magnetic field of 35 mT. One end of the rod is secured to a hinge, such that the rod can rotate around it in a horizontal plane (Figure 24-54). The rod makes five revolutions per second. What is the induced emf along its length?

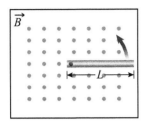

Figure 24-54   Problem 47

48. ✱✱ Two concentric aluminum loops have radii $R_1 = 2.5$ cm and $R_2 = 5$ cm.
(a) The current in the outside loop is changing according to $I(t) = [15\sin(30(\pi t)]$ A, and the resistance of the inside loop is 10 Ω. Derive expressions for the induced emf and the induced electric current in the inside loop.
(b) Compare the frequency of the induced emf and the induced current with the frequency of the current in the outside loop.

49. ✱✱ A copper loop in the shape of an equilateral triangle with sides of 10 cm is placed in a uniform and constant magnetic field, $B = 45.0$ mT, directed perpendicular to the surface of the loop (Figure 24-55). The resistance of the loop is 1 Ω. The loop is pulled out of the magnetic field with a constant velocity of 2 m/s.
(a) What is the magnitude of the emf induced in the loop as it moves out of the magnetic field?
(b) What is the direction of the induced emf?
(c) Find the force that needs to be exerted on the loop to pull it out with the speed of 4 m/s.

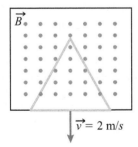

Figure 24-55   Problem 49

50. ✱✱ A rectangular metal loop is located a distance d from a long, straight wire carrying electric current I (Figure 24-56). The short side of the loop is parallel to the wire, and the loop and the wire are located in the same plane. The electric current in the wire changes according to $I(t) = [10\sin(120\pi t)]$ A. Derive an expression that describes the rate of change of the magnetic flux through the loop.

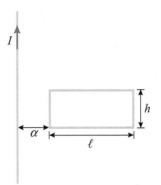

Figure 24-56   Problem 50

51. ✱✱ A circular elastic band is made out of a conducting material. Its initial radius is 5 cm, and it is stretched in a horizontal plane. The band is located in a uniform and constant magnetic field of $B = 50.0$ mT. The band begins expanding uniformly in all directions such that its radius changes at a rate of 0.025 cm/s. What is the induced emf in the band?

52. ✱ A square metal loop 5 cm × 5 cm is located in a region of a nonuniform but constant magnetic field directed perpendicular to the surface of the loop (Figure 24-57). The magnetic field is uniformly decreasing along the direction of motion of the loop at a rate of 5 mT/cm. When the loop is pulled with a velocity of 1 m/s as shown in the figure, what is the emf induced in it?

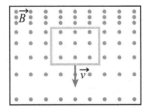

Figure 24-57   Problem 52

53. ✱✱✱ A metal rod with length $L = 0.2$ m, mass 300 g, and cross-sectional area $A = 0.01$ m² slides down friction-less, tilted aluminum rails (Figure 24-58). The rod starts from rest at the top of the rails tilted at a 30° angle to the horizontal. The apparatus is placed in a uniform and constant vertical magnetic field $B = 0.5$ T, and the resistance of the rails and the rod is 2 Ω.
(a) Describe the motion of the rod as it slides down the incline. Indicate all the forces acting on the rod.
(b) Derive an expression for the induced emf across the rod as a function of the rod's velocity.
(c) Derive an expression for the velocity of the rod as a function of time.
(d) Derive an expression of the emf induced across the rod as a function of time.
(e) Find the terminal velocity of the rod as it slides down the incline.

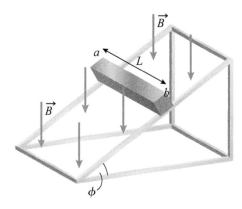

Figure 24-58 Problem 53

(c) If the inner coil is connected to the emf source, and the outer coil is not, how will the value of mutual inductance of these coils change? How can you make sense of your answer?

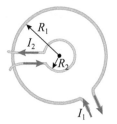

Figure 24-60 Problem 56

54. ✶✶ Two coaxial air-filled solenoids A and B of equal length ($L = 20$ cm) and radii $R_A = 2.5$ cm and $R_B = 5.0$ cm have $N_A = 100$ turns and $N_B = 400$ turns.
(a) When the current in the inner solenoid increases from 0 A to 15 A in 0.01 s, what is the induced emf in the outer solenoid during that time?
(b) After 0.01 s, the current in the inner solenoid becomes constant. What is the induced emf in the outer solenoid at that time?
(c) How will your answer to part (b) change if an iron core is inserted into the solenoids?

55. ✶✶ Toroidal inductors (Figure 24-59) and transformers are electronic components that consist of a ring-shaped magnetic core around which a wire is wound to make an inductor. A toroidal inductor is built by winding 10 000 turns of wire around a soft iron ring with a rectangular cross section of 10 mm × 15 mm. The mean radius of the inductor is 30 cm, and the magnetic permeability of iron used in this particular inductor is $\mu = 1.2 \times 10^{-3}$ H/m.
(a) Calculate the magnetic field inside the toroid when the electric current through it is 10 A.
(b) Calculate the inductance of the toroid.
(c) How will your answers to parts (a) and (b) change if the electric current through the inductor were to double?

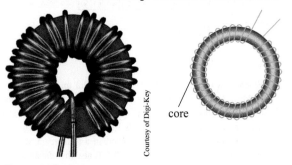

core

Courtesy of Digi-Key

Figure 24-59 Problem 55

56. ✶✶ Two coaxial coils oriented in the same plane are arranged as shown in Figure 24-60. The larger coil has a radius R_1 and N_1 turns, and the smaller coil has a radius R_2 and N_2 turns, where $R_2 \ll R_1$.
(a) Derive an expression for the mutual inductance of these coils.
(b) When the current in the outer coil is changing at the rate of 150 A/s, what is the value of the induced emf in the inner coil?

57. ✶✶ The starter motor in your car has a resistance of 0.40 Ω in its armature windings. (An armature is a conductive coil used in a motor.) The car battery has a voltage of 12 V. When the motor operates at its normal speed, it has a back emf of approximately 10 V. Estimate the amount of current this car motor draws
(a) when running at its operating speed;
(b) during start-up.

58. ✶✶ The switch in the circuit shown in Figure 24-61 has been open for a long time. Then, at $t = 0$ s, the switch is closed.
(a) Derive a relationship that shows how the current through the inductor depends on time.
(b) Derive an expression that shows how the induced emf across the inductor depends on time.
(c) Plot the graphs of the quantities found in parts (a) and (b) as function of time. Assume the inductor is ideal.

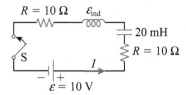

Figure 24-61 Problem 58

59. ✶✶ Faraday's law of electromagnetic induction can be used to measure the speed of a projectile. Imagine a small magnet imbedded into a projectile as shown in Figure 24-62. The apparatus consists of two coils separated by a distance d; each coil is connected to an oscilloscope. When the magnet-carrying projectile passes through a coil, it induces an emf in the coil that is recorded by the oscilloscope. Since the time of the emf pulses can be recorded accurately, the speed of the projectile can be calculated.
(a) Draw what you would see in an oscilloscope connected across the inductor when the projectile is approaching the coils from the left. Denote a current flowing in the clockwise direction as seen by the observer launching the projectile as positive. Clearly indicate the pulse induced in coil 1 and in coil 2.
(b) How will your graphs change if the projectile were to move twice as fast?

170

(c) How will your graphs change if the number of loops in the left coil were to double, and the number of loops in the right coil remained the same?

(d) The time separation between the pulses is 3.5 ms, and the distance between the coils is 2.0 m. What is the speed of the projectile?

(e) The method described above is used to measure the speed of a projectile up to tens of kilometres per second. What are some limitations of this method? Why do you think it is not used to measure speeds of faster projectiles?

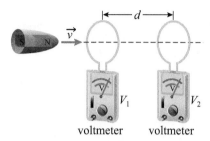

Figure 24-62   Problem 59

60. ✶✶   A loop of wire, shown in Figure 24-63, is placed in a uniform but nonconstant magnetic field. The magnitude and the direction of the magnetic field change continuously with time, such that at times t_1 and t_2 the magnetic flux values are $\Phi_B(t_1)$ and $\Phi_B(t_2)$, respectively.

(a) Prove that the net electric charge that flows through the resistor R during the time $t = t_2 - t_1$ can be expressed as

$$q(t) = \frac{\Phi(t_2) - \Phi(t_1)}{R}$$

(b) Analyze the expression for electric charge for the limiting cases: constant magnetic field, very low resistance, and very high resistance. What does the analysis of these limiting cases tell you?

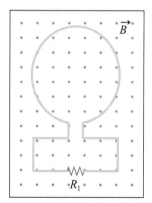

Figure 24-63   Problem 60

61. ✶✶   A piece of insulated conducting wire is shaped as shown in Figure 24-64. The radius of the large circle is twice as large as the radius of the small circle (4 cm and 2 cm, respectively), and the resistance of the small circle is 0.5 Ω. The wire is placed in a uniform but time-varying magnetic field. The rate of change of the magnetic field is 0.5 mT/s. Find the direction and magnitude of the electric current induced in the wires in each case.

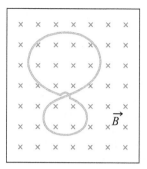

Figure 24-64   Problem 61

62. ✶✶   A series RL circuit consists of a 9 V battery, a 5 Ω resistor, and a 4 H inductor. After the circuit has been turned on, how long will it take for the current in this circuit to reach

(a) 50% of its maximum value;
(b) 75% of its maximum value;
(c) 90% of its maximum value;
(d) 100% of its maximum value?

Supplement your algebraic solution by drawing an $I(t)$ graph for this circuit.

63. ✶✶   A series RL circuit consists of a 12 V battery, a 15 Ω resistor, and a 3 H inductor.

(a) Complete Table 24-3 by calculating the values of the voltage across the resistor, the voltage across the inductor V_L, the current through the battery, and the voltage across it.

(b) How do you know if the values you found are reasonable? Assume the battery is ideal.

(c) How would the answers to the problem change if the battery were not ideal?

Table 24-3   Table for Problem 63

Time	V_R (V)	V_L (V)	I (A)	ε battery (V)
0.001 s				
0.01 s				
0.1 s				
0.2 s				
0.4 s				

64. ✶✶✶   You and your friend decide to design a simple magnetometer. Your device is mounted on your car and consists of a 1 m-long metal pole (a radio antenna, e.g.) and a voltmeter that measures the potential difference across it. When the car is moving due north along a horizontal road at a speed of 60 km/h, your magnetometer measures the potential difference across the antenna to be 1 mV. You know that in the area where you were driving the direction of the magnetic field is approximately 63° below the horizontal. What is the magnitude of the magnetic field there?

65. ✱✱✱ A 60 cm-long bar can slide without friction along the long horizontal rails shown Figure 24-65. The bar and the rails have a resistance of 5 Ω, and the entire setup is placed in a uniform magnetic field of 3.0 mT.
   (a) Derive an expression for the force needed to move the bar to the left at a constant speed.
   (b) Use the expression you derived in part (a) to find the force required to pull the bar with a constant speed of 1.5 m/s.
   (c) Derive the expression for the energy delivered to the resistor in t seconds when the bar is moving to the right with constant speed $\vec{v}$.
   (d) How much energy was delivered to the resistor when the bar was moving with a speed of 1.5 m/s during 3 s?

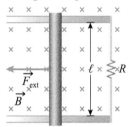

Figure 24-65   Problem 65

66. ✱✱✱ The 60 cm-long metal bar in Figure 24-58 (see problem 53) is given an initial velocity of 2.5 m/s up the incline (up and right) and then let go.
   (a) How long will it take the bar to stop moving, and how far will the bar move along the metal rails provided the friction between the rails and the bar is negligible?
   (b) Provide at least two ways of solving the problem: one solution based on Newton's laws and another solution based on energy considerations.

67. ✱✱ The RL circuit shown in Figure 24-33 is designed such that the switch S is used to choose between having the battery as part of the circuit (the switch is in position a) or having the battery out of the circuit (the switch is in position b). The battery has an emf of 12 V, the resistance of the resistor is $R = 5$ Ω, and the inductance of the inductor is $L = 40$ mH. At first, the switch is moved to position a.
   (a) How long does it take the current to reach 99% of its maximum value? What is this value?
   (b) When the current reaches 99% of its maximum value, what is the emf across the inductor?
   (c) After 25 s, the switch is moved to position b. How long will it take for the current to decrease by 50% of its maximum value?

68. ✱✱ A medium-sized electric generating plant produces electric energy at 50 A and 20 kV. The electricity produced by the power plant has to be transmitted 50 km over transmission lines, which have a resistance of 10.0 Ω/km.
   (a) Compare the power output of this electric generating plant with the electric power output of the Sir Adam Beck #2 Power Plant at Niagara Falls, Ontario (1.29 GW).
   (b) What is the power loss during the transmission when the energy is transmitted at 20 kV?
   (c) To what value should the voltage output value of the generator be stepped up to reduce the energy loss by a factor of 20?
   (d) How many average families can this power plant support? List and justify your assumptions.

69. ✱✱✱ An electric generator consists of a 1000-loop coil formed into a rectangle with sides of 30 cm and 60 cm. The coil is placed in a uniform magnetic field of magnitude $B = 2.5$ T.
   (a) Derive an expression for the emf induced by this generator, provided the coil is spun about the axis perpendicular to the magnetic field with angular velocity ω.
   (b) Find the maximum value of the emf produced by this generator when the coil is rotated about an axis perpendicular to $\vec{B}$ with $f = 1200$ rev/min.
   (c) Use the expression for the induced emf to explain what can be done to the generator to change the frequency of the induced emf and/or its maximum value.

70. ✱✱ The RL circuit in Figure 24-66 consists of an ideal battery, a resistor R, an inductor L, and a switch S that has three different positions: a, b, and N. Initially, the switch is in position N (the circuit is open). After the circuit switch is moved to position a and time Δt elapses, the current in the circuit reaches 50% of its maximum value. The switch remains in position a for the time interval 10τ. After that, the switch is moved into position b.
   (a) What is the time constant of this RL circuit?
   (b) What are the values of the electric current in the circuit, the energy density in the coil, and the emf across the coil when
       (i) the switch is at position a for a long time;
       (ii) after the switch moved to position b and τ seconds elapsed;
       (iii) after the switch moved to position b and 3τ seconds elapsed?
   Support your answers with a graph of electric current in the circuit versus time.

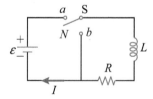

Figure 24-66   Problem 70

71. ✱✱ The value of the electric field at Earth's surface depends on the location on Earth, the time of the day, and the weather, and ranges from 40 V/m to 150 V/m. The magnetic field values at Earth's surface vary from 25 000 nT to 57 000 nT (being the highest at the poles). Compare the energy densities for the electric and magnetic fields near Earth's surface. What does your comparison mean?

72. ✱✱✱ Magnetic resonance imaging (MRI) is a medical technique used widely in modern hospitals to produce images of the interior of the body. During an MRI scan, a patient is placed in a region of a constant magnetic field of up to 5.0 T. While operating properly, the magnetic field is kept constant. However, in case of equipment failure, the magnetic field might be shut off suddenly. This rapidly decreasing magnetic field will generate an induced emf, potentially affecting the charged particles in the body fluids and producing life-threatening electric currents. To prevent this from happening, the engineers make sure that it takes at least the time τ to shut the MRI magnetic field off.

(a) Taking into account that for safety reasons, the maximum induced emf should be kept below 0.010 V and the cross-sectional area of the part of the human body exposed to the magnetic field does not exceed 0.04 m², calculate the value of τ.

(b) One of the important safety regulations for an MRI scan is that a patient or a technician never wear any metal objects. Explain why.

73. ✳✳✳ Baby breathing monitors became popular in the mid–1990s and today are widely used in homes and in hospitals. Although not a life-saving device by itself, the monitor is sensitive to the slightest movement and will sound an alarm if the baby stops breathing for more than 20 s. There are two main types of baby monitor sensors: the mattress pad sensor, placed under the baby's mattress, and the body sensor, which is a thin belt wrapped around the baby's chest. Both detect the changes in Earth's magnetic field flux through a coil as a result of the movement of a patient. The simplest baby body sensor monitor consists of a 300-turn coil wrapped around the baby's chest and connected to a sensitive voltmeter. Estimate the sensitivity of this voltmeter (how accurately it should be able to measure an induced emf) to measure the emf induced by a baby's breathing. Assume that the magnetic field component perpendicular to the coils is 30 μT, the newborn's normal breathing rate is approximately 40 times a minute (much higher than an adult rate), and the smallest increase in the area of a belt around the baby's chest is 5 cm².

74. ✳✳✳ An electric guitar uses a circular pickup coil that detects the vibrations of a steel guitar string. The pickup coil consists of a magnet and a coil with as many as 7000 turns of wire wound around it. A vibrating steel string modulates a changing magnetic flux through the pickup coil. The component of the magnetic field perpendicular to the pickup coil can be described as $B(t) = [45.0 + 3.5\sin(2\pi622t)]$ mT. The diameter of a pickup coil is 5.4 mm. Find the time dependence of the emf induced in the coil.

75. ✳✳✳ Engineers proposed using superconducting materials in the coaxial cables for power transmission lines. A diagram of such a cable is shown in Figure 24-67. The inner and outer wires of such a superconducting cable carry currents in opposite directions. Such a superconducting coaxial cable can carry up to 1 GW of power (1×10^9 W) at 200 kV DC over a distance of 1500 km, almost without a loss in power strength. The radius of an inner wire is 2.5 cm, and the radius of an outer wire if 5.0 cm. Calculate the value of

(a) the magnetic field at the surface of the inner conductor;

(b) the magnetic field at the inner surface of the outer conductor;

(c) the magnetic field at the outer surface of the outer conductor;

(d) the energy density between the conductors;

(e) the energy stored in the space between the conductor over the 1500 km distance;

(f) the pressure exerted on the outer conductor as a result of the power transmission.

76. ✳✳✳ The switch in the circuit shown in Figure 24-68 has been open for a long time. Then, at $t = 0$ s, the switch is closed.

(a) Derive an expression that shows how the current in the inductor, the current in the battery, and the current in the switch depend on time.

(b) Derive an expression that shows how the induced emf across the inductor depends on time.

(c) Plot the graphs for the quantities found in parts (a) and (b) as a function of time. Assume it is an ideal inductor.

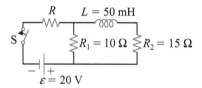

Figure 24-68 Problem 76

77. ✳✳✳ Show that the equivalent inductance of two or more inductors can be calculated as follows:

(a) For inductors connected in series:

$$L_{eq} = L_1 + L_2 + \cdots$$

(b) For inductors connected in parallel:

$$\frac{1}{L_{eq}} = \frac{1}{L_2} + \frac{1}{L_2} + \cdots$$

(c) Use the PhET simulations from the online activities to verify whether these formulas hold.

(d) Design more complex RL circuits, calculate their parameters, and then test your prediction using the PhET simulations.

78. ✳✳✳ A student in a physics lab investigates the operation of an AC generator. He collects data on the emf of the generator as a function of time (Figure 24-69). The generator consists of a 200-turn coil that is spun in a strong magnetic field. The coil has a cross-sectional area of 25 cm².

(a) Determine the frequency of the generated current f (Hz).

(b) Determine the frequency of the rotation of the coil f (Hz) and its angular frequency ω (rad/s).

(c) Find the magnitude of the magnetic field.

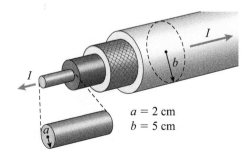

Figure 24-67 Problem 75

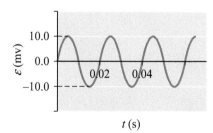

Figure 24-69 Problem 78

79. ✸✸✸ A student in a physics lab investigates the operation of a series RL circuit. She uses a 2 Ω resistor, a battery, an inductor with an unknown value, and a voltmeter. After the inductor is connected to the battery (the switch is in position *a*), she measures the voltage across the inductor at different times. Her observations are recorded in Table 24-4.

(a) Find the inductance value of the inductor.
(b) Find the time constant of the circuit.
(c) Find the values of electric current at each time. (Hint: Use a spreadsheet program to answer the questions.)

Table 24-4 Data for Problem 79

Time (ms)	V_L (V)	Time (ms)	V_L (V)	Time (ms)	V_L (V)
1.0	8.598	3.5	3.737	6.0	1.624
1.5	7.278	4.0	3.163	6.5	1.375
2.0	6.161	4.5	2.678	7.0	1.164
2.5	5.215	5.0	2.267	7.5	0.985
3.0	4.414	5.5	1.919	8.0	0.834

OPEN PROBLEM

80. ✸✸✸ An 8 cm-long bar magnet (Figure 24-70) is dropped into a copper coil from a height of 50 cm above the coil. The coil is 5 cm in radius, consists of 400 turns, is 10 cm long and the bar magnet has a strength of 0.01 T.

(a) Estimate the value of the maximum emf induced in the coil. Clearly list your assumptions.
(b) Draw the graphs of the induced emf in the coil as a function of time and distance.

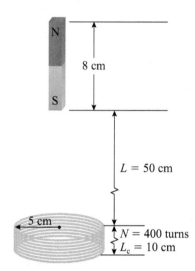

Figure 24-70 Problem 80. Not to scale

See the text online resources at
www.physics1e.nelson.com for Open Problems
and Data-Rich Problems related to this chapter.

Chapter 25
Alternating Current Circuits

Learning Objectives

When you have completed this chapter you should be able to:

1. Derive expressions for the current in alternating current (AC) circuits with resistive, inductive, or capacitive loads.

2. Analyze an LC circuit.

3. Use phasors and phasor diagrams to represent electric current and voltage in AC circuits.

4. Analyze series RLC circuits.

5. Determine the resonant frequency of a series RLC circuit, and describe how the current and component voltages vary with the frequency of the emf.

6. Calculate power dissipated in AC circuits.

According to Natural Resources Canada, the annual energy consumption of an average Canadian household in 2007, including all energy sources except fuel for transportation, was 106×10^9 J $\approx$ 30 000 kW·h (distributed as shown in Figure 25-1). This annual consumption is equivalent to 3.35 kJ of energy per second year-round. Approximately 38% of this energy is electricity supplied in the form of alternating current (AC) through a nation-wide power grid, a gigantic network of AC circuits. This chapter introduces the basic principles of AC circuits.

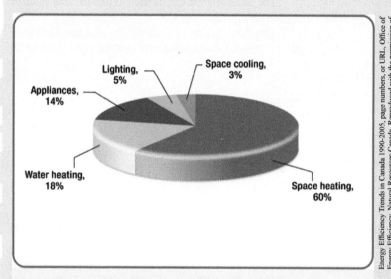

Energy Efficiency Trends in Canada 1990–2005, page numbers, or URL, Office of Energy Efficiency, Natural Resources Canada. Reproduced with the permission of the Minister of Public Works and Government Services Canada, 2012.

Figure 25-1 Domestic energy usage in Canada

For additional Making Connections, Examples, and Checkpoints, as well as activities and experiments to help increase your understanding of the chapter's concepts, please go to the text's online resources at www.physics1e.nelson.com.

ELECTRICITY, MAGNETISM, AND OPTICS

25-1 Simple Loads in AC Circuits

In Chapter 24, we discussed the generation of electrical energy. Most modern power plants generate **alternating current** (AC), which is electric current that changes direction and magnitude many times a second. In North America, the frequency of AC oscillation is 60 Hz; in the European Union and many other countries, the AC frequency is 50 Hz.

Due to the dependence of AC current and voltage on time, we cannot describe these quantities the same way we did for DC circuits. However, we can apply the major concepts and relationships of DC circuits, such as potential difference, electric current, resistance, and Ohm's law, to AC circuits by using some additional techniques and terminology. Unlike a DC circuit, an AC power supply produces an oscillating emf (voltage) that continually changes its magnitude and direction. Therefore, the voltage across the power supply changes with time. For AC circuits, we denote instantaneous values of current and voltage using lower case letters: $i(t)$ and $v(t)$, respectively.

ONLINE ACTIVITY

Exploring AC Circuits

The e-resource that accompanies every new copy of this textbook contains an Online Activity using the PhET simulation "Exploring AC circuits." Work through the simulation and accompanying questions to gain an understanding of more types of AC circuits.

In this chapter, we discuss AC power supplies with an emf that can be described using a sine function:

KEY EQUATION $\quad \varepsilon(t) = \varepsilon_{max}\sin(\omega t) = \varepsilon_{max}\sin(2\pi f t)$ (25-1)

where ε_{max} is the maximum value of the emf, and ω and f are the angular frequency and frequency, respectively.

This emf oscillates between $\pm\varepsilon_{max}$ and has an average value of zero. As you will see below, the current in a sinusoidal AC circuit oscillates between $\pm i_{max}$ and also has an average value of zero. Generally, the **root-mean-square** (rms) values of AC emfs and currents are much more useful for circuit calculations. An rms value of a physical quantity is the square root of the mean value of the square of the mathematical function describing the quantity. For sinusoidal quantities we can take the root-mean over one period, or cycle. If emf $\varepsilon = \varepsilon_{max}\sin(\omega t)$, the period of oscillation is $T = \dfrac{1}{f} = \dfrac{1}{\omega/2\pi} = \dfrac{2\pi}{\omega}$. So, we can substitute the sine function into the expression for an rms value and then integrate over one period:

$$\varepsilon_{rms} = \sqrt{(\varepsilon^2)_{avg}}$$

$$= \sqrt{(\varepsilon_{max}^2\sin^2(\omega t))_{avg}}$$

$$= \varepsilon_{max}\sqrt{(\sin^2(\omega t))_{avg}}$$

$$= \frac{\varepsilon_{max}}{\sqrt{2}}$$

$$(\sin^2(\omega t))_{avg} = \frac{\displaystyle\int_0^T \sin^2(\omega t)\,dt}{T}$$

$$= \frac{1}{T}\int_0^T \frac{1}{2}(1 - \cos(2\omega t))\,dt$$

$$= \frac{1}{T}\frac{T}{2}$$

$$= \frac{1}{2} \tag{25-2}$$

The same method can be used to find the rms value of AC current or any other sine or cosine quantity.

Therefore, the rms values for the emf and current in an AC circuit, with a sinusoidal emf, can be expressed as follows:

KEY EQUATION $\qquad \varepsilon_{rms} = \dfrac{\varepsilon_{max}}{\sqrt{2}}$ (25-3)

KEY EQUATION $\qquad i_{rms} = \dfrac{i_{max}}{\sqrt{2}}$

✓ CHECKPOINT

C-25-1 The rms Value of a Square Wave

Is the rms value of a square wave greater or less than the rms value of a sine wave?

C-25-1 Greater. The rms is defined as the square root of the area under one full waveform squared, divided by the period of the waveform. Since a square wave has an amplitude that is either $\pm \varepsilon_{max}$, the square of that is ε_{max}^2, and the area is $\varepsilon_{max}^2 T$. When we divide by the period and take the square root, we obtain $\varepsilon_{rms} = \varepsilon_{max}$ for a square wave.

Resistive Load

Let us start with an AC circuit that consists simply of an AC power supply connected to a resistor, as shown in Figure 25-2.

Figure 25-2 An AC circuit with a resistive load

Just as with DC circuits, we can apply Kirchhoff's loop rule to obtain

$$\varepsilon(t) - iR = 0 \qquad (25\text{-}4)$$

Solving for i and using Equation 25-1 for the emf we find

$$i(t) = \frac{\varepsilon(t)}{R} = \frac{\varepsilon_{max}}{R}\sin(\omega t) = i_{max}\sin(\omega t) \qquad (25\text{-}5)$$

Not surprisingly, the current in this circuit is also sinusoidal, and the amplitude of the current is related to the amplitude of the emf:

$$i_{max} = \frac{\varepsilon_{max}}{R} \qquad (25\text{-}6)$$

Equation (25-6) has the same form as Ohm's law, $I = \dfrac{V}{R}$: current equals voltage divided by resistance. Figure 25-3 shows a plot of the emf and the resulting current versus time.

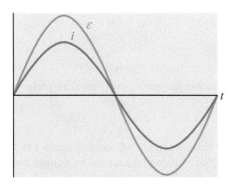

Figure 25-3 The emf and current in an AC circuit with only a resistor. Note that they are in phase.

The voltage that appears across the resistor is given by

$$V_R(t) = i(t) = i_{max}R\sin(\omega t) \qquad (25\text{-}7)$$

From this equation we can identify the maximum value of the voltage across the resistor:

KEY EQUATION
$$V_{R,\,max} = i_{max}R \qquad (25\text{-}8)$$

 EXAMPLE 25-1

Current in a Resistor

A 1.0 kΩ resistor is connected across an emf where $\varepsilon(t) = 20\sin(50t)$. Find the maximum current.

SOLUTION

From the given emf, we identify $\varepsilon_{max} = 20$ V. We can then use Equation (25-6) to find the maximum current:

$$i_{max} = \frac{\varepsilon_{max}}{R} = \frac{20\text{ V}}{1000\ \Omega} = 20\text{ mA}$$

Making sense of the result:

We have a 1000 Ω resistor. With a 1 volt source, we would expect 1 mA.

Inductive Load

We now consider an AC emf connected to just an inductor, as shown in Figure 25-4.

Figure 25-4 An AC circuit with an inductive load

Again applying Kirchhoff's loop rule, we obtain

$$\varepsilon(t) - L\frac{di}{dt} = 0 \qquad (25\text{-}9)$$

Solving for the derivative of the current, we find

$$\frac{di}{dt} = \frac{\varepsilon(t)}{L} = \frac{\varepsilon_{max}}{L}\sin(\omega t) \qquad (25\text{-}10)$$

A solution to this differential equation is

$$i(t) = -\frac{\varepsilon_{max}}{\omega L}\cos(\omega t) = -i_{max}\cos(\omega t) \qquad (25\text{-}11)$$

We note that $i_{max} = \dfrac{\varepsilon_{max}}{\omega L}$, has the form of Ohms's Law—a current is given by a voltage divided by another quantity. The quantity ωL does indeed have units of ohms and we define the **inductive reactance** as

KEY EQUATION
$$X_L = \omega L \qquad (25\text{-}12)$$

If we plot the emf and the current through the inductor, as shown in Figure 25-5, we can see the current peaks a quarter cycle after the emf. Thus, the current *lags* the emf.

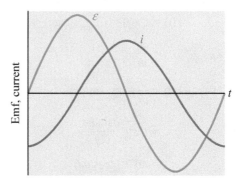

Figure 25-5 Plot of the emf and the current for an AC circuit with an inductive load. Note that the voltage leads the current.

Since $\sin\left(\omega t - \dfrac{\pi}{2}\right) = -\cos(\omega t)$, we can rewrite the current as

$$i(t) = i_{max}\sin\left(\omega t - \frac{\pi}{2}\right) \qquad (25\text{-}13)$$

The maximum voltage that appears across the inductor is given by

$$V_{L, max} = i_{max} X_L \qquad (25\text{-}14)$$

 CHECKPOINT

C-25-2 Inductor Current

How can you verify that the inductor current really is a cosine function of time?

C-25-2 Differentiate Equation (25-11) and substitute it into Equation (25-10).

Capacitive Load

We now consider an AC voltage source connected to just a capacitor, as shown in Figure 25-6.

Figure 25-6 An AC circuit with a capacitive load

Applying Kirchhoff's loop rule, we obtain

$$\varepsilon(t) - \frac{q}{C} = 0 \qquad (25\text{-}15)$$

Solving for q, the charge on the capacitor, gives

$$q(t) = C\varepsilon(t) = C\varepsilon_{max} \sin(\omega t) \qquad (25\text{-}16)$$

Since $i(t) = \dfrac{dq}{dt}$,

$$i(t) = \frac{d}{dt}(C\varepsilon_{max} \sin(\omega t))$$

$$= C\varepsilon_{max} \frac{d\sin(\omega t)}{dt}$$

$$= \omega C\varepsilon_{max} \cos(\omega t) \qquad (25\text{-}17)$$

We now define **capacitive reactance** as

$$X_C = \frac{1}{\omega C} \qquad (25\text{-}18)$$

We can then write

$$i_{max} = \frac{\varepsilon_{max}}{X_C} \qquad (25\text{-}19)$$

 EXAMPLE 25-2

Current in an Inductor

A 10 mH inductor is connected across an emf $\varepsilon(t) = 50\sin(20t)$. Find

(a) the inductive reactance;
(b) the maximum current through the inductor.

SOLUTION

(a) We will use Equation (25-12) for the inductive reactance. From the given emf, we see that $\omega = 20$ rad/s; thus,

$$X_L = \omega L = (20 \text{ rad/s})(10 \text{ mH}) = 0.20 \ \Omega$$

(b) Noting that $\varepsilon_{max} = 50$ V, we can find the maximum current:

$$i_{max} = \frac{\varepsilon_{max}}{X_L} = \frac{50 \text{ V}}{0.20 \ \Omega} = 250 \text{ A}$$

Making sense of the result:

The inductive reactance is very small so we have a very large current.

The expression for AC current again has the same form as Ohm's law, and the maximum voltage that appears across the capacitor is given by

$$V_{C, max} = i_{max} X_C \qquad (25\text{-}20)$$

When we plot the emf and the current through the capacitor, as shown in Figure 25-7, we again see that the emf and the current are not in phase. However, now the current *leads* the emf by a quarter cycle.

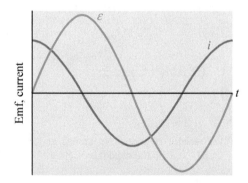

Figure 25-7 Plot of the emf and the current for an AC circuit with a capacitive load. Note that the current leads the emf.

Again, we can rewrite the current in terms of a sine function. Since $\sin\left(\omega t + \dfrac{\pi}{2}\right) = \cos(\omega t)$,

$$i(t) = i_{max} \sin\left(\omega t + \frac{\pi}{2}\right) \qquad (25\text{-}21)$$

In contrast to the inductor current, the phase difference in the argument of the sine function of the current is positive.

 EXAMPLE 25-3

Current in a Capacitor

A 1 nF capacitor is connected across an emf $\varepsilon(t) = 30\sin(40t)$. Find

(a) the capacitive reactance;
(b) the maximum current through the capacitor.

SOLUTION

(a) We will use Equation (25-18) for the capacitive reactance. From the emf, we can see that $\omega = 40$ rad/s; thus,

$$X_C = \frac{1}{\omega C} = \frac{1}{(40\text{ rad/s})(1\text{ nF})} = 25\text{ M}\Omega$$

(b) Noting from the emf that $\varepsilon_{max} = 30$ V, we can find the maximum current:

$$i_{max} = \frac{\varepsilon_{max}}{X_C} = \frac{30\text{ V}}{25\text{ M}\Omega} = 1.2\ \mu A$$

Making sense of the result:

In this case the capacitive reactance is quite large as we therefore have a small current.

The introduction of either an inductor or a capacitor into an AC circuit produces the interesting result that the current is not in phase with the emf. Such components are called **reactive circuit elements**, and the phase difference between the emf and the current is called the **phase shift**.

 LO 2

25-2   The LC Circuit

We will now consider the simple combination of a capacitor and an inductor, called an **LC circuit**, shown in Figure 25-8. Instead of using an AC emf, we will charge the capacitor with a battery. We will remove it

 EXAMPLE 25-4

An LC Circuit

A 1.0 μF capacitor charged with 10 μC is connected across a 10 mH inductor.

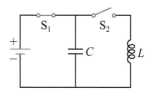

Figure 25-8   An LC circuit with the capacitor fully charged

from the battery and connect it to an inductor. We will assume that the conductors and components in this circuit have no resistance. Once the capacitor has been fully charged to some initial charge q_0 by the battery, we open switch S_1 to disconnect the battery. At time $t = 0$ we then close switch S_2 to connect the inductor across the capacitor.

We apply Kirchhoff's law around the loop containing the capacitor and the inductor to find

$$\frac{q}{C} - L\frac{di}{dt} = 0 \qquad (25\text{-}22)$$

Since $i = -\dfrac{dq}{dt}, \dfrac{di}{dt} = -\dfrac{d^2q}{dt^2}$, which we substitute into Equation (25-22):

$$\frac{q}{C} + L\frac{d^2q}{dt^2} = 0 \qquad (25\text{-}23)$$

$$\frac{d^2q}{dt^2} = -\frac{1}{LC}q$$

This equation has the same form as a simple harmonic oscillator:

$$a(t) = -\omega^2(A\cos(\omega t + \phi)) = -\omega^2 x(t) \qquad (13\text{-}18)$$

Just as for simple harmonic oscillators (Chapter 13), Equation (25-23) has a solution of the form

$$q(t) = q_0\cos(\omega_0 t) \qquad (25\text{-}24)$$

where $\omega_0 = \dfrac{1}{\sqrt{LC}}$

So, the charge on the capacitor, and hence the current in the circuit, oscillates with a frequency that is determined by the value of the inductor and the capacitor.

The LC circuit is analogous to the oscillating mass–spring system in Chapter 13. Inductance plays the role

(a) What is the initial voltage across the capacitor?
(b) What is the angular frequency of the oscillation?
(c) Plot the voltage across the capacitor and the voltage across the inductor versus time.

(continued)

SOLUTION

(a) We use $CV = q$ for a capacitor to solve for V:

$$V = \frac{q}{C} = \frac{10 \; \mu C}{1 \; \mu F} = 10 \text{ V}$$

(b) We calculate the angular frequency of oscillation using Equation (25-24):

$$\omega_0 = \frac{1}{\sqrt{LC}} = \frac{1}{\sqrt{10 \text{ mH} \times 1 \; \mu F}} = 1.0 \times 10^4 \text{ s}^{-1}$$

(c) The voltage across the capacitor is found from

$$v_C(t) = \frac{q(t)}{C} = \frac{10 \; \mu C \cos(\omega_0 t)}{1 \; \mu F} = 10 \cos(1.0 \times 10^4 \text{ s}^{-1} \cdot t) \text{ V}$$

The voltage across the inductor is given by

$$v_L(t) = L\frac{d^2 q}{dt^2}$$

$$= -Lq_0\omega_0^2 \cos(\omega_0 t)$$

$$= -10 \text{ mH} \cdot 10 \; \mu C \cdot (1.0 \times 10^4 \text{ s}^{-1})^2 \cos(1.0 \times 10^4 \text{ s}^{-1} \, t)$$

$$= -10 \cos(1.0 \times 10^4 \text{ s}^{-1} \, t)$$

The plot of these voltages in Figure 25-9 shows that they are exactly out of phase.

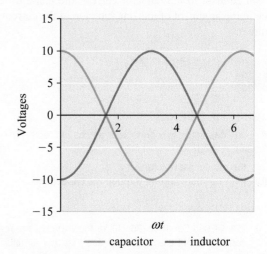

Figure 25-9 Capacitor and inductor voltages versus time

Making sense of the result:

At any instant in time, the voltage across the capacitor is exactly opposite to the voltage across the inductor. This must be the case in order for Kirchoff's Loop rule to be satisfied.

---

of the mass, and the reciprocal of the capacitance plays the role of the spring constant. We can see the similarity between the two systems by comparing Equations 25-23 and 13-18.

✓ CHECKPOINT

C-25-3 How to Change the Resonant Frequency

How does the resonant frequency of an LC circuit change when we increase the capacitance?

C-25-3 The resonant frequency decreases when we increase the capacitance because the capacitance is in the denominator of the expression.

LO 3

25-3 Phasors

As we saw in Section 25-1, the phases of the AC current and voltage sine functions can shift relative to each other depending on the nature of the load in the circuit. We will use phasors to represent and manipulate the various quantities in an AC circuit. Phasors are well suited to this task because they can describe the amplitude and phases of these quantities as well as the phase relationships between them.

A phasor is a vector in two dimensions. The tail of the vector is located at the origin of the coordinate system and the vector has a length that is equal to the amplitude of the quantity we wish to represent. The angle that the phasor makes with the horizontal axis is time dependent and as a consequence, the phasor rotates in a counterclockwise fashion about the origin. The rate at which it rotates is determined by the angular frequency, ω. We can determine the instantaneous value of the quantity the phasor is being used to represent by taking the projection of the phasor onto the vertical axis. For example, the phasor representing the emf in an AC circuit would have a length of ε_{max} and would make an angle of $\theta = \omega t$ with the x-axis. The projection of the phasor on the vertical axis is then $\varepsilon_{max}\sin(\omega t)$ which is $\varepsilon(t)$, as given by Equation (25-1).

When we examined an AC circuit with just an inductor, we found that the current in the circuit was given by $i_{max} \sin\left(\omega t - \frac{\pi}{2}\right)$. We would represent this with a phasor with length of i_{max} that makes an angle of $\theta = \omega t - \frac{\pi}{2}$ with the positive x-axis.

In general, the values of voltage across and current through a circuit element can be represented mathematically as follows:

KEY EQUATION
$$\begin{cases} \varepsilon(t) = \varepsilon_{max}\sin(\omega t) \\ i(t) = i_{max}\sin(\omega t - \phi) \end{cases} \quad (25\text{-}25)$$

where ϕ is the phase shift.

C-25-4 Phase Shift

Which statement correctly describes the electric circuit represented in Figure 25-10(b)?

(a) The phase shift between the current and the voltage is π (current lags voltage).

(b) The phase shift between the voltage and the current is $\dfrac{\pi}{2}$ (current lags voltage).

(c) The phase shift between the current and the voltage is $\dfrac{\pi}{4}$ (current lags voltage).

(d) The phase shift between the current and the voltage is $-\dfrac{\pi}{2}$ (voltage lags current).

(a)

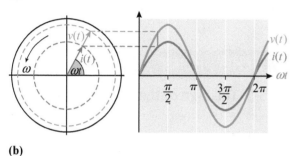

(b)

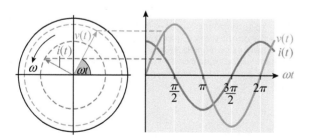

(c)

Figure 25-10 Phasor diagrams representing the instantaneous values of voltage and current with (a) zero phase shift (resistor), (b) current lagging voltage (inductor), and (c) voltage lagging current (capacitor).

C-25-4 (b) From the diagram, we see that voltage reaches its maximum value for the first time at $t_{v_{max}} = \dfrac{\pi}{2}$, and current reaches its maximum value at $t_{i_{max}} = \pi$. Therefore, current lags voltage, and the phase shift between the current and voltage in this circuit is

$$\phi = t_{v_{max}} - t_{i_{max}} = \frac{\pi}{2} - \pi = -\frac{\pi}{2}$$

25-4 Series RLC Circuits

We now consider a circuit with an AC emf, a resistor, an inductor, and a capacitor in series, as shown in Figure 25-11. This type of circuit is called a **series RLC circuit**.

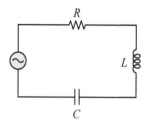

Figure 25-11 A series RLC circuit

Kirchhoff's loop rule (Chapter 22, Section 22-4) requires that the instantaneous voltages around the circuit loop add to zero. We can use phasors in this process to determine the magnitude and phase of the current in the circuit. We know the phase of the voltages across the resistor, inductor, and capacitor relative to the current. Specifically, the resistor voltage is in phase with the current, the inductor voltage leads the current, and the capacitor voltage lags the current. Because all the circuit elements are connected in series, the same current flows through them. Consequently, we can draw a phasor diagram for the circuit by first placing a phasor that represents the current on the circuit. This phasor makes an angle of $\omega t - \phi$ with respect to the positive x-axis, as shown in Figure 25-12.

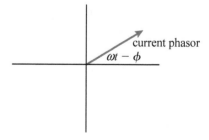

Figure 25-12 A current phasor for the series RLC circuit

Next, we use the voltage–current phase relationships to place phasors for the resistor, inductor, and capacitor voltages, as shown in Figure 25-13.

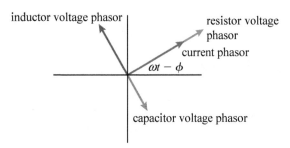

inductor voltage phasor

resistor voltage phasor

current phasor

$\omega t - \phi$

capacitor voltage phasor

Figure 25-13 Current and voltage phasors diagrams for the RLC circuit

By Kirchhoff's loop rule, the vector sum of the voltage phasors must equal the AC emf phasor, as shown in Figure 25-14.

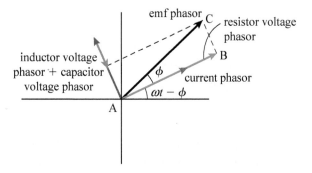

emf phasor

resistor voltage phasor

inductor voltage phasor + capacitor voltage phasor

ϕ

current phasor

$\omega t - \phi$

A

B

C

Figure 25-14 The sum of the phasors for the resistor, inductor, and capacitor voltages gives the AC emf phasor.

In the right-angled triangle ABC in Figure 25-14, the emf phasor is the hypotenuse. The other two sides are given by the magnitude of the resistor voltage phasor and the difference in magnitude of the inductor voltage phasor and the capacitor voltage phasor. Applying Pythagoras' theorem gives

$$\varepsilon_{max}^2 = v_{R,\,max}^2 + (v_{L,\,max} - v_{C,\,max})^2 \qquad (25\text{-}26)$$

Substituting from Equations (25-8), (25-14), and (25-20), we get

$$\varepsilon_{max}^2 = (i_{max}R)^2 + (i_{max}X_L - i_{max}X_C)^2 \qquad (25\text{-}27)$$

Solving for i_{max} gives

$$i_{max} = \frac{\varepsilon_{max}}{\sqrt{R^2 + (X_L - X_C)^2}} \qquad (25\text{-}28)$$

EXAMPLE 25-5

Analyzing a Series RLC Circuit

A series RLC circuit consists of an emf $\varepsilon = 100\sin(8000t)$, a 100 Ω resistor, 1.00 mH inductor, and a 1.00 μF capacitor. Determine

(a) the maximum current flow;
(b) the phase shift;
(c) the maximum voltages across the three components.

Equation (25-28) gives us the magnitude of the maximum current in the circuit as a function of the magnitude of the maximum AC emf, the resistance, the capacitive reactance, and the inductive reactance. Note that both the capacitive and inductive reactance depend on the frequency of the AC emf; consequently, so does the magnitude of the maximum current.

We can see that Equation (25-28) looks similar to Ohm's law in that a current is given by a ratio of a voltage to a quantity that has units of ohms. We define **impedance**, Z, as

KEY EQUATION
$$Z = \sqrt{R^2 + (X_L - X_C)^2} \qquad (25\text{-}29)$$

Now that we have found an expression for the magnitude of the maximum current, we turn our attention to the phase angle. From Figure 25-14 we can see that the tangent of the angle ϕ is given by

KEY EQUATION
$$\tan \phi = \frac{i_{max}(X_L - X_C)}{i_{max}R} = \frac{X_L - X_C}{R} \qquad (25\text{-}30)$$

✓ CHECKPOINT

C-25-5 The Sign of the Phase Angle

In Figure 25-15, is the phase angle positive or negative? Explain.

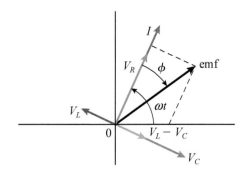

I

V_R

ϕ

emf

V_L

ωt

$V_L - V_C$

V_C

0

Figure 25-15 C-25-5

C-25-5 Negative. The current is leading the emf in the circuit; that is, it is farther counterclockwise than the emf. The emf makes an angle of ωt with the x-axis, and the current makes an angle of $\omega t - \phi$ with the x-axis. The only way for $\omega t - \phi > \omega t$ is if $\phi < 0$. Another way of telling is by noting that $V_C > V_L$, means that $X_C > X_L$. Then, from Equation (25-30) the phase angle must be negative.

SOLUTION

(a) We will first determine the impedance using Equation (25-29):

$$Z = \sqrt{R^2 + (X_L - X_C)^2}$$

$$= \sqrt{100^2 + \left(8000\text{ s}^{-1} \cdot 1\text{ mH} - \frac{1}{8000\text{ s}^{-1} \cdot 1\,\mu\text{F}}\right)^2} = 154\ \Omega$$

Using this result, we can determine i_{max}:

$$i_{max} = \frac{\varepsilon_{max}}{Z} = \frac{100}{154 \ \Omega} = 0.650 \ A$$

(b) The phase shift can be determined using Equation (25-30):

$$\tan \phi = \frac{X_L - X_C}{R} = \frac{(8000 \ s^{-1})(1 \ mH) - \dfrac{1}{(8000 \ s^{-1})(1 \ \mu F)}}{100} = -1.17$$

Therefore $\phi = \tan^{-1}(-1.17) = -49.5°$

(c) We find the maximum voltages across the resistor, the inductor, and the capacitor from Equations (25-8), (25-14), and (25-20), respectively:

$$v_{R, \, max} = i_{max} R = (0.650 \ A)(100 \ \Omega) = 65.0 \ V$$

$$v_{L, \, max} = i_{max} X_L = (0.650 \ A)(8000 \ s^{-1})(1 \ mH) = 5.20 \ V$$

$$v_{C, \, max} = i_{max} X_C = (0.649 \ A) \frac{1}{(8000 \ s^{-1})(1 \ \mu F)} = 81.2 \ V$$

The maximum voltages that appear across the components in an AC circuit reflect their reactances. The maximum voltage across the inductor in Example 25-5 is quite small, and the maximum voltage that appears across the capacitor is relatively large. When we add the maximum voltages, we get

$$v_{R, \, max} + v_{L, \, max} + v_{C, \, max} = 65.0 \ V + 5.20 \ V + 81.2 \ V$$

$$= 151 \ V$$

This total is much greater than the maximum applied voltage of 100 V. How can this be? Remember that the voltages that appear across these elements are time-dependent and are not in phase. The three voltages do not all reach their maximum voltage simultaneously, as we can see from a plot of the voltages versus time. The time-dependent voltages across the RLC circuit elements are given by

KEY EQUATION

$$v_R(t) = Ri(t) = Ri_{max} \sin(\omega t - \phi)$$

KEY EQUATION

$$v_L(t) = L \frac{di}{dt} = \omega L i_{max} \cos(\omega t - \phi)$$
$$= X_L i_{max} \cos(\omega t - \phi) \qquad (25\text{-}31)$$

KEY EQUATION

$$v_C(t) = \frac{q(t)}{C} = -\frac{1}{\omega C} i_{max} \cos(\omega t - \phi)$$
$$= -X_C i_{max} \cos(\omega t - \phi)$$

In Figure 25-16, we plot the voltages versus time along with the AC emf. The voltages are indeed out of phase, and the component voltages do sum to the AC emf at any given instant.

Making sense of the result:

We can get a sense of what is going on in the circuit from the reactances:

$$X_L = \omega L = (8000 \ s^{-1})(1 \ mH) = 8.00 \ \Omega$$

$$X_C = \frac{1}{\omega C} = \frac{1}{(8000 \ s^{-1})(1 \ \mu F)} = 125 \ \Omega$$

The capacitive reactance is much larger than the inductive reactance but comparable to the resistance. As such, we would expect the circuit to behave somewhere in between a purely resistive circuit and a purely capacitive circuit. In a purely resistive circuit, the current is in phase with the applied emf. In a purely capacitive circuit, the current leads the applied emf. For this particular circuit, we found a phase angle of $-49.5°$. The minus sign indicates that the current is leading the emf, and the 49.5° angle indicates that the circuit is somewhere between a purely resistive circuit ($\phi = 0$) and a purely capacitive circuit ($\phi = -90°$), as we predicted from the reactances.

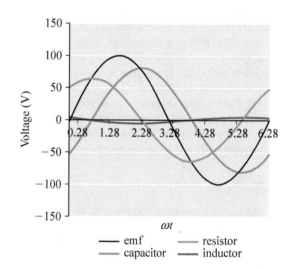

Figure 25-16 Voltages versus time for the RLC circuit of Example 25-5

LO 5

25-5 Resonance

We will now consider how the maximum current and the phase shift vary in a series RLC circuit as we change the frequency of the emf. The inductive reactance increases as we increase the frequency. On the other hand, the capacitive reactance increases when we decrease the frequency. At low frequencies, we would expect the capacitor to dominate the behaviour of the circuit, while at high frequencies, we would expect the inductor to dominate. In Figure 25-17, we plot i_{max} and ϕ versus angular frequency for a series RLC circuit with

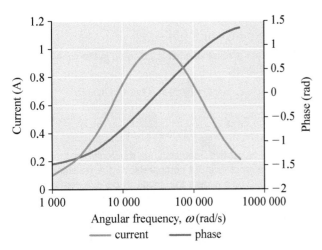

Figure 25-17 Current (left axis) and phase (right axis) versus angular frequency for an RLC circuit

$R = 100\ \Omega$, $L = 1$ mH, and $C = 1\ \mu$F. The applied emf has an amplitude of 100 V.

We can see that the current tends to small values at low and high angular frequencies and peaks at some intermediate frequency. The phase starts off at $-\pi/2$ at low angular frequency and approaches $\pi/2$ at high angular frequency. The phase goes through zero at the same angular frequency that the peak in the current occurs. The point at which the phase goes to zero is determined by the numerator in Equation (25-30), that is when $X_L = X_C$. The angular frequency at which the inductive and capacitive reactances are equal is the **resonance frequency**, ω_0, for this circuit. We can equate the expressions for these reactances and solve for the resonant frequency:

KEY EQUATION
$$\omega_0 = \frac{1}{\sqrt{LC}} \qquad (25\text{-}32)$$

Note that the resonant frequency is the same as the oscillation frequency of the LC circuit with no resistance in Section 25-2. The driven RLC circuit is analogous to a driven damped harmonic oscillator, with the resistance acting as the damping term. In Figure 25-18, we plot the

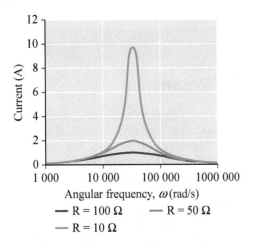

Figure 25-18 Current versus angular frequency in a driven RLC circuit. The different curves correspond to different values of the resistance.

current in a driven RLC circuit with various values of resistance while holding the inductance and the capacitance constant. As the resistance decreases, the resonance peak gets taller and narrower.

Now consider what happens to the voltages that appear across the various circuit elements as we vary the frequency. We plot the maximum resistor, capacitor, and inductor voltages versus frequency for R = 50 Ω, L = 1 mH, and C = 1 μF in Figure 25-19. We can see that the voltage across the resistor has the same shape as the current, which we would expect from Ohm's law. At low frequencies, the voltage across the capacitor becomes large, which is reasonable because the capacitive reactance gets large at low frequencies. Conversely, at high frequencies, the voltage across the inductor becomes relatively large because the inductive reactance gets large at high frequencies.

Remember that Figure 25-19 shows voltage *amplitudes*, which do not generally add to the applied emf of 100 V. However, at resonance, the voltage across the resistor is exactly 100 V, and the voltages across the inductor and the capacitor add to zero because they have equal magnitudes and opposite phases.

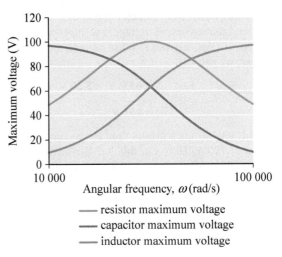

Figure 25-19 Voltage amplitudes versus angular frequency in an RLC circuit with $R = 50\ \Omega$

If we reduce the value of the resistor, the resonance sharpens. We plot the maximum resistor, capacitor, and inductor voltage versus frequency for $R = 10\ \Omega$, L = 1 mH, and $C = 1\ \mu$F in Figure 25-20. The maximum resistor voltage remains unchanged. At low frequency, the capacitor voltage is approximately 100 V, and the inductor voltage is small. At high frequencies, the inductor voltage is approximately 100 V, and the capacitor voltage is small. In the resonance region, the capacitor and inductor voltages are quite large and substantially exceed the applied voltage. We must again remind ourselves that the graphs shows amplitudes and the voltages are not in phase.

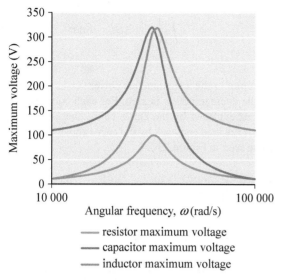

Figure 25-20   Maximum voltages in an RLC circuit for $R = 10 \ \Omega$

We characterize the width of a resonance by a **quality factor**, or **Q-factor**, defined as

$$Q = \frac{f_0}{\Delta f} \qquad (25\text{-}33)$$

where f_0 is the centre frequency of the peak, and Δf is the half-power bandwidth of the peak.

The **half-power bandwidth** is the difference between the two frequencies at which the power in the circuit is equal to half the power at the centre frequency (Figure 25-21). A circuit with a high Q-factor has a narrow, tall resonance peak. The Q-factor can be determined from the power dissipated in the resistor of the circuit, which we will examine more closely in the next section.

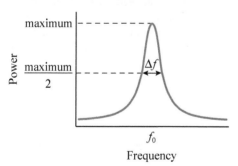

Figure 25-21 f_0 and Δf on a resonance peak

radios with manual tuning. Turning the knob on the capacitor changes the overlap between the interleaved stationary bottom plates and the moving top plates, changing the effective area of the capacitor plates.

Figure 25-22   A variable tuning capacitor

LO 6

25-6   Power in AC Circuits

The individual voltages and currents in an AC circuit all have an average value of zero, because they oscillate symmetrically about zero. However, the power dissipated in a circuit element is the time average of the product of the voltage and the current, and, as we will see, this product generally does not average to zero.

We first consider the power dissipated by a resistor in an RLC circuit. The current through the resistor is given by the following equation:

$$i(t) = i_{max}\sin(\omega t - \phi) \qquad (25\text{-}34)$$

where i_{max} is given by Equation (25-28), and ϕ is given by Equation (25-30).

The time-dependent voltage across the resistor is given by

$$v_R(t) = Ri(t) = Ri_{max}\sin(\omega t - \phi) \qquad (25\text{-}35)$$

The instantaneous power dissipated by the resistor is thus given by

$$P_R(t) = v_R(t)i(t) = Ri_{max}\sin(\omega t - \phi)i_{max}\sin(\omega t - \phi)$$
$$= i_{max}^2 R \sin^2(\omega t - \phi) \qquad (25\text{-}36)$$

Recall from Section 25-1 that the average value of $\sin^2(x) = \frac{1}{2}$. So, averaging the instantaneous power over one cycle gives

KEY EQUATION $P_{R,\,avg} = \dfrac{i_{max}^2}{2} R = \left(\dfrac{i_{max}}{\sqrt{2}}\right)^2 R = i_{rms}^2 R \qquad (25\text{-}37)$

$$= \frac{X_L i^2_{max}}{T} \int_0^T \frac{1}{2} \sin(2(\omega t - \phi))dt \qquad (25\text{-}39)$$

$$= 0$$

A plot of the instantaneous power versus time verifies that the average power is zero. For each complete cycle, the area enclosed by the curve below the *x*-axis exactly cancels the area enclosed by the curve above the *x*-axis, as can be seen in Figure 25-24.

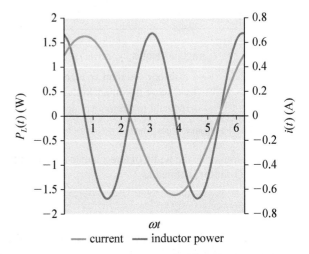

— current — inductor power

Figure 25-24 Power (red) and current (blue) in an inductor in an RLC circuit with $R = 100\ \Omega$, $L = 1$ mH, $C = 1\ \mu$F and $\varepsilon_{max} = 100$ volts. Note that as the magnitude of the current increases, the inductor absorbs energy. As the current returns to zero, the inductor delivers energy back to the circuit.

When the power is positive the inductor is absorbing energy. Unlike the resistor, this energy is not dissipated, but is stored in the magnetic field of the inductor. While the current is increasing, the inductor absorbs energy. When the current starts to decrease, the inductor returns the stored energy to the circuit, and the power is negative.

 EXAMPLE 25-6

Power and the Capacitor

Find the average power in the capacitor in an RLC circuit.

SOLUTION

The instantaneous power in the capacitor is given by

$$P_C(t) = v_C(t)i(t) = -X_C i_{max}\cos(\omega t - \phi)i_{max}\sin(\omega t - \phi)$$

$$= -X_C i^2_{max}\cos(\omega t - \phi)\sin(\omega t - \phi)$$

Averaging this power over one complete cycle, we find

$$P_{C,avg} = \frac{1}{T}\int_0^T -X_C i^2_{max}\cos(\omega t - \phi)\sin(\omega t - \phi)dt$$

$$= \frac{-X_C i^2_{max}}{T}\int_0^T \cos(\omega t - \phi)\sin(\omega t - \phi)dt = 0$$

Heating with Electricity

A heater element toaster (Figure 25-23) is a simple example of resistive power dissipation in an AC circuit. Similar elements are found in electric water heaters, electric clothes dryers, blow dryers, and electric baseboard heaters. Heating elements are made of metals with low resistance and high melting points. The low resistance of heating elements enables them to heat rapidly and efficiently.

Yiargo/Shutterstock

Figure 25-23 Heater elements in a toaster

For the inductor, we also calculate the power as the product of the voltage and the current. We get the voltage across the inductor from Equation (25-31):

$$P_L(t) = v_L(t)i(t) = X_L i_{max}\cos(\omega t - \phi)i_{max}\sin(\omega t - \phi)$$

$$= X_L i^2_{max}\cos(\omega t - \phi)\sin(\omega t - \phi) \qquad (25\text{-}38)$$

When we average this power over one complete cycle, we can use the trigonometric identity $\sin(2\theta) = 2\sin(\theta)\cos(\theta)$ to get

$$P_{L,avg} = \frac{1}{T}\int_0^T X_L i^2_{max}\cos(\omega t - \phi)\sin(\omega t - \phi)dt$$

$$= \frac{X_L i^2_{max}}{T}\int_0^T \cos(\omega t - \phi)\sin(\omega t - \phi)dt$$

Making sense of the result:

The instantaneous power in the capacitor is exactly out of phase with the instantaneous power in the inductor. When the inductor is absorbing energy, the capacitor is releasing energy and vice versa.

Thus, we find that the only element in the driven RLC circuit that dissipates power is the resistor. Total energy must be conserved, so all the power dissipated by the resistor comes from the emf source. The amount of power that the resistor absorbs depends on the frequency. Figure 25-25 shows a plot of power transfer versus frequency for an RLC circuit with $R = 10\ \Omega$, $C = 1\ \mu F$, and $L = 10$ mH.

Frequency dependence is an important general result for all oscillating systems. The maximum energy transfer between the driving emf and the oscillator occurs when the frequency of the driver matches the resonance frequency of the oscillator.

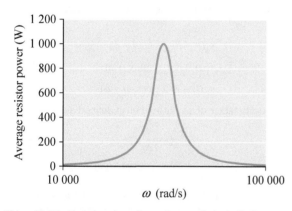

Figure 25-25 Frequency dependence of power dissipated in the resistor of an RLC circuit

Now, we will examine how the quality factor is related to the power curve and the parameters of the RLC circuit. We can use Equation (25-37) to find the power in the resistor:

$$P_{R,\text{avg}} = i_{\text{rms}}^2 R = \frac{\varepsilon_{\text{rms}}^2 R}{Z^2} = \frac{\varepsilon_{\text{rms}}^2 R}{R^2 + (X_L - X_C)^2} \quad (25\text{-}40a)$$

Since the Q factor is defined by the half-power points, we need to find the frequencies at which the power is half the peak value. The peak occurs at resonance when $Z = R$; thus, $P_{R,\text{avg, max}} = \dfrac{\varepsilon_{\text{rms}}^2}{R}$. At the half-power points, the denominator in Equation (25-40a) must be $2R^2$, which requires $(X_L - X_C)^2 = R^2$. Substituting expressions for the reactances, we find

$$\left(\omega L - \frac{1}{\omega C}\right)^2 = R^2$$

or

$$\left(\omega L - \frac{1}{\omega C}\right) = \pm R \quad (25\text{-}40b)$$

This equation yields a quadratic for the angular frequency:

$$L\omega^2 \mp R\omega - \frac{1}{C} = 0 \quad (25\text{-}40c)$$

There are two possible solutions for $+R$ and two for $-R$:

$$\omega = -\frac{\sqrt{C}\sqrt{CR^2 + 4L} - CR}{2CL}$$

$$\omega = \frac{-\sqrt{C}\sqrt{CR^2 + 4L} - CR}{2CL}$$

$$\omega = \frac{\sqrt{C}\sqrt{CR^2 + 4L} + CR}{2CL}$$

$$\omega = \frac{\sqrt{C}\sqrt{CR^2 + 4L} - CR}{2CL} \quad (25\text{-}40d)$$

Since the angular frequency must have a positive value, we reject the two negative roots. The half-power bandwidth is equal to the difference between the two positive roots:

$$\Delta\omega = \frac{\sqrt{C}\sqrt{CR^2 + 4L} + CR}{2CL} - \frac{\sqrt{C}\sqrt{CR^2 + 4L} - CR}{2CL}$$

$$= \frac{R}{L} \quad (25\text{-}40e)$$

Therefore, for a series RCL circuit, the quality factor can be expressed as follows:

KEY EQUATION $\quad Q = \dfrac{f_0}{\Delta f} = \dfrac{\omega_0}{\Delta\omega} = \dfrac{\sqrt{\dfrac{1}{LC}}}{\dfrac{R}{L}} = \dfrac{1}{R}\sqrt{\dfrac{L}{C}} \quad (25\text{-}41)$

EXAMPLE 25-7

The Q-factor from the Resistor Power

Find the quality factor for the RLC circuit with the power curve shown in Figure 25-25.

SOLUTION

The component values are $R = 10\ \Omega$, $C = 1\ \mu F$, and $L = 10$ mH. Therefore,

$$Q = \frac{1}{R}\sqrt{\frac{L}{C}} = \frac{1}{10\ \Omega}\sqrt{\frac{10\ \text{mH}}{1\ \mu F}} = 10$$

Making sense of the result:

We can compare this value to what we would expect for a radio receiver. FM radios receive signals with a frequency on the order of 100 MHz and the channels are separated by 0.2 MHz. The Q-factor for the tuner must therefore be on the order of 100 MHz/0.2 MHz = 500. So, a value of 10 is not a particularly high Q value.

A driven series RLC circuit has a response that depends strongly on the frequency of the emf. In general, the current in the circuit is not in phase with the emf. If the frequency is near the resonance frequency of the circuit, there is a large power transfer from the emf to the resistor in the circuit.

In an AC circuit, the emf and the current have the general forms

$$\varepsilon(t) = \varepsilon_{max} \sin(\omega t) \tag{25-1}$$

and

$$i(t) = i_{max} \sin(\omega t - \phi) \tag{25-34}$$

We express their effective values with rms quantities, which for sine and cosine functions are

$$\varepsilon_{rms} = \frac{\varepsilon_{max}}{\sqrt{2}} \quad \text{and} \quad i_{rms} = \frac{i_{max}}{\sqrt{2}} \tag{25-3}$$

In a purely resistive circuit, the current is in phase with the emf and is given by

$$i(t) = \frac{\varepsilon_{max}}{R} \sin(\omega t) = i_{max} \sin(\omega t) \tag{25-5}$$

In a purely inductive circuit, the voltage leads the current by 90°, and the current is given by

$$i(t) = -\frac{\varepsilon_{max}}{\omega L} \cos(\omega t) = \frac{\varepsilon_{max}}{X_L} \sin\left(\omega t + \frac{\pi}{2}\right)$$

We define the inductive reactance as follows:

$$X_L = \omega L \tag{25-12}$$

In a purely capacitive circuit, the voltage lags the current by 90°, and the current is given by

$$i(t) = \varepsilon_{max} \omega C \sin\left(\omega t - \frac{\pi}{2}\right) = \frac{\varepsilon_{max}}{X_C} \sin\left(\omega t - \frac{\pi}{2}\right)$$

The capacitive reactance is defined as

$$X_C = \frac{1}{\omega C} \tag{25-18}$$

In an LC circuit, with the capacitor initially charged we see oscillations, and the charge on the capacitor is given by

$$q(t) = q_0 \cos(\omega_0 t) \tag{25-24}$$

where

$$\omega_0 = \frac{1}{\sqrt{LC}}$$

Phasors can be used to represent voltages in AC circuits. The magnitude of a phasor is given by the magnitude of the signal we are representing. The phasor makes an angle with the x-axis that varies with time. The instantaneous value of the signal can be found by taking the projection of the phasor onto the y-axis.

In an AC series RLC circuit, the current has the form

$$i(t) = i_{max} \sin(\omega t - \phi) \tag{25-34}$$

where

$$i_{max} = \frac{\varepsilon_{max}}{\sqrt{R^2 + (X_L - X_C)^2}} \tag{25-28}$$

and

$$\tan \phi = \frac{X_L - X_C}{R} \tag{25-30}$$

The time-dependent voltages across the circuit elements are given by

$$v_R(t) = R i_{max} \sin(\omega t - \phi)$$
$$v_L(t) = X_L i_{max} \cos(\omega t - \phi) \tag{25-31}$$
$$v_C(t) - X_C i_{max} \cos(\omega t - \phi)$$

The quality factor of an RLC circuit is defined as

$$Q = \frac{f_0}{\Delta f} \tag{25-33}$$

where Δf is the half-power width and f_0 is the centre frequency.

In a series RLC circuit, the only element that dissipates power is the resistor. The instantaneous power dissipated is

$$P_R(t) = i_{max}^2 R \sin^2(\omega t - \phi) \tag{25-36}$$

and the average power dissipated is

$$P_{R,avg} = i_{rms}^2 R \tag{25-37}$$

APPLICATIONS

Applications: energy consumption, power plants, electric circuits, radio and TV tuners, home heater elements

Key Terms: alternating current, capacitive reactance, half-power bandwidth, impedance, inductive reactance, LC circuit, phase shift, phasors, quality factor, Q-factor, reactive circuit elements, resonance frequency, root-mean-square, series RLC circuit

QUESTIONS

1. An RLC circuit is driven at a certain frequency. When the frequency is increased, the maximum current decreases. Is the circuit above or below resonance?
2. What is the phase angle of a series RLC circuit at resonance?
3. At very low frequencies, an inductor has little effect on a series RLC circuit. Why?
4. Two circuits with identical inductors and capacitors have quality factors of 10 and 100. Which has the smaller resistor?
5. Does capacitive reactance increase or decrease with frequency?
6. When we add the maximum voltages that appear across the elements in a series RLC circuit, we usually get a voltage that is greater than the applied emf. Does this violate Kirchhoff's loop rule?
7. Can the rms values of a voltage ever exceed the maximum value? Equal it?
8. What is the limit on the maximum voltage that can appear across the capacitor (or inductor) in a series RLC circuit?
9. What does the phase angle in a series RLC circuit tend toward as the frequency increases significantly?
10. For fixed L and C, how does one increase the quality factor of a series RLC circuit?

PROBLEMS BY SECTION

For problems, star ratings will be used, (✶, ✶✶, or ✶✶✶), with more stars meaning more challenging problems.

Section 25-1   Simple Loads in AC Circuits

11. ✶ Show that the rms value for a triangular wave is $\dfrac{1}{\sqrt{3}}\varepsilon_{max}$.
12. ✶ The wall outlets in many North American homes provide 110 V rms. What is the maximum amplitude of this emf? In Europe, it is 220 V rms. What is this maximum amplitude?
13. ✶ A 60 W light bulb is connected to 120 V rms.
    (a) What is the rms current?
    (b) What is the resistance of the bulb filament?
14. ✶ A 200 Ω resistor is connected across a 20 V emf with a frequency of 440 Hz.
    (a) What is the amplitude of the current?
    (b) What is the angular frequency of the emf?
    (c) Write an expression for the current through the resistor as a function of time.
15. ✶ A 1 mH inductor is connected across a 20 V rms emf with an angular frequency of 1000 rad/s.
    (a) What is the inductive reactance?
    (b) What is the amplitude of the resulting current?
    (c) Write an expression for the current through the inductor as a function of time.
16. ✶ An inductor is connected across a 100 V emf (RMS) with an angular frequency of 2000 rad/s. The resulting current is given by $i(t) = 0.001 \sin\left(\omega t - \dfrac{\pi}{2}\right)$.
    (a) What is the amplitude of the current?
    (b) What is the inductive reactance?
    (c) What is the inductance?

17. ✶ A 1.0 nF capacitor is connected across a 20 V rms emf with an angular frequency of 100 rad/s.
    (a) What is the capacitive reactance?
    (b) What is the amplitude of the current in the circuit?
    (c) Write an expression for the current in the circuit as a function of time.
18. ✶ A 1 nF capacitor is connected across an emf with a frequency of 200 Hz. A current with an amplitude of 10 μA results.
    (a) What is the capacitive reactance?
    (b) What is the amplitude of the emf?

Section 25-2   The LC Circuit

19. ✶✶ A 10 μF capacitor is charged and connected across an inductor. The resulting current has a frequency of 10 kHz. What is the value of the inductor?
20. ✶ A 1 nF capacitor is charged and connected across a 0.1 mH inductor. What is the angular frequency of the resulting oscillation?
21. ✶ By what factor does the resonance frequency increase when the capacitance of a capacitor is doubled in value?

Section 25-3   Phasors

22. ✶ The voltage across a circuit element is represented by a phasor with an amplitude of 100 V that makes an angle of $\theta = 200t$ with respect to the positive x-axis. What is the value of the voltage across the element at $t = 10$ s?
23. ✶✶ The current in a circuit is represented by a phasor with an amplitude of 20 mA that makes an angle of $\theta = 5000t$ with respect to the positive x-axis.
    (a) At what time(s) is the current zero?
    (b) At what times is the current at its maximum positive value?
    (c) At what times is the current at its maximum negative value?
24. ✶✶ A circuit has three elements and an emf. The phasors representing the voltages across the elements are given by $v_1 = 20 \sin(\omega t)$, $v_2 = 40\cos(\omega t)$, and $v_3 = -60\cos(\omega t)$. Add the three phasors to find
    (a) the amplitude of the emf;
    (b) the angle between the emf and v_1.

Section 25-4   Series RLC Circuits

25. ✶✶ A 10 Ω resistor, a 5.0 nF capacitor, and a 20 mH inductor are connected in series across an emf $\varepsilon(t) = 25 \sin(33\,000t)$.
    (a) Find the capacitive reactance.
    (b) Find the inductive reactance.
    (c) Find the impedance.
    (d) Find the phase angle.
    (e) Find the amplitude of the current, i_{max}.
26. ✶✶ A 25 nF capacitor and a 30 mH inductor are connected in series with an unknown resistor across an emf $\varepsilon(t) = 25 \sin(33\,000t)$. The current has amplitude of 0.10 A.
    (a) What is the value of the resistor?
    (b) What is the phase angle?
27. ✶✶ A 100 Ω resistor and a 5.0 nF capacitor are connected in series with an unknown inductor across an emf $\varepsilon(t) = 250 \sin(9000t)$. The phase angle is −0.79 rad.
    (a) What is the inductive reactance?
    (b) What is the inductance?
    (c) What is the amplitude of the current?

Section 25-5 Resonance

28. ✶ An RLC circuit has an inductor of 23 mH, a capacitor of 1.0 μF, and a resistor of 20 Ω. What is the resonance frequency?

29. ✶ An RLC circuit has a quality factor of 15, a capacitor of 0.10 μF, and a resistor of 100 Ω. What is the value of the inductor?

30. ✶✶✶ A circuit has a quality factor of 200. By what factor, compared to the value at resonance, does the maximum current change when the frequency is changed to 90% of the resonance frequency?

Section 25-6 Power in AC Circuits

31. ✶ A 110 V rms house circuit is fused for 15 A. How many 100 W light bulbs can go on the circuit?

32. ✶ How much power is dissipated in a 100 Ω resistor connected across an emf with an amplitude of 10 V?

33. ✶✶ A series LC circuit is connected across an emf. At $t = 0$, the capacitor is uncharged and there is no current flowing in the circuit. The emf is then turned on. Does the emf deliver any energy to the circuit?

COMPREHENSIVE PROBLEMS

34. ✶✶ A 20 Ω resistor, a 1.0 nF capacitor, and a 20 mH inductor are in series with an emf $\varepsilon(t) = 50\sin(6000)t$. Find the maximum current and the phase angle.

35. ✶✶ A 40 Ω resistor, a 200 μF capacitor, and an inductor are in series with an emf $\varepsilon(t) = 25\sin(4000)t$. The current is observed to have an amplitude of 45 mA. Find the inductance and the phase angle.

36. ✶✶✶ RLC circuits can be used as filters. Plot the amplitude of the maximum voltage versus frequency across the resistor, capacitor, and inductor for a series RLC circuit with a 500 Ω resistor, 1.0 μF capacitor, and a 100 mH inductor. Assume that the emf has an amplitude of 1.0 V, and plot in the range $0 < \omega < 20\,000$ rad/s.

37. ✶ At an angular frequency of 1000 rad/s, a capacitor has a reactance of 300 Ω. What is its capacitance value?

38. ✶✶ A series RLC circuit is observed to have a phase angle of $-45°$. The amplitude of the voltage across the capacitor is twice the amplitude of the voltage across the resistor. Relative to the capacitor, what is the amplitude of the voltage across the inductor?

39. ✶✶ The windings in electric motors have an electrical resistance from the wire as well as an inductance from the fact that they are wound in coils. A motor that is operated at 110 V rms, 60 Hz, draws 2.0 A of current. The windings have a resistance of 30 Ω. What is the inductance of the motor?

40. ✶✶ A 0.10 μF capacitor and a 10 mH inductor are connected together. The current in the circuit is observed to have a maximum amplitude of 10 mA. What is the frequency of oscillation, and what is the maximum charge on the capacitor?

41. ✶✶ A 0.10 μF capacitor is in an LC circuit that oscillates at 200 kHz. The capacitor is initially charged to 200 nC. What is the value of the inductor, and what is the amplitude of the current?

42. ✶✶ In an RLC circuit, the resistor, inductor, and capacitor have a voltage amplitude of 10 V, 20 V, and 30 V, respectively. What are the phase angle and the amplitude of the emf generator?

43. ✶✶ In an RLC circuit, the voltage amplitude across the resistor is 20 V, the frequency is 2000 Hz, and the phase angle is $-45°$. What is the instantaneous voltage across the resistor at $t = 10$ s?

44. ✶✶ A series circuit contains a resistor and an inductor. The inductance is 10 mH, and the emf has a frequency of 2.0 kHz. The phase angle is 45°. What is the value of the resistance?

45. ✶ A series circuit contains a resistor and a capacitor. The emf is $\varepsilon(t) = 45\sin(5000t)$, and the current is $i(t) = 0.001\sin(5000t + 0.7 \text{ rad})$. Find the resistance and the capacitance.

46. ✶ A 20 Ω resistor, a 1.0 nF capacitor, and a 20 mH inductor are in series with an emf $\varepsilon(t) = 50 \sin(6000t)$. How much power does the resistor dissipate?

47. ✶✶ What should the phase angle be in a circuit to deliver maximum power from the emf (source) to the circuit (load)?

48. ✶✶ The emf and current in an RLC circuit are shown in Figure 25-26. What are the phase angle and resistance?

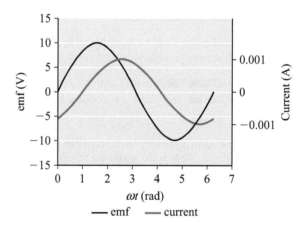

Figure 25-26 Problem 48

49. ✶✶ A filter motor on a swimming pool draws 5.0 A from a 110 V, 60 Hz wall socket and dissipates 500 W rms of power. Find the resistance of the motor and the phase angle.

50. ✶ The receiver in an FM radio has to be tuned from a low frequency of 88 MHz up to 108 MHz. A fixed inductor of 3.0 nH is used. What range must the variable tuning capacitor have to tune across this frequency band?

51. ✶✶✶ FM radio stations are typically separated by 200 kHz in frequency. Each individual station transmits energy in a frequency range from approximately 20 kHz below to 20 kHz above its centre frequency. Design a tuner circuit for an FM radio receiver, using 101.5 MHz as the centre frequency. Your tuning circuit should have a half-power bandwidth of 40 kHz and use a 10 nH inductor.

DATA-RICH PROBLEM

52. ✱✱✱ The markings have worn off the resistor in a series RLC circuit. The circuit has a 1.0 μF capacitor and a 100 mH inductor. You measure the voltage across the resistor as you vary the frequency of the emf and obtain the results in Table 25-1. Use some fitting software to determine the amplitude of the emf and the unknown resistance.

Table 25-1 Voltage versus frequency Data for Problem 52

Angular frequency (rad/s)	Resistor voltage (V)
1 000	11.0
2 000	31.6
3 000	94.9
4 000	55.5
5 000	31.6
6 000	22.5
7 000	17.7
8 000	14.7
9 000	12.6
10 000	11.0
11 000	9.9
12 000	8.9
13 000	8.1
14 000	7.5
15 000	7.0
16 000	6.5
17 000	6.5

OPEN PROBLEM

53. ✱✱✱ You wish to design a very sensitive thermometer that is based on a capacitor whose capacitance changes with temperature. Consider using a driven RLC circuit, and outline the strategy you would take.

See the text online resources at www.physics1e.nelson.com for Open Problems and Data-Rich Problems related to this chapter.

ELECTRICITY, MAGNETISM, AND OPTICS

Learning Objectives

When you have completed this chapter you should be able to:

1. Explain how a changing electric field induces a magnetic field and how a changing magnetic field induces an electric field.

2. Explain why Maxwell needed to add a displacement current to Ampère's law.

3. Write Maxwell's equations in integral form, and explain the terms in these equations.

4. Classify the electromagnetic spectrum according to the range of wavelengths (or frequencies).

5. Describe how electromagnetic waves carry energy and momentum, and calculate the intensity and momentum of a plane electromagnetic wave.

6. Calculate the pressure that electromagnetic radiation exerts on a surface.

7. Explain how electromagnetic waves are generated by accelerating charges.

8. Describe the polarization of electromagnetic waves, explain how a polarizer works, and calculate the intensity of light that passes through two polarizers.

For additional Making Connections, Examples, and Checkpoints, as well as activities and experiments to help increase your understanding of the chapter's concepts, please go to the text's online resources at www.physics1e.nelson.com.

Chapter 26
Electromagnetic Waves and Maxwell's Equations

The radio waves transmitted by local radio stations, the red laser light used to scan a product's bar code, the radiation that cooks food in a microwave oven, the sunlight that makes life possible on Earth, the X-rays used to detect hidden cavities in your teeth, and the gamma rays emitted by quasars are all electromagnetic waves with different frequencies.

Along with Newton's laws of motion, relativity theory, and quantum mechanics, the theory of electromagnetic waves forms the backbone of modern science and our understanding of the universe. In this chapter, we explore some of the important properties of electromagnetic waves.

NASA, ESA, ESO, CXC & D. Coe (STScI/J. Merten (Heidelberg/Bologna)

Figure 26-1 The galaxy cluster Abell 2744 emits visible light and X-rays.

26-1 The Laws of Electric and Magnetic Fields

So far, we have used electric and magnetic fields to describe the forces that act on stationary and moving charges. In 1862, Scottish physicist James Clerk Maxwell (1831–1879) showed that electric and magnetic fields are two components of a single field, which he called the **electromagnetic field**. Maxwell had noted the strong similarities between the key laws that describe electric and magnetic fields, and developed a unified model of the fields. Maxwell's theory also predicts that oscillating electromagnetic waves can exist in free space and can travel without any medium.

Chapters 20, 23, and 24 discussed two laws that govern electric fields and two similar laws for magnetic fields. Table 26-1 lists the equations for these four laws, and the laws themselves are summarized below.

Table 26-1 Four laws of electric and magnetic fields (for steady currents)

Gauss's law for electric fields	Faraday's law for electric fields
$\oint \vec{E} \cdot d\vec{A} = \dfrac{q_{enc}}{\varepsilon_0}$ (20-14)	$\oint \vec{E} \cdot d\vec{l} = -\dfrac{d\Phi_B}{dt}$
Gauss's law for magnetic fields	**Ampère's law for magnetic fields**
$\oint \vec{B} \cdot d\vec{A} = 0$	$\oint \vec{B} \cdot d\vec{l} = \mu_0 \sum I_{enc}$ (23-39)

Gauss's Law for Electric Fields

Gauss's law for electric fields relates the net flux of an electric field $\vec{E}$ through a closed surface, S, to the net electric charge, q_{enc}, enclosed within that surface. The quantity $\oint \vec{E} \cdot d\vec{A}$ is the electric flux through the surface S and is denoted Φ_E. The area vector element $d\vec{A}$ is normal to the surface and directed outward (Figure 26-2).

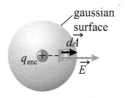

Figure 26-2 Gauss's law for electric fields. The total electric flux through a closed surface is proportional to the total charge enclosed within the surface.

Gauss's Law for Magnetic Fields

Gauss's law for magnetic fields states that the net flux of a magnetic field $\vec{B}$ through a closed surface, S, is zero. The quantity $\oint \vec{B} \cdot d\vec{A}$ is the magnetic flux through the surface S and is denoted by the symbol Φ_B.

Faraday's Law for Electric Fields

Faraday's law for electric fields states that a changing magnetic flux produces an electric field and therefore induces an electromotive force (emf) in a closed circuit. The magnitude of the induced emf is equal to the rate of change of the magnetic flux through the circuit bounded by a closed loop, C.

Ampère's Law for Magnetic Fields

A steady electric current generates a magnetic field that encircles the current. Ampère's law for magnetic fields states that the line integral of a magnetic field $\vec{B}$ around a closed loop that encloses the current is equal to the permeability times the electric current passing through the loop.

As you can see from Table 26-1, the equations for these four laws are quite similar. The left sides of the equations for both of Gauss's laws describe the flux of the field through a closed surface. For the electric field, the flux depends on the quantity of the charge enclosed by that surface. When the net charge within the surface is positive, a net electric flux *emerges* through the surface. When the net charge is negative, a net flux *enters* the surface. However, the net magnetic flux through a closed surface is zero because sources that produce magnetic fields always have both a north pole and a south pole. An isolated magnetic monopole (a single north pole or a single south pole) has never been observed. Therefore, magnetic field lines that originate from the north pole of a magnet eventually have to reenter the magnet's south pole. Consequently, the magnetic flux leaving a closed surface equals the flux reentering the surface. If magnetic monopoles are ever discovered, a nonzero term will have to be added to the right side of the equation for Gauss's law for magnetic fields, making it completely symmetric with Gauss's law for electric fields.

The left sides of the equations for Faraday's law for electric fields and Ampère's law for magnetic fields are both line integrals of a field around a closed loop. However, the right sides of these two equations look quite different. The equation for Faraday's law has no term proportional to a current because there are no magnetic monopoles. (If monopoles did exist, then the right side of Faraday's law would have a term describing a magnetic current due to the flow of magnetic monopoles.) The right side of the equation for Faraday's law indicates that the induced electric field is proportional to the rate of change of the magnetic flux, but Ampère's law has no corresponding term. Does a changing electric flux produce a magnetic field?

Maxwell realized that Ampère's law as stated in Table 26-1 holds only when the electric current I is constant. When a current changes with time, the equation for Ampère's law needs an additional term.

C-26-1 Gauss's Law for Electric Fields

Rank each charge configuration in Figure 26-3 in decreasing order of the amount of net electric flux passing through each closed spherical surface. Use the equality sign if needed.

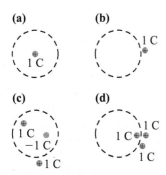

Figure 26-3 C-26-1

C-26-1 (a) = (b) < (d) = (c)

26-2 Displacement Current and Maxwell's Equations

Consider the process of charging a parallel plate capacitor by passing a current $I(t)$ through a connecting wire. As the capacitor charges, a charge $q(t)$ accumulates on its plates and an instantaneous electric field $\vec{E}(t)$ begins to build up between the two plates of the capacitor. We know that a magnetic field exists around a current-carrying wire. Let us apply Ampère's law to the circular loop a of radius R

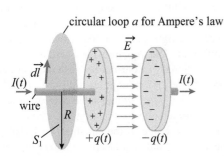

Figure 26-4 A parallel-plate capacitor being charged. The conduction current $I(t)$ induces a magnetic field around the wire, which can be calculated by applying Ampère's law to the flat surface S_1.

that is centered on the wire, as shown in Figure 26-4. The loop a encloses the planar surface S_1 that is being penetrated by the current $I(t)$. So the magnitude of the magnetic field around the path is $B(t) = (\mu_0/2\pi R)\, I(t)$. Now let us distort the surface S_1 (still bounded by the same circular loop a) to a surface S_2 such that the surface S_2 passes through the space between the plates of the capacitor, as shown in Figure 26-5. In this case, no current is penetrating through the surface S_2 (because there is no flow of current between the two plates) and hence the line integral of $\vec{B}$ around the circular path vanishes. So Ampère's law, as given by (23-39) is ambiguous. It gives different results depending upon how the surface bounding the circular loop is chosen. Notice that this ambiguity arises only when the capacitor is being charged (or discharged). When the capacitor is fully charged, current flow through the wire stops and the line integral of $\vec{B}$ is zero for any choice of surface bounding the circular path.

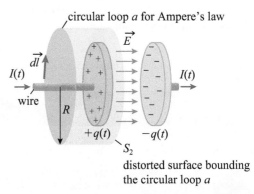

distorted surface bounding the circular loop a

Figure 26-5 There is no conduction current through the surface S_2, however, there is a displacement current through this surface due to a changing electric flux as the charge builds up on the capacitor plates.

Maxwell noted that as the capacitor is being charged, the flux of the electric field between the capacitor plates increases with time. So the *changing* electric field must generate a magnetic field that has exactly the same magnitude as the magnetic field generated when the electric current passes through surface S_1. Using this insight, Maxwell extended Ampère's law:

KEY EQUATION
$$\oint \vec{B} \cdot d\vec{l} = \mu_0 I + \mu_0 \left(\varepsilon_0 \frac{d\Phi_E}{dt} \right) \qquad (26\text{-}1)$$

where Φ_E denotes electric flux, $\dfrac{d\Phi_E}{dt}$ is the rate of change of electric flux with time, and $I = \sum I_{enc}$. Equation (26-1) is called the Ampere-Maxwell equation. The quantity $\varepsilon_0 \dfrac{d\Phi_E}{dt}$ has units of current as shown below and is called the **displacement current**, I_{disp}:

$$[I_{disp}] = \frac{C^2}{N \cdot m^2} \times \frac{1}{s} \times \frac{N \cdot m^2}{C} = \frac{C}{s}$$

Note that no current is actually displaced; the name simply distinguishes the quantity $\varepsilon_0 \dfrac{d\Phi_E}{dt}$ from the current I that is due to a flow of charges. With the addition of the displacement current term, Ampère's law gives an unambiguous result for the magnetic field generated around any closed loop when the current is not steady. This is how it works for the two surfaces of Figures 26-4 and 26-5.

- Surface S_1: A current I flows through the surface, but there is no electric flux through S_1. Hence, the displacement current is zero, and the magnetic field is generated by the conduction current I.

- Surface S_2: There is no conduction current through the surface, but there is a changing electric flux through it. The magnetic field is generated by the displacement current (i.e., by the changing electric flux). As will be shown below, this magnetic field is exactly the same as the magnetic field generated by the conduction current I.

- When the capacitor is fully charged, the conduction current stops. There is an electric flux through the surface S_2, but it is now constant. So the displacement current is zero, and there is no magnetic field in the circuit.

We showed that the dimension of the displacement current is the same as that of the conduction current (due to the flow of electrons). Now we will show that it has the same magnitude. Let $q(t)$ be the charge on a capacitor plate at time t. The charge density (charge per unit area) on a plate of cross-sectional area A is

$$\sigma(t) = \frac{q(t)}{A}$$

Therefore, the magnitude of the electric field between the two plates of the capacitor, ignoring edge effects, is

$$E(t) = \frac{\sigma(t)}{\varepsilon_0} = \frac{q(t)}{A\varepsilon_0}$$

Assuming that the electric field between the plates is uniform, the electric flux, Φ_E, between the plates is the product of the electric field and the area of a single plate:

$$\Phi_E(t) = E(t) \times A = \frac{q(t)}{\varepsilon_0}$$

The rate of change of the electric flux is

$$\frac{d\Phi_E(t)}{dt} = \frac{1}{\varepsilon_0}\frac{dq(t)}{dt}$$

Since the rate of change of charge on the plates is equal to the conduction current,

$$I_{disp}(t) = \varepsilon_0 \frac{d\Phi_E(t)}{dt} = \frac{dq(t)}{dt} = I(t)$$

Thus, *the magnitude of the displacement current is the same as the magnitude of the conduction current.*

We emphasize that no electrons are flowing across the gap between the capacitor plates. The changing electric flux between the plates generates a magnetic field that is exactly the same as the magnetic field generated by the conduction current in the wires (Figure 26-6). If the circuit were enclosed in a sealed box, you would detect a magnetic field around the box, but you would not be able to do any experiment to determine whether the magnetic field is due to a conduction current or a displacement current.

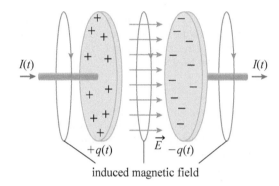

Figure 26-6 As a capacitor is charged, the induced magnetic field around the wire is due to the conduction current, and the field induced between the plates is due to the displacement current.

✓ CHECKPOINT

C-26-2 Displacement Currents

The graph in Figure 26-7 shows the magnitudes of four changing uniform electric fields, all with the same direction. Consider a square loop of area 5 cm² perpendicular to the electric fields. Rank the displacement currents from the changing fields from least to greatest.

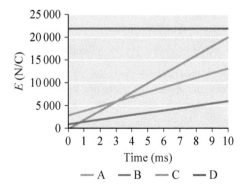

Figure 26-7 A graph of magnitudes of four electric fields as a function of time.

C-26-2 C > A > B > D

EXAMPLE 26-1

Magnetic Field Due to the Displacement Current

D.F. Bartlett and T.R. Cole measured the induced magnetic field inside a charging capacitor in 1984 using a very sensitive magnetometer. They used a capacitor with two circular plates that were 1.22 cm apart. Instead of using direct current to charge the capacitor, they charged the capacitor using a generator that produced a 1.25 kHz sinusoidal voltage with an amplitude of 340 V. The arrangement is similar to the one shown in Figure 26-6. Calculate the peak strength of the magnetic field around a loop of radius 2.00 cm centred on the central axis of the capacitor. Assume that the radius of the capacitor plates is 6.00 cm so that the edge effects can be ignored.

SOLUTION

As the capacitor is being charged, the electric flux between the plates increases and generates a magnetic field. The magnitude and direction of the induced magnetic field are given by the Ampère–Maxwell Equation (26-1). Since there is no conduction current in the region between the plates,

$$\oint \vec{B} \cdot d\vec{l} = \mu_0 \left(\varepsilon_0 \frac{d\Phi_E}{dt} \right)$$

We now evaluate each side of this equation.
Right side:

The electric field is perpendicular to the surface of the plates and has the same magnitude, $E(t)$, anywhere between the plates at a given time t. The electric flux, Φ_E, through a disk of radius r centred on the central axis of the plates is given by

$$\Phi_E(t) = E(t) \times \pi r^2$$

The rate of change of this flux is

$$\frac{d\Phi_E(t)}{dt} = \pi r^2 \frac{dE(t)}{dt} \qquad (1)$$

The potential difference, V, between the two plates has a maximum value of 340 V and varies sinusoidally with a frequency of 1.25 kHz. Therefore,

$$V(t) = V_{max} \sin(2\pi f t) = (340 \text{ V}) \sin(2\pi \times 1250t)$$

The electric field between the plates is related to the potential difference between the plates and their separation, L:

$$E(t) = \frac{V(t)}{L} = \frac{(340 \text{ V}) \sin(2\pi \times 1250t)}{L}$$

Inserting this expression for $E(t)$ into the right side of Equation (1), we get

$$\mu_0 \varepsilon_0 \frac{d\Phi_E(t)}{dt} = \mu_0 \varepsilon_0 \frac{\pi r^2}{L} (340 \text{ V}) \frac{d \sin(2500\pi t)}{dt}$$

$$= 85 \times 10^4 \left(\frac{\pi^2 r^2 \mu_0 \varepsilon_0}{L} \right) \cos(2500\pi t) \frac{\text{C}}{\text{s}}$$

Left side:
We need to calculate the line integral around the circular amperian loop of radius r shown in Figure 26-6. The magnetic field is tangent to the loop, and the loop is centred symmetrically on the central axis. Therefore, the magnetic field has the same magnitude at every point around the loop. Taking $\vec{B}$ and the path element $d\vec{l}$ parallel to each other, we get

$$\oint \vec{B} \cdot d\vec{l} = \oint B \cos(0) \, dl = B \oint dl = B(2\pi r)$$

Equating the left and the right sides, we get the magnitude of the induced magnetic field around a circular loop of radius r that lies inside the two plates:

$$B(t) = 85 \times 10^4 \left(\frac{\pi r \mu_0 \varepsilon_0}{2L} \right) \cos(2500\pi t) \text{ T}$$

Notice that both the electric field and the induced magnetic field oscillate with the same frequency. The amplitude of the magnetic field is equal to the factor multiplying the cosine term. Substituting the known values $r = 2.00 \times 10^{-2}$ m, $L = 1.22 \times 10^{-2}$ m, $\mu_0 = 4\pi \times 10^{-7}$ T·m/A, and $\varepsilon_0 = 8.85 \times 10^{-12}$ C^2/N·m^2, we get

$$B(t) = (2.5 \times 10^{-11}) \cos(2500\pi t) \text{ T}$$

The peak strength of the magnetic field occurs when $\cos(2500\pi t) = \pm 1$ and is therefore $\pm 2.5 \times 10^{-11}$ T.

Making sense of the results:

The magnitude of Earth's magnetic field ranges between 3×10^{-5} T and 6×10^{-5} T, which is much larger than the induced magnetic field in even a large capacitor. Physicists in the time of Faraday and Ampère were unable to detect such small magnetic fields due to changing electric flux in their experiments.

The four equations in Table 26-1, with Ampère's law replaced by Equation (26-1), are collectively called Maxwell's equations. **Maxwell's equations** describe the physics of all phenomena that involve electric and magnetic fields, including the attraction between nuclei and electrons, van der Waals forces between molecules, friction, viscosity, and the propagation of electromagnetic waves. Maxwell's equations are to electromagnetism what Newton's laws are to mechanics.

Maxwell's Equations in a Vacuum

There is no matter in a vacuum and therefore there are no charges or currents. Consequently, Maxwell's equations become much simpler in a vacuum:

$$\oint \vec{E} \cdot d\vec{A} = 0 \quad \text{(Gauss's law for electric fields)} \quad (26\text{-}2)$$

$$\oint \vec{B} \cdot d\vec{A} = 0 \quad \text{(Gauss's law for magnetic fields)} \quad (26\text{-}3)$$

$$\oint \vec{E} \cdot d\vec{l} = -\frac{d\Phi_B}{dt} \quad \text{(Faraday's law)} \quad (26\text{-}4)$$

$$\oint \vec{B} \cdot d\vec{l} = \mu_0 \varepsilon_0 \frac{d\Phi_E}{dt} \quad \text{(Ampère's law)} \quad (26\text{-}5)$$

In a vacuum, Gauss's laws for electric and magnetic fields are identical in form. There are no charges in a vacuum, so the net flux of the electric field through any closed surface is zero. Similarly, the net magnetic flux through a closed surface is zero because there are no magnetic monopoles.

Other than a multiplying factor, Faraday's and Ampère's laws also have identical forms in a vacuum. A changing magnetic flux produces an electric field, and any change in electric flux produces a magnetic field. The minus sign on the right side of Faraday's law is equivalent to Lenz's law, which states that the direction of the induced electric field is such that the induced current produces a magnetic field that opposes the original change in the magnetic flux.

Equations (26-4) and (26-5) indicate that the electric and magnetic fields in a vacuum are coupled. If the strength of the electric field changes with time, the changing electric flux produces a magnetic field that also changes with time. A changing magnetic field means that magnetic flux is changing; hence, a changing electric field is produced. This electric field, in turn, produces a changing magnetic field, and so on, as shown in Figure 26-8. The coupling of the electric and the magnetic fields continuously produces electric and magnetic fields and sets up an electromagnetic wave that propagates in the vacuum. We will study such propagation in the next section.

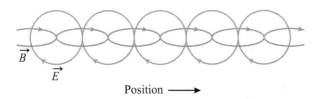

Figure 26-8   An electric field that changes with time produces a magnetic field that also changes with time, and vice versa.

Equations (26-2) to (26-5) contain integrals of electric and magnetic fields and are called "Maxwell's equations in integral form." We can also write Maxwell's equations in terms of derivatives of electric and magnetic fields, and those equations are called "Maxwell's equations in differential form."

Maxwell published his work in 1873. Although relativity and quantum theory were developed in the next century, Maxwell's equations are consistent with both of these theories. Maxwell's careful synthesis of a large amount of seemingly unrelated experimental data produced one of the most elegant theories in physics.

26-3   Electromagnetic Waves

An **electromagnetic wave** consists of coupled electric and magnetic fields that vary with time. Electromagnetic waves are generated by accelerating charges and by quantum-mechanical processes (see Section 26-7). Once an electromagnetic wave is generated, it propagates on its own and does not require any physical medium to continue its propagation. The wave generates itself because a time-varying electric field generates a time-varying magnetic field, which in turn generates a time-varying electric field. This process is continuously repeated.

Electromagnetic waves have the following properties:

- They are *three-dimensional* because the electric field, the magnetic field, and the propagation direction of the wave are all perpendicular to each other.

- Electromagnetic waves are *transverse*. The direction of motion of the wave is perpendicular to the direction of oscillation of the wave's electric and magnetic fields.

- In a vacuum, all electromagnetic waves travel at the speed of light.

The existence of electromagnetic waves can be derived from Maxwell's equations using vector calculus. However, here we will simply show that a sinusoidal plane electromagnetic wave in a vacuum satisfies Maxwell's equations.

Recall from Chapter 15 that a plane wave is a wave with a fixed frequency whose wave fronts are parallel planes of constant amplitude and propagate perpendicular to the direction of motion of the wave. Therefore, the properties of a plane wave are the same when observed at any point on a given plane perpendicular to the direction of motion of the wave (Figure 26-9). A plane wave

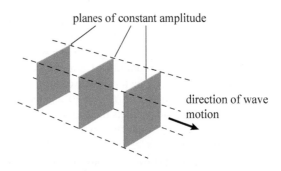

Figure 26-9   A three-dimensional plane wave

is an approximation of a spherical wave that propagates outward from a source. At distances that are much larger than the wavelength of the emitted wave, a spherical wave can be accurately approximated as a plane wave.

Figure 26-10 shows a sinusoidal plane electromagnetic wave travelling in the positive x-direction. The directions of oscillation of the electric field and the magnetic field are chosen as the y-axis and z-axis, respectively. Recall from Chapter 14 that a sinusoidal wave travelling in the positive x-direction is described by the function $\sin(kx - \omega t)$. Here, $k = \dfrac{2\pi}{\lambda}$ is the wave number, and $\omega = 2\pi f$ is the angular frequency of the wave. The components of the electric and magnetic fields of the plane electromagnetic wave in Figure 26-10 are as follows:

$$E_x(x,t) = 0;\ E_y(x,t) = E_0\sin(kx - \omega t);\ E_z(x,t) = 0 \quad (26\text{-}6)$$

$$B_x(x,t) = 0;\ B_y(x,t) = 0;\ B_z(x,t) = B_0\sin(kx - \omega t) \quad (26\text{-}7)$$

where E_0 is the amplitude of the electric field (measured in V/m), and B_0 is the magnitude of the magnetic field (measured in T).

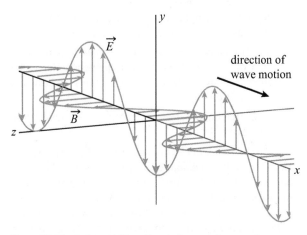

Figure 26-10 A sinusoidal travelling electromagnetic wave at a moment when the wave crests are at the origin of the coordinate system

Note that the electric and magnetic fields have the same wavelength, frequency, and phase constant (which we have chosen to be zero). According to Equation (26-6), the magnitude of the electric field at $x = 0$ varies with time as $E_0\sin(-\omega t) = -E_0\sin(\omega t)$, and the direction of the electric field parallels the y-axis. A charge $+q$ at $x = 0$ would experience a force of magnitude $qE_0\sin(-\omega t)$ directed along the y-axis. Similarly, the magnitude of the magnetic field at $x = 0$ varies with time as $B_0\sin(-\omega t)$, and the direction of the magnetic field parallels the z-axis.

For a plane electromagnetic wave travelling along the x-axis, the magnitudes of the electric and magnetic fields are the same everywhere on a given yz-plane. If the yz-plane is the plane of the page with the x-axis pointing

toward the reader, then at any given instant the electric field has the same magnitude and direction at all points in the plane of the page of the paper. The same is true for the magnetic field. The magnitudes of the electric and magnetic fields oscillate with time, reaching maximum and minimum values in unison (Figure 26-11).

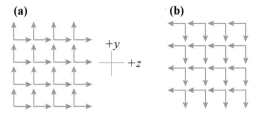

Figure 26-11 (a) A sinusoidal plane electromagnetic wave at an instant when the electric fields (red arrows) and the magnetic fields (green arrows) reach their maximum strengths in the positive y- and z-directions, respectively. The electric and magnetic fields are in the plane of the paper, and the wave is travelling toward the reader. (b) The electric and magnetic fields of the wave half a time period later

✓ **CHECKPOINT**

C-26-3 Field Orientation of Electromagnetic Waves

Figure 26-12 shows four orientations of electric (red) and magnetic (green) fields in a vacuum at a given instant of time. Which orientation could represent an electromagnetic wave? Explain why, and determine the direction in which the wave is travelling.

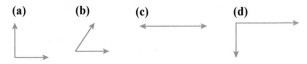

Figure 26-12 C-26-3

C-26-3 (a) and (d) The electric and magnetic fields are perpendicular to each other. These waves are travelling in a direction that is perpendicular to the plane of the page.

We will now consider each of Maxwell's equations as they apply to a plane electromagnetic wave travelling in a vacuum.

Gauss's Law for Electric Fields

Since there are no charges in a vacuum, the net flux of the electric field through any closed surface must be zero. Imagine a cubical Gaussian surface of length h, like the one in Figure 26-13(a), in the presence of a plane electromagnetic wave described by Equations (26-6) and (26-7). Since the electric field does not depend on the y-coordinate, the magnitude of the electric field entering the cube through the bottom surface is equal to the magnitude of the field that leaves the top surface of the cube.

Therefore, the electric flux entering the bottom surface is equal to the flux leaving the top surface. The electric flux through the surfaces in the xy- and yz-planes of the cube is zero because the direction of the electric field is parallel to these surfaces. Therefore, the net electric flux through the box is zero, and Gauss's law for electric fields is satisfied.

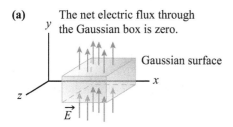

(a) The net electric flux through the Gaussian box is zero.

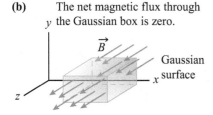

(b) The net magnetic flux through the Gaussian box is zero.

Figure 26-13 (a) The electric flux entering the bottom surface in the xz-plane of the cube is equal to the flux leaving through the corresponding top surface. (b) Similarly, the magnetic flux entering from the back xy-surface of the cube is equal to the flux leaving from the corresponding front surface.

Gauss's Law for Magnetic Fields

Consider the magnetic flux through the cubical Gaussian surface in Figure 26-13(b). The magnetic flux through the surfaces in the xz- and yz-planes of the cube is zero because the direction of the magnetic field is parallel to these surfaces. The magnetic field does not depend on the z-coordinate, so the magnetic flux entering the back surface in the xy-plane is equal to the flux leaving through the parallel front surface. Thus, the net magnetic flux through the Gaussian surface is zero, and Gauss's law for magnetic fields is satisfied.

Faraday's Law

According to Faraday's law, a changing magnetic flux through a closed loop induces an electric field around that loop. The loop may be an imaginary surface or a part of a physical circuit, like a loop of wire. Consider an infinitesimally narrow, rectangular strip in the xy-plane, with height h and width Δx (Figure 26-14) in the presence of a plane electromagnetic wave described by Equations (26-6) and (26-7). The left edge of the strip is at x, and the right edge is at $x + \Delta x$. The width is sufficiently small that the magnitude of the magnetic field passing through the strip can be assumed to remain constant over the entire width. Both the magnetic field and the normal to the strip are pointing along the z-axis. Therefore, the magnetic flux

through the strip is the product of the magnitude of the magnetic field $B_z(x, t)$ and the area of the strip:

$$\Phi_B(x, t) = B_z(x, t)(h\Delta x)$$

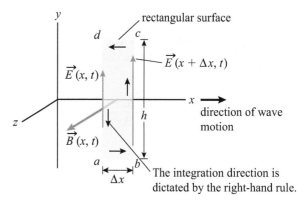

Figure 26-14 The closed rectangular surface in the xy-plane has an infinitesimally small width. The surface is placed in the path of an electromagnetic wave that has $\vec{E}$ along the y-axis and $\vec{B}$ along the z-axis.

The magnetic field is a function of time, so the magnetic flux passing through the strip changes with time, and

$$\frac{\partial}{\partial t}\Phi_B(x, t) = \frac{\partial}{\partial t}[B_z(x, t)(h\Delta x)] = (h\Delta x)\frac{\partial B_z(x, t)}{\partial t} \quad (26\text{-}8)$$

The changing magnetic flux induces an electric field around the strip. *This induced electric field is the electric component of the electromagnetic wave.* The magnetic field points along the positive z-axis; therefore, according to the right-hand rule, the circulation of the electric field is in the counterclockwise direction, as shown in Figure 26-14:

$$\oint \vec{E} \cdot d\vec{l} = \int_a^b \vec{E} \cdot d\vec{l} + \int_b^c \vec{E} \cdot d\vec{l}$$
$$+ \int_c^d \vec{E} \cdot d\vec{l} + \int_d^a \vec{E} \cdot d\vec{l} \quad (26\text{-}9)$$

The electric field has only a y-component. The first and third line integrals therefore vanish because the line elements $d\vec{l}$ for these sections point along the x-axis, perpendicular to the direction of the electric field. The line integral along the path bc is

$$\int_b^c \vec{E} \cdot d\vec{l} = \left(E_y(x + \Delta x, t)\hat{y}\right) \cdot (h\hat{y}) = hE_y(x + \Delta x, t)$$

Here, the electric field is evaluated at $x + \Delta x$, the location of the bc edge of the strip. The path da is traversed in the negative y-direction, from top to bottom (counterclockwise). Therefore,

$$\int_d^a \vec{E} \cdot d\vec{l} = \left(E_y(x, t)\hat{y}\right) \cdot \left((h)(-\hat{y})\right) = -hE_y(x, t)$$

Combining contributions from all the sides, the line integral of the electric field around the rectangular strip is

$$\oint \vec{E} \cdot \vec{dl} = E_y(x + \Delta x, t)h - E_y(x, t)h \quad (26\text{-}10)$$

The expression on the right side is related to the derivative of $E_y(x, t)$ with respect to x. By definition, the derivative of a function $f(x)$ of a variable x is related to its values at two nearby points by

$$\frac{df(x)}{dx} = \lim_{\Delta x \to 0} \left(\frac{f(x + \Delta x) - f(x)}{\Delta x} \right)$$

Therefore, as the width $\Delta x \to 0$,

$$E_y(x + \Delta x, t) - E_y(x, t) \Rightarrow \Delta x \frac{dE_y(x, t)}{dx}$$

and

$$\oint \vec{E} \cdot \vec{dl} = (h\Delta x)\frac{dE_y(x, t)}{dx} \quad (26\text{-}11)$$

Inserting Equations (26-11) and (26-8) into Equation (26-4), we get

$$\frac{\partial E_y(x, t)}{\partial x} = -\frac{\partial B_z(x, t)}{\partial t} \quad (26\text{-}12)$$

In Equation (26-12), we have replaced the total derivative of the electric field by the partial derivative because the electric field depends on both position and time. Equation (26-12) emphasizes that while taking the derivative of $E_y(x, t)$ with respect to x, we must keep t constant. Similarly, while taking the derivative of $B_z(x, t)$ with respect to t, we must keep x constant.

When applied to plane electromagnetic waves, Faraday's law requires that *the rate of change of the electric field with position in the neighbourhood of a given point be equal and opposite to the rate at which the magnetic field changes with time at that point*. Therefore, if the electric field changes with position, then the magnetic field must change with time.

So far, we have not used the fact that the plane electromagnetic wave is a sinusoidal travelling wave. We can evaluate both sides of Equation (26-12) using Equations (26-6) and (26-7):

$$\frac{\partial E_y(x, t)}{\partial x} = \frac{\partial}{\partial x}(E_0 \sin(kx - \omega t)) = kE_0 \cos(kx - \omega t)$$

and

$$-\frac{\partial B_z(x, t)}{\partial t} = -\frac{\partial}{\partial t}(B_0 \sin(kx - \omega t)) = \omega B_0 \cos(kx - \omega t)$$

Dividing out the cosine term, we get

$$kE_0 = \omega B_0 \quad (26\text{-}13)$$

Thus, Faraday's law requires that the amplitude of the magnetic field be equal to the amplitude of the electric field divided by the speed of the electromagnetic waves:

$$B_0 = \frac{k}{\omega} E_0 = \frac{E_0}{v_{em}} \quad (26\text{-}14)$$

where $v_{em} = \omega/k$ is the speed of the electromagnetic waves in a vacuum.

Ampère's Law

The magnetic field of the plane electromagnetic wave points along the z-axis (Equation (26-7)). We therefore choose a closed rectangular strip in the xz-plane, as shown in Figure 26-15.

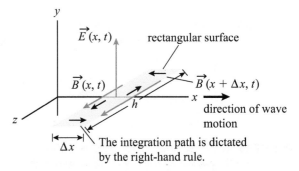

Figure 26-15 The closed rectangular surface has an infinitesimally small width in the xz-plane. The electromagnetic wave has $\vec{E}$ along the y-axis and $\vec{B}$ along the z-axis.

The electric field is normal to the plane of the strip, and the electric flux passing through the strip is the product of the magnitude of the electric field $E_y(x, t)$ and the area of the strip:

$$\Phi_E(x, t) = E_y(x, t)(h\Delta x)$$

The rate at which the electric flux passing through the strip varies with time is given by

$$\frac{\partial}{\partial t}\Phi_E(x, t) = \frac{\partial}{\partial t}[E_y(x, t)(h\Delta x)] = (h\Delta x)\frac{\partial E_y(x, t)}{\partial t} \quad (26\text{-}15)$$

The changing electric flux induces a magnetic field around the rectangular strip. *The induced magnetic field forms the magnetic field component of the electromagnetic wave.* The calculation of the line integral of the magnetic field around the strip is similar to the calculation for the electric field. The result is

$$\oint \vec{B} \cdot \vec{dl} = (h\Delta x)\frac{\partial B_z(x, t)}{\partial x} \quad (26\text{-}16)$$

Inserting Equations (26-15) and (26-16) into Equation (26-5) for Ampère's law we get

$$\frac{\partial B_z(x, t)}{\partial x} = -\varepsilon_0 \mu_0 \frac{\partial E_y(x, t)}{\partial t} \quad (26\text{-}17)$$

When applied to plane electromagnetic waves, Ampère's law requires *that the rate of change of the magnetic field* with position in the neighbourhood of a given point be proportional and opposite to the rate at which the electric field changes with time at that point.

Inserting Equations (26-6) and (26-7) and evaluating the partial derivatives with respect to x and t, we get the following constraint imposed by Ampère's law on electric and magnetic fields of a plane electromagnetic wave:

$$kB_0 = \varepsilon_0 \mu_0(\omega E_0) \qquad (26\text{-}18)$$

The Speed of Electromagnetic Waves

When we combine the constraints of Equations (26-14) and (26-18), we get a remarkable result. Equation (26-18) can be written as

$$B_0 = \varepsilon_0 \mu_0\left(\frac{\omega}{k}\right)E_0 = \varepsilon_0 \mu_0 v_{em} E_0 \qquad (26\text{-}19)$$

Combining Equations (26-19) and (26-14), we get

$$v_{em} = \frac{1}{\sqrt{\varepsilon_0 \mu_0}} \qquad (26\text{-}20)$$

This equation shows that the speed of electromagnetic waves in a vacuum depends *only* on the electric permittivity and magnetic permeability of the vacuum. The speed does not depend on the frequency, wavelength, or amplitude of the waves. Substituting the known values for ε_0 and μ_0 into Equation (26-20) gives

$$
\begin{aligned}
v_{em} &= \frac{1}{\sqrt{\varepsilon_0 \mu_0}} \\
&= \frac{1}{\sqrt{(8.85 \times 10^{-12}\,\text{C}^2/\text{N}\cdot\text{m}^2)(4\pi \times 10^{-7}\,\text{T}\cdot\text{m/A})}} \\
&= 3.00 \times 10^8\,\text{m/s} \qquad (26\text{-}21)
\end{aligned}
$$

which is precisely the speed of light, c. Therefore,

KEY EQUATION
$$v_{em} = c$$

So, Maxwell's equations predict that *all electromagnetic waves in a vacuum travel at the speed of light*. From Equation (26-19), using $k = 2\pi/\lambda$ and $\omega = 2\pi f$, we get

$$c = \frac{\omega}{k} = \lambda f \qquad (26\text{-}22)$$

To summarize, Maxwell's equations predict the existence of electromagnetic waves with the following properties:

1. Electromagnetic waves travel in a vacuum at the speed of light. The wavelength and frequency of an electromagnetic wave are related to its speed by $\lambda f = c$.

2. The electric and magnetic fields are perpendicular to the direction of propagation of the wave. Electromagnetic waves are therefore transverse waves.

3. The electric and magnetic fields are perpendicular to each other.

4. The amplitudes of electric and magnetic fields of an electromagnetic wave are related such that

$$B_0 = \frac{E_0}{v_{em}} = \frac{E_0}{c}$$

We have shown that sinusoidal plane electromagnetic waves satisfy Maxwell's equations. Electromagnetic waves with complex waveforms can be produced by the superposition of sinusoidal waves of various frequencies and amplitudes, similar to the way that complex sound waves can be formed by a combination of harmonics. Since Maxwell's equations are linear in electric and magnetic fields, such complex electromagnetic waves also satisfy Maxwell's equations.

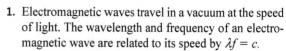

C-26-4 Plane Electromagnetic Waves

The four plots in Figure 26-16 show the directions of electric (red) and magnetic (green) fields at a given instant. Determine whether the electric and magnetic fields in each plot correspond to those of a plane electromagnetic wave. If yes, determine the direction of motion of the wave.

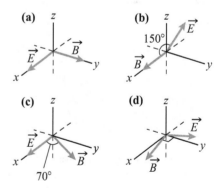

Figure 26-16 C-26-4

C-26-4 (a) Yes, z; (b) no; (c) no; (d) yes, z.

EXAMPLE 26-2

A Helium–Neon Laser

A helium–neon laser produces a beam of light with a wavelength of 633 nm and an electric field strength of 1000 V/m.

The direction of motion of the beam is taken to be along the z-axis, and the electric field is parallel to the x-axis. A laser beam is an electromagnetic plane wave.

(continued)

ELECTRICITY, MAGNETISM, AND OPTICS

(a) Find the frequency of the laser beam.
(b) What are the amplitude and the direction of the magnetic field of the beam?

SOLUTION

(a) The wavelength and the frequency of this wave are related by Equation (26-22). Rearranging and solving for f, we get

$$f = \frac{c}{\lambda} = \frac{3.00 \times 10^8\,\text{m/s}}{633 \times 10^{-9}\,\text{m}} = 4.74 \times 10^{14}\,\text{Hz}$$

(b) The amplitude of the magnetic field is related to the amplitude of the electric field by Equation (26-14). Solving for B_0 gives

$$B_0 = \frac{E_0}{c} = \frac{1000\,\text{V/m}}{3.00 \times 10^8\,\text{m/s}} = 3.33 \times 10^{-6}\,\text{T}$$

The direction of the magnetic field is perpendicular to the direction of motion of the laser beam and that of the electric field; therefore, the direction of the magnetic field must be parallel to the y-axis.

LO 4

26-4 The Electromagnetic Spectrum

The wavelength (and, hence, the frequency) of an electromagnetic wave can have any positive value. The largest possible wavelength is limited only by the size of the universe. The shortest wavelength can tend to zero. This range of allowed wavelengths is called the **electromagnetic spectrum**. As shown in Figure 26-17, regions of the electromagnetic spectrum have their own names. We outline below the properties and some applications of electromagnetic waves in each region. Note, however, that the boundaries of these regions are not precisely defined.

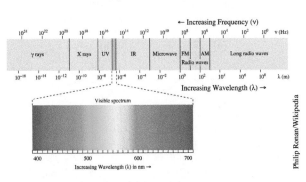

Figure 26-17 The electromagnetic spectrum

Radio Waves

Radio waves ($\lambda \approx 100$ km to 0.3 m, $f \approx 3 \times 10^3$ Hz to 1×10^9 Hz) have the longest wavelengths in the electromagnetic spectrum. Radio waves are used for radio and TV signals, radar, and numerous other applications. Some properties of radio waves depend on the wavelength. For example, the shorter-wavelength radio waves can reflect off the ionosphere and thus travel beyond the horizon. Consequently, shortwave radio broadcasts (1.8 to 30 MHz) can be received at long distances from the transmitter.

Many galaxies, including the Milky Way, emit radio waves as well as visible light. The radio emissions from galaxies are generated by fast-moving electrons that spiral around the magnetic field lines of the galaxy. The branch of astronomy that studies radio waves from space is called **radio astronomy**. The study of radio wave emission from galaxies provides extremely useful information that cannot be obtained by observing only visible light. Figure 26-18 shows a radio image of the central region of the Milky Way. The arrow in the image indicates a supernova remnant at the location of a newly discovered source of low-frequency radio waves.

Figure 26-18 A radio frequency image of the central region of the Milky Way

Microwaves

Applications of microwaves ($\lambda \approx 0.3$ m to 0.3 mm, $f \approx 1 \times 10^9$ Hz to 1×10^{12} Hz) include wireless communications (Bluetooth and IEEE 02.11 devices use 2.4 GHz microwaves), cellphone networks, satellite radio (2.3 GHz), garage door openers, the Global Positioning System (GPS), and microwave ovens. Microwaves are also generated by stars, including the Sun.

Infrared Radiation

The infrared region ($\lambda \approx 0.3$ mm to 700 nm, $f \approx 1 \times 10^{12}$ Hz to 4.3×10^{14} Hz) of the electromagnetic spectrum lies between microwaves and visible light. The part of the region closest to microwaves is called **far infrared**, and the part closest to visible light is called **near infrared**. All objects emit some infrared radiation. Even cold objects, like snow, emit infrared radiation. The hotter an object, the more infrared radiation it emits. The heat from the Sun and from a fire is transmitted largely in the form of infrared radiation. Although human eyes cannot detect infrared radiation, many organisms have infrared receptors that allow them to see warm-blooded animals in the dark. Images taken with sensors and photographic emulsions that respond to infrared radiation are called **thermograms**. Figure 26-19 shows a thermogram that has been processed so that the red colour corresponds to higher temperatures and the blue colour to lower temperatures. The red colour on the roof and the middle window indicates heat escaping from the house, a sign of poor insulation in these areas.

Near-infrared radiation is used in TV remote controls and similar devices. A near-infrared wave causes much less heating than a far-infrared wave.

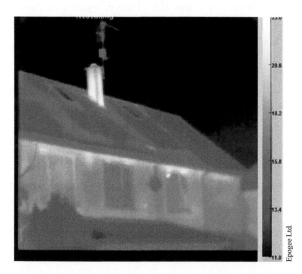

Figure 26-19   A thermogram of a house at night. The scale at the right shows the temperatures corresponding to the various colours.

Visible Light

The narrow band of the electromagnetic spectrum that our eyes can detect is called the **visible spectrum** ($\lambda \approx 750$ nm to 400 nm, $f \approx 4.0 \times 10^{14}$ Hz to 7.5×10^{14} Hz). Although we divide the visible spectrum into colours (often listed as red, orange, yellow, green, blue, indigo, and violet), the wavelength changes continuously within the region, as shown in the enlarged section of Figure 26-17. Human eyes are most sensitive to light with a wavelength of 555 nm, which has a green colour.

Ultraviolet Light

The ultraviolet (UV) region ($\lambda \approx 400$ nm to 10 nm, $f \approx 7.5 \times 10^{14}$ Hz to 3×10^{16} Hz) lies between visible light and X-rays. Ultraviolet radiation has sufficient energy to ionize atoms and cause chemical reactions. Many minerals absorb ultraviolet light and then emit radiation of longer wavelengths, often in the visible spectrum (Figure 26-20). This process is called **fluorescence**. UV lamps are commonly used in suntanning salons.

Figure 26-20   Various coloured light emitted by different minerals when exposed to ultraviolet radiation

The Sun is a major source of UV radiation, which is divided into three bands: UV-A, UV-B, and UV-C.

- The UV-A band contains wavelengths between 320 nm and 400 nm. Radiation in the UV-A band is not absorbed by the atmosphere and is not particularly harmful to living organisms.

- The UV-B band contains wavelengths between 320 nm and 280 nm. Radiation in this band is partly absorbed by the atmosphere. UV-B radiation is harmful to human skin, and prolonged exposure can cause skin cancer.

- The UV-C band contains wavelengths between 280 nm and 100 nm. Radiation in this band is mostly absorbed by the atmosphere. UV-C radiation is more energetic and harmful to human skin. Prolonged exposure can cause sunburn and eventually skin cancer.

 MAKING CONNECTIONS

What Is the UV Index?

The UV index is a numbering system that indicates the level of harm to human skin due to the intensity of UV radiation (Table 26-2). This index was first developed by Environment Canada, and Canada was the first country to issue UV level forecasts for the public. The UV index is now standardized by the World Health Organization and used worldwide. The higher the category, the more harmful the effect of the UV radiation. A color is associated with each risk category.

Table 26-2   The UV Index

UV index	Risk category	Associated colour
0–2	Low	Green
3–5	Moderate	Yellow
6–7	High	Orange
8–10	Very high	Red
11 and higher	Extreme	Violet

X-rays

Electromagnetic waves with wavelengths between 3 nm and 0.003 nm are called X-rays ($\lambda \approx 3$ nm to 0.003 nm, $f \approx 1 \times 10^{17}$ Hz to 1×10^{20} Hz). Wavelengths between 10 nm and 0.10 nm are classified as **soft X-rays**, and wavelengths between 0.10 nm and 0.010 nm are classified as **hard X-rays**. Hard X-rays easily penetrate skin and soft body tissue but are absorbed by dense material such as bones and teeth. Hard X-rays are used for making diagnostic images of the interior of the human body, studying the structure of crystals, and nondestructive testing of objects such as structural materials. The X-ray image is either recorded on a film (a **radiograph**) or stored as an electronic image. Different materials appear light or dark depending on the proportion of the X-rays the materials absorb. Calcium in bones absorbs large amounts of X-rays; therefore, bones look white on the radiograph, which is viewed as a negative image. Fat and other soft tissue absorbs less and look grey. Air absorbs very few X-rays, so lungs look black. X-rays are high-energy radiation, and overexposure to them can cause severe damage to human tissue.

Gamma Rays

Gamma rays ($\lambda \approx 0.003$ nm and smaller, $f \approx 1 \times 10^{20}$ Hz and greater) are the most energetic electromagnetic waves. Gamma rays are emitted by nuclei and can also be produced by collisions of particles and antiparticles. Gamma rays are highly penetrating radiation, and in recent years they have been used in different industries, for example: cancer therapy (destroying cancerous cells), food preservation (killing bacteria and other microorganisms in food), sterilizing medical equipment (killing bacteria), and testing structural materials. Gamma ray detectors are also used in seaports and border crossings to image the insides of containers (Figure 26-21).

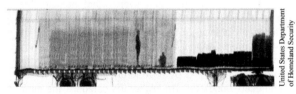

United States Department of Homeland Security

Figure 26-21 A gamma ray image of the inside of a truck. The image clearly shows the boxes and human figures (dummies) inside the truck.

LO 5

26-5   The Energy and Momentum of Electromagnetic Waves

Like all waves, electromagnetic waves carry energy and momentum. The energy and momentum flow in the direction of motion of the wave. In this section, we will explore how the energy and momentum of an electromagnetic wave depend on the amplitudes of the wave's electric and magnetic fields.

We know from electrostatics that electric and magnetic fields store energy. Recall that the magnitude of the *electric energy density* (the electric potential energy per unit volume) stored in any electric field $\vec{E}$ is

$$u_E = \frac{1}{2}\,\varepsilon_0 E^2 \qquad (21\text{-}18)$$

Similarly, the magnitude of the *magnetic energy density* of a magnetic field $\vec{B}$ is

$$u_B = \frac{1}{2\mu_0}\,B^2 \qquad (24\text{-}51)$$

Consider a sinusoidal electromagnetic wave described by Equations (26-6) and (26-7) travelling in a vacuum in the positive *x*-direction. Substituting Equations (26-6) and (26-7) into the equations for the energy densities gives

$$u_E(x,\,t) = \frac{1}{2}\,\varepsilon_0 E_y^2 = \frac{1}{2}\,\varepsilon_0 E_0^2 \sin^2(kx - \omega t)$$

$$u_B(x,\,t) = \frac{1}{2\mu_0}\,B_z^2 = \frac{1}{2\mu_0}\,B_0^2 \sin^2(kx - \omega t) \qquad (26\text{-}23)$$

Note that the energy densities for a travelling wave are position- and time-dependent. Since $B_0 = E_0/c$ for an electromagnetic wave and $c = \dfrac{1}{\sqrt{\varepsilon_0 \mu_0}}$, the magnetic energy intensity can be written as follows:

$$u_B(x,\,t) = \frac{1}{2\mu_0}\left(\frac{E_0}{c}\right)^2 \sin^2(kx - \omega t)$$

$$= \frac{1}{2}\,\varepsilon_0 E_0^2 \sin^2(kx - \omega t) \qquad (26\text{-}24)$$

Thus, *in a travelling electromagnetic wave, the energy density of the magnetic field is equal to the energy density of the electric field.* In any given region of space, the total energy of the electromagnetic field is equally shared between the electric and the magnetic fields. This result is a consequence of the symmetry of Maxwell's equations with respect to electric and magnetic fields in a vacuum.

The total energy density of the wave, $u(x, t)$, is the sum of the electric and magnetic energy densities and can be written in several equivalent ways:

$$u(x,\,t) = u_E(x,\,t) + u_B(x,\,t)$$

$$= 2u_E(x,\,t) = \varepsilon_0 E_0^2 \sin^2(kx - \omega t)$$

$$= \varepsilon_0 c E_0 B_0 \sin^2(kx - \omega t) \qquad (26\text{-}25)$$

The amount of energy flowing per unit time per unit area perpendicular to the direction of the wave propagation is called the **energy flux** (*S*) or the **intensity** of the wave. Imagine a 1.0 m^2 rectangular area perpendicular to the path of an electromagnetic wave in a vacuum. Since an electromagnetic wave travels with the speed of light, c, the energy that passes through the rectangular area in one second is equal to the energy contained in a cube of volume $1.0 \text{ m}^2 \times c \times 1.0 \text{ s}$ (Figure 26-22). Therefore,

$$S(x, t) = u(x, t)c = \varepsilon_0 c^2 E_0 B_0 \sin^2(kx - \omega t)$$

$$= \frac{E_0 B_0}{\mu_0} \sin^2(kx - \omega t) \qquad (26\text{-}26)$$

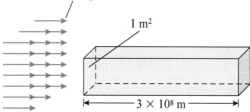

incident electromagnetic wave

1 m²

3×10^8 m

Figure 26-22 The energy flux, S, is defined as the amount of electromagnetic energy that passes through a unit cross-sectional area perpendicular to the path of the incident wave, in one second.

The units of energy flux are W/m², which we can confirm by considering the dimensions of the quantities in Equation (26-26):

$$[\mu_0] = \frac{\text{kg} \cdot \text{m}}{\text{C}^2}; \qquad [E_0] = \frac{\text{N}}{\text{C}}; \qquad [B_0] = \text{T} = \frac{\text{kg}}{\text{C} \cdot \text{s}}$$

So,

$$[S] = \frac{\text{C}^2}{\text{m} \cdot \text{kg}} \times \frac{\text{N}}{\text{C}} \times \frac{\text{kg}}{\text{C} \cdot \text{s}} = \frac{\text{N}}{\text{m} \cdot \text{s}} = \frac{\text{N} \cdot \text{m}}{\text{m}^2 \cdot \text{s}} = \frac{\text{W}}{\text{m}^2}$$

The energy flow varies with the frequency of the electric and magnetic fields. We do not notice these fluctuations in visible light because the frequency ($\sim 10^{14}$ Hz) is far too fast for us to perceive. The time and position average of the

function $\sin^2(kx - \omega t)$ over one oscillation is $\frac{1}{2}$. Therefore, we can define the **average intensity** ($\bar{S}$), or **irradiance**, as

$$\bar{S} = \frac{E_0 B_0}{2\mu_0} = \frac{E_0^2}{2\mu_0 c} = \frac{\varepsilon_0 c E_0^2}{2} \qquad (26\text{-}27)$$

From Equations (26-26) and (26-27) the total average energy density, $\bar{u}$ of an electromagnetic wave is related to the average intensity of the wave by

$$\bar{S} = c\bar{u} \qquad (26\text{-}28)$$

Notice that as for mechanical waves, the energy carried by an electromagnetic wave is proportional to the square of its amplitude.

Consider a source of power that is emitting spherical electromagnetic waves, for example, a light bulb or an omnidirectional radio antenna. The waves emerging from the source spread outward at the speed of light. At a distance r from the source, the power, P, is distributed over a surface area, $4\pi r^2$. Therefore, the average intensity of the waves, $\bar{S}$, at a distance r from the source is

$$\bar{S} = \frac{P}{4\pi r^2} \qquad (26\text{-}29)$$

The intensity of electromagnetic waves falls off as the square of the distance from the source (Figure 26-23).

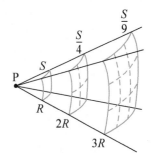

Figure 26-23 The intensity of the three-dimensional spherical waves falls off as the square of the distance from the point source producing the waves.

EXAMPLE 26-3

Solar Power Reaching Earth

The average intensity of sunlight, $\bar{S}$, at the upper atmosphere is approximately 1400 W/m². The average distance between Earth and the Sun is 150 million kilometres, and the mean radius of Earth is 6370 km.

(a) What are the amplitudes of the electric and magnetic fields in the sunlight?
(b) What is the average power generated by the Sun?
(c) What is the total power intercepted by Earth?

SOLUTION

(a) From Equation (26-27), the amplitude of the electric field is related to the average intensity by

$$E_0 = \sqrt{2\mu_0 c \bar{S}}$$

$$= [2(4\pi \times 10^{-7} \text{ T} \cdot \text{m/A})(3.00 \times 10^8 \text{ m/s})(1400 \text{ W/m}^2)]^{1/2}$$

$$= 1030 \text{ V/m}$$

(continued)

The amplitude of the magnetic field is

$$B_0 = \frac{E_0}{c} = \frac{1030 \text{ V/m}}{3.00 \times 10^8 \text{ m/s}} = 3.4 \times 10^{-6} \text{ T}$$

(b) The average power of the Sun can be calculated from Equation (26-29):

$$P = 4\pi r^2 \bar{S} = 4\pi (150 \times 10^9 \text{ m})^2 (1400 \text{ W/m}^2) = 4.0 \times 10^{26} \text{ W}$$

(c) The total power intercepted by Earth is the product of the incident intensity and the cross-sectional area of Earth. At such a large distance from the Sun, electromagnetic waves reaching Earth are plane waves.

Earth projects a disk with a radius of 6370 km to these waves. Therefore, the power intercepted by Earth is

$$P_{\text{Earth}} = (\pi r_{\text{Earth}}^2)\bar{S} = \pi (6370 \times 10^3 \text{ m})^2 \times (1400 \text{ W/m}^2)$$

$$= 1.8 \times 10^{17} \text{ W}$$

Making sense of the results:

In 2008, the average power consumption of the world was approximately 1.5×10^{13} W. So, the Sun could provide all of this power if sufficiently efficient and cost-effective ways to harness Solar power can be developed.

MAKING CONNECTIONS

How Do Microwave Ovens Heat Food?

A microwave oven produces electromagnetic radiation with a frequency of approximately 2.45 GHz ($\lambda \cong 0.12$ m). This radiation is absorbed by water, fats, and sugar molecules contained in the food, thus heating and cooking the food. A water molecule consists of one oxygen and two hydrogen atoms and is electrically neutral overall. However, within the water molecule the oxygen atom is slightly negatively charged, and the hydrogen atoms are slightly positively charged. Therefore, the water molecules act like tiny dipoles. In the presence of an electric field, the positive end of a dipole experiences a force in the direction of the electric field, and the negative end experiences a force in the opposite direction, thus twisting the dipole. When an alternating electromagnetic field is applied to a water molecule, as in a microwave oven, the molecule continuously twists about its centre of charge (Figure 26-24). In a microwave oven, water molecules absorb electromagnetic energy from the microwaves and convert it to thermal energy (molecular motion). The molecules then transfer this thermal energy to adjacent nonpolar molecules by colliding with them and this heating the food. Microwave radiation heats food quickly and effectively because it is absorbed throughout the food. Longer wavelengths would pass through the food, and shorter wavelengths would be absorbed, mainly at the surface. Microwave radiation does not have sufficient energy to remove electrons from the atoms, so it cannot chemically change the food.

(a)

no electric field

(b)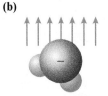

electric field pointing upwards

(c)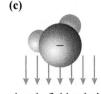

electric field pointing downwards

Figure 26-24 Orientations of a water molecule with (a) no electric field, (b) the electric field directed upward, and (c) the electric field directed downward

ONLINE ACTIVITY

Microwave Ovens

The e-resource that accompanies every new copy of this textbook contains an Online Activity using the PhET simulation "Microwaves." Work through the simulation and accompanying questions to gain an understanding of how microwave ovens work.

The Poynting Vector and Wave Momentum

Recall that the cross product of vectors $\vec{a}$ and $\vec{b}$ is a vector that is perpendicular to the plane containing the two vectors. Since the direction of energy flow of an electromagnetic wave is perpendicular to the direction of the electric and magnetic fields, we define a vector, $\vec{S}$, called the **Poynting vector**, as

$$\vec{S} = \frac{1}{\mu_0} \vec{E} \times \vec{B} \qquad (26\text{-}30)$$

The magnitude of $\vec{S}$ is the energy flux S as defined by Equation (26-26), and the direction of $\vec{S}$ is that of the wave propagation, as shown in Figure 26-25. The magnitude of the Poynting vector oscillates with the frequency of the wave. The Poynting vector was introduced by the English physicist John Henry Poynting (1852–1914).

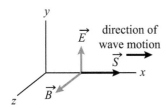

direction of wave motion

The electric and magnetic fields are in the *yz*-plane.

Figure 26-25 The Poynting vector $\vec{S}$ of an electromagnetic wave

Electromagnetic Wave momentum

Consider an electromagnetic wave incident on a collection of charges. Even if all the charges are initially at rest the electromagnetic wave exerts a force on the charges causing them to move and hence gain momentum. By the law of conservation of momentum an increase in the momentum of the charges is equal to the loss in the wave's momentum. Therefore, in addition to energy an electromagnetic wave must also carry momentum.

According to quantum theory, electromagnetic waves are made of massless particles, called photons (see Chapter 33). The relationship between the energy and momentum of a fast moving particle is given by Einstein's relativistic energy-momentum relationship (Chapter 27),

$$E = \sqrt{m^2c^4 + p^2c^2}$$

where E is the energy, p the momentum, m is the rest-mass of the particle and c is the speed of light in vacuum. The energy E and the magnitude of momentum p of a photon ($m = 0$) are therefore related by,

$$p = \frac{E}{c} \qquad (26\text{-}31)$$

Because electromagnetic waves are made of photons the relationship (26-31) also applies to these waves. The momentum carried by an electromagnetic wave is equal to the energy of the wave divided by the speed of light. It follows from the above equation that the magnitude of time-averaged **radiation momentum density** (momentum per unit volume) $\bar{g}_{rad}$ of an electromagnetic wave equals its time-averaged **energy density** $\bar{u}$ (Equation 26-28), divided by c.

$$\bar{g}_{rad} = \frac{\bar{u}}{c} = \frac{1}{c}\left(\frac{\varepsilon_0 E_0^2}{2}\right) \qquad (26\text{-}32)$$

As the direction of energy and momentum flow of a particle is along its direction of motion, therefore the momentum of an electromagnetic wave points along the direction of the energy flow. As defined in Equation (26-30) the Poynting vector $\vec{S}$ describes the direction of energy flow of an electromagnetic wave. Therefore the radiation momentum density $\vec{g}_{rad}$ (a vector quantity that describes both the magnitude of the momentum density as well as the direction of the momentum flow) of an electromagnetic wave is related to $\vec{S}$ by

$$\vec{g}_{rad} = \frac{\vec{S}}{c^2} \qquad (26\text{-}33)$$

The momentum density equals the energy flux divided by c^2. This relationship between the energy flux of a wave and its momentum density is also true for other types of waves, for example sound waves.

The relationship (26-33) can also be derived using Maxwell's equations and was known before the advent of quantum theory. However, that derivation involves the use of vector calculus, a branch of mathematics that you may not have yet studied.

26-6 Radiation Pressure

Radiation pressure is defined as the force per unit area exerted by electromagnetic waves on an object. Light falling on the surface of an object, such as black paper, is absorbed by the surface. As the light is absorbed, it transfers its momentum to the object, thus exerting a force on the object. By definition, the force per unit area on a surface is the pressure exerted on that surface. Therefore, light exerts pressure on an absorbing surface.

Now consider electromagnetic radiation with average intensity $\bar{S}$ incident on a surface of area A that absorbs all the incident radiation. The energy Δu absorbed by the surface in time Δt is given by,

energy absorbed = average intensity × surface area × Δt

$$\Delta\bar{u} = \bar{S}A\Delta t$$

Since all the radiation is absorbed, the total momentum transferred to the surface, Δp, is equal to the time-averaged **radiation momentum**, $\bar{g}_{rad}$, given by Equation (26-32):

$$\Delta p = \frac{\Delta\bar{u}}{c} = \frac{1}{c}\left(\bar{S}A\Delta t\right)$$

The rate of change of momentum per unit area of the surface is therefore,

$$\frac{1}{A}\left(\frac{\Delta p}{\Delta t}\right) = \frac{\bar{S}}{c}$$

The quantity on the left side is the pressure exerted on the surface by the radiation, P_{rad}. Therefore, radiation pressure on a perfectly absorbing surface is

$$P_{\text{rad}} = \frac{\bar{S}}{c} \text{ (for a perfectly absorbing surface) (26-34)}$$

If the surface is a perfect reflector, then the change in the momentum of the reflected waves is $2\Delta p$ for normal incidence (just like the change in the momentum of a ball

when it rebounds off a perfectly elastic surface is twice the incident momentum). The pressure exerted on a perfectly reflecting surface is

$$P_{\text{rad}} = 2\frac{\bar{S}}{c} \text{ (for a perfectly reflecting surface) (26-35)}$$

EXAMPLE 26-4

Radiation Pressure at Earth's Surface

Estimate the radiation pressure at Earth's surface. Is this pressure uniformly distributed over Earth's entire surface at any given time?

SOLUTION

The intensity of solar radiation at Earth's surface is approximately 1000 W/m². It is less than the intensity at the top of Earth's atmosphere due to absorption in the atmosphere. Assuming that most of the sunlight is reflected from Earth's surface, the radiation pressure exerted on Earth's surface is approximately

$$P_{\text{rad}} = 2\frac{1000 \text{ W/m}^2}{3.00 \times 10^8 \text{ m/s}} = 6.7 \times 10^{-6} \text{ Pa}$$

The amount of sunlight reflected by Earth's surface varies considerably across the surface and depends on the presence of cloud cover, snow, and other variables. Our assumption that all incident sunlight is reflected overestimates the radiation pressure. The radiation pressure is only exerted on the side of Earth that is facing the Sun.

Making sense of the result:

The atmospheric pressure at sea level is 1.01×10^5 Pa, so the radiation pressure is approximately 7×10^{-11} times smaller than the atmospheric pressure. That is why we do not feel radiation pressure.

EXAMPLE 26-5

Solar Sailing: IKAROS

On May 21, 2010, the Japan Aerospace Exploration Agency launched a spacecraft, called IKAROS (Interplanetary Kite-craft Accelerated by Radiation of the Sun), toward Venus to demonstrate propulsion by a solar sail. The sail of the spacecraft (Figure 26-26(a)) consists of 200 m² of a reflective polyimide resin membrane as thin as 0.0075 mm. The mass of the solar sail is 15 kg, and the total mass of the spacecraft is 315 kg. Once clear of Earth, the spacecraft is propelled toward Venus by pressure from solar radiation. Estimate the magnitude of acceleration generated by radiation pressure on the sail.

SOLUTION

Let $\bar{S}_{\text{E}}$ be the solar radiation intensity just above Earth's atmosphere. When the spacecraft is at a distance r from the Sun, the solar intensity at this distance, $\bar{S}(r)$, can be related to $\bar{S}_{\text{E}}$ using Equation (26-29):

$$\bar{S}(r) = \bar{S}_{\text{E}}\left(\frac{r_{\text{E}}^2}{r^2}\right)$$

where r_{E} is the distance between Earth and the Sun. Assuming that all incident radiation is reflected, the radiation pressure at the distance r from the Sun is

$$P_{\text{rad}}(r) = \frac{2\bar{S}(r)}{c}$$

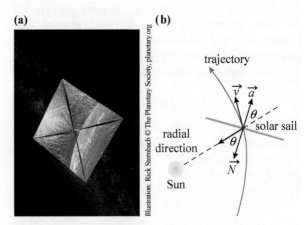

Figure 26-26 (a) The IKAROS solar sail (b) The orientation of the solar sail with respect to the Sun. The normal to the sail ($\vec{N}$) makes an angle θ with respect to the radial direction. The red curve shows the trajectory of the spacecraft.

For a solar sail with cross-sectional area A perpendicular to the incident radiation, the magnitude of the force exerted by the radiation is

$$F_{\text{rad}}(r) = A \times P_{\text{rad}}(r) = \frac{2A\bar{S}(r)}{c}$$

For a general trajectory (Figure 26-26(b)), the sail makes an angle θ with respect to the radial direction between the Sun and the spacecraft. So, the effective area perpendicular to the direction of the incident radiation is $A \cos\theta$ (normal incidence corresponds to $\theta = 0°$). The magnitude of acceleration generated by the radiation pressure is

$$a(r) = \frac{F_{rad}(r)}{m} = \bar{S}_E \left(\frac{r_E^2}{r^2}\right) \frac{2(A \cos\theta)}{mc} \cos\theta$$

where m is the total mass of the spacecraft.

The extra factor of $\cos\theta$ is due to the fact that the acceleration is directed perpendicular to the plane of the sail, at an angle θ with respect to the radial direction.

Let us assume that $r = r_E$, $\theta = 0°$ (normal incidence), and $\bar{S}_E = 1400$ W/m². Then the acceleration due to

radiation pressure when the spacecraft is close to Earth is approximately

$$a(r_E) = \frac{(1400 \text{ W/m}^2)2(200 \text{ m}^2)}{(315 \text{ kg})(3.00 \times 10^8 \text{ m/s})} = 5.9 \times 10^{-6} \text{ m/s}^2$$

Making sense of the result:

The acceleration from solar radiation is very small. The effects of gravity from Earth and the Sun would have to be included when calculating the trajectory of the spacecraft.

 CHECKPOINT

C-26-5 Solar Sail

Assume that the speed of the IKAROS spacecraft when it leaves the atmosphere is 7 km/s and that the acceleration due to solar radiation pressure remains constant at 6×10^{-6} m/s². How long would it take the spacecraft to double its speed?

(a) approximately 6 months
(b) between 5 and 10 years
(c) between 10 and 50 years
(d) over 100 years

C-26-5 (c)

LO 7

26-7 How Are Electromagnetic Waves Generated?

To generate electromagnetic waves, a source must lose energy. The waves carry this energy away from the source. Electromagnetic waves are generated during two types of processes: quantum-mechanical processes and acceleration of a charged particle.

Quantum-Mechanical Processes

When an electron in an atom makes a transition from a state of higher energy to a state of lower energy, it radiates the energy difference as electromagnetic waves. Infrared light, visible light, ultraviolet light, and X-rays can be generated by this process. We will discuss the process of emission of light from atoms in Chapter 31.

Protons and neutrons in a nucleus can also make transitions from a state of higher energy to a state of lower energy, emitting gamma rays in the process. We will discuss the process of emission of gamma rays from a nucleus in Chapter 33.

In matter–antimatter annihilation, a charged particle can combine with its antiparticle (which has an equal

but opposite charge), and the mass of both particles can be converted to energy in the form of electromagnetic radiation. Conversion of mass to energy is discussed in Chapter 29, but the details of annihilation processes are beyond the scope of this book.

Acceleration of a Charged Particle

Electromagnetic waves cannot be generated by stationary charges or charges that are moving with a constant velocity. A stationary charge has an electric field but no magnetic field. Therefore, it cannot generate an electromagnetic wave. The electric field of a stationary charge remains *attached* to the charge, never leaving it.

Now consider a charge moving with a constant velocity. In a frame of reference in which the charge is moving with a uniform velocity, it generates both electric and magnetic fields. However, in the frame of reference of the charge, the charge is at rest and therefore has only an electric field. So, in its own frame of reference, a charge cannot emit an electromagnetic wave. The laws of physics must be the same in all frames that move with a uniform velocity with respect to each other. So, if a charge cannot emit electromagnetic radiation in its own reference frame, it cannot emit electromagnetic radiation in any frame moving with uniform velocity with respect to the charge.

Thus, a charge can emit electromagnetic radiation in free space *only when accelerating*. Note the qualifier "in free space." A charge moving with a uniform velocity through a dielectric medium can emit electromagnetic radiation. Such radiation is called **Cerenkov radiation**.

We briefly discuss a few examples of electromagnetic radiation emitted during accelerated motion of charged particles.

A Charge (or an Electric Current) Undergoing Simple Harmonic Motion Simple harmonic motion is accelerated motion. Therefore, a charged particle or an electric current undergoing oscillatory motion emits electromagnetic waves. The frequency of the radiated wave is equal to the oscillation frequency of the motion. Harmonic motion of charges underlies the generation of electromagnetic waves for radio, TV, and other types of communication signals.

ELECTRICITY, MAGNETISM, AND OPTICS

A Charged Particle Moving in a Curved Orbit Motion along a curved path is accelerated motion. Therefore, a charged particle moving in a curved trajectory radiates electromagnetic waves, called **synchrotron radiation** or **cyclotron radiation**. The term "synchrotron radiation" is generally used for radiation emitted by a charged particle rapidly moving in a magnetic field. In the presence of a magnetic field, a charged particle experiences a force that is perpendicular to both the particle's velocity and the direction of the magnetic field. This force causes the particle to spiral in the direction of the magnetic field (Figure 26-27), continuously emitting electromagnetic radiation. Synchrotron radiation is also generated when fast-moving electrons spiral through the intense magnetic fields of astronomical objects.

A Charged Particle Stopping Abruptly When a fast-moving charged particle stops abruptly, it undergoes large deceleration and emits electromagnetic radiation. Such radiation is called **bremsstrahlung**, a German word meaning "braking radiation." The X-ray machine in a dentist's office generates X-rays by firing a beam of fast-moving electrons at a metal plate. When electrons collide with the plate, they come to an abrupt stop, emitting X-rays. The electrons actually follow a curved path as they decelerate, as shown in Figure 26-28. The electric fields of nuclei of the metal atoms deflect the electrons.

Figure 26-27 is shown with labels: magnetic field line, synchrotron radiation, spiraling electrons.

Ricky Leon Murphy, MSc (http://astronomyonline.org)

Figure 26-27 The spiral motion of a charged particle in a magnetic field generates synchrotron radiation.

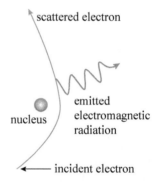

Figure 26-28 is shown with labels: scattered electron, emitted electromagnetic radiation, nucleus, incident electron.

Figure 26-28 An electron moving within the vicinity of a nucleus is deflected by the electric and magnetic forces between the two.

Half-Wave Dipole Antennas

A dipole antenna consists of two conducting metal wires (or rods) of equal length, separated by a narrow insulating gap. Dipole antennas can be used both for generating and receiving electromagnetic waves. To generate waves, the two wires are powered, often by connecting them to an RLC circuit as shown in Figure 26-29. (An RLC circuit is an electrical circuit consisting of a resistor, an inductor, and a capacitor.) The current and voltage in the wires vary sinusoidally with frequency f_0, the resonant frequency of the RLC circuit. The sinusoidal output of the RLC circuit forces electrons in the antenna to undergo harmonic motion, and the accelerated electrons emit electromagnetic waves at frequency f_0, which then propagate away from the antenna. The frequency of the emitted waves can be changed by changing the inductance or the capacitance in the RLC circuit.

For maximum efficiency, the total length of the antenna should be approximately half the wavelength of the electromagnetic waves emitted. So, for example, if the frequency of the RLC circuit is 98 MHz (which is approximately in the middle of the FM radio band in North America), the wavelength of the emitted waves is

$$\lambda_0 = \frac{c}{f_0} = \frac{3 \times 10^8 \text{ m/s}}{98 \times 10^6 \text{ Hz}} = 306 \text{ cm}$$

Therefore, the optimal total length of the antenna is 153 cm, and each wire would be approximately 75 cm long (depending on the length of the gap between the two wires). The exact length for the antenna is also affected by other factors, such as the thickness of the wires and the height of the antenna above the ground.

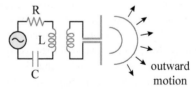

Figure 26-29 shows a circuit with R, L, C labels and outward motion arrows.

Figure 26-29 A dipole antenna connected to an RLC circuit emits electromagnetic waves at the resonant frequency of the RLC circuit.

26-8 Polarization

The **polarization** of a transverse wave at a given point is defined as the direction of oscillation of the wave at that point. For example, for the transverse wave moving along the string in Figure 26-30, the motion of the string is taken to be along the y-axis, so the wave is said to be polarized along the y-axis.

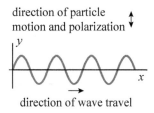

Figure 26-30 A wave on a string is polarized perpendicular to its direction of motion.

By convention, the polarization of electromagnetic waves is described by specifying the orientation of the wave's *electric* field at a given point over one time period. The electric field of the plane electromagnetic wave in Figure 26-31(a) is oriented along the y-axis, so the wave is polarized along the y-axis. When the electric field is oriented along a single line, the polarization is called **linear polarization**, and the wave is **linearly polarized**. The plane containing the electric field and the direction of motion of the wave is called the **plane of polarization**. The wave shown in Figure 26-31(a) is linearly polarized along the y-axis, and its plane of polarization is the yz-plane.

Since the electric and magnetic fields of electromagnetic waves are always perpendicular to the direction of motion, these waves are always polarized perpendicular to their direction of motion. Figure 26-31(b) shows a wave linearly polarized at an angle of $45°$ in the xy-plane.

✓ CHECKPOINT

C-26-6 Polarization

A linearly polarized electromagnetic wave is travelling along the x-axis, and its magnetic field is oscillating along the y-axis. Which of the following statements is correct?

(a) The wave is polarized along the y-axis, and its plane of polarization is the xy-plane.

(b) The wave is polarized along the x-axis, and its plane of polarization is the xy-plane.

(c) The wave is polarized along the z-axis, and its plane of polarization is the xz-plane.

(d) The wave is polarized along the y-axis, and its plane of polarization is the xz-plane.

C-26-6 (c) As the wave is moving along the x-axis the electric and magnetic fields are in y-z plane. Since the magnetic field is along the y-axis, the electric field must be along the z-axis. Therefore, the wave is polarized along the z-axis and its plane of polarization is the xz plane.

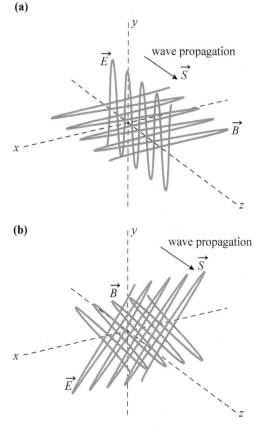

Figure 26-31 (a) A linearly polarized electromagnetic wave with its electric field along the y-axis (b) An electromagnetic wave linearly polarized at an angle of $45°$ in the xy-plane

Unpolarized Light

Light from the Sun and from a common light bulb consists of a large number of waves emitted by individual atoms. In general, an electromagnetic wave emitted by one atom has no correlation with the waves emitted by other atoms, and the electric fields of individual waves point in random directions. For example, in a 50 W light bulb, approximately 10^{19} atoms emit individual electromagnetic waves with randomly oriented electric fields every second. Such light is **unpolarized**. The electric field vector of unpolarized light consists of a random superposition of a very large number of linearly polarized waves (Figure 26-32).

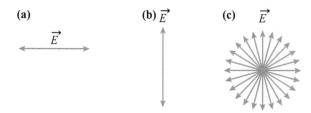

Figure 26-32 (a) An electromagnetic wave polarized along the x-axis (b) An electromagnetic wave polarized along the y-axis (c) An unpolarized electromagnetic wave consisting of random superposition of linearly polarized waves. The waves are travelling perpendicular to the page.

ELECTRICITY, MAGNETISM, AND OPTICS

Polarization by Absorption

We can produce polarized light from a beam of unpolarized light by filtering out all but one of the polarizations. **Polarizers** are materials that allow the electric field only with a particular orientation to pass through. The electric field of the transmitted light is oriented in that direction and is therefore polarized.

A commonly used polarizer is Polaroid film, which is a flexible, plastic sheet made of polyvinyl alcohol (PVA). The sheet is heated and stretched to align the PVA molecules into long, parallel rows. The sheet is then dipped into an iodine dye. The iodine atoms, which have loosely bound outer electrons, bond to the long chains of PVA molecules, making them conductive. The PVA chains can then act as long, extremely thin, closely spaced metal wires. When unpolarized light falls on the plastic film, the electric field of the light exerts a force on the free-moving iodine electrons. The electrons can move along the length of the stretched chains of molecules, so the component of the electric field that is parallel to the direction of these chains is easily absorbed by the electrons. However, the iodine electrons cannot readily move perpendicular to the stretched chains and therefore cannot absorb the component of the electric field in this direction. Consequently, this perpendicular component of the electric field passes through the material. The direction along which the electric field is transmitted is called the **transmission axis**, or **polarizing axis**. Note that the transmission axis of Polaroid film is perpendicular to the axis of long-chained molecules.

Figure 26-33 shows unpolarized light incident on a polarizer that lies in the plane of the page. The red arrow shows the direction of the electric field, $\vec{E}$, of one of the randomly polarized light waves. The transmission axis of the polarizer is along the y-axis, and the electric field makes an angle θ with respect to the transmission axis. The electric field can be resolved into a component along the transmission axis ($E_y = E\cos\theta$) and a component perpendicular to the transmission axis ($E_x = E\sin\theta$). Only the E_y component passes through the polarizer.

When a polarized beam of light passes through a polarizer, the intensity of the transmitted light depends on the angle between the light's initial polarization direction and the transmission axis of the polarizer. Let I_0 be the intensity of a polarized beam of light that falls on a polarizer. We denote the angle between the polarization direction of the light and the transmission axis of the polarizer as θ and the intensity of light that is transmitted through the polarizer as $I(\theta)$. Then

KEY EQUATION
$$I(\theta) = I_0 \cos^2\theta \qquad (26\text{-}36)$$

This relationship was discovered experimentally by Étienne-Louis Malus in 1809 and is called the **Malus' Law**. We can derive Malus' law from the properties of electromagnetic waves.

Consider the arrangement shown in Figure 26-34. A beam of unpolarized light is incident on polarizer P_1, which polarizes the light along its transmission axis. Let the amplitude of the electric field that is transmitted through P_1 be E_0, and the intensity of the transmitted light be I_0. A second polarizer, P_2 (called an **analyzer**), is placed in front of the polarized beam with its polarization axis at an angle θ with respect to the transmission axis of P_1. The amplitude of the electric field transmitted through P_2 is $E_0 \cos\theta$. The intensity of light is proportional to the square of the amplitude of the electric field (Equation (26-27)); therefore, the intensity of the light transmitted through P_2 is

$$I(\theta) = \frac{1}{2}c\varepsilon_0(E_0\cos\theta)^2 = \left(\frac{1}{2}c\varepsilon_0 E_0^2\right)\cos^2\theta$$
$$= I_0\cos^2\theta \qquad (26\text{-}37)$$

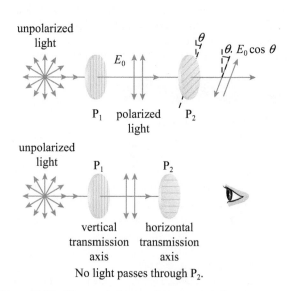

Figure 26-34 When an electromagnetic wave passes through a polarizer, only the component of the electric field that is parallel to the transmission axis of the polarizer is transmitted. The component that is perpendicular to the transmission axis is blocked.

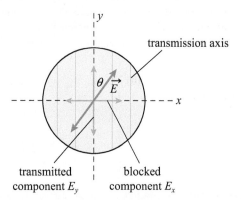

Figure 26-33 Only the component of the electric field that is parallel to the transmission axis of the polarizer is transmitted. The component that is perpendicular to the transmission axis is blocked.

Note these consequences of Malus' law (see Figure 26-34):

■ When the polarizing axes of two polarizers are parallel to each other ($\theta = 0°$ or $\theta = 180°$), the intensity of the light passing through the analyzer remains I_0. The analyzer does not block any light that is polarized along its transmission axis.

■ When the polarizing axes of two polarizers are perpendicular to each other ($\theta = 90°$), the intensity of the light passing through the analyzer is zero. The analyzer completely blocks the light that is polarized perpendicular to its transmission axis.

 CHECKPOINT

C-26-7 Malus' Law

A beam of light is polarized along the vertical axis and passes through two polarizers. The transmission axis of the first polarizer (P_1) is inclined at 45° with respect to the light's polarization direction. The transmission axis of the second polarizer (P_2) is inclined at 45° with respect to P_1 so that it is perpendicular to the polarization direction of the incident beam. The intensity of the initial beam is I_0. What is the intensity of the beam after it passes through P_2?

(a) zero (b) $\dfrac{I_0}{4}$ (c) $\dfrac{I_0}{2}$ (d) I_0

C-26-7 (c) The transmission axes of the two polarizers are inclined at 45° and $\cos(45°) = 1/\sqrt{2}$.

Polarization by Reflection

A wave travelling in a medium divides into two parts when it encounters the boundary of another medium. The part that is reflected into the original medium is called the **reflected wave**. The part that is transmitted into the second medium is the **transmitted wave**. The plane containing the direction of the incident wave and the normal to the surface between the two media is called the **plane of incidence** (Figure 26-35).

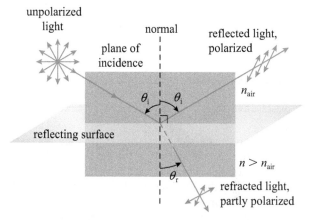

Figure 26-35 The incident, reflected, and transmitted waves at the boundary between two media. Here θ_i is the angle of incidence with respect to the normal to the reflecting surface and θ_r is the angle of refraction.

Consider a beam of unpolarized light incident at an angle to the surface of a flat glass plate in air. The electric field of the incident beam can be resolved into two components: one in the plane of incidence and the other

EXAMPLE 26-6

Beam Intensity Through Two Polarizers

A beam of unpolarized light, with intensity I_0, is incident on a polarizer with a vertical transmission axis. The beam then passes through a second polarizer, the transmission axis of which is at an angle of 60° to the vertical.

(a) What is the intensity of the light after it passes through the first polarizer?
(b) What is the intensity of the beam that emerges from the second polarizer in terms of I_0?

SOLUTION

(a) We can resolve the electric field of the unpolarized light into two perpendicular components. We choose one component to be in the vertical direction and the other component to be in the horizontal direction. For unpolarized light, these two components have equal magnitudes. When the light passes through the first

polarizer, the vertical component is transmitted and the horizontal component is absorbed. Therefore, half the incident intensity passes through the first polarizer:

$$I_1 = \frac{I_0}{2}$$

(b) The light that passes through the first polarizer is linearly polarized. We can now apply Malus' law to find its intensity after transmission through the second polarizer:

$$I_2 = I_1(\cos(60°))^2 = \frac{I_0}{2} \times \left(\frac{1}{2}\right)^2 = \frac{I_0}{8}$$

Making sense of the result:

Only 12.5% of the initial intensity emerges from the second polarizer.

perpendicular to it, as shown in Figure 26-36. For unpolarized light, both components have the same amplitude.

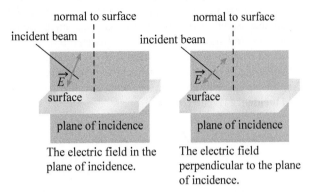

The electric field in the plane of incidence.

The electric field perpendicular to the plane of incidence.

Figure 26-36 The electric field of the incident beam of light can be resolved into a component in the plane of incidence (the plane of the page) and a component perpendicular to the plane of incidence.

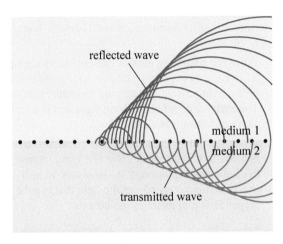

Figure 26-37 When subjected to an incident electromagnetic wave the atomic electrons at the interface of two surfaces act as sources of spherical electromagnetic waves that form the reflected and the transmitted waves.

The reflected and transmitted waves are generated by electrons on the surface of the glass plate. The incident electric field exerts an oscillatory force on the electrons, causing them to oscillate. Each oscillating electron becomes a source of electromagnetic waves that propagate outward, forming the reflected and transmitted waves (Figure 26-37).

When an incident wave hits the surface of the glass plate, the component of the electric field perpendicular to the plane of incidence lies in the plane of the glass plate. Electrons oscillating in response to the perpendicular component do so in the plane of the plate; they therefore radiate in a direction perpendicular to the surface of the plate. Hence, the electric field of this part of the reflected and transmitted waves is polarized perpendicular to the plane of incidence.

The component of the electric field that is in the plane of incidence is perpendicular to the surface of the glass plate. Electrons responding to this component oscillate perpendicular to the surface of the glass plate and therefore emit radiation in the plane of the plate (like waves propagating on the surface of a pond when a stone is thrown into it). Virtually all of this radiation transmits into the body of the glass plate. Therefore, the transmitted wave has an electric field with substantial components parallel and perpendicular to the plane of incidence, and the reflected wave is predominantly polarized perpendicular to the plane of incidence (Figure 26-36).

Maxwell's Equations

Maxwell discovered that a varying electric flux produces a magnetic field. To incorporate this phenomenon, he added a displacement current term, $\varepsilon_0 \dfrac{d\Phi_E}{dt}$, to Ampère's law.

Maxwell's equations describe how electric charges, electric currents, electric fields, and magnetic fields interact with each other; the equations also predict the existence of travelling electromagnetic waves.

Properties of Electromagnetic Waves

Electromagnetic waves sustain themselves once generated, travel in a vacuum at the speed of light, and have electric and magnetic fields in phase with each other with amplitudes related by $E_0 = cB_0$.

In a travelling electromagnetic wave, the electric field, the magnetic field, and the direction of motion of the wave are all perpendicular to each other.

Electromagnetic waves span a broad spectrum, from very large to extremely small wavelengths. Radio waves, TV waves, microwaves, infrared radiation, visible light, ultraviolet radiation, X-rays, and gamma rays are all electromagnetic waves.

Electromagnetic waves are generated by quantum-mechanical processes and by accelerating charged particles.

Electromagnetic waves carry energy and momentum. The rate at which energy is transported per unit area per unit time is called the energy flux or intensity. The Poynting vector, $\vec{S}$, describes the magnitude of energy flux and the direction of the energy flow in electromagnetic waves:

$$\vec{S} = \frac{1}{\mu_0} \vec{E} \times \vec{B} \qquad (26\text{-}29)$$

The average intensity flow in one cycle is given by the time-averaged energy flux, $\bar{S}$:

$$\bar{S} = \frac{E_0 B_0}{2\mu_0}$$

In an electromagnetic wave, the energy density of the electric field is equal to the energy density of the magnetic field.

The intensity of a three-dimensional spherical wave varies inversely as the square of the distance from the source.

Electromagnetic waves exert radiation pressure on objects:

$$P_{\text{rad}} = \frac{\bar{S}}{c} \text{ (when absorbed)} \qquad (26\text{-}34)$$

$$P_{\text{rad}} = 2\frac{\bar{S}}{c} \text{ (when reflected)} \qquad (26\text{-}35)$$

Polarization describes the orientation of the electric field of an electromagnetic wave. The plane of polarization is a plane that contains the direction of motion of the wave and the direction of the electric field of the wave.

When polarized light with intensity I_0 falls on a polarizer, which has its transmission axis inclined at an angle θ with respect to the direction of polarization of the incident light, the intensity of the emitted light, I_1, is related to I_0 by Malus' law:

$$I_1 = I_0 \cos^2 \theta \qquad (26\text{-}36)$$

APPLICATIONS

Applications: wireless communications, astronomical research, food preservation, security, GPS, UV index, medical applications

Key Terms: average intensity, bremsstrahlung, Cerenkov radiation, cyclotron radiation, displacement current, electromagnetic field, electromagnetic spectrum, electromagnetic wave, energy flux, far infrared, fluorescence, hard X-rays, intensity, irradiance, linear polarizer, linearly polarized, Malus' law, Maxwell's equations, momentum density, near infrared, plane of incidence, plane of polarization, polarization axis, polarization, polarizer, Poynting vector, radiation momentum, radiation pressure, radio astronomy, radiograph, reflected wave, soft X-rays, synchrotron radiation, thermograms, transmission axis, transmitted wave, unpolarized, visible spectrum

QUESTIONS

1. Explain why a displacement current is needed to explain the propagation of electromagnetic waves.
2. An electromagnetic wave is travelling along the positive z-axis. If at a given instant and position the magnetic field is pointing along the negative y-axis, the electric field at that instant and position points along the
   (a) negative y-axis;
   (b) positive y-axis;
   (c) negative x-axis;
   (d) positive x-axis.
3. Which of the following sets of equations for electric and magnetic fields do *not* represent a travelling electromagnetic wave? Why not?

   (a) $\vec{E}(x, t) = E_0 \sin(x - ct)\vec{z}$; $\quad \vec{B}(x, t) = \dfrac{E_0}{c} \sin(x - ct)\vec{z}$

   (b) $\vec{E}(x, t) = E_0 \sin(x - ct)\vec{z}$; $\quad \vec{B}(x, t) = \dfrac{E_0}{c} \sin(x - ct)\vec{y}$

   (c) $\vec{E}(x, t) = E_0 \sin(x - ct)\vec{y}$; $\quad \vec{B}(x, t) = \dfrac{E_0}{c} \cos(x - ct)\vec{z}$

   (d) $\vec{E}(x, t) = E_0 \sin(x - ct)\vec{y}$; $\quad \vec{B}(x, t) = E_0 \sin(x - ct)\vec{z}$

4. Give several examples of electromagnetic waves from very large to very small frequencies. Compare and contrast your examples.
5. Compare and contrast sound and electromagnetic waves.
6. (a) A dipole antenna transmits electromagnetic waves at a frequency of 1130 kHz. Determine the length of the antenna.
   (b) A dipole antenna transmits radio waves at a frequency of 98.8 MHz. Determine the length of the antenna.
7. Describe various ways that a charged particle can emit electromagnetic radiation.
8. Unpolarized light is incident on two polarizers (Figure 26-34). Their transmission axes are oriented so that no light is transmitted through the second polarizer. A third polarizer with its transmission axis oriented at 45° with respect to that of the first polarizer is inserted between the two. Can the light now pass through the second polarizer? Explain your reasoning.
9. Can an isolated charged particle move in a circular orbit of constant radius while emitting electromagnetic radiation? Explain your reasoning.
10. Can a laser beam be used to levitate a small and perfectly reflecting object? Explain your reasoning.
11. Is the radiation pressure greater on a surface that absorbs all incident radiation or a surface that is a perfect reflector? Explain your reasoning.

PROBLEMS BY SECTION

For problems, star ratings will be used, (✶, ✶✶, or ✶✶✶), with more stars meaning more challenging problems.

Section 26-2   The Displacement Current and Maxwell's Equations

12. ✶ A uniform electric field is increasing at a rate of 2.0×10^6 V/m·s. What is the displacement current through an area of 5.0×10^{-4} m² that is perpendicular to the direction of the field?

13. ✶ A parallel-plate capacitor has circular plates of radius 0.01 m each that are 0.10 m apart. The capacitor is being charged at a rate of 100 V/m·s. What is the displacement current in the capacitor?
14. ✶✶ Circular plates of a capacitor are 5.0 cm in radius, 2.0 mm apart, and have air between them. The voltage across the plates is changing at a rate of 60.0 V/s. Determine
    (a) the rate of change of the electric field between the plates;
    (b) the displacement current between the plates.
15. ✶ A uniform displacement current of magnitude 1.00 A, directed out of the plane of the paper, passes through a circular region of radius 5.00 cm. Determine the magnitude of the magnetic field due to the displacement current at the radial distances (a) 2.00 cm and (b) 10.00 cm.
16. ✶✶ A parallel-plate capacitor with circular plates of radius 10 cm is being charged. Consider a circular loop of radius 20 cm centred at the central axis of the plates. The displacement current through the loop is 1.0 A. What is the rate of change of the magnitude of the electric field between the plates?
17. ✶✶ A 100 pF capacitor has circular plates of 10.0 cm radius that are 5.0 mm apart and have air between them. The capacitor is charged by connecting it to a 12.0 V battery through a 1.0 Ω resistor.
    (a) Determine the current through the plates at $t = 0$ (when the battery is connected).
    (b) What is the current through the plates at $t = 60$ s?
    (c) Determine the rate at which the electric field between the plates changes at $t = 0$ and at $t = 60$ s.
    (d) Determine the magnetic field between the plates at $t = 0$ and at $t = 60$ s.
18. ✶✶ The rate of change of a uniform electric field through a region of space is shown in Figure 26-38. Determine the displacement current through a 0.25 m² area perpendicular to the direction of the electric field during the time intervals $0 < t < 12$, $12 < t < 22$, and $22 < t < 30$, where t is in milliseconds.

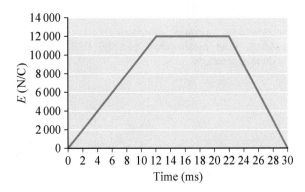

Figure 26-38   Problem 18

Section 26-3   Electromagnetic Waves

19. ✶ Determine the direction of propagation of the electromagnetic wave for each of the following cases.
    (a) $\vec{E}$ is in the z-direction; $\vec{B}$ is in the x-direction.
    (b) $\vec{E}$ is in the y-direction; $\vec{B}$ is in the x-direction.
    (c) $\vec{E}$ is in the x-direction; $\vec{B}$ is in the y-direction.
    (d) $\vec{E}$ is in the z-direction; $\vec{B}$ is in the x-direction.

20. ✳ The amplitude of the magnetic field of an electromagnetic wave is 2.0×10^{-2} T. What is the amplitude of the electric field of the electromagnetic wave? If the magnetic field is pointing along the positive z-axis, what are the possible directions of the electric field?

21. ✳ What is the amplitude of the magnetic field of an electromagnetic wave that has a electric field of amplitude 5.0×10^{-3} V/m? When the magnetic field is pointing along the positive x-axis, what are the possible directions of the electric field?

22. ✳ The electric field of an electromagnetic wave in a vacuum is given by

$$\vec{E}(x, t) = (100 \text{ V/m}) \sin(2.00 \times 10^9 x - \omega t)\hat{z}$$

(a) What are the wavelength and frequency of this wave?
(b) Write an equation for $\vec{B}(x, t)$.
(c) In which direction is the wave travelling?

23. ✳ The magnetic field of an electromagnetic wave is given by

$$\vec{B}(x, t) = (5.0 \times 10^{-6} \text{ T}) \sin(4.00 \times 10^9 x - \omega t)\hat{k}$$

(a) Determine the wavelength and the frequency of the wave.
(b) What is the amplitude of the wave's electric field?
(c) Write an the equation for $\vec{E}(x, t)$.
(d) What is the direction of propagation of the wave?

24. ✳ A plane electromagnetic wave with a wavelength of 500 nm is travelling in the positive x-direction, and its electric field points along the z-axis. The amplitude of the electric field is 2.0 V/m. Write the equations for the electric and magnetic fields of this wave as a function of position and time.

25. ✳ A sinusoidal electromagnetic field is travelling in the $+y$-direction. At a certain position and time its electric field has a magnitude of 1.0 V/m and is pointing along the $-x$-direction. What are the magnitude and direction of the wave's magnetic field at that position and location?

26. ✳ The electric field of an electromagnetic wave is given by

$$\vec{E}(y, t) = (5.0 \text{ V/m}) \sin\left(\frac{2\pi}{10^6} y - 2\pi f t\right)\hat{i}$$

(a) Determine the frequency of the wave.
(b) In which direction is the wave travelling?
(c) Write an equation for $\vec{B}(y, t)$.

Section 26-4 The Electromagnetic Spectrum

27. ✳ Rank the following electromagnetic waves in the order of their frequencies from smallest to largest: infrared light, gamma rays, yellow light, blue light, microwaves, and X-rays.

28. ✳ What is the wavelength of gamma rays that have a frequency of 10^{20} Hz?

29. ✳ Determine the frequency of light of wavelengths (a) 450 nm, (b) 533 nm, and (c) 700 nm.

30. ✳ Which of the following combinations of wavelength and frequency are not allowed for electromagnetic waves in a vacuum? Why? For the speed of light, use $c = 3.0 \times 10^8$ m/s.
(a) $\lambda = 100.0$ m; $f = 3.0 \times 10^6$ Hz
(b) $\lambda = 0.1$ m; $f = 3.0 \times 10^8$ Hz
(c) $\lambda = 6.0 \times 10^{-7}$ m; $f = 5.0 \times 10^{14}$ Hz
(d) $\lambda = 2.0 \times 10^{-15}$ m; $f = 3.0 \times 10^{-23}$ Hz

Sections 26-5 and 26-6 Energy and Momentum of Electromagnetic Waves, and Radiation Pressure

31. ✳ A 100 W point source produces light with a wavelength of 550 nm. Determine the amplitudes of the electric and magnetic fields of the light at (a) 10 m, (b) 100 m, and (c) 10^5 m from the source. What is the intensity of the electromagnetic wave at the three distances?

32. ✳ The intensity of the sunlight on top of Earth's atmosphere is approximately 1400 W/m². Calculate the amplitudes of the electric and magnetic fields corresponding to this intensity.

33. ✳ A laser beam delivers 0.10 J/m² of energy in 5.0 s to a surface that is placed normal to the direction of motion of the beam. What is the irradiance of the beam?

34. ✳✳ A laser pointer has a radius of 2.0 mm and delivers 3.2×10^{-3} W of power.
(a) What is the intensity of the laser light?
(b) For a beam length of 5.0 m, how much energy is contained in the beam?

35. ✳ The cosmic microwave background (CMB) radiation is the electromagnetic radiation that is left over from the Big Bang and fills the universe. It has an average energy density of 4×10^{-14} J/m³. What are the peak values (i.e., the amplitudes) of the electric and magnetic fields of the CMB radiation?

36. ✳✳ The National Ignition Facility in California fired the world's most powerful laser in March 2012. The pulse from the laser lasted for 23×10^{-9} s and delivered 4.11×10^{14} W of power.
(a) What was the total energy delivered by the laser?
(b) What were the amplitudes of the electric and magnetic fields?
(c) If the laser beam was focused on an area of 1.0 mm², what was the radiation pressure on this area?

37. ✳ The irradiance at 1.0 m from a light bulb is 2.0 W/m². What is the irradiance from this bulb at a distance of 5.0 m?

38. ✳ A point source emits lights uniformly in all directions. At 10.0 m from the source, the electric field strength of the light is 50 N/C. Determine the average power emitted by the source.

39. ✳ The average solar power that reaches Earth's surface is 1000 W/m². What is the magnitude of the force exerted by the sunlight on a free electron that is moving with a speed of 1.1×10^5 m/s?

40. ✳✳✳ Radiation pressure of a laser beam can be used to levitate a small particle. What should be the minimum power of a laser beam to levitate a particle of mass 1.0×10^{-6} kg? Assume that the beam is totally reflected from the particle and that the cross-sectional area of the particle is greater than the cross-sectional area of the beam.

41. ✳✳ Photovoltaic cells convert electromagnetic radiation into electricity. A solar panel consists of an assembly of photovoltaic cells (Figure 26-39). A typical efficiency of these cells is approximately 15%, which means that 15% of the incident radiation is converted into electricity. For solar panels that cover an area of 16 m² on the roof of a house, how many kilowatt hours of energy will the panels generate in one year? Assume that the average solar intensity at Earth's surface is approximately 200 W/m². This takes into account the fact that Earth represents a disk of radius 6370 km to the incoming sunlight and that a fraction of the incident energy is either absorbed or reflected by the atmosphere.

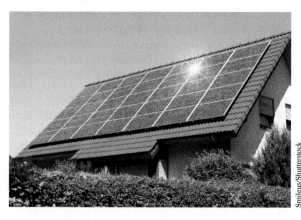

Figure 26-39 Problem 41. Solar panels on a rooftop

42. ✳✳ A sinusoidal electromagnetic wave from a satellite passes perpendicularly through a window with a cross-sectional area of 0.75 m². The amplitude of the electric field of the wave entering the window is 4.0×10^{-3} V/m. How much energy passes through the window in one hour?

43. ✳✳ A laser has a power of 5.00 mW and produces a spot with a radius of 1.00 mm on a white screen.
   (a) What is the intensity of the laser light on the spot?
   (b) When all the light reflects from the white screen, what are the radiation pressure and the magnitude of the force exerted by the light on the screen?

44. ✳✳ The power emitted by the Sun is approximately 3.8×10^{26} W.
   (a) What is the average intensity of the Sun's electromagnetic waves at Earth's location? (The average distance between the Sun and Earth is approximately 1.5×10^{11} m.)
   (b) What is the radiation pressure exerted on Earth by the sunlight?

Section 26-8 Polarization

45. ✳ An electromagnetic wave is moving in the direction of the positive *x*-axis. At a given instant the magnetic field of the wave is pointing toward the negative *z*-axis. What is the direction of polarization of the wave?

46. ✳ In a certain setup, light is polarized in the vertical direction, and only 75% of the incident light is transmitted through the polarizer. What angle does the transmission axis of the polarizer make with the vertical?

47. ✳ In a certain setup, light is polarized in the horizontal direction, and only 25% of the incident light is transmitted through the polarizer. What angle does the transmission axis of the polarizer make with the vertical?

48. ✳ Linearly polarized light is incident on a polarizer (see Figure 26-33). The intensity of the incident light is 1.0 W/m². Calculate the intensity of the transmitted light when the angle between the transmission axis and the direction of the electric field is (a) 30°, (b) 60°, and (c) 90°.

49. ✳ Unpolarized light passes through two polarizers (see Figure 26-34), and the transmission axis is inclined at an angle of 45° with respect to each other. The initial light has an intensity of 1.0 W/m². What is the intensity of the light that emerges from the second polarizer?

50. ✳✳ Linearly polarized light with an intensity of 5.0 W/m² passes through two polarizers. The transmission axis of the first polarizer is inclined at 45°, and the transmission axis of the second polarizer is inclined at 90° with respect to the polarization direction. What is the intensity of the transmitted light?

51. ✳✳ The transmission axes of two polarizers are inclined at 90° with respect to each other. For the following cases, determine the ratio of incident to transmitted intensity of the light that passes through the two polarizers.
   (a) The initial light is unpolarized.
   (b) The initial light is linearly polarized with its polarization axis along the transmission axis of the first polarizer it encounters.
   (c) The initial light is linearly polarized with its polarization axis perpendicular to the transmission axis of the first polarizer it encounters.
   (d) The initial light is linearly polarized with its polarization axis inclined at 45° with respect to the transmission axis of the first polarizer it encounters.

52. ✳✳ Vertically polarized light is incident on two polarizers, as shown in Figure 26-40. The transmission axis is indicated by the solid black line. The incident intensity is 5.0 W/m². Calculate the transmitted intensity for each configuration.

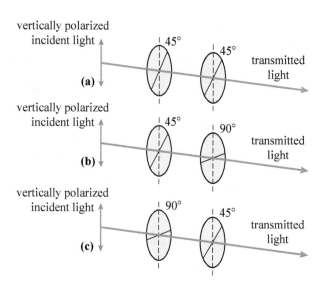

Figure 26-40 Problem 52

53. ✳✳ Unpolarized light from a laser is incident on three polarizers, as shown in Figure 26-41. The intensity of the incident light is I_0. Determine the intensity of the light at points A, B, and C.

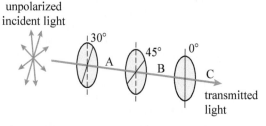

Figure 26-41 Problems 53 and 54

54. ✳✳ Consider the transmission of unpolarized light through three polarizers (Figure 26-41). Determine the ratio of incident to transmitted intensity for the following combinations of the directions of the transmission axes of the polarizers. The angles are with respect to the horizontal direction.
(a) 90°; 45°; 0°
(b) 90°; 45°; 90°
(c) 90°; 0°; 45°
(d) 0°; 45°; 45°

55. ✳✳✳ Five identical polarizers are placed in a straight line next to each other with their transmission axes inclined at angles θ, 2θ, 3θ, 4θ, and 5θ from left to right, with respect to the vertical direction. Unpolarized light is incident from the left. What must the angle θ be so that only 10% of the incident light is transmitted through the polarizers?

COMPREHENSIVE PROBLEMS

56. ✳✳✳ Two identical circular disks of radius 1.00 cm and mass 2.00 g each are attached to the opposite ends of a thin wire of length 10.0 cm and mass 1.00 g. The wire is free to rotate about an axis that passes through its centre (Figure 26-42). One of the disks is coloured black to absorb all the incident radiation, and the other disk is a perfect reflector. The arrangement is placed in the sunlight, which falls perpendicular on one face of each disk.
(a) Will the wire rotate in the presence of the sunlight? Explain your reasoning.

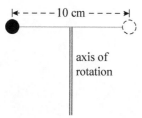

Figure 26-42 Problem 56

(b) If yes, determine the angular acceleration of the wire.
(c) Will the wire rotate if both disks are perfect reflectors or coloured black? Ignore the effect of air drag in this problem. The intensity of the sunlight is 1000 W/m².

57. ✳✳✳ As a comet approaches the Sun, the solar radiation causes some materials within the comet to vaporize and form an atmosphere around the comet. The force due to solar radiation pressure pushes lighter particles in the atmosphere away from the Sun, forming a tail (Figure 26-43). Assume that the particles in the comet's atmosphere are spherical and have a density of 2500 kg/m³.
(a) For what size would the force due to radiation pressure be equal to the gravitational force of the Sun on a particle? Assume that a particle reflects all incident radiation.
(b) What would happen to the particles smaller than the size you calculated in part (a)? Would you expect the comet's tail to become longer as the comet approaches the Sun?

Figure 26-43 Problem 57. Comet Hyakutake

See the text online resources at www.physics1e.nelson.com for Open Problems and Data-Rich Problems related to this chapter.

Learning Objectives

When you have completed this chapter you should be able to:

1. Understand nuclear terminology, including atomic mass number, atomic number, nucleon, nuclide, isotopes, isobars, isotones, and atomic mass.

2. Calculate the size and density of nuclei, and describe the properties of the strong force.

3. Calculate nuclear binding energies from nuclear masses and vice versa, and calculate atomic masses and average nuclear masses.

4. Calculate radioactive decay rates.

5. Explain what a Q-value is, and calculate Q-values for simple nuclear reactions.

6. Explain alpha, beta, and gamma radiation.

7. Explain nuclear fission and fusion, and calculate the energy released during nuclear fission and fusion reactions.

8. Explain the difference between the absorbed dose and the equivalent dose of radiation, and calculate the daily equivalent dose of radiation for various radioactive materials.

9. Describe some common applications of nuclear physics.

For additional Making Connections, Examples, and Checkpoints, as well as activities and experiments to help increase your understanding of the chapter's concepts, please go to the text's online resources at www.physics1e.nelson.com.

Chapter 33
Introduction to Nuclear Physics

On March 11, 2011, a 9.0 magnitude earthquake struck off the northeast coast of Japan near the city of Fukushima. The earthquake was followed by a 14 m-high tsunami that devastated the coastal area. The tsunami flooded the buildings that housed the six nuclear reactors at the Fukushima 1 Power Plant, causing the emergency generators and cooling systems to fail. Although three of the reactors had been shut down for maintenance, the other three overheated catastrophically (Figure 33-1). Two of the reactor cores melted, and hydrogen gas produced by the high temperatures caused massive explosions that destroyed the outer containment buildings and damaged the vessels containing the nuclear fuel. Radioactive cesium, iodine, strontium, and barium were released into the air, forcing the evacuation of the surrounding area. Today, there is still concern over possible radioactive contamination of food and water supplies.

How do nuclear reactors generate energy? What is radioactivity, and why is it harmful? How does radioactive cesium differ from ordinary cesium? This chapter introduces nuclear physics and examines some of the applications and dangers of nuclear technology.

Figure 33-1 Smoke billowing from the damaged nuclear reactors at Fukushima

DigitalGlobe/Contributor/Getty Images

33-1 Nuclear Terminology and Nuclear Units

As described in Chapter 30, experiments by Ernest Rutherford and others at the beginning of the 20th century determined that all the positive charge in an atom and most of the mass of an atom are localized in an extremely small central region called the nucleus. Later research showed that nuclei are made up of positively charged particles called **protons** and electrically neutral particles called **neutrons**. A neutron is slightly more massive than a proton, and both particles have about 1840 times the mass of an electron (see Table 33-2). The charge of a proton is $+1.602 \times 10^{-19}$ C, which is equal and opposite to the charge of an electron. An atom has an equal number of protons and electrons. The number of protons in a nucleus is called the **atomic number**, Z. For example, a carbon nucleus has six protons. Therefore, the atomic number of carbon is 6. The chemistry of an element is determined by its atomic number.

The number of neutrons in a nucleus is called the **neutron number**, N. The total number of protons and neutrons in a nucleus is called the **mass number**, A. By definition,

$$A = Z + N \tag{33-1}$$

Each element in the periodic table has a fixed number of protons and is represented by a symbol. For example, helium has $Z = 2$ and is represented by the symbol He, and iron has $Z = 26$ and is represented by the symbol Fe. In general, a nucleus is represented by a symbol with the form $^A_Z X$, where

X = the symbol for the element
Z = the atomic number of the element
A = the mass number of the element

For a given atomic number, Z, the number of neutrons in a nucleus may vary. Atoms with the same number of protons but a different number of neutrons are called the **isotopes** of an element. Isotopes have different masses because they contain a different number of neutrons. For example, naturally occurring carbon has three isotopes, as listed in Table 33-1.

Nuclei that have the same number of neutrons but a different number of protons are called **isotones**. Nuclei that have the same mass number, A, but a different number of protons and neutrons are called **isobars**. The term **nuclide** refers to a nucleus with any number of protons and neutrons.

✓ CHECKPOINT

C-33-1 Nuclei with Properties in Common

Identify the isotopes, isotones, and isobars in the following set of nuclei:

$$^{16}_8O;\ ^{15}_6C;\ ^{14}_7N;\ ^{18}_9F;\ ^{20}_{10}Ne;\ ^{15}_7N;\ ^{18}_8O.$$

C-33-1 Isotopes: $^{16}_8O$, $^{18}_8O$; $^{15}_7N$, $^{14}_7N$; Isotones: $^{15}_6C$, $^{18}_9F$; $^{16}_8O$, $^{15}_7N$; $^{18}_8O$, $^{20}_{10}Ne$; Isobars: $^{18}_9F$, $^{18}_8O$.

Units for Nuclear Quantities

The size of a nucleus is of the order of 10^{-15} m. Therefore, in the study of nuclear physics, a convenient unit of length to use is the femtometre (symbol fm). A femtometre is also called a fermi in honour of Italian American physicist Enrico Fermi:

$$1\ \text{fm} = 10^{-15}\,\text{m}$$

When dealing with energies involved in nuclear processes, a convenient unit to use is mega (million) electron volts:

$$1\ \text{MeV} = 10^6\,\text{eV}$$

The Atomic Mass Unit (u) An atomic mass unit (u) is defined as exactly 1/12 of the rest mass of one atom of the isotope $^{12}_6C$:

$$1\ \text{u} = 1.6605 \times 10^{-24}\,\text{g} = 1.6605 \times 10^{-27}\,\text{kg} \tag{33-2}$$

Table 33-1 Isotopes of carbon

Isotope name	Symbol	Atomic number, Z	Neutron number, N	Occurrence in nature
Carbon-12	$^{12}_6C$	6	6	98.93%
Carbon-13	$^{13}_6C$	6	7	1.07%
Carbon-14	$^{14}_6C$	6	8	10^{-10}%

EXAMPLE 33-1

Molar Mass and Atomic Mass

How many atoms are in 12 g of $^{12}_{6}$C?

SOLUTION

Mass of one $^{12}_{6}$C atom = 12 u = $12 \times 1.6605 \times 10^{-24}$ g = 19.926×10^{-24} g

Number of atoms in 12 g of $^{12}_{6}$C = $\dfrac{12 \text{ g}}{19.926 \times 10^{-24} \text{ g}}$ = 6.022×10^{23}

Making sense of the result:

The answer, 6.022×10^{23}, equals Avogadro's number, the number of atoms in one mole of a substance.

In nuclear physics it is convenient to express masses in the unit of energy/c^2, using Einstein's energy–momentum relationship, $E = \sqrt{p^2c^2 + m_0^2c^4}$, where p is the momentum of a particle and m_0 is its rest mass. The energy equivalent of 1 u of mass at rest is

$E = m_0c^2$

$= (1.6605 \times 10^{-27} \text{ kg})(2.9979 \times 10^8 \text{ m/s})^2$

$= 14.9236 \times 10^{-11}$ J

$= \dfrac{14.9236 \times 10^{-11} \text{ J}}{1.6021 \times 10^{-19} \text{ J/eV}}$

$= 9.3150 \times 10^8$ eV

$= 931.50$ MeV

Therefore,

$$1 \text{ u} = 931.50 \text{ MeV}/c^2 \qquad (33\text{-}3)$$

Table 33-2 lists the basic properties of protons, neutrons, and electrons.

33-2 Nuclear Size and Nuclear Force

By bombarding a nucleus with a beam of fast-moving electrons and then observing how the electrons are deflected by the nucleus, scientists can determine the shape and the size of the nucleus. Several experiments using various elements have shown that, to a high degree of accuracy, most nuclei can be approximated as closely packed spherical clusters of protons and neutrons. The volume of the nucleus is proportional to the number of nucleons in the nucleus. A **nucleon** is a particle in an atomic nucleus—a proton or a neutron. The radius, r, of a nucleus is related to the number of nucleons, A:

$$r = r_0A^{1/3} \qquad (33\text{-}4)$$

where $r_0 = 1.2$ fm is a constant, determined from experiments. Table 33-3 lists the radii of nuclei of some common elements, using Equation (33-4).

Nuclear Density

The relationship between the radius and the mass number of a nucleus in Equation (33-4) indicates that the nuclear density remains constant as A changes, that is, all nuclei

Table 33-2 Some physical properties of atomic particles

Particle	Symbol	Spin	Charge	Atomic mass units, u	Mass MeV/c^2
Electron	e	1/2	$-e$	5.4858×10^{-4}	0.5110
Proton	p	1/2	$+e$	1.007 276	938.29
Neutron	n	1/2	0	1.008 665	939.57

Table 33-3 Radii of some common isotopes, assuming a spherical nuclear shape

Nucleus	Mass number, A	Radius, $r = r_0A^{1/3}$ (fm)
Helium, $^4_2$He	4	1.9
Oxygen, $^{16}_8$O	16	3.0
Iron, $^{56}_{26}$Fe	56	4.6
Lead, $^{208}_{82}$Pb	208	7.1

have the same density. To calculate this density, we start with the volume of a spherical nucleus of radius r:

$$V = \frac{4\pi}{3} r^3 = \frac{4\pi}{3} \left(r_0 A^{1/3} \right)^3 = \frac{4\pi}{3} r_0^3 A \qquad (33\text{-}5)$$

Next, we need to determine the mass of a nucleus that has A nucleons. From Table 33-2 we see that the mass of a nucleon is approximately equal to 1.0 u. Therefore, to a good approximation, the mass of a nucleus (M_{nuc}) with A nucleons is

$$M_{nuc} \approx A\,\text{u} \qquad (33\text{-}6)$$

This approximation is accurate to within 1% of the actual mass. The nuclear density, ρ_{nuc}, is then given by

$$\rho_{nuc} = \frac{M_{nuc}}{V} = \frac{A\,\text{u}}{\dfrac{4\pi}{3} r_0^3 A} = \frac{\text{u}}{\dfrac{4\pi}{3} r_0^3}$$

$$= \frac{1.6605 \times 10^{-27}\ \text{kg}}{\dfrac{4\pi}{3}(1.2 \times 10^{-15}\ \text{m})^3} = 2.3 \times 10^{17}\ \text{kg/m}^3 \quad (33\text{-}7)$$

This density is fantastically large. A nucleus with a volume of 1.0 mm³ would have a mass of 2.3×10^8 kg, that is, 230 thousand tonnes! In comparison, the mass of the same volume of iron is only 0.0078 g.

The Strong (or the Nuclear) Force

Protons are positively charged and exert a repulsive Coulomb force on each other. The magnitude of the Coulomb force between two protons that are a distance r apart is

$$F_{Coulomb} = \frac{1}{4\pi\varepsilon_0} \frac{(+e)(+e)}{r^2}$$

$$= \left(8.99 \times 10^9\ \frac{\text{N} \cdot \text{m}^2}{\text{C}^2}\right) \left(\frac{(1.602 \times 10^{-19}\ \text{C})^2}{r^2}\right) (33\text{-}8)$$

Consider two protons inside a helium nucleus. If the average distance between the two protons is taken to be 2.0 fm, the repulsive force between the protons is

$$F_{Coulomb} = \left(8.99 \times 10^9\ \frac{\text{N} \cdot \text{m}^2}{\text{C}^2}\right) \frac{(1.602 \times 10^{-19}\ \text{C})^2}{(2.0 \times 10^{-15}\ \text{m})^2}$$

$$= 58\ \text{N}$$

This is an enormous amount of repulsion. For comparison, the magnitude of the gravitational attraction between the protons at this distance is

$$F_{grav} = G \frac{(m_p)^2}{r^2}$$

$$= \left(6.674 \times 10^{-11}\ \frac{\text{N} \cdot \text{m}^2}{\text{kg}^2}\right) \left(\frac{(1.673 \times 10^{-27}\ \text{kg})^2}{(2.0 \times 10^{-15}\ \text{m})^2}\right)$$

$$= 5 \times 10^{-35}\ \text{N} \qquad (33\text{-}9)$$

where m_p is the proton mass.

Obviously, gravitational attraction is not sufficient to overcome the enormous Coulomb repulsion between the protons and keep them within the helium nucleus. There must be some very strong attractive force that keeps the protons confined within the nucleus. This force is called the **strong force** or the **nuclear force**. The strong force exists not only between two protons but also between two neutrons and between a proton and a neutron, as shown in Figure 33-2. There is another force, called the **weak force**, that acts between the nucleons, but it does not play any role in binding the nuclei. We will ignore the weak force in this chapter. The origin of the strong and weak forces is discussed in the next chapter.

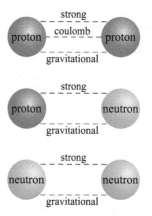

Figure 33-2 The forces acting between pairs of nucleons. There is also a weak force between two nucleons, but it is not shown in this figure.

Despite considerable research, the complicated nature of the strong force between two nucleons is still not completely understood. Experiments have shown that this force has the following properties:

- The strong force is repulsive when the distance between the two nucleons is less than approximately 0.7 fm. The repulsion prevents a nucleus from collapsing to a point.

- For distances larger than 0.7 fm, the strong force is attractive and reaches a maximum when the separation between the nucleons is approximately 1.2 fm. At this separation the strong force is approximately 10 times stronger than the Coulomb force. This attraction holds the nucleus together.

- At distances beyond 1.2 fm, the strength of the strong force decreases exponentially, and it becomes negligible for separations of more than 3.0 fm. Thus, the strong force acts *only* at a very short range, in marked contrast to the gravitational and electrostatic forces.

- The strong force only exists between nucleons. There is no strong force between an electron and a nucleon or between two electrons.

A plot of the strength of the strong force as a function of distance between two nucleons is shown in Figure 33-3.

The scale for the magnitude of the force is not specified in this plot because the exact magnitude for a given separation depends on the model used to describe the force.

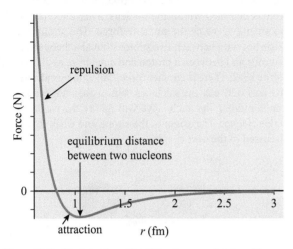

Figure 33-3 The behaviour of the strong force as a function of the distance between two nucleons. The force is repulsive for positive values and attractive for negative values.

LO 3

33-3 Nuclear Binding Energy

It is customary to express the nuclear mass in terms of A and Z. The rest mass of a nucleus that has Z protons and $N = A - Z$ neutrons is denoted by $M_{\text{nuc}}(A, Z)$. From Einstein's mass–energy relationship, the rest mass energy of this nucleus is $M_{\text{nuc}}(A, Z)c^2$.

Since a nucleus is bound by the strong force, separating it into its constituent protons and neutrons requires energy to overcome the attractive strong force, just as removing an electron from an atom requires energy to overcome the electrostatic force binding the electron to the nucleus. By the law of conservation of energy, *the rest mass energy of a nucleus together with the energy required to separate all the nucleons of the nucleus must be equal to the total rest mass energy of all the separated nucleons.* The energy required to separate a nucleus into individual nucleons is called the **nuclear binding energy** or simply the **binding energy**. The binding energy is therefore the difference between the total rest mass energy of constituent nucleons and the rest mass energy of the nucleus. The binding energy of a nucleus with A nucleons and Z protons is denoted by $B(A, Z)$:

$$B(A, Z) = Zm_pc^2 + (A - Z)m_nc^2 - M_{\text{nuc}}(A, Z)c^2 \quad (33\text{-}10)$$

Equivalently, we can write the nuclear mass in terms of the nuclear binding energy and proton and neutron masses:

$$M_{\text{nuc}}(A, Z) = Zm_p + (A - Z)m_n - \frac{B(A, Z)}{c^2} \quad (33\text{-}11)$$

The **atomic mass** of a neutral atom, $M_{\text{atom}}(A, Z)$, is equal to the sum of the mass of its nucleus and the masses of its Z electrons. Since the binding energies of the electrons in an atom are relatively small compared to the nuclear energies, they are often neglected in nuclear calculations. Therefore,

$$M_{\text{atom}}(A, Z) = M_{\text{nuc}}(A, Z) + Zm_e \quad (33\text{-}12)$$

The **average atomic mass** is the weighted average of the masses of the naturally occurring isotopes for a given element. For example, the two naturally occurring isotopes of nitrogen are $^{14}_{7}\text{N}$ (99.634%, atomic mass = 14.003 074 u) and $^{15}_{7}\text{N}$ (0.366%, atomic mass = 15.000 109 u), so the average atomic mass of nitrogen is

(14.003 074 u $\times$ 0.996 34) + (15.000 109 u $\times$ 0.003 66)

= 14.006 7 u

EXAMPLE 33-2

The Binding Energy of Helium

The atomic mass of helium ^4_2He is 4.002 603 u. Calculate the binding energy of the nucleus.

SOLUTION

The atomic mass includes the mass of the electrons. Since a helium atom has two electrons, we subtract two electron masses from the atomic mass to find the nuclear mass:

Mass of a ^4_2He nucleus = $M_{\text{nuc}}(4, 2)$ = 4.002 603 u − (2 × 0.000 548 u) = 4.001 507 u

The binding energy of a helium nucleus is

$$B(4, 2) = 2m_pc^2 + (4 - 2)m_nc^2 - M_{\text{nuc}}(4, 2)c^2$$

$$= (2 \times 1.007\ 276\ \text{u} + 2 \times 1.008\ 665\ \text{u} - 4.001\ 507\ \text{u})c^2$$

$$= (0.030\ 375\ \text{u})c^2$$

$$= (0.030\ 376\ \text{u} \times 931.5\ \text{MeV}/c^2)c^2$$

$$= 28.3\ \text{MeV}$$

From the above example, we see that it takes 28.3 MeV of energy to separate a ^4_2He nucleus into two protons and two neutrons. The same amount of energy will be released if two protons and two neutrons are combined to form a ^4_2He nucleus. Therefore, the nuclear binding energy can also be defined as the amount of energy released when a nucleus is assembled from individual nucleons.

By itself, the binding energy of a nucleus does not tell us how tightly bound the nucleons are in the nucleus. To compare how tightly various nuclei are bound, we define the **binding energy per nucleon**, $B_{\text{per}}(A, Z)$:

$$B_{\text{per}}(A, Z) = B(A, Z)/A \quad (33\text{-}13)$$

From experiments, the total binding energy of a gold nucleus ($^{184}_{79}$Au) is determined to be 1484 MeV. Comparing the binding energy per nucleon of helium ($^{4}_{2}$He) and gold nuclei, we find that the nucleons in gold are somewhat more tightly bound than those in helium:

$$B_{per}(4, 2) = \frac{28.3 \text{ MeV}}{4 \text{ nucleons}} = 7.07 \text{ MeV/nucleon}$$

$$B_{per}(184, 79) = \frac{1484 \text{ MeV}}{184 \text{ nucleons}} = 8.06 \text{ MeV/nucleon}$$

Since nuclear masses of all stable nuclei have been experimentally determined to a high degree of accuracy, we can plot $B_{per}(A, Z)$ as a function of A, as shown in Figure 33-4. This plot is called the **binding energy curve**. Notice that the binding energy per nucleon first sharply increases with A, reaches a maximum near $A = 60$, and then gradually decreases with increasing A. The shape of

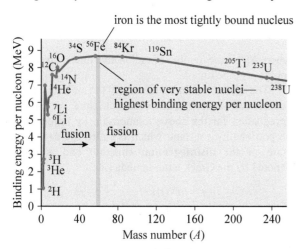

Figure 33-4 A plot of binding energy per nucleon as a function of mass number A for stable nuclei

the binding energy curve is mainly caused by the interplay between the repulsive electrostatic force and the attractive strong force.

The elements with low mass numbers are weakly bound because each nucleon in these nuclei has relatively few adjacent nucleons exerting attractive forces on it. For example, a **deuteron**, the nucleus of deuterium $^{2}_{1}$H, consists of one proton and one neutron and a binding energy per nucleon of only 1.1 MeV (the total binding energy of a deuteron is 2.2 MeV). A helium-3 nucleus, $^{3}_{2}$He, which has one more proton, has a binding energy per nucleon of 2.5 MeV. Adding an additional neutron to $^{3}_{2}$He forms a $^{4}_{2}$He nucleus, which has a binding energy per nucleon of approximately 7.0 MeV. The $^{4}_{2}$He nucleus is the most tightly bound of all nuclei with $A \leq 8$.

The binding energy per nucleon increases gradually as the mass number increases from 12 to 55. It peaks in the range $55 \leq A \leq 65$. Nuclei in this range are the most tightly bound and, therefore, the most stable. Iron-56 ($^{56}_{26}$Fe) has the largest binding energy per nucleon, 8.8 MeV. The binding energy per nucleon decreases steadily for $A \geq 65$. The strong force is a short-range force, so each additional nucleon interacts only with the nucleons that are very close it. However, the Coulomb force has an infinite range, so each additional proton repels *all* other protons in the nucleus, thus making the nucleus less stable as Z increases.

Neutrons are electrically neutral, and adding a neutron does not increase repulsion; however, when the number of neutrons in a nucleus increases above a critical value, it becomes energetically possible for a neutron to convert into a proton. Therefore, it is not possible to form heavier nuclei by keeping the number of protons fixed and just adding more and more neutrons.

Most nuclei beyond $A = 208$ are unstable and decay into smaller nuclei by a process, called alpha decay, that we will discuss in the next section.

 EXAMPLE 33-3

The Fusion of Two Deuterons

(a) How much energy is gained when two deuterons combine to form a helium-4 nucleus?
(b) How many joules of energy are released when one mole of deuterium (2 g) combines to form $^{4}_{2}$He?

SOLUTION

(a) A nuclear reaction releases energy by converting some of the mass of the original nuclei into energy. From Equation (33-10), the rest mass energy of a deuteron is

$$M_{nuc}(2, 1)c^2 = m_p c^2 + m_n c^2 - B(2, 1)$$

where $B(2, 1)$ is the binding energy of the deuteron. Similarly, the rest mass energy of the $^{4}_{2}$He nucleus is

$$M_{nuc}(4, 2)c^2 = 2m_p c^2 + 2m_n c^2 - B(4, 2)$$

where $B(4, 2)$ is the binding energy of $^{4}_{2}$He.

The energy released (ΔE) when two deuterons combine to form a helium nucleus is equal to the difference in the rest mass energies of the two deuterons and the helium nucleus:

$$\Delta E = 2 \times M_{nuc}(2, 1)c^2 - M_{nuc}(4, 2)c^2$$
$$= 2(m_p c^2 + m_n c^2 - B(2, 1)) - (2m_p c^2 + 2m_n c^2 - B(4, 2))$$
$$= B(4, 2) - 2 \times B(2, 1)$$

So, the released energy is equal to the difference between the binding energy of the final nucleus ($^{4}_{2}$He) and the sum of the binding energies of the initial deuterons. From Figure 33-4, the binding energy *per nucleon* for a deuteron is approximately 1.1 MeV, so $B(2, 1) = 2 \times 1.1 \text{ MeV} = 2.2 \text{ MeV}$. Similarly, $B(4, 2) = 4 \times 7.0 \text{ MeV} = 28.0 \text{ MeV}$. Therefore,

$$\Delta E = 28.0 \text{ MeV} - (2 \times 2.2 \text{ MeV}) = 23.6 \text{ MeV}$$

(continued)

(b) There are 6.02×10^{23} nuclei in one mole of a substance. Therefore, the energy released when one mole of deuterium is converted into helium is

$$(23.6 \text{ MeV}) \left(\frac{1.60 \times 10^{-13} \text{ J}}{\text{MeV}} \right) \left(\frac{6.02 \times 10^{23}}{2} \right) = 1.14 \times 10^{12} \text{ J}$$

Making sense of the result:

Burning one barrel (about 159 L) of oil produces approximately 6.12×10^9 J of energy. So, the fusion of 2 g of deuterium produces as much energy as burning 186 barrels of oil. The energy released per unit mass is vastly greater for a nuclear fuel than for a chemical fuel.

LO 4

33-4 Nuclear Decay and Radioactivity

In 1896, French physicist Antoine Becquerel (1852–1908) discovered that a mineral, later identified as uranyl potassium sulfate, continuously emits invisible radiation. The emitted radiation was not visible light and could easily penetrate a sheet of black paper. Further experiments by Becquerel, Marie Curie, Pierre Curie, and other scientists showed that invisible radiation is also emitted by some other elements, including thorium, radon, and radium. Furthermore, it was discovered that these elements emitted three different types of invisible radiations, which were called alpha (α), beta (β), and gamma (γ) radiation after the first three letters of the Greek alphabet.

α, β, and γ radiations are collectively called **nuclear radiation** and, as we now know, are emitted by nuclei. An element that emits nuclear radiation is called **radioactive**, and the process of emission of nuclear radiation is called **radioactive decay** or **nuclear decay**.

Like electromagnetic radiation, nuclear radiation carries energy. Only an unstable nucleus emits nuclear radiation. By emitting nuclear radiation, a nucleus transforms into either a nucleus of a lighter element or a lower-energy state of the original nucleus. The nucleus that emits the radiation is called the **parent nucleus**, and the final nucleus is called the **daughter nucleus**. A daughter nucleus always has less energy (including the rest mass energy) than the parent nucleus.

α-radiation consists of helium-4 ($^4_2$He) nuclei, which were originally called **alpha** (α) **particles**. Thus, a nucleus that emits an α-particle loses two protons and two neutrons and becomes a different element. β-radiation consists of either electrons or positrons. A **positron** is the antiparticle of an electron; it has the same mass as an electron but the opposite charge of an electron. γ-radiation is high-energy electromagnetic radiation. In Section 33-6 we will discuss these radiations in detail.

A general law applies to the emission of nuclear radiation: *at any given time, the amount of radiation emitted by a material depends only on the number of radioactive nuclei present.* For example, the uranium-238 ($^{238}_{92}$U) nucleus is radioactive and emits an α-particle. The compound uranyl potassium sulfate contains uranium, potassium, sulfur, and oxygen. The number of α-particles emitted in each second by a sample of this compound only depends on the number of uranium-238 nuclei in the sample. As the uranium nuclei decay, fewer of the radioactive nuclei remain; therefore, fewer α-particles are emitted by the sample each second. The rate at which this number decays is proportional to $N(t)$, and

$$-\frac{dN(t)}{dt} \propto N(t) \qquad (33\text{-}14)$$

where $N(t)$ is the number of radioactive nuclei present in a source at some time t.

The minus sign in Equation (33-14) indicates that the number of nuclei, $N(t)$, decreases with time. We can write an equation for the above relationship by introducing a proportionality constant, which is called the **decay constant** or the **disintegration constant** and is usually denoted by the Greek letter lambda (λ):

$$-\frac{dN(t)}{dt} = \lambda N(t) \qquad (33\text{-}15)$$

The unit of λ is decays per second, or simply, s^{-1}. The decay constant is a measure of how quickly a radioactive element decays with time. A large value of λ means that the nuclide will decay rapidly.

The decay constant is a characteristic of each radioactive nuclide. For a radioactive nuclide that can emit α-, β-, and γ-radiation, the decay constant has a different value for each type of radiation.

Suppose a radioactive nuclide has a decay constant of 0.10 s^{-1}, and at $t = 0$ we have 1.0×10^6 nuclei. After 1.0 s, the number of nuclei that have decayed is $\lambda N(0) = 0.10 \times 10^6 = 1.0 \times 10^5$, and 9.0×10^5 nuclei are left. During the next second, another $\lambda N(1) = 0.10 \times 9.0 \times 10^5 = 9.0 \times 10^4$ nuclei decay, leaving 8.1×10^5 of the original nuclei. After a third second, $\lambda N(2) = 0.1 \times 8.1 \times 10^5 = 8.1 \times 10^4$ more nuclei have decayed, and 7.29×10^5 are left. In each one second interval, 10% of the nuclei present at the start of that interval decay. The decreases in the number of radioactive nuclei by *an equal percentage in equal intervals of time* is a property of an exponential function. Figure 33-5 shows a plot of the number of remaining nuclei as a function of time for the above example. Obviously, this number decreases exponentially. So *radioactive decay is an exponential process.*

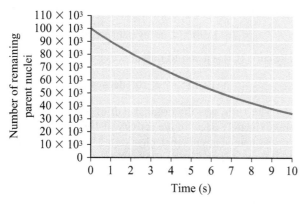

Figure 33-5 A plot of the number of parent nuclei as a function of time for a radioactive nuclide with a decay constant of 0.10 s^{-1}

The Exponential Decay Law

From Equation (33-15), we can derive an expression for the number of parent nuclei remaining at any time, given the number of parent nuclei at some initial time. Equation (33-15) shows that the derivative of the function $N(t)$ is directly proportional to its value, which is a characteristic property of exponential functions. Therefore, this function can be written as follows:

$$N(t) = ae^{bt} \qquad (33\text{-}16)$$

where a and b are constants that we need to determine. Substituting this form into Equation (33-15), we get

$$\text{Left-hand side: } -\frac{dN(t)}{dt} = -a\frac{d}{dt}(e^{bt}) = -b(ae^{bt})$$

$$\text{Right-hand side: } \lambda N(t) = \lambda(ae^{bt}) \qquad (33\text{-}17)$$

Therefore, $b = -\lambda$, and

$$N(t) = ae^{-\lambda t} \qquad (33\text{-}18)$$

To determine a, we need additional information, such as the number of radioactive nuclei present at some given time. Suppose there are N_0 radioactive nuclei at $t = 0$. Evaluating Equation (33-18) at $t = 0$ gives $N(0) = a = N_0$. So,

KEY EQUATION
$$N(t) = N_0 e^{-\lambda t} \qquad (33\text{-}19)$$

where $N(t)$ is the number of undecayed nuclei at time t, N_0 is the initial number of radioactive nuclei, and λ is the decay constant of the nuclide.

The greater the decay constant of a nuclide, the more quickly its nuclei decay. For stable nuclei, $\lambda = 0$ and the number of parent nuclei does not change with time.

Half-life

A **half-life**, $t_{1/2}$, is the time it takes for the number of radioactive nuclei in a sample to decrease to half the original value. Suppose a sample contains N_0 nuclei of a given radioactive nuclide at $t = 0$, and this number reduces to $N_0/2$ at a later time, $t = t_{1/2}$. Then from Equation (33-19),

---

✓ **CHECKPOINT**

C-33-2 Decay Constants

Figure 33-6 shows the number of remaining nuclei for four radioactive nuclides as a function of time.

(a) Arrange the nuclides, from high to low, in order of the decay constants.

(b) Each decaying nucleus of the nuclides emits the same amount of energy. Arrange the nuclides in the order of power emitted, from high to low, between $t = 1$ s and $t = 2$ s.

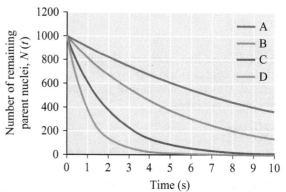

Figure 33-6 C-33-2

C-33-2 (a) D, C, B, A; (b) D, C, B, A. A higher decay constant means that the number of remaining parent nuclei will decrease faster with time.

$$N(t_{1/2}) = \frac{N_0}{2} = N_0 e^{-\lambda t_{1/2}} \qquad (33\text{-}20)$$

and

$$\frac{1}{2} = e^{-\lambda t_{1/2}}$$

Taking the natural logarithm on both sides and using the identities $\ln(e^x) = x$ and $\ln\left(\frac{1}{a}\right) = -\ln(a)$, we get the following relationship between the decay constant and the half-life:

$$t_{1/2} = \frac{\ln(2)}{\lambda} \simeq \frac{0.693}{\lambda} \qquad (33\text{-}21)$$

The SI unit for half-life is the second. If a sample has 1000 radioactive nuclei at some time, then it will have 500 nuclei after one half-life, 250 after two half-lives, 125 after three half-lives, and so on. A nuclide with a long half-life decays more slowly than a nuclide with a shorter half-life. For example, $^{238}_{92}\text{U}$ has a half-life of 4.468×10^9 y, so it decays slowly, and a sample containing this nuclide remains radioactive for a long time. Only half of the $^{238}_{92}\text{U}$ present at the formation of Earth has decayed so far. In contrast, radium-224 ($^{224}_{88}\text{Ra}$) has a half-life of 3.632 days, and any $^{224}_{88}\text{Ra}$ present at the time Earth was

Table 33-4 The decay constants and half-lives for a few radioactive nuclides

Nuclide	Type of decay	Decay constant, λ (s^{-1})	Half-life, $t_{1/2}$
$^{238}_{92}$U	α-decay	4.92×10^{-18}	4.46×10^9 y
$^{224}_{88}$Ra	α-decay	2.21×10^{-6}	3.63 days
$^{224}_{86}$Rn	β-decay	1.07×10^{-4}	1.8 h
$^{135}_{55}$Cs	β-decay	9.55×10^{-15}	2.30×10^6 y
$^{40}_{19}$K	β-decay	1.72×10^{-17}	1.28×10^9 y
$^{14}_{6}$C	β-decay	3.83×10^{-12}	5730 y

formed decayed into other nuclides long ago. Table 33-4 lists decay constants and half-lives for a few radioactive nuclides. A more comprehensive list is available at the text's online resources.

Decay Rate

It is easier to measure emitted radiation than to count the number of radioactive nuclei in a sample. The decay rate, or **activity**, R, of a sample is the number of nuclei that decay per unit time. The activity equals the magnitude of the time derivative of $N(t)$. From Equation (33-19), we have

$$R(t) = \left| \frac{dN(t)}{dt} \right| = \left| \frac{d}{dt} \left(N_0 e^{-\lambda t} \right) \right| = \lambda N_0 e^{-\lambda t} = \lambda N(t) \quad (33\text{-}22)$$

The more radioactive nuclei in a source, the greater its activity. Equation (33-22) shows that we can determine the number of radioactive nuclei in a sample simply by measuring the activity of a sample and knowing its decay constant. The SI unit of activity is the becquerel (Bq):

$$1 \text{ Bq} = 1 \text{ decay/s}$$

A commonly used abbreviation for decay/s is dps.

$$1 \text{ dps} = 1 \text{ decay per second}$$

The curie (Ci) is a non-SI unit of activity and is defined as

$$1 \text{ Ci} = 3.7 \times 10^{10} \text{ decays/s}$$

The curie was the original unit of activity, and it is approximately equal to the activity of 1 g of radium. The curie is named after French physicists Marie Curie (1867–1934) and Pierre Curie (1859–1906), whose pioneering research on radioactivity includes the discovery of the elements radium and polonium. From Equation (33-22),

$$R(0) = \lambda N_0 \quad (33\text{-}23)$$

Therefore, we can write

$$R(t) = R(0)e^{-\lambda t} \quad (33\text{-}24)$$

The activity of a nuclide decays exponentially with time. For example, in one half-life, the decay rate of a nuclide decreases to half of its original value.

☑ **CHECKPOINT**

C-33-3 A Radioactive Nuclide

A radioactive nuclide has a half-life of two days. On a certain day, its activity at 9:00 a.m. is measured to be 1000 Bq. The next day at 9:00 a.m. its activity is approximately

(a) 750 Bq;
(b) 700 Bq;
(c) 500 Bq;
(d) 250 Bq.

C-33-3 (b)

EXAMPLE 33-4

Radioactive Gallium

Gallium-67 ($^{67}_{31}$Ga), a radioactive isotope of gallium with a half-life of 3.26 days, is used for some types of medical imaging. A source containing $^{67}_{31}$Ga is calibrated to emit 3.7×10^7 Bq of radiation.

(a) How many gallium-67 atoms are there in the source?
(b) It takes one day to deliver the source to a hospital. What is the activity of the source when it arrives?

SOLUTION

(a) We have already derived all the required relationships between various quantities. We will measure time in seconds so that all quantities are converted in the correct units.

$$R(0) = 3.7 \times 10^7 \text{ Bq}$$

The number of radioactive nuclei is related to activity by Equation (33-22). Therefore, the number of gallium-67 atoms in the source at $t = 0$ is

$$N(0) = \frac{R(0)}{\lambda}$$

The decay constant of gallium-67 is

$$\lambda = \frac{\ln(2)}{t_{1/2}} = \frac{\ln(2)}{(3.26 \text{ days} \times 24 \text{ h/day} \times 3600 \text{ s/h})}$$

$$= 2.46 \times 10^{-6}\ \mathrm{s}^{-1}$$

Therefore,

$$N(0) = \frac{3.7 \times 10^7\ \text{decay/s}}{2.46 \times 10^{-6}\ \mathrm{s}^{-1}} = 1.5 \times 10^{13}\ \text{atoms}$$

33-5 Nuclear Reactions

When a fast-moving nucleus or a particle such as a proton, neutron, or photon collides with a nucleus, the collision rearranges the nucleons. In such **nuclear reactions**, the nuclei in the final states may be different from the initial nuclei. A nuclear reaction can be represented by the following equation:

$$a + X \rightarrow Y + b \qquad (33\text{-}25)$$

where a is the incoming nucleus or a particle, X is the target nucleus, and Y and b are the final products.

The left side of Equation (33-25) is called the initial state of the reaction, and the right side is called the final state of the reaction. There can be more than two products in the final state. If the projectile a is a nucleus or a positively charged particle, then it must have sufficient kinetic energy to overcome the Coulomb repulsion and come within the range of the strong force of the target nucleus X.

Examples of Nuclear Reactions

- When a beryllium-9 nucleus absorbs a fast-moving helium-4 nucleus, it transforms into a carbon-12 nucleus and emits a neutron:

$$\,^4_2\mathrm{He} + \,^9_4\mathrm{Be} \rightarrow \,^{12}_6\mathrm{C} + \,^1_0\mathrm{n} \qquad (33\text{-}26a)$$

A schematic diagram for this nuclear reaction is shown in Figure 33-7. Note that the number of nucleons is conserved in the reaction. This reaction was used by the British physicist James Chadwick (1891–1974) to prove the existence of neutrons in 1932.

- A neutron is absorbed by a nitrogen-14 nucleus, resulting in a carbon-14 nucleus and a proton in the final state. This reaction occurs in Earth's atmosphere

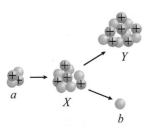

Figure 33-7 A nuclear reaction of beryllium-9 with a helium-4 nucleus. Protons are represented by red circles with a plus sign and neutrons by blue circles.

by cosmic rays and is responsible for replenishing carbon-14 which is present in natural carbon.

$$\,^1_0\mathrm{n} + \,^{14}_7\mathrm{N} \rightarrow \,^1_1\mathrm{p} + \,^{14}_6\mathrm{C} \qquad (33\text{-}26b)$$

- Two fast-moving oxygen-16 nuclei fuse together. One of the possible final states consists of a neon-20 nucleus and a carbon-12 nucleus. The oxygen-fusion reaction occurs in massive stars that have used up the lighter elements in their core.

$$\,^{16}_8\mathrm{O} + \,^{16}_8\mathrm{O} \rightarrow \,^{20}_{10}\mathrm{Ne} + \,^{12}_6\mathrm{C} \qquad (33\text{-}26c)$$

Conservation Laws for Nuclear Reactions

There are several physical quantities that are conserved in all nuclear reactions. These quantities include some that we are already familiar with from classical mechanics and electrodynamics, and there are others that are unique to nuclear physics.

Energy Conservation Total energy—the sum of kinetic and rest mass energies—is conserved in a nuclear reaction. Note that neither kinetic energy nor the rest mass energy is conserved by itself. Consider the nuclear reaction

$$a + b \rightarrow c + d$$

where a, b, c, and d represent nuclei or particles. The energy of each body in the above reaction is the sum of its kinetic energy and the rest mass energy. The conservation of energy requires that

$$K_a + M_a c^2 + K_b + M_b c^2 = K_c + M_c c^2 + K_d + M_d c^2$$

where K is kinetic energy, and Mc^2 is the rest mass energy. The total gain in the kinetic energy in this reaction is equal to the total loss of rest mass energy:

$$\Delta K = (K_f - K_i) = (M_i - M_f)c^2$$

where K_i and K_f denote, respectively, the initial and final total kinetic energies, and $M_i c^2$ and $M_f c^2$ are the corresponding total rest mass energies. The gain ΔK in the kinetic energy is called the **Q-value** of the reaction and is denoted by Q. Thus

KEY EQUATION $$Q = (M_i - M_f)c^2 \qquad (33\text{-}27)$$

If the rest mass energy in the final state is less than the rest mass energy in the initial state, the Q-value is positive and kinetic energy is released in the nuclear reaction. In this case, the reaction would occur even if $K_i = 0$ (e.g., in a nuclear decay). If the rest mass energy in the final state is greater the rest mass energy in the initial state, the Q-value

(b) Given the activity at $t = 0$, the activity at a later time is given by $R(t) = R(0)e^{-\lambda t}$. Using $1 = 24\ \mathrm{h/day} \times 3600\ \mathrm{s/h} = 86\,400\ \mathrm{s}$, the activity of the source when it arrives is

$$R(86\,400) = (3.7 \times 10^7\ \mathrm{Bq})e^{-2.461 \times 10^{-6} \times 86\,400} \approx 3.0 \times 10^7\ \mathrm{Bq}$$

is negative. In this case, the bodies in the initial state must have sufficient kinetic energy for the reaction to occur.

By writing the nuclear mass energy in terms of the nuclear binding energy, Equation (33-10), we can write the Q-value of a nuclear reaction in terms of the nuclear binding energies as follows:

$$Q = B_f - B_i$$

where B_i and B_f denote the total binding energies of the bodies in the initial and the final state. Here, we have used the fact that the total number of nucleons (protons plus neutrons) in the initial and the final state of a nuclear reaction remains the same.

Charge Conservation Total charge is conserved in a nuclear reaction. For example, in the beryllium–helium reaction above in Equation (33-26a), the total charge is $6e$ (six protons) in both the initial and final states.

Momentum Conservation Momentum is conserved in all nuclear reactions. For the reaction of Equation (33-25),

$$\vec{p}_a + \vec{p}_X = \vec{p}_b + \vec{p}_Y$$

Angular Momentum Conservation The total angular momentum (the sum of the orbital angular momentum and the spin) is conserved in all nuclear reactions.

Conservation of Nucleons The total number of nucleons (protons and neutrons) in a nuclear reaction remains the same. A proton can change into a neutron and vice versa, but the total number of neutrons plus protons remains constant before and after the reaction. For example, in

reaction (33-26a) above, there are a total of 13 nucleons in both the initial state and in the final state.

There are other physical quantities that are conserved in nuclear reactions; however, that discussion is beyond the scope of this introduction.

LO 6

33-6 α, β, and γ Decays

In a **nuclear decay**, a nucleus transforms into another nucleus or rearranges its constituents on its own, without an interaction with an external particle, nucleus, or radiation.

Alpha (α) Decay

From Figure 33-4, we can observe that a large nucleus can increase its binding energy, and hence become more stable, by reducing its atomic number and thus transforming into a different nucleus. For example, a nucleus could emit neutrons or protons. Since a helium-4 nucleus has a large binding energy, a heavy nucleus can increase its binding energy more by emitting a helium-4 nucleus than by emitting separate protons and neutrons. When a parent nucleus X with Z protons and N neutrons decays by emitting an α-particle ($^4_2$He), the resulting daughter nucleus Y has $Z - 2$ protons and $N - 2$ neutrons. Energy is released in an **alpha decay** (α-decay) and appears in the form of the kinetic energy of the α-particle and the daughter nucleus. We can represent an α-decay as

EXAMPLE 33-5

Proton Absorption on Lithium

In 1932, English physicist John Cockroft and Irish physicist Ernest Walton produced the first nuclear reaction by bombarding lithium with 600 keV protons and producing helium in the following process:

$$^1_1H + ^7_3Li \rightarrow ^4_2He + ^4_2He$$

Determine the Q-value of the reaction.

SOLUTION

From Table 33-5, the atomic masses of hydrogen lithium, and helium atoms are as follows:

Atomic mass of $^1_1$H = 1.007 825 u

Atomic mass of $^7_3$Li = 7.016 003 u

Atomic mass of $^4_2$He = 4.002 603 u

Table 33-5 Table of selected atomic masses

Z	A	Symbol	Name	Atomic mass (u)
0	1	n	Neutron	1.008 665
1	1	p	Proton	1.007 276
1	1	H	Hydrogen	1.007 825
1	2	H	Deuterium	2.014 102
1	3	H	Tritium	3.016 049
2	3	He	Helium-3	3.016 029
2	4	He	Helium-4	4.002 603

Z	A	Symbol	Name	Atomic mass (u)
3	6	Li	Lithium	6.015 121
3	7	Li	Lithium	7.016 003
4	9	Be	Beryllium	9.012 182
5	10	B	Boron	10.012 937
5	11	B	Boron	11.009 305
6	12	C	Carbon	12
6	13	C	Carbon	13.003 355
6	14	C	Carbon	14.003 242
7	14	N	Nitrogen	14.003 074
7	15	N	Nitrogen	15.000 109
8	16	O	Oxygen	15.994 915
8	17	O	Oxygen	16.999 131
8	18	O	Oxygen	17.999 160
10	20	Ne	Neon	19.992 436
19	39	K	Potassium	38.963 708
19	40	K	Potassium	39.964 000
19	41	K	Potassium	40.961 827
26	56	Fe	Iron	55.934 939
36	90	Kr	Krypton	89.919 517
37	93	Rb	Rubidium	92.922 042
38	88	Sr	Strontium	87.905 619
40	102	Zr	Zirconium	101.922 980
52	134	Te	Tellurium	131.911 369
55	141	Cs	Cesium	140.920 046
56	144	Ba	Barium	143.922 953
82	208	Pb	Lead	207.976 627
83	208	Bi	Bismuth	297.979 717
84	210	Po	Polonium	209.982 848
84	218	Po	Polonium	218.008 965
86	222	Rn	Radon	222.017 571
90	231	Th	Thorium	231.036 298
90	232	Th	Thorium	232.038 051
90	234	Th	Thorium	234.043 593
92	232	U	Uranium	232.037 129
92	235	U	Uranium	235.043 924
92	238	U	Uranium	238.050 783

The Q-value of the reaction is equal to the difference in the rest mass energies of the bodies in the initial and the final states.

$Q = ((1.007\,825\ \text{u} + 7.016\,003\ \text{u}) - 2 \times (4.002\,603\ \text{u})) = 0.018\,6\ \text{u}$

$\quad = \left(\dfrac{931.5\ \text{MeV}}{\text{u}}\right) \times 0.0186\ \text{u} = 17.3\ \text{MeV}$

With their rudimentary instrumentation Cockroft and Walton measured that 17.2 MeV of energy is released in this reaction. This was the first experimental verification of Einstein's mass-energy relation.

$$_Z^A X \rightarrow \; _{Z-2}^{A-4} Y + \; _2^4 He + Q_\alpha \qquad (33\text{-}28)$$

Here, $_Z^A Y$ is the parent nucleus, $_{Z-2}^{A-4} Y$ is the daughter nucleus, and Q_α represents the energy released in the decay and is called the **Q-value** of the decay.

From the definition of Q-value, the energy released in α-decay is

$$Q_\alpha = M_X c^2 - (M_Y + M_\alpha)c^2 \qquad (33\text{-}29)$$

where M_X, M_Y, and M_α are the atomic masses of the parent nucleus, the daughter nucleus, and the α-particle, respectively.

By the law of conservation of energy, α-decay can happen only if the rest mass of the parent nucleus is *greater* than the combined rest masses of the daughter nucleus and the α-particle. Therefore, Q_α must be positive for a nucleus to undergo α-decay. We can express Q_α in terms of the binding energies of the nuclei, using Equation (33-10):

$$M_X c^2 = Z m_p c^2 + (A - Z)m_N c^2 - B(A, Z)$$

$$M_Y c^2 = (Z - 2)m_p c^2 + (A - Z - 2)m_N c^2 - B(A - 4, Z - 2)$$

$$M_\alpha c^2 = 2 m_p c^2 + 2 m_N c^2 - B(4, 2) \qquad (33\text{-}30)$$

Note that the daughter nucleus has $Z - 2$ protons and $A - 4 - (Z - 2) = A - Z - 2$ neutrons. By inserting Equation (33-30) into Equation (33-29), we obtain an expression for Q_α in terms of binding energies:

$$Q_\alpha = B(A - 4, Z - 2) + B(4, 2) - B(A, Z) \quad (33\text{-}31)$$

We see that the Q-value is the difference in the binding energies of the final products and the initial parent nucleus. From experiments we know that the binding energy of a helium nucleus is 28.2 MeV, so $B(4, 2) = 28.2$ MeV.

Most of the energy released in the α-decay in Example 33-6 is carried away by the α-particle in the form of kinetic energy. Approximately 5% of the energy appears as the kinetic and excitation energy of the polonium nucleus. When formed in this decay process, the polonium nucleus is initially in an excited state (just like an atom can be in an excited state when not all of its electrons are in their lowest energy states). The excited polonium nucleus reaches its ground state by emitting a γ-ray, a high-energy photon.

Decay Diagrams

A nuclear decay can be graphically represented by plotting the atomic numbers (charge) of parent and daughter nuclei along the horizontal axis and their energies along the vertical axis. Such a diagram is called a **decay diagram**. Energy is always released in a nuclear decay, so the daughter nucleus is lower in energy than the parent nucleus. In these diagrams a short horizontal line, centred at a given Z, represents a nucleus with a fixed charge and in a particular energy state. An arrow with its tail at the parent nucleus and its head at the daughter nucleus represents the decay process. The vertical distance between the parent and the daughter nuclei represents the energy released in the decay, that is, the Q-value of the decay (Figure 33-8(a)). Figure 33-8(b) shows a decay diagram for the α-decay of uranium-238.

EXAMPLE 33-6

The α-Decay of Radon

Radon-222 ($_{86}^{222}$Rn) has a half-life of 3.8235 days and decays by emitting an α-particle.

(a) What is the daughter nucleus in this decay?
(b) Using the atomic masses from Table 33-5, determine the Q-value of this decay.
(c) Find the difference in the binding energies of the parent and the daughter nuclei.

SOLUTION

(a) For the parent nucleus, $A = 222$ and $Z = 86$. For the daughter nucleus, $A = 222 - 4 = 218$ and $Z = 86 - 2 = 84$.
From a periodic or atomic table, we find that the nucleus with $Z = 84$ is polonium (Po) and the daughter nucleus is $_{84}^{218}$Po. Therefore, the equation for α-decay is

$$_{86}^{222}Rn \rightarrow \; _{84}^{218}Po + \; _2^4 He + Q_\alpha$$

(b) Looking up the known atomic masses of the isotopes (Table 33-5) in the reaction, we find the following:

$$\text{Atomic mass of } _{86}^{222}Rn = 222.017\ 571\ u$$

$$\text{Atomic mass of } _{84}^{218}Po = 218.008\ 965\ u$$

$$\text{Atomic mass of } _2^4 He = 4.002\ 603\ u$$

Now we can use Equation (33-29) to determine Q_α:

$$Q_\alpha = (222.0175\ 71\ u - 218.008\ 965\ u - 4.002\ 603\ u)\left(\frac{931.5\ MeV}{u}\right)$$

$$= 5.59\ MeV$$

(c) From Equation (33-31):

$$Q_\alpha = B(218, 84) + B(4, 2) - B(222, 86)$$

and

$$B(222, 86) - B(218, 84) = B(4, 2) - Q_\alpha$$

$$= 28.2\ MeV - 5.59\ MeV$$

$$= 22.6\ MeV$$

(a)

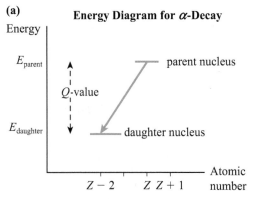

Energy Diagram for α-Decay

(b)

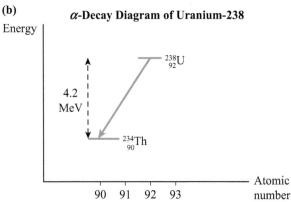

α-Decay Diagram of Uranium-238

Figure 33-8   (a) A decay diagram for α-decay (b) A decay diagram for the α-decay of $^{238}_{92}$U

Beta (β) decay

Nuclei are most stable in the lowest energy state. Figure 33-9 shows a plot of the rest mass as a function of the number of protons (Z) for various nuclei with $A = 16$. Notice that oxygen-16, with 8 protons and 8 neutrons, has the lowest rest mass and therefore the lowest rest mass energy. The rest mass of $^{16}_{7}$N is 16.006 102 u, and the rest mass energy of $^{16}_{8}$O is 15.994 914 u. Therefore, the energy of $^{16}_{8}$O is lower by

$$(16.006\,102\,\text{u} - 15.994\,914\,\text{u})(931.5\,\text{MeV/u}) = 10.4\,\text{MeV}$$

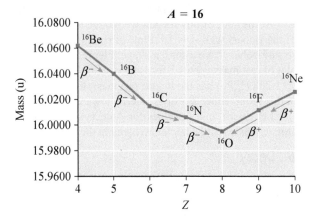

Figure 33-9   The rest masses as a function of the number of protons for various nuclei with $A = 16$

Therefore a $^{16}_{7}$N nucleus could transform into a $^{16}_{8}$O, a nuclide of lower rest-mass energy, by transforming one neutron into a proton.

Now we look at conservation of charge. The initial neutron has no charge, but the final proton has a charge of $+e$. So, there must be another particle, with charge $-e$, that is created when a neutron changes into a proton—this particle is an electron. We can write the process as follows:

$$\text{neutron} \rightarrow \text{proton} + \text{electron}$$

or

$$^{1}_{0}\text{n} \rightarrow {}^{1}_{1}\text{p} + {}^{0}_{-1}\text{e} \qquad (33\text{-}32)$$

In using the symbol $^{1}_{0}$n to represent a neutron, we have used the same convention as that for a nucleus. A neutron has no charge ($Z = 0$), and the atomic mass number is $A = 1$. Similarly, an electron has zero atomic mass number and has a charge of -1. The proton remains inside the nucleus; only the electron comes out. The emitted electron is called a beta (β) ray, and the decay process in which a nucleus changes its charge by one unit is called **beta decay** (β-decay).

Let us examine the conservation of energy and momentum during this process. We assume that the neutron is at rest. The Q-value of the neutron decay process is

$$Q = m_{\text{n}}c^2 - (m_{\text{p}}c^2 + m_{\text{e}}c^2) \qquad (33\text{-}33)$$

Using $m_{\text{n}}c^2 = 939.565\,56\,\text{MeV}$, $m_{\text{p}}c^2 = 938.2720\,\text{MeV}$, and $m_{\text{e}}c^2 = 0.510\,999\,\text{MeV}$, $Q = 0.782\,\text{MeV}$. The Q-value is positive; therefore, the decay of a neutron into a proton is allowed by the law of conservation of energy. A free neutron is indeed unstable. It decays into a proton with a half-life of 614 s.

Since the neutron is at rest, the proton and the electron momenta must be equal and opposite so that the total momentum of the final state is zero. We leave it as an end-of-chapter exercise (problem 46 in Chapter 34) to show that the magnitude of the proton and electron momentum, p, is given by

$$\frac{p^2}{c^2} = \left(\frac{m_{\text{n}}^2 + m_{\text{p}}^2 - m_{\text{e}}^2}{2m_{\text{n}}}\right)^2 - m_{\text{p}}^2$$

Inserting values for the masses of the three particles, we get $p = 1.188\,\text{MeV}/c$. So the proton and electron have a well-defined momentum. The kinetic energy of an electron, KE_{e}, corresponding to this momentum is the difference between its total energy and the rest mass energy:

$$KE_{\text{e}} = \sqrt{p^2c^2 + m_{\text{e}}^2c^4} - m_{\text{e}}c^2 = 0.782\,\text{MeV}$$

When we observe decays of neutrons, the emerging electrons should all have 0.782 MeV of kinetic energy. But almost all electrons in neutron decay experiments have less kinetic energy, as shown in Figure 33-10. Where is the rest of the energy going? Could neutron decay somehow violate conservation of energy?

This problem puzzled physicists until Wolfgang Pauli suggested that a neutron decays into three particles: a proton, an electron, and a third particle, which he called a **neutrino** (ν). Neutrino is Italian for "small neutral one."

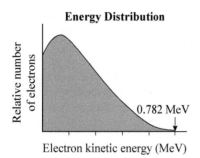

Energy Distribution

Relative number of electrons

0.782 MeV

Electron kinetic energy (MeV)

Figure 33-10 The kinetic energy of electrons emitted in the β-decay of a neutron

Since the particle had not been previously detected, Pauli assumed that it interacts with matter only by the weak force.

Pauli argued that the neutrino and the electron share the energy available in the decay. Since a proton is approximately 1836 times more massive than an electron, the speed of the proton is quite small; consequently, its kinetic energy can be ignored. The sum of kinetic energies of the electron and the neutrino must be equal to the Q-value calculated in Equation (33-33). So the electron's kinetic energy can have any value between zero and 0.782 MeV. The neutrino must be close to massless because some electrons in the β-decay of neutrons are emitted with kinetic energy nearly equal to the Q-value, leaving almost no energy for the neutrino. So, Pauli predicted that the neutrino has no charge, no mass, and an intrinsic spin of $\frac{1}{2}$, making it a fermion.

Neutrinos were discovered in 1952 by American physicists Frederick Reines (1918–98) and Clyde Lorrain Cowan (1919–74), for which they shared a Nobel Prize in 1995. However, 50 years after Pauli's original hypothesis, it was determined that the third particle emitted in neutron β-decay is actually an antiparticle of the neutrino, called the antineutrino, $\bar{\nu}$. (We will discuss the nature of antiparticles in Chapter 34.) The β-decay of a neutron can then be written as follows:

$$_0^1n \rightarrow {_1^1}p + {_{-1}^0}e + \bar{\nu} \qquad (33\text{-}34)$$

Similarly, the β-decay of a nucleus in which a neutron converts into a proton, for example, the transformation of $_7^{16}N$ into $_8^{16}O$, is written as

$$_7^{16}N \rightarrow {_8^{16}}O + {_{-1}^0}e + \bar{\nu} + Q \qquad (33\text{-}35)$$

The decay specified by Equation (33-35) is called the β-decay of $_7^{16}N$. The half-life of $_7^{16}N$ for β-decay to $_8^{16}O$ is 7.13 s, and that is why nitrogen-16 is not seen in nature. The Q-value in Equation (33-35) is not the same as the Q-value for the β-decay of a free neutron. The neutron that converts into a proton in $_7^{16}N$ β-decay is not free and is bound to the nucleus by the strong force. Similarly, the final proton is bound to the $_8^{16}O$ nucleus. We will show how to calculate the Q-value for β-decay of a nucleus later in this section.

All $A = 16$ elements with $Z < 8$ eventually β-decay into $_8^{16}O$: $_4^{16}Be$ β-decays into $_5^{16}B$, which then β-decays into $_6^{16}C$, which β-decays to $_7^{16}N$, and then finally to $_8^{16}O$. The half-lifes and the Q-values for the decays at each stage are different. The process stops at oxygen-16 because it is stable and does not decay.

How about the nuclei with $Z > 8$? From Figure 33-9 we observe that $_9^{16}F$ has a higher rest mass energy than $_8^{16}O$. So $_9^{16}F$ can decay to $_8^{16}O$, which requires transforming a proton into a neutron. To conserve electric charge, a particle with a charge equal to the charge of a proton must be emitted during this decay. This particle is the positron, the antiparticle of the electron. A positron has the same mass as an electron but opposite charge. The positron is denoted by the symbol $_{+1}^0e$. The energy of positrons emitted during proton decay has a distribution similar to that for electrons emitted in β-decay, indicating that a third particle is also produced when a proton decays into a neutron. The emitted particle is the neutrino. So, the β-decay of a proton can be represented as

$$_1^1p \rightarrow {_0^1}n + {_{+1}^0}e + \nu \qquad (33\text{-}36)$$

There is a crucial difference between neutron decay and proton decay. The rest mass of a proton is *less* than the rest mass of a neutron. Therefore, a free proton cannot decay into a neutron. Proton decay into a neutron is possible only inside a nucleus where other protons and neutrons can provide the required energy. Otherwise, all hydrogen atoms would have decayed a long time ago.

The decay of $_9^{16}F$ into $_8^{16}O$ can be represented as

$$_9^{16}F \rightarrow {_8^{16}}O + {_{+1}^0}e + \nu + Q \qquad (33\text{-}37)$$

$_9^{16}F$ is extremely unstable and has a half-life of the order of 10^{-20} s.

When a neutron converts into a proton, a negatively charged particle (electron) is emitted from the nucleus. This process is called **beta-minus (β^-) decay**. Similarly, the process during which a proton converts into a neutron and a positively charged particle (positron) is emitted from the nucleus is called **beta-plus (β^+) decay**. So we say "nitrogen-16 β^- decays and transforms into oxygen-16."

At the start of this section we plotted the rest masses of the isobars with $A = 16$. Plots of rest masses for other sets of isobars have a similar shape. Figure 33-11 shows a plot of rest mass versus Z for isobars with $A = 208$. Since lead-208 ($_{82}^{208}Pb$) has the lowest rest mass, the other nuclei in this group either β^-- or β^+-decay toward lead-208.

Let us see how Q-values for β-decays are related to atomic masses of the nuclei involved in the decay.

β^- Decay

The following equation represents the β^--decay of a parent nucleus $_Z^AX$:

$$_Z^AX \rightarrow {_{Z+1}^A}Y + {_{-1}^0}e + \bar{\nu} + Q_{\beta^-} \qquad (33\text{-}38)$$

where Q_{β^-} is the Q-value of the β-decay.

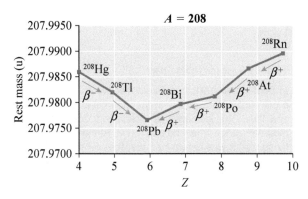

Figure 33-11 The rest masses as a function of the number of protons for various nuclei with $A = 208$

For example, sulfur-35 has a half-life of 87.9 days for the β-decay into chlorine-35:

$$^{35}_{16}S \rightarrow {}^{35}_{17}Cl + {}^{0}_{-1}e + \bar{\nu} + 0.167 \text{ MeV}$$

From the definition of Q-value,

$$Q_{\beta^-} = M_X c^2 - (M_Y + m_e)c^2 \quad (33\text{-}39)$$

Here, m_e is the electron mass, and M_X and M_Y are the nuclear masses of the parent and the daughter nuclei, respectively. We can also write the Q-value in terms of atomic masses of corresponding atoms by adding the rest mass energy of Z electrons to both terms on the right side of Equation (33-39):

EXAMPLE 33-7

The β-Decay of Carbon-14

Carbon-14 ($^{14}_{6}C$) is an unstable isotope that undergoes β^--decay.

(a) What is the daughter nucleus for the decay?
(b) Write an equation that describes the decay.
(c) Calculate the Q-value for the decay.
(d) Draw a decay diagram for the decay.

SOLUTION

(a) A carbon-14 nucleus has 6 protons and 8 neutrons. In a β^--decay a neutron converts into a proton. Therefore, the daughter nucleus has 7 protons and 7 neutrons. The daughter nucleus is nitrogen-14 ($^{14}_{7}N$).

(b) The decay equation is

$$^{14}_{6}C \rightarrow {}^{14}_{7}N + {}^{0}_{-1}e + \bar{\nu} + Q_{\beta^-}$$

(c) To calculate the Q-value of this decay, we use Equation (33-41). From Table (33-5),

Atomic mass of $^{14}_{6}C$ = 14.003 242 u
Atomic mass of $^{14}_{7}N$ = 14.003 074 u

The Q-value of the β^- decay is

$$Q_{\beta^-} = (M_X + Zm_e)c^2 - (M_Y + m_e + Zm_e)c^2 \quad (33\text{-}40)$$

The parent nucleus has Z protons so its atom has Z electrons. The daughter nucleus has $Z + 1$ protons, and its atom has $Z + 1$ electrons. Therefore, the terms in the parentheses in Equation (33-40) add to the atomic masses of the parent and daughter elements, and Q_{β^-} is equal to the energy equivalent of the difference between these atomic masses:

$$Q_{\beta^-} = \tilde{M}_X c^2 - \tilde{M}_Y c^2 \quad (33\text{-}41)$$

If the atomic mass of the parent nucleus is greater than the atomic mass of the daughter nucleus, the parent nucleus will β^--decay into the daughter nucleus.

In a β^--decay, the charge of the nucleus increases by e. The corresponding decay diagram is shown in Figure 33-12.

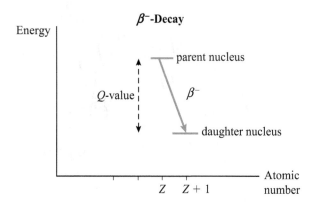

Figure 33-12 A decay diagram for β^--decay

$$Q_{\beta^-} = (\tilde{M}_{\text{parent}} - \tilde{M}_{\text{daughter}})c^2$$

$$= (14.003\ 242\ \text{u} - 14.003\ 074\ \text{u})c^2$$

$$= (1.68 \times 10^{-4}\ \text{u})\left(\frac{931.5\ \text{MeV}/c^2}{\text{u}}\right)c^2$$

$$= 0.156\ \text{MeV}$$

(d) The decay diagram is shown in Figure 33-13.

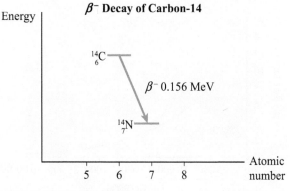

Figure 33-13 The β^- decay of $^{14}_{6}C$

Radiocarbon Dating

Radiocarbon dating (also called **carbon dating**) uses the naturally occurring carbon-14 ($^{14}_{6}$C) to estimate the age of carbon-rich materials. Carbon has two stable isotopes, carbon-12 and carbon-13. All other isotopes of carbon are radioactive. Carbon-14 has a half-life of 5730 ± 40 y and β-decays to nitrogen-14 ($^{14}_{7}$N), a stable element:

$$^{14}_{6}\text{C} \rightarrow {}^{14}_{7}\text{N} + \text{e}^- + \bar{\nu}_\text{e}$$

Carbon-14 is continuously formed in the upper atmosphere by high-energy neutrons that are produced by cosmic rays. The neutrons displace a proton from a nitrogen-14 nucleus, converting it into a carbon-14 nucleus:

$$^{1}_{0}\text{n} + {}^{14}_{7}\text{N} \rightarrow {}^{14}_{6}\text{C} + {}^{1}_{1}\text{p}$$

Carbon-14 is chemically identical to carbon-12 and reacts with oxygen to form carbon dioxide gas, which diffuses through the atmosphere, biosphere, and oceans. Living organisms (plants, trees, and animals) continuously exchange carbon dioxide with their environment, so they absorb a small amount of carbon-14: one atom of carbon-14 for every 1.2×10^{12} atoms of carbon. The absorbed carbon eventually decays to nitrogen-14. The activity due to carbon-14 decay is approximately 15 decays per minute per gram of carbon.

As long as an organism is alive, its interactions with the environment keep the ratio of carbon-14 in the organism the same as in the environment. When an organism dies, it stops exchanging carbon, and the number of carbon-14 atoms in it begins to decrease. Since the activity of a radioactive element is proportional to the number of undecayed nuclei, the activity of a dead organism decreases with time, reducing by 50% every 5730 y (Figure 33-14). By measuring the activity of carbon-14 in organic matter, scientists can determine the age of an animal bone, a wooden object, or a piece of cloth that was made from plant or animal fibres. The length of the half-life of carbon-14 makes this method of dating organic matter reasonably reliable for ages less than 60 000 years.

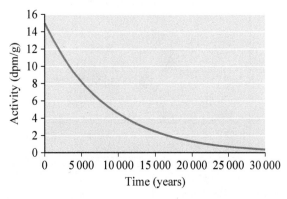

Figure 33-14 The activity of a sample of carbon-14 as a function of time

EXAMPLE 33-8

The Age of Iceman Ötzi

In September 1991, two hikers discovered the body of a man frozen in a glacier in the mountains near Austria and Italy. The iceman was nicknamed Ötzi, after the mountain range where he was found. At the University of Innsbruck, it was determined that the carbon-14 activity of the body was 53% of the activity of living organisms. How old is the Ötzi iceman?

SOLUTION

Let $N(0)$ be the number of carbon-14 atoms in a living organism and $N(t)$ be the number of carbon-14 atoms in an organism that has been dead for t years. From Equation (33-19),

$$N(t) = N(0)e^{-\lambda t}$$

where λ is the decay constant of carbon-14.
Dividing the above equation by $N(0)$, taking the natural logarithm on both sides, and using $\ln(e^x) = x$ gives

$$\ln\left(\frac{N(t)}{N(0)}\right) = -\lambda t$$

and

$$t = -\frac{1}{\lambda} \ln\left(\frac{N(t)}{N(0)}\right) = -\frac{t_{1/2}}{\ln(2)} \ln\left(\frac{N(t)}{N(0)}\right)$$

Since the activity is proportional to the number of undecayed nuclei,

$$\frac{\lambda N(t)}{\lambda N(0)} = \frac{N(t)}{N(0)} = 0.53$$

and

$$t = -\frac{5730 \text{ y}}{\ln(2)} \ln(0.53) = 5250 \text{ y}$$

Making sense of the result:

Several corrections and approximations are required in such analysis, for example, to adjust for historical variations in the concentration of carbon-14 in the atmosphere. It is generally agreed that iceman Ötzi died approximately 5300 y ago.

β^+ Decay

The following equation describes the β^+-decay of a parent nucleus $^{A}_{Z}X$:

$$^{A}_{Z}X \rightarrow {}^{A}_{Z-1}Y + {}^{0}_{+1}\text{e} + \nu + Q_{\beta^+} \qquad (33\text{-}42)$$

Here, Q_{β^+} is the Q-value for β^+-decay. For example, the β-decay of fluorine-17 ($^{17}_{9}$F) into oxygen-17 ($^{17}_{8}$O) is given by

$$^{17}_{9}\text{F} \rightarrow {}^{17}_{8}\text{O} + {}^{0}_{+1}\text{e} + \nu + 1.74 \text{ MeV}$$

Similarly, sodium-22 ($^{22}_{11}$Na) β-decays into neon-22:

$$^{22}_{11}\text{Na} \rightarrow {}^{22}_{10}\text{Ne} + {}^{0}_{+1}\text{e} + \nu + 0.167 \text{ MeV}$$

Similar to Equation (33-39), for β^+-decay,

$$Q_{\beta^+} = M_X c^2 - (M_Y + m_e)c^2 \qquad (33\text{-}43)$$

where m_e is the positron mass (same as the electron mass).

We can write Q_{β^+} in terms of the atomic masses by allowing for the rest mass energy of the electrons in the atoms. The parent nucleus has Z protons, so its atom has Z electrons. The daughter nucleus has $Z - 1$ protons, and its atom has $Z - 1$ electrons. So, the Q-value for a β^+-decay can be written as

EXAMPLE 33-9

The Q-Value of the β^+-Decay of Bismuth-208

Calculate the Q-value for the β^+-decay of bismuth-208 ($^{208}_{83}$Bi) using the atomic masses given in Table 33-5.

SOLUTION

In the β^+-decay of bismuth-208 ($^{208}_{83}$Bi), the daughter nucleus has one less proton than the parent nucleus. The nucleus with 82 protons is lead, so the decay process is

$$^{208}_{83}\text{Bi} \rightarrow {}^{208}_{82}\text{Pb} + {}^{0}_{+1}\text{e} + \nu + Q_{\beta^+}$$

The Q-value of the decay is given by Equation (33-44). From Table 33-5,

$$Q_{\beta^+} = \tilde{M}_X c^2 - \tilde{M}_Y c^2 - 2m_e c^2 \qquad (33\text{-}44)$$

Notice that in terms of atomic masses, the Q-value for β^+-decay differs from the Q-value for β^--decay by twice the electron rest mass energy, $2m_e c^2$, or 1.022 MeV. Since Q_{β^+} must be greater than zero for β^+-decay to occur, the atomic mass of the parent nucleus must be greater than the atomic mass of the daughter nucleus by at least 1.022 MeV.

Atomic mass of $^{208}_{83}$Bi = 207.979 717 u

Atomic mass of $^{208}_{82}$Pb = 207.976 627 u

Rest mass of an electron = 0.000 548 u

The Q-value of the decay is therefore

$$Q_{\beta^+} = \tilde{M}_X c^2 - \tilde{M}_Y c^2 - 2m_e c^2$$
$$= (207.979\ 717\ \text{u} - 207.976\ 627\ \text{u} - (2 \times 0.000\ 548\ \text{u}))c^2$$
$$= (0.001\ 994\ \text{u})\left(\frac{931.5\ \text{MeV}/c^2}{\text{u}}\right)c^2$$
$$= 1.86\ \text{MeV}$$

EXAMPLE 33-10

Neutrinos from Bananas!

An average banana has approximately 450 mg of potassium. Naturally occurring potassium consists of three isotopes: $^{39}_{19}$K (93.3%), $^{40}_{19}$K (0.012%), and $^{41}_{19}$K (6.73%). Both $^{39}_{19}$K and $^{41}_{19}$K are stable, and $^{40}_{19}$K undergoes both β^-- and β^+-decays with a half-life of 1.248×10^9 y:

$$^{40}_{19}\text{K} \rightarrow {}^{40}_{18}\text{Ar} + {}^{0}_{+1}\text{e} + \nu \quad (11.2\%)$$

$$^{40}_{19}\text{K} \rightarrow {}^{40}_{20}\text{Ca} + {}^{0}_{-1}\text{e} + \bar{\nu} \quad (88.8\%)$$

How many neutrinos and antineutrinos are emitted from a typical banana each second?

SOLUTION

To determine how many neutrinos and antineutrinos are emitted from a banana, we need to know the number of $^{40}_{19}$K atoms in a banana. We first calculate the average atomic mass of potassium. From reference tables, we find that the atomic masses of the potassium isotopes are as follows:

$^{39}_{19}$K: 38.963 708 u; $^{40}_{19}$K: 39.964 000 u; $^{41}_{19}$K: 40.961 827 u

The average atomic mass of naturally occurring potassium is

$$m_K = (38.963708\ \text{u} \times 0.933) + (39.964000\ \text{u} \times 0.00012)$$
$$+ (40.961827\ \text{u} \times 0.0673) = 39.1147\ \text{u}$$

Therefore, 39.111 47 g of potassium contains 6.02×10^{23} atoms, and the number of potassium atoms in 450 mg is

$$\frac{6.02 \times 10^{23}\ \text{atoms}}{39.1147\ \text{g}} \times 450 \times 10^{-3}\ \text{g} = 6.93 \times 10^{21}\ \text{atoms}$$

Since 0.012% of naturally occurring potassium is $^{40}_{19}$K, the number of $^{40}_{19}$K atoms in a typical banana is

$$6.93 \times 10^{21}\ \text{atoms} \times \frac{0.012}{100} = 8.31 \times 10^{17}\ \text{atoms}$$

The half-life of $^{40}_{19}$K is the same for β^-- and β^+-decays. The activity of the potassium in a typical banana is

$$R = \text{number of atoms} \times \text{decay rate}$$
$$= \text{number of atoms} \times \frac{\ln(2)}{\text{half-life}}$$
$$= 8.31 \times 10^{17}\ \text{atoms} \times \frac{\ln(2)}{1.248 \times 10^9\ \text{y} \times 31\ 557\ 600\ \text{s/y}}$$
$$= 14.6\ \text{atoms/s}$$

On average, 14.6 atoms of $^{40}_{19}$K decay each second. Since 88.8% of these decays are β^- decays producing an antineutrino, and 11.2% are β^+ decays producing a neutrino, an average banana emits approximately 13 antineutrinos and 2 neutrinos each second.

237

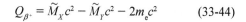

MODERN PHYSICS

Gamma (γ) Decay

The nucleons in a nucleus are not stationary. They move with speeds of approximately 1/10 the speed of light in orbits of well-defined energies. This motion is similar to the orbital motion of electrons around the centre of a nucleus. However, electrons move in the Coulomb potential generated by the positive charge of the nucleus, and the nucleons move in a potential, called the **nuclear potential**, generated by the strong force between the nucleons. The details of the nuclear potential and the calculation of resulting eigenstates of nucleons are very complicated. To introduce the main concepts of γ-decay, we introduce a very simple model of the energy eigenstates of nucleons bound in a nucleus.

Let us assume that the protons and neutrons in a nucleus move in equally spaced energy states (or orbitals). The lowest-energy state is denoted by E_0, and successively higher-energy states are E_1, E_2, E_3, ... The energy difference between adjacent states is ΔE. In addition to the attractive strong force, protons also exert a repulsive Coulomb force on each other. Consequently, the orbitals of protons are shifted to slightly higher energies than the orbitals of neutrons; however, we will ignore this difference. Figure 33-15 shows the energy levels of our simple model.

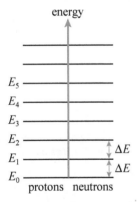

Figure 33-15 Energy levels of protons and neutrons in a nucleus (the Coulomb interaction between protons has been ignored in this energy-level diagram)

Protons and neutrons are fermions with a spin quantum number of $\frac{1}{2}$. The Pauli exclusion principle prohibits two fermions with identical quantum numbers from simultaneously occupying the same energy state. Therefore, no more than two protons (or neutrons) can be in a given energy level, one with spin-up ($\uparrow$) and the other with spin-down ($\downarrow$). A single nucleon in an energy level can have its spin projection either up or down.

Consider the ground state of $^{12}_6$C, which has six protons and six neutrons. Two protons fill energy level E_0, two go in E_1, and two go in E_2. Neutrons fill their corresponding levels in the same way (Figure 33-16).

A nucleus in its excited state is indicated by an asterisk. For example, $^{12}_6$C* denotes a carbon-12 nucleus with at least one nucleon in an energy level higher than the ground state.

Figure 33-17 shows two possible excited states of the $^{12}_6$C nucleus. In Figure 33-17(a), a proton has jumped from level E_2 to level E_3, thereby increasing the energy of the whole nucleus by an amount ΔE. In Figure 33-17(b), a proton and a neutron have jumped from E_2 to E_3, so the energy of this excited state is $2\Delta E$ above the ground-state energy.

A nucleus in an excited state releases its excess energy by emitting a photon, or a γ-ray. This process is called a **gamma decay** (γ-decay) and is represented as

$$^A_Z X^* \rightarrow \, ^A_Z X + \gamma + Q_\gamma \qquad (33\text{-}45)$$

The decay diagram for γ-decay is shown in Figure 33-18.

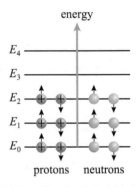

Figure 33-16 The configuration of protons and neutrons in the ground state of $^{12}_6$C (the Coulomb interaction between protons has been ignored)

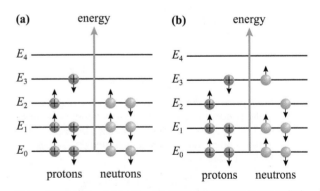

Figure 33-17 The configuration of protons and neutrons in two excited states of $^{12}_6$C (a) A proton has jumped to a higher-energy level. (b) A proton and a neutron have moved to higher-energy levels.

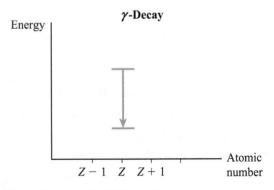

Figure 33-18 The decay diagram for γ-decay

When a nucleus decays by emitting an α-particle or a β-particle, the daughter nucleus is usually left in an excited state. The nucleus then jumps to a lower-energy state by emitting a γ-ray. Two nuclides that differ only in energy state are called **isomers**. For example, $^{12}_{6}C^*$ and $^{12}_{6}C$ are isomers. Usually, a nucleus stays in its excited state for a very short period of time of the order of 10^{-19} s. However, an excited state can exist for seconds, hours, or even years. Such excited states are called **metastable** states.

The energy difference between nuclear levels is of the order millions of electron volts. In contrast, atomic energy levels are only tens of electron volts apart. Consequently, γ-rays have much higher energies than the electromagnetic radiation typically emitted by electrons in atoms. For example, boron-12 ($^{12}_{5}B$) β-decays to various excited states of carbon-12. In one of the excited states, the $^{12}_{6}C^*$ nucleus decays to the ground state by emitting a γ-ray of 4.44 MeV.

Since γ-rays are highly penetrating, they can be used to inspect welds, structural materials, and sealed containers (see Figure 26-20).

33-7 Nuclear Fission and Nuclear Fusion

From Figure 33-4 we can see that the binding energy per nucleon for $A \geq 200$ is approximately 7.5 MeV, and for $A \simeq 100$ it is approximately 8.5 MeV. So, if a large nucleus ($A > 200$) with a binding energy per nucleon of 7.5 MeV were to split into two nuclei of approximately equal size, the binding energy per nucleon would increase to about 8.5 MeV. The two final nuclei are more tightly bound, so the difference in the total binding energy between the initial and the two final nuclei would be approximately 1 MeV/nucleon. Thus, the total energy released when the large nucleus splits is about 200 MeV. **Nuclear fission** is the process in which a heavy nucleus splits into two nuclei. The final nuclei are called **fission products**. Usually, a few neutrons are emitted during nuclear fission. Fission processes can be either spontaneous fission or neutron-induced.

Spontaneous Fission

In spontaneous fission, a large nucleus undergoes fission on its own (Figure 33-19). This process can be represented as follows:

$$^{A}_{Z}X \rightarrow ^{A_1}_{Z_1}Y_1 + ^{A_2}_{Z_2}Y_2 + m\,^{1}_{0}n \qquad (33\text{-}46)$$

where Y_1 and Y_2 are fission products, and m is the number of emitted neutrons, usually from 0 to 3.

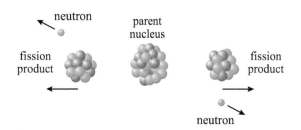

Figure 33-19 During spontaneous fission, a nucleus with a large atomic number spontaneously breaks into two nuclei of similar atomic numbers, accompanied by the emission of a few neutrons.

A large nucleus can split into various combinations of fission products. As in decay processes, the number of nucleons and the total charge must be conserved. Therefore,

$$A = A_1 + A_2 + m \qquad (33\text{-}47)$$

and

$$Z = Z_1 + Z_2 \qquad (33\text{-}48)$$

For example, uranium-238 ($^{238}_{92}U$) undergoes spontaneous fission. Here are two ways that uranium-238 fissions:

$$^{238}_{92}U \rightarrow ^{134}_{52}Te + ^{102}_{40}Zr + 2\,^{1}_{0}n + Q_f$$

$$^{238}_{92}U \rightarrow ^{134}_{50}Sn + ^{102}_{42}Mo + 2\,^{1}_{0}n + Q_f \qquad (33\text{-}49)$$

Here, Q_f denotes the Q-value for the fission decay and is different for the two reactions.

Energy Released in Spontaneous Fission The energy released during the spontaneous fission of a nucleus appears mainly as the kinetic energy of the fission products. Some of the energy also appears as the emission of γ-rays and electrons, as well as excitation energy of the final nuclei. The total energy released is equal to the difference between the rest mass energy of the parent nucleus and the total rest mass energies of the fission products, including neutrons:

$$Q_f = M_X c^2 - (M_{Y_1} + M_{Y_2} + mm_n)c^2 \qquad (33\text{-}50)$$

By accounting for Z electron masses, Equation (33-50) can be rewritten in terms of atomic masses:

$$Q_f = \tilde{M}_X c^2 - (\tilde{M}_{Y_1} + \tilde{M}_{Y_2} + mm_n)c^2 \qquad (33\text{-}51)$$

Why do all heavy nuclei not fission immediately? Why is lead-208 a stable nucleus when it could split into two more tightly bound nuclei? The reason is that an energy barrier, due to Coulomb repulsion, prevents fission. Consider the Coulomb potential energy between a proton and a nucleus as a function of the distance of the proton from the centre of the nucleus. If the charge Ze of the nucleus is distributed uniformly in a sphere of radius R,

EXAMPLE 33-11

The Fission of Uranium-238

Calculate the energy released during the spontaneous fission of uranium-238 into tellurium-134 and zirconium-102.

SOLUTION

We determine the Q-value of this reaction by using the atomic masses listed in Table 33-5:

$$\text{Atomic mass of } {}^{238}_{92}U = 238.050\,783 \text{ u}$$

$$\text{Atomic mass of } {}^{134}_{52}Te = 133.911\,369 \text{ u}$$

$$\text{Atomic mass of } {}^{102}_{40}Zr = 101.922\,981 \text{ u}$$

$$\text{Mass of two neutrons} = 2 \times 1.008\,665 \text{ u} = 2.017\,330 \text{ u}$$

The difference between the mass of the parent nucleus and the total mass of the products including the two neutrons is

$$\Delta m = 238.050\,783 \text{ u} - (133.911\,369 \text{ u} + 101.922\,981 \text{ u}$$

$$+ 2 \times 1.008\,665 \text{ u}) = 0.1991 \text{ u}$$

Converting this mass difference into energy, we have

$$Q_f = 0.1991 \text{ u} \times \frac{931.5 \text{ MeV}}{\text{u}} = 185.3 \text{ MeV}$$

Making sense of the result:

Although 185 MeV is an enormous amount of energy compared to the energy released in a chemical reaction, the half-life of uranium-238 for spontaneous fission is approximately 8×10^{15} y. Therefore, the rate at which energy is released by the spontaneous fission of a sample of uranium-238 is as small as very few nuclei fissions per second.

then the Coulomb potential energy, $V_c(r)$, between the proton and the nucleus is

$$V_c(r) = \begin{cases} \dfrac{Ze^2}{4\pi\varepsilon_0} \dfrac{r^2}{R^3} & r \leq R \\[2mm] \dfrac{Ze^2}{4\pi\varepsilon_0} \dfrac{1}{r} & r > R \end{cases} \quad (33\text{-}52)$$

A plot of $V_c(r)$ is shown in Figure 33-20. The Coulomb potential energy is positive because like charges repel each other. The potential energy is zero at the centre of the nucleus and maximum at the surface of the nucleus; outside the nucleus it falls off as $1/r$.

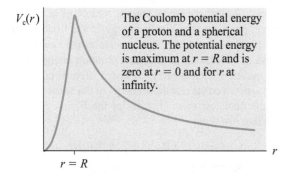

$V_c(r)$

The Coulomb potential energy of a proton and a spherical nucleus. The potential energy is maximum at $r = R$ and is zero at $r = 0$ and for r at infinity.

$r = R$

Figure 33-20 A plot of the Coulomb potential energy between a proton and a spherical nucleus, as a function of the distance between the two

Now, consider the spontaneous fission of uranium-238 into tellurium-134 and zirconium-102 (Equation (33-49)). We can imagine the uranium nucleus to be made up of a tellurium and zirconium nucleus, plus two neutrons. As the tellurium and zirconium nuclei begin to separate, the Coulomb potential energy between the two increases, opposing the separation. From Example 33-11 we know

that 185 MeV of energy is released by this separation. Is this energy sufficient to overcome the Coulomb repulsion and cause the fission? At the point where the ${}^{134}_{52}Te$ and ${}^{102}_{40}Zr$ nuclei are just touching at their surfaces, the Coulomb potential energy is

$$V_c(R_1 + R_2) = \frac{1}{4\pi\varepsilon_0} \frac{(52e)(40e)}{r_0(134^{1/3} + 102^{1/3})}$$

Here, we have used Equation (33-4) for nuclear radii. Using $r_0 = 1.2$ fm and $e^2/4\pi\varepsilon_0 = 1.44$ MeV fm, we get

$$V_c(R_1 + R_2) = 255 \text{ MeV}$$

The daughter nuclei need 255 MeV of energy to overcome the Coulomb barrier, but only 185 MeV of energy is released in the decay process. So the energy released during the spontaneous fission of uranium-238 is not sufficient for the daughter nuclei to overcome the Coulomb barrier and separate from the parent nucleus. The fact that the Q-value is less than the energy barrier explains why the probability of the spontaneous fission of uranium-238 is so small and the half-life is so long. So, why do ${}^{238}_{92}U$ nuclei undergo spontaneous nuclear fission at all? Nuclear fission, like all other decays, is a quantum-mechanical phenomenon and is possible because of quantum tunnelling, the same phenomenon that allows α-decay to occur.

Neutron-Induced Fission

Large A nuclides can be induced to fission by bombarding them with neutrons. This process is called **neutron-induced fission** and can be represented by

$${}^{1}_{0}n + {}^{A}_{Z}X \rightarrow {}^{A_1}_{Z_1}Y_1 + {}^{A_2}_{Z_2}Y_2 + m\,{}^{1}_{0}n \quad (33\text{-}53)$$

For example, neutrons can cause uranium-235 to fission in several different ways, including

$${}^{1}_{0}n + {}^{235}_{92}U \rightarrow {}^{93}_{37}Rb + {}^{141}_{55}Cs + 2\,{}^{1}_{0}n + 180 \text{ MeV} \quad (33\text{-}54)$$

and

$$_{0}^{1}n + _{92}^{235}U \rightarrow _{36}^{92}Kr + _{56}^{141}Ba + 3_{0}^{1}n + 173 \text{ MeV} \quad (33\text{-}55)$$

The calculation of the energy released in neutron-induced fission is similar to the calculation for spontaneous emission, but the total energy of the incident neutron must be included in the energy of the initial state. Generally, the kinetic energy of the incident neutron is less than a few MeV.

Chain Reactions Consider a large number of uranium-235 nuclei and a single neutron that initiates the fission reaction described by Equation (33-53). Let us assume that two neutrons are emitted in this fission reaction. The neutrons emitted in the initial fission can be absorbed by two other uranium nuclei, causing these nuclei to fission and emit four neutrons. These four neutrons can then induce four more nuclei to fission, generating eight neutrons, and so on (Figure 33-21). If each neutron induces another uranium nucleus to fission, the number of nuclei that fission doubles at each stage. It takes approximately 10^{-4} s for a neutron to be emitted and then absorbed again. Within one-hundredth of a second of the start of the process, $1 + 2 + 2^2 + \cdots + 2^{100} \cdots \approx 2.5 \times 10^{30}$ uranium nuclei decay. Since 185 MeV of energy is released per decay, approximately 4.6×10^{32} MeV, or 7.3×10^{19} J, of energy is released in this short time. This amount of energy is equivalent to the detonation of about 15 gigatonnes of TNT.

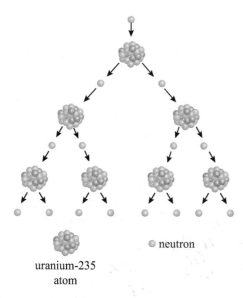

Figure 33-21 An ideal chain reaction. Each fission reaction produces two neutrons, each of which then causes another nucleus to fission.

Such a sequence of self-propagating nuclear reactions is called a **chain reaction**. Chain reactions are the basis of nuclear power generating plants and nuclear bombs. In reality, not all neutrons produced in the fission process act as triggers for other fission reactions. Many neutrons escape through the material, scatter off parent nuclei, or cause other types of reactions.

How a Nuclear Reactor Works As described above, approximately 200 MeV of energy is released when a heavy nucleus with $A > 200$ fissions into two smaller nuclei. Most nuclear reactors use uranium-235 ($_{92}^{235}U$) as the nuclear fuel. As discussed earlier, a uranium-235 nucleus can fission by absorbing a slow-moving neutron. Some of the possible outcomes of this fission process are

$$_{0}^{1}n + _{92}^{235}U \rightarrow _{56}^{140}Ba + _{36}^{93}Kr + 3_{0}^{1}n$$

$$_{0}^{1}n + _{92}^{235}U \rightarrow _{55}^{134}Cs + _{37}^{100}Rb + 2_{0}^{1}n$$

$$_{0}^{1}n + _{92}^{235}U \rightarrow _{53}^{131}I + _{39}^{104}Y + _{0}^{1}n$$

On average, 2.4 neutrons are produced in the fission of each uranium-235 nucleus. These neutrons, called **prompt neutrons**, can be used to fission other uranium-235 nuclei. The key to generating continuous energy in a nuclear power plant is to establish a self-sustaining chain reaction so that, on average, the same number of uranium-235 nuclei fission each second. For this, we need a sufficient number of uranium-235 nuclei available to fission, and we need to control the fission process so that the number of fission prompt neutrons does not go out of control.

Naturally occurring uranium ore consists mostly of uranium-238 with only 0.72% uranium-235. Uranium-238 does not fission by absorbing slow neutrons. To be used as a **nuclear fuel**, uranium must contain at least 4% uranium-235 (an exception is the Canadian CANDU reactor that uses natural uranium as the nuclear fuel). To produce this **enriched uranium**, uranium hexafloride, a compound consisting of uranium and fluorine is vaporized and rapidly spun in a tall, cylindrical **centrifuge**. The uranium-235 atoms are lighter than uranium-238 atoms (which have three more neutrons) and tend to stay in the middle of the centrifuge, and the uranium-238 atoms move closer to the outer wall. Thus, some of the uranium-238 can be separated out, leaving an increased proportion of uranium-235. Enriched uranium is pressed into thumb-sized pellets, which are stacked in long hollow cylinders made of zirconium, called **fuel rods** (Figure 33-22). Several fuel rods are bundled together, parallel to each other, with space between them.

With a sufficient concentration of uranium-235 nuclei, a chain reaction can occur, and the number of prompt neutrons increases quickly. Uncontrolled, the number of fissions per second would increase quickly, generating enough heat to melt the nuclear fuel and cause a **nuclear meltdown**. The number of neutrons in the reactor core is controlled by **control rods**, which are long, thin cylinders made of an element that readily absorbs neutrons, such as boron-10. The control rods are positioned between the fuel rods, and they can be either fully or partially inserted. This assembly is called a **nuclear core**. When the control rods are pulled out, the reactor runs at its maximum power. When the rods are completely inserted, most of the prompt neutrons are absorbed, and the chain reaction largely stops.

Energy released by fission is carried out of the nuclear core by a **coolant**, usually water, because water is readily available and inexpensive. However, other types of

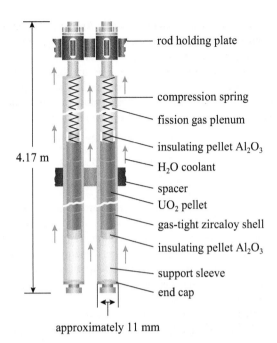

Figure 33-22 A nuclear fuel rod consists of enriched uranium oxide pellets that are packed in a thin cylinder made of zirconium alloy.

Labels in figure:
- rod holding plate
- compression spring
- fission gas plenum
- insulating pellet Al_2O_3
- H_2O coolant
- spacer
- UO_2 pellet
- gas-tight zircaloy shell
- insulating pellet Al_2O_3
- support sleeve
- end cap
- 4.17 m
- approximately 11 mm

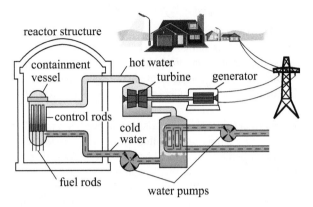

Figure 33-23 A boiling water reactor

Labels in figure:
- reactor structure
- containment vessel
- control rods
- fuel rods
- hot water
- turbine
- generator
- cold water
- water pumps

coolants are also used. Canadian-made nuclear reactors, called CANDU reactors, use heavy water as a coolant. In heavy water, the hydrogen atom is replaced by a deuterium atom (a deuterium atom contains one proton and one neutron in its nucleus).

The average energy of prompt neutrons is approximately 1.0 MeV. A neutron with this energy is moving at approximately 4.5% of the speed of light. The probability of a $^{235}_{92}U$ nucleus absorbing such a fast-moving neutron is very small. Therefore, these neutrons are slowed down by letting them lose energy during collisions with a **moderator**. In many reactors, water is also used as a moderator. The whole assembly consisting of the fuel rods, control rods, and the coolant is housed in a thick steel vessel called the **containment vessel**. All radioactive elements produced during the operation of the power plant remain within the containment vessel.

Steel pipes bring water into the containment vessel and bring heated water out of it. In boiling water reactors (BWRs), the type used in the Fukushima nuclear plant, the heated water is kept at a high pressure, usually 50 to 100 times atmospheric pressure. Water under pressure boils at a higher temperature, so the water temperature in BWRs reaches between 200°C and 250°C. The heated water is then turned into steam, which drives a steam turbine to generate electricity (Figure 33-23). Approximately 30% of the energy produced during fission is converted into electricity, and the rest is lost to the cooling water.

Over 90 different isotopes are produced when $^{235}_{92}U$ fissions. Most of these fission products are unstable and decay into stable elements by emitting high-energy electrons, neutrons, and γ-rays. Some of the common fission products in a nuclear reactor are iodine-131 ($^{131}_{53}I$, half-life

8.025 days), cesium-136 ($^{136}_{55}Cs$, half-life 13.04 days), cesium-137 ($^{137}_{55}Cs$, half-life 30.08 years), and barium-140 ($^{140}_{56}Ba$, half-life 12.75 days).

About one percent of the fission products decay by emitting neutrons, which are called **delayed neutrons** to distinguish them from the prompt neutrons. The delayed neutrons are also absorbed by uranium-235, causing it to fission. So, a nuclear reactor cannot be completely shut off by inserting control rods. Its energy production decreases, but it remains hot for a long time.

When the concentration of uranium-235 in fuel rods decreases below 1%, the rods need to be replaced. The spent rods are placed in large pools of water for a number of years until the radioactivity has fallen to a level where they can be stored. Dealing with radioactive waste products is a major technological challenge.

The fission products are harmful. For example, iodine-131 ($^{131}_{53}I$), a radioactive isotope of iodine, β-decays into xenon-131, a stable isotope of xenon, in two steps:

$$^{131}_{53}I \rightarrow {}^{131}_{54}Xe^* + e^- + \bar{\nu}_e + 606 \text{ keV}$$

$$^{131}_{54}Xe^* \rightarrow {}^{131}_{54}Xe + \gamma + 364 \text{ keV}$$

Most of the 606 keV energy produced in β-decay (the first step) is shared between the electron and the antineutrino. Xenon-131 produced in the β-decay is in an excited state and decays to its ground state by emitting a 364 keV photon (the second step). The electron and the photon have sufficiently high energy to penetrate human tissue to a depth of a few millimetres and cause cell mutation and destruction. Stable iodine-127 and radioactive iodine-131 are chemically identical. The body absorbs iodine and concentrates it in the thyroid gland, which uses it for the production of thyroxin hormones. If radioactive iodine-131 is present in the food or the air, it will be absorbed by the body and may lead to thyroid cancer. During the Fukushima disaster (and other accidental releases of fission products into the atmosphere), people nearby were advised to take natural (and stable) iodine-127 pills to saturate their thyroid glands with the stable isotope and make them less likely to absorb radioactive iodine-131.

Nuclear Fusion

From Figure 33-4, we observe that the binding energy per nucleon can also be increased by combining two lighter nuclei, thus releasing energy. The combination of two nuclides to form a heavier nuclide is called **nuclear fusion**. Fusion is the source of energy in all stars, including the Sun. A key series of fusion reactions in the core of relatively cooler stars, like the Sun, turns four hydrogen nuclei (protons) into a helium nucleus. In the first stage, two protons ($^1_1H + {}^1_1H$) combine to form a hydrogen-2 nucleus (deuteron) with the emission of a positron and a neutrino. The hydrogen-2 nucleus then combines with a proton to form a helium-3 nucleus with the emission of a γ-ray. Two helium-3 nuclei then combine to form a helium-4 nucleus with the emission of two protons. Energy is released in each stage of this cycle:

$$^1_1H + {}^1_1H \rightarrow {}^2_1H + {}^0_{+1}e + \nu + 0.42 \text{ MeV} \qquad (33\text{-}56a)$$

$$^1_1H + {}^2_1H \rightarrow {}^3_2He + \gamma + 5.49 \text{ MeV} \qquad (33\text{-}56b)$$

$$^3_2He + {}^3_2He \rightarrow {}^4_2He + 2({}^1_1H) + 12.86 \text{ MeV} \qquad (33\text{-}56c)$$

The positron ($_{+1}^{0}e$) produced in reaction (33-56a) combines with a surrounding electron (in the core of a star the electrons are knocked out from the hydrogen atoms). When an electron combines with a positron, both are annihilated into two photons with a total energy of 1.022 MeV (equal to the combined rest mass energies of the two):

$$_{+1}^{0}e + {}_{-1}^{0}e \rightarrow 2\gamma$$

Thus, in the reactions of Equation (33-56), four protons combine to form a helium-4 nucleus, and the overall reaction can be written as

$$6({}^1_1H) \rightarrow {}^4_2He + 2({}^1_1H) + 2{}^0_{+1}e + 2\nu + 26.7 \text{ MeV} \quad (33\text{-}57)$$

Reaction (33-57) is called the **proton–proton cycle**. Of the 26.7 MeV of energy released in this cycle, approximately 25 MeV is used to heat the star, and the rest is carried away by the two neutrinos.

For two nuclei to fuse together, they must have sufficient kinetic energy to overcome the Coulomb repulsion between them. In reaction (33-56a), the two protons must overlap (be within 1.2 fm of each other) to form a deuteron. At this distance, the Coulomb repulsion between the protons is approximately 1.2 MeV. So, the average kinetic energy of the protons must be at least 1.2 MeV to overcome the repulsion. From the kinetic theory of gases, we know that the average kinetic energy, $\overline{K}$, of a gas particle is related to the absolute temperature T by $\overline{K} = \dfrac{3}{2} k_B T$, where $k_B = 1.38 \times 10^{-23}$ J/K $= 8.62 \times 10^{5}$ eV/K is Boltzmann's constant, and T is measured in kelvins. Taking the average kinetic energy to be 1.2 MeV, the required temperature is

$$T = \frac{2\overline{K}}{3k_B} = \frac{2 \times 1.2 \times 10^6 \text{ eV}}{3 \times 8.62 \times 10^{-5} \text{ eV/K}} \approx 9 \times 10^9 \text{ K}$$

If all the kinetic energy is due to thermal motion, the protons must be in an environment that is at a temperature of approximately 9 billion kelvins (9 GK). Such high temperatures exist in the interiors of stars. The temperature of the Sun's core is approximately 15 MK, high enough to ionize the hydrogen gas into electrons and protons. The kinetic energies of the protons are distributed about a mean value corresponding to this temperature. A tiny fraction of protons in the Sun's interior have kinetic energies equivalent to the temperature of 9 GK and can fuse to form a deuteron. Even if the energies of colliding protons are below 1.2 MeV, quantum tunnelling can cause two protons to tunnel through the Coulomb barrier and form a deuteron.

EXAMPLE 33-12

Energy Released in the Proton–Proton Cycle

Using the Q-values given in reactions (33-56), show that approximately 26.7 MeV of energy is released in the proton–proton cycle of reaction (33-57).

SOLUTION

In reaction (33-56c), two helium-3 nuclei fuse to form a helium-4 nucleus and two protons. To form these two helium-3 nuclei, reactions (33-56a) and (33-56b) need to happen twice. Also, the positron emitted in reaction (33-56a) combines with an electron to produce two photons of energy 1.022 MeV. Therefore, the energy released in the proton–proton cycle is as follows:

$2 \times$ the energy released in proton − proton fusion
$= 2 \times 0.42$ MeV $= 0.84$ MeV

$2 \times$ the energy released in proton − deuteron fusion
$= 2 \times 5.49$ MeV $= 10.98$ MeV

$2 \times$ the energy released in electron − positron annihilation
$= 2 \times 1.022$ MeV $= 2.044$ MeV

Energy released in the fusion of two helium-3 nuclei
$= 12.86$ MeV

Total energy released: 0.84 MeV + 10.98 MeV + 2.044 MeV + 12.86 MeV = 26.7 MeV

LO 8

33-8 Ionizing Radiation

Ionizing radiation is electromagnetic radiation or particle radiation with sufficient energy to ionize atoms and molecules by removing bound electrons from them. The types of radiation in **ionizing electromagnetic radiation** are

X-rays and γ-rays. **Ionizing particle radiation** generally consists of α-particles, protons, neutrons, β-particles, or other elementary particles. The sources of ionizing radiation are radioactive materials, X-ray machines, nuclear reactors, particle accelerators, and cosmic rays.

To become free, a bound electron must absorb energy greater than its binding energy. The binding energies of electrons in outer atomic orbits are of the order of several eV. Therefore, ionizing radiation must have energy greater than a few eV to interact with electrons. Usually, only a fraction of the energy of the ionizing radiation is transferred to a single electron. As ionizing radiation passes through matter, it loses energy due to collisions with electrons. Therefore, to consistently ionize atoms, the energy of the radiation needs to be greater than 100 eV. For example, an average of 33.85 eV is required to ionize an air molecule. So a 5.0 MeV α-particle could ionize approximately 150 000 air molecules. For particle radiation, the rate of energy loss is proportional to the charge of the particle and the number of electrons per unit volume of the material, and is inversely proportional to the speed of the particle (slower particles have more time to interact with electrons and to transfer energy).

Absorbed Dose and Equivalent Dose

The amount of ionizing radiation incident on an object is called **exposure**. As a result of exposure, the object will absorb some of the incident energy. The energy absorbed per unit volume by an object is called the **absorbed dose** (D). The SI unit of absorbed radiation is the gray (Gy), which is defined as the absorption of 1 J of radiation energy per kilogram of the absorbing material:

$$1 \text{ Gy} = 1 \text{ J/kg}$$

An older unit of absorbed radiation is the rad (radiation absorbed dose):

$$1 \text{ Gy} = 100 \text{ rad}$$

For a given exposure, the amount of energy transferred to biological tissue and the resulting damage to the tissue depend on the type of radiation. Because α-particles are positively charged and have a relatively large size, they are very effective in ionizing atoms. When passing through matter, α-particles transfer their energy within a short distance, causing intense damage to the DNA structure of the tissue. β-particles and γ-rays lose their energy more slowly, and the resulting damage to biological tissue is more diffuse. To account for different interactions of radiation with the human body, we define the **equivalent dose** (H) to be a measure of the amount of damage caused to biological tissue by ionizing radiation. An equivalent dose is the absorbed dose multiplied by the **radiation weighting factor** (W_R), which is a measure of how damaging the radiation is:

$$\text{Equivalent dose} = \text{absorbed dose}$$
$$\times \text{ radiation weighting factor}$$

$$H = D \times W_R$$

The SI unit of equivalent dose is the sievert (Sv). Since the radiation weighting factor is a dimensionless number, the sievert and the gray have the same dimensions, joules per kilogram. Table 33-6 lists radiation weighting factors for various ionizing radiations. Notice that α-particles cause 20 times more damage to biological tissue than the same absorbed dose of γ-rays and β-particles. The equivalent dose is therefore a measure of the risk associated with absorbed ionizing radiation.

Table 33-6 Radiation weighting factors

Radiation	Radiation weighting factor (W_R)
Electrons, positrons, X-rays, γ-rays	1
Protons	2
Slow neutrons (10 keV) (depends on the neutron's energy)	5–10
Medium energy neutrons (100 keV–2 MeV)	20
α-particles, medium and heavy nuclei	20

In daily usage, equivalent dose is often referred to simply as "dose." The old unit of equivalent dose was the rem (röntgen equivalent (in) man), which is equal to a hundredth of a sievert:

$$1 \text{ Sv} = 100 \text{ rem}$$

EXAMPLE 33-13

Equivalent Dose

Find the equivalent dose for a person who has absorbed 10 mGy of α particles.

SOLUTION

$$H = D \times W_R$$
$$= 0.010 \text{ Gy} \times 20 = 0.20 \text{ Sv} = 20 \text{ rem}$$

Making sense of the result:

Absorbing a dose of 0.010 Gy of α-particles is equivalent to absorbing a dose of 0.20 Gy of X-rays.

For an average adult, the recommended "safe limit" of ionizing radiation is 50 mSv per year. For minors, this limit is 5 mSv. People living in Canada and the United States are continually exposed to natural and human-made ionizing radiation from a variety of sources, with an average yearly dose of 3.5 mSv. Figure 33-24 shows the average annual radiation exposure in the United States. Notice that approximately half the exposure results from inhaling radon gas, which is produced naturally by the α-decay of uranium, which is typically present in soil in concentrations from 0.7 to 11 parts per million. Radon is odourless, chemically inert, and highly radioactive. It decays into other radioactive elements and it is these products which stick in the lungs and can cause lung cancer. The U.S. Environmental Protection Agency estimates that approximately 21 000 lung cancer deaths every year can be attributed to radon poisoning, a statistic second only to cigarette smoking.

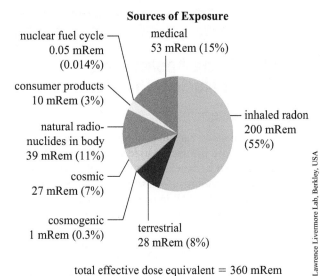

Sources of Exposure

nuclear fuel cycle 0.05 mRem (0.014%)
medical 53 mRem (15%)
consumer products 10 mRem (3%)
natural radio-nuclides in body 39 mRem (11%)
inhaled radon 200 mRem (55%)
cosmic 27 mRem (7%)
cosmogenic 1 mRem (0.3%)
terrestrial 28 mRem (8%)

total effective dose equivalent = 360 mRem

Figure 33-24 The average annual radiation exposure in the United States from various radioactive sources

EXAMPLE 33-14

The Equivalent Dose of Polonium

Polonium-210 ($^{210}_{84}$Po) α-decays to lead-206 ($^{206}_{82}$Pb) and releases 5.307 MeV of energy in the process. The half-life of $^{210}_{84}$Po is 138.376 days, and its atomic mass is 209.983 u.

(a) What is the equivalent dose received by an average adult lung (mass approximately 5.0 kg) from 10 μg of polonium-210?

(b) What is the approximate daily equivalent dose?

SOLUTION

(a) We know the energy released in a single decay, so we need to determine how many nuclei of 10 μg of polonium-210 decay in one second. The atomic mass of polonium-210 is 209.983 u. Therefore, 209.983 g of polonium-201 contains 6.02×10^{23} atoms, and

$$\text{Number of atoms in 10 } \mu g = \frac{6.02 \times 10^{23} \text{ atoms}}{209.983 \text{ g}} \times 10^{-6} g$$

$$= 2.87 \times 10^{16} \text{ atoms}$$

Since the initial activity, R_0, of the polonium equals the number of atoms times the decay constant,

$$R_0 = 2.87 \times 10^{16} \text{ atoms} \times \frac{\ln(2)}{138.376 \times 24 \times 3600 \text{ s}}$$

$$= 1.66 \times 10^9 \text{ Bq}$$

The energy, E, released per second equals the number of decays per second times the energy released in a single decay:

$$E = (1.66 \times 10^9 \text{ decay/s})(1 \text{ s})(5.307 \text{ MeV/decay})$$

$$= 8.81 \times 10^9 \text{ MeV}$$

To express the absorbed dose in sieverts, we need to express the incident energy in joules:

$$E = 8.81 \times 10^9 \text{ MeV} \times 1.60 \times 10^{-13} \text{ J/MeV}$$

$$= 1.41 \times 10^{-3} \text{ J}$$

Since the mass of the lung is 5.0 kg, the absorbed dose is

$$D = \text{energy absorbed per unit mass} = \frac{1.41 \times 10^{-3} \text{ J}}{5.0 \text{ kg}}$$

$$= 2.8 \times 10^{-4} \text{ Gy}$$

The radiation weighting factor for α-particles is 20. So, the equivalent dose per second is

$$H = D \times W_R = 2.8 \times 10^{-4} \text{ J/kg} \times 20 = 5.7 \times 10^{-3} \text{ Sv}$$

(b) The half-life of polonium-210 is 138 days, so its activity does not change substantially in one day. Therefore, a reasonable approximation for the equivalent dose per day is

$$5.7 \times 10^{-3} \text{ Sv/s} \times 24 \text{ h/d} \times 3600 \text{ s/h} = 490 \text{ Sv}$$

Making sense of the result:

An equivalent dose of 490 Sv is approximately 10 000 times the recommended maximum annual dose. Clearly, $^{210}_{84}$Po is extremely dangerous. Ingesting even in a tiny amount can cause fatal damage to internal organs.

33-9 Some Applications of Nuclear Physics

Explosive Detectors

Nitrate compounds, such as ammonium nitrate and potassium nitrate, are commonly used in explosives. Nitrates can be detected by bombarding an object with neutrons. Some of the neutrons are absorbed by nitrogen nuclei, forming the isotope $^{15}_{7}\text{N}^*$ in an excited state. This isotope then decays to its ground state by emitting a γ-ray with a characteristic energy unique to the $^{15}_{7}\text{N}^*$ nucleus:

$$^{14}_{7}\text{N} + ^{1}_{0}\text{n} \rightarrow ^{15}_{7}\text{N}^* \rightarrow ^{15}_{7}\text{N} + \gamma$$

This process is called a (n, γ) reaction, meaning "neutron in, photon out." A detector tuned to the characteristic frequency of the nitrogen-15 γ-rays can then determine when an object contains enough nitrogen to suggest the presence of explosives. Such neutron-activated explosive detectors are becoming common at seaports, airports, and border crossings.

Smoke Detectors

As described in the previous section, α-particles are very efficient at ionizing matter. Most household smoke detectors use this property to detect smoke and combustion products. Such detectors contains a small amount of synthetically produced radioactive americium-241 ($^{241}_{95}\text{Am}$), which emits α-particles with about 5.5 MeV of kinetic energy. These α-particles ionize air molecules and lose all of their energy within 4 to 5 cm.

In a smoke detector, α-particles from $^{241}_{95}\text{Am}$ enter the space between two electrodes that are approximately 1 cm apart and are kept at a potential difference by a battery (Figure 33-25). As the air between the electrodes is ionized, the negatively charged electrons are attracted toward the positive plate of the electrode, and positively charged ions are attracted toward the negative plate. The resulting tiny continuous electric current between the electrodes is sensed by an electronic circuit. When a fire starts, smoke particles and invisible combustion products get between the electrodes and neutralize some of the ions, thus reducing the current flowing between the electrodes. If the current falls below a threshold value, the electronic circuit triggers an alarm.

Americium-241 is chosen because it has a half-life of 433 y, which is long enough that the rate of emission of α-particles does not decrease significantly during the lifetime of a smoke detector. It also emits very few γ-rays. The half-life is also short enough that only approximately 0.2 μg of the americium is needed to generate a current detectable by a simple and inexpensive circuit.

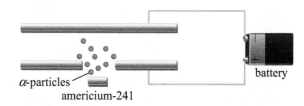

Figure 33-25 An ionization chamber of a smoke detector

- Atomic nuclei consist of protons and neutrons. The atomic number, Z, is the number of protons in the nucleus. The atomic mass number, A, is the number of protons and neutrons in the nucleus. Nuclei with the same number of protons but a different number of neutrons are called isotopes.

- Nuclei are approximately spherical. The radius of a nucleus is approximately

$$r_0 A^{1/3} \qquad (33\text{-}4)$$

where $r_0 = 1.2$ fm and A is the mass number.

- The nucleons are bound within a nucleus by the attractive strong force, which has a range of approximately 2.0 fm. Nuclear density is approximately 2.8×10^{17} kg/m³.

- Nuclear masses are usually given in atomic mass units (u). One atomic mass unit equals 1.6605×10^{-27} kg and is equivalent to 931.5 MeV of energy.

- The binding energy of a nucleus is the energy required to separate the nucleus into its constituent protons and neutrons. The binding energy $B(A, Z)$ of a nucleus is related to the nuclear mass, $M_{nuc}(A, Z)$, the proton mass, m_p, and the neutron mass, m_n:

$$B(A, Z) = Z m_p c^2 + (A - Z) m_n c^2 - M_{nuc}(A, Z) c^2 \quad (33\text{-}10)$$

- The Q-value of a nuclear reaction is the difference between the rest mass energies of initial nuclei and the rest mass energies of the final nuclei.

- Unstable nuclei spontaneously emit energy in the form of α-, β-, and γ-rays. The rate of radioactive decay is proportional to the decay constant, λ, and the number of unstable nuclei present:

$$-\frac{dN(t)}{dt} = \lambda N(t) \qquad (33\text{-}15)$$

- The number of unstable nuclei remaining after time t is given by

$$N(t) = N_0 e^{-\lambda t} \qquad (33\text{-}19)$$

where N_0 is the number of nuclei present at $t = 0$.

- The half-life, $t_{1/2}$, of a radioactive nuclide is the time it takes for half of the radioactive nuclei in a given sample to decay. The half-life of a nuclide is related to its decay constant:

$$t_{1/2} = \frac{\ln(2)}{\lambda} \qquad (33\text{-}21)$$

- The general form for α-decay is

$$^A_Z X \rightarrow {}^{A-4}_{Z-2} Y + {}^4_2 He + Q_\alpha \qquad (33\text{-}28)$$

where $^A_Z X$ denotes a parent nuclide, $^{A-4}_{Z-2} Y$ is the daughter nuclide, and Q_α is the energy released in α-decay.

- Beta-minus (β^-) particles are electrons. In a β^--decay, a neutron converts into a proton:

$$^A_Z X \rightarrow {}^A_{Z+1} Y + {}^0_{-1} e + \bar{\nu} + Q_{\beta^-} \qquad (33\text{-}38)$$

where $\bar{\nu}$ is an antineutrino, and Q_{β^-} is the energy released in the decay.

- Beta-plus (β^+) particles are positrons. In a β^+-decay, a proton converts into a neutron:

$$^A_Z X \rightarrow {}^A_{Z-1} Y + {}^0_{+1} e + \nu + Q_{\beta^+} \qquad (33\text{-}42)$$

where ν is a neutrino, and Q_{β^+} is the energy released in the decay.

- Gamma (γ) rays are high-energy photons. A radioactive nuclide emits a γ-ray when a proton or neutron moves to a lower-energy state:

$$^A_Z X^* \rightarrow {}^A_Z X + \gamma + Q_\gamma \qquad (33\text{-}45)$$

where $^A_Z X^*$ denotes an excited energy state, $^A_Z X$ is the lower-energy state of the same nuclide, and Q_γ is the energy released in γ-decay.

- Spontaneous nuclear fission is the splitting of a nucleus with large A into two nuclei, usually associated with the emission of one or more neutrons. Induced nuclear fission is caused by the absorption of a neutron by a large nucleus.

- Nuclear fusion is the merging of two light nuclei into a single nucleus. Nuclear fusion is the basic process responsible for energy generation in stars.

- The SI unit for nuclear radiation is the becquerel, 1 Bq = 1 nuclear decay/s. The SI unit for absorbed radiation is the gray: 1 Gy = 1 J/kg.

APPLICATIONS

Applications: nuclear reactors, medical imaging, carbon dating, explosive detectors, smoke detectors, security inspection

Key Terms: absorbed dose, activity, alpha particles, atomic mass, atomic number, average atomic mass, beta decay, beta-minus decay, beta-plus decay, binding energy curve, binding energy per nucleon, binding energy, carbon dating, centrifuge, chain reaction, containment vessel, control rods, coolant, daughter nucleus, decay constant, decay diagram, delayed neutrons, deuteron, disintegration constant, enriched uranium, equivalent dose, exposure, fission products, fuel rods, gamma decay, half-life, ionizing electromagnetic radiation, ionizing particle radiation, ionizing radiation, isobars, isomers, isotones, isotopes, mass number, metastable, moderator, neutrino, neutron number, neutron-induced fission, neutrons, nuclear binding energy, nuclear core, nuclear decay, nuclear fission, nuclear force, nuclear fuel, nuclear fusion, nuclear meltdown, nuclear potential, nuclear radiation, nuclear reactions, nucleon, nuclide, parent nucleus, positron, prompt neutrons, proton–proton cycle, protons, Q-value, radiation weighting factor, radioactive decay, radioactive, radiocarbon dating, strong force, weak force

QUESTIONS

1. Define the following terms: nucleon, nuclide, isotope, decay constant, half-life, decay diagram, Q-value, spontaneous fission, radioactive dating, and proton–proton cycle.

2. What are the main differences between the strong and the electromagnetic forces between two protons?

3. Describe the three main processes by which unstable nuclei decay.

4. Estimate Earth's radius if the atoms were compressed to the size of a nucleus.

5. In a nuclear decay series, a $^{238}_{92}$U nucleus decays into a $^{206}_{82}$Pb nucleus, which is stable. What is the maximum number of α-particles that can be emitted in this decay?

6. The mass distribution of the human body is approximately 65% oxygen, 18% carbon, 10% hydrogen, 3% nitrogen, and 1.4% calcium, the rest being other elements. Estimate the number of protons and neutrons in your body.

7. What is the ratio of the coulomb energy and the gravitational potential energy of two protons that are 2.0 fm apart?

8. The half-life of $^{8}_{4}$Be is 6.7×10^{-17} s. What is the most likely decay product of its decay? Explain your reasoning.

9. How many half-lives must pass until 75% of the atoms of a radioactive nuclide have decayed?

10. Why is energy released in the fusion of light nuclei?

11. Why is energy released in the fission of heavier nuclei? Would energy be released if two iron ($Z = 26$) nuclei were to fuse into a tellurium ($Z = 52$) nucleus?

12. What is a coulomb barrier?

13. How would nuclei decay if the mass of a proton were slightly larger than the mass of a neutron?

14. A free neutron has a half-life of 881 s, but a neutron in a carbon-12 nucleus does not decay. Why?

Section 33-1 Nuclear Terminology and Nuclear Units

15. ✳ Express the rest mass energy of 1 g of matter in J and MeV.

16. ✳ Approximately 1.2×10^{17} J of solar energy is intercepted by Earth every second. If all of this energy is absorbed by Earth, what is the increase in Earth's mass in one year?

17. ✳ The mass of a baseball is 145 g. Calculate the rest mass energy of a baseball in
    (a) J;
    (b) eV.

18. ✳ Assuming that nuclei are spherical, calculate the Coulomb repulsion between two carbon-12 nuclei that are
    (a) just touching each other;
    (b) 1.0 cm apart.

19. ✳✳ A free neutron (mass 939.55 MeV/c^2) decays into a proton (mass 938.26 MeV/c^2), an electron (mass 0.511 MeV/c^2), and an antineutrino (zero mass). The initial neutron is at rest. Calculate the maximum possible momentum for the electron. Compare this momentum with the maximum momentum that the antineutrino could have.

20. ✳✳ Consider the fission of a uranium-232 nucleus into two palladium nuclei:

$$^{232}_{92}\text{U} \rightarrow \, ^{116}_{46}\text{Pa} + \, ^{116}_{46}\text{Pa}$$

    (a) How much Coulomb energy is released?
    (b) How many uranium nuclei need to fission each second to produce 1.0 W of power?

21. ✳✳ Two stable isotopes of carbon are $^{12}_{6}$C (98.89%) and $^{13}_{6}$C (1.11%). Using Table 33-5, calculate the average atomic mass of carbon.

22. ✳✳ Calculate the average atomic mass of oxygen from the data in Table 33-7.

Table 33-7 Data for Problem 22

Isotope	Atomic mass (u)	Abundance
Oxygen-16	15.994 914 6	99.757%
Oxygen-17	16.999 131 54	0.038%
Oxygen-18	17.999 160 44	0.205%

Section 33-3   Nuclear Binding Energy

23. ✹✹ Using Table 33-5, calculate the total binding energy and the binding energy per nucleon for the following nuclei:
 (a) ^2_1H;
 (b) ^4_2He;
 (c) ^6_3Li;
 (d) $^{56}_{26}Fe$;
 (e) $^{208}_{82}Pb$.

24. ✹✹ Use the binding energy per nucleon provided in the table below to determine the nuclear masses of the following nuclei. Compare these values to the masses given in Table 33-8.

Table 33-8 Data for Problem 24

Isotope	Binding energy per nucleon (MeV)
^8_4Be	7.06
$^{12}_6C$	7.68
$^{84}_{38}Sr$	8.68
$^{208}_{82}Pb$	7.87
$^{238}_{92}U$	7.57

25. ✹✹ Using Table 33-5, calculate the nuclear masses of the following atoms:
 (a) ^2_1H;
 (b) $^{12}_6C$;
 (c) $^{16}_8O$;
 (d) $^{56}_{26}Fe$;
 (e) $^{238}_{92}U$.

26. ✹✹ Using Table 33-5, calculate the binding energy per nucleon for $A = 100$ nuclei with $Z = 42, 43, 44, 45,$ and 46. Plot these binding energies as a function of Z. Which nuclide is the most tightly bound?

27. ✹✹ Even-even nuclei have an even number of protons and neutrons. In the liquid drop model of a nucleus, the total binding energy of an even-even nucleus can be approximated using the following formula.

$$B(A, Z) = a_V A - a_S A^{2/3} - a_C \frac{Z^2}{A^{1/3}} - a_A \frac{(A - 2Z)^2}{A} + a_P \frac{1}{\sqrt{A}}$$

where

$a_V = 15.8$ MeV, $a_S = 18.3$ MeV, $a_C = 0.72$ MeV,

$a_A = 23.2$ MeV, $a_P = 12.0$ MeV

Using the above formula, calculate the binding energies of the nuclei in problem 24. Compare the two sets of binding energies.

Section 33-4   Nuclear Decay and Radioactivity

28. ✹✹ In natural carbon, one atom in 10^{12} is $^{14}_7C$ ($t_{1/2} = 5730$ y).
 (a) What is the activity of 1 g of natural carbon?
 (b) After 17 190 y, what is the activity?
 (c) Approximately 18% of the atoms in the human body consists of carbon. Estimate the activity of carbon-14 in your body.

29. ✹✹ The half-life for carbon-14 is 5730 y. Determine its decay constant.

30. ✹✹ A radioactive isotope decays to one-tenth of its original amount in two days. How long did it take for half of it to decay?

31. ✹✹ The half-life of $^{28}_{12}Mg$ is 21 h. At a certain time, the activity of magnesium-28 is 2.2×10^8 Bq. What is its activity two days later?

32. ✹✹ A radioactive nuclide had an activity of 3.0×10^4 Bq 10 h ago. Now it has an activity of 2.0×10^4 Bq. What is the half-life of the nuclide?

33. ✹✹ What mass of carbon-14 must be in a sample to have an activity of 10^6 Bq?

34. ✹✹ What mass of $^{226}_{88}Ra$ has an activity of 3.7×10^{10} Bq?

35. ✹✹ A radioactive sample contains 3.0×10^{20} atoms and has an activity of 2.0×10^{10} Bq. Find the half-life of the sample.

36. ✹✹ Strontium-90 has a half-life of 25 y.
 (a) Determine its decay constant.
 (b) How long will it take for 80% of the original amount of strontium-90 to decay?

37. ✹✹ A certain radioactive source has an activity of 1000 Bq at $t = 0$. The half-life of the source is 10 h.
 (a) What is its activity after 30 min?
 (b) After 3 days?

38. ✹✹ A sample of cloth contains 20 g of carbon, and the measured carbon-14 decay rate from the cloth is 120 counts/min. Estimate the age of the cloth.

39. ✹✹ At $t = 0$, the activity for a radioactive source is 20.0 MBq. At $t = 240$ s, its activity is 15.0 MBq. What is the half-life of the source?

40. ✹✹ A radioactive source has a half-life of 8 h. At $t = 0$, the activity is 900 decays/min. What is the activity 24 h later?

41. ✹✹ Table 33-9 lists the activities of a radioactive element as a function of time.
 (a) Plot the natural logarithm of the activity as a function of time.
 (b) Determine the slope of the resulting curve.
 (c) Calculate the half-life of the element.

Table 33-9 Data for Problem 41

Time (s)	R (decay/s)	Time (s)	R (decay/s)
0.0	1000	20.0	387
5.0	785	25.0	303
10.0	620	30.0	240
15.0	485	35.0	190

Section 33-5 Nuclear Reactions

42. ✶✶ Identify the missing particle in the following decays:
(a) $^{22}_9\text{F} \rightarrow {}^{22}_{10}\text{Ne} + ?;$
(b) $^{12}_6\text{C} \rightarrow {}^{12}_5\text{B} + ?;$
(c) $^8_4\text{Be} \rightarrow {}^4_2\text{He} + ?;$
(d) $^{239}_{94}\text{Pu} \rightarrow {}^{235}_{92}\text{U} + ?;$
(e) $^{60}_{28}\text{Ni}^* \rightarrow {}^{60}_{28}\text{Ni} + ?.$

43. ✶✶ Which of the following decays are not possible? Why not?
(a) $^{18}_8\text{O} \rightarrow {}^{17}_8\text{O} + {}^0_{-1}\text{e} + \nu$
(b) $^{14}_6\text{C} \rightarrow {}^{14}_7\text{N} + \nu$
(c) $^9_5\text{B} \rightarrow {}^9_4\text{Be} + {}^0_{+1}\text{e} + \gamma$
(d) $^{239}_{94}\text{Pu} \rightarrow {}^{239}_{94}\text{Pu} + {}^0_{-1}\text{e} + \bar\nu$
(e) $^{222}_{86}\text{Rn} \rightarrow {}^{220}_{84}\text{Po} + {}^4_2\text{He}$

44. ✶✶ What are the atomic number (Z) and atomic mass (A) of the unknown nuclei, marked as X, in the following reactions?
(a) $^6_2\text{He} \rightarrow X + \text{e}^- + \bar\nu_\text{e}$
(b) $^7_4\text{Be} \rightarrow X + \text{e}^+ + \nu_\text{e}$
(c) $^1_1\text{p} + {}^{12}_6\text{C} \rightarrow X + {}^1_0\text{n}$
(d) $^1_0\text{n} + X \rightarrow {}^{31}_{15}\text{P} + 2{}^1_0\text{n}$
(e) $^{27}_{16}\text{Al} \rightarrow X + \gamma$

45. ✶✶ In a nuclear reaction, slow-moving neutrons (ignore the neutrons' kinetic energy) are absorbed on a parent nucleus (X), which then decays into a daughter nucleus (Y) and a helium nucleus:

$$^1_0\text{n} + {}^A_Z X \rightarrow {}^{A-3}_{z-2} Y + {}^4_2\text{He}$$

(a) What is the Q-value of the above reaction in terms of the nuclear masses?
(b) The parent nucleus is $^{17}_8\text{O}$. Calculate the energy released using the table of masses. Take the binding energy of a helium nucleus to be 28.2 MeV.

46. ✶✶ A common nuclear reaction, called electron capture, is the capture of a k-shell electron by a nucleus:

$$^A_Z X + {}^0_{-1}\text{e} \rightarrow {}^A_{z-1} Y + \nu$$

(a) Write an expression for the Q-value of the above process in terms of the nuclear masses of the parent (X) and the daughter (Y) nuclei.
(b) Write the expression for the Q-value in terms of atomic masses of the parent and the daughter nuclei.

47. ✶✶ Can a $^{12}_6\text{C}$ nucleus decay into three ^4_2He nuclei? If yes, how much energy will be released in such a decay? If not, why not?

48. ✶✶ Berillium-8 (^8_4Be) is an unstable nucleus that decays into two helium nuclei. Given the following data, determine why ^8_4Be is not stable:

Atomic mass of ^8_4Be = 8.005305 u

Atomic mass of ^4_2He = 4.002603 u

Section 33-6 α-, β-, and γ-Decays

49. ✶ Write equations to describe the α-decay of the following nuclei. Use a periodic table to identify the daughter nuclei.
(a) $^{32}_{14}\text{Si}$
(b) $^{56}_{25}\text{Mn}$
(c) $^{60}_{26}\text{Fe}$

50. ✶ Write equations to describe the β^--decay of the following nuclei. Use a periodic table to identify the daughter nuclei.

(a) $^{32}_{14}\text{Si}$
(b) $^{56}_{25}\text{Mn}$
(c) $^{60}_{26}\text{Fe}$

51. ✶ Write the equations to describe the β^+-decay of the following nuclei. Use a periodic table to identify the daughter nuclei.
(a) $^{52}_{25}\text{Mn}$
(b) $^{55}_{27}\text{Co}$
(c) $^{59}_{28}\text{Ni}$

52. ✶ Using the table of atomic masses (Table 33-5), calculate the Q-value of the following α-decay reactions:
(a) $^{238}_{92}\text{U} \rightarrow {}^{234}_{90}\text{Th} + {}^4_2\text{He};$
(b) $^{235}_{92}\text{U} \rightarrow {}^{231}_{90}\text{Th} + {}^4_2\text{He};$
(c) $^{210}_{84}\text{Po} \rightarrow {}^{206}_{82}\text{Pb} + {}^4_2\text{He}.$

53. ✶ Tritium is an isotope of hydrogen with two neutrons. It has a half-life of 12.3 y and β-decays into helium-3.
(a) Write the reaction that describes the β-decay of tritium into helium-3.
(b) Calculate the energy released in this decay, using the atomic masses from Table 33-5.

54. ✶✶ Lead-212 ($^{212}_{82}\text{Pb}$) is a radioactive isotope of lead. It decays to the stable lead-208 through the following decay chain: β^-, β^-, α. Draw a decay diagram showing the decay process, and identify the intermediate daughter nuclei at each step.

55. ✶✶ Thorium-232 ($^{232}_{90}\text{Th}$) decays to lead-208 ($^{208}_{82}\text{Pb}$). How many α- and β-particles are emitted in this process?

Section 33-7 Nuclear Fission and Nuclear Fusion

56. ✶✶ In one of the possible reactions involving the neutron-induced fission of $^{239}_{94}\text{Pu}$, the two daughter elements $^{141}_{56}\text{Ba}$ and $^{92}_{36}\text{Kr}$ are produced.
(a) Write an equation describing this reaction.
(b) Find the energy released in the process, ignoring the kinetic energy of the incident neutron.

57. ✶✶ Using the table of atomic masses (Table 33-5), calculate the Q-values for the following fission reactions:
(a) $^1_0\text{n} + {}^{235}_{92}\text{U} \rightarrow {}^{90}_{36}\text{Kr} + {}^{144}_{56}\text{Ba} + 2{}^1_0\text{n};$
(b) $^1_0\text{n} + {}^{235}_{92}\text{U} \rightarrow {}^{93}_{37}\text{Rb} + {}^{141}_{55}\text{Cs} + 2{}^1_0\text{n}.$

58. ✶✶ The half-life for the spontaneous fission of uranium-238 is approximately 8×10^{15} y, and the half-life of uranium-238 for α-decay is 4.5×10^9 y. Given 1 g of uranium-238, how many nuclei undergo spontaneous fission in one day? How many nuclei α-decay in a day?

59. ✶✶✶ Even–even nuclei have an even number of protons and neutrons. Odd–odd nuclei have an odd number of protons and neutrons. Even–even nuclei are more tightly bound than odd–odd nuclei. There are only five stable odd–odd nuclei: ^2_1H, ^6_3Li, $^{10}_5\text{B}$, $^{14}_7\text{N}$, and $^{180}_{73}\text{Ta}$.
(a) Using Table 33-5 of nuclear masses, calculate the binding energy per nucleon of odd–odd nuclei.
(b) Using the same method, calculate the binding energy per nucleon of the following even–even nuclei obtained by adding one neutron and one proton to the odd–odd nuclei:
(i) ^4_2He;
(ii) ^8_4Be;
(iii) $^{12}_6\text{C}$;
(iv) $^{16}_8\text{O}$;
(v) $^{182}_{74}\text{W}$.
(c) How much binding energy is gained in each case?

60. ✷✷✷ Show that the Q-value for spontaneous nuclear fission can be written in terms of the binding energies of the parent nucleus (A, Z) and daughter nuclei (A_1, Z_1) and (A_2, Z_2) as follows:

$$Q_f = B(A_1, Z_1) + B(A_2, Z_2) - B(A, Z)$$

Using the binding energy formula for the liquid drop model (problem 27), determine the energy released in the following fission processes.

$$^{238}_{92}U \rightarrow ^{134}_{52}Te + ^{102}_{40}Zr + 2^1_0n + Q_f$$

$$^{238}_{92}U \rightarrow ^{134}_{50}Sn + ^{102}_{42}Mo + 2^1_0n + Q_f$$

COMPREHENSIVE PROBLEMS

61. ✷✷✷ The binding energy of an α-particle (a $^4_2$He nucleus) is 28.2 MeV. Use the liquid drop model (problem 27) to answer the following questions.
(a) A $^8_4$Be nucleus can decay into two α-particles. How much energy is released in this process?

(b) Can a $^{12}_6$C nucleus decay into three α-particles? Explain your answer.

62. ✷✷✷ In an (n, α) nuclear reaction, slow-moving neutrons (ignore the neutrons' kinetic energy) are absorbed on a target nucleus (X), which then decays into a daughter nucleus (Y) and a helium nucleus:

$$^1_0n + ^A_ZX \rightarrow Y + ^4_2He$$

The target nucleus is hafnium-180 ($^{180}_{72}$Hf). Calculate the energy released in the above process using the liquid drop model of problem 27. Take the binding energy of a helium nucleus to be 28.2 MeV.

63. ✷✷✷ Using the liquid drop model in problem 27, show that the energy (S_n) required to separate a neutron from a nucleus with Z protons and $A - Z$ neutrons, with large A ($A \gg 1$), is approximately given by

$$S_n = a_V - \frac{2}{3}a_s A^{-1/3} - a_A\left(1 - \frac{4Z^2}{A(A-1)}\right)$$

 See the text online resources at www.physics1e.nelson.com for Open Problems and Data-Rich Problems related to this chapter.

Chapter 34
Introduction to Particle Physics

On July 4, 2012, scientists at the Large Hadron Collider (LHC) announced the discovery of the Higgs particle, bringing an end to the most expensive and long-awaited search for a particle in the history of humankind (Figure 34-1). The Higgs particle was the last yet-to-be-discovered member of the Standard Model, a model that forms the basis of our current understanding of the nature of matter and the fundamental forces that exist between the particles. What is the Standard Model? What are the other particles in the Standard Model? How do particles interact with each other? Why does the LHC need to be so large? The subject of particle physics is fascinating as well as intriguing.

Figure 34-1   A section of the Large Hadron Collider

34-1 Classification of Particles

The electron was discovered by J.J. Thomson in 1896, the proton by Ernest Rutherford in 1919, and the neutron by James Chadwick in 1932. These discoveries led to a model of the atom with electrons orbiting a central nucleus made of protons and neutrons. The three particles in this atomic model were thought to be the only building blocks of matter. However, as technology developed and it became possible to collide extremely fast-moving particles and nuclei with each other, physicists began to discover a range of new types of particles. Most of the new particles exist for only a very short time and decay into other particles. To date, physicists have discovered more than 200 different subatomic particles. The branch of physics that deals with the study of particles is called **particle physics.**

Particles are classified as either elementary or composite. **Elementary** (or **fundamental**) **particles** are thought to be point particles with no internal structure. Electrons, neutrinos, photons, and quarks (which we will discuss later) are examples of elementary particles. A list of all known elementary particles is given in Table 34-1. **Composite particles** are made of elementary particles. For example, protons and neutrons are made of quarks and are therefore composite particles. The physical properties of a composite particle are determined by the properties of its constituents and depend on how the constituents interact with each other to form the composite particle (similar to how the properties of a nucleus are determined by the number of protons and neutrons that make up the nucleus and how they interact to form the nucleus).

A particle is classified in terms of

- its physical properties, such as mass, charge, and magnetic moment;

- its quantum numbers, including spin, and a few other properties, such as baryon number and lepton number;

- the type of forces that the particle exerts on other particles.

Table 34-1   The Fundamental Particles

Type of particle	Symbol	Name	Mass (MeV/c^2)	Charge (e)	Spin quantum number	Baryon number	Lepton number
Quarks*	u	Up quark	2.5	+2/3	1/2	1/3	0
	d	Down quark	5.0	−1/3	1/2	1/3	0
	s	Strange quark	125	−1/3	1/2	1/3	0
	c	Charm quark	1.3×10^3	+2/3	1/2	1/3	0
	b	Bottom quark	4.2×10^3	−1/3	1/2	1/3	0
	t	Top quark	171×10^3	+2/3	1/2	1/3	0
Leptons	e^-	Electron	0.511	−1	1/2	0	1
	μ^-	Muon	105.7	−1	1/2	0	1
	τ^-	Tau	1.777×10^6	−1	1/2	0	1
	ν_e	Electron neutrino	$<2.2 \times 10^{-6}$	0	1/2	0	1
	ν_μ	Muon neutrino	<0.17	0	1/2	0	1
	ν_τ	Tau neutrino	<15.5	0	1/2	0	1
Gauge bosons	W^+	W-plus boson	80.4×10^3	+1	1	0	0
	W^-	W-minus boson	80.4×10^3	−1	1	0	0
	Z^0	Z-zero boson	91.2×10^3	0	1	0	0
	γ	Photon	0	0	1	0	0
	g	Gluon	0	0	1	0	0
Higgs boson	H^0	Higgs boson	Estimated to be approximately 125×10^3	0	0	0	0

* Here the mass implies the rest-mass of the particle. The spin is the intrinsic spin quantum number and the baryon and lepton numbers are explained in the text. An isolated quark has never been detected. Therefore, the given values are the best estimates of the quark masses.
Source: Data from "Wuark Masses," updated Jan 2010 by A.V. Manohar (University of California, San Diego) and C.T. Sachrajda (University of Southampton, http://pdg.lbl.gov/2011/reviews/rpp2011-rev-quark-masses.pdf

Mass

The rest masses of the elementary particles vary over a wide range, as can be seen from Table 34-1. For example, a photon has zero rest mass, and the rest mass of the top quark is approximately 170 GeV/c^2, which is approximately 340 000 times the rest mass of an electron. The rest mass of a composite particle depends on both the rest mass of its constituent elementary particles and the nature of the forces between them to form the composite particle.

Electric Charge

A particle can have an electric charge or it can be electrically neutral. The electric charge is measured in units of the electron charge ($e = 1.602 \times 10^{-19}$ C). Until the 1960s, it was believed that the charge of a particle must be an integer multiple of e. However, with the discovery of quarks it was realized that quarks come in two charges: $+\frac{2}{3}e$ and $-\frac{1}{3}e$. The charge of a composite particle is equal to the sum of the charges of its constituents.

Intrinsic Spin

All elementary particles are assigned a spin quantum number, s. The electron has $s = \frac{1}{2}$, and the photon has $s = 1$. The intrinsic spin of a composite particle is obtained by adding the intrinsic spins of its constituents using the rules for the addition of angular momenta as discussed in Section 31-9. Recall that particles with half-integer values of s are called fermions and the particles with integral values of s are called bosons.

Fundamental Forces

The four known forces (or interactions) in nature are the strong force, the weak force, the electromagnetic force, and the gravitational force. These forces vary greatly in relative strengths, as shown in Table 34-2.

Table 34-2 Relative strengths of the four known forces

Force	Relative Strength (N)
Strong force	1
Electromagnetic force	10^{-2}
Weak force	10^{-7}
Gravitational force	10^{-38}

For example, if the strong force between two protons at a certain distance is 1 N, the strength of the electromagnetic force between them at the same distance is approximately 10^{-2} N, the weak force approximately 10^{-7} N, and the gravitational force approximately 10^{-38} N.

All particles with mass exert a gravitational force on each other. We will ignore the gravitational force in the rest of this chapter. The electromagnetic force always

exists between all charged particles (elementary and composite). The strong force exists only between quarks and is responsible for binding quarks into composite particles (composite particles are discussed in Section 34-5). The weak force is responsible for processes such as β-decay. Particles that interact with other particles only through the weak force and the electromagnetic force (if charged) are called **leptons**.

Quarks

Quarks are the building blocks of all composite particles. Quarks are charged fermions with $s = \frac{1}{2}$. There are six types of quarks (called **flavours**): the **up quark** (u), the **down quark** (d), the **strange quark** (s), the **charm quark** (c), the **bottom quark** (b), and the **top quark** (t). Quarks interact with each other through the strong, electromagnetic, and weak forces. We will discuss the quantum properties of quarks further in Section 34-6.

Leptons

Leptons are also fermions with $s = \frac{1}{2}$. There are six types of leptons: the electron (e^-), the **electron neutrino** (ν_e), the **muon** (μ^-), the **muon neutrino** (ν_μ), the **tau** (τ^-), and the **tau neutrino** (ν_τ). The charged leptons interact with each other and with other particles through the weak and electromagnetic forces. Neutrinos are electrically neutral, so they interact only through the weak force. An electron is stable and does not decay. The muon and tau are considerably more massive than an electron and are unstable. For example, a muon has a half-life of 2.26×10^{-6} s and decays into an electron and two neutrinos.

Gauge Bosons

According to the theory of relativity and quantum physics, elementary particles exert forces on each other by exchanging other particles, called **gauge bosons**. Photons mediate the electromagnetic force, gluons mediate the strong force, and $W^\pm$ and Z^0 bosons mediate the weak force. It is possible that the gravitational force is mediated by elementary particles called gravitons, but gravitons have not been observed. Gauge bosons have $s = 1$.

Higgs Bosons

In 1964, a group of scientists proposed that the elementary particles quarks, leptons, and gauge bosons gain mass by interacting with a field, which is called the Higgs field after one member of the group, British physicist Peter Higgs. In quantum theory, the Higgs field is quantized with the corresponding particles called **Higgs bosons**, just as the electromagnetic field is quantized with photons as the associated particles. The Higgs boson was predicted to be a neutral particle with an intrinsic spin quantum number 0 and a mass of approximately 125 GeV/c^2. On July 4, 2012, scientists at the LHC announced the long-awaited discovery of the Higgs boson.

C-34-1 Particle Classification

Particles that interact only through the weak and electromagnetic forces are called

(a) bosons;

(b) quarks;

(c) gauge bosons;

(d) leptons;

(e) gluons.

C-34-1 (d)

LO 2

34-2   Gauge Bosons

How do two electrons repel each other? If one electron suddenly moves away from another electron, would the electromagnetic force between the two decrease instantaneously? A consequence of the theory of relativity and quantum physics is that particles exert forces on each other by exchanging other particles. The rules of adding angular momentum in quantum mechanics require that an exchanged particle have an integer spin; therefore, it must be a boson. The carrier of the electromagnetic force between two charged particles is the photon, the particle that results when electromagnetic radiation is quantized. Two electrons therefore repel each other by exchanging a photon. A photon travels at the speed of light, so if the distance between two electrons suddenly changes, the force between them will take a finite time to adjust. The process of the exchange of a photon between two electrons is represented by the two diagrams in Figure 34-2. These diagrams are called **Feynman diagrams**, and they will be discussed in greater detail in Section 34-9.

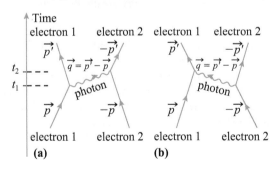

Figure 34-2   Feynman diagrams for the exchange of a photon between two electrons (a) Electron 1 emits a photon, which is later absorbed by electron 2. (b) Electron 2 emits a photon, which is later absorbed by electron 1.

In Figure 34-2(a), electron 1 emits a photon, which travels to electron 2. At a later time, electron 2 absorbs the photon. Let us consider this process using the centre-of-mass coordinate system of the two electrons. In this coordinate system, the two electrons have equal and opposite momenta in the initial state, and their energies E_1 and E_2 are

$$E_1 = \sqrt{\vec{p} \cdot \vec{p} c^2 + m_e^2 c^4} \; ;$$

$$E_2 = \sqrt{(-\vec{p}) \cdot (-\vec{p}) c^2 + m_e^2 c^4}$$

Let the momentum of the emitted photon be $\vec{q}$. After emitting the photon, the momentum of the first electron is $\vec{p} - \vec{q} = \vec{p}'$. When electron 2 absorbs the photon, its momentum changes to $-\vec{p} + \vec{q} = -\vec{p}'$. Therefore, the energies of the two electrons in the final state (after the photon has been absorbed by the electron 2) are

$$E_1' = \sqrt{\vec{p}' \cdot \vec{p}' c^2 + m_e^2 c^4} \; ;$$

$$E_2' = \sqrt{(-\vec{p}') \cdot (-\vec{p}') c^2 + m_e^2 c^4}$$

Note that in the centre-of-mass coordinate system, $E_1 = E_2$ and $E_1' = E_2'$. Since the total energy must be conserved before and after the two electrons exchange a photon, we must have

$$E_1 + E_2 = E_1' + E_2'$$

This implies that in the centre-of-mass coordinate system, $E_1 = E_1'$ and $E_2 = E_2'$. Before electron 1 emits the photon, the total energy of the two electrons is

$$E = E_1 + E_2$$

Let the energy of the emitted photon be E_γ. After the photon is emitted *but before it is absorbed*, the total energy of the two electrons and the photon is

$$E_1' + E_2 + E_\gamma = E_1 + E_2 + E_\gamma$$

Thus, we see that while the photon is travelling between the two electrons, the total energy is not conserved. Is the nonconservation of energy allowed? According to Heisenberg's uncertainty principle, nonconservation of energy by an amount ΔE cannot be observed if it occurs for a time Δt such that

$$\Delta t \leq \frac{\hbar}{2\Delta E} \tag{34-1}$$

The energy of a photon with frequency f is hf. Therefore, the energy of a photon with frequency f cannot be determined to an accuracy hf if the photon exists for a time less than $\Delta t = \dfrac{\hbar}{2hf} = \dfrac{1}{4\pi f}$. During this time, the photon travels the distance $R = c\Delta t = \dfrac{c}{4\pi f} = \dfrac{\lambda}{4\pi}$. Photons are massless, so the energy of a photon can be arbitrarily small; therefore, the distance R over which a photon can transmit the electromagnetic force is arbitrarily large. Figure 34-2(b) shows the process in which the photon is emitted by electron 2 and is later absorbed by electron 1. Instead of showing both diagrams, it is common to represent a photon exchange between two electrons by a single diagram with a horizontal line (Figure 34-3).

An exchanged photon exists for a limited time, and is called a **virtual photon**. Its energy is uncertain by an amount that is inversely proportional to its time

MODERN PHYSICS

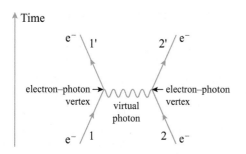

Figure 34-3 The exchange of a virtual photon between two electrons

of existence. A virtual particle does not satisfy Einstein's energy–momentum relation. Therefore a virtual photon can carry momentum without carrying energy. A photon emitted by a candle or a light bulb is a real photon. Its energy can be determined to a very high degree of accuracy, and its momentum (p) and energy (E) are related by $E = pc$.

The point where the electron emits a photon is called a **vertex**. Each electron–photon vertex is assigned a **coupling strength**, $\dfrac{e}{\sqrt{4\pi\varepsilon_0\hbar c}}$. The strength of the electromagnetic interaction is obtained by multiplying the coupling strength at both vertices of the diagram:

$$\frac{e}{\sqrt{4\pi\varepsilon_0\hbar c}} \times \frac{e}{\sqrt{4\pi\varepsilon_0\hbar c}} = \frac{e^2}{4\pi\varepsilon_0\hbar c}$$

Similar arguments can be applied to the strong and the weak interactions. Gluons are the carriers of the strong force. Quarks interact with each other by exchanging gluons. Like photons, gluons have no mass. The weak force is due to the exchange of W^+, W^-, and Z^0 bosons between elementary particles. Unlike the photon and the gluon, these bosons are very massive. Following the same arguments as discussed above, we can show that the range R of a force between two particles that is due to the exchange of a boson of mass m is approximately

$$R = \frac{\hbar c}{2mc^2} \qquad (34\text{-}2)$$

For example, the Z^0 and $W^\pm$ bosons have masses of 91.2 GeV/c^2 and 80.4 GeV/c^2 respectively, so the range of the weak force is approximately $\dfrac{200\ \text{MeV}\cdot\text{fm}}{160\ \text{GeV}} \simeq$ 0.001 fm, an extremely short distance.

Figure 34-4 summarizes the carriers of the electromagnetic, strong, and weak forces.

LO 3

34-3 Antiparticles

As discussed in Chapter 31, Schrödinger's equation satisfies the nonrelativistic energy–momentum equation $E = \dfrac{p^2}{2m} + V(x)$. But a particle moving with a relativistic speed must satisfy Einstein's energy and momentum relation, $E^2 = p^2c^2 + m^2c^4$. In 1928, British physicist Paul Dirac developed an equation that is consistent with the theory of relativity as well as quantum mechanics. Dirac used his equation to calculate many properties of atomic electrons, such as intrinsic spin and hyperfine splitting of hydrogen levels. Since the relativistic energy–momentum relationship is quadratic in energy, solutions to Dirac's equation allow the electron's energy to have both positive and negative values: $E = \pm\sqrt{p^2c^2 + m_e^2c^4}$, where m_e is the mass of the electron. Dirac interpreted the negative-energy solutions as corresponding to particles that have exactly the same mass as an electron but are positively charged. These particles are called **antiparticles**. The antiparticle of an electron is the **positron** (e^+). Dirac predicted that an electron–positron pair can be created by bombarding nuclei with photons with energy greater than $2m_ec^2$:

$$\gamma + \text{nucleus} \rightarrow e^- + e^+ + \text{nucleus}$$

Such a process, called **pair production**, requires the presence of a nucleus or another charged particle to conserve energy and momentum. Dirac also noted that when an electron and a positron combine, they can annihilate each other into two photons. This process is called **pair annihilation** and is written as follows:

$$e^- + e^+ \rightarrow \gamma + \gamma$$

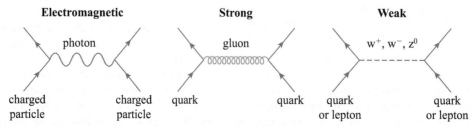

Figure 34-4 The carriers of the electromagnetic, strong, and weak forces

The existence of positrons was confirmed by the American physicist Carl Anderson, in 1932. He used a cloud chamber to study properties of cosmic rays. A cloud chamber consists of an enclosed chamber filled with a supersaturated vapour, often alcohol. When a charged particle passes through the chamber, it ionizes some vapour atoms along its path. The ionized atoms trigger the condensation of droplets in the supersaturated vapour, creating a visible track of the path of the charged particle. Placing the chamber in a magnetic field causes the tracks of positively and negatively charged particles to curve in opposite directions. Thus, the charge and the mass of a particle can be determined from measurements of the curvature and thickness of its track.

Some of the tracks observed by Anderson looked like the tracks in Figure 34-5. At the vertex of the curved upside-down V-shaped trail, a fast-moving photon created by a cosmic ray collides with a nucleus, producing an electron–positron pair. The curvature is due to the magnetic field applied at right angles to the plane of the photograph. One of the tracks corresponds to the electron, and the other track corresponds to a particle that has the same mass as an electron but opposite charge—a positron.

CARL ANDERSON/SCIENCE PHOTO LIBRARY

Figure 34-5 Tracks of several charged particle–antiparticle pairs in a cloud chamber

Experiments have shown that each quark and charged lepton has an antiparticle with the same mass and opposite charge. It is now assumed that every particle has a corresponding antiparticle. A neutral particle either has an antiparticle with some opposite quantum property or is its own antiparticle. Table 34-3 lists the elementary antiparticles. Note that the antiparticles for quarks and neutrinos are denoted by adding a bar over the symbol for the particle.

Table 34-3 The Elementary Particles and Antiparticles

Particle	Antiparticle	Name/Description
u	$\bar{u}$	u-bar
d	$\bar{d}$	d-bar
s	$\bar{s}$	s-bar
c	$\bar{c}$	c-bar
b	$\bar{b}$	b-bar
t	$\bar{t}$	t-bar
e^-	e^+	Positron
μ^-	μ^+	Mu-plus
τ^-	τ^+	Tau-plus
ν_e	$\bar{\nu}_e$	Electron antineutrino
ν_μ	$\bar{\nu}_\mu$	Muon antineutrino
ν_τ	$\bar{\nu}_\tau$	Tau antineutrino
γ	γ	A photon is its own antiparticle.
W^-	W^+	W^+ is the antiparticle of W^-.
W^+	W^-	W^- is the antiparticle of W^+.
Z^0	Z^0	Z^0 is its own antiparticle.
H^0	H^0	The Higgs boson is its own antiparticle.

✓ CHECKPOINT

C-34-3 Classifications of Particles

Which of the following statements are true?
(a) A lepton may be a boson.
(b) All quarks are fermions.
(c) Quarks and electrons can interact through the strong force.
(d) All gauge bosons are virtual particles.
(e) A photon is its own antiparticle.
(f) An elementary particle cannot decay into other particles.

C-34-3 (b), (e)

LO 4

34-4 Quarks and the Standard Model

The Standard Model postulates that the known universe is made of four types of fundamental particles: quarks, leptons, gauge bosons, and the Higgs boson (Figure 34-6), as well as their antiparticles. The particles interact with each other through the four known forces: the strong

MODERN PHYSICS

Three Families of Matter

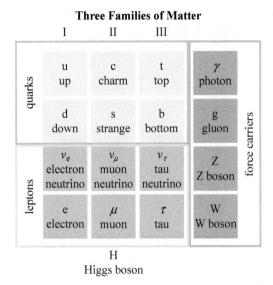

Figure 34-6 Elementary particles of the Standard Model

force, the electromagnetic force, the weak force, and the gravitational force. The Standard Model describes how the particles interact with each other through three of the four forces, the exception being the gravitational force. As noted earlier, the forces between the particles are mediated through the exchange of gauge bosons, $W^{\pm}$, Z^0, γ, and g (gluons). The Higgs boson is an additional boson that gives mass to fundamental particles. It is not a gauge boson (i.e., it is not a force carrier).

The six quarks and the six leptons are divided into three **particle families** or **generations**. The first generation consists of the up quark, the down quark, the electron, and the electron neutrino. The first generation is the most stable and least-massive family of particles. Protons, neutrons, and all atoms are made up of the first-generation particles.

The second generation consists of the strange quark, the charm quark, the muon, and the muon neutrino. The third generation consists of the bottom quark, the top quark, the tau, and the tau neutrino. Particles in the second and third generations are more massive than particles in the first generation, and they decay quickly when produced in high-energy collisions of first-generation particles. The fact that there are six quarks and six leptons that can be grouped into three families is required for the Standard Model to be consistent.

The Standard Model accurately describes how particles interact with each other and correctly predicted the existence of a number of particles. The up, down, and strange quarks were known to exist quite early in the development of the quark model of hadrons. The existence of the charm quark was predicted on the basis that the second family needs a quark with a charge of $+2e/3$. The charm quark was discovered in 1974 at the Stanford Linear Accelerator by colliding beams of electrons and positrons. Similarly, the Standard Model also predicted the existence of $W^{\pm}$ and Z^0 and bosons, which were discovered in 1983 with the particle accelerator at CERN. The

model also predicts the existence of many new composite particles made up of the more massive charm, bottom, and up quarks. Many of these composite particles have been observed in high-energy collisions, and the observed masses and other physical properties are consistent with the predictions of the Standard Model.

LO 5

34-5 Composite Particles

All the particles, which can interact via the strong force are collectively called hadrons. This includes protons and neutrons. Hadrons that are fermions are called **baryons**, and hadrons that are bosons are called **mesons**. By early 1960's a large number of baryons and mesons had been discovered. The existence of quarks was first postulated by an American physicist, Murray Gell-Mann (1929 –), in an attempt to understand whether this large number of particles have an underlying structure. Just as protons and neutrons bind to form a large number of nuclei, Gell-Mann proposed that baryons and mesons are made up of only three types of elementary particles, which were named quarks. These were the up (u), the down (d) and the strange (s) quark. The charm (c), the bottom (b) and the top (t) quarks were discovered later.

Baryons

Baryons are made of three quarks and have half-integer spin because all the quarks have $s = \dfrac{1}{2}$. A proton is a combination of two up quarks and one down quark, and a neutron consists of one up quark and two down quarks (Figure 34-7):

$$\text{proton} = (uud) \qquad \text{charge} = \left(\frac{2}{3} + \frac{2}{3} - \frac{1}{3}\right)e = +e$$

$$\text{neutron} = (udd) \qquad \text{charge} = \left(\frac{2}{3} - \frac{1}{3} - \frac{1}{3}\right)e = 0$$

Quarks are confined within a proton (or a neutron); therefore, their energies are quantized. The proton and the

MODERN PHYSICS

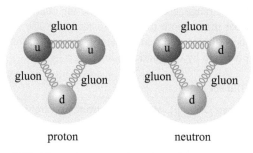

proton   neutron

Figure 34-7   The quark structure of a proton and a neutron

neutron are the lowest-energy bound states made of up and down quarks. As a proton (or a neutron) has spin $s = \dfrac{1}{2}$, one of the three quarks must have its spin oriented opposite to the spin of the other two. A proton with spin-up, written as $p\uparrow$, has the following possible quark structures:

$$p\uparrow = (u\uparrow\, u\uparrow\, d\downarrow + u\uparrow\, u\downarrow\, d\uparrow + u\downarrow\, u\uparrow\, d\uparrow)$$

Baryons can also have quarks with their spins all pointing in the same direction. For example, the delta-plus-plus (Δ^{++}) particle contains three up quarks. The resulting particle has a rest mass of 1230 MeV/c^2 and a spin quantum number of $s = \dfrac{3}{2}$:

$$\Delta^{++} = (u\uparrow\, u\uparrow\, u\uparrow)$$

There are three other delta particles with quark spins aligned in the same direction:

$$\Delta^{+} = (u\uparrow\, u\uparrow\, d\uparrow);\ \ \Delta^{0} = (u\uparrow\, d\uparrow\, d\uparrow);\ \ \Delta^{-} = (d\uparrow\, d\uparrow\, d\uparrow)$$

The superscript on each particle indicates its charge. Delta particles are excited states of three quarks and therefore are more massive than a proton or a neutron.

The quark model predicted the existence of particles that had not yet been observed. Consider particles containing the three lowest-mass quarks, up, down, and strange. We have seen how combinations of up and down quarks provide internal structures for the proton, neutron, and delta particles. The addition of the strange quark provides the internal structure of other particles, some of which had not yet been discovered.

Particles that contain one strange and two up or down quarks are called sigma baryons (symbol Σ). There are three sigma baryons:

$$\Sigma^{+} = (uus);\ \ \ \Sigma^{0} = (uds);\ \ \ \Sigma^{-} = (dds)$$

With two strange and one up or down quark, we can construct two baryons. These particles had previously been discovered and are called xi baryons (symbol Ξ):

$$\Xi^{0} = \ (uss);\ \ \Xi^{-} = (dss)$$

Finally, the model predicts the existence of a baryon that is made of three strange quarks. Gell-Mann called this baryon the omega (symbol Ω) baryon:

$$\Omega^{-} = (sss)$$

The omega baryon had not been discovered, and its discovery in 1964 was a great triumph of the quark model.

Table 34-4 lists some of the lowest-mass baryons made of up, down, and strange quarks. Note that some of the particles have the same quark structure.

Mesons

Mesons are hadrons that are composed of one quark and one antiquark. A quark and an antiquark both have intrinsic spin $\dfrac{1}{2}$, so the total intrinsic spin of a quark–antiquark system can either be 0 or 1. Mesons with $s = 0$ are called **scalar mesons**, and mesons with $s = 1$ are called **vector mesons**.

The lightest scalar meson made of up and down quarks and antiquarks is called the pion (symbol π). The three possible combinations of pions are the following:

Table 34-4   Some lowest-mass baryons made of u, d, and s quarks

Symbol	Name	Quark structure	Mass (MeV/c^2)	Spin	Mean life (s)
p	Proton	uud	938.3	1/2	Stable
n	Neutron	udd	939.6	1/2	886
Λ	Lambda	uds	1115.6	1/2	2.52×10^{-10}
Σ^{+}	Sigma-plus	uus	1189.4	1/2	0.80×10^{-10}
Σ^{0}	Sigma-zero	uds	1192.5	1/2	1.0×10^{-14}
Σ^{-}	Sigma-minus	dds	1197.3	1/2	1.48×10^{-10}
Ξ^{0}	Xi-zero	uss	1314.9	1/2	2.98×10^{-10}
Ξ^{-}	Xi-minus	dss	1321.3	1/2	1.67×10^{-10}
Ω^{-}	Omega-minus	sss	1672.5	3/2	1.3×10^{-10}

$$\pi^+ = (u\,\bar{d}); \quad \text{charge} = \left(\frac{2}{3} + \frac{1}{3}\right)e = e$$

$$\pi^- = (d\,\bar{u}); \quad \text{charge} = \left(-\frac{1}{3} - \frac{2}{3}\right)e = -e$$

$$\pi^0 = \frac{1}{\sqrt{2}}(u\,\bar{u} + d\,\bar{d}); \quad \text{charge} = \left(\frac{2}{3} - \frac{2}{3} + \frac{1}{3} - \frac{1}{3}\right)e = 0$$

The electrically neutral pion is made of a $u\bar{u}$ and a $d\bar{d}$ combination. The factor of $1/\sqrt{2}$ implies that both combinations are present with an equal probability. The spins of the quark and antiquark of a pion are aligned antiparallel to each other.

The lightest vector meson is the rho meson (ρ), with a mass of 775 MeV/c^2. The quark structure of a rho meson is the same as the quark structure of the correspondingly charged pion; however, the spins of its quark and antiquark are aligned parallel to each other. As yet, there is no clear explanation why the mass of a rho meson is more than five times the mass of a pion.

With strange, charm, bottom, and top quarks, we can construct many more mesons. So far, over 120 mesons have been discovered. The existence of many mesons was first predicted by the quark model.

Antimatter

The antiproton ($\bar{p}$) and antineutron ($\bar{n}$) are made of antiquarks:

$$\bar{p} = (\bar{u}\,\bar{u}\,\bar{d}); \quad \bar{n} = (\bar{u}\,\bar{d}\,\bar{d})$$

Notice that although an antineutron is electrically neutral, it clearly has a different quark structure than a neutron. Some composite particles are their own antiparticles. For example, a π^0 meson is made of equal amounts of $u\bar{u}$ and $d\bar{d}$ pairs. The anti-π^0 meson is obtained by replacing each quark of π^0 with its antiquark. Thus, the quark structure of an anti-π^0 meson is exactly the same as the quark structure of the π^0 meson:

$$\bar{\pi}^0 = \frac{1}{\sqrt{2}}(\bar{u}\,u + \bar{d}\,d) = \pi^0$$

EXAMPLE 34-1

Constructing Mesons

List all the mesons that have one antibottom ($\bar{b}$) quark. What is the charge of each meson? Assuming that the rest mass energy of a meson is the sum of the rest mass energies of its constituent quarks, predict the rest mass energy of each meson. Compare your prediction with the experimental values given in Table 34-5. Use the quark masses in Table 34-1.

SOLUTION

Since mesons contain one quark and one antiquark, we can construct six mesons by combining a $\bar{b}$ antiquark with any of the quarks. A meson constructed from an up quark and a $\bar{b}$ quark (called a B meson) has the following properties:

Quark structure: $u\,\bar{b}$

Charge: $2e/3 + e/3 = +e$

Estimated mass: $m_{\bar{b}} + m_u = 4.2 \times 10^3\,\text{MeV}/c^2 + 2.5\,\text{MeV}/c^2$
$$= 4.2\,\text{GeV}/c^2$$

Experimental mass from Table 34-5: 5.28 GeV/c^2

Charges and estimated masses of the other five mesons that contain a $\bar{b}$ quark can be determined in the same way. The results, along with the experimental masses, are listed in Table 34-5.

Making sense of the result:

Note that the meson masses calculated by simply adding the rest masses of the constituent quarks are always lower than the experimentally determined values. The bound quarks have a considerable amount of energy, and a proper theoretical determination of a meson's mass requires information about the forces that bind the quarks in the meson.

Table 34-5 Mesons that include a $\bar{b}$ quark

Quark content	Given name	Charge (e)	Estimated mass (MeV/c^2)	Experimental mass (MeV/c^2)
$u\,\bar{b}$	B^+ (B-plus meson)	+1	4.2×10^3	5.28×10^3
$d\,\bar{b}$	B^0 (neutral B meson)	0	4.2×10^3	5.28×10^3
$s\,\bar{b}$	B^0_s (strange B meson)	0	4.3×10^3	5.36×10^3
$c\,\bar{b}$	B^+_c (charm B meson)	+1	5.5×10^3	6.27×10^3
$b\,\bar{b}$	η_b (bottom eta meson)	0	8.4×10^3	9.4×10^3
$t\,\bar{b}$	No given name	+1	175×10^3	Not yet discovered

MODERN PHYSICS

Ordinary matter consists of electrons, protons, and neutrons. Can we construct antimatter made of positrons, antiprotons, and antineutrons? Antiparticles can be produced in high-energy accelerators. For example, antiprotons are created in proton–proton collisions in the following process:

$$p + p \rightarrow p + p + p + \bar{p}$$

In 1995, a team of scientists working at CERN created the first antihydrogen atom (symbol $\bar{H}$) by bringing positrons and antiprotons together. When an $\bar{H}$ atom interacts with ordinary matter, its positron annihilates with an electron to create two photons, and the antiquarks of the antiproton combine with quarks of a proton (or a neutron) to create pions. Therefore, the $\bar{H}$ atoms need to be isolated in a vacuum, away from matter. By trapping $\bar{H}$ atoms in a magnetic field, scientists have been able to keep them isolated for several minutes, long enough to study their properties. According to a fundamental theorem in physics, a universe made of antimatter must behave exactly the same as our universe. So the emission spectrum of $\bar{H}$ should be exactly the same as the emission spectrum of the ordinary hydrogen atom. Any difference between the two spectra would require radical changes to currently accepted theories.

MAKING CONNECTIONS

Antihydrogen and the Big Bang

There is another important reason to study antimatter. Most scientists think that particles and antiparticles should have been created in equal numbers at the start of the Big Bang. However, our universe is dominated by particles. Antiparticles are only created during high-energy collision of particles and photons. What has happened to the antiparticles that were created at the start of the Big Bang? Scientists hope that a study of antihydrogen can help answer this question.

 CHECKPOINT

C-34-5 Baryon Mass and Charge

Assume that the rest mass of a baryon is approximately equal to the sum of the masses of its constituent quarks, and rank the following baryons in order of increasing rest mass. Determine the charge of each baryon.

(a) tdd
(b) tbs
(c) ttu
(d) bss
(e) bbb
(f) ccc

C-34-5 (c); +2e; (b) 0; (a), 0; (e), −e; (d), −e; (f), +2e. The highest mass quark is the t quark, followed by b, c, s, d, and u quarks.

34-6 Colour Quantum Number and Quark Confinement

Just as electrons in an atom have quantized energy levels, the energies of quarks in baryons and mesons are quantized. As described in the previous section, a Δ^{++} baryon is made of three up quarks with spins pointing in the same direction. Experiments indicate that all three up quarks of a Δ^{++} are in the lowest-energy state. However, quarks are fermions, and according to the Pauli exclusion principle, two or more identical quarks cannot simultaneously occupy the same energy state. Therefore, physicists speculated that quarks have an additional internal quantum property that can take on three values. This property is called **colour** (or **colour charge**), and the three possible values are called red (R), blue (B), and green (G). Thus, there are three up quarks: up-red, up-blue, and up-green. The Δ^{++} baryon is therefore made of three up quarks of different colour quantum numbers (Figure 34-8). Since the three up quarks are not identical anymore (they have different colours), there is no conflict with the Pauli exclusion principle in them occupying the same energy state:

$$\Delta^{++} = (u_R\uparrow \ u_G\uparrow \ u_B\uparrow)$$

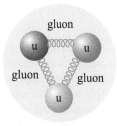

Figure 34-8 A Δ^{++} consists of three up quarks with different colour quantum numbers.

The colour property of quarks is not an actual colour. An up-red quark does not look red. The names for this quantum property were chosen because the colour quantum numbers of a baryon and a meson must add to zero (neutral colour), somewhat like the way the primary colours red, green, and blue can combine to form white light. Experiments have verified that quarks do indeed possess an internal property with three possible values. The colour quantum numbers for antiquarks are anti-red ($\bar{R}$), anti-green ($\bar{G}$), and anti-blue ($\bar{B}$). Baryons and mesons, although made of quarks, do not have the colour property because the colour numbers of the possible states of the constituent quarks add to zero, similar to the way an up-spin and a down-spin add to zero.

Colour is an additive quantum number, and a colour and its anticolour cancel just as equal and opposite electric charges cancel. Like the conservation of electric charge in a process, the total colour of the initial and final states must be the same. Consequently, gluons must have colour charge. For example, if a red quark emits a gluon and changes into a blue quark (Figure 34-9), then

Colour of the initial quark = colour of the final quark
+ colour of the gluon

R = B + colour of the gluon

Colour of the gluon = red + anti-blue = $R\bar{B}$

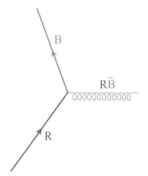

Figure 34-9 A red quark can change into a blue quark by emitting a gluon of colour red-anti-blue.

Gluons can have eight possible combinations of colours. Because gluons have colour charge, they interact with each other, unlike photons, which have no charge or colour.

Quark Confinement

We can break up a nucleus and observe its individual protons and neutrons. If a proton is constructed from quarks, then we should be able to break it apart and observe individual quarks. Despite numerous attempts using various techniques, no fractionally charged particles have ever been observed. Bombarding a hadron with very high-energy particles does not separate a quark from it; instead, the collisions create additional quark–antiquark pairs, which combine to form other hadrons. It is now believed that quarks are permanently confined within hadrons, and it is impossible to detach a single quark from a hadron. This **quark confinement** hypothesis is not yet fully understood.

Consider the strong force between a quark and an antiquark pair ($q\bar{q}$) due to the exchange of gluons between the two. Since gluons are coloured, they also interact with each other, which causes the field lines to be confined in the region directly between the quark and the antiquark, forming what is called a **flux tube** (Figure 34-10). The potential energy therefore increases as the distance r between the pair increases. At large distances the potential between the pair can be approximated as follows:

$$V_{q\bar{q}}(r) = -\lambda r \qquad (34\text{-}3)$$

each line represents a gluon

Figure 34-10 The exchange of gluons between a quark and an antiquark forms a flux tube.

Here, λ is a constant that depends on the strength of the strong force; its exact value is not needed for this discussion. The situation is similar to stretching a rubber band. The more the band is stretched, the greater the force needed to stretch it farther until the band breaks into two bands. Beyond a certain separation, enough energy has been put into the $q\bar{q}$ pair to produce an additional $q\bar{q}$ pair. The original meson then fissions into two mesons (Figure 34-11) rather than splitting into a quark–antiquark pair.

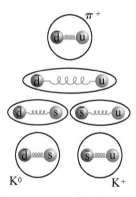

Figure 34-11 As energy is pumped into a pion to separate the quark–antiquark pair, the internal energy of the pion increases until there is sufficient energy to form two kaons.

If quarks are confined within a hadron, then how do nucleons exert a strong force on each other to form a nucleus? Gluons are coloured and a nucleon has no colour; therefore, a nucleon cannot emit a gluon and remain colourless. An exchange of a $q\bar{q}$ pair between the two nucleons is, however, allowed. This $q\bar{q}$ pair exchange represents the exchange of a virtual meson between two nucleons. So, the model of the strong force is as follows: The strong force between quarks arises due to the exchange of gluons. This force confines quarks within the hadrons. The strong force between hadrons arises due to the exchange of virtual mesons.

C-34-6

Which of the following statements are incorrect
(a) Just like quarks, leptons are also assigned a color quantum number.
(b) The green quarks emit light of green color.
(c) A meson can be made of a green quark and a blue antiquark.
(d) All three quarks of a proton can have the same color.

C-34-6 All of these statements are incorrect.

LO 7

34-7 Conservation Laws

The conservation laws of classical physics apply to interactions between particles. So, total energy, charge, and momentum are conserved when particles interact with each other. In addition, a numbers of other quantum number are also conserved. We can use conservation laws to determine whether specific reactions are possible without having to consider the details of the interactions between particles.

Conservation of Energy

The total energy of the initial state must be equal to the total energy of the final state. The total energy includes the rest mass energy of the particles. Consider the decay of a neutron into a proton, an electron, and an antineutrino:

$$n \rightarrow p + e^- + \bar{\nu}_e$$

In the rest frame of the neutron, there is no kinetic energy, so the total energy in the initial state is simply the rest mass energy of the neutron. The total energy in the final state is the sum of the rest mass energy and the kinetic energy of all three product particles and must equal $m_n c^2$.

Conservation of energy explains why a free proton cannot spontaneously decay into a neutron, as follows:

$$p \rightarrow n + e^+ + \nu_e$$

The total energy in the initial state is equal to the rest mass energy of the proton. Since the rest mass energy of the neutron alone is greater than the rest mass energy of the proton, the reaction cannot occur by itself.

Conservation of Momentum

The total momentum of the initial state must be equal to the total momentum of the final state. For example, for neutron decay in the rest frame of the neutron, conservation of momentum requires that

$$\vec{0} = \vec{p}_p + \vec{p}_e + \vec{p}_{\bar{\nu}}$$

where $\vec{p}_p$, $\vec{p}_e$, and $\vec{p}_{\bar{\nu}}$ are the momenta of the proton, electron, and antineutrino, respectively.

For relativistic kinematics, energy and momentum are combined into a single quantity called the **four-momentum**, p_μ. The laws of conservation of energy and momentum can then be combined into the law of conservation of four-momentum. For neutron decay,

$$p_{\mu,n} = p_{\mu,p} + p_{\mu,e} + p_{\mu,\nu}$$

Conservation of Angular Momentum

As described in Chapter 31, the total angular momentum $\vec{J}$ of a particle is the sum of its orbital angular momentum $\vec{L}$ and its intrinsic spin $\vec{S}$:

$$\vec{J} = \vec{L} + \vec{S}$$

According to the law of conservation of angular momentum, in the absence of net external torque, the total angular momenta of the initial and the final states are equal. So, for neutron decay,

$$\vec{J}_n = \vec{J}_p + \vec{J}_e + \vec{J}_\nu$$

Note that the *total* angular momentum is conserved, but the orbital angular momentum and spin are not conserved individually.

Conservation of Charge

The total charge in the initial and final states must be the same. The process $p + p \rightarrow p + n + \pi^+$ is allowed by charge conservation because the total charges of the initial and final states are both $+2e$. Conservation of energy requires that the protons in the initial state have at least enough kinetic energy to create a pion and make up the difference in rest mass between a proton and a neutron. However, the process $p + p \rightarrow p + n + \pi^0$ is prohibited because the total charge of the initial state is $+2e$, and the total charge of the final state is $+e$.

Conservation of Lepton Number

It is experimentally observed that the number of leptons minus the number of antileptons is conserved in all reactions. Therefore, leptons are assigned a **lepton number**, L, of $+1$, and antileptons are assigned a value of -1. The lepton number of all other particles is 0. With this assignment, the total lepton number is conserved in any interaction. For example, the lepton number in the initial and final states in the decay of a neutron is 0:

$$n \rightarrow p + e^- + \bar{\nu}_e$$
$$L: \quad 0 = 0 + 1 + (-1)$$

Similarly, the reaction $e^+ + e^- \rightarrow \pi^+ + \pi^-$ conserves a lepton number of zero. In contrast, the following two decay processes cannot happen because the lepton number is not conserved:

$$\pi^- \rightarrow e^- + \gamma \qquad \mu^- \rightarrow e^- + \bar{\nu}_e$$
$$L: \quad 0 \neq 1 + 0 \qquad L: \quad +1 \neq 1 + (-1)$$

Neither of these prohibited decays has ever been observed.

MODERN PHYSICS

Conservation of Baryon Number

The law of conservation of **baryon number**, B, is also an experimental fact. It states that the number of baryons minus the number of antibaryons is the same in the initial and final states of a reaction. A baryon number of $+1$ is assigned to each baryon and -1 to each antibaryon. Since baryons are made up of three quarks, all quarks are assigned a baryon number of 1/3, and antiquarks are assigned a value of $-1/3$. All other particles (including mesons and leptons) have a baryon number of 0.

For example, in the β-decay of a neutron the baryon number before and after the decay is the same:

$$n \rightarrow p + e^- + \bar{v}_e$$
$$B: \ +1 = +1 + 0 + 0$$

However, a proton cannot decay into a positron and a neutrino even though energy, momentum, charge, and lepton number would be conserved in this reaction:

$$p \rightarrow e^+ + v_e + \gamma$$
$$B: \ +1 \neq 0 + 0 + 0$$
$$L: \ \ \ 0 = -1 + 1 + 0$$

The process $p + p \rightarrow p + p + n$ is not possible, regardless of the total energy of the initial state, because the baryon number of the initial state is 2 and the baryon number of the final state is 3. Similarly, the decay process $p \rightarrow e^+ + \gamma$ conserves energy, momentum, angular momentum, and charge but is still prohibited because it does not conserve baryon number.

✓ CHECKPOINT

C-34-7 Conservation Laws

Indicate whether the reactions listed in Table 34-6 are possible. If not, indicate which conservation law forbids the reaction. Assume that when there are two particles in the initial state they have enough kinetic energy to conserve total energy in the process.

Table 34-6 Reactions for C-34-3

Reaction	Yes/No	Reason (if No)
(a) $p \rightarrow n + e^+ + v_e$		
(b) $p \rightarrow \pi^+ + \pi^0$		
(c) $n + p \rightarrow p + p + \pi^-$		
(d) $n + p \rightarrow p + p + \pi^0$		
(e) $e^- + p \rightarrow n + \gamma$		
(f) $n \rightarrow e^- + e^+$		
(g) $e^- + p \rightarrow n + v_e$		
(h) $e^- + e^+ \rightarrow \mu^- + \mu^+$		

C-34-7 (a) No, energy conservation; (b) no, baryon number; (c) yes; (d) no, charge conservation; (e) no, lepton number; (f) no, baryon number; (g) yes; (h) yes.

LO 8

34-8 The Production and Decay of Particles

Scientists create new particles by colliding beams of high-energy particles, usually electrons or protons, with other particles or nuclei. In such collisions, the kinetic energy of the colliding particles is transformed into the mass of the new particles, in accordance with Einstein's mass–energy equation, $E = mc^2$. For example, pions can be produced by colliding fast-moving protons with other protons in the following processes:

$$p + p \rightarrow p + n + \pi^+$$
$$p + p \rightarrow p + p + \pi^0$$
$$p + p \rightarrow p + p + \pi^0 + \pi^+ + \pi^-$$

One of the protons on the left side of each reaction arrow represents a fast-moving **incident proton**, and the other is the **target proton**, usually at rest. How much kinetic energy does the incident proton need to produce one charged pion? The mass of π^+ is 139.6 MeV/c^2, so one might think that the incident proton must have at least 139.6 MeV of kinetic energy. However, the kinetic energy of the incident proton must be at least twice this amount.

Consider a collision between two particles of masses m_1 and m_2. We will assume one-dimensional motion and not use vector notation. Assume that particle 1 (mass m_1) is moving along the positive x-axis with velocity $v_{lab} \ll c$, and particle 2 (mass m_2) is initially at rest. In this frame of reference, called the **laboratory frame of reference**, the total kinetic energy of the two particles is (here we have used non-relativistic kinematics to simplify the calculation)

$$K_{lab} = \frac{1}{2} m_1 v_1^2 + \frac{1}{2} m_2 v_2^2 = \frac{1}{2} m_1 v_{lab}^2 \qquad (34\text{-}4)$$

It is easier to analyze the collision in a frame of reference that is moving with the centre of mass of the colliding particles. If at some instant particle 1 is located at x_1 and particle 2 is at x_2, the centre of mass x_{cm} of the two particles is located at

$$x_{cm} = \frac{m_1 x_1 + m_2 x_2}{m_1 + m_2} \qquad (34\text{-}5)$$

Differentiating with respect to time,

$$\frac{dx_{cm}}{dt} = \frac{m_1 \dfrac{dx_1}{dt} + m_2 \dfrac{dx_2}{dt}}{m_1 + m_2}$$

In the above equation, $\dfrac{dx_{cm}}{dt} = v_{cm}$ is the velocity of the centre of mass, $\dfrac{dx_1}{dt} = v_{lab}$ is the velocity of the incident particle in the laboratory frame, and $\frac{dx_2}{dt} = 0$ because particle 2 is at rest. Therefore,

$$v_{cm} = \left(\frac{m_1}{m_1 + m_2}\right)v_{lab} \qquad (34\text{-}6)$$

Notice that the centre of mass moves in the same direction as the incident particle but with a slower speed. According to an observer moving with the centre of mass, particle 1 is incident from the left with velocity $v_{lab} - v_{cm}$, and particle 2 is approaching from the right with velocity $-v_{cm}$. Before the collision, the total momentum of the two particles is zero in the centre-of-mass frame:

$$m_1(v_{lab} - v_{cm}) + m_2(-v_{cm})$$
$$= m_1 v_{lab} + (m_1 + m_2)(-v_{cm}) = 0 \qquad (34\text{-}7)$$

By the law of conservation of momentum, the total momentum remains zero after the collision. In the centre-of-mass frame, the total kinetic energy, K_{cm}, of the two colliding particles is

$$K_{cm} = \frac{1}{2}m_1(v_{lab} - v_{cm})^2 + \frac{1}{2}m_2(-v_{cm})^2$$
$$= \left(\frac{m_2}{m_1 + m_2}\right)K_{lab} \qquad (34\text{-}8)$$

The total kinetic energy in the centre-of-mass frame is not the same as in the laboratory frame because the centre of mass of the two particles also moves and there is a kinetic energy associated with this motion. Using Equation (34-6),

$$K_{cm} + \frac{1}{2}(m_1 + m_2)v_{cm}^2 = K_{lab} \qquad (34\text{-}9)$$

In the centre-of-mass frame, the colliding particles can come to rest after the collision and still conserve momentum. In this case, since the total kinetic energy is zero after the collision, all the initial kinetic energy becomes either mass–energy of the new particles or excitation energy of the particles. Therefore, the *maximum* possible energy available to create a new particle is

$$K_{cm} = \left(\frac{m_2}{m_1 + m_2}\right)K_{lab} \qquad (34\text{-}10)$$

The greater the kinetic energy of the incident particle, the more energy is available to produce new particles. To create particles with very large masses, the incident particle must have a very large kinetic energy. This is the reason for building large particle accelerators such as the LHC.

Particle Decay

Particles can decay into particles of lower mass provided no conservation laws are violated. Particle decay follows the exponential decay law described in Chapter 33:

$$N(t) = N(0)\, e^{-\frac{t}{\tau}} \qquad (34\text{-}11)$$

EXAMPLE 34-2

Producing Pions

Bombarding a stationary hydrogen target with a beam of fast-moving protons can produce positively charged pions (π^+, rest mass 139.6 MeV/c^2) in the reaction $p + p \rightarrow p + n + \pi^+$. What is the minimum kinetic energy required for the proton beam to produce the charged pions?

SOLUTION

The minimum energy required to create a π^+ is equal to its rest mass energy, $(139.6 \text{ MeV}/c^2)c^2 = 139.6 \text{ MeV}$. This energy has to come at the expense of a decrease in the centre-of-mass kinetic energy. For proton–proton collisions,

$$\frac{m_2}{m_1 + m_2} = \frac{m_p}{m_p + m_p} = \frac{1}{2}$$

Therefore, from Equation (34-10),

$$K_{cm} = 139.6 \text{ MeV} = \frac{1}{2}K_{lab}$$

$$K_{lab} = 2 \times 139.6 \text{ MeV} = 279.2 \text{ MeV}$$

Thus, the minimum kinetic energy for the proton beam incident on a hydrogen target to create positively charged pions is about 280 MeV. The final state contains a neutron and its rest mass is 1.2 MeV/c^2 greater than that of a proton. So some additional kinetic energy is needed to create this extra mass.

Making sense of the result:

As colliding particles have the same mass, half of the incident kinetic energy goes into the centre of mass motion and the other half is converted into the rest mass of the new particle.

where $N(0)$ is the number of particles present at $t = 0$, $N(t)$ is the number remaining after time t, and τ is the mean lifetime of the particle.

Approximate values of lifetimes for decays through the strong, electromagnetic, and weak interactions are the following:

Decay through the strong interaction	10^{-23} s
Decay through the electromagnetic interaction	10^{-18} s
Decay through the weak interaction	10^{-10} s

The exact values of the lifetimes depend on detailed calculations. A particle can decay in several different ways. For example, a negatively charged pion can decay into a muon and an muon antineutrino, or into an electron and an electron antineutrino:

$$\pi^- \rightarrow \mu^- + \bar{\nu}_\mu \qquad (34\text{-}12)$$
$$\pi^- \rightarrow e^- + \bar{\nu}_e \qquad (34\text{-}13)$$

Consider the decay of particle a with a mass of m_a into particle b with a mass of m_b and particle c with a mass of m_c:

$$a \rightarrow b + c$$

MODERN PHYSICS

Conservation of energy and momentum requires that

$$E_a = E_b + E_c \quad \text{and} \quad \vec{p}_a = \vec{p}_b + \vec{p}_c$$

If particle a is at rest, conservation of momentum gives

$$\vec{p}_b = -\vec{p}_c$$

Using the relativistic energy–momentum relation, the conservation of energy requires that

$$m_a c^2 = \sqrt{p^2 c^2 + m_b^2 c^4} + \sqrt{p^2 c^2 + m_c^2 c^4}$$

Solving for p, the magnitude of momentum of particles b and c is

$$p = \frac{m_a c}{2} \sqrt{\left(1 - \frac{m_b^2 + m_c^2}{m_a^2}\right)^2 - 4\frac{m_b^2 m_c^2}{m_a^4}} \quad (34\text{-}14)$$

EXAMPLE 34-3

The Decay of the Higgs Boson

The rest mass of a Higgs boson is approximately $125\ \text{GeV}/c^2$. It has a very short lifetime and decays into other particles. One possible decay mode is the decay into two photons. Find the momentum, energy, and wavelength of the two photons after the decay of a Higgs boson.

SOLUTION

This is the case of a single particle decaying into two particles. The momentum of the decay products in the center of mass frame of the initial particle is given by Equation (34-14). As photons are massless, in this case:

$$m_b = m_c = m_\gamma = 0 \quad \text{and} \quad m_a = m_{\text{H}} = 125\ \text{GeV}/c^2$$

Inserting these values in Equation (34-14), we obtain for the momenta of the emitted photons,

$$p = \frac{m_{\text{H}} c}{2} = \frac{1}{c}\left(\frac{m_{\text{H}} c^2}{2}\right) = 62.5\ \text{GeV}/c$$

The energy E of a photon is related to its momentum p by $E = pc$. Therefore the energy of each of the emitted photons is

$$E = pc = 62.5\ \text{GeV}$$

So each photon carries half the rest mass energy of the Higgs boson. The wavelength λ of a photon is related to its momentum p by, $\lambda = \dfrac{h}{p}$, where h is Planck's constant. Therefore,

$$\lambda = \frac{h}{p} = \frac{4.14 \times 10^{-21}\ \text{MeV} \cdot \text{s}}{62.5 \times 10^3\ \text{MeV}/c}$$

$$= \frac{(4.14 \times 10^{-21}\ \text{MeV} \cdot \text{s}) \times (3.00 \times 10^8\ \text{m/s})}{62.5 \times 10^3\ \text{MeV}}$$

$$= 2.0 \times 10^{-17}\ \text{m}$$

 CHECKPOINT

C-34-8 Energy of the Centre of Mass

Consider the following two situations:

1. A proton with kinetic energy of $100\ \text{GeV}$ collides with a stationary target proton.
2. Two protons, each with $50\ \text{GeV}$ of kinetic energy, are moving toward each other and collide.

The total energy available to produce new particles in these two situations is

(a) the same;
(b) greater for situation 1;
(c) greater for situation 2.

C-34-8 (a) In a proton-proton collision where one of the initial protons is at rest, only half of the kinetic energy of the incident proton is available to produce new particles.

LO 9

34-9 Feynman Diagrams

American physicist Richard Feynman introduced an ingenious method for describing interactions of particles (elementary and composite) by means of position versus time graphs, called **Feynman diagrams**. Each diagram represents a possible way that a particular process can occur, and a given process can be represented by several diagrams. There is a well-defined mathematical procedure to calculate the probability amplitude corresponding to each diagram. The probability for a certain process to occur is proportional to the square of the sum of all the probability amplitudes for that process.

Here are the rules for drawing simple Feynman diagrams for scattering or decay of particles.

- The initial and final states of a process contain only free particles or antiparticles. Particles and antiparticles satisfy the energy–momentum equation $E^2 = p^2 c^2 + m^2 c^4$.
- An arrow that has one free end and points in the direction of increasing time represents a free particle.
- An arrow that has one free end and points in the direction of decreasing time represents a free antiparticle.
- Lines with both ends connected represent virtual particles. Virtual particles do not satisfy the energy–momentum relation and do not appear in the initial or the final states.

- Usually, dashed or wavy lines represent bosons, and solid lines represent fermions. Each line is assigned a four-momentum representing the four-momentum of the particle.

- The point at which two or more particles come together is called a vertex. Electric charge, colour, baryon number, lepton number, and four-momentum are conserved at each vertex.

In Section 34-2, we used a Feynman diagram (Figure 34-2) to represent a process in which two electrons scatter from each other by exchanging a single photon. The wavy photon line represents both a photon emitted by electron 1 and absorbed by electron 2 and a photon emitted by electron 2 and absorbed by electron 1. The exchanged photon is a virtual photon.

Now, consider a process in which an electron and a positron scatter from each other by exchanging a photon. This process is represented by the two Feynman diagrams in Figure 34-12. Figure 34-12(a) corresponds to the case where a virtual photon is exchanged between the electron and the positron and the two then scatter into the final states. Figure 34-12(b) represents a quite different mechanism: the electron and positron annihilate each other into a single photon, which at a later time converts back into an electron–positron pair. Both processes contribute to the probability that an electron and a positron scatter from each other. In diagram (a), the electron and the positron are present at all times, whereas in diagram (b), there is a time interval when only a photon is present.

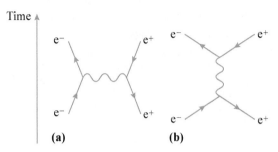

Figure 34-12 Feynman diagrams representing electron–positron scattering. Electron-positron scattering through (a) the exchange of a virtual photon, and (b) electron-positron annihilation into a photon.

EXAMPLE 34-4

Muon Pair Production

Muon (μ^-) and antimuon (μ^+) pairs can be produced by colliding a beam of positrons with electrons that are bound to atoms in the following process:

$$e^+ + e^- \rightarrow \mu^- + \mu^+$$

Draw a Feynman diagram representing this process, and calculate the minimum energy of the positron beam needed for this process to occur. The rest mass energy of a muon is 105.7 MeV.

SOLUTION

To create a μ^-, μ^+ pair in the final state, an electron and the positron pair in the initial state must annihilate into a photon, which then converts into a μ^-, μ^+ pair. The Feynman diagram for this process is shown in Figure 34-13.

The total energy required in the centre-of-mass coordinate system of the electron–positron pair must be must at least twice the rest mass energy of the muon, 2 × 105.7 MeV = 211.4 MeV. In the experimental arrangement, a beam of positrons strikes electrons that are bound to a stationary target, for example, hydrogen atoms. Since the binding energy of electrons in an atom is very small, it can be ignored. So, to a very good approximation, the beam of positrons collides with electrons that are at rest. From Equation (34-10), for $m_1 = m_2 = m_e$

$$K_{cm} = \frac{1}{2} K_{lab}$$

Therefore, in the laboratory coordinate system, the kinetic energy of the positron beam must be at least 2 × 211.4 MeV = 422.8 MeV.

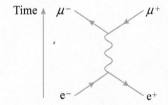

Figure 34-13 The Feynman diagram for an electron–positron annihilation that produces a muon and an antimuon

EXAMPLE 34-5

Neutron Decay

Draw a Feynman diagram for the decay of a neutron into a proton, an electron, and an electron antineutrino. Assume that the neutron and proton are elementary particles. Then modify your diagram to include the quark structure of the proton and the neutron.

(continued)

MODERN PHYSICS

SOLUTION

The neutron decay reaction can be represented as $n \rightarrow p + e^- + \bar{\nu}_e$. Figure 34-14(a) shows the Feynman diagram for this decay.

The quark structure of a neutron is (udd), and the quark structure of a proton is (uud). Therefore, in a neutron decay, a down quark must convert into an up quark. The charge of a down quark is $-\frac{1}{3}e$, and that of an up quark $+\frac{2}{3}e$. Therefore, for an up quark to convert to a down quark, it must emit a particle of charge $-e$. This particle happens to be the W^- boson. The final state also includes an electron and an electron antineutrino, which are created by the decay of the W^- boson. The Feynman diagram for this process is shown in Figure 34-14(b). Circles around the quark arrows for the neutron and proton indicate that the quarks are bound.

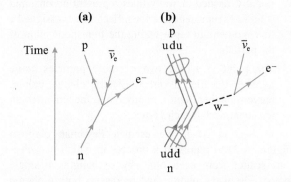

Figure 34-14 Feynman diagrams for neutron decay. (a) The decay process assuming that neutrons and protons are elementary particles. (b) The decay mechanism using the quark structure of the neutron and proton.

✓ CHECKPOINT

C-34-9 The Decay of a π^+ Meson

A π^+ meson consists of an up quark and a $\bar{d}$ quark. It has mean lifetime of 2.6×10^{-8} s and decays into an antimuon (μ^+) and a muon neutrino. The Feynman diagram for the decay is shown in Figure 34-15. Which of the following intermediate bosons is allowed in this decay?

(a) photon
(b) W^- boson
(c) W^+ boson
(d) Z^0 boson

Figure 34-15 Pion decay into a muon and a neutrino

C-34-9 (c) As charge must be conserved at each vertex the charge of the intermediate particle must be $+e$, hence a W^+ particle.

LO 10

34-10 Pions and Muons

Both the pion (or the π meson) and the muon were discovered decades before the introduction of the quark model.

The Discovery of Pions

In 1935, Japanese physicist Heidi Yukawa (1907–81) proposed the existence of a new particle to explain how nucleons exert a strong force on each other by exchanging this particle, in analogy with how charged particles exert the electromagnetic force by exchanging photons. Yukawa named the particle mesotron, which was later changed to pion, or a π meson. By that time, it was known through the work of Lord Rutherford and others that the range of the strong force between nucleons is of the order of a femtometer. Assuming that the uncertainty in the energy of the exchanged pion is of the order of its rest mass energy (see Section 34-2), Yukawa argued that such a pion could exist for a time $\Delta t \leq \dfrac{\hbar}{2^* mc^2}$ before being absorbed. Here, m is the rest-mass of the pion. The maximum distance that a pion can travel in this time is therefore of the order of

$$R = c\Delta t = \frac{\hbar c}{2mc^2} \qquad (34\text{-}15)$$

Using $R \approx 1$ fm, Yukawa estimated the rest mass of the pion to be

$$m = \left(\frac{\hbar c}{2R}\right)\frac{1}{c^2} = \frac{200 \text{ MeV} \cdot \text{fm}}{2 \text{ fm}}\frac{1}{c^2} = 100 \text{ MeV}/c^2$$

The range of the nuclear force was only approximately known, so the predicted mass of the exchanged particle was approximate, too. Since charge is conserved during the exchange of a virtual particle, there are three different pions: a positively charged pion (π^+), a negatively charged pion (π^-), and an electrically neutral pion (π^0). Two protons (or neutrons) can only exchange a π^0. A proton–neutron pair can exchange either a π^+ or a π^-.

Feynman diagrams describing the exchange of pions between two nucleons are shown in Figure 34-16. Note that charge is conserved at each vertex.

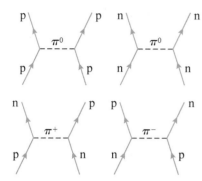

Figure 34-16   Feynman diagrams for one pion exchange between two nucleons

The exchanged pions are virtual and absorbed within a very short time:

$$\Delta t \le \frac{\hbar}{2mc^2} = \left(\frac{\hbar c}{2mc^2}\right)\frac{1}{c} \approx \left(\frac{200 \text{ MeV} \cdot \text{fm}}{200 \text{ MeV}}\right)\frac{1}{c}$$

$$= 1\frac{\text{fm}}{c} = \frac{10^{-15} \text{ m}}{3 \times 10^8 \text{ m/s}} \approx 3 \times 10^{-24} \text{ s}$$

Real pions can be produced in high-energy collisions of protons through the following processes, provided sufficient energy is available in the centre-of-mass coordinate system of the colliding protons:

$$\text{p} + \text{p} \rightarrow \text{p} + \text{n} + \pi^+$$
$$\text{p} + \text{p} \rightarrow \text{p} + \text{p} + \pi^0 \qquad (34\text{-}16)$$

Cosmic rays consist mainly of high-energy protons, with some electrons and helium nuclei, created in deep space. When high-energy protons collide with nuclei in the upper atmosphere, they produce both charged and neutral pions as described above. In 1947, a team of researchers led by British physicist Cecil Powell (1903–69) placed specially designed photographic plates at high-altitude locations in Europe. Just as light produces an image on light-sensitive film, charged pions interact with the nuclei of the photographic plates and produce a visible track. An analysis of these plates confirmed the existence of charged particles of mass 134.5 MeV/c^2, confirming Yukawa's prediction. With the development of high-energy proton accelerators, the production of pions has become straightforward. Neutral pions were discovered in 1950. Some basic properties of pions are listed in Table 34-7. The three pions are the lightest known mesons.

The Discovery of Muons

The muon (μ^-) is an unstable, negatively charged elementary particle with a mass of 105.6 MeV/c^2. Other than being 200 times more massive than an electron, in most respects muons and electrons are identical. A muon

Table 34-7   Some properties of pions

Property	Charged pions	Neutral pions
Mass	139.6 MeV/c^2	135.0 MeV/c^2
Mean lifetime	2.6×10^{-8} s	8.4×10^{-17} s
Spin	0	0

is a lepton and interacts with other matter only through the electromagnetic and weak forces. Its antiparticle is a positively charged muon, μ^+. It was discovered by Carl Anderson in 1936 while searching for pions. Since its rest mass is approximately the same as was predicted by Yukawa for the particle responsible for the strong nuclear force, it was thought to be a meson. However, it was soon discovered that muons do not interact through the strong force because they pass through matter easily.

Approximately 99.99% of charged pions decay into muons and neutrinos through the following processes:

$$\pi^- \rightarrow \mu^- + \bar{\nu}_\mu$$
$$\pi^+ \rightarrow \mu^+ + \nu_\mu \qquad (34\text{-}17)$$

Neutrinos emitted in pion decay are different from neutrinos emitted in neutron decay (n $\rightarrow$ p or p $\rightarrow$ n) and are called muon neutrinos. Pions quickly decay into muons; the pions created by cosmic rays cause a flow of approximately 10 000 muons/m²/min at Earth's surface.

Muons have a mean lifetime of 2.26×10^{-6} s and decay into an electron or a positron and a neutrino–antineutrino pair:

$$\mu^- \rightarrow \text{e}^- + \bar{\nu}_e + \nu_\mu$$
$$L: \quad +1 \rightarrow \quad +1 + (-1) + \quad 1$$

$$\mu^+ \rightarrow \text{e}^+ + \nu_e + \bar{\nu}_\mu$$
$$L: \quad -1 \rightarrow \quad -1 + \quad 1 + (-1) \qquad (34\text{-}18)$$

Notice that the lepton number is conserved in μ^- and μ^+ decays.

LO 11

34-11   Particle Accelerators

How do we create beams of fast-moving particles? The basic technique is to accelerate charged particles by passing them through electric and magnetic fields. A particle of charge q and mass m passing through a region where the electric field is $\vec{E}$ and the magnetic field $\vec{B}$ experiences a force given by

$$\vec{F} = m\vec{a} = q\vec{E} + q\vec{v} \times \vec{B} \qquad (34\text{-}19)$$

As described in earlier chapters, an electric field accelerates a charged particle in the direction of the field, and the force exerted by a magnetic field is perpendicular to both the magnetic field and the velocity of the particle. Therefore, a constant magnetic field changes the direction of motion of a particle without doing any work on it. In this section, we discuss a few common types of accelerators.

Cyclotrons

The simplest form of a cyclotron consists of two hollow semi-circular electrodes (called **dees**) with a small gap between them (Figure 34-17). A high-frequency alternating voltage is applied across the electrodes so that the electrodes change polarity at a fixed frequency. The electrodes are placed in a vacuum, and a constant magnetic field, perpendicular to the plane of the electrodes, is applied. A source of ions is connected to the centre of the electrodes.

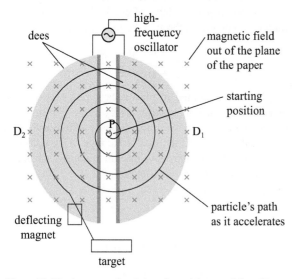

Figure 34-17 A cross-sectional view of a cyclotron consisting of two dees

Imagine that a slow-moving proton emerges from the ion source at P. The voltage between the two electrodes accelerates the proton toward the negatively charged electrode with a force $q\vec{E}$. Once through the gap and inside the hollow electrode, the proton does not experience any force because the electric field is shielded by the conductive metal. However, the proton does experience the magnetic field, which causes it to move in a circular path of radius r. The speed of the proton as it enters the electrode is v and the magnitude of the magnetic field is B, yielding

$$qvB = \frac{mv^2}{r}$$

and

$$r = \frac{mv}{qB} \qquad (34\text{-}20)$$

The alternating frequency is set so that the polarity of the electrodes reverses when the proton emerges from the electrode back into the gap. Now, the electrode at the opposite end of the gap is negatively charged and the proton accelerates toward it. The proton enters the electrode with a greater speed, and once inside moves in a path of greater radius. Each time the proton passes into the gap between the two electrodes, it is accelerated by the voltage across the electrodes, and the radius of its circular path within the dees increases. The proton's speed increases only when it is passing through the gap. Once inside the electrodes, the proton moves with a constant speed. The time, t, required for the proton to travel a distance πr with a constant speed v is given by

$$t = \frac{\pi r}{v} = \frac{\pi}{v}\left(\frac{mv}{qB}\right) = \frac{\pi m}{qB}$$

Thus, the time that a proton spends inside the electrodes is independent of its speed. The polarity of the electrodes must reverse with the same timing. Therefore, the frequency of the applied voltage must be

$$f = \frac{1}{2t} = \frac{qB}{2\pi m} \qquad (34\text{-}21)$$

This frequency is called the **cyclotron frequency**. The cyclotron frequency depends on the charge-to-mass ratio of the accelerated particle and the magnitude of the applied magnetic field. When the proton reaches the outer edge of the electrode, it is deflected into an evacuated pipe, called the beam line, by a small magnet. The fast-moving protons can then be made to strike a target placed at the other end of the beam line.

MAKING CONNECTIONS

The TRIUMF Cyclotron

The largest cyclotron in the world, TRIUMF (Tri-University Meson Facility), is at the University of British Columbia in Vancouver, British Columbia. The six magnets in this cyclotron have a radius of 18 m and a total mass of 4000 tonnes (Figure 34-18). The magnets can generate a magnetic field of 6000 G (0.60 T). The cyclotron frequency of TRIUMF is 23 MHz. Instead of protons, TRIUMF accelerates negatively charged hydrogen ions (hydrogen atoms with an extra electron). When high-energy hydrogen ions are taken out of the cyclotron, they are passed through a very thin metal film that strips the electrons, thus creating a high-energy proton beam. TRIUMF can accelerate protons to 0.75 times the speed of light.

Figure 34-18 The six magnets of the TRIUMF cyclotron are clearly visible in this photograph, which was taken at the completion of the cyclotron in 1971.

EXAMPLE 34-6

Designing a Cyclotron

You need to design a cyclotron that can produce protons with 10 MeV of kinetic energy. The design parameters limit the radius of the electrodes to 0.50 m. Determine the magnitude of the applied magnetic field and the frequency of the power supply. The rest mass energy of a proton is approximately 938.3 MeV.

SOLUTION

First, determine the speed of protons with 10 MeV of kinetic energy. The rest mass energy, mc^2, of a proton is 938.3 MeV, so its kinetic energy is much less than its rest mass energy. Therefore, nonrelativistic kinematics can be used as a good approximation. The speed of the protons is given by

$$K = 10 \text{ MeV} = \frac{1}{2} mv^2 = \frac{1}{2} (mc^2)\left(\frac{v^2}{c^2}\right)$$

$$v = \sqrt{\frac{2 \times K}{mc^2}}\, c = \sqrt{\frac{20 \text{ MeV}}{938.3 \text{ MeV}}}\, c = 0.146\, c$$

Therefore, $v = 4.38 \times 10^7$ m/s. The magnitude of the required magnetic field can now be calculated using Equation (34-20):

$$B = \frac{mv}{rq} = \frac{(1.67 \times 10^{-27} \text{ kg})(4.38 \times 10^7 \text{ m/s})}{(0.50 \text{ m})(1.60 \times 10^{-19} \text{ C})}$$

$$= 0.91 \text{ T}$$

The frequency of the power supply must be the same as the cyclotron frequency. Therefore, using Equation (34-21):

$$f = \frac{qB}{2\pi m} = \frac{(1.60 \times 10^{-19} \text{ C})(0.91 \text{ T})}{(6.28)(1.67 \times 10^{-27} \text{ kg})}$$

$$= 1.4 \times 10^7 \text{ Hz} = 14 \text{ MHz}$$

MODERN PHYSICS

Equation (34-20) is valid only for low-energy particles. At higher energies, relativistic kinematics must be used. When the mass in Equation (34-20) is replaced by the relativistic mass, $\dfrac{m_0}{\sqrt{1 - v^2/c^2}}$ where m_0 is the rest mass of the particle, the equation for the cyclotron frequency, Equation (34-21), changes to

$$f = \frac{qB}{2\pi m_0}\sqrt{1 - \frac{v^2}{c^2}} \qquad (34\text{-}22)$$

Therefore, at energies where relativistic kinematics are important, the cyclotron frequency depends on the particle's speed, which greatly complicates the design of a cyclotron.

MAKING CONNECTIONS

Cyclotrons in Medical Physics

Radioactive isotopes are used for both the diagnosis of the condition of a person's bones and internal organs (such as thyroid, liver, and heart) and the treatment of various types of cancers. Medically important radioisotopes include technetium-99, nitrogen-13, fluorine-18, and iodine-123. For example, fluorine-18 is used in fludeoxyglucose to detect cancer and to monitor the effectiveness of cancer treatment. Many large hospitals have their own cyclotrons to produce these radioisotopes (Figure 34-19). Using a nuclear reactor at Chalk River, Ontario, Canada produces approximately two-thirds of the technetium-99 required worldwide. Research is underway to develop large-scale production of technetium-99 with cyclotrons as an alternative source. Proton beams from cyclotrons are also used to treat cancer. A beam of high-energy protons is targeted at the tumour. The protons deposit their energy in the tumour, killing the cancer cells.

© BSIP SA/Alamy

Figure 34-19 A cyclotron made by IBA (Belgium) for medical use.

Linear Accelerators

A **linear accelerator** (also called a **linac**) accelerates charged particles by passing the particles through large potential differences along a straight path. In contrast to a cyclotron, where charged particles move in circular orbits of increasing radii, particles make a single pass through a linear accelerator. Therefore, the high-power linear accelerators tend to be long and therefore costly. The largest linear accelerator in the world is SLAC, an acronym for its original name, the Stanford Linear Accelerator Center. Located at Stanford University in California, the SLAC accelerator is 3.2 km long and can accelerate electrons and positrons up to energies of 50 GeV.

The two main types of linear accelerators are distinguished by whether they use a DC or an AC voltage for acceleration. Consider two oppositely charged plates a distance d apart with a constant potential difference V_0 between them. The magnitude of the electric field between the plates is V_0/d. The magnitude of the force exerted on a particle of charge e and mass m in this electric field is

$$F = (e)(E) = \frac{eV_0}{d}$$

Therefore, the acceleration of the particle is

$$a = \frac{F}{m} = \frac{eV_0}{md} \qquad (34\text{-}23)$$

If the particle was at rest initially, its speed after travelling the distance d between the plates is given by (ignoring relativistic effects)

$$v = \sqrt{\frac{2eV_0}{m}} \qquad (34\text{-}24)$$

For electrons that accelerate through a 20000 V potential difference,

$$v = \sqrt{\frac{2 \times (1.60 \times 10^{-19}\text{ C})(20000\text{ V})}{(9.11 \times 10^{-31}\text{ kg})}} = 8.38 \times 10^7 \text{ m/s}$$

This speed is approximately 28% of the speed of light. Acceleration with a DC voltage works well when required energies are of the order of tens of kilo-electron volts. For example, cathode ray tubes typically accelerate electrons with a potential difference of the order of 10 kV. To accelerate particles close to the speed of light, the potential difference needs to be increased substantially. High voltages cause electric arcs even in a vacuum chamber, so using a constant electric field (DC voltage) to accelerate charged particles to very high speeds is not feasible.

Alternating electric fields can accelerate charged particles to much higher speeds. This is done by passing the particles through an arrangement of spatially separated electrodes in such a way that the particles are accelerated during one-half of the AC cycle and are shielded from the electric field by the electrodes when the electric field reverses direction during the other half of the cycle. As in a cyclotron, the frequency of the alternating field must be matched to the motion of the particles. The shielding

MODERN PHYSICS

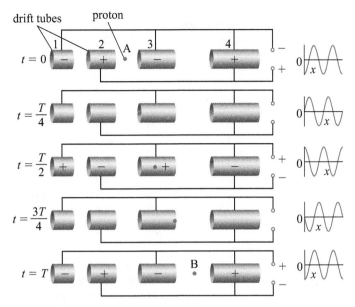

Figure 34-20 The cycle of voltages applied to the drift tubes in a linear accelerator

electrodes consist of cylindrical metal tubes, called **drift tubes**. As a particle accelerates, it gains speed and therefore travels longer and longer distances during each half cycle of the electric field. Therefore, each successive drift tube must be longer than the one before it (Figure 34-20).

Consider the motion of a proton as it travels from point A to point B in Figure 34-20. Let $t = 0$ when the proton is midway between tubes 2 and 3, and the voltage (and therefore the electric field) is at its maximum. At this instant, tube 3 is negatively charged, and the proton experiences a maximum forward acceleration. Over the next quarter cycle, the voltage drops, reaching zero at $t = T/4$, where T is the period of the AC cycle. Tube 3 is placed such that at $t = T/4$, the proton enters the tube. For the next half cycle, the electric field reverses direction, and the proton would decelerate if it is not shielded by the drift tube. However, the electric field is zero inside the metal tube, so the proton moves within it with

a constant velocity, the velocity with which it entered the tube. At $t = 3T/4$, the voltage is zero, and the electric field reverses again. The length of drift tube 3 is such that the proton emerges from it at this time. Between $t = 3T/4$ and $t = T$, the electric field does work on the proton, accelerating it forward. This process is repeated during the next cycle.

We can approximate the required length of a drift tube: Let f be the frequency of the AC voltage and v be the average speed of the proton during a given cycle. The proton travels a distance v/f in one cycle. Since the proton is to be shielded for half a cycle, the length L_d of the drift tube should be half this distance:

$$L_d = \frac{v}{2f} \tag{34-25}$$

This length is approximate because the proton gains kinetic energy, and its speed increases during the cycle.

 EXAMPLE 34-7

Drift Tube Lengths

The LHC at CERN is the largest proton accelerator in the world. Before entering the main circular accelerator, protons are accelerated to a kinetic energy of 50 MeV in a linear accelerator. The frequency of the AC power supply for this linear accelerator is 202 MHz. Calculate the length of the drift tubes when the kinetic energy of the protons is
(a) 10.0 MeV;
(b) 30.0 MeV;
(c) 50.0 MeV.

SOLUTION

The length of the drift tube can be calculated using Equation (34-25) once we know the speed of the protons.

We can use Einstein's relationship between mass and energy to determine the proton's speed for a given value of its kinetic energy. Let K be the kinetic energy of the proton. Then

Kinetic energy + rest mass energy = total energy

$$K + m_0c^2 = \frac{m_0c^2}{\sqrt{1 - \dfrac{v^2}{c^2}}}$$

Solving the above equation for v we get

$$v = c\sqrt{1 - \left(\frac{m_0c^2}{K + m_0c^2}\right)^2} = c\,\frac{\sqrt{K^2 + 2Km_0c^2}}{K + m_0c^2} \tag{34-26}$$

(continued)

By substituting the known values for the rest mass of the proton (938.3 MeV/c^2) and the speed of light, we can calculate the proton speed and hence the length of the drift tube for a given K.

(a) 10.0 MeV

$$v = c\sqrt{1 - \left(\frac{m_0c^2}{K + m_0c^2}\right)^2}$$

$$= (3.00 \times 10^8 \text{ m/s})\sqrt{1 - \left(\frac{938.3 \text{ MeV}/c^2}{10.0 + 938.3 \text{ MeV}}\right)^2}$$

$$= 4.34 \times 10^7 \text{ m/s}$$

$$L_d = \frac{v}{2f} = \frac{4.34 \times 10^7 \text{ m/s}}{2 \times 202 \times 10^6 \text{ Hz}}$$

$$= 10.8 \times 10^{-2} \text{ m} = 10.8 \text{ cm}$$

(b) 30.0 MeV

$$v = 7.41 \times 10^7 \text{ m/s}; \quad L_d = 18.3 \times 10^{-2} \text{ m} = 18.3 \text{ cm}$$

(c) 50.0 MeV

$$v = 9.42 \times 10^7 \text{ m/s}; \quad L_d = 23.3 \times 10^{-2} \text{ m} = 23.3 \text{ cm}$$

Making sense of the result:

The length of the drift tube increases with increasing kinetic energy of the proton.

 CHECKPOINT

C-34-10 Drift Tubes for Electrons

When electrons with the same kinetic energy as protons are accelerated in a linear accelerator with a frequency of 200 MHz, the length of the drift tube required for the electrons should be
(a) less than the length for protons;
(b) the same as the length for protons;
(c) greater than the length for protons.
(d) The electrons are negatively charged, so they do not require drift tubes for shielding.

C-34-10 (c)

Synchrotrons

A synchrotron accelerates charged particles by continuously moving the particles in a circle of constant radius. A **synchrotron** is essentially a cyclotron in which the electric and magnetic fields are adjusted to keep the radius of the path of the accelerating particles constant as the speed of the particles increases. From Equation (34-20), the strength of the magnetic field required to rotate a particle with speed v in a circle of radius R_0 is

$$B = \frac{m_0}{\sqrt{1 - \frac{v^2}{c^2}}}\left(\frac{v}{qR_0}\right) \qquad (34\text{-}27)$$

where q is the charge of the particle, and m_0 is its rest mass.

For circular motion, $v = \omega R_0 = (2\pi f_0)R_0$. Therefore, as particle speed increases, the frequency of the synchrotron must also increase, along with the strength of the magnetic field.

Accelerating particles to very high energies requires strong, energy-efficient magnets and other relevant technologies. The LHC uses superconducting electromagnets to force the particles to move in a circular path. These electromagnets are more powerful and more compact than electromagnets using ordinary conductors.

 EXAMPLE 34-8

Magnets for the Super Collider

The LHC can accelerate protons to energies of 7.0 TeV. Given that the accelerator ring is 27 km in circumference, calculate the strength of the magnetic field needed to keep the protons in the synchrotron ring.

SOLUTION

The strength of the required magnetic field can be calculated from Equation (34-27). We are given the kinetic energy of the proton. It is convenient to write Equation (34-27) in terms of the kinetic energy. From Equation (34-26) in Example 34-7:

$$v = c\sqrt{1 - \left(\frac{m_0c^2}{K + m_0c^2}\right)^2} = c\frac{\sqrt{K^2 + 2Km_0c^2}}{K + m_0c^2}$$

Since

$$\sqrt{1 - \frac{v^2}{c^2}} = \frac{m_0c^2}{K + m_0c^2}$$

we can write Equation (34-27) as

$$B = \frac{m_0}{\sqrt{1 - \frac{v^2}{c^2}}}\left(\frac{v}{qR_0}\right) = \frac{\sqrt{K^2 + 2Km_0c^2}}{qR_0c}$$

We have the following data:

$$m_0c^2 = 938.3 \times 10^6 \text{ eV}; \quad K = 7.0 \text{ TeV} = 7.0 \times 10^{12} \text{ eV}$$

$$q = 1.60 \times 10^{-19} \text{ C}; \quad c = 3.00 \times 10^8 \text{ m/s}; \quad R_0 = 27\,000 \text{ m}/2\pi$$

Substituting the known values, we get

$$B = \frac{\sqrt{(7.0 \times 10^{12}\ \text{eV})^2 + 2(7.0 \times 10^{12}\ \text{eV})(938.3 \times 10^6\ \text{eV})}}{(1.60 \times 10^{-19}\ \text{C})(27\ 000\ \text{m}\ /2\pi)(3.00 \times 10^8\ \text{m/s})}$$

$$\times (1.60 \times 10^{-19}\ \text{J/eV}) = 5.4\ \text{T}$$

Making sense of the result:

Earth's magnetic field is approximately 5×10^{-5} T, and the field strength close to a very strong niobium magnet is approximately 0.2 T. CERN lists the actual strength of their superconducting magnets as 8.36 T. Our calculated value is lower because we assumed that the magnetic field is uniform around the 27 km ring. To create room for equipment, some sections of the LHC ring have no magnetic field, so a stronger field is required for the rest of the ring.

 CHECKPOINT

C-34-11 Synchrotron Magnetic Fields

Electrons and protons with the same speeds are travelling in circular orbits of equal radii. The strength of the magnetic field required to keep the electrons in the circular orbit is

(a) less than the strength of the magnetic field required for protons;

(b) the same as the strength of the magnetic field for protons;

(c) greater than the strength of the magnetic field required for protons;

C-34-11 (a)

LO12

34-12 Beyond the Standard Model

The Standard Model has successfully explained all high-energy experimental results, and all of its predictions about the existence of new particles have proven to be correct. Until now, there has not been a single experimental result that has contradicted the Standard Model. The discovery of the Higgs boson at LHC has provided a very convincing argument that the Standard Model is indeed correct. However, there still are many questions that puzzle scientists:

- The mass of the up quark is estimated to be 2.5 MeV/c^2, and the mass of the top quark is 171 GeV/c^2. Why is one elementary particle approximately 70 000 times more massive than another?

 MAKING CONNECTIONS

Synchrotron Radiation

An accelerating charged particle emits electromagnetic radiation. The radiation emitted when a charged particle moves at a speed that is close to the speed of light in a curved path is called **synchrotron radiation**. The spectrum of synchrotron radiation ranges from microwaves to hard X-rays, and its intensity can be very high. Electrons, being lighter, emit much more synchrotron radiation than protons. Industrial uses of synchrotron radiation include determining the crystalline structure of proteins, designing faster computer chips, testing properties of materials under conditions of high temperature and pressure, and identifying environmental contaminants by X-ray absorption.

The Canadian Light Source (CLS) at the University of Saskatchewan in Saskatoon is one of the most advanced synchrotron radiation facilities in the world. CLS uses a 2.9 GeV electron beam to generate extremely intense beams of synchrotron radiation. The accelerator is the size of a football field (Figure 34-21).

Kevin Van Paassen-The Globe and Mail/The Canadian Press

Figure 34-21 The Canadian Light Source at the University of Saskatchewan, Saskatoon

- Quarks and leptons are fermions, and gauge particles are bosons. Are there quarks and leptons that are bosons and gauge particles that are fermions? In other words, is the universe symmetric between fermions and bosons, such that for every fermion there is a corresponding boson and vice versa? These additional particles are not part of the Standard Model. So far, all attempts to discover the boson partner of the electron have been unsuccessful.

- The graviton is the gauge boson that is assumed to be the carrier of the gravitational force. Why has the graviton not been discovered?

- Observations of very distant supernovas has shown that the universe is expanding faster now than it was in the distant pass. Since the gravitational force is pulling all the matter in the universe together, we would expect the rate of expansion to decrease with time. So, what is causing the accelerated expansion? Some scientists think that a presently unknown type of energy, called dark energy, is pushing the galaxies apart. What is the nature of dark energy? How does it exert a repulsive force on galaxies? Is there a quantum particle corresponding to dark energy, and how would addition of this particle modify the Standard Model? Some scientists prefer to think of dark energy as a feature of space time and not due to particles per se.

- The existence of the quarks was envisaged in order to find a common structure for a large number of elementary particles. Are quarks and leptons made of more elementary particles? In other words, do quarks and leptons have a substructure? So far, there is no experimental proof of such a substructure. But that may change in future as particle accelerators of higher energies are constructed.

Classification of Particles

There are 18 elementary particles: Six quarks, six leptons, five gauge bosons, and the Higgs boson. These particles interact with each other through four forces: the strong, the weak, the electromagnetic, and the gravitational force.

Particles that exert the strong force on each other are called hadrons. Hadrons that are fermions are called baryons, and hadrons that are bosons are called mesons. Leptons interact with each other and other particles through the weak and electromagnetic forces.

Gauge Bosons as the Carriers of the Forces

Particles interact with each other by exchanging gauge bosons. The range of a force is inversely proportional to the mass of the exchanged boson.

- Gluons are the carriers of the strong force.
- Photons are the carriers of the electromagnetic force.
- W^+, W^-, and Z^0 bosons are the carriers of the weak force.
- The carrier of the gravitational force has not been observed.

Antiparticles

An antiparticle of a particle has the same mass and spin but opposite values for other properties, such as charge, lepton number, and baryon number. Each charged particle has an antiparticle. A neutral particle either has an antiparticle (such as an antineutrino) or is its own antiparticle (such as a photon). Particle–antiparticle pairs can be produced in collisions of particles.

The Standard Model

The Standard Model groups the six quarks and six leptons into three generations (Figure 34-6). Most of the matter in the known universe is made of the particles in the first generation: the up quark, the down quark, and the electron. Higher-mass particles can decay into lower-mass particles provided the conservation laws are not violated.

Composite Particles

Hadrons are bound states of quarks and antiquarks. A baryon consists of three quarks, and a meson consists of a quark and an antiquark. The charge of a hadron is equal to the sum of the charges of the constituent quarks. The mass of a hadron depends on the masses of the constituent quarks. A proton is made of two up quarks and one down quark, and a neutron is made up of one up quark and two down quarks.

Colour Quantum Number and Quark Confinement

Quarks have an additional quantum number called colour, which has three values, usually called red, blue, and green. There are eight possible colours for gluons. All composite particles are colour-neutral.

Conservation Laws

Charge, energy, momentum, angular momentum, baryon number, and lepton number are conserved in all particle reactions and decays. Conservation laws are a powerful tool to determine whether a reaction is possible.

Production of Particles

New particles can be produced by colliding fast-moving particles. Energy available in the centre-of-mass coordinate system of the colliding particles is transformed into the rest mass energy of the new particles in accordance with Einstein's mass–energy relation.

Feynman Diagrams

Feynman diagrams are graphical ways of representing a particular reaction or a decay process.

Muons and Pions

A muon is a charged lepton. Its mass is 210 times the mass of an electron; otherwise, it is identical to an electron. It has a half-life of $1.5 \times 10^{-6}\,\text{s}$ and decays into an electron and two neutrinos.

The existence of pions was predicted by Japanese physicist Hideki Yukawa to explain the origin of the strong nuclear force.

Particle Accelerators

In a linear accelerator, charged particles are accelerated in a straight-line path by potential differences between successive drift tubes. In cyclotrons, charged particles follow a spiral path as they accelerate. In a synchrotron, the electric and magnetic fields vary to keep the accelerating particles moving along a circular path of constant radius.

QUESTIONS

1. Explain whether each of the following statements is true or false.
   (a) Quarks can only exchange gluons.
   (b) The strong interaction is mediated by gluons.
   (c) The strong interaction is mediated by photons
   (d) Two quarks can exchange a neutrino.
   (e) A neutron and a proton can exchange a gluon.

2. Explain whether each of the following statements is true or false.
   (a) A quark and an electron can annihilate into two photons.
   (b) A quark and an antiquark can annihilate into two photons.
   (c) Two photons can annihilate into a proton–antiproton pair.
   (d) Two photons can annihilate into a neutron–antineutron pair.
   (e) Any elementary particle and its antiparticle can annihilate into two photons.

3. Explain whether each of the following statements is true or false.
   (a) All baryons are hadrons.
   (b) All mesons are baryons.
   (c) The lightest hadron is a proton.
   (d) The lightest baryon is a pion.
   (e) An electron is an antiparticle of a positron.
   (f) A positron is an antiparticle of an electron.

4. Explain whether each of the following statements is true or false.
   (a) The total spin quantum number of an electron–positron pair can be either 0 or 1.
   (b) The spin quantum number of a meson can be 2.
   (c) The spin quantum number of a baryon can be 3.
   (d) Mesons can have nonzero baryon number.

5. Explain whether each of the following statements is true or false.
   (a) When a proton collides with a stationary proton, all the kinetic energy of the incident proton can be used to create new particles.
   (b) An electron moving in a straight trajectory can emit photons.
   (c) An electron moving in a circular path emits photons.
   (d) A constant magnetic field can increase the speed of a charged particle.
   (e) A constant magnetic field can increase the velocity of a charged particle.

6. Calculate the ratio of gravitational and electromagnetic forces between two protons that are 10^{-15} m apart. How large would the gravitational constant have to be for the two forces to be equal?

7. It is estimated that the radius of a carbon nucleus is between 4×10^{-15} m and 5×10^{-15} m. What is the minimum required energy of an electron beam to resolve distances of this length?

PROBLEMS BY SECTION

For problems, star ratings will be used, (✱, ✱✱, or ✱✱✱), with more stars meaning more challenging problems.

Section 34-1 Classification of Particles

8. ✱ Which of the following particles do not interact through the strong force?
   (a) electron
   (b) photon
   (c) neutrino
   (d) quark
   (e) W^+
   (f) gluon
   (g) Higgs boson

9. ✱ Which of the following particles are fermions?
   (a) electron
   (b) photon
   (c) neutrino
   (d) quark
   (e) W^+
   (f) gluon
   (g) Higgs boson

10. ✱ Which of the following particles possess a colour quantum number?
   (a) electron
   (b) photon
   (c) neutrino
   (d) quark
   (e) W^+
   (f) gluon
   (g) Higgs boson

11. ✱ Which of the following particles are gauge bosons?
   (a) photon
   (b) Z^0

(c) neutrino
(d) gluon
(e) top quark
(f) Higgs boson

Section 34-2   Gauge Bosons

12. ✳   In 1986, a group of scientists claimed the existence of a fifth force that had a range of approximately 100 m. The claim was not correct. Had it been, what would be the mass of the gauge boson mediating such a force?

13. ✳   What would be the range of the weak force if the $W^\pm$ and Z^0 gauge bosons were massless?

14. ✳   Estimate the range of strong force between two protons due to the exchange of a meson of mass $1.0 \text{ GeV}/c^2$.

Section 34-5   Composite Particles

15. ✳✳   Construct all the baryons that are made of up, down, and strange quarks and contain at least one strange quark. Determine the masses of the baryons, assuming that the mass of a baryon is equal to the sum of the masses of the constituent quarks. Assume that the masses for the three quarks are $m_u = 300 \text{ MeV}/c^2$, $m_d = 310 \text{ MeV}/c^2$, and $m_s = 500 \text{ MeV}/c^2$. These masses are called "constituent quark masses" and are different from the masses listed in Table 34-1.

16. ✳   What are all the possible values of the intrinsic spin quantum number of a baryon that is composed of three quarks?

17. ✳   Find the charge, baryon number, and possible values of the spin quantum number for the baryons with the following quark combinations:
(a) uus;
(b) uds;
(c) dds;
(d) uss;
(e) dss;
(f) sss.

18. ✳   Assume that baryon masses are proportional to the sum of the masses of the constituent quarks, with the same proportionality constant for all baryons. Rank the baryons in problem 17 from light to heavier mass using the quark masses in Table 34-1.

19. ✳   Perform the same calculations as in problems 17 and 18 for the following quark combinations:
(a) ttb;
(b) tts;
(c) tbs;
(d) tbd;
(e) tuu.

20. ✳   Find the charge and all possible values of the spin quantum number for mesons with the following quark combinations:
(a) s ū;
(b) s d̄;
(c) s s̄;
(d) u s̄;
(e) d s̄;
(f) c̄ d.

21. ✳   Assume that meson masses are proportional to the sum of the masses of constituent quarks, with the same proportionality constant for all mesons. Rank the mesons in problem 20 from light to heavy mass using the quark masses in Table 34-1.

22. ✳   Perform the same calculations as in problem 17 for the following quark combinations:
(a) c ū;
(b) c d̄;
(c) c s̄;
(d) c c̄;
(e) c̄ u;
(f) c̄ d;
(g) c̄ s.

Section 34-7   Conservation Laws

23. ✳✳   Explain why the following reactions are not possible. Which conservation law is violated in each case?
(a) $p \rightarrow n + e^- + \nu_e$
(b) $n \rightarrow p + \gamma$
(c) $p \rightarrow p + \gamma$
(d) $\mu^- \rightarrow e^- + \nu_e$
(e) $p \rightarrow \pi^+ + \pi^-$
(f) $n + n \rightarrow p + e^-$
(g) $n + \bar{\nu}_e \rightarrow p + e^-$
(h) $p \rightarrow e^- + \nu_e$

24. ✳✳   Identify the particle denoted by the ? symbol in the reactions listed below.
(a) $\mu^- \rightarrow e^- + \nu_\mu + ?$
(b) $\pi^- + p \rightarrow \pi^0 + ?$
(c) $e^- + p \rightarrow n + ?$
(d) $\pi^- + \pi^+ \rightarrow p + ?$
(e) $\pi^+ \rightarrow \mu^+ + ?$

25. ✳✳   Use the laws of conservation of energy and momentum to show that the reaction $e^- + e^+ \rightarrow \gamma$ is not allowed.

26. ✳✳✳   Consider a particle of mass m and velocity $\vec{v}_0$ that makes an elastic collision with a particle of mass M that is at rest in the laboratory frame of reference. Show, using non-relativistic kinematics, that the kinetic energy of the target particle (in the lab frame) is given by

$$K_M = \left(\frac{4mM}{(m + M)^2} \cos^2 \theta \right) K_i$$

where $K_i = \frac{1}{2} m v_0^2$ is the kinetic energy of the incident particle and $\theta (\leq \pi/2)$ is the angle that the target particle makes after the collision with respect to the direction of the incident particle.

27. ✳✳   What is the minimum energy of a neutrino in the laboratory frame of reference for the reaction $\nu_e + p \rightarrow n + e^+$ to occur?

28. ✳✳   Electron–positron annihilation occurs according to the reaction

$$e^- + e^+ \rightarrow \gamma + \gamma$$

Calculate the energies, momenta, and frequencies of the two photons in the final state when
(a) the kinetic energies of the electron and the positron are ignored compared to their rest mass energies;
(b) each has a kinetic energy of 50 MeV, and they have equal and opposite momenta.

29. ✳✳   A proton and an antiproton can annihilate into a π^+ and a π^- meson according to the reaction

$$p + \bar{p} \rightarrow \pi^+ + \pi^-$$

What are the energies and momenta of the two pions in the final state when the kinetic energies of the proton and antiproton are ignored?

30. ✳ Consider the reaction in which a fast-moving negatively charged pion is absorbed by a proton to produce two neutrons

$$\pi^- + p \to n + n$$

Is the following reaction allowed? If not, which conservation law(s) are violated?

31. ✳✳ The proton is the lightest known baryon, and it does not decay. Which conservation law will be violated if we observe the decay of a proton?

32. ✳ Which conservation law will be violated if we observe the decay of an electron?

33. ✳✳ Use the laws of conservation of energy and momentum to show that a free photon cannot decay into an electron–positron pair. (This process can happen only in the presence of another charged particle.)

Section 34-8 The Production and Decay of Particles

34. ✳✳ Calculate the momentum and energy of emitted photons in the decay of a π^0 meson:

$$\pi^0 \to \gamma + \gamma$$

35. ✳✳ Calculate the momenta and energies of the final particles in the following decays:
(a) $\pi^- \to e^- + \bar{\nu}_e$;
(b) $\pi^- \to \mu^- + \bar{\nu}_\mu$.

Section 34-9 Feynman Diagrams

36. ✳✳ Draw Feynman diagrams for the following processes:
(a) $e^- + \mu^- \to e^- + \mu^-$
(b) $p \to n + e^+ + \nu_e$
(c) $e^- + e^+ \to e^- + e^+$

37. ✳✳ A positively charged pion (u$\bar{\text{d}}$) decays into a μ^+ and ν_μ. Draw a Feynman diagram to represent this decay.

38. ✳✳ Consider the process in which an electron neutrino (ν_e) is absorbed by a neutron resulting in a proton and an electron in the final state:

$$\nu_e + n \to p + e^-$$

What really happens is that a d quark converts into a u quark by emitting a W$^-$ gauge boson. Write a Feynman diagram to represent the above process.

39. ✳✳ Draw a Feynman diagram to represent the scattering of a photon from an electron through the following process:

$$e^- + \gamma \to e^- + \gamma$$

40 ✳✳ When drawing Feynman diagrams, would it make a difference if time were plotted along the horizontal direction and position along the vertical direction?

Section 34-10 Pions and Muons

41. ✳ (a) In the meson-exchange model, the strong force between two nucleons arises due to the exchange of several mesons between the nucleons. Determine the approximate range of the nuclear force between two protons due to the exchange of the following neutral mesons:
   (i) pi-zero (π^0, mass 135 MeV/c^2)
   (ii) omega (ω, mass 783 MeV/c^2)
   (iii) phi (ϕ, mass 1.02 GeV/c^2)
(b) Can two protons exchange an electron? Explain your answer.

42. ✳✳ The mass of a lambda-zero (Λ^0) particle is 1115.7 MeV/c^2, and its half-life is 2.6×10^{-10} s. The Λ^0 particle quickly decays into a proton and a negatively charged pion:

$$\Lambda^0 \to p + \pi^-$$

Assume that Λ^0 is initially at rest. Determine the kinetic energies of the proton and the pion in this decay.

Section 34-11 Particle Accelerators

43. ✳✳ (a) A proton linear accelerator works at a frequency of 200 MHz. Calculate the length of the drift tubes at the sections where the average kinetic energy of the proton is
   (i) 10 MeV;
   (ii) 100 MeV;
   (iii) 200 MeV.
(b) The protons need to be accelerated to 2 GeV kinetic energy. Should the frequency of the applied AC voltage be increased or decreased? Explain.
(c) Repeat for an electron linear accelerator.

44. ✳✳ A proton beam is to be accelerated to an energy of 30 GeV in a synchrotron ring with a circumference of 1000 m. Calculate the strength of the magnetic field needed to keep the beam in a circular path of this circumference.

45. ✳✳✳ You are asked to design a synchrotron that can accelerate protons to 500 MeV. The magnets available for the project can produce a maximum magnetic field of 2 T.
(a) What is the speed of the 500 MeV protons at this energy? (Use relativistic kinematics.)
(b) How long would a 500 MeV proton take to complete one revolution around the synchrotron ring?
(c) What is the circumference of the synchrotron?

COMPREHENSIVE PROBLEMS

46. ✳✳✳ Before the discovery of the neutrino, it was assumed that a neutron can decay into a free proton and an electron, $n \to p + e^-$. Consider this process in the laboratory frame of reference in which the neutron is at rest. By applying the laws of conservation of energy and momentum, show that the magnitude of an electron's momentum, p_e, is

$$p_e = \sqrt{\frac{(m_n^2 - m_p^2 - m_e^2)^2}{4m_n^2} - \frac{m_p^2 m_e^2}{m_n^2}} = 1.26 \text{ MeV}/c$$

47. ✳✳ Some scientists estimate that at 10^{16} GeV of energy, the four fundamental forces unify into a single force. To test this hypothesis, you are asked to design a synchrotron that can accelerate protons to 10^{16} GeV. The strongest available magnets can generate a magnetic field of 10 T. What is the radius of the synchrotron? Is there any hope of building a synchrotron with this energy with current technology? What is the strength of the magnetic field if the design requires the radius of the synchrotron to be 100 km?

48. ✳✳✳ Antiprotons can be produced in the following reaction:

$$p + p \to p + p + p + \bar{p}$$

The target proton is at rest. Determine the minimum energy of the incident proton for this reaction to occur.

Appendix A
ANSWERS TO SELECTED QUESTIONS

Chapter 1—Introduction to Physics

1. c
3. $\mu = 4$ m, $\sigma = 0.9$ m
5. a
7. c
9. The graph does not state the difference between the measurement points represented by dots and those represented by circles. Since both distance and velocity measurements have associated uncertainties, the corresponding x and y error bars should be included. There is no indication on the graph as to what the two solid and dashed lines represent.
11. The duration of 9 192 631 770 periods of the radiation corresponding to the transition between the two hyperfine levels of the ground state of a caesium 133 atom at rest at 0 K.
13. Ampere is a measure of the amount of electric charge passing a point in an electric circuit per unit time with 6.241×10^{18} electrons (one coulomb) per second constituting one ampere. References include the *Bureau international des poids et mesures* (BIPM, the standards agency for SI units), the *Guide for the Use of the International System of Units* (*SI*) published by the National Institute of Standards and Technology, and general reference books.
15. d
17. d
19. 3
21. (a) 4   (b) 2   (c) 4   (d) 2   (e) 3   (f) 4
23. (a) 2.452×10^{-3} (b) 5.95×10^{-1} (c) 1.2×10^{4}
    (d) 4.5×10^{-5}
25. 25.7
27. (a)

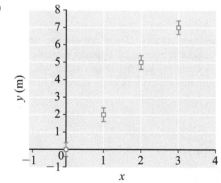

(b)

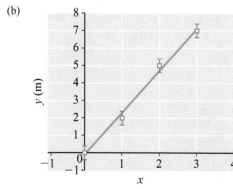

(c) 7.2 m (or ± 3.6 m)

29. mgh
31. V = IR
33. kg/s
35. About 7.5×10^{11} assuming the space between the cells is negligible
37. Roughly 50–150 thousand (varies with assumptions made)
39. 1.15×10^{6} pg
41. Years 1990–1999: mean win percentage 0.513 with SDOM of 0.020
    Years 2000–2009: mean win percentage 0.497 with SDOM of 0.012
    Although the teams in years 1990–999 had a somewhat better win-loss record, the difference is within the range of the SDOMs, so these data do not prove any significant difference between the two sets of teams.
43. (a) 3.9×10^{-8} kg m^{-2} y^{-1} (b) about 330
45. (a) $\sqrt{\dfrac{Gh}{c^5}}$ (b) 5.39×10^{-44} s

Chapter 2—Scalars and Vectors

1. (a) $r = 30$ N, $\theta = 315°$
   (b) $(21.21, -21.21)$ N
   (c) $21.21\hat{i} - 21.21\hat{j}$
3. $(2.53, -7.59)$, $(-2.53, 7.59)$ There are two possible answers due to quadratic equation obtained from the Pythagorean theorem.
5. 5.74 m
7. (a) $(4, -2, 11)$
   (b) $(-4, 2, -11)$
   (c) $(-24, 11, 22)$
   (d) $(-20, 5, 10)$
9. c. Vector magnitudes are invariant under coordinate transformation.
11. Student 2: Consider a vector in each plane directed such that they both form a 45° angle with the line of intersection of the two orthogonal planes. These two vectors are not perpendicular to each other.
13. (a) For $\vec{A}$: $(2, 0, 0)$, $(0, 2, 0)$ and $(0, 0, -2)$ For $\vec{B}$: $(-1, 0, 0)$, $(0, 3, 0)$ and $(0, 0, -2)$
    (b) 8
    (c) $2\hat{i} + 6\hat{j} + 8\hat{k}$
15. Disagree; if more than one component equals 1, the magnitude will be greater than 1.
17. $F_1 = \sqrt{11}$ $\vec{F_2} = -2\hat{i} - 4\hat{j} + 3\hat{k}$, $F_2 = \sqrt{29}$
    $\vec{F_3} = 4\hat{i} + 2\hat{j} - 6\hat{k}$, $F_3 = \sqrt{56}$
    $\vec{F_R} = 3\hat{i} - 5\hat{j} - 2\hat{k}$, $F_R = \sqrt{38}$
19. Disagree. The magnitude of the resultant is not equal to the sum of the radius vectors of individual vectors. Similarly, the resultant angle is not equal to the sum of the individual vector angles.
21. Mathematically, head-to-tail rule is equivalent to addition of vectors in Cartesian form. The associative property of vector addition, that is, $\vec{V_1} + \vec{V_2} + \vec{V_3} = (\vec{V_1} + \vec{V_2}) + \vec{V_3} = \vec{V_1} + (\vec{V_2} + \vec{V_3})$, proves the head-to-tail rule for more than two vectors.

23. A vector product represents rotation, which is not commutative.

25. $4.33\hat{i} + 3.83\hat{j} + 2.50\hat{k}$ N

27. $5.9\hat{i} + 0.4\hat{j} + 4.3\hat{k}$. It is difficult to accurately draw the vectors head-to-tail in three dimensions by hand.

29. 21.9 m

31. (a) $\vec{A}$: $19.3\hat{i} - 5.18\hat{j}$, $\vec{B}$: $12.3\hat{i} + 8.60\hat{j}$,
$\vec{C}$: $-14.3\hat{i} + 20.5\hat{j}$
(b) $17.3\hat{i} + 23.9\hat{j}$, $(29.5, 54.1°)$
(c) $(20.1, 51.2°)$

33. (a) $(3\hat{i} - 5\hat{j} + 6\hat{k})/\sqrt{70}$
(b) Any unit vector $\hat{u}$ that satisfies the condition $\hat{u} \cdot (3\hat{i} - 5\hat{j} + 6\hat{k}) = 0$ is perpendicular to the given vector. This question has infinite number of answers, such as $(3\hat{i} + 3\hat{j} + \hat{k})/\sqrt{19}$
(c) There are infinite number of unit vectors parallel to the plane. Any unit vector $\hat{u} = a\hat{i} + b\hat{j} + c\hat{k}$ satisfying the relation $3a + 2b - 4c = 0$ is a vector parallel to the given plane.
(d) $\dfrac{1}{\sqrt{29}}(3\hat{i} + 2\hat{j} - 4\hat{k})$

35. (a) $F_x = -\sqrt{2}$, $F_y = 3$, $F_z = 5$
(b) $F_x = -3$, $F_y = -5/2$, $F_z = 3$

37. Two possible solutions since the vector in the plane is a unit vector: $\dfrac{2}{\sqrt{13}}\hat{i} + \dfrac{3}{\sqrt{13}}\hat{j}$ and $-\dfrac{2}{\sqrt{13}}\hat{i} - \dfrac{3}{\sqrt{13}}\hat{j}$.

39. 46.98

41. $-\sqrt{5}$

43. $6\hat{i} - 22\hat{j} - 14\hat{k}$

45. $|\vec{A} \times \vec{B}| = 17.1$ pointing in $+y$ or $-y$ direction

47. (a) $F_x = 2\sqrt{2}$; $F_y = 14$
(b) $F_x = -\dfrac{20}{\sqrt{3}}$; $F_z = -\dfrac{80}{\sqrt{3}}$

49. (a) $\begin{pmatrix} \cos(60°) & -\sin(60°) & 4 \\ \sin(60°) & \cos(60°) & 5 \\ 0 & 0 & 1 \end{pmatrix} \begin{pmatrix} x' \\ y' \\ 1 \end{pmatrix} = \begin{pmatrix} x \\ y \\ 1 \end{pmatrix}$
(b) $x = x'\cos(60°) - y'\sin(60°) + 4$,
$y = x'\sin(60°) + y'\cos(60°)$

51. See online resources.

53. See online resources.

55. 0

57. See online resources.

59. See online resources.

61. (a) $s = s_0 - gt$
(b)

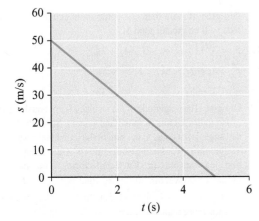

63. (c) $t = \dfrac{s_0}{g}$
(d) An object thrown straight up in the air.

63. (a) 178 m/s²
(b) $\dfrac{\pi}{2}$, 51.8°, 38.2°
(c) $\vec{a} = 110\hat{j} - 140\hat{k}$
(d) $110\hat{j}$, $-140\hat{k}$, $110\hat{j} - 140\hat{k}$

65. See online resources.

67. 109.5°

Chapter 3—Motion in One Dimension

1. (a) Both objects have same average velocity.
(b) B at $t = 30$ s; A at $t = 90$ s
(c) Yes, when the slopes of their position-time graphs are equal, around $t = 55$ s.

3. (a) No
(b) Yes, at $t = 0$.
(c) A. Maximum accelerations: A, about 100 m/s²; B, 25 m/s²

5. (a) B
(b) B
(c) Same magnitude for both (opposite signs)
(d) A
(e) Same acceleration at around $t = 130$ s

7. (a) Yes, at the maxima and minima of the curve
(b) Highest at $t = 200$ s, lowest at $t = 30$ s and $t = 140$ s

9. b

11. a

13. b

15. a

17. d

19. In the limit of infinitesimally small time change, average acceleration becomes equal to the instantaneous acceleration.

21. At a point where tangent is parallel to displacement, the average velocity is equal to the instantaneous velocity.

23. a

25. d

27. Only momentarily. If you are moving one direction but have acceleration in the opposite direction, you will have zero speed for just the instant when you come to a stop before starting to move in the direction of the acceleration.

29. d

31. d

33. a

35. c

37. (a) 2400 m
(b) -200 m

39. $d = 230$ cm, $\vec{d} = 80$ cm [down]

41. $v_{av} = 2.2$ m/s, $\vec{d} = 20$ m [down], $\vec{v}_{av} = 2.0$ m/s [down]

43. $v_{av} = 1.3$ m/s, $\vec{v}_{av} = 1.3$ m/s [down]

45. 6.2 h

47. 29.8 km/s

49. 1.0 km

51. (a) 5 km
(b) 15 km
(c) (i) 40 km/h, (ii) 120 km/h

53. (a) 105 m, 70 m, 40 m
(b) -10 m/s²

55. (a) 8.3 s
(b) 4890 years
(c) about 100 000 years

57. $v = 800$ m/s, $\vec{v} = -800$ m/s

59. 12.6 m/s

61. (a) -22.3 m/s
(b) -22.3 m/s

63. (a) 10.70 m/s² (b) 1713 km

65. See online resources.

67. 9.8 m/s²

69. 1.95 s

71. $\vec{a}_{av} = 9.8$ m/s² [down], $v_{av} = 16$ m/s, $\vec{v}_{av} = 0$

73. (a) 11.29 m/s²
(b) 381.3 m
(c) 9.19 s

75. (a) 1.4 s
(b) 7.4 m/s
(c) 8.4 m/s, 14.5 m

77. 38 m/s, 84 ms

79. 1.6×10^2 m/s

81. (a) 2.818 km/s
(b) 3816 km
(c) 480 km

83. 17.7 h

85. $v_{av} = 17.2$ m/s, $\vec{a}_{av} = 9.8$ m/s² [down], $d = 120$ m, $\vec{d} =$ zero

87. 4.5 m/s

89. (a) 45 m/s (b) 45 m/s

91. 33.1 m/s

93. (a) 1.77 s
(b) 4.28 m, apple will be caught before it reaches its maximum height
(c) 1.22 s

95. 77.6 m

97. (a) $\dfrac{n\pi}{2}$; $n = 1,3,5, \ldots \ldots$
(b) (i)

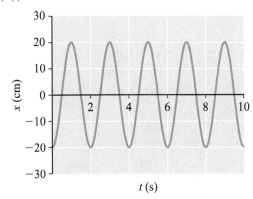

(ii)

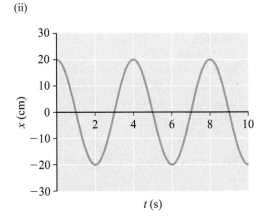

(iii)

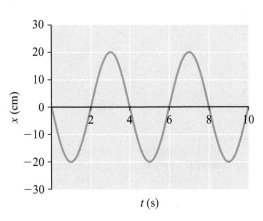

(c) $v = -x_0 \omega \sin(\omega t + \phi)$
(d) $a = -x_0 \omega^2 \cos(\omega t + \phi)$
(e) $a = -\omega^2 x$

99. (a) 5.1 min (b) 5.71 km toward the dock, 14.29 km

101. 51.1 m, 31.6 m/s

103. 90.5 m/s

105. 0.9 s

107. 37 m/s

109. (a) Less than 0.5 km/s per kilometre of altitude at 120 km; about 2.9 km/s per kilometre of altitude at 92 km
(b) Since the meteor fragment is slowing, the force of atmospheric friction must be somewhat greater than the force of Earth's gravity at an altitude of 120 km, and much greater at an altitude of 90 km.
(c) The density of the atmosphere increases substantially as your descend in altitude from 120 to 85 km.

111. (a) About 30 m/s², 20 m/s², and 25 m/s²
(b) About 13 m/s²
(c) About 15 m/s², 14 m/s², and 13 m/s²

113. Approximate shape shown below. Since this acceleration graph is based on values estimated from a small velocity graph, the resulting graph does not exactly match Figure 3-41 and does not show the details of the sudden changes in acceleration between the stages of the launch.

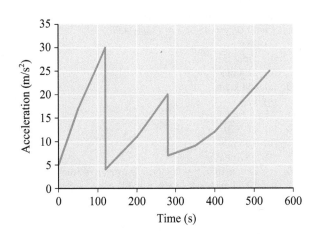

Chapter 4—Motion in Two and Three Dimensions

1. b
3. a
5. b
7. d
9. d
11. b
13. d
15. d
17. a
19. a
21. Both will hit the ground at the same time.
23. Tangential acceleration: tangent to the bowl and pointing in the direction of motion, radial acceleration: pointing towards the center of the bowl
25. (a) 1.4m/s (b) 2.2m/s (c) 1.7m/s (d) 2.0m/s (e) No, these average speeds apply for only part of the time elapsed.
27. (a) $v_x = -7.99r$, $v_y = -0.23r$
    (b) $7.99r$
    (c) circular motion, $y = \pm\sqrt{r^2 - x^2}$, $v_y = \pm\sqrt{64r^2 - v_x^2}$, $a_y = \pm\sqrt{4096r^2 - a_x^2}$
29. Straight line, 8 m/s, 0.005 m/s²
31. (a) 248 m [37.0° up and 35.9° towards the end of the curve]
    (b) 12.2 m/s [37.0° up and 35.9° towards the end of the curve]
    (c) 0.40 m/s² [37.0° up and 35.9° towards the end of the curve]
33. 5.9 m/s
35. 17 m/s
37. (a) 2 h
    (b) 1285 km/h
39. 417 m
41. $a_t = 2.5$ m/s², $a_r = 2.7$ m/s², $\vec{a} = 3.7$ m/s² 43.7° with respect to radial direction
43. About 21 krad/s
45. $\vec{a} = 16$ m/s² 13.1° with respect to radial direction
47. 0.18 s
49. The acrobat will land in the car; 7.9 m
51. 1.8 m/s
53. 1.5 m
55. 11 m/s
57. 23 m/s
59. 29°
61. 19.6 m/s, 24.5 m/
63. (a) 796 m
    (b) 2436.7 m/s², 1442 m
    (c) Right before hitting the ground
65. $x = 52.0t, y = 43.6t, z = 122t - 4.9t^2$
67. (a) 26.6 m
    (b) 125.2 m
    (c) 22.4 m/s
69. (a) 954 km/h
    (b) 13 h
71. About 1400 km/h
73. (a) $2\hat{i} + 3\hat{j}$
    (b) 0.85 m/s
    (c) 3.87 m/s²
75. $x = 3r - 0.167r, y = 0.986r, v = 6\pi r^2, a = 36\pi^2 r^3$
77. $h = 12.6$ km, $R = 8.13$ km, $v = 301$ m/s, $a = 20.0$ m/s²

79. (a) 4.0 m (b) 21 m/s (c) 26°, 34°
81. 86.7°
83. (a) 8.0 m/s tangent to the circle
    (b) 5.0 m/s 96.7° with respect to x-axis, 0
85. 29.8°
87. 85.2° up from the ground
89. (a) 0.36 km/s (b) 0.42 km/s, 0.14 km/s, 2.0 km/s, 2.5 km/s
    (c) The small increase in the slope of the graph for the next 250 s indicates some radial acceleration; after that the curve is almost straight, so there is little or no radial acceleration after 1750 s.
    (d) Since the graph shows altitude versus time, the slope does not reflect any tangential component of the velocity.
91. 23.4 m/s; yes, the negative root of the quadratic is spurious since it corresponds to a negative speed.

Chapter 5—Forces and Motion

1. d
3. b
5. b
7. c
9. 16 kg mass accelerates down while 4 kg mass accelerates up
11. d
13. b
15. b
17. c
19. b
21. c
23. b
25. (a) 588 N (b) 13.6 kN (c) 13.6 kN (d) 13.6 kN (e) 13.3 kN
27. a
29. c
31. a
33. b
35. a
37. (a) $6N$: $\vec{F} = 5.14\hat{i} + 3.09\hat{j}$
    $8N$: $\vec{F} = -4.93\hat{i} + 6.30\hat{j}$
    $5N$: $\vec{F} = -1.87\hat{i} - 4.64\hat{j}$
    (b) 5 N $\angle 109°$
39. (a) $(-\hat{i} + 3\hat{j} - 3.5\hat{k})$ N
    (b) $(6.2\hat{i} + 1.1\hat{j})$ N
    (c) $(-5\hat{i} + 16\hat{j} + 6\hat{k})$ N
    (d) $(22.6\hat{i} - 0.2\hat{j} + 25.9\hat{k})$ N
41. 20.1 m/s
43. 0.54 m
45. (a) 21.49 kN
    (b) 1.05 kN
    (c) 21.49 kN
47. (a) along the slope, $v_f = v_i + gt\sin\theta$
    (b) along the slope, $v_f = v_i + gt(\sin\theta - \mu\cos\theta)$
    (c) radial acceleration directed towards pivot,
    $t = 2\pi\sqrt{\dfrac{L\cos\theta}{g}}$
    (d) along the slope, $v_f = v_i + \dfrac{Ft}{m}\cos\theta - gt\sin\theta$

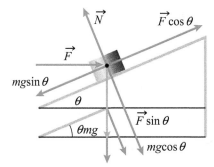

(e) parallel to the plane,

$$v_f = v_i + \frac{Ft}{m}\cos\theta - \mu t\left(g - \frac{F}{m}\sin\theta\right)$$

(f) radial acceleration directed towards the centre

(i) $v_{top} = \sqrt{gr}$ (ii) $v_{bottom} = \sqrt{5gr}$

(g) radial acceleration directed towards the centre, $v = \sqrt{rg\tan\theta}$

(h) radial acceleration directed towards the centre,

$$v = \sqrt{\frac{rg(\sin\theta - \mu_s\cos\theta)}{\cos\theta + \mu_s\sin\theta}}$$

49. (a) 8.2×10^2 N
   (b) 24 kN
   (c) 1.6 kN
   (d) 23 kN
51. 35 N
53. 2°
55. 0.08
57. (a) $T = \dfrac{M_1 M_2 g}{M_1 + M_2}$, $M_2 > M_1$
   (b) $T = M_2 g$
   (c) 16.8 N, 19.6 N
59. (a) $\dfrac{m_2 g}{2(m_1 + m_2)}$
   (b) 0
61. 8.2 cm
63. 272 N/m
65. (a) 3.6 m/s
   (b) 0
67. (a) 62.3 km/h
   (b) 300 N, outward
69. 0.51
71. 4.5×10^2 N
73. 12.9 m/s
75. 2.7°
77. 69 km/h
79. (a) m_1: 2.45 m/s, m_2: −2.45 m/s
   (b) 127 N
81. $\dfrac{5.29}{R}$
83. $(M + m)g\tan\theta$
85. $\mu_k(M + m)g\sin\theta\cos\theta$
87. $7.35m$ N
89. (a) 68.6 N
   (b) 39.2 N, 19.6 N, 9.8 N; due to other masses
91. (a) $Mg\cos\theta$

(b) $Mg\cos\theta + \dfrac{mv^2}{R}\sin\theta$

(c) $Mg\dfrac{\cos\theta\sin\theta(1 - \mu_s) + \cos^2\theta - \sin^2\theta}{\cos\theta - \mu_s\sin\theta}$

(d) Downward parallel to the surface, towards the center, towards the center, resolved components are used to determine the net force

93. $mg\dfrac{(\sin\theta - \mu_s\cos\theta)}{(\cos\theta + \mu_s\sin\theta)}$
95. 6.74 m/s²
97. $mg\dfrac{\sqrt{R^2 - h^2}}{h}$
99. 7.26 m/s², 3.63 m/s², 16.6 m/s
101. (a) 1.5×10^2 N
   (b) 6.8×10^2 N
   (c) 1.5×10^2 N
103. 0.40

Chapter 6—Energy

1. Yes
3. T
5. Negative
7. Yes, if the displacement is in a direction opposite to the applied force
9. Can increase or decrease depending on the direction of movement and the applied force
11. zero, zero
13. zero
15. 0.98 J
17. d
19. c
21. b
23. $\theta = \tan^{-1}(\mu_k)$; equal and opposite, so total work done is zero
25. b
27. e
29. d
31. c
33. c
35. (a) −0.45 J
   (b) 0.45 J
   (c) zero
37. −18 J
39. (a) −36 J
   (b) 36 J
41. (a) 1.37 kJ
   (b) −1.37 kJ
43. (a) $\sqrt{(4.9 - 0.019k)}$
   (b) 2.2 m/s
   (c) 1.8 m/s
45. (a) $\dfrac{F}{mg}$

(b) Fd

(c) $F = mg\sin\theta$; more work is done since now force is acting against the gravitational pull.

(d) $F = mg\sin\theta + ma$ (More work than in part (c))

(e) $F = mg\sin\theta + ma + \mu mg\cos\theta$ (More work than in part (c))

47. 1.4×10^2 J, 1.8×10^2 N

49. 0.19

51. (a) 3.1×10^2 J, 24 m/s
(b) 3.0×10^2 J

53. mgh

55. 86.5 cm

57. (a) 13 kJ
(b) 1.9 J

59. 6.85 cm

61.

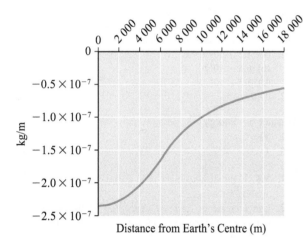
Distance from Earth's Centre (m)

63. (a) $\sqrt{2K\dfrac{Qq}{mR}\left(1 - \dfrac{\Delta r}{R}\right)}$
(b) 1.6×10^2 m/s

65. 800 kN

67. 4.1 kN

69. (a) 89.5°
(b) 1.17 m/s

71. $\dfrac{5}{2}r$

73. $\dfrac{2}{3}r$ from bottom of the bowl; mg, where m is the mass of the bead

75. 45 cm

77. (a) $mg\cos(23°)$
(b) $mgL\cos(23°)$
(c) zero

79. (a) $\dfrac{mg}{k}$
(b) $\sqrt{2h\left(g - \dfrac{kh}{m}\right)}$

81. 54 J

83. (a) 0.94 m/s
(b) $\sqrt{\dfrac{2gh(m - \mu_k M)}{(m + M)t^2}}$

85. (a) $\dfrac{A}{2}\left(\dfrac{1}{r_1^2} - \dfrac{1}{r_2^2}\right)$
(b) $-\dfrac{A}{2}\left(\dfrac{1}{r_1^2} - \dfrac{1}{r_2^2}\right)$

(c) $\dfrac{A}{2}\left(\dfrac{1}{r_1^2} - \dfrac{1}{r_2^2}\right)$
(d) attractive
(e) $21.3\sqrt{A}$ m/s

87. $\dfrac{14r}{(r^2 + 6)^2}$, $v_i + \dfrac{42r}{m(r^2 + 6)^2}$

89. 2.3 m

91. See online resources.

93. $\theta = \cos^{-1}\left(\dfrac{2R}{3R + 0.4}\right)$

95. An increase of about 5.0 GJ assuming plane starts from sea level, no significant change in g with altitude, and mass of fuel used during the climb is negligible.

Chapter 7—Linear Momentum, Collisions, and Systems of Particles

1. a

3. d

5. d

7. a

9. b

11. The centre of mass moves down as the pieces of the firecracker fall away from the needle. If the explosion is not symmetrical, the centre of mass also shifts to one side.

13. Yes, if air resistance is negligible

15. 14.48 m/s, due to momentum lost during impulse

17. c

19. a

21. d

23. a

25. b

27. c

29. b

31. T

33. c

35. b

37. a

39. 1.2 kg m/s

41. 3.3 kN

43. (a) 1.7 N   (b) 0.043 kg m/s

45. (a) 6.3 m/s
(b)

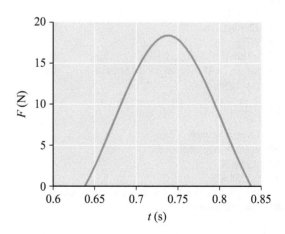

(c) 9.18 N

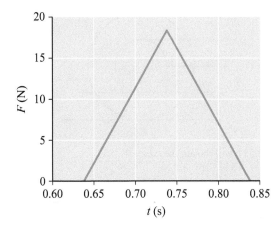

(d) 18.4 N

47. $\dfrac{14}{15}R$

49. $(0, -L/5)$ from centre

51. 3.9 m

53. 0.99 m away from the child

55. 4.2 m/s

57. 8.7 km/s

59. $1 - \dfrac{\cos^2\theta}{\cos^2\theta'}$

61. $0.42\,v$

63. 13 m/s

65. 5:1

67. 1:1.09, $20.9\,v$

69. 328.9 kg m/s^2, 84.1 m/s

71. (a) 7.9 cm/s^2 (b) 34 cm/s   (c) 9.6 cm/s^2

73. 7×10^7 km, 5×10^7 km

75. 39.6 cm

77. 0.016 m/s, 9.8 m/s^2 [down]

79. (a) 1.1 m   (b) 0.97 m/s

81. 5.9 m/s

83. 29 cm

85. 141 km/s

87. 180°

89. $\dfrac{v}{3}\sqrt{1 + 9\sin^2\theta}$

91. $\dfrac{2m + M}{m}\left(\dfrac{k}{m + M}\right)^{1/2} X$

93. 4.4×10^2 J, 1.3 m/s

95. (a) 0.02 mm   (b) 8×10^{-7} m/s   (c) 8×10^{-7} m/s

97. $\dfrac{2L}{3}$

99. 2.7 m/s (with respect to moving frame of reference)

101. 2.0 m

103. (a) $L + v_1\sqrt{\dfrac{m_1 m_2}{k(m_1 + m_2)}}$ (b) 51.7 cm

105. (a) $(v + u)\sqrt{\dfrac{mM}{k(m + M)}}$

(b) $\dfrac{mv - Mu}{m + M}$

(c) $\dfrac{mv - Mu}{m + M}$

(d) $\dfrac{mv - Mu}{m + M}$

107. $\dfrac{2v \pm \sqrt{4v^2 + \dfrac{2}{m}(kx^2 - 2mv^2)}}{2}$

109. (a) 2.1 kg   (b) zero

111. (a) 0.482 m/s   (b) 55.1 cm

Chapter 8—Rotational Dynamics

1. Solid

3. All three quantities for the point on the rim are higher since the radius is larger.

5. Smaller disk has higher angular speed. Radial acceleration at the circumference of the smaller disk is smaller. The disks have the same tangential speed.

7. Increase

9. Shorter rod

11. The equation is still valid if other units (such as degrees) are used for all of the angular quantities.

13. (a) No.   (b) The dot has radial acceleration but no tangential acceleration.

15. Negative, positive, equal

17. See online resources.

19. 1.8 mm/s

21. Tilting the axis of rotation changes the direction of the angular velocity vector, and hence changes the angular momentum vector.

23. Tension is the same when there is no acceleration.

25. Yes, at the moment when the angular acceleration reverses the direction of rotation of the wheel

27. Yes, as long as they are not pushing the car straight toward the tree

29. No, torque is defined about a pivot. Force is a vector quantity, so its magnitude is independent of the frame of reference.

31. 393 m/s

33. 46.4 cm

35. 1.45×10^{-4} rad/s

37. (a) 69 rad/s

(b) 0.43 km/s^2

(c) 2.8 m/s^2

(d) 2.8 m/s^2

39. 8.4 rad/s

41. (a) 0.41 rad   (b) 1.0 rad/s

43. (a) 0.97 m/s^2 (b) 5.2 m/s^2

45. $16.78\hat{k}$ N·m

47. $(-112\hat{i} + 49\hat{j} + 67\hat{k})$ N·m

49. 806 N·m

51. $(-28\hat{i} + 13\hat{j} - 19\hat{k})$ N·m, $(36.25, 140.6°, 69.0°, 121.6°)$ N·m

53. 0.48 kg m^2

55. 0.23 kg m^2

57. $\dfrac{2MR^2}{5}$

59. $\dfrac{m_1 gr \sin\theta}{I + r^2(m_1 + m_2)}$

61. 5.18×10^4 kg·m^2/s, 5.18×10^4 kg·m^2/s

63. 19.2°

65. (a) 0.27 rad/s   (b) 0.032 J

NEL

287

APPENDIX A | ANSWERS TO SELECTED QUESTIONS   A-7

67. $-28\hat{i} + 39\hat{j} - 20\hat{k}$

69. (a) 12 m/s (b) 4.1×10^5 J, 123 km/h

71. 0.31 rad/s

73. (a) 1.7 s (b) 14 rad

75. 42 kJ

77. (a) $\dfrac{mL^2}{3}, \dfrac{mL^2}{3}, \dfrac{mL^2}{3}, mL^2, I_{\text{total}} = 2mL^2$

(b) Yes

(c) Each thin bar is treated as having its mass distributed in only one dimension.

79. $\dfrac{mL^2}{12}; \dfrac{M}{12}(L^2 + T^2)$ if T not negligible

81. (a) 1.2 m/s

(b) 1.2 m/s

(c) 1.2 m/s

(d) 2.3 rad/s

(e) 0.32

83. (a) (i) 4.3 m/s, (ii) 6.0 m/s (b) 4.5 m/s

85. 3.8 m/s

87. 13 N

89. $\left[\dfrac{2d(m_2 g - m_1 g\sin\theta - \mu m_1 g \cos\theta)}{m_1 + m_2 + I/r^2}\right]^{1/2}$

91. (a) 11 rad/s (b) 1.7×10^2 J

93. (a) 1.9 rad/s (b) 0.80 rad/s

95. 0.2 rev

97. (a) 49 rad/s (b) 6.3 m/s²

99. (a) negative

(b) increase

(c) 1.3 rad/s

(d) decrease

(e) 22 kJ

Chapter 9—Rolling Motion

1. Solid disk

3. (a) solid cylinder (b) same angular speed

5. To prevent locking up of wheels that may cause skidding

7. Static

9. Sphere

11. $2mr^2$

13. Both disks will reach the bottom of the hill at the same time.

15. Both shells will reach the bottom of the hill at the same time.

17. Not possible.

19. 1:10

21. Friction and air resistance

23. Opposite to the direction of motion.

25. (a) 30 m/s, 1.2 km/s² (b) 15.0 m/s, 304.1 m/s²

27. (a) 18 m/s (b) no

29. (a) 7.98 m/s² (b) 117 m/s², 91.7° with respect to direction of motion

31. The apparent acceleration is due to change in frame of reference and not a real effect.

33. $\cos^{-1}\left[\dfrac{I\alpha + R(F + ma)}{rF}\right]$

35. $\dfrac{g}{2}$

37. F_1 and F_3 right; F_2 and F_4 left

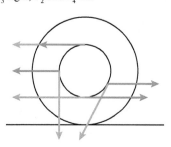

39. 2.5 N, will remain the same

41. (a) 3.8 N (b) 3.8 N

43. $\dfrac{F}{\dfrac{3}{4}m + M}$

45. (a) No, since $f > \mu_s N$ (b) 137.0 rad/s² (c) 4.45 J

47. 46.4°

49. 2.5 N

51. (a) $K_{\text{rot}} = 13$ J, $K_{\text{trans}} = 27$ J (b) $K_{\text{rot}} = 20$ J, $K_{\text{trans}} = 20$ J

53. (a) 5 m

(b) Yes, the ball spins (not rolls) as it moves up the incline.

(c) 1.6×10^2 rad/s

55. (a) $\dfrac{5}{7}h$, energy is conserved

(b) zero

(c) $\dfrac{2}{7}mgh$

(d) A ring of the same mass has a higher moment of inertia, so more of the total energy will go towards rotational motion as it moves down. Less translational kinetic energy means that the ring will move up to a smaller height on the right hand side as compared to the solid sphere.

57. (a) 0.69 N (b) 6.5 m/s² (c) 1.1×10^2 rad/s

59. $\dfrac{g(M_c \sin\theta_2 - M_s \sin\theta_1)}{m + M_c + M_s + \dfrac{I_1}{r_1^2} + \dfrac{I_2}{r_2^2}}$

61. (a) In the direction of the force

(b) $\left(\dfrac{3\mu_s g R I}{F}\right)^{1/3}$ where μ_s is the coefficient of static friction between the object and the surface

63. -6.8 m/s

65. (a) $mg\left[1 - \dfrac{10}{7(1 - r/R)}\right]$

(b) $-\dfrac{3}{7}mg$

(c) -2.9 N; the approximation differs from the actual value by about 2.3%.

67. (a) 3.4 m/s² opposite to the direction of the velocity

(b) 1.87 s

(c) 41.6 J

69. $\dfrac{mg}{m + \dfrac{3}{8}m_c + \dfrac{I}{r^2}}$

71. Only if the object is already rolling without slipping. Otherwise the object will slip because there is no frictional torque to change the angular speed.

73. If the marble a perfectly rigid sphere and the horizontal surface is totally frictionless, the marble will not lose any energy to the surface. However, air resistance will cause the marble to gradually come to a stop.

75. See online resources.

77. (a) $F = 6.86\dfrac{M^2}{m} - 16.42\,M - 16.17m$ where F is in newtons and the masses are in kilograms

(b) $\dfrac{F}{\frac{3}{4}m + M}$

79. See online resources.

81. (a) $\sqrt{g\dfrac{(r-h)(r+h-2R)}{R-h}}$

(b) Above: marble will move down. Below: marble will move up.

83. (a) 3.1 rad/s^2 (b) 6.3 N

Chapter 10—Equilibrium and Elasticity

1. No, even when the object is at its highest point an unbalanced force (gravity) acts on it.

3. c

5. c

7. b

9. No, an unbalanced centripetal force is acting on the object.

11. Yes. For example, the centre of gravity of a V-shaped object lies outside the object.

13. no

15. $\dfrac{r}{5}$ away from the planet in the middle, toward the outer planet

17. No

19. Steel

21. Compression

23. d

25. c

27. b

29. a

31. 0.42

33. 2.7 kN

35. $F_1 = F_2 = 240$ kN

37. At least 0.49

39. $T_{21°} = 4.1$ kN, $T_{37°} = 2.4$ kN

41. 0.16 kN

43. $\dfrac{L}{2}\left[\dfrac{1 - e^{-L/120}}{1 + e^{-L/120}}\right]$

45. 110 m away from the mass on the surface toward the second mass

47. 1.4 kN

49. $m_2 = \frac{1}{2}m_1$

51. 8.1×10^2 N

53. $A_x = 35.4$ kN, $A_y = 30.0$ kN, $B_x = 35.4$ kN, $B_y = 2.6$ kN, $C_x = 35.4$ kN, $C_y = 23.2$ kN

55. $f_A = 3.7$ kN, $f_B = 1.2$ kN, $C_x = 2.5$ kN, $C_y = 6.8$ kN

57. 1.6 t

59. 1.8×10^2 kg

61. 2.9 MPa

63. (a) 7.2×10^4 kg   (b) 1.3×10^5 kg   (c) 4.0 cm

65. 0.016

67. about 31 000

69. (a) 4.7×10^5 J   (b) 2.4 t

71. Surface: $F_n = 6.7$ kN, Hinge: $F_R = 4.3\hat{\imath} + 5.6\hat{\jmath}$ kN

73. 9.6°

75. 0.53 kg

77. $T = 11$ kN, $R_x = 8.3$ kN, $R_y = 1.6$ kN

79. $r(1 + \mu)$

81. 0.27

83. 1.24

85. (a) 0.31 kN   (b) tip   (c) 112 cm

87. 28 N

89. (a) 13 GPa

(b)

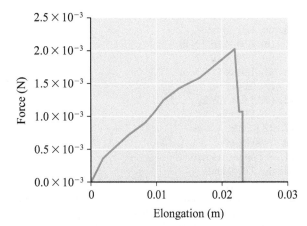

(c) 1.3×10^{-7} J

(d) around (1.5%, 200 MPa)

(e) 5 cm/s, yes

91. About 1.1 N/m

93. 0.36 MPa, 1.8×10^{-6}

95. 1.0 cm

97. (a) 11 m   (b) 5.8 mm

99. Longitudinal: 0.14 MN compression, 92 kN tension; transverse: 0.28 MN compression, 1.0–1.1 MN tension

101. (a) The ultimate tensile strength increases as the steel passes through subsequent cycles. From the graph we see that the ultimate tensile strength of the steel was about 850 MPa. The UTS increased to about 860 MPa after first pass and to about 1140 MPa after four passes.

(b) The pressing process increases the ultimate tensile strength of the steel, and hence increases the energy required to break the steel.

Chapter 11—Gravitation

1. b

3. Weight is a force and should be measured in units such as newtons.

5. c

7. c

9. a

11. Atmospheric drag slows it down, but it speeds up as it loses altitude. In general, the drag slows down the satellite.

13. d

15. a

17. a

19. 1.4×10^{-20} N

21. 0.005%

23. 3.7 m/s^2

25. 9.801 m/s^2
27. (a) 8.0 m/s^2
    (b) 20.5 m/s^2
    (c) $7.68 \times 10^{24} \text{ kg}$
29. $2.04 \times 10^6 \text{ J}$
31. $F_x = 0, F_y = -2ky$
33. 2.4 km/s
35. (a) 4 years
    (b) $5 \times 10^{-8} \text{ rad/s}$
37. 1680 m/s
39. (a) 488 km
    (b) 0.000645
41. (a) 23.4 s
    (b) $9.12 \times 10^{15} \text{ kg}, 6.4 \times 10^{21} \text{ kg}$
43. (a) 1.31 kg m^2
    (b) $2.94 \times 10^{-1} \text{ N m}$
    (c) $1.79 \times 10^{-7} \text{ N}$
    (d) $1.61 \times 10^{-7} \text{ N m}$
    (e) 0.0011 rad
45. (a) $5.0 \times 10^{23} \text{ kg}$
    (b) 3.9 km/s
47. 42.1 km/s
49. 1400 kg/m^3
51. See online resources.
53. (a) 73000 km/s
    (b) 4.7 ms
55. The simulation shows enhanced numbers of asteroids that have orbital radii and periods similar to Jupiter, but travel approximately 60° ahead or behind Jupiter. These locations are two of the Lagrange points (L4 and L5).
57. (a) The planet with the 10 day period is closer.
    (b) The one with the 10 day period is slightly more massive.
59. 505 m/s
61. $\dfrac{3kMm}{r^4}$
63. (a) $1.1 \times 10^{41} \text{ J}$
    (b) 10^7 years
65. (a) 22 m/s
    (b) 396.78097 to 396.78103 nm
67. (a) 72 km/s
    (b) 10^{13} kg
    (c) $2.6 \times 10^{22} \text{ J}, 6.2 \times 10^6 \text{ Mt}$

Chapter 12—Fluids

1. c
3. d
5. ABC
7. (a) When the iron cube is in the boat, the water displaced is due to the weight of the cube. However, when it is dropped in the water, it displaces water equal to its volume. Therefore the water level will fall.
9. b
11. b
13. Yes, the pressure at the bottom depends on the height of the water, not on the surface area at the bottom.
15. a
17. $3.1 \times 10^{-8} \text{ cm}$
19. 69 kN/m^2
21. (a) $4.10 \times 10^{20} \text{ kg/m}^3$
    (b) $4.1 \times 10^{15} \text{ N}$, absolutely not
23. about 1100 kg/m^3; no

25. 57 kN
27. 6.0 kPa
29. 349 N
31. a
33. 27 m
35. 880 kg/m^3
37. 0.4 N
39. 2.78 g/cm^3
41. (a) 0.69
    (b) 27
    (c) Yes, some of the weight of the survivors would be offset by the buoyant force corresponding to the volume of water displaced by their legs.
43. 6.2 m/s^2. Acceleration will decrease as drag from the water increases with speed. Although drag is the dominant factor, the density of the water increases slightly with depth due to the greater pressure. This increase in density increases the buoyance force, and decreases the acceleration correspondingly.
45. 650 m^3
47. 1.3 m
49. (a) $3.3 \times 10^{-5} \text{ m}^3\text{/s}$
    (b) 0.11 m/s
    (c) 2.0 m/s
    (d) $1.7 \times 10^{-5} \text{ m}^2$
51. (a) 45.6 m/s (b) 468 kPa
53. (a) 13 kPa (b) 1.5%
55. (a) 47 kPa (b) 5.5 m
57. Bernoulli's equation indicates that the pressure increases when the speed of water is reduced.
59. $A_2\sqrt{\dfrac{2(P_t + \rho g y_2)}{\rho(A_2^2 - A_1^2)}}$
61. See online resources.
63. 6.3 kPa
65. See online resources.
67. 1.9 N m
69. b

Chapter 13—Oscillations

1. $4A$, zero
3. Since force is proportional to distance from equilibrium point, acceleration increases with amplitude, keeping the period constant.
5. Increased
7. The system has to be treated as a physical pendulum, and the period will be $2\pi\sqrt{\dfrac{I}{MgR}}$.
9. a
11. Decreases
13. c
15. a, b
17. d
19. (a) 0.3 m
    (b) 0.47 m/s
    (c) 0.75 m/s^2
    (d) $x(t) = 0.3 \cos(1.58t)$
21. (a) 7.7 rad/s
    (b) 15.0 cm
    (c) 0
    (d) $x(t) = (-10 \text{ cm}) \cos(0.3t)$

23. (a) $x(t) = 0.40 \cos\left(\pi t + \dfrac{\pi}{2}\right)$

(b) 1.3 m/s, 4.0 m/s²

(c) 0.079 J

25. No, since $x(0) = A\cos\phi = -x(T/2)$ we have only one independent equation, so we cannot solve for the two unknowns.

27. (a) CBDAE

(b) EADBC

(c) BDACE

(d) EADBC

29. 7.27×10^{-5} rad/s, 24 h

31. DABEFC

33. (a) 32 rad/s, 0.20 s

(b) 6.3 m/s, 0.20 km/s²

(c) 2.0 J

35. (a) 200 N/m

(b) 1.6 s⁻¹

(c) $x(t) = 0.050 \cos(10t + 1.283)$

(d) 0.49 m

37. (a) 0.31 s

(b) No change since period does not depend on spring compression.

39. (a) 4.7×10^4 N/m (b) 1.8 Hz

41. (a), (b), (c): See online resources.

(d) No. At the instant when the oscillating mass passes through its initial position, both springs are in their equilibrium positions. When the mass is at any other position, it exerts a force on spring 1, which in turn exerts a somewhat lesser force on spring 2. These forces either stretch both springs or compress both of them.

43. 6.2 cm

45. (a) 9.9 N/m

(b) 0.012 J

(c) 0.64

(d) $y(t) = 0.050 \cos(\pi t)$

47. (a) 63 J (b) 65 m/s

49. $\dfrac{1}{14.1}\sqrt{\dfrac{k}{m}}$

51. ADBCEF

53. (a) 200.6 s (b) 200.9 s, yes

55. (a) See online resources. (b) increase by $L/360$

57. See online resources.

59. (a) 0.6 m, 3 s

(b) $\dfrac{\pi}{2}$

(c) $\dfrac{7\pi}{6}, \dfrac{11\pi}{6}$

(d) $x(t) = 0.6 \cos\left(\dfrac{2\pi}{3}t + \dfrac{\pi}{2}\right)$

(e) 0.63 m/s

(f) 2.3 m/s²

61. (a) 0.20 m, 3.0 s

(b) 1.0 m

(c) $\pi/3$ rad

(d) $x(t) = (0.20\text{ m})\cos\left(\dfrac{2\pi}{3}t + \dfrac{\pi}{3}\right) + 1.0\text{ m}$

(e) $x(t) = (0.20\text{ m})\cos\left(\dfrac{2\pi}{3}t + \dfrac{5\pi}{6}\right) + 1.0\text{ m}$

$= (0.20\text{ m})\sin\left(\dfrac{2\pi}{3}t + \dfrac{4\pi}{3}\right) + 1.0\text{ m}$

(f) 0.88 m/s²

63. (a) 312 (b) 132 (c) 321 (d) 123

65. (a) 6.4×10^{-3} kg/s (b) 15.8 (c) No

67. ACB

69. $\phi = \tan^{-1}\left[-\dfrac{x(t = T/4)}{x(t = 0)}\right]$, $A = \dfrac{x(t = 0)}{\cos\phi}$

71. 34.2 min. The object will be oscillating between the two poles with a period given by $T = 2\pi\sqrt{\dfrac{R_{\text{earth}}}{g}}$, which is independent of the mass of the object. Therefore the time to reach the other pole does not depend on the mass of the object.

73. See online resources.

75. (a) $\dfrac{2m}{m + M}v$ (b) $\dfrac{2mv}{m + M}\sqrt{\dfrac{M}{k}}$

Chapter 14—Waves

1. (a) F. For a transverse wave, the particles of the medium vibrate perpendicular to the direction of wave. For a longitudinal wave, the particles move back and forth in the direction of the wave.

(b) F. Wave speed of a mechanical wave in a medium depends on the elastic and inertial properties of the medium.

(c) T. The speed of waves in a medium often varies somewhat with wavelength.

(d) F. Mechanical waves depend on the movement of particles of the medium through which they pass.

(e) F. Since the speed of the wave depends on the properties of the medium, the speed will be constant in a uniform medium.

(f) F. A traveling wave always carries energy.

(g) F. The maximum amplitude cannot be greater than the sum of the amplitudes of individual waves.

(h) F. To produce a standing wave, the waves must be traveling in opposite directions.

3. Light wave

5. No

7. The wave propagates outward from the point where the stone hits the water surface. As the wavefront expands the energy per unit length decreases, and therefore the amplitude decreases.

9. b

11. The two waves must have same frequency and amplitude to produce a standing wave. If the two waves have same amplitude but different frequencies, interference will occur but standing waves will not be produced. (b) If the two waves have same frequency but different amplitudes, a pattern similar to a standing wave will be produced but without any nodes.

13. No, a difference in linear mass density could be offset by a difference in tension.

15. (a) π rad/m (b) 20π rad/s (c) 20 m/s

17. (a) 143 Hz (b) 6.98 ms (c) 1.05 m

19. 17 mm to 17 m

21. 10 mm to 6 m in ocean water; 2.3 mm to 1.4 m in air

23. $D(1.5, 2.0) = 6.9$ mm, $D_{\text{min}} = 0$, $D_{\text{max}} = 25$ cm

25. (a) 3.0 m/s, traveling left

(b) -23.6 mm

(c) -0.5 mm

(d) 1.2 cm/s

(e)

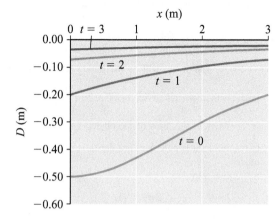

27. (a)

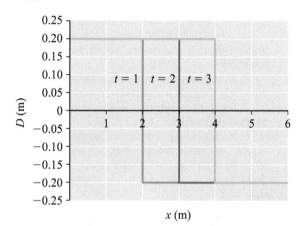

(b) 1.0 m/s, right
(c) 0.2 m
(d) $D(x, t) = \begin{cases} +0.2 \text{ m} & \text{if } |x + t| > 4 \\ -0.2 \text{ m} & \text{if } |x + t| \leq 4 \end{cases}$

29. (a)

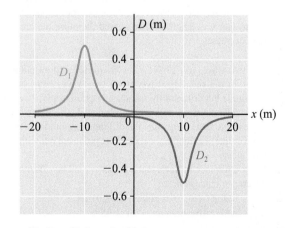

(b) D_1: −10.0 m, D_2: 10.0 m
(c) $t = 2$ s
(d) No, there is no such point.
31. 25 N
33. 0.22 km/s
35. 11.6 m from the end of string B

37. (a) See online resources.

(b) $\dfrac{2\pi v}{g}$

(c) 19 m/s
39. $\lambda_b < \lambda_a = \lambda_c < \lambda_d$, $f_a = f_b = f_d < f_c$; all waves moving toward increasing x.

41. $D_1(x, t) = \sin\left(\dfrac{4\pi}{3}x - 2\pi t - \dfrac{\pi}{4}\right)$,

$D_2(x, t) = \sin\left(2\pi x - 3\pi t + \dfrac{\pi}{2}\right)$

43. (a) 0.626 m, 1.19 Hz, 0.750 m/s
(b) $D(x, t) = 0.05 \sin(10.0x - 7.50t)$

45. (a) 3.0 m, $\dfrac{1}{6}$ Hz, 0.50 m/s

(b) Toward decreasing x.
(c)

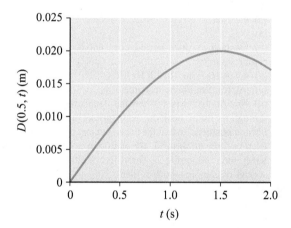

(d) 2.2 mm/s
47. (a) 8.0 m
(b) 40 m/s

(c) $\dfrac{21\pi}{2}$, which is equivalent to $\dfrac{\pi}{2}$

(d) $D(x, t) = 1.5 \sin\left(\dfrac{\pi}{4}x - 10\pi t + \dfrac{21\pi}{2}\right)$

49. (a) 0.50 Hz
(b) 8.0 m

(c) $\dfrac{3\pi}{8}$ rad

(d) $D(x, t) = 1.5 \sin\left(\dfrac{\pi}{4}x - \pi t + \dfrac{3\pi}{8}\right)$

51. (a) $D(x, t) = 1.5 \sin\left(\dfrac{\pi}{4}x - 2\pi t + \dfrac{\pi}{2}\right)$

(b) $D(x, t) = 1.5 \sin\left(\dfrac{\pi}{4}x + 2\pi t - \dfrac{\pi}{2}\right)$

53. (a) $D(x, t) = 0.10 \sin\left(\dfrac{2\pi}{3}x - \dfrac{\pi}{3}t - 5.5\right)$

(b) 0.50 m/s, toward decreasing x
55. (a) 0.2 rad
(b) 1.2 rad
(c) Yes, the phase changes linearly with time.
(d) 0.4 rad
(e) Yes
(f) 2π rad, which is equivalent to 0 rad

57. 0.88 J

59. (a)

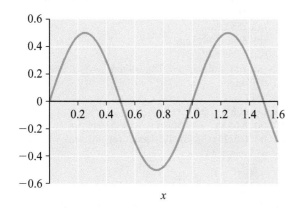

(b) $A = 0.50$, $\lambda = 1.0$

(c) The two component waves have the same frequency and wavelength, so these waves have the same speed. Consequently, the resultant wave will also have the same speed.

(d) Travelling

61. −0.42 rad

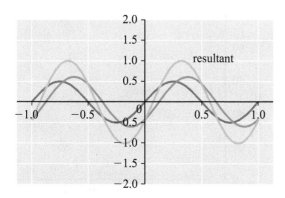

63. 2.636 rad, 1.318 rad

65. (a) $|A_1 - A_2|$ (b) $A_1 + A_2$

67. See online resources

69. (a) $D(x, t) = 0.2 \sin(3x - 4t + \pi)$

(b) $D(x, t) = 0.2 \sin(3x - 4t)$

71. (a) $\dfrac{10\pi}{3}$ m, 10 Hz

(b) $\dfrac{5\pi}{3}$, $\dfrac{5\pi}{6}$

(c) $D_1(x, t) = 0.0075 \sin(0.6x - 20\pi t)$,
$D_2(x, t) = 0.0075 \sin(0.6x + 20\pi t)$

(d) 1.8 mm

73. (a) $D(x, t) = (2.0 \text{ mm}) \sin(\pi x) \cos(0.5\pi t)$

(b) Nodes: ± 1.0 m, ± 2.0 m, ± 3.0 m,
Antinodes: ± 0.5 m, ± 1.5 m, ± 2.5 m

(c) 1.0 m

75. See online resources.

77. 265 Hz

79. (a) 4.0 m

(b) 50.0 Hz

(c) No, all frequencies of standing waves are integer multiples of the fundamental frequency.

(d) 100.0 Hz, 200.0 Hz

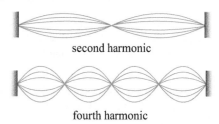

81. (a) 98.0 Hz

(b) 196 Hz, 294 Hz

(c) 196 m/s

(d) 116 Hz

Chapter 15—Interference and Sound

1. T

3. 0.5

5. T

7. T

9. F

11. 3.01 dB

13. c

15. 34.32 cm

17. 0.040 s

19. $s(x, t) = s_m \cos(6.9x - 377t)$

21. 1.08×10^{-5} m

23. 2

25.

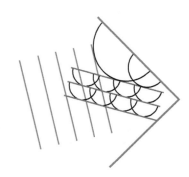

27. 1.7 kHz, 1.1 kHz, 0.86 kHz

29. 2 Hz

31. 90 Hz

33. 90 dB

35. 749 Hz

37. 9.8 cm/s

39. 1.4 km

41. 28 nm

43. 3.2×10^{-6} W/m², 21 mW

45. 2.4 kHz

47. 1.3 m

49. 24 m/s

51. Intensity reduces by a factor of 10^6 to 0.2 μW/m².

53. 35.6 m

55. 61 Hz

57. (a) 2.4 m (b) 2.68 kHz

59. See online resources.

61. 252 m

Chapter 16—Temperature and the Zeroth Law of Thermodynamics

1. Only if both thermometers are linear between the calibration temperatures

3. The most probable and mean values are the same only for symmetric distributions with a central peak. If a distribution is skewed, the mean differs from the most probable value.

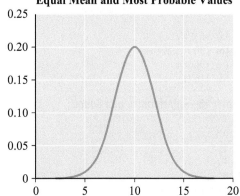

(a) Symmetric Probability Distribution with Equal Mean and Most Probable Values

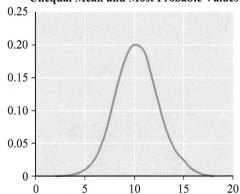

(b) Skewed Probability Distribution with Unequal Mean and Most Probable Values

5. The triple point of water exists at exactly 0.01°C or 273.16 K. If liquid water did not expand when cooled, the melting point of ordinary ice would not decrease as a function of pressure and the triple point would be the limit below which water would not exist in liquid state.

7. No, the gases would have to have equal low-density concentrations (N/V).

9. No

11. As the Sun rises, the temperature of the land increases more rapidly than that of the water, and the air just above the land becomes warmer than the air above the water. As a result the air pressure on land is lower than the pressure above water. This pressure difference forces the cooler air above the water to move toward the land.

13. For an ideal gas the relationship between pressure, volume and temperature is given by $PV = NkT$. Therefore, if the temperature increases while the volume is reduced by half, the pressure will more than double.

15. 3.71×10^{-26} m³, 3.34 nm

17. No, when a system is in thermodynamic equilibrium, all macroscopic properties, including temperature, remain constant.

19. (a) 758 kPa
    (b) 8.80×10^{-4} cm³
    (c) 0.267 mol
    (d) 7.51 g nitrogen, 1.07 g helium

21. 0.68 mm

23. $-40°$C

25. (a) 136°F   (b) 331 K

27. (a) 8.65 kg   (b) 52.2 m³   (c) 530 moles

29. (a) 0.0224 m³   (b) 493.1 m/s   (c) 461.4 m/s   (d) 1:1.069

31. 433 m/s, 0.54 km/s

33. $\sqrt{\dfrac{8kT}{\pi m}}$

35. Water, oxygen and carbon dioxide in solid phase; nitrogen in liquid phase

37. 0.60 m, for example, 48 kg of water for a body mass of 80 kg

39. 4×10^{-4} m/s

41. 180 K

43. 3.3×10^{27} m^{-2} s^{-1}

45. (a) 8.5×10^{15} Pa   (b) 4.1×10^5 m/s

47.

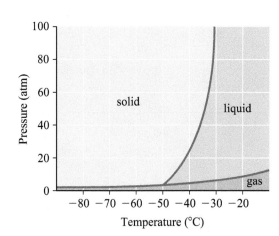

49. $R = 193\ \Omega$ at $T = 400$ K

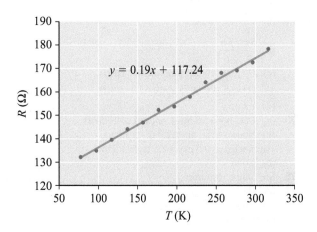

$y = 0.19x + 117.24$

Chapter 17—Heat, Work, and the First Law of Thermodynamics

1. Constant volume
3. A solid; B solid and liquid; C liquid; D liquid and gas; E gas
5. All surfaces, including our skin, lose heat through radiant heat transfer with rates that differ in winter and summer months. The reason is the unequal temperature differentials that exist between objects and their surroundings in winter and summer months. Hence in winter months we lose heat at a faster rate than in summer months.
7. Positive
9. 2
11. The food has reached an equilibrium state.
13. The heat capacities of the objects are equal (i.e., the product cm is the same).
15. 8.0×10^2 s
17. 13.8°C
19. 130 J kg^{-1} K^{-1}
21. 11°C
23. 2.4 kJ
25. 100 J
27. 21 kW/m^2
29. 9.6 kW
31. 8.0 kJ/K, 80.0 kJ kg^{-1} K^{-1}
33. 1.3 kJ/s assuming that all of the perspiration was evaporated by heat from the athlete's body
35. −3.74 kJ
37. About 0.15 W (assuming 0.5 emissivity and cylindrical shape with 1 cm radius)
39. 505 kJ, 495 kJ
41. −7.6 kJ, 1.5 J, 7.6 kJ (out of the gas)
43. 61 kJ
45. 696°C, 13.4 kJ, 5.37 kJ, 8.06 kJ

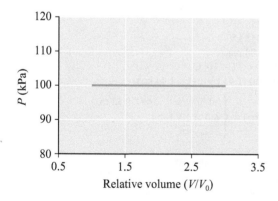

47. 11.5 kg

Chapter 18—Heat Engines and the Second Law of Thermodynamics

1. No, more heat will be added to the room than extracted as refrigeration is not a perfectly efficient process.
3. The efficiency would still be governed by the Carnot cycle efficiency, which depends only on the temperature difference between the hot and cold reservoirs.
5. No. If the temperature difference between the waste energy source and the heat reservoir of the heat engine is too great, the heat pump will use more energy than it transfers to the heat reservoir.

7. The reasoning is not entirely correct since moving around to clean up the room increases the entropy of the Universe even though the things in the room become more ordered.
9. An object falling to the ground.
11. (a) about 1.6 mL/s   (b) about 53 kJ/s
13. (a) about 12.5 W   (b) about 12.5 W   (c) 0.29 kJ/s   (d) 0.30 kJ/s
15. (a) 39.3%   (b) 39.3 kJ
17. 3.9 MJ
19. (a) 10 $m_{mol}c$, where m_{mol} is the molar mass of the gas, and c is the specific heat
    (b) 0.05 mc, where m is the mass of the gas
    (c) −0.0488 mc
    (d) 0.0012 mc
    (e) no
21. (a) 63 kJ/s
    (b) −82 J K^{-1} s^{-1}
    (c) 0.22 kJ K^{-1} s^{-1}
    (d) 0.14 kJ K^{-1} s^{-1}
23. 85
25. (a) −0.77 J/K
    (b) −8.1 J/K
    (c) −53 J/K
    (d) −53 J/K
27. No. Heat engines and heat pumps are never 100% efficient. The amount of work that the heat pump could do would always be less than the energy input into the engine.
29. The data supplied indicate that the engine would have an efficiency of 55.5%, which is greater than the maximum possible efficiency of 50% for the given temperatures. Since the data are erroneous, the application should be rejected.
31. See online resources.
33. 7.0 kJ/K
35. about -2.6×10^7 J/K, 6.8×10^7 J/K, 4.2×10^7 J/K
37. 35.9 J/K
39. about 1.2
41. (a) $\dfrac{23}{d}$ J m^{-2} s^{-1} where d is the thickness of the ice in metres
    (b) $\dfrac{0.0812}{d}$ J m^{-2} s^{-1} K^{-1}
    (c) $-\dfrac{0.0842}{d}$ J m^{-2} s^{-1} K^{-1}
    (d) 5.9 mm/day
    (e) See online resources.
43. $\dfrac{mc\Delta T}{T} - \dfrac{mgh}{T}$
45. No, at the smaller scale, the entropy of the Universe is constantly increasing.
47. See online resources.
49. Answers will vary. For a sea with a temperature around 22°C at the surface and 4°C at some depth below the surface, the maximum theoretical efficiency would be about 6%. Extracting energy would lower the water temperature, and could affect local sea life. Large-scale operations could alter ocean currents, and affect coastal erosion, silt deposits, and possibly even Earth's climate. The core of Earth has a temperature of about 5430°C, so the theoretical efficiency with a surface temperature of about 22°C is around 95%. Large-scale operations could affect aquifers and local wildlife habitat.

Chapter 19—Electric Charges and Forces

1. c
3. b
5. c
7. b
9. a
11. c
13. c
15. b
17. 40 nA
19. (a) 8.22×10^{-8} N
    (b) 2.19×10^{6} m/s
21. 4.24 cm to the left of $+1.00 \ \mu C$ charge
23. 1.60×10^{-12} N
25. 0.0365 nm
27. 8.99×10^{-2} N directed away from the rod
29. 2.9 ms
31. 5.71×10^{13} C
33. Each charge experiences a force of 0.922 N directed away from the centre of the triangle.
35. zero
37. 4.2 N/C in $+x$ direction
39. 0.27 μm to the right of the negative charge
41. 3.79×10^{-14} C
43. 2.4×10^{-22} N m pointing in $-z$ direction
45. 1.80×10^{7} N/C directed upward
47. -2.0 mC located at $x = -6.0$ m.

Chapter 20—Electric Potential and Gauss's Law

1. a
3. c
5. a
7. b
9. d
11. d
13. a
15. a
17. -27.2 eV
19. 509 V
21.

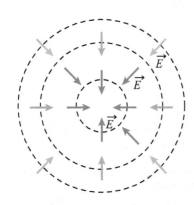

23. (a) $E_x = 0$, $E_y = -25.0$ N/C, $E_z = 0$
    (b) -25.0 V/m
25. (a) Parallel to yz-plane
    (b) 2.5 m away from origin in x-direction
27. (a) 3.93×10^{-19} J (b) 9.38×10^{-20} cal
29. 657 μC/m
31. 3.44×10^{-2} C/m^3

33. $\pi R^2 |\vec{E}|$, where R is the radius of the hemisphere

35. $E = \begin{cases} \dfrac{\rho r}{3\varepsilon_0}\hat{r}, & r \leq r_0 \\[2mm] \dfrac{\rho R^3}{3\varepsilon_0 r^2}\hat{r}, & r > r_0 \end{cases}$

37. $E = \begin{cases} 0 & r < 0.045 \text{ m} \\[2mm] \dfrac{2.70 \times 10^5}{r} & 0.0450 \text{ m} < r < 0.085 \text{ m} \\[2mm] \dfrac{8.99 \times 10^4}{r} & r > 0.085 \text{ m} \end{cases}$

where E is measured in volts per metre and r is measured in metres

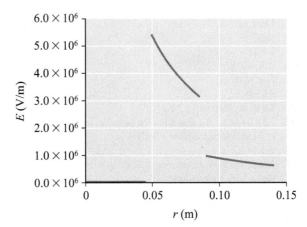

39. 7.69×10^{-14} J
41. $v_1 = v_2 = 179$ m/s
43. 256 mV
45. 555 kV
47. 488 pm
49. -6.77×10^5 C
51. (a) 1.44 kV (b) 1.44 keV
53. $E(r) = \begin{cases} 0 & r < 0.12 \text{ m} \\[2mm] \dfrac{6.0 \times 10^{-8}}{\pi\varepsilon_0 r^2} & r > 0.12 \text{ m} \end{cases}$

$V(r) = \begin{cases} \dfrac{5.0 \times 10^{-7}}{\pi\varepsilon_0} & r \leq 0.12 \text{ m} \\[2mm] \dfrac{6.0 \times 10^{-8}}{\pi\varepsilon_0 r} & r \geq 0.12 \text{ m} \end{cases}$

where E is measured in volts per metre, V in volts, and r in metres

55. (a) $\dfrac{2.70 \times 10^5}{r}$ N/C directed outward
    (b) $\dfrac{1.44 \times 10^5}{r}$ N/C directed outward
    (c) 0
57. (a) 11.6 V/m
    (b) zero
    (c) 28.1 V/m
    (d) 15.0 V/m

59. 5.33×10^5 V/m

61. (a) 5.39×10^6 V

(b) 1.12×10^7 V

(c) small drop: 2.16×10^{10} N/C; large drop: 3.11×10^{10} N/C

63. $V(a/2) = \dfrac{\mu}{2\pi\varepsilon_0} \ln 2$, $V(2a) = -\dfrac{\mu}{2\pi\varepsilon_0} \ln 2$

65. $V(z) = \dfrac{\sigma}{2\varepsilon_0}\left[\sqrt{z^2 + a^2} - z\right]$

67. (a) 3.0×10^6 V/m

(b), (c), (d) Answers will vary.

Chapter 21—Capacitance

1. b

3. d

5. a

7. c

9. b

11. d

13. b

15. b

17. 0.500 mF

19. (a) 4.80 V (b) 11.7 μF

21. 1.36 mm

23. (a) Connect 4 in parallel.

(b) Connect 5 in series

(c) Connect two in parallel with each other and with another pair connected in series.

25. Dielectric could be mica since $\kappa = 6.91$.

27. (a) 180 μJ (b) 720 μJ

29. 70.7 V

31. See online resources.

33. (a) 300 fC

(b) 1.9×10^6

35. 60.7 pF/m

37. $C = \dfrac{\varepsilon_0 A}{2d}(k_1 + k_2)$

39. (a) 3.60 μC

(b) 1.80 V

(c) 3.24 μJ

41. (a) 39.8 kV/m

(b) 159 V

(c) higher

(d) 3.57 ns

(e) 4.46 cm, no

43. $C_1 = 2\ \mu\text{F}$, $C_2 = 4\ \mu\text{F}$, $C_3 = 8\ \mu\text{F}$, $C_4 = 8\ \mu\text{F}$, $C_5 = 2\ \mu\text{F}$

45. (a) 2.50 nF

(b) 28 μm

(c) 4.5 μJ

(d) 2.1 MV/m

47. $2.92 \times$ mJ/m³

49. (a) 0.545 pF (b) 40.7 fC (c) 2.55×10^5

51. 5.59 mF

53. Answers will vary.

Chapter 22—Electric Current and Fundamentals of DC Circuits

1. (a) FALSE: Historically, the direction of electric current is defined as the direction of the flow of positive charge.

(b) FALSE: The resistance depends also on wire dimensions.

(c) FALSE: Free electron density is a characteristic of the metal crystal that is independent of temperature

(d) TRUE: $\rho = \rho_0(1 + \alpha\Delta T)$, $\rho = \dfrac{1}{\sigma}$.

(e) TRUE: Combining equations 22-7 and 22-1 gives

$v_d = \dfrac{E}{n_e e} \cdot \dfrac{1}{\rho}$

3. (b) For circuit I, $R_e = R$; for circuit II $R_e = 10\,R$, and for circuit III, $R_e = R/10$. Hence, $P = \dfrac{V^2}{R_e}$ for circuit III is 10 times greater than for circuit I and 100 times greater than for circuit II.

5. e

7. d

9. b

11. c

13. c

15. e

17. d

19. b

21. a

23. (a) 1.3×10^{19} per second

(b) 6.4×10^5 A/m²

(c) 4.0 C

25. (a) $\rho = 1.7 \times 10^{-8}\ \Omega\cdot\text{m}$, $\sigma = 5.9 \times 10^7\ \Omega^{-1}\text{m}^{-1}$

(b) 4.7×10^{-5} m/s

(c) 25 fs

(d) 11×10^{-3} mV/m

(e) Resistivity, conductivity, and mean time between collisions will not change; drift velocity and electric field inside the wire will double.

(f) None

(g) The resistivity and the electric field inside the wire will increase; the conductivity and the mean time between collisions will decrease; the drift velocity will not change.

27. 20 m, 0.010 mm²

29. 8.3 A; only one

31. (a) 2.0 Ω

(b) 1.5 A

33. See online resources.

35. (a) about 44 MJ

(b) about 79 cents

(c) Answers will vary. Answers could include using CFl or LED bulbs, replacing fridge with high-efficiency model if over 15 years old, unplugging computer, printer, TV, and other electronic devices when not in use for long periods.

37. (a) 4 in parallel

(b) 2 pair in parallel connected in series

(c) 2 in series with each other and a pair in parallel (or just 3 in series)

(d) 4 in series

39. (a) 21 Ω, 6.9 W

(b) $I_A = 0.57$ A, $I_B = I_C = I_D = I_H = I_G = I_I = 0.29$ A, $I_E = 0.34$ A, $I_F = 0.23$ A

(c) $V_A = V_D = V_I = 2.9$ V, $V_B = V_C = V_H = V_G = 1.4$ V, $V_E = V_F = 3.4$ V

(d) $P_A = 1.6$ W, $P_B = P_C = P_H = P_G = 0.4$ W, $P_D = P_I = 0.8$ W, $P_E = 1.2$ W, $P_F = 0.8$ W

(e) $P_{total} = P_A + P_B + P_C + P_D + P_E + P_F + P_G + P_I = 6.9\,W$, which is equal to the power calculated in question (a), confirming that equivalent resistance does accurately model the circuit.

41. $\dfrac{12}{7}R$

43. $2.4\,\Omega$

45. (a) 6.9τ

(b) $q(\tau) = 2.3\,mC$, $q(2\tau) = 3.1\,mC$, $q(3\tau) = 3.4\,mC$

(c) $I(\tau) = 0.88\,mA$, $I(2\tau) = 0.32\,mA$, $I(3\tau) = 0.12\,mA$

47. (a) If the energy were taken from the electrical outlet it would cost about 0.05 cents, 2000 times less than power from the battery.

(b) Answers will vary. For the energy listed on the bill in Figure 22-10, the cost would be about \$93 000.

49. $V_{AB} = V_{FG} = V_{EF} = 0\,V$

$V_{AG} = V_{BE} = V_{CF} = 10\,V$

$V_{BH} = V_{HF} = 5\,V$

$V_{CD} = 4\,V$

$V_{DE} = 6\,V$

$V_{HD} = -1\,V$

51. (a) $\dfrac{I_a}{I_b} = \dfrac{2}{3}$

(b) Circuit (a): 4 V; circuit (b): 6 V

(c) In circuit (b) bulb O will not light at all and bulbs M and N will be markedly brighter than the bulbs in circuit (a).

53. (a) When the two wires are connected in parallel, the potential difference across them is equal. Since the heat produced by each wire is given by $P = V^2/R$, the wire with the lesser resistance will produce more heat, and hence have a higher equilibrium temperature. The aluminum wire has the lesser thermal coefficient. At any temperature above room temperature, the aluminum wire has less resistance and produces more heat than the tungsten wire at the same temperature. Thus, the aluminum wire will have the higher equilibrium temperature.

(b) When the two wires are connected in series, the current through them is equal. Since the heat produced is given by $P = I^2R$, the wire with the greater resistance will produce more heat, and hence have a higher equilibrium temperature. The tungsten wire will have the greater resistance because it has the greater thermal coefficient.

55. (a) $I_1 = 0.615\,A$

$I_2 = 1.27\,A$

$I_3 = -0.650\,A$

$I_4 = 0.675\,A$

$I_5 = 0.590\,A$

(b) $V_{R_1} = 6.15\,V$

$V_{R_2} = -6.50\,V$

$V_{R_3} = 8.85\,V$

$V_{R_4} = 13.5\,V$

$V_{R_5} = 0.50\,V$

$V_{R_6} = 0.25\,V$

(c) If the batteries are real, small resistances will be connected in series with R_1 and R_2. Consequently, the currents through these resistors will decrease.

57. $I_1 = 7.32\,A$

$I_2 = 1.75\,A$

$I_3 = -0.284\,A$

$I_4 = 0.100\,A$

$I_5 = 1.65\,A$

$V_{R_1} = 14.6\,V$

$V_{R_2} = 8.74\,V$

$V_{R_3} = -4.26\,V$

$V_{R_4} = 2.00\,V$

$V_{R_5} = 14.6\,V$

59. (a) Zero potential difference across the three resistors on the right side of the circuit.

$V_C = V_{700\,\Omega} = 73.0\,V$

$V_{250\,\Omega} = 26.1\,V$

$V_{100\,\Omega} = 10.4\,V$

$V_{150\,\Omega} = 10.4\,V$

$V_{300\,\Omega} = 10.4\,V$

(b) 3.60 ms

61. (a) $40.0\,\Omega$

(b) 41.5 mF

(c) 2.07 J

(d) 41.3 mJ

Chapter 23—Magnetic Fields and Magnetic Forces

1. Yes, there could be nonzero B, if it is parallel to the velocity of the particle.

3. See the text online resources

5. The charge carriers are positive.

7. b

9. f

11. c

13. a

15. c

17. $(e) > (d) = (b) > (a) = (c) = f$.

19. $\vec{F} = (7.68\hat{i} + 10.24\hat{j} + 3.84\hat{k}) \times 10^{-15}\,N$

$F = 13.4 \times 10^{-15}\,N$

21. $F \cong 4.5\,mN$

$\vec{F}$ along $\hat{j}$ direction

23. (a) $r_\alpha > r_p > r_e$

(b) $T_\alpha > T_p > T_e$

25. (a) $V_p \cong 1.6 \times 10^7\,m \cdot s^{-1}$

(b) $\omega_p = 1.6 \times 10^{11}\,rad \cdot s^{-1}$

27. (a) $r_d = \sqrt{2}\,r_p$

(b) $r_\alpha = \sqrt{2}\,r_p$

29. $r_1 = 2.8\,pm$

$r_2 = 5.7\,pm$

$r_3 = 11\,pm$

$F_{B1} = 72\,\mu N$

$F_{B2} = 140\,\mu N$

$F_{B3} = 290\,\mu N$

31. For figure and notations see the text online resources.

$\Delta = R - \sqrt{R^2 - d^2} \cong 9.9\,mm$

33. (a) $\dfrac{F}{l} = 18\,N/m$

(b) $\dfrac{F'}{l} = \dfrac{F}{l} = 18\,N/m$

35. $B = 0$ T

37. $B(10 \text{ m}) = 200 \ \mu\text{T}$

$B(100 \text{ m}) = 20 \ \mu\text{T}$

$B(1 \text{ km}) = 2 \ \mu\text{T}$

Earth's magnetic field strength is roughly $50 \ \mu\text{T}$.

39. (a) $B(2 \text{ mm}) = 0.4$ mT

$B(5 \text{ mm}) = 1$ mT

(b) $B(r) = \begin{cases} 0.2 \ r \text{ (mm) mT}, & r \leq 5 \text{ mm}, \\ \dfrac{5}{r \text{ (mm)}} \text{ mT}, & r > 5 \text{ mm} \end{cases}$

For plot of $B(r)$, see the text online resources.

(c) $E(r) = \begin{cases} \dfrac{Q}{4\pi\varepsilon_0 R^2} \cdot \dfrac{r}{R}, & r \leq R, \\ \dfrac{Q}{4\pi\varepsilon_0 r^2}, & r > R \end{cases}$

where R is the radius of the uniformly charged ball. By comparison,

$B(r) = \begin{cases} \dfrac{\mu_0 I}{2\pi R} \cdot \dfrac{r}{R}, & r \leq R \\ \dfrac{\mu_0 I}{2\pi r}, & r > R \end{cases}$

For plots of $E(r)$ and $B(r)$ see the text online resources.

41. $F_1 = 30 \ \mu N$

$F_2 = 4/313 \ \mu N$

43. (a) $\vec{\mu}_{\text{loop}} = -0.1\pi \ A \cdot m^2 \ \hat{k}$

(b) $\vec{\mu}_{\text{coil}} = -10\pi \ A \cdot m^2 \ \hat{k}$

(c) $\vec{\tau} = 10\pi \ N \cdot m \ \hat{i}$

(d) The magnitude of $\vec{\mu}_{\text{loop}}$, $\vec{\mu}_{\text{coil}}$, and $\vec{\tau}$ do not change, just their directions will be opposite to those indicated in parts (a), (b), and (c).

(e) If $\vec{B} = 1.0 \ T \ \hat{i}$, the answers to parts (a) and (b) do not change and $\vec{\tau} = -10\pi \ N \cdot m \ \hat{j}$.

If $\vec{B} = 1.0 \ T \ \hat{k}$, the answers to parts (a) and (b) do not change and $\tau = 0 \ N \cdot m$.

(f) $\Delta U = \pm \mu_{\text{coil}} B = \pm 10\pi \ J$

45. (a) $F_B = 1.2 \times 10^{-16}$ N

Direction of $\vec{F}_B$ is perpendicular and away from the wire.

(b) $F_B = 1.2 \times 10^{-16}$ N

Direction of $\vec{F}_B$ is perpendicular and towards the wire.

(c) The radius of the electron's curved trajectory increases as it moves away from the wire.

The radius of the proton's curved trajectory decreases as it moves towards the wire.

See the text online resources for plotted trajectories.

47. $\vec{B} = \dfrac{\mu_0 I}{6} \left(\dfrac{1}{R_1} - \dfrac{1}{2R_2} \right) \hat{k}$,

where $\hat{k}$ is the unit vector going into the page.

49. (a) $B(\text{centre}) = 50\pi \ \mu\text{T}$

(b) $B_x = \dfrac{\mu_0 n I}{2} \left(\dfrac{x - x_1}{\sqrt{(x - x_1)^2 + R^2}} - \dfrac{x - x_2}{\sqrt{(x - x_2)^2 + R^2}} \right)$

$B(15 \text{ cm}) = 1.32 \times 10^{-4}$ T

(c)

Dependence of Magnetic Field Along the Axis of a Solenoid B_x (mT) on the Distance From its Centre Measured in Metres

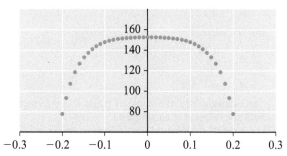

(d) One can see that 15 cm away from the centre, T decreased by about 12%. So we can estimate from the graph that it will decrease by about 5% around 10 cm off its centre. The more exact value is 12 cm.

51. See solutions manual for answer.

53. $F_{\text{loop}} = 0$ N

55. (a) $\dfrac{F_{\text{AB}}}{l} = 30 \ \mu\text{N/m}$

(b) $\dfrac{F_{\text{BA}}}{l} = \dfrac{F_{\text{AB}}}{l} = 30 \ \mu\text{N/m}$

(c) $F_{\text{AB}} = F_{\text{BA}}$

The forces calculated in questions parts (a) and (b) are equal as expected from Newton's third law.

57. (a) $\vec{F}_B = 14.4 \ fN \ \hat{j}$

$G = 1.6 \times 10^{-26}$ N

(b) Trajectory of the proton is an upward spiral of constant radius.

(c) $\omega = 43 \times 10^6$ rad/s

$T = 0.15 \ \mu s$

(d) $R = 4.6$ mm

Pitch $= 2.3$ cm

59. (a) The electron moves on circular trajectory upwards. See the text online resources for diagram.

(b) $R = 0.29$ m

(c) The gravitational force can be neglected due to the very small mass of the electron.

61. (a) $I_{\text{max}} = 83$ A

(b) $I_{\text{max}} = 41$ A

63. $r = 2$ mm

The magnetic field is zero on a line 2 mm above the wire.

65. $B = 13$ mT

$B' = B(\chi_{\text{iron}} + 1) \cong 50$ T

67. (a) $\dfrac{\Delta B}{B} \ (\%) = \dfrac{K_{\text{water}} - K_{\text{air}}}{K_{\text{air}}} \times 100$

(b) See solutions manual for answer.

(c) See solutions manual for answer.

69. See the text online resources for derivation.

71. (a) See the text online resources for derivation.

(b) $B(P_1) = \dfrac{\mu_0 I}{2\pi R}$ for $L \to \infty$, as expected when applying Ampère's law for an infinitely long wire.

(c) $B(P_2) = \dfrac{\mu_0 I}{4\pi R} \cdot \dfrac{L}{(L^2 + R^2)^{1/2}}$

73. (a) $B_{in} = \dfrac{\mu_0 NI}{2\pi R}$,

$B_{out} = 0$ T

(b) For solenoid:

$B_{in} = \dfrac{\mu_0 NI}{L}$,

$B_{out} = 0$ T

The magnetic field of a toroid of radius R is the magnetic field of a solenoid of length $2\pi R$.

(c) A toroid is a solenoid bent into a circular shape.

(d) $B = 6$ mT

(e) $B = 6\pi$ mT

$\dfrac{B(e)}{B(d)} = \pi$, as expected.

75. From the paper of Howard Bassen, magnetic fields less than 0.2 μT were measured at 1 cm away from the iPod case. Since magnetic fields are inversely proportional to the distance, it would be recommended for people with pacemakers to wear their iPod devices as far away from their pacemakers as possible.

Chapter 24—Electromagnetic Induction

1. h

3. e

5. a

7. d

9. d

11. b

13. a

15. $L_b > L_a = L_c > L_d > L_e$

17. $u_{B,b} = u_{B,c} > u_{B,a} = u_{B,d} > u_{B,e}$

19. $1 = 2 = 3 > 4 = 5$

$(\tau = L/R)$

21. c

23. (a) $\dfrac{d\Phi_B}{dt} = 0.55$ mWb

(b) $\dfrac{d\Phi_B}{dt} = 0.67$ mWb

(c) $N = 20$ loops:

(a) $\dfrac{d\Phi_B}{dt} = 11$ mWb

(b) $\dfrac{d\Phi_B}{dt} = 13$ mWb

25. $\left(\dfrac{dB}{dt}\right)_o = 30$ μT/s

27. $emf = 0.6$ V,

29. $B = 75$ mT

31. See the text online resources for derivation.

33. (a) The induced current flows counter-clockwise and the magnetic force acts upwards on the metal rod.

$F(t = 0\ s) = 0.84$ μN

The magnetic field decreases to 0 T in 50 s. The magnetic force acting upwards on the metal rod decreases from $F(t = 0\ s)$ to 0 N according to the equation:

$F(t) = \dfrac{B(t)L^2}{R}\left[x(t)\dfrac{dB}{dt} + B(t)v(t)\right]$,

where $B(t) = B(t = 0\ s) + t\dfrac{dB}{dt}$.

(b) $a(t = 0\ s) = 3.4$ μm$\cdot$s^{-2}

$a(t) = \dfrac{B(t)L^2}{mR}\left[x(t)\dfrac{dB}{dt} + B(t)v(t)\right]$

(c) See solutions manual for answer.

35. (a) $emf_{max} = 110$ mV

(b) $emf_{max} = 11$ V

(c) $emf(t) = emf_{max}\cos(2\pi ft)$

37. (a) $N_s = 100$ turns

(b) $(I_{max})_p = 80$ mA

$(I_{max})_s = 800$ mA

$(I_{rms})_p = 57$ mA

$(I_{rms})_s = 570$ mA

(c) $(I_{max})_p = 80$ mA

$(I_{max})_s = 720$ mA

$(I_{rms})_p = 57$ mA

$(I_{rms})_s = 510$ mA

39. (a) $E(r) = \dfrac{1}{r} \cdot \dfrac{\mu_o \pi N^2 R^2 f I_{max}\cos(2\pi ft)}{L}$

(b) $E(r) = r \cdot \dfrac{\mu_o \pi N^2 f I_{max}\cos(2\pi ft)}{L}$

(c) See the text online resources for the graph.

41. $M = 0.1$ H

43. (a) $M = 62$ mH

(b) $emf_{coil} = 0.62$ V

45. (a) $U = 5.9$ mJ

(b) $U = 1.5$ mJ

(c) $U = 0$ J

47. $emf = 5.5$ mV

49. (a) $emf(t = 0\ s) = 10$ mV

(b) The induced current flows counter-clockwise.

(c) See solutions manual for answer.

51. $emf(t) = -3.9$ μV $- 0.02$ μV$\cdot$s$^{-1}t(s)$

53. (a) $a = g\sin\phi - \dfrac{F_B}{m}\cos\phi$,

where a is the downward acceleration on the incline plane.

(b) $emf = Blv\cos\phi$

(c) $v(t) = g\tau\sin\phi\left(1 - e^{-\frac{t}{\tau}}\right)$,

where

$\tau = \dfrac{mR}{B^2L^2(\cos\phi)^2}$,

or, numerically,

$v(t) = 392(1 - e^{-0.0125\cdot s^{-1}t(s)})$ m/s

(d) $emf(t) = \dfrac{mgR\tan\phi}{BL}\left(1 - e^{-\frac{t}{\tau}}\right)$,

Or, numerically,

$emf(t) = 34(1 - e^{-0.0125\ s^{-1}t(s)})$ V

(e) $v_t = 392$ m/s

55. (a) $B = 64$ T

(b) $L = 9.6$ H

(c) $B = 130$ T

$L = 9.6$ H

57. (a) $I_A = \dfrac{v - emf}{R} = 5.0$ A

(b) $I_A = 30$ A

59. (a) See the text online resources for sketches of the pulses observed on the oscilloscope.

(b) The time between pulses is half as much as that in question (a), their widths are half the size, and their amplitudes are twice as large.

(c) The amplitude and width of the pulse corresponding to the left coil are twice as large as those of the pulse from the right coil.

(d) $v = 570$ m/s

(e) For higher speeds the two pulses merge since a high speed reduces the time separation of the recorded pulses below the width of the pulse. Increasing the distance between the two coils may affect the accuracy of the speed measurement.

61. $I = 1\ \mu$A

The current flows counterclockwise in the large loop and clockwise in the small loop if $\dfrac{dB}{dt} > 0$; the directions are opposite if $\dfrac{dB}{dt} < 0$.

63. (a)

Time (s)	V_R (V)	V_L (V)	I (A)	ε (V)
0.001	0.06	11.94	0.004	12
0.01	0.59	11.41	0.040	12
0.1	4.72	7.28	0.315	12
0.2	7.59	4.41	0.506	12
0.4	10.38	1.62	0.692	12

(b) $V_R + V_L = \varepsilon = 12$ V

$I = \dfrac{V_R}{R}$

(c) Add battery resistance to R.

65. (a) $F_{ext} = \dfrac{B^2 l^2 v}{R}$

(b) $F_{ext} = 1\ \mu$N

(c) $E_R = \dfrac{B^2 l^2 v^2 t}{R}$

(d) $E_R = 4\ \mu$J

67. (a) $t = 37$ ms

$I_{max} = 2.4$ A

(b) $V_L = 0.12$ V

(c) $t = 5.5$ s

69. (a) $emf(t) = NBlw\,\omega \sin(\omega t)$

(b) $emf_{max} = 57$ kV

(c) The frequency of the emf can only be changed by modifying the rotation frequency of the coil.

The maximum emf can be increased by increasing the following quantities: N, B, l, w, or ω.

71. $u_B = 0.25$ mJ$\cdot$m^{-3}

$u_E = 7.1$ nJ$\cdot$m^{-3}

The magnetic field energy density at Earth's surface is more than 10,000 times larger than the electric field energy density. Hence, the Earth is a better magnetic field dynamo than an electric field dynamo.

73. $\delta V = 3\ \mu$V

75. (a) $B_{inner} = 40$ mT

(b) $B_{outer-in} = 13$ mT

(c) $B_{outer-out} = 0$ T

(d) $u_B = 0.92$ kJ$\cdot$m^{-3}

(e) $U_B = 2.6$ MJ

(f) $p = 0.2$ kPa

77. (a) $L_{eq} = L_1 + L_2 + \cdots$

(b) $(L_{eq})^{-1} = (L_1)^{-1} + (L_2)^{-1} + \cdots$

79. (a) $L = 6.0$ mH

(b) $\tau = 3.0$ ms

(c)

Time (ms)	V_L (V)	ln V_L	I (A)
1.0	8.598	2.152	1.701
1.5	7.278	1.985	2.361
2.0	6.161	1.818	2.919
2.5	5.215	1.652	3.392
3.0	4.414	1.485	3.793
3.5	3.737	1.318	4.132
4.0	3.163	1.152	4.418
4.5	2.678	0.985	4.661
5.0	2.267	0.818	4.867
5.5	1.919	0.652	5.041
6.0	1.624	0.485	5.188
6.5	1.375	0.318	5.313
7.0	1.164	0.152	5.418
7.5	0.985	−0.015	5.507
8.0	0.834	−0.182	5.583

Chapter 25—Alternating Current Circuits

1. The RLC circuit is above resonance.

3. Mathematically, the inductive reactance X_L is directly proportional to the AC frequency ω: $X_L \overset{\text{def}}{=} \omega L$. Therefore, a low frequency ω translates into a low inductive reactance X_L. Qualitatively, the inductor's emf depends on how fast the magnetic flux varies. Therefore, the induced emf is directly proportional to the AC frequency ω.

5. $X_C = \dfrac{1}{\omega C}$

Capacitive reactance decreases with frequency.

7. The rms value of a voltage can never exceed its maximum value, but they are equal for a constant DC voltage.

9. The phase angle approaches $\pi/2$ as the frequency increases significantly.
11. See the online resources for the derivation.
13. (a) $i_{rms} = 0.50\,A$

    (b) $R = 240\,\Omega$

15. (a) $X_L - \omega L = 1\,\Omega$

    (b) $i_{max} = 30\,A$

    (c) $i(t) = i_{max} \sin\left(\omega t + \dfrac{\pi}{2}\right)$

17. (a) $X_C = 10\,M\Omega$

    (b) $i_{max} = 2.8\,\mu A$

    (c) $(t) = i_{max} \sin\left(\omega t - \dfrac{\pi}{2}\right)$

19. $L = 0.25\,\mu H$

21. $\dfrac{1}{\sqrt{2}}$

23. (a) $t = \dfrac{k\pi}{2500}\,s,$

    $k = 0, 1, 2, \ldots$

    (b) $t = \dfrac{(2m + 1)\pi}{10000}\,s,$

    $m = 0, 2, 4, \ldots$

    (c) $t = \dfrac{(2n + 1)\pi}{10000}\,s,$

    $n = 1, 3, 5, \ldots$

25. (a) $X_C = 100\,k\Omega$

    (b) $X_L = 40\,\Omega$

    (c) $Z = 100\,k\Omega$

    (d) $\phi - 90°$

    $i_{max} = 0.5\,mA$

27. (a) $X_L = 22\,k\Omega$

    (b) $L = 2.5\,H$

    (c) $i_{max} = 1.8\,A$

29. $L = 0.23\,H$
31. $N = 11$
33. Yes, the energy delivered by the emf is equal to the magnetic energy stored in the magnetic field of the coil and in the electric field energy associated with the charge stored by the capacitor.
35. $L = 140\,mH$

    $\phi = 89.9°$

37. $C = 3.3\,\mu F$
39. $\Rightarrow L = 120\,mH$
41. $L = 6.3\,\mu H$

    $i_{max} = 0.25\,A$

43. $V_R(t = 10\,s) = 14\,V$
45. $R = 160\,\Omega$

    $C = 1.5\,\mu F$

47. $\phi = 0°$
49. $R = 20\,\Omega$

    $\phi = 25°$

51. $\Delta f = 2.5\,m\Omega$

    $C = 0.25\,nF$

53. Answers may vary.

Chapter 26—Electromagnetic Waves and Maxwell's Equations

1. It explains the generation of varying magnetic fields from varying electric fields.
3. (a) $\vec{E}$ and $\vec{B}$ waves are on the same axis.
   (c) $\vec{E}$ and $\vec{B}$ waves have different phases.
   (d) $\vec{E}$ and $\vec{B}$ waves have the same amplitude.
5. Sound waves do not propagate in vacuum.
   Sound waves are not transverse waves.
   Microscopically, massless particles called photons are associated with electromagnetic waves; quasi-particles called phonons are associated with sound waves.
7. Deceleration and acceleration in a straight line, curved trajectory, oscillations.
9. No, it cannot because of energy loss that is associated with the emission of electromagnetic radiation.
11. The radiation pressure is twice greater on a surface that is a perfect reflector than on a surface that is a perfect absorber. The difference is due to the change of total momentum of the system (radiation + surface) which is equal to twice the initial momentum of the radiation for the perfect reflector surface, and equal to the initial momentum for the perfect absorber surface.
13. $I_d = 0.3\,pA$
15. (a) $B = 0.320\,\mu T$
    (b) $B = 2.00\,\mu T$
17. (a) $I(t = 0\,s) = 12\,A$

    (b) $I(t = 60\,s) = 0\,A$

    (c) $\dfrac{dE}{dt}(t = 0\,s) = 43 \times 10^{12}\,V/m \cdot s$

    $\dfrac{dE}{dt}(t = 60\,s) = 0\,V/m \cdot s$

    (d) $B(t = 0\,s) = 24\,\mu T$
    $B(t = 60\,s) = 0\,\mu T$
19. (a) $\vec{S}$ is in the y-direction
    (b) $\vec{S}$ is in the $(-z)$-direction
    (c) $\vec{S}$ is in the z-direction
    (d) $\vec{S}$ is in the $(-x)$-direction
21. $B_0 = 17\,pT$
23. (a) $\lambda = 1.57\,nm$

    (b) $f = 1.91 \times 10^{17}\,Hz$

    (c) $E_0 = 1500\,V/m$

    (d) $\vec{E}(x, t) = (1500\,V/m) \sin(4.00 \times 10^9 x - \omega t)(-\hat{y})$
    The wave travels in the x-direction.
25. $B(t) = 3.3 \times 10^{-9}\,T$ in the $(-z)$-direction.
27. Microwaves $<$ infrared light $<$ yellow light $<$ blue light $<$ X-rays $<$ gamma rays
29. (a) $f = 6.67 \times 10^{14}\,Hz$

    (b) $f = 5.63 \times 10^{14}\,Hz$

    (c) $f = 4.29 \times 10^{14}\,Hz$

31. (a) $E_0 = 7.8\,V/m$

    $B_0 = 4.5 \times 10^{-4}\,T$

    (b) $E_0 = 0.78\,V/m$

    $B_0 = 4.5 \times 10^{-5}\,T$

(c) $E_0 = 7.8 \times 10^{-4}$ V/m

$B_0 = 4.5 \times 10^{-8}$ T

33. $\bar{S} = 0.50$ W/m^2

35. $E_0 = 0.1$ V/m

$B_0 = 3 \times 10^{-10}$ T

37. $\bar{S} = 0.08$ W/m^2

39. $F = 6.0 \times 10^{-14}$ N

41. $E = 4000$ kW·h

43. (a) $\bar{S} = 1.59 \times 10^3$ W/m^2

(b) $P_{rad} = 10.6 \times 10^{-6}$ Pa

$F = 3.33 \times 10^{-11}$ N

45. The electromagnetic wave is polarized along the y-axis.

47. 30°

49. $I_2 = 0.25$ W/m^2

51. (a) $I_2 = 0$ W/m^2

(b) $I_2 = 0$ W/m^2

(c) $I_2 = 0$ W/m^2

(d) $I_2 = 0$ W/m^2

53. $I_A = \dfrac{1}{2} I_0$

$I_B = \left(\dfrac{1}{4} + \dfrac{\sqrt{3}}{8} \right) I_0$

$I_C = \left(\dfrac{1}{8} + \dfrac{\sqrt{3}}{16} \right) I_0$

55. 35°

57. (a) 0.5 μm

(b) $\dfrac{F_g}{F_{rad}} = \dfrac{r}{r_{(a)}} \Rightarrow r < r_{(a)} \Rightarrow F_{rad} > F_G$

Hence, if the particles have a diameter smaller than 1 μm, the force due to the radiation pressure of the Sun will exceed its gravitational attraction force.

Yes, the tail will be longer as the comet approaches the Sun. For particles below the radius value calculated in question (a) the radiation pressure will exceed the gravitational attraction of the Sun. Thus, these particles will be further apart from the core of the comet and away from the Sun, forming a longer tail.

Chapter 27—Geometric Optics

1. $d'_{oi} - d_{oi} = 2d'_o - 2d_o = 1$ m

3. For plane mirrors, the image and object distances are equal, which lies at the heart of the reason behind why images in plane mirrors display depth inversion. Plane mirrors effect depth inversion; they do not exchange left and right, nor do they exchange up and down.

The word "AMBULANCE" is written from right to left at the front of an ambulance so that drivers can easily read it in their rear-view mirrors.

5. (c)

7. The side-view mirrors of cars are convex mirrors where the image of the object is smaller than the object (magnification $M < 1$). Because the magnification is less than one, objects appear further away than they really are. Convex mirrors are used because the image is upright and magnification

less than one allows the driver a larger field of view of the road behind the car.

9. (a) Yes, an image of the rose will be formed.

(b) To see the image of the rose in the mirror the observer has to be located on the left-lower corner of the rose-mirror assembly.

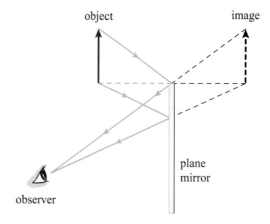

11. The maximum number of images that could be viewed is 3. The number of images is equal to the number of times a ray of light parallel to the axis of symmetry between the two mirrors is reflected. See also the solution and the ray diagram of Problem 30.

13. The answer for Problem 12 is based on the fact that a reflected ray of light from the toe of the observer has to reach his/her eye as in the ray diagram from Figure 27-12. Based on Table 27-1 the correct answer is (f) for a spherical mirror.

15. A concave mirror has to be chosen that magnifies for $R/2 < d_o < R$, where R is the radius of the mirror.

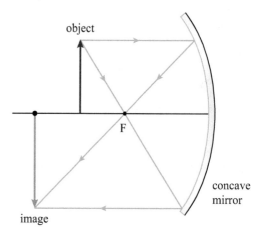

17. All three rays of light emitted simultaneously arrive at the screen in the same time following Fermat's principle. The two rays of light undergoing the longer path have a shorter path through the lens than the central ray of light has a longer path through the lens where the speed of light is smaller than in air.

19. You will get a fainter image because half of the rays from all parts of the image are blocked.

21.

convergent lens

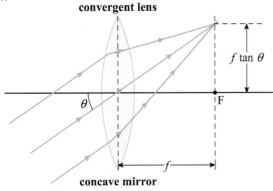

$f \tan \theta$

F

θ

f

concave mirror

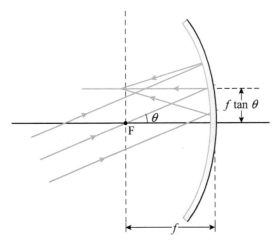

$f \tan \theta$

θ

F

f

(b)

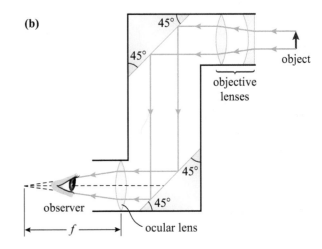

45°

45°

object

objective lenses

45°

45°

observer

f

ocular lens

(c) Using curved mirrors would not be a viable design because these mirrors distort the object-observer distance due to varying magnification. The object-observer distance is important in many applications of the periscope.

33. (a) $f = 3.5$ cm (b) Image is real and inverted

35. $f = -7.7$ cm (b) $M = 0.04$. The image is real, upright, and reduced

37. Assuming critical angle, area $= 7$ m^2

39.

23. 34.3 m

25. (a) Observers at A will see a total solar eclipse (the Sun is entirely eclipsed by the Moon), observers at B will see a partial solar eclipse (the Sun is partially eclipsed by the Moon), and observers at C will not see an eclipse.

(b) The Earth rotates about its axis from West to East in geographical terms. The rotation is counterclockwise in the Cartesian reference frame of the Earth with its z-axis oriented from South to North. An observer on Earth perceives this motion through the position of the Sun in the sky from sunrise (East) to sunset (West). During the time of a total solar eclipse the region in which this astronomical event can be observed will move from West to East.

27. Angle $= 31°$

29. $\Delta h = 0.24$ m

31. (a) The image is not inverted as the ray diagram indicates.

(a)

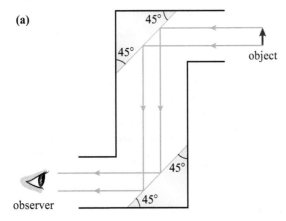

45°

45°

object

45°

45°

observer

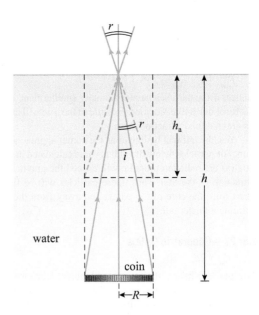

r

r

i

h_a

h

water

coin

R

From the geometry indicated in the ray diagram the following relationships can be derived:

$$\tan i = \frac{R}{h}$$

$$\tan r = \frac{R}{h_a}$$

From the two equations it can be deducted that:

$$\frac{h_a}{h} = \frac{\tan i}{\tan r} \approx \frac{\sin i}{\sin r} = \frac{1}{n} \Rightarrow h_a \approx \frac{h}{n} = 60 \text{ cm}$$

The used approximation is valid for small angles. The observation angles are small because the radius of the coin $R \ll h$.

41. (a) $n = 1.41$ (b) $n = 2.08$

43. (a) 45 mm   (b) $M = 0.008$

45. $d_i = -3.4$ cm   (b) diverging lens   (c) Virtual, erect and reduced

47. (a) $M = 0.8$ (b) $M = 0.5$

49. $R = 1.14\ H$

51. Angle of deflection = 169°; decreases

53.

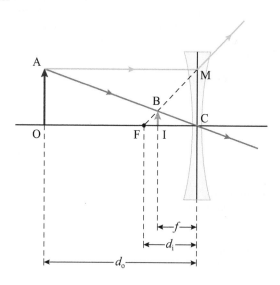

$d_i = 10$ cm

The image is formed in front of the divergent lens; it is virtual, upright, and reduced. The image of the object cannot be seen on a screen because it is virtual.

55. (a) 0.45 cm   (b) 4.5 cm

57. (a) Through the base   (b) 80°   (c) 0, because the ray exits through the base

59. (a) $f(4D) = 25$ cm, $f(5D) = 20$ cm   (b) $d_i = 40$ cm from the second lens   (c) No, the combined power of the two lenses cannot be used to solve this problem because the distance between them is large relative to their focal lengths. The combined optical power describes a system where lenses are very close together.

61.

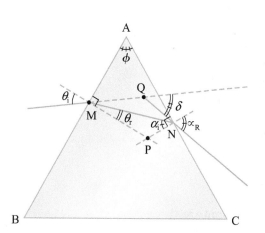

From the ray diagram the following relationships between all the angles can be derived:

In $\triangle MQN$:

$(\theta_i - \theta_r) + (\alpha_i - \alpha_r) = \delta$

Using quadrilateral AMPN and $\triangle MPN$:

$\theta_r + \alpha_i = \phi = 180° - \angle MPN$

The refraction law applied at the entry and exit boundaries of the prism gives:

$\sin\theta_i = n \sin\theta_r$

$n \sin\alpha_i = \sin\alpha_r$

Using all these equations it follows that the deflection angle δ is given by:

$\delta = \theta_i + \phi - 2\theta_r - \sin^{-1}[n \sin(\phi - \theta_r)]$,

where

$\theta_r = \sin^{-1}\left(\dfrac{\theta_i}{n}\right)$

63. (a) From the ray diagram the distance between lenses is:

$d = F_2 - |F_1| = 2|F_1|$

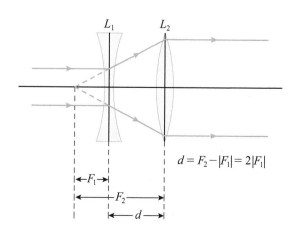

$d = F_2 - |F_1| = 2|F_1|$

(b) From the ray diagram the distance between lenses is:

$d = F_2 + |F_1| = 4|F_1|$

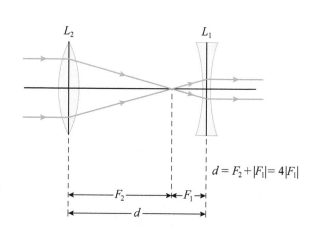

$d = F_2 + |F_1| = 4|F_1|$

65. (a)

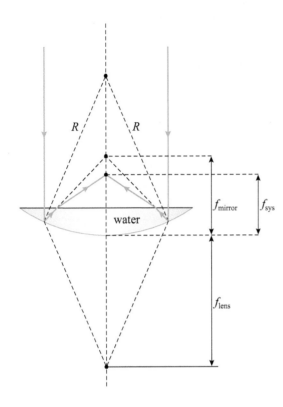

(b) $f_{mirror} = 25$ cm $\Rightarrow P_{mirror} = 4\ D$

$\Rightarrow f_{lens} = 1.5$ m $\Rightarrow P_{lens} = 0.67\ D$

(c) $P_{sys} = 4.7$

67. $t_{total} = 33$ ms

69. Let f_1 and f_2 be the focal lengths characterizing the two lenses. The focal length of one lens, say, f_1 will be the object-lens distance for the other lens and the image distance will then be the focal length of the pair of lenses f_{pair}. Because the lenses are very close, the object-lens distance is negative and equal to $-f_1$ which corresponds to a virtual object. Hence, using the thin lens equation for mirror of focal length f_2,

$$\frac{1}{f_2} = \frac{1}{-f_1} + \frac{1}{f_{pair}} \Rightarrow P_{pair} = P_1 + P_2$$

71. $\omega = 8$ rad/s

73. (a) $d_{o1} = 6.1$ cm

(b) $M = -7.7$

(c) Yes, the compound microscope can produce an upright final image if the image produced by the first lens (L_1) is between the two lenses. That is,

5 cm $< d_{i1} <$ 10 cm

(d) Use a graphing software and the equations you derived or a virtual microscope simulation (such as http://www.udel.edu/biology/ketcham/microscope/scope.html) to explore how the change in each one of the parameters of the compound microscope (distance between the lenses, power of each one of the lenses, and the distance between the object and the objective lens) will affect the magnification.

75. (a) No, it is not possible to confine all the light from a large source into a significantly reduced image of the light source. This would mean that all the light of a source would have to be confined in a smaller volume. This would correspond to a decrease in entropy of an isolated system (no light loss or gain) which contradicts the second law of thermodynamics. (b) Only an ideal system would project all the light from a smaller source into a magnified image. Such a system does not exist due to light-matter interactions; there are no perfect mirrors and lenses. Real mirrors and lenses do not reflect or transmit, respectively, 100% of the incident light.

77. Answers will vary.

Chapter 28—Physical Optics

1. d
3. c
5. b
7. d
9. b
11. b
13. b
15. (a) valid
(b) valid (although less precisely so)
(c) valid
(d) not valid
17. (a) constructive
(b) 50 m
19. (a) 0.145°
(b) 2.28 mm
21. (a) 381 lines/cm
(b) 1.14 cm
23. (a) 226 nm
(b) 624 nm
25. 29.3 μm
27. 17 fringes
29. 6.16 km
31. 1.00018
33. 0.151°
35. 84.6 μm
37. (a) 12.1°, 36.9°
(b) 28.7 mm
(c) 53.5 mm
39. 282 fringes
41. (a) 1.07×10^{-5} degrees
(b) 0.039″
43. 7.0×10^{-8} degrees
45. 8.39 cm
47. 41.7 μm

Chapter 29—Relativity

1. c
3. c
5. d
7. c
9. d
11. c
13. c
15. 1.26×10^{-6} N/A²
17. (a) 0.31 s (b) 0.27 s
19. (a) 1.85×10^8 s (b) 1.22×10^8 s
21. 3.0×10^8 m/s
23. 0.783 MeV
25. 1.33 μs

27. 35.4 km

29. 9.47×10^{15} m

31. (a) 1.60×10^9 s
    (b) 1.62×10^9 s
    (c) 2.80×10^8 s

33. (a) 2.60×10^8 m/s
    (b) 0.023 s

35. (a) 1.1×10^8 m/s
    (b) 1.0×10^8 m/s
    (c) No

37. No, this is not in conflict with special relativity. Neutrinos, having very small interaction probabilities, can pass through dense matter more freely than photons. Therefore they leave the supernova before the photons. The photons leave with the shockwave and reach Earth a few hours after the neutrinos.

39. (a) 4.28×10^9 kg/s
    (b) 2.05×10^{19} kg/y
    (c) 9.78×10^9 y

41. For the second observer, the events will also be 3.0 m apart in space.

43. (a) 14.9 ns
    (b) $0.667c$

45. 0.916μs

47. $0.86 c$

49. 7.36×10^9 kg/m³

51. (a) $0.999 c$
    (b) 1.11×10^4 s⁻¹
    (c) 7.0×10^6 MeV/c $= 3.7 \times 10^{-15}$ kg m/s

53. (a) $0.976 c$
    (b) $0.67 m_0 c^2$
    (c) $3.59 m_0 c^2$

55. $m_0' = \dfrac{m_0}{2} \sqrt{\dfrac{(3c)^2 - V^2}{c^2 - V^2}}$

57. $\dfrac{1}{f} df = \dfrac{GM}{c^2 r^2} dr$

59. Answers may vary.

Chapter 30—Fundamental Discoveries of Modern Physics

1. In 1897, J. J. Thomson postulated the existence of particles smaller than atoms while trying to explain the existence of "cathode rays" that he produced in a glass tube. He postulated that these smaller particles were minuscule pieces of atoms. Later on Philipp Lenard performed more experiments on these cathode rays and showed that if cathode rays were particles, their mass must be smaller than the mass of an atom.

3. Atoms have concentrated positive charge, a large empty space and negative charges. Some atoms can spontaneously produce positive, negative and neutral rays. When subjected to external light, some atoms produce light of different wavelength.

5. Electron's angular momentum.

7. A blackbody spectrum is continuous whereas a discharge spectrum has peaks at certain wavelengths characteristic of the material.

9. The thermometer works by detecting infrared radiation from the eardrum through a device such as a thermopile.

11. H: 9.570×10^7 C/kg;   O: 4.823×10^7 C/kg

13. (a) The object with higher intensity (black line) is at a higher temperature.
    (b) No.

15. (a) 5.333×10^5 m⁻¹
    (b) $n_1 = 4$
    (c) A wavelength of 1875 nm corresponds to infrared light.

17. (a) 6.4×10^7 m/s
    (b) 1.2×10^5 V/m
    (c) 1.3 mm

19. (a) 15 000 V/m
    (b) 2.4×10^{-15} N
    (c) 8.927×10^{-30} N
    (d) Yes, it is reasonable to neglect gravity because the electric and magnetic forces on the electron are greater than the gravitational force by a factor of $\sim 10^{14}$.

21. (a) 0.147%
    (b) 0.127%

23. (a) $dU = \dfrac{3kQ^2 r^4 dr}{R^6}$

    (b) $U = \dfrac{3kQ^2}{5R}$

    (c) 8.6×10^{-16} J

25. (a) 1.5×10^{-13} m
    (b) 3.6×10^{-14} m

27. (a) 1.602×10^{-16} J
    (b) 1.875×10^7 m/s
    (c) 1000 eV

29. (a) 3.65×10^{-19} J
    (b) 5.51×10^{14} Hz
    (c) 544 nm

31. (a) $f = \dfrac{c}{\lambda}$

    Calculated values are listed in table below.

    (b) $K_{max} = e\Delta V$

    Calculated values are listed in table below.

Wavelength (nm)	Stopping Potential (v)	Frequency (Hz)	K_{max} (J)
260	0.46	1.154×10^{15}	7.369×10^{-20}
250	0.66	1.200×10^{15}	1.057×10^{-19}
240	0.87	1.250×10^{15}	1.394×10^{-19}
230	1.09	1.304×10^{15}	1.746×10^{-19}

(c)

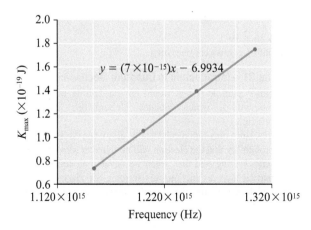

$y = (7 \times 10^{-15})x - 6.9934$

(d) 7×10^{-34} J s

(e) 4.37 eV

33. 2.19×10^6 m/s

35. 2.52×10^{-16} s

37. (a) 302 keV

(b) 48.3 keV

39. 1.95×10^{-18} C

41. 7.42×10^{-13} m

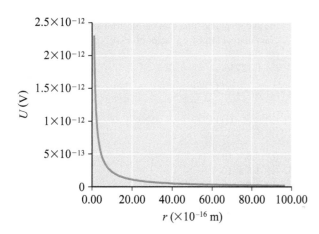

43. 3.75×10^5 m/s

45. 4.18 cm

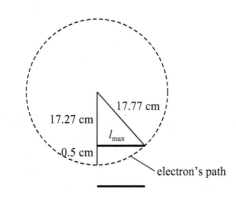

47. $f_{max} = \dfrac{2.82\,kT}{h}$

49. $E > 1.988 \times 10^{-8}$ J, or, equivalently $E > 124.1$ GeV

51. $\dfrac{B_p^2}{E_p} = 1835.84\,\dfrac{B_e^2}{E_e}$

53. 1.26×10^{21}

55. 6680 kg; answers may vary

Chapter 31—Introduction to Quantum Mechanics

1. No. A particle at rest would have a definite position and momentum, which violates Heisenberg's uncertainty principle.

3. Yes, since quantum mechanically, all we can do is calculate a probability that the electron will be found at some place and time. Having said that, when we develop an equation for a particle's wave function, we use some boundary conditions, which may confine the wave function to a certain region.

5. Infinite

7. (a) No, since the energy of an incident photon is less than the difference between the energy of the ground state and first excited state of hydrogen.

(b) Yes, since the energy of an incident photon is greater than the difference between the energy of the ground state and first excited state of hydrogen.

(c) Yes, since the energy of an incident photon is greater than the difference between the energy of the ground state and first excited state of hydrogen.

9. For $n = 4$ to $n = 2$: $\Delta E = 2.55$ eV

For $n = 6$ to $n = 3$: $\Delta E = 1.13$ eV

For $n = 3$ to $n = 1$: $\Delta E = 12.09$ eV

For $n = 5$ to $n = 3$: $\Delta E = 0.97$ eV

Hence $\Delta E_d < \Delta E_b < \Delta E_a < \Delta E_c$

11. All are possible.

13. (a) 1.17×10^{-12} m

(b) 3.46×10^{-13} m

15. 4.18 μV

17. $\Delta p = 5.25 \times 10^{-25}$ kg m/s, $K = 1.51 \times 10^{-19}$ J

19. 2.63×10^{-31} m

21. (a) $\Delta t = 1.44 \times 10^{-12}$ s, $\Delta E = 3.64 \times 10^{-23}$ J

(b) $\Delta t = 1.44 \times 10^{-23}$ s, $\Delta E = 3.64 \times 10^{-12}$ J

23. $E = 4.55 \times 10^{-21}$ J, $\Delta E = 9.1 \times 10^{-26}$ J, $\Delta t = 5.77 \times 10^{-10}$ s

25. Since the square of the wave function integrated over the whole length for the one-dimensional case must be a dimensionless quantity, therefore the units of the wave function should be $m^{-1/2}$.

27. $E_1 = 5.97 \times 10^{-18}$ J

$E_2 = 2.39 \times 10^{-17}$ J

$E_3 = 5.37 \times 10^{-17}$ J

The probability density is given by

$$\psi_n^*(x)\,\psi_n(x) = \frac{2}{L}\,\sin^2\!\left(\frac{n\pi}{L}x\right)$$

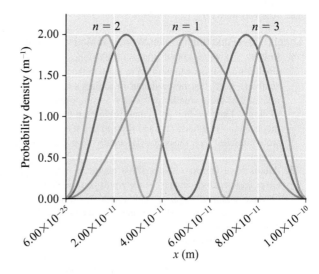

29. $\Delta E = 2.39 \times 10^{-23}\,(n_2^2 - n_1^2)$

(a) 7.17×10^{-23} J

(b) 1.91×10^{-22} J

(c) 1.20×10^{-22} J

(d) 2.39×10^{-17} J

31. $P = 0.5$

33. 3.33×10^{-8} m

35. See solutions manual for answer.

37. $\psi(x) = \begin{cases} \sqrt{\dfrac{15}{512}}\,(4 - x^2) & \text{for } -2 \le x \le 2 \\ 0 & \text{everwhere else} \end{cases}$

39. $\psi(x) = \begin{cases} \sqrt{\dfrac{15}{512}}\,(4 - x^2)\, e^{-i\frac{p^2 t}{2mh}} & \text{for } -2 \le x \le 2 \\ 0 & \text{everywhere else} \end{cases}$

41. 0.62

43. (a) $E_2 = 80$ eV
$E_3 = 180$ eV
$E_4 = 320$ eV

(b) 1.36×10^{-10} m

(c) 2.05×10^{-8} m

45. 0.36

47. $1.13 \times 10^{278}\, y$

49. -0.544 eV

51. $L = \hbar, \sqrt{2}\hbar, \sqrt{6}\hbar, \sqrt{12}\hbar$ and $L_z = -3\hbar, -2\hbar, -\hbar, 0, \hbar, 2\hbar, 3\hbar$

53. (a) $l = 3$ and $n = 4$
(b) $l = 0$ and $n = 1$
(c) $l = 4$ and $n = 5$

55. $r = a_B$, that is, the most probable distance is equal to the Bohr radius.

57. (a) $E_n = -\dfrac{2847.5}{n^2}$ eV

(b) 949.2 eV

(c) 2.54×10^{13} m

59. 2.50×10^{14} m/s

61. (a) $j = 3, 2, 1, 0$
(b) For $j = 3$: $J_z = 3\hbar, 2\hbar, \hbar, 0, -\hbar, -2\hbar, -3\hbar$
For $j = 2$: $J_z = 2\hbar, \hbar, 0, -\hbar, -2\hbar$
For $j = 1$: $J_z = \hbar, 0, -\hbar$
For $j = 0$: $J_z = 0$

63. For $n = 1$, maximum number of electrons $= 2(1)^2$
For $n = 2$, maximum number of electrons $= 2(2)^2$
For $n = 3$, maximum number of electrons $= 2(3)^2$

Chapter 32—Introduction to Solid-State Physics

1. Decrease

3. d

5. d

7. b

9. Silicon

(a) $V = a^3$

11. (b) $V = \dfrac{a^3}{4}$

13. 94.9%

15. 3

17. (a) Positive
(b) Negative
(c) Positive

19. (a) 10^{13}
(b) 10^{-13} J/s

21. 7.05×10^{-21}

23. $0.22\ \mu$g

25. 4.0×10^5

27. 0.07 W

29. (a) 3.4×10^{-17} F
(b) 510

31. 90 %

33. (a) 1000 V/m
(b) 1.8×10^{14} m/s^2
(c) $1.8 \times 10^{14}\, t$ m/s
(d) $0.014\, t^2$ J
(e) $0.028\, t$ J/s
(f) 3.57×10^{-12} s
(g) 1.12 nm

35. 10^{47} J/m^3

37. (a) 0
(b) 9.1×10^{-6}

39. (a) 8.6 eV
(b) 8.5 eV

41. 2.50×10^{-14} s

43. 4.4 nm

45. 0.27 m
This distance between the circuit elements on a chip does not seem reasonable as chips are much smaller than this. Therefore the signal takes much less time to propagate than 1ns.

47. 100 s

49. The Fermi wave number depends on the number of electrons that each atom contributes to conduction, that is $\dfrac{N}{N^*}$, for a certain lattice parameter.

51. $\lambda = 2a$

53. (a) Since the Fermi energy for metals is fairly high, only a tiny fraction of electrons close to the Fermi level have their energies increased when the metal is heated.

(b) $\dfrac{N}{N^*} = 0.0055$

(c) No, only the electronic contribution to heat capacity in metals is very small because only a fraction of the electrons are within thermal enegry of the Fermi energy.

Chapter 33—Introduction to Nuclear Physics

1. Nucleon: A proton or neutron in an atomic nucleus.
Nuclide: Nuclide refers to a particular type of nucleus with a specific number of neutrons and protons.
Isotope: Species of nuclei with same number of protons and different number of neutrons.
Decay Constant: Proportionality constant that characterizes the relation between the decay rate and the amount of a radioactive substance.
Half Life: Time it takes for half of the atoms of the sample to decay.
Decay Diagram: A diagram that specifies the sequence in which some nuclide decays.
Q–value: Net energy released or absorbed in a nuclear reaction.
Spontaneous Fission: Spontaneous breaking up of a heavy and unstable nucleus with release of neutrons.
Radioactive Dating: A process through which the age of a substance is estimated based on comparison of abundance of some radio-isotope and its decay products.

Proton-Proton Cycle: Fusion of hydrogen nuclei resulting in production of hydrogen, helium, electrons, neutrinos and release of energy.

3. α-decay: In this process, the parent nucleus gives off an α-particle and transforms into a lighter nucleus.

β^--decay: In this process, a neutron in the nucleus of the parent transforms into a proton and gives off an electron and an anti-neutrino.

β^+-decay: In this process, a proton in the nucleus of the parent transforms into a neutron and gives off a positron and a neutrino.

5. 7

7. 1.2×10^{36}

9. $t = 2t_{1/2}$

11. The binding energy per nucleon for heavy nuclei ($A \geq 200$) is less than the binding energy for nuclei in the range $50 \leq A \leq 120$. Therefore when a heavier nucleus fissions into two lighter nuclei there is an increase in the total binding energy. This excess energy is released in the fission process.

The iron nucleus has a larger binding energy per nucleon than any other nucleus. Therefore, if two iron nuclei were to fuse into a heavier nucleus (tellurium), the total binding energy of the tellurium nucleus will be less than that of the two iron nuclei. Therefore, there is no release of energy in this process.

13. Then all the protons would get converted into neutrons. In fact if this were the case at the beginning of the big bang, there wouldn't be any protons and the universe would have been simply a large collection of neutrons.

15. 5.6×10^{26} MeV

17. 8.146×10^{34} eV

19. 0.78 MeV/c

21. $m_C = 12.011137$ u $= 1.9944 \times 10^{-26}$ kg

23. (a) $B_{per}(2, 1) = 1.1$ MeV/nucleon
(b) $B_{per}(4, 2) = 7.1$ MeV/nucleon
(c) $B_{per}(6, 3) = 5.3$ MeV/nucleon
(d) $B_{per}(56, 26) = 8.8$ MeV/nucleon
(e) $B_{per}(208, 82) = 7.9$ MeV/nucleon

25. (a) 2.013554 u
(b) 11.996712 u
(c) 15.990531 u
(d) 55.920691 u
(e) 238.000369 u

27. (a) 89.87 MeV
(b) 85.82 MeV
(c) 722.44 MeV
(d) 1611.77 MeV
(e) 1790.76 MeV

29. 3.833×10^{-12} m^{-1}

31. 4.5×10^7 Bq

33. $N = 2.609 \times 10^{17}$ atoms of carbon-14, $m = 6.06$ μg

35. $\lambda = 6.67 \times 10^{-11}$ s^{-1}, $t_{1/2} = 1.04 \times 10^{10}$ s

37. (a) 970 Bq
(b) 6.8 Bq

39. 578 s

41. (a)

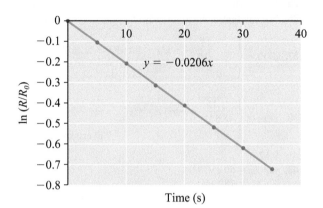

(b) 0.0206 s^{-1}
(c) 33.6 s

43. (a) Not possible since charge must be conserved.
(b) Not possible since charge must be conserved.
(c) Possible.
(d) Not possible since charge must be conserved.
(e) Not possible since mass number must be conserved.

45. (a) $Q = (m_n + m_X - m_Y - m_{He})c^2$
(b) 4.54 MeV

47. $Q = -7.27$ MeV
Since the Q-value is negative, carbon-12 cannot decay through this channel spontaneously.

49. (a) $^{32}_{14}\text{Si} \rightarrow {}^{28}_{12}\text{Mg} + {}^4_2\text{He}$
(b) $^{56}_{25}\text{Mn} \rightarrow {}^{52}_{23}\text{V} + {}^4_2\text{He}$
(c) $^{60}_{26}\text{Fe} \rightarrow {}^{56}_{24}\text{Cr} + {}^4_2\text{He}$

51. (a) $^{52}_{25}\text{Mn} \rightarrow {}^{52}_{24}\text{Cr} + e^+ + \nu$
(b) $^{55}_{27}\text{Co} \rightarrow {}^{55}_{26}\text{Fe} + e^+ + \nu$
(c) $^{59}_{28}\text{Ni} \rightarrow {}^{59}_{27}\text{Co} + e^+ + \nu$

53. (a) $^3_1\text{H} \rightarrow {}^3_2\text{He} + e^- + \bar{\nu}$
(b) 18.6 keV

55. Thorium-232 goes through 4 β-decays and 6 α-decays before converting into a stable lead-208 as shown in the decay diagram below.

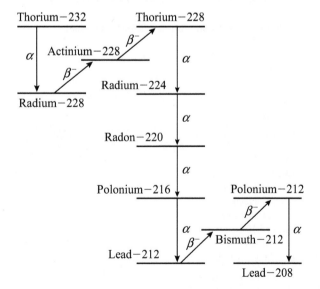

57. (a) 179.6 MeV
(b) 179.9 Mev

59. (a) $B_{per}(2, 1) = 1.1$ MeV/nucleon, $B_{per}(6, 3) = 5.3$ MeV/nucleon, $B_{per}(10, 5) = 6.5$ MeV/nucleon, $B_{per}(14, 7) = 7.5$ MeV/nucleon, $B_{per}(180, 73) = 8.0$ MeV/nucleon
(b) $B_{per}(4, 2) = 7.1$ MeV/nucleon, $B_{per}(4, 8) = 7.1$ MeV/nucleon, $B_{per}(12, 6) = 7.7$ MeV/nucleon, $B_{per}(16, 8) = 8.0$ MeV/nucleon, $B_{per}(182, 74) = 8.0$ MeV/nucleon

61. (a) 9.0 MeV
(b) this spontaneous decay mode is not possible

63. $S_n = a_V - a_S \dfrac{2}{3} A^{-\frac{1}{3}} - a_A \left[1 - \dfrac{4Z^2}{A(A-1)} \right]$

Chapter 34—Introduction to Particle Physics

1. (a) This is incorrect as quarks can interact with each other through any of the fundamental forces and can therefore exchange other force mediating particles as well.
(b) True
(c) False, since the strong force is mediated by gluons.
(d) False, since neutrinos are not force carriers.
(e) True, since gluons carry the strong force.

3. (a) True
(b) False, since mesons contain a quark and an antiquark, whereas baryons are made up of three quarks.
(c) True
(d) False, since a pion is a meson and not a baryon.
(e) True
(f) True

5. (a) True
(b) True, if the electron decelerates.
(c) True
(d) False, since a charged particle cannot gain energy in a constant magnetic field.
(e) True, since even a constant magnetic field would curve the path of a charged particle.

7. 380 MeV

9. electron, neutrino, quark

11. photon, Z^0, gluon

13. $R \propto \dfrac{1}{m}$; therefore if these particles were massless, the range of the weak force would be infinite

15. uds: $m = 1110$ GeV/c²
uus: $m = 1100$ GeV/c²
dds: $m = 1120$ GeV/c²
uss: $m = 1300$ GeV/c²
dss: $m = 1310$ GeV/c²
sss: $m = 1500$ GeV/c²

17. The u, d and s quarks have the following quantum numbers.

	Charge	Baryon Number	Spin
u	⅔	⅓	½
d	−⅓	⅓	½
s	−⅓	⅓	½

This table can be used to find the charge, baryon number, and spin of the baryons.

	Charge	Baryon Number	Spin
uus	+1	+1	½
uds	0	+1	½
dds	−1	+1	½
uss	0	+1	½
dss	−1	+1	½

19. Quarks have the following quantum numbers:

	Charge	Baryon Number	Spin
u	⅔	⅓	½
d	−⅓	⅓	½
c	⅔	⅓	½
s	−⅓	⅓	½
t	⅔	⅓	½
b	−⅓	⅓	½

	Charge	Baryon Number	Spin	(Mass × C MeV/c²)	Mass Rank
ttb	+1	+1	½	346200	5
tts	+1	+1	½	342125	4
tbs	0	+1	½	175325	3
tbd	0	+1	½	175205	2
tuu	+2	+1	½	141005	1

21. $m_{s\bar{u}} = C(125.0 + 2.5) = 127.5C$ MeV/c², where C is the proportionality constant.
$m_{s\bar{d}} = C(125.0 + 5.0) = 130.0C$ MeV/c²
$m_{s\bar{s}} = C(125.0 + 125.0) = 250.0C$ MeV/c²
$m_{u\bar{s}} = C(2.5 + 125.0) = 127.5C$ MeV/c²
$m_{d\bar{s}} = C(5.0 + 125.0) = 130.0C$ MeV/c²
$m_{c\bar{d}} = C(1300.0 + 5.0) = 1305.0C$ MeV/c²
$\Rightarrow m_{s\bar{u}} = m_{u\bar{s}} < m_{s\bar{d}} = m_{d\bar{s}} < m_{s\bar{s}} < m_{c\bar{d}}$

23. (a) $C: +1 \neq 0 - 1 + 0 \Rightarrow$ conservation of charge violated
(b) $C: 0 \neq +1 + 0 \Rightarrow$ conservation of charge violated
(c) conservation of energy violated
(d) $L: -1 \neq -1 + 1 \Rightarrow$ conservation of lepton number violated
(e) $B: +1 \neq 0 + 0 \Rightarrow$ conservation of baryon number violated
(f) $B: +1 + 1 \neq +1 + 0 \Rightarrow$ conservation of baryon number violated
(g) $L: -1 + 0 \neq 0 + 1 \Rightarrow$ conservation of lepton number violated
(h) $B: +1 \neq 0 + 0 \Rightarrow$ conservation of lepton number violated

25. The production of a single photon in electron-positron annihilation is impossible, because linear momentum would not be conserved.

27. 1.8 MeV

29. $E_\pi = 931.5$ MeV, $p_\pi = 921.0$ MeV/c

31. Because the proton is the lightest baryon, it cannot decay into another baryon; if it decays into a meson, the law of conservation of baryon number will be violated.

33. The reaction is not possible because it would require $v_e \geq c$.

35. (a) $p = 69.8$ MeV/c, $E_v = 69.8$ MeV, $E_e = 69.8$ MeV
    (b) $p = 29.9$ MeV/c, $E_v = 29.9$ MeV, $E_\mu = 109.7$ MeV

37.

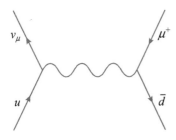

39.

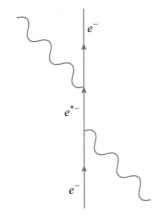

41. (a) (i) $R = 7.3 \times 10^{-16}$ m
        (ii) $R = 1.3 \times 10^{-16}$ m
        (ii) $R = 9.6 \times 10^{-17}$ m

43. (a) (i) 10.9 cm
        (ii) 32.2 cm
        (iii) 42.6 cm
    (b) frequency must be increased to achieve greater kinetic energies
    (c) (i) 74.9 cm
        (ii) 74.9 cm
        (iii) 74.9 cm

45. (a) 2.28×10^8 m/s
    (b) $t = 50$ ns
    (c) circumference $= 11.4$ m

47. Circumference $> 10^{32}$ m; building a synchrotron of this size is impossible

Appendix B
SI UNITS AND PREFIXES

Base SI Units

Unit name	SI symbol	Measures
Ampere	A	Electric current
Candela	cd	Luminous intensity
Kelvin	K	Temperature
Kilogram	kg	Mass
Metre	m	Length
Mole	mol	Amount of a substance
Second	s	Time

The Most Common Derived SI Units

Unit name	SI symbol	Measures	In base units
Coulomb	C	Electric charge	$A \cdot s$
Farad	F	Electric capacitance	C/V
Henry	H	Electromagnetic inductance	$V \cdot s/A$
Hertz	Hz	Frequency	/s
Joule	J	Energy and work	$N \cdot m$
Newton	N	Force	$kg \cdot m/s^2$
Ohm	Ω	Electric resistance	V/A
Pascal	Pa	Pressure	N/m^2
Radian	rad	Angle	dimensionless
Tesla	T	Magnetic field strength	$V \cdot s/m^2$
Volt	V	Electric potential difference	J/C
Watt	W	Power	J/s

Common Prefixes

Prefix	Abbreviation	Power
Zepto-	z	10^{-21}
Atto-	a	10^{-18}
Femto-	f	10^{-15}
Pico-	p	10^{-12}
Nano-	n	10^{-9}
Micro-	μ	10^{-6}
Milli-	m	10^{-3}
Centi-	c	10^{-2}
Deci-	d	10^{-1}
Kilo-	k	10^{3}
Mega-	M	10^{6}
Giga-	G	10^{9}
Tera-	T	10^{12}
Peta-	P	10^{15}
Exa-	E	10^{18}
Zetta-	Z	10^{21}

Appendix C
GEOMETRY AND TRIGONOMETRY

Arc Length and Angle

$$s = \text{arc length} = r\theta$$

Angle θ is in radians.

$$2\pi \text{ rad} = 360°$$

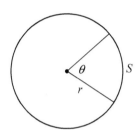

Trigonometric Functions
Right-angled Triangle

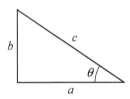

Pythagoras' Theorem: $a^2 + b^2 = c^2$

$$\sin\theta = \frac{\text{opposite}}{\text{hypotenuse}} = \frac{b}{c}; \quad \csc\theta = \frac{\text{hypotenuse}}{\text{opposite}} = \frac{c}{b}$$

$$\cos\theta = \frac{\text{adjacent}}{\text{hypotenuse}} = \frac{a}{c}; \quad \sec\theta = \frac{\text{hypotenuse}}{\text{adjacent}} = \frac{c}{a}$$

$$\tan\theta = \frac{\text{opposite}}{\text{adjacent}} = \frac{b}{a}; \quad \cot\theta = \frac{\text{adjacent}}{\text{opposite}} = \frac{a}{b}$$

General Triangle

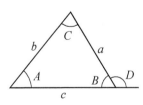

Angles: A, B, C Opposite sides: a, b, c

$$A + B + C = 180° \quad A + C = D$$

Law of cosines $c^2 = a^2 + b^2 - 2ab\cos C$

Law of sines $\dfrac{\sin A}{a} = \dfrac{\sin B}{b} = \dfrac{\sin C}{c}$

Trigonometric Identities

$$\tan\theta = \frac{\sin\theta}{\cos\theta}; \quad \sin^2\theta + \cos^2\theta = 1$$

$$\sin(A \pm B) = \sin A \cos B \pm \cos A \sin B$$

$$\cos(A \pm B) = \cos A \cos B \mp \sin A \sin B$$

$$\tan(A \pm B) = \frac{\tan A \pm \tan B}{1 \mp \tan A \tan B}$$

$$\sin(\theta \pm \pi/2) = \pm\cos\theta \quad \cos(\theta \pm \pi/2) = \mp\sin\theta$$

$$\sin(\theta \pm \pi) = -\sin\theta \quad \cos(\theta \pm \pi) = -\cos\theta$$

$$\sin(2\theta) = 2\sin\theta\cos\theta \quad \cos(2\theta) = \cos^2\theta - \sin^2\theta$$

$$\sin A \pm \sin B = 2\sin\left(\frac{A \pm B}{2}\right)\cos\left(\frac{A \mp B}{2}\right)$$

$$\cos A + \cos B = 2\cos\left(\frac{A + B}{2}\right)\cos\left(\frac{A - B}{2}\right)$$

$$\cos A - \cos B = -2\sin\left(\frac{A + B}{2}\right)\sin\left(\frac{A - B}{2}\right)$$

Expansions and Approximations
Trigonometric Expansions

$$\sin x = x - \frac{x^3}{3!} + \frac{x^5}{5!} - \frac{x^7}{7!} + \ldots \quad (x \text{ is in radians})$$

$$\cos x = 1 - \frac{x^2}{2!} + \frac{x^4}{4!} - \frac{x^6}{6!} + \ldots \quad (x \text{ is in radians})$$

$$\tan x = x + \frac{x^3}{3} + \frac{2x^5}{15} + \frac{17x^7}{315} + \ldots \quad (x \text{ is in radians})$$

Small-angle Approximation

If $x \ll 1$ rad, then $\sin x \approx \tan x \approx x$. The small-angle approximation is generally good for $x < 0.2$ rad.

Appendix D
KEY CALCULUS IDEAS

Derivatives

Given a function $f(x)$, the derivative is defined to be

$$f'(x) = \frac{df}{dx} = \lim_{h \to 0} \frac{f(x+h) - f(x)}{h}$$

The derivative can be interpreted as the instantaneous rate of change of the function at x. We can also think of the derivative as the slope of the tangent to the curve as shown in the figure.

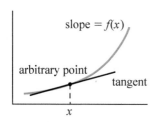

From a physics perspective, if the function $f(t)$ describes the position of an object, the derivative is the velocity of the object.

Basic Properties

For two functions $f(x)$ and $g(x)$ whose derivatives exist, the following properties apply:

1. $\frac{d}{dx}(cf(x)) = c\frac{df}{dx}; \quad c = \text{constant}$

2. $\frac{d}{dx}(f \pm g) = \frac{df}{dx} \pm \frac{dg}{dx}$

3. $\frac{d}{dx}(fg) = f\frac{dg}{dx} + g\frac{df}{dx}$ (Product Rule)

4. $\frac{d}{dx}\left(\frac{f}{g}\right) = \frac{\frac{df}{dx}g - f\frac{dg}{dx}}{g^2}$ (Quotient Rule)

5. $\frac{d}{dx}f(g(x)) = \frac{df}{dg}\frac{dg}{dx}$ (Chain Rule)

Common Derivatives

1. $\frac{d}{dx}x = 1$

2. $\frac{d}{dx}x^n = nx^{n-1}$

3. $\frac{d}{dx}\sin x = \cos x$

4. $\frac{d}{dx}\cos x = -\sin x$

5. $\frac{d}{dx}\tan x = -\sec^2 x$

6. $\frac{d}{dx}\sec x = \sec x \tan x$

7. $\frac{d}{dx}\csc x = -\csc x \cot x$

8. $\frac{d}{dx}\cot x = -\csc^2 x$

9. $\frac{d}{dx}\sin^{-1} x = \frac{1}{\sqrt{1-x^2}}$

10. $\frac{d}{dx}\cos^{-1} x = -\frac{1}{\sqrt{1-x^2}}$

11. $\frac{d}{dx}\tan^{-1} x = \frac{1}{\sqrt{1+x^2}}$

12. $\frac{d}{dx}a^x = a^x \ln(a)$

13. $\frac{d}{dx}e^x = e^x$

14. $\frac{d}{dx}\ln x = \frac{1}{x}$

Integrals

Definition: Suppose that $f(x)$ is continuous on the interval $[a, b]$. We divide $[a, b]$ into N subintervals of width $\Delta x = \frac{b-a}{N}$, with centre $x_i = \left(i + \frac{1}{2}\right)\Delta x$. We then define the definite integral as follows:

$$\int_a^b f(x)\,dx = \lim_{N \to \infty} \sum_{i=0}^{N} f(x_i)\Delta x$$

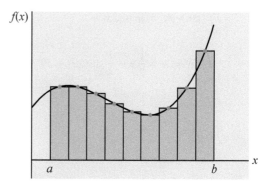

We define the antiderivative of $f(x)$ as $g(x)$ such that $\frac{dg}{dx} = f$.

The indefinite integral is defined as $\int f(x)\,dx = g(x) + C$, where

$$\frac{dg}{dx} = f \quad \text{and} \quad C = \text{constant}$$

We interpret the integral as the area bounded by the function $f(x)$ and the x-axis, where the areas above the axis are positive, and the areas below the axis are negative.

Some Properties of Integrals

$$\int (f(x) \pm g(x))\,dx = \int f(x)\,dx \pm \int g(x)\,dx$$

$$\int c f(x)\,dx = c \int f(x)\,dx; \quad c = \text{constant}$$

$$\int_a^b f(x)\,dx = -\int_b^a f(x)\,dx$$

$$\int u\frac{dv}{dx}\,dx = uv - \int v\frac{du}{dx}\,dx$$

Some Indefinite Integrals

$$\int b\,dx = bx + c; \quad b, c \text{ are constants}$$

$$\int x^n\,dx = \frac{1}{n+1}x^{n+1} + c$$

$$\int \frac{dx}{x} = \ln(x + c)$$

$$\int e^x\,dx = e^x + c$$

$$\int \sin x\,dx = -\cos x + c$$

$$\int \cos x\,dx = \sin x + c$$

$$\int \tan x\,dx = \ln|\sec x| + c$$

$$\int \sin^2 x\,dx = \frac{1}{2}x - \frac{1}{4}\sin(2x) + c$$

$$\int \frac{dx}{\sqrt{x^2 + a^2}} = \ln\left(x + \sqrt{x^2 + a^2}\right) + c$$

$$\int \frac{x\,dx}{(x^2 + a^2)^{3/2}} = -\frac{1}{(x^2 + a^2)^{1/2}} + c$$

$$\int \frac{dx}{(x^2 + a^2)^{3/2}} = \frac{x}{a^2(x^2 + a^2)^{1/2}} + c$$

$$\int \frac{x\,dx}{x + a} = x - a\ln(x + a) + c$$

$$\int e^{-ax}\,dx = -\frac{1}{a}e^{-ax} + c$$

$$\int xe^{-ax}\,dx = -\frac{1}{a^2}(ax + 1)e^{-ax} + c$$

$$\int x^2 e^{-ax}\,dx = -\frac{1}{a^3}(a^2x^2 + 2ax + 2)e^{-ax} + c$$

Partial Derivatives

We sometimes need to take the derivative of a function that depends on more than one variable. For example, the displacement amplitude of a wave depends on both position and time, and in one dimension is thus a function of both x and t. When we need to find the derivatives of such functions, we can use partial derivatives.

Consider a function $f(x, y, z)$. We denote the partial derivatives by $\frac{\partial f}{\partial x}$, $\frac{\partial f}{\partial y}$ and $\frac{\partial f}{\partial z}$ (pronounced die f by die x, etc.). We calculate a partial derivative by differentiating with respect to the variable of interest while treating all other variables as constants. For example, for the function $f(x, y, z) = ax^2 + bxy + cz$, the partial derivatives are given by

$$\frac{\partial f}{\partial x} = 2ax + by, \quad \frac{\partial f}{\partial y} = bx, \quad \text{and} \quad \frac{\partial f}{\partial z} = c.$$

Appendix E

USEFUL MATHEMATICAL FORMULAS AND MATHEMATICAL SYMBOLS USED IN THE TEXT AND THEIR MEANING

Lengths, Areas, and Volumes

Rectangle

$$\text{Area} = ab$$

$$\text{Perimeter} = 2(a + b)$$

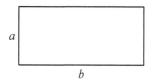

Rectangular Cuboid

$$\text{Surface Area} = 2(ab + bc + ac)$$

$$\text{Volume} = abc$$

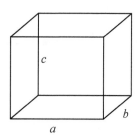

Triangle

$$\text{Area} = \frac{1}{2}bh$$

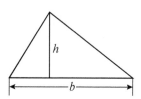

Circle

$$\text{Circumference} = 2\pi r$$

$$\text{Area} = \pi r^2$$

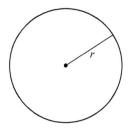

Sphere

$$\text{Surface area} = 4\pi r^2$$

$$\text{Volume} = \frac{4}{3}\pi r^3$$

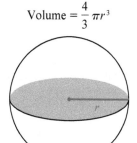

Cylinder

$$\text{Surface area} = 2\pi rh + 2\pi r^2$$

$$\text{Volume} = \pi r^2 h$$

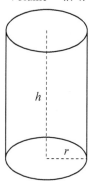

Quadratic Equation

An equation of the form $ax^2 + bx + c = 0$ has as its solution

$$x = \frac{-b \pm \sqrt{b^2 - 4ac}}{2a}$$

Linear Equation

A linear equation is of the form $y = mx + b$, where b is the intercept of the line with the y-axis, and m is the slope of the line;

$$m = \frac{y_2 - y_1}{x_2 - x_1} = \frac{\Delta y}{\Delta x}$$

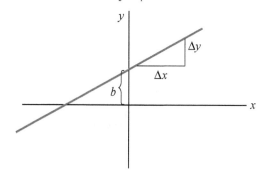

Logarithms

These identities apply to all bases:

$$\log a + \log b = \log (ab)$$

$$\log a - \log b = \log\left(\frac{a}{b}\right)$$

$$\log a^b = b \log a$$

Expansions

$$(1 + x)^n = 1 + \frac{nx}{1!} + \frac{n(n-1)x}{2!} + \cdots \qquad (x^2 \ll 1)$$

$$e^x = 1 + x + \frac{1}{2!} x^2 + \frac{1}{3!} x^3 + \cdots$$

$$\ln(1 + x) = x - \frac{1}{2} x^2 + \frac{1}{3} x^3 - \frac{1}{4} x^4 \qquad (|x| < 1)$$

$$\sin \theta = \theta - \frac{1}{3!} \theta^3 + \frac{1}{5!} \theta^5 - \cdots$$

$$\cos \theta = 1 - \frac{1}{2!} \theta^2 + \frac{1}{4!} \theta^4 - \cdots$$

Mathematical Symbols Used in the Text and Their Meaning

Symbol	Meaning	Sample expression	How it is read
$+$	Addition sign	$7 + 14 = 21$	7 plus 14 equals 21 The sum of 7 and 14 equals 21.
$\cdot$ $\times$	Multiplication signs	$7 \cdot 3 = 21$ $7 \times 3 = 21$	7 times 3 equals 21 The product of 7 and 3 equals 21
$\cdot$	Dot product sign	$\vec{A} \cdot \vec{B} = 32$ $(1, 2, 3) \cdot (4, 5, 6) = 32$	Vector A dot vector B equals 32 The dot (scalar) product of vector A and vector B equals 32.
$\times$	Cross product sign	$\vec{A} \times \vec{B} = \vec{C}$ $(1, 2, 0) \times (3, 4, 0) = (0, 0, -2)$	Vector A cross vector B equals vector C The cross (vector) product of vector A and vector B equals vector C
$-$	Subtraction sign Minus sign	$7 - 3 = 4$ $-(3 + 5) = -8$	7 minus 3 equals 4 The difference of 7 and 3 equals 4 Negative of three plus five equals minus 8 The opposite of three plus five equals minus 8
$\div$ $/$ $-$	Division signs	$21 \div 3 = 7$ $^3/_4 = 3/4 = 0.75$ $\frac{3}{4} = 0.75$	21 divided by 3 equals 7 The quotient of 21 and 7 equals 3 3 over 4 equals three quarters equals point 75
$\%$	Percent symbol	$58\% \equiv 0.58$ $30\%(\$200) = \$60$	58 percent equals point 58 30 percent of $200 equals $60
$:$	Ratio	$1 : 5 = 100 : 500$	1 is to 5 as 100 is to 500
$\pm$ $\mp$	Plus/minus sign Minus/plus sign	$50\ \Omega \pm 10\%$ $(a \pm b)^2 = a^2 \pm 2ab + b^2$ $\cos(\alpha \pm \beta) = \cos^2\alpha \mp \sin^2\beta$	Fifty Ohms plus minus 10 percent a plus minus b squared equals… cos alpha plus minus beta equals cos squared alpha minus plus sin squared beta
$=$	Two values are the same	$-(-7) = 7$ $x + 3y = 57$	The opposite of minus seven equals seven
$\equiv$	A definition	$\sqrt{x} \equiv x^{1/2}$	Square root of x is defined as x to the power of one half
$\neq$	Two values are different	$-1 + 5 \neq -6$	Minus 1 plus 5 is not equal to minus 6
$\approx$	Two values are close to each other (of the same order of magnitude)	$x + y \approx z;\ 2^{10} \approx 1000$	x plus y is approximately equal to z 2 to the power of 10 is approximately equal to 1000

~	Two objects are geometrically similar	$\triangle ABC \sim \triangle ABD$	Triangle ABC is similar to triangle ABD.
$\propto$	Two variables change in direct proportion	$y \propto x$	y is proportional to x
$>(<)$	greater than (less than)	$2^{10} > 10^2$ and $2^3 < 3^2$	Two to the power of 10 is greater than ten to the power of two. Two cubed is less than three squared.
$\gg (\ll)$	much greater than (much less than)	$2^{20} \gg 20^2$ and $10^{-5} \ll 10^5$	Two to the power of twenty is much greater than twenty squared. Ten to the power of minus five is much less than ten to the power of five.
$\geq (\leq)$	greater than or equal to (less than or equal to)	$x \geq 10^2$ and $y \leq 2^3$	x is greater than or equal to ten squared y is less than or equal to two cubed
∞	Infinity	$x \rightarrow \infty$	x approaches infinity
$\ldots$	Continuation	$1 + \dfrac{1}{2} + \dfrac{1}{4} + \dfrac{1}{8} + \cdots + \dfrac{1}{1024}$ $1 + \dfrac{1}{2} + \dfrac{1}{4} + \dfrac{1}{8} + \cdots$	... and so on up to ... ... and so on indefinitely
$\Rightarrow$	Logical implication	$A \Rightarrow B$	A implies B If A then B
$\Leftrightarrow$	Logical equivalence	$A \Leftrightarrow B$	A is logically equivalent to B
$\therefore$	Logical following	$A = B$ and $B = C$ $\therefore A = C$	A equals B and B equals C, therefore (it follows that), A equals C
() [] {}	Parentheses Square brackets Curly brackets	$[(a+b)^2 + 3c]^2$ $\vec{A} = (3, 4, 5)$ $\{a_i\}_{i=1}^{100} = \{a_1, a_2, a_3, \ldots, a_{100}\}$	... quantity, list, set of coordinates, open interval ( ) or closed interval [ ], set { }
$|x|$	Absolute value (a magnitude of a vector). It is always a non-negative quantity.	$|\vec{F}| = 5\ \text{N}$ $|-37| = 37$	The magnitude of force F equals 5 Newtons The absolute value of negative 37 equals 37
$\sqrt{\ }$	Square root symbol	$\sqrt{25} = 5$	The square root of twenty five equals five
$\sqrt[n]{\ }$	Root symbol	$\sqrt[4]{81} = 3$	The fourth root of eighty one equals three
!	Factorial	$3! = 1 \times 2 \times 3 = 6$	Three factorial equals six
°	Degree symbol	$\angle ABC = 60°$ $\cos(90°) = 0$	Angle ABC has a value of sixty degrees
$\perp$	Perpendicularity symbol	$\vec{A} \perp \vec{B}$	Vector A is perpendicular to vector B
$\|$	Parallel symbol	$\vec{A} \| \vec{B}$	Vector A is parallel to vector B
$\angle$ or $\sphericalangle$	Angle symbols	$\angle ABC$, $\sphericalangle ABC$	Angle ABC
$\rightarrow$	An object is a vector	$\vec{F}, \vec{v}$	Vector F, vector v
$\displaystyle\sum_{i=1}^{N} x_i$	Finite summation	$\displaystyle\sum_{i=1}^{N} x_i = 345$	The summation of N quantities x_i equals 345. The sum of all quantities x_i from $i = 1$ to $i = N$ equals 345.
$\displaystyle\sum_{i=1}^{\infty} x_i$	Infinite summation	$\displaystyle\sum_{n=1}^{\infty} \dfrac{1}{2^n} = 1$	The summation of an infinite number of quantities, ... the sum of all quantities x_i from $i = 1$ to $i = \infty$ (infinity)

(continued)

Mathematical Symbols Used in the Text and Their Meaning (continued)

Symbol	Meaning	Sample expression	How it is read
Δ	The change in ... The vertices of a triangle	Δx ΔABC	Delta x (the change in x) Triangle ABC
$\rightarrow$	Approaching	$\Delta x \rightarrow 0$	Delta x approaches zero
$\dfrac{d\dots}{dt}$	Time derivative	$\dfrac{dx}{dt}$; $\dfrac{d\vec{v}}{dt}$	The derivative of x with respect to time The derivative of vector v with respect to time
$\dfrac{\partial\dots}{\partial t}$	Partial time derivative	$\dfrac{\partial f(x,t)}{\partial t}$	The partial derivative of function f with respect to time
$\displaystyle\int$	Indefinite integral	$\displaystyle\int x^2 dx = \dfrac{x^3}{3} + \text{const}$	The integral of x squared dx equals ...
$\displaystyle\iint$	Indefinite double integral	$\displaystyle\iint f(x,y)dxdy$	The double integral of of $f(x,y)dxdy$
$\displaystyle\iiint$	Indefinite triple integral	$\displaystyle\iiint f(x,y,z)dxdydz$	The triple integral of of $f(x,y,z)dxdydz$
$\displaystyle\int_a^b$	Definite integral	$\displaystyle\int_0^2 x^3 dx = 2\dfrac{2}{3}$	The integral of x squared dx equals 2 and 2/3.
$\displaystyle\oint$	Line (path) integral	$\displaystyle\oint \vec{B}\cdot d\vec{l}$	The line integral of B dl
$\displaystyle\oint$	Line integral around a closed path of	$\displaystyle\oint_L \vec{B}\cdot d\vec{l}$	The line integral of B dl around a close path L
$\displaystyle\oiint$	A surface integral over a closed surface of	$\displaystyle\oiint_S \vec{E}\cdot d\vec{A}$	The surface integral of E dA over a closed surface S

Periodic Table of the Elements

Legend

- MAIN GROUP METALS
- TRANSITION METALS
- METALLOIDS
- NON-METALS

Uranium
92 ---- Atomic number
U ---- Symbol

At the date of publication, elements 113–118 had not been named and have been given temporary names.

Group 1	2	3	4	5	6	7	8	9	10	11	12	13	14	15	16	17	18
Hydrogen 1 H																	Helium 2 He
Lithium 3 Li	Beryllium 4 Be											Boron 5 B	Carbon 6 C	Nitrogen 7 N	Oxygen 8 O	Fluorine 9 F	Neon 10 Ne
Sodium 11 Na	Magnesium 12 Mg											Aluminum 13 Al	Silicon 14 Si	Phosphorus 15 P	Sulfur 16 S	Chlorine 17 Cl	Argon 18 Ar
Potassium 19 K	Calcium 20 Ca	Scandium 21 Sc	Titanium 22 Ti	Vanadium 23 V	Chromium 24 Cr	Manganese 25 Mn	Iron 26 Fe	Cobalt 27 Co	Nickel 28 Ni	Copper 29 Cu	Zinc 30 Zn	Gallium 31 Ga	Germanium 32 Ge	Arsenic 33 As	Selenium 34 Se	Bromine 35 Br	Krypton 36 Kr
Rubidium 37 Rb	Strontium 38 Sr	Yttrium 39 Y	Zirconium 40 Zr	Niobium 41 Nb	Molybdenum 42 Mo	Technetium 43 Tc	Ruthenium 44 Ru	Rhodium 45 Rh	Palladium 46 Pd	Silver 47 Ag	Cadmium 48 Cd	Indium 49 In	Tin 50 Sn	Antimony 51 Sb	Tellurium 52 Te	Iodine 53 I	Xenon 54 Xe
Cesium 55 Cs	Barium 56 Ba	Lanthanum 57 La	Hafnium 72 Hf	Tantalum 73 Ta	Tungsten 74 W	Rhenium 75 Re	Osmium 76 Os	Iridium 77 Ir	Platinum 78 Pt	Gold 79 Au	Mercury 80 Hg	Thallium 81 Tl	Lead 82 Pb	Bismuth 83 Bi	Polonium 84 Po	Astatine 85 At	Radon 86 Rn
Francium 87 Fr	Radium 88 Ra	Actinium 89 Ac	Rutherfordium 104 Rf	Dubnium 105 Db	Seaborgium 106 Sg	Bohrium 107 Bh	Hassium 108 Hs	Meitnerium 109 Mt	Darmstadtium 110 Ds	Roentgenium 111 Rg	Copernicium 112 Cn	Ununtrium 113 Uut	Ununquadium 114 Uuq	Ununpentium 115 Uup	Ununhexium 116 Uuh		

Lanthanides

Cerium 58 Ce	Praseodymium 59 Pr	Neodymium 60 Nd	Promethium 61 Pm	Samarium 62 Sm	Europium 63 Eu	Gadolinium 64 Gd	Terbium 65 Tb	Dysprosium 66 Dy	Holmium 67 Ho	Erbium 68 Er	Thulium 69 Tm	Ytterbium 70 Yb	Lutetium 71 Lu

Actinides

Thorium 90 Th	Protactinium 91 Pa	Uranium 92 U	Neptunium 93 Np	Plutonium 94 Pu	Americium 95 Am	Curium 96 Cm	Berkelium 97 Bk	Californium 98 Cf	Einsteinium 99 Es	Fermium 100 Fm	Mendelevium 101 Md	Nobelium 102 No	Lawrencium 103 Lr

Atomic Masses of the Elements[†] (IUPAC 2007), Based on relative atomic mass of $^{12}C = 12$ exactly

Name	Symbol	Atomic Number	Atomic Mass	Name	Symbol	Atomic Number	Atomic Mass
Actinium*	Ac	89	(227)	Molybdenum	Mo	42	95.96(2)
Aluminum	Al	13	26.9815386(8)	Neodymium	Nd	60	144.242(3)
Americium*	Am	95	(243)	Neon	Ne	10	20.1797(6)
Antimony	Sb	51	121.760(1)	Neptunium*	Np	93	(237)
Argon	Ar	18	39.948(1)	Nickel	Ni	28	58.6934(4)
Arsenic	As	33	74.92160(2)	Niobium	Nb	41	92.90638(2)
Astatine*	At	85	(210)	Nitrogen	N	7	14.0067(2)
Barium	Ba	56	137.327(7)	Nobelium*	No	102	(259)
Berkelium*	Bk	97	(247)	Osmium	Os	76	190.23(3)
Beryllium	Be	4	9.012182(3)	Oxygen	O	8	15.9994(3)
Bismuth	Bi	83	208.98040(1)	Palladium	Pd	46	106.42(1)
Bohrium	Bh	107	(272)	Phosphorus	P	15	30.973762(2)
Boron	B	5	10.811(7)	Platinum	Pt	78	195.084(9)
Bromine	Br	35	79.904(1)	Plutonium*	Pu	94	(244)
Cadmium	Cd	48	112.411(8)	Polonium*	Po	84	(209)
Cesium	Cs	55	132.9054519(2)	Potassium	K	19	39.0983(1)
Calcium	Ca	20	40.078(4)	Praseodymium	Pr	59	140.90765(2)
Californium*	Cf	98	(251)	Promethium*	Pm	61	(145)
Carbon	C	6	12.0107(8)	Protactinium*	Pa	91	231.03588(2)
Cerium	Ce	58	140.116(1)	Radium*	Ra	88	(226)
Chlorine	Cl	17	35.453(2)	Radon*	Rn	86	(222)
Chromium	Cr	24	51.9961(6)	Rhenium	Re	75	186.207(1)
Cobalt	Co	27	58.933195(5)	Rhodium	Rh	45	102.90550(2)
Copernicium	Cn	112	(285)	Roentgenium	Rg	111	(280)
Copper	Cu	29	63.546(3)	Rubidium	Rb	37	85.4678(3)
Curium*	Cm	96	(247)	Ruthenium	Ru	44	101.07(2)
Darmstadtium	Ds	110	(281)	Rutherfordium	Rf	104	(267)
Dubnium	Db	105	(268)	Samarium	Sm	62	150.36(2)
Dysprosium	Dy	66	162.500(1)	Scandium	Sc	21	44.955912(6)
Einsteinium*	Es	99	(252)	Seaborgium	Sg	106	(271)
Erbium	Er	68	167.259(3)	Selenium	Se	34	78.96(3)
Europium	Eu	63	151.964(1)	Silicon	Si	14	28.0855(3)
Fermium*	Fm	100	(257)	Silver	Ag	47	107.8682(2)
Fluorine	F	9	18.9984032(5)	Sodium	Na	11	22.98976928(2)
Francium*	Fr	87	(223)	Strontium	Sr	38	87.62(1)
Gadolinium	Gd	64	157.25(3)	Sulfur	S	16	32.065(5)
Gallium	Ga	31	69.723(1)	Tantalum	Ta	73	180.94788(2)
Germanium	Ge	32	72.64(1)	Technetium*	Tc	43	(98)
Gold	Au	79	196.966569(4)	Tellurium	Te	52	127.60(3)
Hafnium	Hf	72	178.49(2)	Terbium	Tb	65	158.92535(2)
Hassium	Hs	108	(270)	Thallium	Tl	81	204.3833(2)
Helium	He	2	4.002602(2)	Thorium*	Th	90	232.03806(2)
Holmium	Ho	67	164.93032(2)	Thulium	Tm	69	168.93421(2)
Hydrogen	H	1	1.00794(7)	Tin	Sn	50	118.710(7)
Indium	In	49	114.818(3)	Titanium	Ti	22	47.867(1)
Iodine	I	53	126.90447(3)	Tungsten	W	74	183.84(1)
Iridium	Ir	77	192.217(3)	Ununhexium	Uuh	116	(293)
Iron	Fe	26	55.845(2)	Ununoctium	Uuo	118	(294)
Krypton	Kr	36	83.798(2)	Ununpentium	Uup	115	(288)
Lanthanum	La	57	138.90547(7)	Ununquadium	Uuq	114	(289)
Lawrencium*	Lr	103	(262)	Ununtrium	Uut	113	(284)
Lead	Pb	82	207.2(1)	Uranium*	U	92	238.02891(3)
Lithium	Li	3	6.941(2)	Vanadium	V	23	50.9415(1)
Lutetium	Lu	71	174.9668(1)	Xenon	Xe	54	131.293(6)
Magnesium	Mg	12	24.3050(6)	Ytterbium	Yb	70	173.054(5)
Manganese	Mn	25	54.938045(5)	Yttrium	Y	39	88.90585(2)
Meitnerium	Mt	109	(276)	Zinc	Zn	30	65.38(2)
Mendelevium*	Md	101	(258)	Zirconium	Zr	40	91.224(2)
Mercury	Hg	80	200.59(2)				

[†]The atomic masses of many elements can vary depending on the origin and treatment of the sample. This is particularly true for Li; commercially available lithium-containing materials have Li atomic masses in the range of 6.939 and 6.996. The uncertainties in atomic mass values are given in parentheses following the last significant figure to which they are attributed.

*Elements with no stable nuclide; the value given in parentheses is the atomic mass number of the isotope of longest known half-life. However, three such elements (Th, Pa, and U) have a characteristic terrestial isotopic composition, and the atomic mass is tabulated for these. http://www.chem.qmul.ac.uk/iupac/AtWt/

Source: © 2009 IUPAC, Pure and Applied Chemistry 81, 2131–2156. Note: The atomic mass referred to in this table is the abundance averaged atomic mass of all the isotopes of the particular element. This quantity is sometimes referred to as the atomic weight of an element.

Carnot, Nicolas Léonard Sadi, 492
Carnot cycle, 492–95, *492f*, *495f*, 503
　efficiency and, 491–96, 498
　in reverse, 493
Carnot's theorem, 493
　violated, 495–96
cars. *See* automobiles
Cartesian vector notation, 27–29, 30, 34–35, 202
　axes, 98, 119
cathode, 875
cathode ray, 814–18, *814f*
　cathode ray tube (CRT), 532, 612, *612f*, 816, 938
Celsius, 455
centre of gravity, 255–256
　balance and, 256
　may not coincide with centre of mass, 255
centre of mass, 175–77, 255, 272, 284
　balance and, 256
　and external force, 178, 189, 211, 255
　and gravity, 255–57
　moment of inertia and, 207–11
　rolling, 231–38
　of a sphere, 284, 360
　system of particles, 174–77
centrifuges, 77, 907
　ultracentrifuge, 77
　　radial acceleration in, *50t*
　Zippe centrifuge, *77f*
centripetal acceleration, 199–200, 289, 295
　gravity as, 288
centripetal force, 114–18, 211, 242
Cerenkov radiation, 715
Ceres, 533, 540
CERN, 809, 918, 927
Chadwick, James
　discovery of the neutron, 819, 895, 919
Chandra X-ray Observatory, 49
charge coupled device (CCD), 3
charge density
　linear, 517–18, 520
　surface, 534–35, 540–42
　uniform, 517–19, 520
Chicxulub crater, *137f*, 288, *288f*
　energy of meteor impact forming, 134
Churchill River Underground Power Plant, *653f*
circular motion, 84, 96
　and centripetal forces, 114–17
　uniform, 76–78
　nonuniform, 78–79
Clausius statement, 490–91, 503
　violated, 495
cloud chamber, 923, *923f*
Cloud Gate, 726, *726f*
coaxial cables, 538, 557, *557f*, 627
　capacitance of, 556–57
COBE satellite, radiation measurements from, *499f*
Cockroft, John, 896–97
collisions
　automotive, 167, 171, 177, 181–83
　cosmic, 181–82
collisions. *See* elastic collisions; inelastic collisions
colour quantum number, 927–28

composite particles, 919, 924–27
　bayrons, 924–25, *924t*
　mesons, 925–26, *926t*
compression, 105, 265, 266
　failure models, 268–69
compressive strength, 268, 269
Compton, Arthur Holly, 824
Compton scattering, 824–26, *824f*, 827
Compton shift, 826
concave mirrors, 733–35, 754
　curvature of, 734
conduction, 480, 509, 515, 520
　conduction density in metals, *572t*
conductivity
　electrical, 574
　and resistivity, 574–79
　of different metals, *575t*
conductors, 515, 520
　electric fields and, 534, 540–42, 544
　metals as, 481, 515
conic section, for orbit identification, 297–98, *297f*
conservation of momentum in moving fluids, 331–32
conservative forces, 148–49, 155, 158
　nonconservative forces, 145, 158
　　and mechanical energy, 148–50, 168
　and potential energy, 145–46, 147, 149, 154
　perpendicular to equipotential surfaces, 154–56
constant acceleration
　in one dimension, 74, 131
　kinematics equations for, 53–56, 58–59, 144
　relative motion with, 59–60, 61
constructive interference of waves
　sound, 407, 434, 444
　light, 765–69, *769f*, *773f*, 774
continuity equation, 324–28, 336
continuity of fluids, 325–28
　equation of, 324–31, 336
continuous distribution equation, 175, 189
convection, 482–83, *483f*, 484
convex mirrors, 733, 736–39
　effect of location on image, 737, *737f*
　virtual focal point, 736, *736f*
coordinate direction angles, 28–29
correspondence principle, 844
cosmic microwave background (CMB) radiation, 499, *499f*
cosmology, 1
Cottrell, Frederick, 543
coulomb, *10t*, 510, 520
Coulomb, Charles Augustin de, 510
Coulomb's law, 511–14, 520, 537, 621, 624, 889
coulombmetres, 516
Cowan, Clyde Lorrain, 900
Crab pulsar, 47, 198
crater, in Yucatan, 137, *137f*, 288
crest of wave, 390, 407, 441–43
　of sound wave, 428, 434–35
　of plane wave, 429, *429f*, *433f*
　shock wave, 443, *443f*
critically damped oscillations, 367–68, *367f*
　tuned-mass damper, 368, *368f*
cross product of vectors, 32–35
　definition, 33, 202

right-hand rule, 32, 202, 216
　and torque, 202
cross-multiplication circle, 33
crumple zones, in cars, 167
crystal structures, 865–68, *865f*, *866t*
　conduction electrons within, 866–70
　energy bands, 871, *871f*, *871t*
　lattice parameter, 865–86
　periodic potential, 870–71, 881
　phonons, 870
　screening, 866
curie, 894
Curie, Marie, 892, 894
Curie, Pierre, 632, 892, 894
Curie's law, 632
current, 509, 520
　electric charges and, 510, 514, 515, 520
cyclotron, 608, 612–14, *613f*, 936–39, 943
　cyclotron radiation, 716
　dees, 613, 93
　frequency, 608, 614
　usc in medicine, 614, 938, *938f*
　synchrotron, 940–42
　TRIUMF, 525, *525f*, 533, 613–14, *613f*, 936–37, *937f*
Cygnus X-1, 799

damped oscillations, 365–70, 372
　critically, 367–68, *367f*
　energy from, 368–69
　envelope of, 366
　overdamped, 368–69
　tuned-mass damper, 368, *368f*
　underdamped, 366–68
　See also drag force
damping
　constant, 368, 370, 372
　electromagnetic, 656
daughter nucleus, 892, *893f*, *901f*
Davisson, Clinton, 833
Davisson–Germer experiment, 833–84, *833f*
Davy, Humphry, 580
DC circuits. *See* direct current circuits
de Broglie, Louis, 832, 860
de Broglie wavelength, 515, 832–34, 835–36, *837f*
debye, 517
Debye, Petrus Josephus Wilhelmus, 517
decay rate, 894
decay time of subatomic particles, 6
deceleration of particle, 716
decibel level, 424, 437–38, 444
　some common sources, *438t*
dees, 613, 936
defibrillators, 551
deformation, 265–71
　elastic, 266
　plastic, 267, 272
　See also tensile strength
density, 308–10, 336
　average, 321, 336
　of atomic particles, 888–89
　of common substances, *309t*
　of ocean water, 320–21
　of various media, *426f*
　SI unit, 309
　of the Sun, 309
derivatives to calculate acceleration, 51

destructive interference of waves, 407, 432,
    434–35, 444
diamagnetism, 632
diamond, *449t*, *453t*
    band gap of, 871
    density of, *309t*, *426t*
    as insulator, 871
    magnetic permeability, *631t*
    refractive index of, *740t*, 741–43, *743f*
    structure of, 449
diastolic pressure, 334
dielectric heating, 517
dielectrics, 450, 515
    and capacitance, 559–60, *559f*, *560t*, 565
    constants in various materials, *560t*
    strengths, *872t*
diffraction of electron beam through graphite,
    779f
diffraction of light waves, 170, 727, *769f*,
    778f, *779f*, 780
    single slit, 773–76, 780
        interference patterns, *775f*
    diffraction grating, 768–69, *768f*
diffraction of x-rays by crystals, 833, *834f*
diffuse reflection, 730, *730f*
dimensional analysis, 11, 16
diodes, 563, 564, 576
    avalanche current, 876
    bias of, 876
    pn junction diode, 875–76, *875f*, 881
    as rectifiers, 876
dipole antennas, 716
dipole moments
    of an atom, 630–32
    electric, 516, 517, 520, 619
    magnetic, 619, 630
direct current (DC) circuits, 563, 578, 581–90
    capacitors and, 563
    compound, 585–87
    sources of emf, 581–82
    and Kirchhoff's laws, 581–82
dispersion of light, 740, *740f*, *742f*, *743f*
displacement, 42, 43, 61, 84, 142, 178–79
    angular, 199, 209, 211–12
    and distance, 42–43
    SI unit, 42
    of a spring, 113
    in two or three dimensions, 72–74, 138–40
    vector, 21, 28–29, 131–32
    and velocity and acceleration, 54–57,
        72–78, 96
displacement amplitude, 426–27, *429f*, *431t*,
    444
    of standing waves, 430, *431t*
displacement current, 700–01, 721
displacement function, 386, 387–88, *397f*
    See also wave function
distance, 42–44
    ranges in nature, *43–44t*
    SI unit, 42
dopants, 874–75, 877
doping semiconductors, 874–75, 881
Doppler, Christian, 441
Doppler effect (Doppler shift), 440–42, 499
    in electromagnetic radiation, 442, 825
    moving source, stationary receiver, 441–42
    moving receiver, stationary source, 442–43
Doppler spectroscopy, 299
Dora rail cannon, 75

dot (scalar) product, 35
    definition, 30
    electric flux as, 535
    and unit vectors, 30–32
drag force, 92, 186, *365f*
    aerodynamic, 292, 294
    in air, 365–66, 817
    constant, 365
    in a fluid, 134, 365–66
    in maglev trains, 667
    magnitude of, 817
    shockwave, 202
    and Stokes' law, 817
    in underdamped oscillations, 366–37
driven harmonic oscillators, 369–70
ductile failure, 268
ductility, 267, 268–69

$E = mc^2$ (mass-energy equivalence equation),
    786, 793–94, 797–98, 803, *897t*, 930
Earth
    escape speed from, 294
    Eratosthenes' estimate of radius, 728
    gravity and, 155
    magnetic field, *604f*, 605, 609, 615, 625, 702
    magnetic poles, 604
    magnetosphere of, 606
    mass of, 291, 786, 800
    orbit, 176
    orbital momentum, *168t*
    orbital speed of, 298, 788
    radiation pressure at surface of, 714
    rotation of, 176, 200, 208
earthquake, 254, 380, 383
    Fukushima, 886, *866f*, 908
    quake-resistant structures, 143, *254f*, 370
        tuned-mass dampers, 368
    waves, 383, *383f*
eccentricity of orbit, 296
ECG, 345–46, *345f*
eclipses, 727
    lunar, *727f*
    solar, 729
eddies, 649–50
Edison, Thomas Alva, 580, 654–55
eigenvalue, 839–40, 860, 904
    eigen wave function, 840
Einstein, Albert, 2, 4, *134t*, *786f*, 788, 796
    particle nature of light (photoelectric
        effect), 170, 822–23, 832
Einstein's theory of relativity, 786
    energy-momentum relationship, 713,
        793–94, 797–98
        virtual particles and, 922
    general, 2, 285
    mass-energy relationship, 786, 793–94,
        797–98, 803, *897t*, 930
    special, 786, 788
        assumptions of, 788
ejection seats, 79
elastic collisions, 172–74, 189
    conservation of energy and momentum,
        172–74, 183–85
    duration, 174
elastic deformation, 266
elastic force, 93
    and Hooke's law, 143
    potential energy, 147–48
elastic limit, 266–67

elasticity, 272
electric batteries, 581
electric cars, 146
electric charges
    current, 510, 514, 515, 520
    direction of, 511
    on hanging mass, 511–12
    magnitude of, 510
    multiple, 512–13
electric circuits
    meters in, 582
    See also alternating current (AC) circuits;
        direct current (DC) circuits
electric current
    density, 572–74
    flow, 573
    macroscopic model of, 574–75
    microscopic model of, 572–74
    Ohm's law, 575–78
    undergoing simple harmonic motion,
        715–16
electric dipoles, 515–17, 520
    and molecular physics, 517
electric field, 513–19, 520, 544
    in capacitors, 565
    and conductors, 534
    determining, 514
    for a dipole, 515–16
    from electric potential, 530–32, 544
    Faraday's law for, 699, 703, 705–06
    Gauss's law for, 537–39, 699, 704–05
    inducing a magnetic field, 699–702
    from infinite plane of charge, 539
    laws of, 699–700, *699t*
    linear charge density, 517–18, 520
    superposition principle, 512, 515, 520,
        528, 544
    uniform charge density, 517–19, 520
electric field lines, 529–30, *529f*, *530f*, 658,
    658f
electric forces, 530
    calculating, 511–12, 513, 516, 518, 520
    conservative, 526
electric guitar, 656–57, *657f*
electric motor, simple DC, 620
    magnetic torque in, 630
electric potential, 527–28, 544
electric potential energy, 544
    calculating, 526–27
    for groups of point charges, 527–29
electric toothbrush, 662
electrical energy, sources of, 653–54
    hand-powered generators, *654f*
electricity
    grounding, 580–81
    household, 579–81, 681, 691–92
electrolysis, 810, 827
    of water, *810f*
electromagnetic field
    induction, 658–59
electromagnetic force, 520, *658t*, 920, *920t*,
    922t, 943
    between molecules, 308, 770
    as fundamental, 93, 920
electromagnetic polarizer, 718–20
electromagnetic waves/radiation, 381, 404,
    480, 703–07, *704f*
    Ampère's law for, 706–07
    Doppler effect with, 442

momentum of, 170, 185
vertex, 922
virtual, 921–22, *922f*, 946, *946f*
photovoltaic effect, 878
physical optics
  compared to geometric optics, 764, 780
  light-wave interference, 764–79, 780, 833
  double slit interference, 766–68, *766f*,
    767f, 780
    actual intensity pattern, 776–77, *776f*,
      780
  diffraction grating, 768–69, *768f*
  resolution limit, 777–79, 780
  single slit diffraction, 773–76, 780
    interference patterns, *775f*
  thin-film interference, 771–73, 780
  See also diffraction; interfering waves;
    thin films
physical pendulum, 359–61
physicists, 2–4, 14–15
physics, distinguishing characteristics of,
  2–3, 16
pions, 857, 925–26, *928f*, 931, 935, 943
  discovery of, 934–35
pipeline, pressure in, 315
PIXE (proton-induced X-ray emission), 2
Planck, Max, 812, 822, 827
Planck's constant, 19, 498, 812, 822–24
  Einstein and, 822–23, 832
  photoelectric effect and, 822
Planck length, 43
plane waves, 429, *433f*
  crest of, 429, *429f*, *433f*
planets
  definition, 285
  exoplanets, 299–300, *300f*
  gravity near the surface of, 286–87
  habitable, 14
  orbits of, 294, 299–300
  Kelper's laws of, 294–96
plasma, 308, 449
plastic deformation, 267, 272
point mass
  angular momentum of, 215–16
  definition, 95, 175, 211
  moment of inertia of, 205–09
  rotational kinetic energy of, 211–12
Poiseuille's law for viscous flow, 333, 337
Poisson, Siméon, 774
Poisson spot, 774, *774f*
polar molecules, 515, 517, 559
polar notation, 21
polarization, 717–20
  by absorption, 718
  Brewster's angle, 752–53
  electromagnetic polarizer, 718–20
  linear, 717
  plane of, 717
  by reflection, 719–20
  unpolarized light, 718–19, *719f*
polarizing sunglasses, 753
Polaroid film, 718
position, 42–3, 61
  derivative of, 49
position vector, 28
positive amplitude, 434
  peak, 433
positive orbital energy, 298
positrons, 892, 922–23

potential energy, 131, 145–46, 148, 158
  change in is path-independent, 147
  conservative forces and, 145–46, 147, 149,
    154
  converted to kinetic energy, 149
  elastic force and, 147–48
  electric, 544
    calculating, 526–27
    for groups of point charges, 527–29
  in fluids, 322–33
  force from, 292–93
  gravitational potential energy, 146, 290–93,
    301
    definition, 290
    and gravitational work, 131, 290
    zero level of, 293, 526, 799
  and reference points, 154–55
  SI units, 322
  in simple harmonic motion, 353–57
  of a spring, 147–48, 154–55
potential energy function, 292–93
power, 156
  SI unit, 156
Poynting, John Henry, 713
Poynting vector, 712–13, 721
Prebus, Albert, 515, 779
precision, need for, 4, 14
pressure, 310, 336
  absolute, 314, 323
  atmospheric, 311–12, *312t*, 336
  calculating, 310
  in fluids, 311
  gauge, 314–15
  hydrostatic, 312–13
  manometer, 314–15, *314f*, *315f*
  measured, 314
  pascal, 310
  reference, 314
  SI unit, 310, 336
principle of the least time, 730, 754
principle quantum number, 852–53
printers, and electric fields, 514, *514f*
probability, 13
probability distribution, 460–61
projectile motion, 74–76, 84
proportional limit, 266–67
proton beams, 525, 533, 938, *938f*
protons, 630, 887, 896, 913, 924–25, 943
  in auroras, 609
  antiproton, 926–27
  charge, 889–91
  in cyclotron, 525, 613, 809, 936, 938, 941
  decay, 930–34, *934f*
  discovery of, 919
  electrostatic potential of, 851
  elementary charge, 510
  emitting gamma rays, 715
  energy levels, *904f*
  in fusion, *794*, 909
  mass of, 820, 890, *925t*
  in MRIs, 628
  momentum of, 168, 837
  not a point particle, 821
  properties of, *888t*, 924, 941
  proton–proton cycle, 909
  rest mass, *794*, *901f*
  spin, 857, 904
pulley, 106–07, 110–11
  angular acceleration of, 212–13, 242

pulsar, 198, *198f*, 299
  pulsar periods, 217–18
pulse, 382–89
  on a hanging string, 389–90
  and harmonic wave, 393
  reflected, *408f*, 408–10
  superposition, 404–05
  travelling in one dimension, 385–87
  two pulses travelling in opposite directions,
    405–07, *405–06f*
Pythagorean theorem, 21–22, 28, 93

Q values, 896–97, 913
quantum logic clock, 217–18
quantum mechanics, 715, 831, 832, 845
quantum number, 843, 852–54
  shells and subshells, 853, *853t*
quantum tunnelling, 846–49, 860, 906, 909
  boundary conditions, 847–49
  through a barrier, 849, 909
quarks, 920, 923–24, *924f*, 927–29
  colour quantum numbers, 927–28
  flavours, 920
  quark confinement, 928, *928f*
  and Standard Model, 923–24
quasars, 698

R value (RSI), 482
radial acceleration, 78, 84, 114, 243, 389
  and tangential acceleration, 199
radial axis, 358
radial velocity spectroscopy, 29
radian
  SI unit, *10t*, 199
radiation weighting factors, *910t*
radio resonance, 691
radio telescope, 763, *763f*, 778
radio waves, 708
radioactivity, 892
radiocarbon dating, 902
radiography, 710
radioisotopes, 614, 938
random errors, 4, 5, 16
Rayleigh, Baron (John William Strutt), 778
Rayleigh criterion, 778–79, 780
Rayleigh–Benard cells, 483
RC circuits, 590–94, *590f*, 595
  time constant of, 591
  capacitors in, 590–94
redshift, 3, 300, 798
  gravitational redshift, 798
reentry speed of space shuttle, 46
reference frames, 21
  inertial and noninertial, 118
  and fictitious forces, 117–18
reflected ray, 730
reflection of light, 730–39
  angle of, 730
  diffuse, *730f*
  hard, 408, *408f*, *771f*, 772, 780
  law of, 730–31, *730f*, 754
  plane mirror, 731–33
  polarization and, 752–53
  soft, *408f*, 409
  specular, *730f*
  spherical mirror, 733–39
  total internal reflection, 742–42, *742f*
reflection of waves, 408–09
refracted ray, 740

refraction of light waves, 739–43
  Fermat's principle and, 736, *736f*
  index of, 739–41, *740t*, 754
  law of, 740, 754
  optical density, 739
  Snell's law, 740–41
  thin lens images, 743–50
  See also thin lenses
  in triangular prism, 743–43, *743f, 744f*
refraction of sound waves, 429–30, *429f,*
    439–40
refrigerators and heat pumps, 490,
    492, 503
  Carnot cycle, 492–95, *492f, 495f*, 503
    efficiency and, 491–96, 498, 503
    in reverse, 493
    theorem violated, 495–96
  operation of, 488, 490, *490f*
Reines, Frederick, 900
relative
  acceleration, 57–58
  motion, 57–61, 84
    notation, 57
    in one dimension, 57
    in two and more dimensions, 80–84
  position, 57–58
  velocity, 57–8
relative permeability of paramagnetic
    materials, 631–32, *631t*
relativistic kinetic energy, 786,
    794–96, 803
relativistic momentum, 793, 803
relativity
  black holes and, 799–800
  equivalence principle, 797
  general, 786
    gravitational time dilation, 797–99, 803
    and GPS, 800–802, *801f*
  gravitational lensing, 800
  gravitational redshift, 798
  mass-energy equivalence, 793–94
  Michelson–Morley experiment and, 765,
    787–88, *787f*
  rest mass, 793
  speed of light, 787–88
  special, 786, 803
    inertial reference frames, 788
    length contraction, 791–93, 803
    proper length, 791
    proper time, 789
    relative speeds, 795–96, 803
    relativistic kinetic energy, 7
      94–95, 803
    relativistic momentum, 793, 803
    spacetime, 786, 796–97, *797f*, 803
  time dilation, 786, 788–90, 803
  twin paradox, 790–91
resistive load in AC circuit, 682–83, *682f*
resistivity, 574–75, 595, 881
  Einstein's theory of, 2, 285
  of different metals, *575t*, 871, 874
  superconductivity, 874–75
resistors, 562–63, 575–79, *576f*, 595
  and Ohm's law, 575–78
  in parallel, 578, 585–94
  potential differences across, 588–89,
    660–61
  in series, 557, 577–85, 663
  See also RC circuits; RL circuits

resonance, 286, 369–70, 372
  in electromagnetism, 369
  radio, 691
  tidal, 344
rest mass, *134t*, 793, 803, 890, 899, *899f,*
    901f, 920, 943
  atomic mass and, 887, 920
  and binding energy, 890
  and energy conservation, 895–96, 929
restoring force, 143, 371
  and Hooke's law, 350
  of a pendulum, 357–58, 371
  of simple harmonic motion, 350
  of a spring, 143, *143f*, 352–56, 366,
    370, 371
  on a string, 388–89
rho meson, 857, 926
right-hand rule for determining
    direction, 32
  of angular velocity, 202, 216
  of cross products, 32, 202, 216
  of a magnetic field, 606–07, 616, 622
rigid bodies, 175, 206–08
  angular momentum of rotating, 216
  moments of inertia of, 207–08
RL circuits, 659, *659f*, 663–66, *663f*
RLC circuit, series, 687–89, *692f*, 694, 716
  half-power bandwidth, 691
  power dissipation in, 691–93
  resonance frequency of, 689–91
rocket equation, ideal, 187–88, 189
rocket propulsion, 186–88, 189
  ideal rocket equation, 187–88, 189
rolling, 231, 245
  down an incline, 234–36
  friction and, 231–40, 244, 245
  ideal/perfect, 231–32
  mechanical energy and, 238–44
  as a rotation about a moving axis, 233–34
  as a rotation about a stationary point, 234
root-mean-square (rms) values, 452,
    655, 682
rotation about a fixed axis
  perfect/ideal rolling, spinning, and
    skidding, 231–32
  and translation, 232–33
rotational and translational motion,
    232–34
rotational kinetic energy, 211–12
Rubin, Clinton, 101
Rumford, Count (Benjamin Thompson),
    470
Rutherford, Ernest, 819, 919
Rutherford scattering, 819–21, 827
Rydberg, Johannes, 813–14, 823
Rydberg's constant, 814

satellite, 285, 296
Saturn, 296
  Titan, 296
scalars
  definition, 21
  used for components of a vector, 72
scanning microscopes
  electron (SEM), 515
  probe (SPM), 879–80
  tunnel (STM), 880
Schrödinger, Erwin, 838

Schrödinger equation, 838–49, 855, 860
  assumptions, 383
  for a hydrogen atom, 851–55, *852t*, 860
  in one dimension, 842–43, *842f, 843t,*
    866, 881
  and quantization, 850
  for simple harmonic oscillators, 840
  in three dimensions, 841
  time independent equation, 840–42
Schumacher, Michael, 78
Schwarzchild, Karl, 799–800, *799f*
Schwarzchild radius, 799–800
scientific notation, 7, 14
screening, 866
seat belts, 50, 171
second law of motion (Newton), 94–97, 114,
    119, 131, 205, 234, 285, 320
  applied to fluids, 320, 331
second law of thermodynamics, 488, 496,
    497, 503
  absolute zero, 498
  Clausius statement of, 490–91, 503
    violated, 495
  consequences of entropy and, 495–96, 503
  heat death, 498–500
  Kelvin–Planck statement of, 490–91,
    498, 503
    violated, 495
  thermodynamic limit, 498, 502
self-assembled monolayers (SAMs), 880
semi-major axis of orbit, 294–96, 301
semiconductors, 872–74
  BJT and FET transistors, 876
  carrier concentration, 874
  donors and acceptors, 875
  doping, 874–75
  holes, 873–74
  integrated circuits, 876–78, *877f*
  n-type or p-type, 875–77
  pn junction diode, 875–76, *875f*
shadows, 727, *727f*
shear force, 265–66, 272
shock absorbers, 183, 367, *367f*
shock wave, 443, *443f*
short circuit, 587
SI (Système international d'unités) units,
    9–11, *10t*, 16, 134
  absorbed radiation, 910, 913
  amplitude, 346
  capacitance, 553
  conversion, 11–12
  decay rate, 894
  density, 309
  displacement, 42
  distance, 42
  electrical charge, 510, 520
  electric current, 573, 629
  electric dipole moments, 516, 517, 520, 619
  electrical field, 530
  equivalent dose, 910
  flow rate, 324
  frequency, 345
  gravitational constant, 284
  half-life, 893
  kelvin, 455
  kinetic energy, 322
  magnetic field, 605
  mass, 95
  nuclear radiation, 894, 913

Pedagogical Colour Chart

MECHANICS AND THERMODYNAMICS

Displacement and position vectors

Displacement and position component vectors

Linear ($\vec{v}$) and angular ($\vec{w}$) velocity vectors

Velocity component vectors

Force vectors ($\vec{F}$)

Force component vectors

Acceleration vectors ($\vec{a}$)

Acceleration component vectors

Energy transfer arrows

W_{eng}

$Q_?$

$Q_?$

Process arrow

ELECTRICITY AND MAGNETISM

Electric fields

Electric field vectors

Electric field component vectors

Magnetic fields

Magnetic field vectors

Magnetic field component vectors

POSITIVE CHARGES

Protons

NEGATIVE CHARGES

Electrons

Neutrons

LIGHT AND OPTICS

Light ray

Focal light ray

Central light ray

Converging lens

Diverging lens

LIGHT AND OPTICS continued

Linear ($\vec{p}$) and angular ($\vec{L}$) momentum vectors

Linear and angular momentum component vectors

Torque vectors ($\vec{\tau}$)

Torque component vectors

Schematic linear or rotational motion directions

Dimensional rotational arrow

Enlargement arrow

Springs

Pulleys

Resistors

Batteries and other DC power supplies

Switches

Capacitors

Inductors (coils)

Voltmeters

Ammeters

AC Sources

Lightbulbs

Ground symbol

Current

Mirror

Curved mirror

Objects

Images

Some Physical Constants

Gravitational constant	G	6.673×10^{-11} N·m/kg^2
Speed of light	c	2.998×10^8 m/s
Fundamental charge	e	1.602×10^{-19} C
Avogadro's number	N_A	6.022×10^{23} particles/mol
Gas constant	R	8.315 J/mol·K 1.987 cal/mol·K
Boltzmann's constant	$k = R/N_A$	1.381×10^{-23} J/K 8.617×10^{-5} eV/K
Unified mass unit	$u = (1/N_A)$	1.661×10^{-24} g
Coulomb's constant	$k = \dfrac{1}{4\pi\varepsilon_0}$	8.988×10^9 N·m^2/C^2
Permittivity of free space	ε_0	8.854×10^{-12} C^2/N·m^2
Permeability of free space	μ_0	$4\pi \times 10^{-7}$ N/A^2 1.257×10^{-6} N/A^2
Planck's constant	h	6.626×10^{-34} J·s 4.136×10^{-15} eV·s
	$h = h/2\pi$	1.055×10^{-34} J·s 6.582×10^{-16} eV·s
Mass of electron	m_e	9.109×10^{-31} kg 511.0 keV/c^2
Mass of proton	m_p	1.673×10^{-27} kg 938.3 MeV/c^2
Mass of neutron	m_n	1.675×10^{-27} kg 939.6 MeV/c^2
Bohr magneton	$m_B = eh/2m_e$	9.274×10^{-24} J/T 5.788×10^{-5} eV/T
Nuclear magneton	$m_n = e\hbar/2m_p$	5.051×10^{-27} J/T 3.152×10^{-8} eV/T
Magnetic flux quantum	$\phi_0 = h/2e$	2.068×10^{-15} T·m^2
Quantized Hall resistance	$R_K = h/e^2$	2.581×10^4 Ω
Rydberg constant	R_H	1.097×10^7 m^{-1}
Josephson frequency–voltage quotient	$2e/h$	4.836×10^{14} Hz/V
Compton wavelength	$\lambda_c = h/m_e C$	2.426×10^{-12} m

NEL

Physical Data Often Used

Mass of Earth, M_E	5.98×10^{24} kg
Radius of Earth, R_E, mean	6.37×10^6 m
Mass of Moon, M_M	7.35×10^{22} kg
Radius of Moon, R_M	1.74×10^6 m
Mass of Sun, M_S	1.99×10^{30} kg
Radius of Sun, R_S	6.96×10^8 m
Earth–Sun distance, $D_{E\text{-}S}$, mean	1.496×10^{11} m
Earth–Moon distance, $D_{E\text{-}M}$, mean	3.844×10^8 m
One light year (the distance light travels in one year)	9.47×10^{15} m
Acceleration of gravity on Earth, g (standard value)	9.81 m/s^2
At sea level, at equator	9.78 m/s^2
At sea level, at poles	9.83 m/s^2
Acceleration of gravity on Moon, g_M	1.62 m/s^2
Orbital speed:	
Earth	2.98×10^4 m/s
Moon	1.02×10^3 m/s
Period:	
Earth (sidereal year)	365.26 days
Moon (sidereal month)	27.3 days
Escape velocity:	
Earth, $v_{E\text{-}esc}$	1.12×10^4 m/s
Moon, $v_{M\text{-}esc}$	2.4×10^3 m/s
Solar constant	1.35 kW/m^2
Time it takes light to travel the distance:	
from Earth to Sun	498 s = 8.3 min
from Earth to Moon	1.28 s
around Earth	0.13 s
equal to one light year	1 year = 3.16×10^7 s
Milky Way Galaxy data:	
Diameter	100 000 to 120 000 light years ($\approx 10^{21}$ m)
Thickness (average)	1 000 light years ($\approx 10^{19}$ m)
Number of stars	100 to 400 billion
Estimated mass	$5.8 \times 10^{11}\, M_S$
Useful ratios	$\dfrac{M_S}{M_E} = 3.33 \times 10^5;\ \dfrac{M_E}{M_M} = 81.3$
	$\dfrac{R_S}{R_E} = 109;\ \dfrac{R_E}{R_M} = 3.66$
	$\dfrac{D_{E\text{-}S}}{D_{E\text{-}M}} = 389;\ \dfrac{D_{E\text{-}M}}{R_E} = 60.4;\ \dfrac{D_{E\text{-}S}}{R_E} = 2.35 \times 10^4;$
	$\dfrac{g_E}{g_M} = 6.1;\ \dfrac{v_{E\text{-}esc}}{v_{M\text{-}esc}} = 4.67$

Solar System Data

	Mass (kg)	Planetary radius (m)	Semi-major axis (m)	Eccentricity
Mercury	3.30×10^{23}	2.44×10^6	5.76×10^{10}	0.206
Venus	4.87×10^{24}	6.05×10^6	1.08×10^{11}	0.00676
Earth	5.97×10^{24}	6.37×10^6	1.50×10^{11}	0.0167
Mars	6.42×10^{23}	3.38×10^6	2.28×10^{11}	0.0933
Jupiter	1.90×10^{27}	7.07×10^7	7.79×10^{11}	0.0488
Saturn	5.68×10^{26}	6.03×10^7	1.43×10^{12}	0.0557
Uranus	8.68×10^{25}	2.53×10^7	2.88×10^{12}	0.0444
Neptune	1.03×10^{26}	2.46×10^7	4.55×10^{12}	0.0112
Ceres (d)	9.43×10^{20}	4.80×10^5	4.13×10^{11}	0.0791
Pluto (d)	1.31×10^{22}	1.15×10^6	5.87×10^{12}	0.249
Eris (d)	1.67×10^{22}	1.2×10^6	1.46×10^{13}	0.436

(d) = dwarf planet

Some Prefixes for Powers of 10

Zepto	(z)	10^{-21}
Atto	(a)	10^{-18}
Femto	(f)	10^{-15}
Pico	(p)	10^{-12}
Nano	(n)	10^{-9}
Micro	(μ)	10^{-6}
Milli	(m)	10^{-3}
Centi	(c)	10^{-2}
Deci	(d)	10^{-1}
Kilo	(k)	10^{3}
Mega	(M)	10^{6}
Giga	(G)	10^{9}
Tera	(T)	10^{12}
Peta	(P)	10^{15}
Exa	(E)	10^{18}
Zetta	(Z)	10^{21}

Standard Abbreviations and Symbols for Units

Unit name	Symbol	Measures	Equal to
Ampere (*)	A	Electric current	C/s
Atmosphere	atm	Pressure	1.01×10^5 Pa
Becquerel	Bq	Radioactive decay	decays/s
Candela (*)	cd	Luminous intensity	
Coulomb	C	Electric charge	A · s
Day	d	Time	8.64×10^4 s
Decibel	dB	Logarithmic ratio of intensities	
Degree	°	Angle	π/180 rad
Degree Celsius	°C	Temperature	K − 273
Farad	F	Electric capacitance	C/V
Henry	H	Electromagnetic inductance	V · s/A
Hertz	Hz	Frequency	cycle/s
Hour	h	Time	3600 s
Joule	J	Energy or work	N · m
Kelvin (*)	K	Temperature	
Kilogram (*)	kg	Mass	
Kilowatt hour	kW·h	Energy	kW · h
Litre	L	Volume	10^{-3} m^3
Lumen	lm	Luminous flux	cd · sr
Lux	lx	Luminous flux per unit area	l m/m^2
Light year	ly	Distance light travels in a year	9.46×10^{15} m
Metre (*)	m	Length	
Mole (*)	mol	Avogadro's number of units	
Newton	N	Force	kg · m/s^2
Ohm	Ω	Electric resistance	V/A
Pascal	Pa	Pressure	N/m^2
Radian	rad	Angle	m/m
Second (*)	s	Time	
Steradian	sr	Solid angle	
Tesla	T	Magnetic field strength	Wb/m^2
Volt	V	Electric potential difference	J/C
Watt	W	Power	J/s
Weber	Wb	Magnetic flux	V·s or T·m^2
Year	yr	Time	3.156×10^7 s

Base SI units are marked with *. The equivalents given in the last column are not the only possibilities. See Chapter 1 for equivalents expressed in terms of the seven SI base units.

Conversions

1 rev = 2π rad = 360°
1 rad = 57.3° = $\pi/180°$
1 d = 8.64×10^4 s
1 yr = 3.16×10^7 s
1 angstrom (Å) = 1.00×10^{-10} m
1 light year (ly) = 9.46×10^{15} m
1 astronomical unit (au) = 1.50×10^{11} m
1 mile = 1.61×10^3 m
1 litre (L) = 1.00×10^{-3} m³
1 unified mass unit (u) = 1.66×10^{-27} kg
1 tonne (t) = 1.00×10^3 kg
1 mile/h (mph) = 0.447 m/s
1 litre (L) = 1.00×10^{-3} m³
1 dyne = 1.00×10^{-5} N
1 lb = 4.45 N
1 erg = 1.00×10^{-7} J
1 kilowatt hour (kW·h) = 3.60×10^6 J
1 cal = 4.18 J
1 Cal = 4.18×10^3 J
1 electron volt (eV) = 1.60×10^{-19} J
1 British thermal unit (Btu) = 1.05×10^3 J
1 horsepower (hp) = 746 W
1 Btu/h = 0.293 W
1 atmosphere (atm) = 1.01×10^5 Pa = 760 mm Hg
1 torr = 133 Pa
1 gauss (G) = 1.00×10^{-4} T
1 curie (Ci) = 3.70×10^{10} Bq
1 rem = 0.0100 Sv
K = °C + 273.15 (for temperatures)

Greek Letters Commonly Used in Physics

alpha	α
beta	β
delta	δ
epsilon	ε
eta	η
gamma	γ
lambda	λ
mu	μ
nu	ν
omega	ω
phi	ϕ
pi	π
psi	ψ
rho	ρ
sigma	σ
tau	τ
theta	θ
Delta	Δ
Gamma	Γ
Omega	Ω
Phi	Φ
Sigma	Σ